# POLITICAL CLEAVAGES AND
# SOCIAL INEQUALITIES

# POLITICAL CLEAVAGES AND SOCIAL INEQUALITIES

A Study of Fifty Democracies, 1948–2020

AMORY GETHIN

CLARA MARTÍNEZ-TOLEDANO

THOMAS PIKETTY

Harvard University Press

Cambridge, Massachusetts   London, England   2021

First published in French as *Clivages politiques et inégalités sociales. Une étude de
50 démocraties (1948–2020)* (Paris: Les Éditions du Seuil, 2021).

*Library of Congress Cataloging-in-Publication Data*
Names: Gethin, Amory, 1995– author. | Martínez-Toledano,
Clara, 1990– author. | Piketty, Thomas, 1971– author.
Title: Political cleavages and social inequalities : a study of fifty democracies,
1948–2020 / Amory Gethin, Clara Martínez-Toledano, Thomas Piketty.
Other titles: Clivages politiques et inégalités sociales. English
Description: Cambridge, Massachusetts : Harvard University Press, 2021. |
First published in French as Clivages politiques et inégalités sociales. Une étude de
50 démocraties (1948–2020) (Paris: Les Éditions du Seuil, 2021). |
Includes bibliographical references and index.
Identifiers: LCCN 2021012242 | ISBN 9780674248427 (cloth)
Subjects: LCSH: Party affiliation—History—20th century. | Party affiliation—
History—21st century. | Equality—Political aspects—History—20th century. |
Equality—Political aspects—History—21st century. | Politics, Practical—History—
20th century. | Politics, Practical—History—21st century. | Democracy—History—
20th century. | Democracy—History—21st century.
Classification: LCC JF2071 .G4813 2021 | DDC 306.209 / 045—dc23
LC record available at https://lccn.loc.gov/2021012242

# CONTENTS

# POLITICAL CLEAVAGES AND
# SOCIAL INEQUALITIES

# Introduction

AMORY GETHIN, CLARA MARTÍNEZ-TOLEDANO, AND THOMAS PIKETTY

### Electoral Democracies, Electoral Surveys: Objectives and Methods

This volume presents the results of a collective research program on the structure of political cleavages and social inequalities in fifty electoral democracies, located on the five continents, from 1948 to 2020. The purpose of this introduction is to succinctly describe the program's objectives and methods, as well as to briefly outline the organization of the volume and its different chapters.

"Electoral democracies": this notion must immediately be clarified so as to circumscribe our object of enquiry. None of the countries studied in this book are perfect democracies, far from it, and some of them notably depart from being so, in particular when it comes to freedom of the press or to neutrality of the state in organizing electoral operations. All these countries, however, have at some point held plural and disputed elections, in the sense that the results were not entirely known in advance and could have determined access to political power. For our purpose, these elections allow us to study how different social groups have decided to cast their votes for existing parties and coalitions, thereby offering an imperfect yet tangible window on citizens' beliefs, their political and ideological visions, and the electoral choices that derive from them, given the limited options they face.

Such is, above all, the central objective of this volume: the study in a systematic manner of how electoral choices vary according to social attributes such as income, education, wealth, occupation, gender, age, national origin, or ethnoreligious identity. To do so, we have relied on a quasi-unique source: electoral surveys conducted in a number of countries that have organized plural elections since the end of World War II. These surveys, carried out on representative samples of generally a few

thousand voters, most often in the days or weeks following the corresponding election, have collected information on both respondents' electoral behaviors and their socioeconomic characteristics. In spite of their imperfections, they constitute one of the most precious sources at our disposal for studying the relationships between the structures of political cleavages and social inequalities.[1]

Thanks to the collaboration of about twenty researchers participating to this project, we have been able to assemble and exploit on a homogeneous and comparable basis nearly all electoral surveys conducted in fifty electoral democracies throughout the world from 1948 to 2020. This has allowed us to establish a global and historical mapping of the ways by which different dimensions of social inequalities are or are not, within a given party or coalition, subject to common political mobilizations.

Among the numerous questions that we have attempted to tackle is the following: to what extent are voters from underprivileged backgrounds—whether in terms of income, education, or wealth—prone to support a common electoral bloc, independent of their other characteristics such as national or regional origin or ethnoreligious identity? In other words, what is the relative importance of "class-based" and "identity-based" factors in structuring political cleavages and determining electoral behaviors? As we shall see, the answers to this question vary considerably across time and space, including within a given country. In practice, these different factors combine in multiple ways, depending on specific historical and political constructions and deconstructions, which should be analyzed as such.

Let us take an example. From the 1950s to the 1980s, the Democratic Party in the United States drew to a large extent the votes of the lower classes, regardless of the criteria adopted to define them (income, education, wealth, or occupation), and independent of their origins or racial affiliations. Over the 2000–2020 period, by contrast, lower classes belonging to Black or Latino "minorities" continue to predominantly vote for the Democratic Party, but White lower classes have clearly shifted toward the Republican Party. Another type of fragmentation also seems

---

1. These surveys are sometimes referred to as "postelectoral surveys." They generally differ from exit polls in that they are conducted some time after the election (rather than outside polling stations), collect more detailed information on the socioeconomic characteristics of voters, and have been developed by academic research centers. All details on the surveys used are provided in the different chapters of this volume.

to have occurred at the top of the social hierarchy: higher-educated voters are now strongly supportive of the Democratic Party, while those with highest levels of wealth (and to a lesser extent those with highest levels of income) continue to support the Republican Party, albeit not as clearly as they used to in the postwar era.

A somewhat comparable transformation seems to have taken place in Europe, where divides related to origins and ethnoreligious identities have recently taken unprecedented importance. As a result, European democracies are now gradually coming closer to the case of the United States, despite extremely different initial configurations, in particular regarding the historically stronger influence of "class-based" cleavages (and correlatively the weaker influence of racial and ethnoreligious divides) in Europe. On the contrary, we shall see that in other parts of the world, notably in Asia, Latin America, or Africa, the "class-based" dimension of political conflicts has in some cases intensified in recent decades. These results call into question the Western view that sometimes favors a narrow "ethnicist" vision of electoral conflicts in non-Western democracies. In reality, it is the West that appears to be undergoing a process of "ethnicization" and "tribalization," at a time where a number of other democracies are moving toward class-based conflicts. These results also and most importantly invite us to take a closer look at the programmatic and politico-ideological platforms allowing specific parties and coalitions to bring together, with varying degrees of success, voters from different origins.

It should, however, be clear that the ambition of this volume is limited and circumscribed. In no way do we pretend to explain in a perfectly convincing way *why* these different voters vote in the way they do or *the reasons* underlying the evolutions we observe. Our primary objective is modestly descriptive: we aim first and foremost to establish a number of factual regularities and transformations in the socioeconomic structure of electoral coalitions, political cleavages, and social inequalities by adopting a historical, transnational, and global perspective.

We also attempt in the chapters of this volume to analyze some of the many potential hypotheses that could explain the observed evolutions, depending on the specific contexts of each country, and following the general principle that the multiplication of case studies and comparisons can contribute to enriching our understanding of the processes at stake. We insist on the fact that the structure of political cleavages is never frozen. It evolves as the result of numerous factors, including the mobilizational strategies pursued by different political movements, which,

depending on the nature of the proffered project, may or may not succeed in gathering large coalitions of voters despite their differences.

It goes without saying that a satisfactory analysis of the conjunction of these processes, for such long periods of time and such a large number of countries, would require piecing together sources, methods, and capacities that go far beyond those mobilized in this volume. We keenly hope that the mainly descriptive and historical work proposed in this book will be used and extended by further research and discussions, so as to allow us to better understand the documented transformations. It is with this collective and participatory perspective in mind that all the data assembled in this volume have been made available to all interested readers (whether researchers, journalists or other citizens), in the form of the World Political Cleavages and Inequality Database (wpid.world).

## Organization of the Volume

Chapter 1 starts by proposing a synthesis of the main results of the different case studies. Among the fifty democracies considered (see Table 1.1), seventeen are located in Western Europe (Austria, Belgium, Denmark, Finland, France, Germany, Iceland, Ireland, Italy, Luxembourg, the Netherlands, Norway, Portugal, Spain, Sweden, Switzerland, and the United Kingdom), three are in postcommunist Eastern Europe (the Czech Republic, Hungary, and Poland), four are in North America and Oceania (Australia, Canada, New Zealand, and the United States), ten are in Asia (Hong Kong, India, Indonesia, Japan, Malaysia, Pakistan, the Philippines, South Korea, Taiwan, and Thailand), seven are in Latin America (Argentina, Brazil, Chile, Colombia, Costa Rica, Mexico, and Peru), and nine are in Africa and the Middle East (Algeria, Botswana, Ghana, Iraq, Israel, Nigeria, Senegal, South Africa, and Turkey). Our choice to study these countries has mainly been dictated by the availability of sufficiently rich electoral surveys, with well enough preserved and documented files, to allow for satisfactory exploitation and homogeneous cross-country comparisons.

The following chapters expose in greater detail the results obtained by approximately following this geographical order. Chapter 2 analyzes the cases of France, the United States, and the United Kingdom, revealing important commonalities between these three countries, notably the reversal of the educational cleavage, the emergence of "multi-elite" party systems, and the evolution of identity-based cleavages in the past decades. The next chapters evaluate to what extent this general scheme applies to

4

other Western democracies. Chapter 3 examines the case of Germany. Chapter 4 delves into the trajectories of northern countries (Denmark, Finland, Iceland, Norway, and Sweden). Chapter 5 studies the similarities and specificities of the dynamics observed in Australia, Canada, and New Zealand. Chapter 6 is dedicated to the cases of Italy, Spain, Portugal, and Ireland. Chapter 7 focuses on the transformations visible in Austria, Belgium, the Netherlands, and Switzerland. Despite noticeable differences between these countries, this exploration of political cleavages in Western democracies (Europe, North America, and Oceania) suggests relatively similar evolutions to those observed in France, the United States, and the United Kingdom.

Chapter 8 broadens the perspective by studying three countries of postcommunist Eastern Europe (the Czech Republic, Hungary, and Poland), unveiling specific yet informative structures of political cleavages, characterized in particular by the nearly complete disappearance of social democratic and socialist parties.

Chapter 9 enlarges even further the perspective by considering the case of India. As the world's largest democracy, with a number of voters exceeding the cumulated total of all the abovementioned countries, India provides a useful counterpoint to the democracies studied in previous chapters. We shall see, for instance, that in contrast to what we observe with increasing clarity in Europe and the United States, lower classes from majority (Hindus) and minority (Muslims) ethnoreligious groups are still inclined to vote for the same parties and coalitions in India. Chapter 10 turns to the case of Pakistan, where the politicization of ethnolinguistic divides and social inequalities has taken equally specific and varying forms. Chapter 11 documents the evolution of electoral divides in Japan, notably insisting on the historical role of the rural-urban cleavage and on the exceptional weakening of class cleavages in recent years. Chapter 12, dedicated to Thailand, the Philippines, Malaysia, and Indonesia, investigates how the structure of regional and ethnic inequalities has contributed to generate diverse and evolving forms of class divides. Chapter 13 compares the cases of South Korea, Hong Kong, and Taiwan, focusing on the articulation between socioeconomic cleavages and diverging attitudes toward the North Korean (South Korea) and Chinese (Hong Kong and Taiwan) regimes.

Chapter 14 examines the case of Brazil and documents a remarkable intensification of class cleavages in the past decades, in the context of the new post-dictatorship democratic system. The Brazilian example

illustrates the role played by the concrete implementation of public policies in fostering class-based electoral divides. Chapter 15 proposes a comparative analysis of several other Latin American countries (Argentina, Chile, Colombia, Costa Rica, Mexico, and Peru), insisting in particular on the interaction between class cleavages, ethnic cleavages, and the personalization of electoral politics.

Chapter 16 is dedicated to the structure of political cleavages in South Africa, in a context marked by extreme racial inequalities but where the politicization of inequalities beyond race has been slowly gaining traction. Chapter 17 studies the processes underlying the political representation of social inequalities and ethnic cleavages in Botswana, Ghana, Nigeria, and Senegal. Unlike what common stereotypes suggest, class-based cleavages appear to some extent in the course of emerging in Africa, in particular in Botswana and Nigeria. Chapter 18 analyzes the transformation of the structure of political cleavages in Israel. Chapter 19 investigates the formation of sociopolitical cleavages in Algeria, Iraq, and Turkey, insisting on the diverse and changing relationships between religious and class mobilizations. It should be stressed that the lack of historical depth and the insufficiencies of available electoral surveys considerably limit the scope of the analyses that can be developed in African and Middle Eastern countries. Nevertheless, we considered it essential to include them in our inquiry to illustrate the specific forms taken by the interactions between political cleavages and social inequalities in these different contexts.

Finally, a brief Conclusion recalls some of the key lessons of this volume and more importantly outlines a number of prospects for future research.

# 1

# Political Cleavages and Social Inequalities in Fifty Democracies, 1948–2020

AMORY GETHIN, CLARA MARTÍNEZ-TOLEDANO, AND THOMAS PIKETTY

## Introduction

Income and wealth inequalities have increased substantially in many regions of the world since the 1980s. This evolution came after a relatively egalitarian period from 1950 to 1980, accompanied by inclusive growth and the expansion of welfare states. Yet, this reversal has not led to widespread demands for redistribution or the revival of class conflicts. The past decades have seen instead the rise of various forms of identity-based politics, embodied by the Brexit vote and the success of xenophobic parties in Europe, Donald Trump in the United States, Jair Bolsonaro in Brazil, and Narendra Modi in India. What explains this remarkable transformation? Why have so many democracies left growing inequalities unchecked and shifted to debates over immigration, national identity, and integration?

This chapter attempts to make some progress in answering these questions by studying the interplay between social inequalities and the long-run evolution of political cleavages in fifty democracies. Drawing on a new dataset of electoral surveys spanning more than six decades, we document how the link between electoral attitudes and the main socioeconomic characteristics of voters varies across countries and over time. This analysis and this new harmonized database serve as a basis for a comparative approach of the politicization of social inequalities, focusing on how political movements have represented different types of conflicts over

We are grateful to Harry Blain, Javier Padilla, and Juliet-Nil Uraz for their useful comments on this chapter. Some of the results presented in this chapter are based on A. Gethin, C. Martínez-Toledano, and T. Piketty, "Brahmin Left versus Merchant Right: Changing Political Cleavages in 21 Western Democracies, 1948–2020," Working Paper, 2021.

inequality and identity. This chapter provides an overview of the main findings of this volume, contrasting the conclusions of its different case studies and drawing parallels between the varieties of electoral regimes it covers. Our full database and all our results are publicly available at http://wpid.world (World Political Cleavages and Inequality Database).

In the first section of this chapter, we start by justifying the interest in linking political cleavages to inequality. Numerous studies have documented how processes of political representation can have major economic and social consequences. Inequalities in political participation, influence, and political finance are well-known mechanisms by which citizens' interests are unequally represented in the electoral arena. The relative salience of distributional issues in the public debate, as well as their intersection with other axes of political conflict, have also been found to matter significantly in shaping political actors' incentives to reduce income and wealth disparities. Nevertheless, few studies have attempted to adopt a global comparative and historical perspective on the interaction between various dimensions of political conflicts and inequality in contemporary democracies. This, we argue, requires turning to the study of political cleavages, which has been the object of considerable research in political science. By bringing new data and new perspectives on the link between inequality and political cleavages, we hope that we can provide novel insights into these two fields of research.

We then turn to outlining the general framework of this volume. In contrast to existing studies focusing on occupation to understand the dynamics of class cleavages, most chapters in this volume are centered on two vertical measures of social inequality, income and education. These two criteria—to which one should add wealth, although existing electoral surveys measure it in only a limited number of countries—have the advantage of being easier to compare between countries and over time. We then propose to study how these two variables have structured political cleavages in comparative and historical perspective, and how other forms of political conflicts have interacted with class divides. To do so, we consider in turn how income and education, religious affiliations, sociocultural identities, rural-urban and spatial inequalities, gender, and generational experiences have differentially shaped political conflicts and inequality in the democracies covered by our dataset.

Our results reveal a striking transformation of the link between income, education, and the vote in Western democracies. From the 1950s to the 1980s, Western party systems were "class-based" in the sense that

social democratic, socialist, democratic, labor, communist, and green parties (a group of parties commonly classified as "left-wing," but which we prefer to refer to as "social democratic" in a broader sense, or by their exact denominations) attracted a significant share of the low-income and lower-educated electorate. By contrast, conservative, republican, Christian democratic, liberal, or nationalist parties (commonly classified as "right-wing," but which we prefer to refer to as "conservative" in a broader sense, or by their exact denominations) obtained better results among high-income and higher-educated voters.[1] As higher-educated voters gradually shifted toward social democratic and affiliated parties, these systems have become "multi-elite party systems," in which conservative parties now represent high-income voters, while social democratic parties have become the new parties of higher-educated voters. This transformation has significantly weakened the political representation of class conflicts, as mirrored by the declining relationship between individuals' self-perceived positions in the social hierarchy and their political behaviors. Such disconnection between the politicization of education and income appears to be rare in comparative and historical perspective, but we document substantial variations in the strength of educational and income divides across contemporary democracies. These variations mirror a variety of modalities of class representation, which we propose to link to the strength of other existing cleavages and to their interaction with the structure of social inequalities and professional careers, which have themselves undergone profound transformations. Among these transformations are the rise of tertiary education and the concomitant development of aspirations and careers not directly oriented toward monetary gain (including occupations related to education, culture, and health), which now coexist with occupations more directly oriented toward for-profit activities but also sometimes relying on higher education (including business, real estate, and finance).

Religious divisions have historically been strong cross-cutting cleavages in Western democracies, splitting voters with similar class profiles along religious lines. We document a high persistence of these divides,

---

1. In the context of this book, we try to avoid as much as possible the polysemic expressions of "left" and "right," whose meanings, political use, and ideological content vary substantially across countries, time periods, and languages. When we do use these terms, we take care to explicitly define the specific, historically situated parties, movements, and political organizations to which we are referring.

with religious voters continuing to be significantly more likely to vote for conservative parties than nonreligious voters, although the past decades have seen their influence wane. Our dataset also reveals the existence of important religious-secular cleavages in other regions of the world. In Latin America, nonreligious voters have been significantly more likely to vote for left-wing parties (or parties commonly designated as such), but the influence of religion is weaker in countries with class-based party systems such as Argentina and Brazil. Muslim-majority countries such as Turkey, Pakistan, and Indonesia also display significant religious divides, with religious minorities and nonreligious citizens being substantially more likely to vote for historically secular parties. India is the country where religious polarization has intensified the most, driven by the rise of Hindu nationalism. At the same time, disadvantaged Hindu and Muslim voters continue to vote for the same parties and coalitions, indicating that the identity dimension has not yet overcome the class dimension, in contrast to what we observe to some extent in Western democracies.

Sociocultural identities, whether linked to national origins, language, or ethnicity, represent major sources of political conflicts in contemporary democracies. Consistently with the growing salience of issues related to immigration and the integration of new minorities, we find that immigrants are significantly more likely to vote for left-wing parties (social democratic in a broad sense) in Western countries today. This gap is exceptionally pronounced in the case of Muslim voters. It is also higher in countries with significant far-right parties, which points to the role of political actors in shaping identity-based conflicts. Turning to a broader comparison of the votes of religious, ethnic, and racial minorities, we find particularly strong cleavages in the cases of Black voters in the United States, Muslim voters in India, Maori voters in New Zealand, and Kurdish voters in Turkey. In countries with particularly high ethnic diversity and ethnic inequalities such as South Africa, Pakistan, and Nigeria, we document a systematic alignment of ethnic cleavages and class cleavages, pointing to the role of ethnic disparities in fostering both ethnic conflicts and the emergence of class-based party systems.

Spatial and rural-urban inequalities also matter significantly in structuring political conflicts. Rural areas have consistently been more likely to vote for conservative parties in Western democracies. As rural areas tend to be poorer, the rural-urban cleavage has also historically weakened class divides. In most non-Western democracies, by contrast, we find

that parties bringing together the low-income and lower-educated electorate tend to perform better in rural areas. This is especially the case with one-party dominant systems (systems in which opposition parties do not have a realistic chance of winning elections against the ruling party in the short run), where incumbents tend to rely on rural clientelistic networks to ensure reelection. Beyond the rural-urban dichotomy, we find that regional cleavages are strongest in countries with high ethnic diversity, a clustering of ethnic groups by region, and/or sharp regional inequalities. In many democracies, including India, Pakistan, and Turkey, these cleavages have steadily deepened in the past decades. Western democracies have also seen the rise of powerful regional separatist movements. These movements have been supported by high-income voters in Belgium (Flanders) and Spain (Catalonia) and by low-income voters in Canada (Québec) and the United Kingdom (Scotland), pointing to the role of both ideological legacies and socioeconomic interests in shaping independentism.

Diverging generational experiences have also been sources of political differentiation in many contemporary democracies. Contrary to a commonly held view, however, we do not find evidence of a rise in left-right generational divides in Western democracies. While green parties do consistently attract younger voters, the age profile of far-right voting has been highly variable, and anti-immigration movements have attracted significant support from younger cohorts in Austria, France, Finland, and Spain. Dominant-party systems often present strong generational divides, as growing opposition to the dominant party tends to be concentrated among the urban, educated youth. The democracies where we observe some of the strongest generational cleavages are those where conflicts over foreign policy and political integration have been the most salient, including the United Kingdom with the Brexit vote, Taiwan and Hong Kong with voters' attitudes to mainland China, and South Korea with citizens' diverging positions on relationships to the North Korean regime. Generational conflicts tend to inhibit class divides, as age is only a weak predictor of socioeconomic status.

Finally, we document a complete reversal of the vote of women in Western democracies, who used to be closer to conservative and religious movements and have gradually become significantly more likely to vote for social democratic parties (in a broad sense). This transition was reinforced by secularization in Catholic countries and the concentration of

women in the public sector in Northern Europe. We find much more variable patterns in non-Western democracies, suggesting that candidate effects and supply-driven dynamics may be more relevant in determining the politicization of gender issues.

In summary, our analysis suggests that socioeconomic factors matter substantially, but that these factors are crucially conditioned by the interaction between social inequalities and the politicization of social identities. This calls for a renewed perspective on the way party systems contribute to representing or obliterating class conflicts, at the intersection of contingent events and long-run historical trajectories. We hope that our new database and the framework we propose will open new avenues for future research on the link between political cleavages and socioeconomic inequalities.

## Democracy and the Politics of Inequality

A large and growing body of social science research has aimed to understand how political factors can affect the distribution of economic resources in democracies. Another area of study, more specific to political science and electoral sociology and following the pioneering work of Lipset and Rokkan, has sought to analyze how social conflicts give rise to political cleavages and how elections allow, or on the contrary obliterate, the representation of these cleavages. This section briefly surveys some key studies and brings together these two strands of research, which motivate the underlying framework of this volume.

### Why Do the Poor Not Expropriate the Rich in Democracies?

According to a simplistic vision of political conflict, sometimes adopted by some economists, electoral cleavages could be reduced to an antagonism between rich and poor, with the implication that the former would risk being expropriated at any time by the latter. This fear, a recurring theme of philosophical debate since antiquity and recently revisited by contemporary politico-economic analysis,[2] synthesizes an obvious yet complex fact. In a perfectly democratic world, in which voters with different income levels would vote over a single tax rate and redistribute government revenue in a way benefiting the poorest individuals, any increase in inequality should lead a majority of citizens to support higher

2. J. E. Roemer, "Why the Poor Do Not Expropriate the Rich: An Old Argument in New Garb," *Journal of Public Economics* 70, no. 3 (1998): 399–424.

redistribution.[3] Why, then, have growing inequalities been left unchecked in many democracies in the past decades? At least three dimensions to this problem have been considered by existing studies.

COLLECTIVE BELIEFS. First, citizens may not always be favorable to reducing socioeconomic inequalities, even when it is in their immediate economic interest. A large body of literature has accordingly studied how "preferences for redistribution" contribute to explaining variations in inequalities and redistribution.[4] Perceptions of expected social mobility, for instance, may lead individuals to be against higher taxation of top incomes if they believe that they will soon climb the social ladder. Diverging beliefs over the relative importance of "effort" versus "luck" in determining income could thus contribute to explaining differences in redistribution across countries, in particular between the United States and Western Europe.[5]

UNEQUAL POLITICAL REPRESENTATION. Even if a majority of citizens believe that inequality should be tackled, however, this is no guarantee that existing political institutions will respond accordingly. In fact, there is little evidence that existing taxes and transfers correspond to citizens' aspirations: in many affluent democracies, a majority of individuals declare that they would favor higher welfare spending, a gap that has been coined the "social welfare deficit."[6] Numerous political science studies have accordingly shifted from studying collective beliefs to analyzing the political representation of these beliefs. There is extensive evidence that contemporary democratic politics are characterized by unequal representation. Wealthy individuals, through political finance, lobbying, or other modalities of influence, have a substantially higher impact on political decision-making than average citizens.[7] Political inequality is also strongly

3. A. H. Meltzer and S. F. Richard, "A Rational Theory of the Size of Government," *Journal of Political Economy* 85, no. 5 (1981): 914–927.

4. For a review, see, for instance, N. McCarty and J. Pontusson, "The Political Economy of Inequality and Redistribution," in *Handbook on Economic Inequality,* ed. B. Nolan, W. Salverda, and T. M. Smeeding (Oxford University Press, 2012), 665–692.

5. T. Piketty, "Social Mobility and Redistributive Politics," *Quarterly Journal of Economics* 110, no. 3 (1995): 551–584; A. Alesina, S. Stantcheva, and E. Teso, "Intergenerational Mobility and Preferences for Redistribution," *American Economic Review* 108, no. 2 (2018): 521–554.

6. L. M. Bartels, "Political Inequality in Affluent Democracies: The Social Welfare Deficit" (working paper 5-2017, Center for the Study of Democratic Institutions, Vanderbilt University).

7. Among numerous studies, see, for instance, J. Cagé, *The Price of Democracy: How Money Shapes Politics and What to Do about It* (Harvard University Press, 2020); T. K.

tied to political participation. When low-income or lower-educated voters do not vote, election candidates have weaker incentives to cater to their needs and, as a result, curtail social transfers and other redistribution mechanisms.[8]

Unequal representation also influences directly political parties' electoral strategies and political programs. Social democratic parties tend to shift to the left on economic matters when inequality increases, but only in cases where voter turnout is sufficiently high.[9] Relatedly, there is evidence that left-wing parties may in some cases reduce their efforts to mobilize low-income voters when income disparities increase.[10] Rising economic inequality, disillusionment with the political process among popular classes, and parties' subsequent detachment from low-income voters may thus generate self-reinforcing cycles of inequality and exclusion.[11]

---

Kuhner, *Capitalism v. Democracy: Money in Politics and the Free Market Constitution* (Stanford Law Books, 2014); M. Gilens, *Affluence and Influence: Economic Inequality and Political Power in America* (Princeton University Press, 2012); M. Gilens and B. I. Page, "Testing Theories of American Politics: Elites, Interest Groups, and Average Citizens," *Perspectives on Politics* 12, no. 3 (2014): 564–581; K. L. Scholzman, S. Verba, and H. E. Brady, *The Unheavenly Chorus: Unequal Political Voice and the Broken Promise of American Democracy* (Princeton University Press, 2012); M. Bertrand, M. Bombardini, R. Fisman, and F. Trebbi, "Tax-Exempt Lobbying: Corporate Philanthropy as a Tool for Political Influence," *American Economic Review* 110, no. 7 (2020): 2065–2102; A. Bonica, N. McCarty, K. T. Poole, and H. Rosenthal, "Why Hasn't Democracy Slowed Rising Inequality?," *Journal of Economic Perspectives* 27, no. 3, (2013): 103–124.

8. S. Ellingsen and Ø. Hernæs, "The Impact of Commercial Television on Turnout and Public Policy: Evidence from Norwegian Local Politics," *Journal of Public Economics* 159 (2018): 1–15; A. Gavazza, M. Nardotto, and T. Valletti, "Internet and Politics: Evidence from U.K. Local Elections and Local Government Policies," *Review of Economic Studies* 86, no. 5 (2019): 2092–2135; E. U. Cascio and E. Washington, "Valuing the Vote: The Redistribution of Voting Rights and State Funds following the Voting Rights Act of 1965," *Quarterly Journal of Economics* 129, no. 1 (2014): 379–433; T. Fujiwara, "Voting Technology, Political Responsiveness, and Infant Health: Evidence from Brazil," *Econometrica* 83, no. 2 (2015): 423–464; F. F. Piven, *Why Americans Don't Vote* (Pantheon, 1988).

9. J. Pontusson and D. Rueda, "The Politics of Inequality: Voter Mobilization and Left Parties in Advanced Industrial States," *Comparative Political Studies* 43, no. 6 (2010): 675–705.

10. C. J. Anderson and P. Beramendi, "Left Parties, Poor Voters, and Electoral Participation in Advanced Industrial Societies," *Comparative Political Studies* 45, no. 6 (2012): 714–746; E. Barth, H. Finseraas, and K. O. Moene, "Political Reinforcement: How Rising Inequality Curbs Manifested Welfare Generosity," *American Journal of Political Science* 59, no. 3 (2015): 565–577.

11. T. Iversen and D. Soskice, "Information, Inequality, and Mass Polarization: Ideology in Advanced Democracies," *Comparative Political Studies* 48, no. 13 (2013): 1781–1813.

INEQUALITY, IDEOLOGY, AND MULTIDIMENSIONAL POLITICS. Parties and coalitions, finally, do more than mechanically translate interests: they are active actors of political change, who may undergo ideological transformations at least partly independent from those experienced by the electorate. Processes of global ideological diffusion, visible for instance in the rise and fall of tax progressivity in many Western and non-Western countries over the course of the twentieth century,[12] should not be understated. This relates to a literature in political science on the role of "political supply," to which we will return below.

Most importantly in the context of this volume, economic issues are not the only ones that matter. Political conflicts have always been much more complex, involving divergent visions over sociocultural values, social progress, and political integration. This multidimensionality of politics has concrete consequences. Rising inequality may lead conservative parties to put greater emphasis on identity-based conflicts, in the hope of attracting voters otherwise favorable to parties oriented further to the left on economic issues.[13] Conflicts over the integration of minorities or immigration, especially if they create divisions within popular classes, can even lead to strategic proposals for lesser redistribution from all parties, including social democratic parties (in a broad sense) constrained to diversify their voting base.[14] This has been a classic explanation of differences between the United States and Western Europe: racial conflicts in the United States, by reducing solidarity, would have eroded mass support for the welfare state.[15]

### From Political Inequality to Political Cleavages

All the evidence at our disposal therefore suggests that political representation matters substantially for democracy and inequality. To understand how politics can influence inequality, we therefore need to better understand how parties interact with voters, and how social conflicts are expressed in the democratic arena. To do so, we need to turn more

---

12. F. Alvaredo, L. Chancel, T. Piketty, E. Saez, and G. Zucman, *World Inequality Report 2018* (Harvard University Press, 2018).

13. M. Tavits and J. D. Potter, "The Effect of Inequality and Social Identity on Party Strategies," *American Journal of Political Science* 59, no. 3 (2015): 744–758.

14. J. E. Roemer, W. Lee, and K. Van der Straeten, *Racism, Xenophobia, and Distribution: Multi-Issue Politics in Advanced Democracies* (Harvard University Press, 2007).

15. A. Alesina and E. Glaeser, *Fighting Poverty in the US and Europe: A World of Difference* (Oxford University Press, 2004).

specifically to the study of political cleavages, which has been the object of considerable research in political science.

DEFINING POLITICAL CLEAVAGES. The modern concept of political cleavage originates in Seymour Martin Lipset and Stein Rokkan's seminal study on the historical formation of party systems in Europe.[16] Lipset and Rokkan argued that four types of fundamental divisions had emerged from the national and industrial revolutions. First, a *center-periphery cleavage,* triggered by the process of nation building, materialized from oppositions between the nascent state and the diverse subject populations subdued by the central authority. Second, a *religious cleavage* developed from the conflict between the nation-state and the church, as the latter gradually lost its ability to exert political power. The Industrial Revolution, finally, was associated with the emergence of two other types of enduring conflicts: a *sectoral cleavage* between opposing agricultural and industrial interests, and a *class cleavage* setting capital owners against workers.

More generally, the Rokkanian concept of political cleavage refers to "a specific type of conflict in democratic politics that is rooted in the social structural transformations that have been triggered by large-scale processes such as nation building, industrialization, and possibly also by the consequences of post-industrialization."[17] While this conception leaves a certain degree of flexibility, it involves dimensions of political conflict that are durable, originated in large historical changes, and are not necessarily still linked to the events that initiated them. This "hysteresis" property was directly visible in the remarkable stability of Western democracies across the twentieth century: the original divides associated with the emergence of democratic competition led to the "freezing" of Western party systems. Stefano Bartolini and Peter Mair thus proposed to define a political cleavage by three necessary components: an observable characteristic distinguishing individuals (such as class or religion), a sense of collective identity linking this characteristic to a specific social group, and an organizational manifestation of this group, translating this identity into collective action.[18]

16. S. M. Lipset and S. Rokkan, *Cleavage Structures, Party Systems, and Voter Alignments: An Introduction* (Free Press, 1967).

17. S. Bornschier, "Cleavage Politics in Old and New Democracies," *Living Reviews in Democracy* 1 (2009).

18. S. Bartolini and P. Mair, *Identity, Competition and Electoral Availability: The Stabilisation of European Electorates 1885–1985* (Cambridge University Press, 1990).

Clearly, the concept of cleavage is of the utmost relevance for understanding the political representation of social inequalities. It encompasses both the mobilization of different social groups in defending their interests and the mediation of these interests by political parties in democratic elections. This allows us to go beyond contingent explanations of the link between politics and inequality and to understand political change with a much larger comparative and historical scope.

DEALIGNMENT AND REALIGNMENT IN WESTERN DEMOCRACIES. Political scientists have dedicated tremendous efforts to documenting the transformation of political cleavages in Western democracies. The systematic collection of dedicated postelectoral surveys gave rise to the multiplication of "voter studies" aiming at measuring the drivers of electoral behaviors across countries and over time.[19] While it would be impossible to summarize all the contributions of this literature here, several key results are worth mentioning.

On the one hand, existing studies have documented a gradual weakening of historical cleavages in many Western democracies, or *dealignment*. As secularization, urbanization, the decline of trade unions, and the tertiarization of the economy unfolded in the decades following World War II, traditional class and religious affiliations were found to have lost much of their original sway. The Alford index (attributed to the work of sociologist Robert Alford),[20] defined as the difference between the share of the "working class" (blue-collar and other manual workers) and the share of the "middle class" (non-manual wage earners and self-employed voters) voting for social democratic parties (in a broad sense), has collapsed in the majority of Western democracies in the past decades.[21] More generally, there is extensive evidence that standard measures of class or religion have lost much of their ability to predict individuals' vote

19. Seminal works include A. Campbell, P. E. Converse, W. E. Miller, and D. E. Stokes, *The American Voter* (University of Chicago Press, 1960); and D. Butler and D. Stokes, *Political Change in Britain: Forces Shaping Electoral Choice* (St. Martin's Press, 1969). Many others are cited in the case studies of this volume.

20. R. Alford, *Party and Society: The Anglo-American Democracies* (Rand McNally, 1963).

21. T. Clark, S. M. Lipset, and M. Rempel, "The Declining Political Significance of Social Class," *International Sociology* 8, no. 3 (1993): 293–316; R. Inglehart, *Modernization and Postmodernization: Cultural, Eonomic, and Political Change in 43 Societies* (Princeton University Press, 1997); S. Bartolini, *The Political Mobilization of the European Left, 1860–1980* (Cambridge University Press, 2000).

choices.[22] In many cases, the decline of party identification, the rise of undecided voters, and the growing influence of short-run campaign factors and candidate appeals have accompanied this transition.[23]

On the other hand, a growing body of evidence has revealed a *realignment* of voters toward new dimensions of political conflicts. Starting in the 1960s and 1970s, new sociocultural issues related to gender equality, the rights of minorities, and the environment took on a growing importance in political debates. Green parties and the "New Left," who were the first to put these issues at the center of their political agenda, embodied the rise of this new cleavage. Ronald Inglehart argued in this context that a "silent revolution" had been on its way in Western societies: unprecedented levels of affluence were changing the political priorities of new generations from "materialism" to "post-materialism."[24] As a result of these changes, the political space of Western democracies was found to have gradually shifted from materializing one to two dominant dimensions: a socioeconomic dimension, reflecting the persistence of conflicts over the distribution of economic resources, and a new "libertarian-authoritarian" or "universalistic-particularistic" dimension, related to preferences over group identity and cultural values.[25] For many analysts, the recent rise of far-right and anti-immigration movements has represented a conservative response to these sociopolitical changes.[26]

The emergence of this new cleavage does not mean the end of class conflicts. Class cleavages have not disappeared; they have undergone a deep

22. M. Franklin, T. Hackie, H. Valen, et al., *Electoral Change: Responses to Evolving Attitudinal Structures in Western Countries* (Cambridge University Press, 1992).

23. R. J. Dalton and M. P. Wattenberg, *Parties without Partisans: Political Change in Advanced Industrial Democracies* (Oxford University Press, 2002); R. J. Dalton, S. C. Flanagan, P. A. Beck, and J. E. Alt, *Electoral Change in Advanced Industrial Democracies: Realignment or Dealignment?* (Princeton University Press, 1984); D. Denver and I. Crewe, *Electoral Change in Western Democracies: Patterns and Sources of Electoral Volatility* (Croom Helm, 1985).

24. R. Inglehart, *The Silent Revolution: Changing Values and Political Styles among Western Publics* (Princeton University Press, 1977).

25. H. Kitschelt, *The Transformation of European Social Democracy* (Cambridge University Press, 1994); H. Kriesi, E. Grande, R. Lachat, M. Dolezal, S. Bornschier, and T. Frey, *West European Politics in the Age of Globalization* (Cambridge University Press, 2008); R. J. Dalton, *Political Realignment: Economics, Culture, and Electoral Change* (Oxford University Press, 2018).

26. S. Bornschier, *Cleavage Politics and the Populist Right* (Temple University Press, 2010); P. Norris and R. Inglehart, *Cultural Backlash: Trump, Brexit, and Authoritarian Populism* (Cambridge University Press, 2019).

process of restructuration. The New Left and Green parties have attracted an increasing share of "sociocultural professionals," a broad category of highly educated workers involved in interactive and nonhierarchical tasks, including health care, social services, and the media. Blue-collar workers, meanwhile, have in many countries shifted away from social democratic, socialist, and communist parties to become the new core supporters of the far right.[27]

To what extent was this remarkable transformation inevitable? A number of studies have attempted to move beyond "demand factors," understood as the set of values held by citizens and shaping social conflicts, to the role of "supply"—that is the ways by which parties *represent* and *construct* political cleavages.[28] Geoffrey Evans and James Tilley notably documented how the decline of class voting in Britain could be attributed to a remarkable depoliticization of class, as the Labour Party and mainstream media gradually shifted to deemphasizing working-class issues, despite huge continuity in class divisions and inequalities in British society.[29] The emergence of a new sociocultural dimension of political conflicts has actively contributed to this transformation, leading some observers to conclude that "class is not dead: it has been buried alive."[30]

These results point to a broader fact: despite the multidimensionality inherent to electoral politics, not all social conflicts are politicized. In contexts of instability or democratic transitions, in particular, parties emerge and come to structure the political space in a limited number of fundamental elections. Some social cleavages can then become entirely obliterated for long periods of time, while others become the dividing points

27. D. Oesch, *Redrawing the Class Map: Stratification and Institutions in Britain, Germany, Sweden and Switzerland* (Palgrave Macmillan, 2006); D. Oesch, "The Class Basis of the Cleavage between the New Left and the Radical Right: An Analysis for Austria, Denmark, Norway and Switzerland," in *Class Politics and the Radical Right,* ed. J. Rydgren (Routledge, 2012), 31–51; S. Bornschier, "The Populist Right, the Working Class, and the Changing Face of Class Politics," in Rydgren, *Class Politics and the Radical Right,* 10–30; P. Beramendi, S. Häusermann, H. Kitschelt, and H. Kriesi, eds., *The Politics of Advanced Capitalism* (Cambridge University Press, 2015).

28. G. Evans and N. D. De Graaf, eds., *Political Choice Matters: Explaining the Strength of Class and Religious Cleavages in Cross-National Perspective* (Oxford University Press, 2013).

29. G. Evans and J. Tilley, *The New Politics of Class: The Political Exclusion of the British Working Class* (Oxford University Press, 2017).

30. J. van der Waal, P. Achterberg, and D. Houtman, "Class Is Not Dead—It Has Been Buried Alive: Class Voting and Cultural Voting in Postwar Western Societies (1956–1990)," *Politics and Society* 35, no. 3 (2007): 403–426.

between parties and voters.[31] Critical junctures and slow processes of realignment thus represent the two forces underlying the "freezing" and "unfreezing" of political systems in contemporary democracies.

### Political Cleavages in Non-Western Democracies

We have already shown how complex it is to analyze the relationship between political parties and their social base in Western democracies. In non-Western countries, this analysis is even more complicated, as the quality of data available is scarce, political parties are often weakly institutionalized, and electoral volatility can be exceptionally high.[32] Institutionalization tends to be especially weak in countries that have gone through long periods of authoritarian rule, even if this depends partly on the strategies chosen by incumbent rulers to maintain power during the initial stages of democratic opening.[33] Furthermore, institutionalization is not necessarily indicative of democratic quality: some of Asia's most institutionalized party systems, such as those of Malaysia or Singapore, are also those where democratic accountability is the weakest.[34] Global ideological shifts, such as the neoliberal turn in Latin America in the 1980s or in the Middle East in the 1990s, can also have dramatic consequences on political stability, power allocation between economic and political actors, and the materialization of class-based party systems.[35]

Many studies analyzing the relationship between political parties and society in Western democracies use as a reference the Lipset and Rokkan model we have introduced above. The question is then whether this model can be useful to understand this relationship in non-Western democracies. Recent studies argue that it is a useful point of departure but that it needs to be extended to capture specific features of new democracies. This implies going beyond the focus on national and industrial revolutions,

31. J. Zielinski, "Translating Social Cleavages into Party Systems: The Significance of New Democracies," *World Politics* 54, no. 2 (2002): 184–211.

32. V. Randall and L. Svåsand, "Party Institutionalization in New Democracies," *Party Politics* 8, no. 1 (2002): 5–29.

33. R. S. Katz and W. J. Crotty, *Handbook of Party Politics* (Sage, 2006); R. B. Riedl, *Authoritarian Origins of Democratic Party Systems in Africa* (Cambridge University Press, 2014).

34. A. Hicken and E. M. Kuhonta, *Party System Institutionalization in Asia: Democracies, Autocracies, and the Shadows of the Past* (Cambridge University Press, 2014).

35. K. Roberts, *Changing Course in Latin America: Party Systems in the Neoliberal Era* (Cambridge University Press, 2014); M. Cammett, I. Diwan, A. Richards, and J. Waterbury, *A Political Economy of the Middle East* (Western Press, 2015).

which in many cases have either not occurred or have not been politicized by existing parties.[36] It also requires reconsidering the concept of cleavage itself, especially in democracies where party-voter linkages are weak. As Andreas Ufen noted when attempting to apply the Lipset-Rokkan model to Indonesian politics, "Cleavages are to a certain extent a given, but also formed by political actors; and the parties that articulate these cleavages are not necessarily European mass integration parties."[37]

Studying electoral divides in non-Western democracies thus involves extending the scope of the analysis beyond Lipset and Rokkan's four traditional cleavages. In particular, church-state and center-periphery cleavages need to be extended to include competing confessional parties and ethnoregional conflicts (which, it should be noted, also exist in Western democracies). Another important source of identification emerged from the division between the oppressed nation and the imperial power, which was behind the emergence of national liberation movements and led to the creation of powerful parties in Latin America, Sub-Saharan Africa, and Asia at the time of decolonization. With high levels of industrialization and urbanization and the important influence of the Roman Catholic Church, Latin America is often considered the region that most closely resembles the Lipsen and Rokkan model.[38] In Africa, ethnic divides, valence issues, and candidate effects have in many cases been found to be more salient than class.[39] In many democracies, clientelism also plays a major role in shaping electoral behaviors, often (though not always) at the expense of political programs and ideology.[40]

In summary, studying the politicization of social inequalities in both Western and non-Western democracies requires rethinking class analysis to consider how other variables, related for instance to ethnicity or

36. Bornschier, "Cleavage Politics."

37. A. Ufen, "Lipset and Rokkan in Southeast Asia: Indonesia in Comparative Perspective," in *Party Politics in Southeast Asia: Clientelism and Electoral Competition in Indonesia, Thailand and the Philippines*, ed. D. Tomsa and A. Ufen (Routledge, 2013), 40–61.

38. Katz and Crotty, *Handbook of Party Politics*.

39. J. Bleck and N. van de Walle, *Electoral Politics in Africa since 1990: Continuity and Change* (Cambridge University Press, 2018).

40. H. Kitschelt and S. I. Wilkinson, eds., *Patrons, Clients and Policies: Patterns of Democratic Accountability and Political Competition* (Cambridge University Press, 2007); S. C. Stokes, T. Dunning, M. Nazareno, and V. Brusco, *Brokers, Voters, and Clientelism: The Puzzle of Distributive Politics* (Cambridge University Press, 2014); E. Kramon, *Money for Votes: The Causes and Consequences of Electoral Clientelism in Africa* (Cambridge University Press, 2017).

regional affiliations, contribute to shape electoral behaviors and interact with socioeconomic concerns. This is what we contribute to undertaking in this volume, by systematically analyzing the roles played by income, education, and other sociopolitical identities in generating durable electoral divides.

## Conceptual Framework and Data Sources

Having reviewed some key areas of previous research, we are now in a position to ask our main research question: What are the factors underlying the politicization of social inequalities in democracies? Our objective is not to provide a definite answer to this problem, but rather to document as precisely as possible the interaction between inequality and political cleavages in comparative and historical perspective. To do so, we introduce the general framework and the dataset underlying our work.

### Inequality and Social Class

Understanding the link between political cleavages and social inequalities involves studying how economic, social, and cultural resources influence voting behaviors. It thus requires adopting a practical definition of *social class*. When studying class, the vast majority of studies in political science have relied on occupation, and for good reason. The class cleavages that emerged in Western countries at the turn of the twentieth century were not, as is sometimes incorrectly said, divisions between the "rich" and the "poor." Social democratic and socialist parties originating from the labor movement attracted mostly blue-collar and other manual workers, but failed to gain support from poor farmers and the self-employed. Researchers accordingly designed "class schemes," from Alford's index to increasingly more complex and refined categories, to study the persistence and transformation of class cleavages in contemporary democracies.[41]

Although this approach has generated invaluable contributions, it is not well suited for our purpose. Studying the link between political cleavages and social inequalities requires introducing simple and comparable measures of inequality. Occupational categories usually incorporate such

41. See, for instance, E. O. Wright, "Class and Occupation," *Theory and Society* 9, no. 1 (1980): 177–214; R. Erikson and J. H. Goldthorpe, *The Constant Flux: A Study of Class Mobility in Industrial Societies* (Clarendon Press, 1992); Kitschelt, *Transformation of European Social Democracy*; Oesch, *Redrawing the Class Map*.

inequality dimensions, but they do so in a way that is hard to compare across time and space. Furthermore, in many non-Western democracies, standard class schemes may be both hard to measure empirically and conceptually meaningless.

For these reasons, much of this book centers on two complementary measures of individuals' positions in the social hierarchy: income and education. While the use of these two variables also has limitations, it has two major advantages. First, they are straightforward measures of *vertical* inequality, in the sense that one can refer to inequalities between people with higher incomes and lower incomes. Second, they are much easier to compare across countries and over time, even if, as we do not deny, this remains a challenging task too. When possible, we also consider two other dimensions of inequality, wealth and self-perceived class, although they are available in only a handful of countries. Taking these four variables together, our definition of social class is inherently multidimensional. We hope that our approach can usefully complement traditional occupational class analyses and enrich the complex analysis of political and economic conflicts.

### From Social Inequalities to Political Identities

Shifting the focus toward a broader conception of class cleavages, emerging from the mobilization of various social identities more or less embedded in the socioeconomic structure, is at the heart of this volume. It is useful in this context to distinguish between *reinforcing* and *cross-cutting* cleavages.[42] Reinforcing cleavages enhance class divides and therefore have a strong socioeconomic component. This was historically the case with "occupational" class cleavages in Western democracies, but this concept can be applied to a number of other cases too. Ethnic cleavages in Nigeria, regional cleavages in Thailand, and caste cleavages in India are three among numerous cases of reinforcing cleavages documented in this volume. Cross-cutting cleavages, on the contrary, contribute to blurring class cleavages, because they "pressure" voters to support parties that a priori do not represent their socioeconomic interests. A classic

42. G. Simmel, *Sociology: Inquiries into the Construction of Social Forms* (1908), trans. A. J. Blasi, A. K. Jacobs, and M. Kanjirathinkal (Brill, 2009); L. A. Coser, *The Functions of Social Conflict* (Routledge, 1956); D. J. Grove, "A Cross-National Examination of Cross-Cutting and Reinforcing Cultural Cleavages," *International Journal of Comparative Sociology* 18, no. 3–4 (1977): 217–227; R. Dahl, *Dilemmas of Pluralist Democracy: Autonomy vs. Control* (Yale University Press, 1982).

example is the religious cleavage in Western democracies, which contributed to reduce class cleavages by splitting the vote of the working class along religious lines. More generally, we are interested in studying *voter alignments,* that is, contexts in which various forms of political conflicts come to be aligned with class.

Doing so requires departing slightly from the strict definition of political cleavage of Lipset and Rokkan or Bartolini and Mair. While political cleavages should entail some element of collective identity and ideological consistency, the stringency of the concept makes it hard to apply when it comes to grasping the full complexity of socioeconomic divides. This is especially true of non-Western and new democracies (though not exclusive to them), where party systems are often weakly institutionalized, and ideological conflicts are sometimes framed by charismatic leaders rather than stable organizations. We thus choose to adopt a flexible conceptualization of political cleavages, which we can define as the set of social conflicts politicized by political parties that produce an enduring alignment of voters along observable social identities. While we acknowledge that this definition is not entirely satisfactory, it is worth bearing in mind that our objective is not to provide a theory of how political cleavages rise and fall. We mainly wish to understand how the transformation of these cleavages contributes to fostering or inhibiting the representation of conflicts over inequality.

### A New Dataset on Political Cleavages and Social Inequalities

The main contribution of this book is to exploit a new database on the structure of political cleavages and social inequalities, which allows a systematic comparison of the link between electoral behaviors and the socioeconomic characteristics of voters. Such an attempt is not new: many researchers and a growing number of dedicated organizations have engaged in considerable efforts to accomplish comparable projects, and we build on such international datasets in many case studies. Nonetheless, we contribute to these efforts in several dimensions.

The database we present in this volume consists in a set of electoral surveys covering approximately 500 elections conducted in fifty democracies from 1948 to 2020. All these surveys have in common that they have collected information on individuals' voting behaviors in national elections, together with data on voters' sociodemographic characteristics such as income, education, religion, ethnicity, regional location, age, and

gender. The contributors of this book, following a similar and reproducible methodology, carefully harmonized each of these surveys one by one.

Besides its geographical and historical scope, our dataset differs from existing ones in the particular effort made to harmonize data on income and education. One reason these two variables are often not exploited in comparative research is that they tend to be difficult to compare. Education systems and educational attainments vary significantly across countries and over time, and they are not always perfectly comparable across surveys. The same limitations apply to income, which is reported only in brackets in the vast majority of existing surveys.

To limit this source of bias, the chapters of this book focus as much as possible on broad education and income groups, decomposing the electorate into, for instance, its poorest half (the "bottom 50 percent"), the next 40 percent (the "middle 40 percent"), and the top decile (the "top 10 percent"). We introduce in the online appendix to this volume the simple statistical method we use to move from discrete categories (education levels or income brackets) to these groups. In order to make existing surveys more representative of election outcomes, we also systematically reweight respondents' answers to match official election results.[43]

Let us stress that we use the term "democracy" for simplicity. None of the countries studied in this volume can be considered perfect or ideal democracies (which by definition remain to be built), and several of them cannot even be considered democracies in a minimalistic sense if one adopts, for instance, a definition of democracy as "a system in which incumbents lose elections and leave when they lose."[44] All countries covered have at some point organized plural and contested elections (otherwise, one simply could not study the structure of electoral behaviors in these elections), which have sometimes contributed to regulating access to political power, but this practice has not always been systematic. Our main objective is to study the socioeconomic determinants of support for

43. See online appendix, World Political Cleavages and Inequality Database, http://wpid.world. In the vast majority of cases, this correction leaves our main results unchanged. Furthermore, for reasons of readability, the figures and tables of this volume do not report statistical confidence intervals. The comparisons conducted in this volume are in the vast majority of cases strongly statistically significant. All the codes and a list of data sources used in this book are fully available in the online appendix, allowing researchers to reproduce and contrast our findings.

44. A. Przeworski, *Crises of Democracy* (Cambridge University Press, 2019), 5. One territory, Hong Kong, also cannot be referred to as a "country."

and opposition to political coalitions in a variety of historical and institutional settings. This can be done with a reasonable degree of confidence in all of these "electoral democracies," which one could also qualify as "semi-electoral political regimes" to insist on the fact that elections often coexist with other mechanisms of access and conservation of power.[45]

Finally, while some chapters do refer to dynamics of political participation, most of the contributions in this book do not study electoral turnout. The reason for this is quite simple: even the best postelectoral surveys at our disposal are well known for strongly undersampling nonvoters, a bias that has grown over time in many countries.[46] While we have attempted to estimate trends in turnout disparity by income and education in some countries,[47] the data at our disposal is simply too scarce to properly do so for all the democracies covered by this volume. We acknowledge that this is an important limitation, and we hope that future research (notably, combining other data sources such as localized election and census data) will complement our work.

A synthetic description of our dataset is provided in Table 1.1. The data covers seventeen Western European democracies, three Eastern European postcommunist democracies, the four English-speaking democracies of North America and Oceania, ten Asian countries, seven Latin American democracies, and nine African and Middle Eastern countries. Available surveys allow us to cover all elections held since the 1960s or 1970s in the vast majority of Western democracies, and in some cases they date to the end of the 1940s or in the 1950s. In some non-Western countries, too, we have had access to historical data sources covering an equally long time span, in particular Japan, India, Pakistan, Costa Rica, Mexico, and Israel. Surveys unfortunately start in the 1980s, 1990s, or 2000s in the majority of the remaining countries, often because these years coincide with democratization, and sometimes because electoral

---

45. On the notion of "electoral democracy," also see the introduction to this volume.

46. See, for instance, C. H. Achen and T. Y. Wang, "Declining Voter Turnout in Taiwan: A Generational Effect?," *Electoral Studies* 58 (2019): 113–124; M. K. Berent, J. A. Krosnick, and A. Lupia, "Measuring Voter Registration and Turnout in Surveys: Do Official Government Records Yield More Accurate Assessments?," *Public Opinion Quarterly* 80, no. 3 (2016): 597–621; B. C. Burden, "Voter Turnout and the National Election Studies," *Political Analysis* 8, no. 4 (2000): 389–398.

47. T. Piketty, *Capital and Ideology* (Harvard University Press, 2020), figure 14.8; A. Gethin, "Cleavage Structures and Distributive Politics" (master's thesis, Paris School of Economics, 2018), figure 6.9.

*Table 1.1*  A New Dataset on Political Cleavages and Social Inequalities

| | Time Period | Elections | Data Quality | Avg. Sample Size | Low-Income Party/Coalition/Candidates |
|---|---|---|---|---|---|
| **Western Europe** | | | | | |
| Austria | 1971–2017 | 10 | Medium | 3,831 | Social Democratic Party, KPÖ, Greens, NEOS, Other left |
| Belgium | 1971–2014 | 14 | High | 4,817 | Socialist Party, Socialist Party Differently, Ecolo, Agalev, PTB |
| Denmark | 1960–2015 | 21 | High | 2,819 | Social Democrats, SF, Social Liberal Party, Red-Green Alliance |
| Finland | 1972–2015 | 11 | High | 2,452 | Social Democratic Party, Green League, Left Alliance, Other left |
| France | 1956–2017 | 17 | High | 3,208 | Socialist Party, Communist Party, Other left |
| Germany | 1949–2017 | 19 | High | 2,782 | Social Democratic Party, Alliance 90 / Greens, Die Linke |
| Iceland | 1978–2017 | 12 | High | 1,488 | Left-Green Movement, Social Democratic Alliance, People's Party |
| Ireland | 1973–2020 | 13 | Medium | 7,115 | Fianna Fáil, Sinn Féin, Other left |
| Italy | 1953–2018 | 14 | High | 2,147 | Democratic Party, Free and Equal |
| Luxembourg | 1974–2018 | 9 | Low | 3,890 | Socialist Workers' Party, Greens, Other left |
| Netherlands | 1967–2017 | 15 | High | 2,068 | Labour Party, Socialist Party, D66, Greens, Other left |
| Norway | 1957–2017 | 15 | High | 1,964 | Labour Party, Green Party, Socialist Left Party |
| Portugal | 1983–2019 | 10 | High | 1,822 | Socialist Party, Left Bloc, Unitary Democratic Coalition |
| Spain | 1979–2019 | 14 | High | 8,996 | Socialist Workers' Party, Podemos, United Left, Other left |
| Sweden | 1956–2014 | 19 | High | 3,088 | Social Democratic Party, Left Party, Green Party |
| Switzerland | 1967–2019 | 14 | High | 3,328 | Social Democrats, Party of Labour, Green Party, Green Liberal Party |
| United Kingdom | 1955–2017 | 16 | High | 5,262 | Labour Party |
| **Postcommunist Eastern Europe** | | | | | |
| Czech Republic | 1990–2017 | 7 | High | 1,565 | Social Democratic Party, Communist Party, Greens, Pirate Party |
| Hungary | 1998–2018 | 6 | High | 1,679 | Fidesz, Jobbik |
| Poland | 1991–2015 | 8 | High | 2,555 | Law and Justice |

(continued)

*Table 1.1* (continued)

| | Time Period | Elections | Data Quality | Avg. Sample Size | Low-Income Party/Coalition/Candidates |
|---|---|---|---|---|---|
| **North America / Oceania** | | | | | |
| Australia | 1963–2019 | 18 | High | 2,382 | Labor Party, Greens |
| Canada | 1963–2019 | 17 | High | 3,302 | Liberal Party, Green Party, New Democratic Party |
| New Zealand | 1972–2017 | 16 | High | 2,555 | Labour Party, Greens, Other left |
| United States | 1948–2020 | 18 | High | 2,179 | Democratic Party |
| **Asia** | | | | | |
| Hong Kong | 1998–2016 | 5 | Low | 864 | Pro-Beijing camp |
| India | 1962–2014 | 10 | High | 13,412 | Indian National Congress, left-wing parties, Other center / left |
| Indonesia | 1999–2014 | 4 | High | 1,850 | Indonesian Democratic Party of Struggle, NasDem, Golkar |
| Japan | 1953–2017 | 14 | Medium | 1,909 | Constitutional Democratic Party, Communist Party, Soc. Dem. Party |
| Malaysia | 2004–2013 | 3 | Low | 1,213 | Barisan Nasional |
| Pakistan | 1970–2018 | 8 | High | 3,682 | Pakistan Peoples Party |
| Philippines | 1998–2016 | 4 | Medium | 1,200 | Grace Poe, Jejomar Binay |
| South Korea | 2000–2016 | 5 | Medium | 1,160 | Liberty Korea Party |
| Taiwan | 1996–2016 | 6 | Medium | 1,744 | Democratic Progressive Party |
| Thailand | 2001–2011 | 3 | Low | 1,431 | Pheu Thai |

## Latin America

| Country | Years | N | Quality | Sample | Parties |
|---|---|---|---|---|---|
| Argentina | 1995–2019 | 6 | Medium | 2,056 | Peronist parties |
| Brazil | 1989–2018 | 8 | High | 10,225 | Workers' Party |
| Chile | 1989–2017 | 7 | Medium | 1,135 | Broad Front, Progressive Party, País |
| Colombia | 2002–2018 | 5 | Medium | 3,340 | Democratic Center, Mejor Vargas Lleras |
| Costa Rica | 1974–2018 | 12 | Medium | 1,083 | National Liberation Party |
| Mexico | 1952–2018 | 9 | Medium | 1,339 | Institutional Revolutionary Party |
| Peru | 1995–2016 | 5 | Medium | 1,592 | Popular Force |

## Africa and Middle East

| Country | Years | N | Quality | Sample | Parties |
|---|---|---|---|---|---|
| Algeria | 2002–2017 | 3 | Low | 1,226 | National Liberation Front, Democratic National Rally |
| Botswana | 1999–2019 | 5 | Low | 1,680 | Botswana Democratic Party |
| Ghana | 2000–2016 | 4 | Low | 2,600 | National Democratic Congress |
| Iraq | 2005–2018 | 5 | Low | 1,984 | Shia lists |
| Israel | 1969–2019 | 15 | High | 1,381 | Likud, Other conservative / ultra-orthodox |
| Nigeria | 1999–2019 | 6 | Low | 2,853 | All Progressives Congress |
| Senegal | 2000–2019 | 4 | Low | 1,800 | Alliance for the Republic |
| South Africa | 1994–2019 | 6 | High | 3,514 | African National Congress |
| Turkey | 1991–2018 | 7 | Medium | 1,564 | Justice and Development Party (AKP) |

*Data Source*: Authors' elaboration using the World Political Cleavages and Inequality Database (see wpid.world).

*Note*: The table presents, for each country, the time coverage of the dataset, the number of elections covered, the quality of electoral surveys, the average sample size of these surveys, and the main significant party or group of parties whose support is concentrated among the bottom 50 percent of income earners in the last election available (see corresponding case studies).

surveys of sufficient quality were not conducted in earlier elections (or because survey data files have not been preserved).

The quality of the available data sources varies significantly. High-quality sources include postelectoral surveys or exit polls specifically dedicated to collecting information on electoral behaviors. Such data have been collected on a regular basis in most Western democracies, often since the 1950s or 1960s, and in a number of non-Western democracies such as India, Pakistan, Brazil, South Africa, and Indonesia. Low-quality sources include surveys not specifically dedicated to elections, which are sometimes not even conducted in the year of the corresponding election, and in some cases only provide rough information on individuals' closeness to or identification with existing parties. This implies that we need to be much more careful when interpreting the dynamics of electoral behaviors, even if we are confident that one can still generally identify broad transformations with such data sources.

### Who Do Low-Income Voters Vote For?

Given the enormous variations in institutional settings, political histories, social conflicts, and party systems observed in the fifty countries studied in this volume, carrying comparisons across countries is an extremely complex task. This requires reducing the complexity of the problem and, inevitably, simplifying it.

To do so, in the context of this summary chapter we restrict the main part of the chapter's analysis to one large party or group of parties for each country: the party or coalition whose support most disproportionately comes from low-income voters, referred to as the "low-income" or "pro-poor" party. More precisely, we define that party as the party or coalition whose support among the poorest 50 percent of voters is higher than among the richest 50 percent in terms of income.[48] This definition has the advantage of providing an objective basis for comparisons across countries and time periods. Nonetheless, it has several important limitations. In particular, the identity of the "pro-poor" party or parties often changes over time. In Western democracies, for instance, social democratic and socialist parties (in a broad sense) achieved significantly higher results among low-income and lower-educated voters from the 1950s to the 1980s, but this was less and less the case from 2000 to 2020. During

---

48. The exceptions are Botswana, Ghana, Nigeria, and Senegal, for which data on income is not available and we exceptionally rely on education.

this period, anti-immigration parties appeared to be pro-poor parties too (and sometimes even more clearly than social democratic parties), in the sense that they drew much of their support from the low-income and lower-educated electorate. In the context of this analysis, we define social democratic parties (in a broad sense) as the only pro-poor parties over the entire 1948–2020 period, which will allow us to study how the structure of their electorate has changed over time. Furthermore, as we already mentioned, income does not always contribute to determining the same electoral affiliations as education or wealth. Despite these limitations, this is in our view the only approach that allows us to take such a broad historical and comparative perspective. It also does not prevent us from studying more carefully these competing coalitions when necessary, which is what we do in the next sections and in a more detailed way in each of the chapters of this volume.

Who, then, do low-income voters vote for? Table 1.1 provides a first answer to this question by listing low-income parties or groups of parties in our fifty democracies of interest, focusing on the last election in our dataset. In Western democracies, for simplicity and coherence with the related case studies, these correspond to social democratic, socialist, democratic, labor, communist, and green parties, commonly classified as "left-wing" but which we prefer to refer to as "social democratic" (in a broad sense) or by their country-specific denominations, for reasons explained above.[49] In non-Western democracies, this classification reveals an even greater diversity of ideological and programmatic orientations. On the one hand, we have parties historically affiliated with social democratic or socialist traditions, such as the Brazilian Workers' Party, the Indian National Congress, and the Mexican Institutional Revolutionary Party. On the other hand, we have many parties often considered unambiguously conservative, including the Liberty Korea Party in South Korea, Law and Justice in Poland, and the Fujimorist Popular Force in Peru. In addition to these two groups, we have a wide diversity of other parties, from catchall coalitions to dominant parties such as the Botswana Democratic Party and the African National Congress in South Africa. This diversity directly

---

49. See Table 1.1. This group also includes a few parties clearly not affiliated with socialist or social democratic traditions, such as the Liberal Party in Canada and Fianna Fáil in Ireland. This choice is motivated by our objective to compare across countries large electoral coalitions obtaining at least 30 percent of the vote in most elections, but the transformations we document are robust to alternative specifications (see corresponding chapters for more detailed decompositions).

mirrors the complexity of political cleavages; it is only by studying the link between socioeconomic status and other axes of political conflicts that one can understand these varieties of class divides.

## Depoliticizing Class: Income, Education, and Multi-elite Party Systems

### The Emergence of Multi-elite Party Systems
### in Western Democracies

We begin our analysis by documenting the transformation of cleavages related to income and education in Western democracies. To do so, we rely on a very simple indicator: the difference between the share of richest 10 percent voters and the share of poorest 90 percent voters voting for social democratic, socialist, democratic, labor, communist, and green parties. This difference is negative when top-income voters have a lower likelihood of voting for these parties, and positive when they have a higher likelihood of doing so. It is equal to zero if they have exactly the same likelihood of supporting the left as the rest of the electorate. Accordingly, we can define the same indicator for education as the difference between the share of top 10 percent most-educated voters and the share of bottom 90 percent least-educated voters voting for social democratic and affiliated parties.[50]

Figure 1.1 depicts the long-run evolution of these two indicators, taking their average values in the twelve Western democracies for which data is available since the 1960s. The bottom line of the figure shows that top-income voters have always been less likely to vote for social democratic and affiliated parties and more likely to vote for conservative and affiliated parties. In the 1960s, the indicator was equal to −15: top-income voters had a probability of voting for social democratic parties that was 15 percentage points lower than that of low-income voters. This gap has decreased slightly until reaching −10 in the last decade, but it remains significantly negative. High-income voters have thus remained closer to conservative parties than low-income voters over the past fifty years.

A dramatically different evolution took place in the case of education. As the upper line of Figure 1.1 shows, highest-educated voters were less

50. We focus here on differences between the top 10 percent and the bottom 90 percent, but the evolutions observed are similar when comparing other groups such as the bottom 50 percent and top 50 percent.

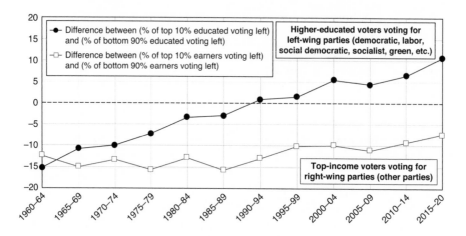

FIGURE 1.1. The emergence of multi-elite party systems in Western democracies
*Data Source:* Authors' computations using the World Political Cleavages and Inequality
Database (see wpid.world).
*Note:* In the 1960s, both higher-educated and high-income voters were less likely to
vote for left-wing (democratic/labor/social democratic/socialist/green) parties than
lower-educated and low-income voters by more than 10 percentage points. The left vote
has gradually become associated with higher-education voters, giving rise to a multi-elite
party system. Figures correspond to five-year averages for Australia, Britain, Canada,
Denmark, France, Germany, Italy, the Netherlands, Norway, Sweden, Switzerland, and
the US. Estimates control for income/education, age, gender, religion, church attendance,
rural/urban, region, race/ethnicity, employment status, and marital status (in country-years
for which these variables are available).

likely to vote for social democratic parties than lowest-educated voters
by 15 percentage points in the 1960s. There has been a striking reversal
in this educational divide. The gap shifted very gradually from being negative to becoming positive, moving from −10 in the 1970s to −5 in the 1980s,
0 in the 1990s, +5 in the 2000s, and finally +10 in 2015–2020. Higher-
educated voters thus moved from being significantly more right-wing than
lower-educated voters to significantly more left-wing.[51]

51. Several studies had already hinted at a renewed role of education in determining electoral behaviors. See, in particular, van der Waal, Achterberg, and Houtman, "Class Is Not
Dead"; S. Bornschier, "The New Cultural Divide and the Two-Dimensional Political Space in
Western Europe," *West European Politics* 33, no. 3 (2010): 419–444; M. Dolezal, "Exploring
the Stabilization of a Political Force: The Social and Attitudinal Basis of Green Parties in the

If we combine these two evolutions, a very clear picture emerges. In the early postwar decades, the party systems of Western democracies were "class-based," meaning that social democratic parties (including socialists, democrats, communists, and so on) represented both the low-education and the low-income electorates, whereas conservative parties (including Christian democrats, republicans, and so on) represented both high-education and high-income voters. These party systems have gradually evolved toward what we can call *multi-elite party systems*: social democratic and affiliated parties have become the parties of higher-educated elites, while conservative and affiliated parties remain the parties of high-income elites.[52]

Notice that this figure accounts for statistical controls, meaning that we are considering the *independent* effects of income and education. The figure reads as follows: at given levels of education and other individual characteristics, top-income voters were less likely to vote for left-wing parties than low-income voters by about 10 percentage points in 2015–2020. If we were not to account for these controls, then we would observe a stronger decline in the influence of income on the vote, from nearly −20 in the 1960s to −5 in 2015–2020.[53] This is because higher-educated voters have on average higher incomes, so the reversal of the educational divide has mechanically led to a reduction in the difference between top-income and low-income voters.

### The Reversal of the Education Cleavage

Although the emergence of a multi-elite party system is common to nearly all Western democracies, it has happened at different speeds and with different intensities, a fact that we will explore in greater detail in the corresponding chapters (see Chapters 2, 3, 4, 5, 6, and 7). For instance, as shown in Figure 1.2, the support of higher-educated voters for social democratic parties was lowest in Norway, Sweden, and Finland from the 1950s to the 1970s; these three democracies are well known for having

---

Age of Globalization," *West European Politics* 33, no. 3 (2010): 534–552; R. Stubager, "The Development of the Education Cleavage: Denmark as a Critical Case," *West European Politics* 33, no. 3 (2010): 505–533; M. Bovens and A. Wille, "Education: The Contours of a New Cleavage? Comparing 23 European Countries," in *Stabiliteit en verandering in Europa*, ed. K. Aarts and M. Wittenberg (DANS, 2012), 35–62.

52. Piketty, *Capital and Ideology*, chapter 15.

53. See appendix Figure A1, wpid.world.

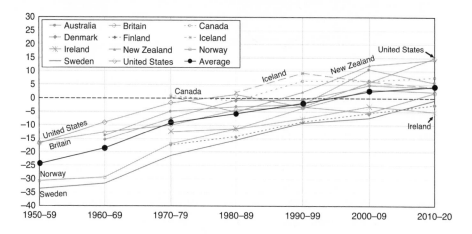

FIGURE 1.2 (a). The reversal of educational divides in Western democracies: English-speaking and Northern European countries

*Data Source:* Authors' computations using the World Political Cleavages and Inequality Database (see wpid.world).

*Note:* The figure represents the difference between the share of higher-educated (top 10%) and lower-educated (bottom 90%) voters voting for democratic/labor/social democratic/socialist/green parties in English-speaking and Northern European countries. In nearly all countries, higher-educated voters used to be significantly more likely to vote for conservative parties and have gradually become more likely to vote for these parties. Estimates control for income, age, gender, religion, church attendance, rural/urban, region, race/ethnicity, employment status, and marital status (in country-years for which these variables are available).

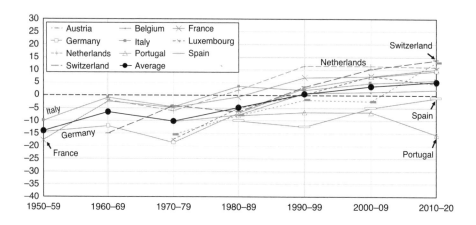

FIGURE 1.2 (b). The reversal of educational divides in Western democracies: Continental and Southern European countries

*Data Source:* Authors' computations using the World Political Cleavages and Inequality Database (see wpid.world).

*Note:* The figure represents the difference between the share of higher-educated (top 10%) and lower-educated (bottom 90%) voters voting for democratic/labor/social democratic/socialist/green parties in Continental and Southern European countries. In nearly all countries, higher-educated voters used to be significantly more likely to vote for conservative parties and have gradually become more likely to vote for these parties. Estimates control for income, age, gender, religion, church attendance, rural/urban, region, race/ethnicity, employment status, and marital status (in country-years for which these variables are available).

stronger historical class-based party systems than most Western democracies (see Chapter 4). The reversal of the education cleavage has not yet been fully completed in these countries, as social democratic parties have managed to keep a non-negligible fraction of the low-income and lower-educated electorate.

This delay is also common to recent democracies such as Spain and Portugal and late industrialized countries such as Ireland, where left-wing parties continue to be more class-based. Portugal and to a lesser extent Ireland represent two major exceptions in our dataset, where we do not observe a clear tendency toward a reversal of the educational divide. This unique trajectory can be explained by, among several factors, the polarization of mainstream parties and the success of new left-wing parties after the onset of the 2008 financial crisis (see Chapter 6). By contrast, the gap in left votes between higher-educated voters and lower-educated voters is today highest in countries such as the United States, New Zealand, Switzerland, and the Netherlands. The particular salience of identity-based concerns, mirrored in the case of the latter two countries by the strength of anti-immigration and green movements, can contribute to explaining these variations (see Chapter 7).

### The Persistence and Attenuation of Income Divides

In all Western democracies, top-income voters have remained significantly more likely than low-income voters to vote for conservative and Christian parties, but with significant variations (Figure 1.3). The impact of income on the vote was the strongest in Northern European countries, Britain, Australia, and New Zealand in the 1950s and 1960s, consistent with their histories of early industrialization and strong class polarization. However, as traditional class divides have collapsed in these countries in the past decades, so has the relationship between income and the vote.

Meanwhile, low-income voters have supported less decisively left-wing parties in countries with weak historical class cleavages and strong cross-cutting religious (Italy) or ethnolinguistic (Canada) cleavages. Overall, despite these variations, the tendency of high-income voters to support the right in contemporary Western democracies has proved remarkably resilient over time, pointing to the persistence of conflicts over economic issues and redistributive policy. The only country where a complete reversal of the income effect could well be underway is the United States

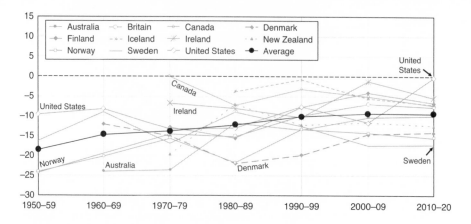

FIGURE 1.3 *(a)*. The stability/decline of income divides in Western democracies: English-speaking and Northern European countries

*Data Source:* Authors' computations using the World Political Cleavages and Inequality Database (see wpid.world).

*Note:* The figure represents the difference between the share of high-income (top 10%) and low-income (bottom 90%) voters voting for democratic/labor/social democratic/ socialist/green parties in English-speaking and Northern European countries. In all countries, top-income voters have remained significantly less likely to vote for these parties than low-income voters. Estimates control for education, age, gender, religion, church attendance, rural/urban, region, race/ethnicity, employment status, and marital status (in country-years for which these variables are available).

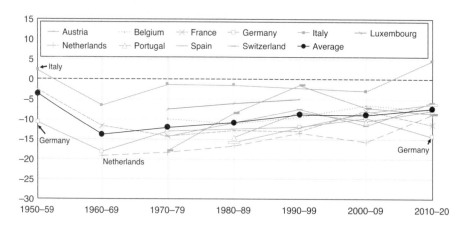

FIGURE 1.3 *(b)*. The stability/decline of income divides in Western democracies: Continental and Southern European countries

*Data Source:* Authors' computations using the World Political Cleavages and Inequality Database (see wpid.world).

*Note:* The figure represents the difference between the share of high-income (top 10%) and low-income (bottom 90%) voters voting for democratic/labor/social democratic/ socialist/green parties in Continental and Southern European countries. In all countries, top-income voters have remained significantly less likely to vote for these parties than low-income voters. Estimates control for education, age, gender, religion, church attendance, rural/urban, region, race/ethnicity, employment status, and marital status (in country-years for which these variables are available).

(and to some extent Italy, due to the recent strength of the Five Star Movement among low-income voters), where in 2016 top 10 percent earners became more likely to vote for the Democratic Party for the first time since World War II (see Chapter 2).

### The Origins of Multi-elite Party Systems in Western Democracies

How can we explain the reversal of educational divides? While answering these questions is arguably a task of too great complexity to be undertaken in the present chapter, we can stress at least three complementary mechanisms underlying this evolution.

The classic explanation for the shift of higher-educated voters toward the left, and conversely the shift of lower-educated voters toward the right, relates to the rise of identity-based conflicts following the cultural revolution of the 1960s and 1970s and more recently the increasing salience of immigration. As questions related to environmentalism, gender equality, and the rights of sexual and ethnic minorities (including the civil rights movements in the United States) took on a growing importance in public debate and civil society, they eventually gave rise to green and "New Left" parties, whose support drew disproportionately from the young, urban middle class.[54] In the 1990s and the 2000s, the rise of far-right and anti-immigration movements advocating for social-conservative policies and tighter immigration controls then reinforced this sociocultural cleavage, representing for some observers a "cultural backlash" to the social progress advocated by the younger generations.[55] In the next section, we demonstrate that indeed, this process strongly contributed to reinforcing multi-elite party systems, as the key dividing variable between anti-immigration and green parties is education.

Nonetheless, this explanation needs to be complemented by other factors. The transformation that we documented did not start in the 1960s or in the 2000s. As we showed above, it instead corresponds to a very gradual process, starting as early as the 1950s in countries for which we have data and developing at a relatively stable pace over the course of the second half of the twentieth century. Furthermore, it has happened with the same magnitude in countries with weak anti-immigration par-

---

54. Kitschelt, *Transformation of European Social Democracy*; Dalton, *Political Realignment*.

55. Norris and Inglehart, *Cultural Backlash*.

ties (such as Australia and New Zealand, see Chapter 5), and there are equally some countries where it simply did not happen (Portugal and Ireland).

A second mechanism that can potentially explain this long-run evolution and does hold even in the absence of identity-based cleavages has to do with the process of educational expansion. In the 1950s and 1960s, it was relatively straightforward to design an egalitarian educational platform, as the majority of voters had at most a primary or secondary education. With the rise of tertiary education, social democratic parties have increasingly been viewed as the parties defending the winners of the competition for higher education, contributing to growing resentment among popular classes. Growing inequalities in access to the education system, by eroding lower-educated citizens' trust in public education institutions, accordingly may have facilitated the emergence of new movements pushing for the contraction of public investments and state intervention.[56] We provide evidence consistent with this hypothesis when we study generational cleavages below: the higher educated have indeed been more left-wing than the lower educated only among voters born after World War II, while prewar generations continue in large part to vote along class lines.

A third, related mechanism involves the transformation of global ideology toward the liberalization of the economy, the sacralization of private property, the decline of progressive taxation, and more generally the abandonment of any perspective supporting the transformation of the economic system and the supersession of capitalism, following the conservative revolution of the 1980s and the collapse of communism at the end of the Cold War. The moderation of traditional left-wing parties' platforms, as well as in some cases their shift to promoting neoliberal policies, arguably contributed to the decline of class cleavages, their subsequent demise, and the rise of identity-based conflicts. This is all the more evident in postcommunist democracies such as Hungary and Poland, where the collaboration of previously ruling communist and socialist parties in the process of market liberalization was followed by growing disillusionment, their near disappearance from the political scene, and the emergence of new powerful right-wing coalitions (see Chapter 8). The cases of Ireland and Portugal, where economic issues

56. Piketty, *Capital and Ideology.*

continue to decisively structure political conflicts and where the left has managed to keep a significant share of the low-income and lower-educated electorate, show, however, that the reversal of educational divides in Western democracies is not an ineluctable or mechanical transition.

### The Expansion of Multiparty Systems in Western Democracies

In two-party systems like that of the United States, the emergence of multi-elite party systems has occurred entirely within existing parties. In many multiparty systems, however, we observe a significant reshuffling of political forces. Traditional socialist and social democratic parties have seen their average vote share across Western democracies decline from about 40 percent to 34 percent since the end of World War II, while that received by Christian and conservative parties has decreased from 38 percent to 30 percent (Figure 1.4). Communist parties, who received 7 percent of the vote in the 1940s, have now almost

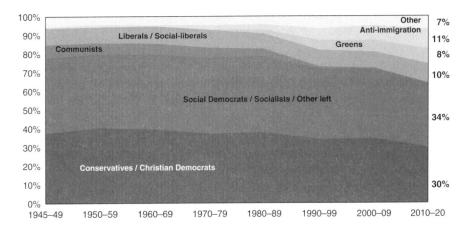

FIGURE 1.4. The transformation of Western party systems, 1945–2020
*Data Source:* Authors' computations using the World Political Cleavages and Inequality Database (see wpid.world).
*Note:* The figure represents the average share of votes received by selected families of political parties in Western democracies between the 1940s and the 2010s. Communist parties saw their average scores collapse from 7% to less than 0.5%, while green and anti-immigration parties have risen until reaching average vote shares of 8% and 11%, respectively. Decennial averages are over all Western democracies except Spain and Portugal (no democratic elections before 1970s) and the United States and the United Kingdom (two-party systems).

completely disappeared from the political scene. Green and anti-immigration parties, meanwhile, made their entry in the political landscape in the 1970s and 1980s and have progressed uninterruptedly since then, reaching on average 8 percent and 11 percent of the votes in the past decade. Support for social-liberal and liberal parties such as NEOS in Austria, the Liberal Party in Norway, and D66 in the Netherlands has remained more stable, although there are important variations across countries.

Figure 1.5 decomposes our previous income and education indicators for each of these families of parties in the past decade, revealing the profound transformation in the structure of political cleavages that took place from the 1960–1980 period (panel a) to the 2000–2020 period (panel b). Strikingly, income appears to be the key variable

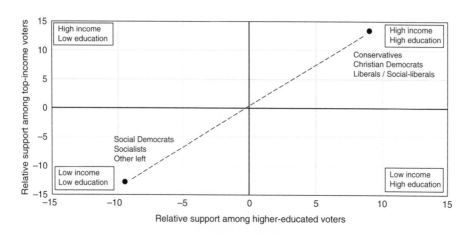

FIGURE 1.5 *(a)*. The fragmentation of Western cleavage structures: 1960–1980
*Data Source:* Authors' computations using the World Political Cleavages and Inequality Database (see wpid.world).
*Note:* The figure represents the difference between the share of high-income (top 10%) and low-income (bottom 90%) voters voting for selected groups of parties on the y-axis, and the same difference between higher-educated (top 10%) and lower-educated (bottom 90%) voters on the x-axis. In the 1960s–1980s, socialist and social democratic parties were supported by both low-income and lower-educated voters, while conservative, Christian, and liberal parties were supported by both high-income and higher-educated voters. Averages over all Western democracies. Estimates control for income/education, age, gender, religion, church attendance, rural/urban, region, race/ethnicity, employment status, and marital status (in country-years for which these variables are available).

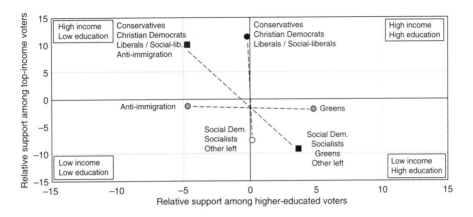

FIGURE 1.5 *(b)*. The fragmentation of Western cleavage structures: 2000–2020
*Data Source:* Authors' computations using the World Political Cleavages and Inequality Database (see wpid.world).
*Note:* The figure represents the difference between the share of high-income (top 10%) and low-income (bottom 90%) voters voting for selected groups of parties on the *y*-axis, and the same difference between higher-educated (top 10%) and lower-educated (bottom 90%) voters on the *x*-axis. Education most clearly distinguishes anti-immigration from green parties, while income most clearly distinguishes conservative and Christian parties from socialist and social democratic parties. Averages over all Western democracies. Estimates control for income/education, age, gender, religion, church attendance, rural/urban, region, race/ethnicity, employment status, and marital status (in country-years for which these variables are available).

distinguishing social democrats and socialists from conservative, Christian, and social-liberal parties today, while education is the determining factor when it comes to differentiating anti-immigration and green parties. The increasing support for green and anti-immigration parties has thus clearly contributed to the reversal of the education cleavage previously documented.

We stress that behind these averages, however, there are significant variations across countries.[57] In particular, while nearly all green parties in our dataset achieve better results among higher-educated voters than among the lower educated, they differ in their tendency to attract low- or high-income voters. Similarly, anti-immigration parties have attracted a particularly high share of the lower-educated vote in several

57. See appendix Figure A16, wpid.world.

Western democracies in the past decade, but we also observe significant variations in the income profile of far-right voting. The Austrian Freedom Party, the French National Front, and the Danish People's Party stand out as parties whose support has been most concentrated among the low-income electorate. Meanwhile, the Lega in Italy and VOX in Spain have achieved significant results among high-income voters, which can be explained by the interaction between immigration issues and other dimensions of political conflicts (the Catalan independence movement in Spain, and the concentration of Lega votes in the richer northern region in Italy; see Chapter 6). Overall, these variations call for nuance of the idea that green parties would be systematically oriented toward high-income earners, while far-right parties would be oriented toward the least privileged sections of society.

Beyond these decompositions, however, we find that most traditional left-wing parties in Western democracies have also attracted a growing share of the higher-educated electorate. It is the combination of these two transformations, the reversal of the educational cleavage within old parties and the rise of new green and far-right parties, which has led to a decisive shift of higher-educated voters to the left in recent years.

### The Erosion of Perceived Class Cleavages

Our analysis has revealed a gradual decoupling of two complementary measures of social class in Western democracies, income and education, as individuals ranking at the top of the social hierarchy in each of these dimensions have increasingly voted for different parties and coalitions. In some countries, existing postelectoral surveys have also collected information on individuals' self-perceived class positions, asking respondents whether they identify themselves as belonging to categories such as "the working class," "the lower classes," "the middle class," or "the upper class." While the wording of these questions and the scales used vary significantly across countries and sometimes over time, they can still be particularly useful in giving a complementary view on the long-run dynamics of class cleavages.

In Figure 1.6, we represent the difference between the share of voters identifying with the "working class" or "lower class" and the share of voters identifying with the "middle class," the "upper class," or "no class" voting for social democratic and affiliated parties in all countries in which such data is available. This difference was large and positive in the 1950s: voters self-ranking at the bottom of the social ladder were more likely to

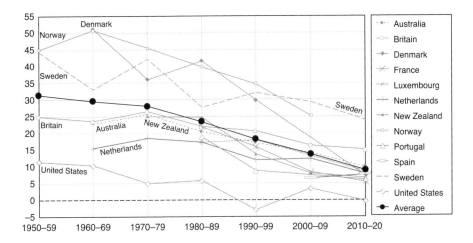

FIGURE 1.6. The decline of self-perceived class cleavages in Western democracies
*Data Source:* Authors' computations using the World Political Cleavages and Inequality Database (see wpid.world).
*Note:* The figure shows the difference between the share of voters self-identifying as belonging to the "working class" or the "lower class" and the share of voters identifying with the "middle class," the "upper class," or "no class" voting for democratic/labor/social democratic/socialist/green parties. Self-perceived class cleavages have declined significantly over the past decades. Estimates control for income, education, age, gender, religion, church attendance, rural/urban, region, race/ethnicity, employment status, and marital status (in country-years for which these variables are available).

vote for left-wing parties by over 30 percentage points on average. This gap has very gradually declined until falling below 10 percentage points in the past decade. Self-perceived class divides were historically strongest in Northern European countries, consistent with what we found for education and income, and weakest in the United States. In every single country, these cleavages have diminished significantly.

Together, our results on income, education, and subjective social positioning uncover the complexity and multidimensionality of class cleavages. While the effect of income on support for social democratic and affiliated parties has remained relatively stable in the past decades, the impact of education has completely reversed. Self-perceived class divides arguably capture the joint influence of these two dimensions, exhibiting a consistent decline but not a complete reversal to the present day.

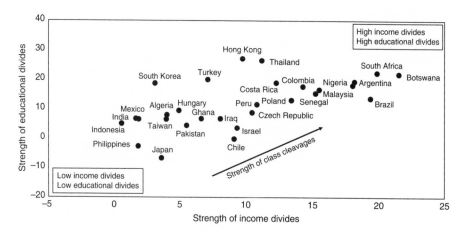

FIGURE 1.7. Income and educational divides in non-Western democracies
*Data Source:* Authors' computations using the World Political Cleavages and Inequality Database (see wpid.world).
*Note:* The figure represents the difference between the share of low-income (bottom 50%) and high-income (top 50%) voters voting for selected "pro-poor parties" (see table 1.1) on the *x*-axis, and the same difference between lower-educated (bottom 50%) and higher-educated (top 50%) voters on the *y*-axis in non-Western democracies. South Africa and Argentina display particularly strong income and educational divides, while education and income only play a minor role in determining electoral behaviors in Japan, the Philippines, and Indonesia. Income and education are shown as identical for Botswana, Ghana, Nigeria, and Senegal given lack of data on income.

## Class Cleavages in Non-Western Democracies

How strong are relative effects of income and education in determining electoral behaviors in non-Western democracies? To answer this question, we compare in Figure 1.7 two indicators for all the countries available in our dataset: on the x-axis, the difference between the shares of top 50 percent and bottom 50 percent voters in terms of income who support low-income parties and coalitions, and on the y-axis the same difference in terms of education.

Strikingly, education and income appear to be closely aligned in nearly all countries—that is, lower-educated and low-income voters tend to vote for the same parties or coalitions, revealing that multi-elite party systems comparable to those visible in Western democracies today are rare in

comparative and historical perspective.[58] There are, however, two other multi-elite party systems identified in this volume that are worth mentioning. The first is in postwar Japan, where the dominant Liberal Democratic Party used to be supported by economic elites, while socialists and communists, who were fiercely opposed to remilitarization and cooperation with the United States, achieved better results among the higher-educated urban middle class (see Chapter 11). A comparable decoupling was also visible in Turkey in the 1990s, when the opposition between center-right and center-left parties materialized a cleavage between secular and business elites (see Chapter 19). In each case, the separation between the income and education dimensions was made possible by the existence of a particularly strong cross-cutting sociocultural cleavage (attitudes toward foreign policy in Japan, secular-religious divides in Turkey).

Just as in Western democracies, there are, nonetheless, significant variations in the importance of income and educational divides across countries, which in many cases can be explained by the relative strength of other political cleavages and their interactions with the socioeconomic structure. In Hong Kong, for instance, the educational divide is exceptionally high mainly because of its interaction with age, as young educated voters are much more supportive of the pro-democracy camp (see generational cleavages section below). In South Africa, meanwhile, racial inequalities appear to largely structure the relationship between income and the vote. In other words, understanding these variations requires carefully studying how socioeconomic concerns interact with other political and social identities. This is what we do in the remaining sections of this chapter and in the dedicated chapters of this volume.

### Ethnoreligious and Sociocultural Cleavages

We now turn to the analysis of cleavages related to sociocultural identities, defined as broad sociopolitical categories encompassing a variety of affiliations related to religion, national identity, language, culture, and historical traditions. We first discuss the strength and evolution of religious-secular cleavages and the vote of religious minorities in Western

---

58. The strength of this alignment is partly driven by the correlation between education and income, but is robust to controls in the vast majority of countries. See appendix Figure A30, wpid.world.

and non-Western democracies and their interactions with class. We then analyze political cleavages related to immigration and new minorities in Western democracies by looking at the voting behaviors of foreign-born and Muslim voters. Finally, we expand our analysis to discuss how political parties and socioeconomic concerns articulate the political representation of disadvantaged sociocultural groups in a larger set of countries.

### Religious-Secular Cleavages and Religious Minorities

Historically, religious cleavages have strongly influenced the content of political discourse in Western democracies. Social democratic parties, as well as their secularist and radical predecessors, were always more favorable to preserving the secular aspect of the state, while conservative and Christian parties traditionally represented the interests of the church and religious voters. As secularization advanced in the decades following World War II, traditional religious affiliations progressively lost importance, leading to the collapse of Christian democratic parties in many countries.

Figure 1.8 depicts the difference in the share of voters belonging to the religious majority—Protestants in historically Protestant countries (panel a), Catholics in historically Catholic countries, and both Catholics and Protestants in mixed countries (panel b)—and the share of non-religious voters or religious minorities voting for left-wing parties from the 1950s to the 2010s. In all Western democracies with available data, this difference has remained consistently negative: voters belonging to the religious majority have always been significantly less likely to vote for left-wing parties. This gap has, however, declined, suggesting a gradual weakening of traditional religious-secular divides. The difference was historically larger in Catholic countries and in countries with both Catholics and Protestants, but it has also declined faster than in Protestant-majority countries. These historical differences have been explained by the establishment of national churches under state authority in Protestant countries, which limited the importance of religion as a significant source of political conflict.[59]

59. R. J. Dalton, "Political Cleavages, Issues, and Electoral Change," in *Comparing Democracies: Elections and Voting in Global Perspective*, ed. L. LeDuc, R. G. Niemi, and

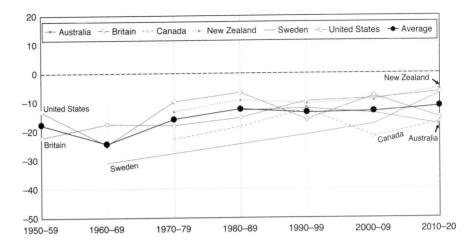

FIGURE 1.8 *(a)*. Religious-secular cleavages in Western democracies: English-speaking and Northern European countries

*Data Source:* Authors' computations using the World Political Cleavages and Inequality Database (see wpid.world).

*Note:* The figure displays the difference between the share of Protestants declaring going to church at least once a year and the share of other voters voting for democratic/labor/social democratic/socialist/green parties. In all countries, Protestants have remained significantly less likely to vote for these parties than other voters.

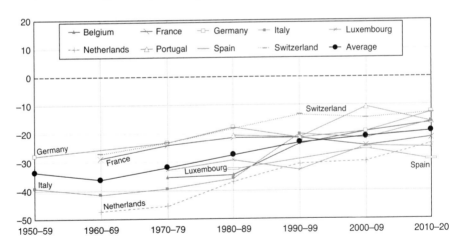

FIGURE 1.8 *(b)*. Religious-secular cleavages in Western democracies: Continental and Southern European countries

*Data Source:* Authors' computations using the World Political Cleavages and Inequality Database (see wpid.world).

*Note:* The figure displays the difference between the share of Catholics (or Catholics and Protestants in mixed countries) declaring going to church at least once a year and the share of other voters voting for democratic/labor/social democratic/socialist/green parties. In all countries, religious voters have remained significantly less likely to vote for these parties than other voters.

Given that religion is generally only weakly linked to socioeconomic status, religious cleavages have historically been strongly cross-cutting, dividing voters with similar levels of income or education along religious lines. As Catholic countries have had more pronounced religious cleavages, in particular, religion has acted as a more important neutralizer of class cleavages than in Protestant countries. Italy stands out as the country where income and education have had the weakest influence on electoral behaviors overall (see Figure 1.3 above), due in part to the exceptional importance of these religious-secular divides.

In addition to this cleavage between religious and nonreligious voters, several Western democracies were historically characterized by significant divides between the religious majority and a religious minority. Examples of such minorities included French-speaking Catholics in Canada, Catholics in Australia and New Zealand, and Protestants in Ireland. In both Protestant and Catholic countries, these religious minorities were much less likely to vote for conservative parties in the 1960s and 1970s.[60] One interesting exception to this alignment between the vote of religious minorities and the vote of low-income voters is Ireland, where both high-income voters and the Protestant minority have voted disproportionately more for the center-right party Fine Gael. This can be explained by the particular legacy of the civil war cleavage, as well as by the historical overrepresentation of the Protestant minority at the top of the social hierarchy (see Chapter 6).

Conflicts over state secularism and the integration of religious minorities in the national polity have not been specific to Western countries; they have also generated electoral cleavages in many other democracies throughout the world.

In Latin America, we find evidence of a religious-secular cleavage and a Catholic-Protestant cleavage, but with substantial variations across countries. In the Latin American countries we have studied, voters declaring no religion have been more likely to vote for left-wing or secular parties (Figure 1.9). Interestingly, however, and in line with Western democracies, this gap was generally greater in countries with strong Christian democratic parties (for instance, Costa Rica) and smallest in countries with pronounced class cleavages (for instance, Brazil and Argentina).

---

P. Norris (Sage, 1996), 189–209; O. Knutsen, *Social Structure and Party Choice in Western Europe: A Comparative Longitudinal Study* (Springer, 2004).

60. See appendix Figure B1, wpid.world.

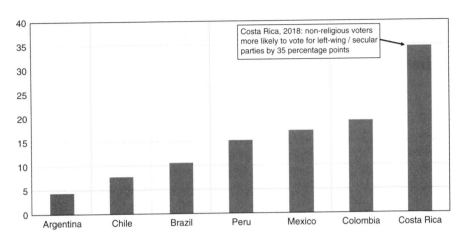

FIGURE 1.9. Religious-secular cleavages in Latin America
*Data Source:* Authors' computations using the World Political Cleavages and Inequality Database (see wpid.world).
*Note:* The figure represents the difference between the share of voters declaring belonging to no religion and the share of other voters voting for left-wing/secular parties (Peronist parties in Argentina) in the last election available (Argentina 2015, Brazil 2018, Chile 2017, Colombia 2018, Costa Rica 2018, Mexico 2018, Peru 2016). Non-religious voters are more likely to vote for left-wing/secular parties in all countries, but this gap is large in Costa Rica and almost insignificant in Argentina. See the corresponding chapters for more details on the classification of parties.

The emergence of a religious-secular divide in Latin America has been a relatively recent phenomenon, enabled by the secularization process starting in the 1980s and by the increasing importance of Protestantism as a competing religious affiliation to Catholicism.[61]

Unlike in Western democracies, in Latin America the Catholic-Protestant cleavage has not systematically pushed voters to the left or right, but has mostly represented identity voting in elections featuring non-Catholic candidates. Costa Rica, where, for instance, the National Restoration Party gained support from a substantial share of the Protestant electorate in the 2018 elections, stands out as one of the Latin American countries where this cleavage has been the clearest (see Chapter 15).

61. R. E. Carlin, M. M. Singer, and E. J. Zechmeister, *The Latin American Voter: Pursuing Representation and Accountability in Challenging Contexts* (University of Michigan Press, 2015).

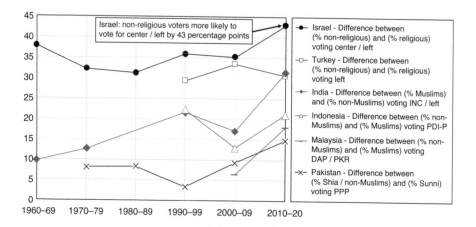

FIGURE 1.10. Religious-secular cleavages in Israel, Turkey, India, Indonesia, Pakistan, and Malaysia

*Data Source:* Authors' computations using the World Political Cleavages and Inequality Database (see wpid.world).

*Note:* The figure represents the evolution of the vote of religious minorities or non-religious voters in Israel, Turkey, India, Indonesia, Pakistan, and Malaysia. In the past decades, religious cleavages have risen in India, Pakistan, and Malaysia, while they have remained stable at high levels in Indonesia, Turkey, and Israel. INC: Indian National Congress; PDI-P: Indonesian Democratic Party of Struggle; DAP: Democratic Action Party; PKR: People's Justice Party; PPP: Pakistan Peoples Party.

Religious divides may also be playing a growing role in Brazilian politics, exemplified by the popularity of Jair Bolsonaro among the evangelical electorate in the 2018 presidential election (see Chapter 14).

We also find strong evidence of significant and persistent religious-secular cleavages in Muslim-majority countries, as well as in India and in Israel (Figure 1.10). The Turkish secular center-left, the Indonesian Democratic Party of Struggle, the Pakistan Peoples Party, and the Malaysian Democratic Action Party have all been substantially more popular among nonreligious voters or religious minorities. Senegal, a country well known for its weak politicization of religious issues, stands out among Muslim-majority countries as having no marked electoral divide along religious lines (see Chapter 17). In India, the Indian National Congress and left-wing parties have always achieved better results among Muslim voters than among the Hindu majority. This cleavage has risen dramatically in the past decades, as the Hindu nationalist Bharatiya Janata Party

attracted a growing share of votes from upper-caste and, more recently, lower-caste Hindus (see Chapter 9). Finally, in Israel, we observe one of the strongest and most stable religious-secular cleavages: nonreligious voters have been consistently more likely to vote for left-wing and centrist parties, by 30 to 40 percentage points since the 1960s. In all these countries, religious-secular cleavages have therefore represented deep historical divides, which often emerged immediately after the constitution of the modern nation-state and have proved to be highly resilient over time.

### The Emergence of a New Nativist Cleavage: Immigrants and the Muslim Vote in Western Democracies

Starting at the end of the twentieth century, a number of Western democracies saw the rise of a new cleavage related to national identity, which, as we showed in Figure 1.4, coincided with the emergence of new anti-immigration parties. Following the decolonization process, the opening of international borders, the shocks induced by globalization, and the influx of refugees from war-ridden countries, Western democracies saw a gradual increase in migration inflows in the past decades. Many of these immigrants and their descendants acquired citizenship, allowing them to vote in national elections. Figure 1.11 shows that social democratic and affiliated parties have attracted a significant share of these new minorities in many Western democracies, but with substantial variations. In particular, the strength of this new "nativist" cleavage strongly correlates to the salience of immigration issues and the way they are represented politically. Many of the countries at the top of this figure have seen the emergence of powerful anti-immigration parties in the past decades, including Austria, Denmark, France, and Switzerland. Meanwhile, countries with the weakest differences in voting behaviors between natives and immigrants from non-Western democracies, notably Iceland, Portugal, Australia, and New Zealand, have seen anti-immigration parties achieve lower results at the national level or simply have no such party at all. Together, these results point to the role of the politicization of immigration in generating new cleavages over national identity.[62]

---

62. It should be noted that the voting behaviors of European immigrants follow a completely different logic from those of non-European immigrants. In France, immigrants originating from European countries (mainly Southern European countries such as Spain, Portugal, and Italy) do not vote significantly differently from the rest of the population. In Germany, European migrants (mainly from Eastern Europe and Russia) are more likely than the rest of the electorate to support Christian democrats.

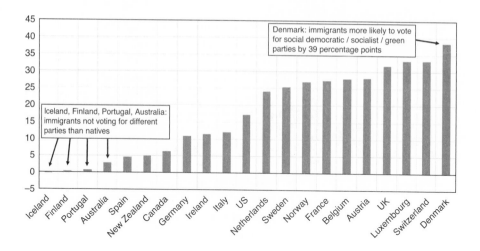

FIGURE 1.11. The native-immigrant cleavage in Western democracies
*Data Source:* Authors' computations using the World Political Cleavages and Inequality
Database (see wpid.world) and the European Social Survey for Denmark, Finland,
Germany, Italy, Norway, Spain, Sweden, Switzerland, and the United Kingdom.
*Note:* The figure represents the difference between the share of voters born in non-
Western countries (all countries excluding Europe, Australia, New Zealand, Canada,
and the United States) and the share of natives (voters born in the country considered)
voting for democratic/labor/social democratic/socialist/green parties over the 2010–
2020 period. In nearly all Western countries, immigrants are much more likely to vote
for these parties than natives. US and Iceland figures include voters born in Western
countries given lack of data on exact country of origin. Excludes Fianna Fáil in Ireland.

Following 9/11 and the rise of Islamist extremism in the Middle East
and other parts of the world, many Western countries faced deadly terrorist attacks and saw terrorism take on a growing importance in public
debate and the media. At the same time, many anti-immigration and conservative parties gradually shifted from opposing immigration in general
terms to emphasizing the specific threat that Islam and Muslim minorities would represent to Western culture.[63] Figure 1.12 documents that in
every single country for which data is available, Muslim voters have been
substantially more likely than other voters to vote for social democratic

63. A. Kallis, "The Radical Right and Islamophobia," in *The Oxford Handbook of
the Radical Right,* ed. J. Rydgren (Oxford University Press, 2018), 42–60; F. Perocco,
"Anti-migrant Islamophobia in Europe: Social Roots, Mechanisms and Actors," *Revista
Interdisciplinar da Mobilidade Humana* 26, no. 53 (2018): 25–40.

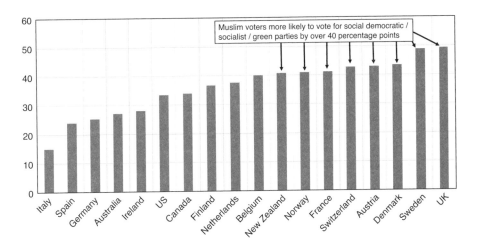

FIGURE 1.12. The Muslim vote in Western democracies
*Data Source:* Authors' computations using the World Political Cleavages and Inequality Database (see wpid.world) and the European Social Survey for Denmark, Finland, Germany, Italy, Norway, Spain, Sweden, Switzerland, and the United Kingdom.
*Note:* The figure represents the difference between the share of Muslim voters and the share of non-Muslims voting for democratic/labor/social democratic/socialist/green parties over the 2010–2020 period. In all Western countries, Muslims are substantially more likely to vote for these parties than non-Muslims. This cleavage is stronger in countries with strong far-right parties (e.g., Sweden, Denmark, Austria, Switzerland, France). Excludes Fianna Fáil in Ireland.

and affiliated parties. The gap is much larger than for immigrants as a whole, exceeding 40 percentage points in several countries, which points to the particular strength of cleavages linked to Muslim communities. Even if cross-country comparisons should be interpreted with care given the low number of observations,[64] significant variations across countries are still visible, and in many cases they follow the ranking observed in the case of the immigrant-native cleavage. This is consistent with the idea that Muslim voters are less likely to vote for the right when conservative and anti-immigration parties are perceived as particularly hostile to their integration in the national polity.

64. In particular, Muslim voters represent only a tiny minority in countries like New Zealand or the United States, which increases the uncertainty of estimates.

What does the emergence of this new cleavage mean for the representation of class conflicts? On the one hand, many social-nativist movements and parties have been increasingly capable of attracting the votes of the low-income and lower-educated electorate in several countries, and they could well become the first parties of the least privileged social groups in the future. On the other hand, given the support for social democratic and affiliated parties from immigrants and new minorities, minorities who tend to be overrepresented at the lower end of the social hierarchy, these parties are likely to continue to draw at least some sections of the low-income electorate. In other words, nativist conflicts could well contribute to further blurring class divides, as social democratic parties would shift to increasingly represent higher-educated voters and disadvantaged minorities, while anti-immigration parties would concentrate the votes of lower-educated and low-income voters of the native majority.

### Sociocultural and Ethnic Cleavages in Comparative Perspective

We now extend our analysis to a broader comparison of ethnoreligious, ethnolinguistic, ethnoregional, and racial cleavages, focusing on the vote of specific disadvantaged sociocultural groups in a selected number of countries in our dataset. This has the advantage of shedding light on striking variations across countries, but we stress that it remains insufficient to grasp the complexity of these divides. Racial cleavages in the United States, ethnic cleavages in Nigeria, and caste cleavages in India are undoubtedly extremely different in their historical origins, their modes of reproduction, and the ways they are politicized. Our main objective in this short overview is to provide a stylized comparison of how these different identities interact with socioeconomic inequalities and contribute to reinforcing or blurring class divides.

To capture the diversity of historical and political trajectories, we propose to consider in turn three groups of countries, corresponding to three ideal-typical forms of sociocultural conflicts: countries with a disadvantaged minority, countries with a historically dominant minority, and countries with high sociocultural fragmentation.

DISADVANTAGED MINORITIES. Many countries in the world are home to ethnic, religious, or racial minorities who, because of histories of oppression, marginalization, or prejudice, continue to display significantly lower levels of economic and human capital. We have seen in the previous section that this was the case with immigrants and Muslim voters in

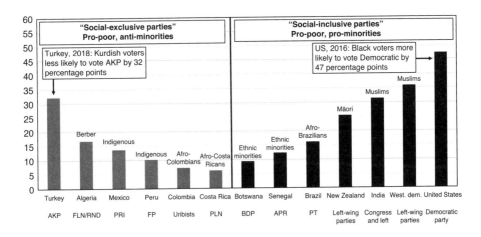

FIGURE 1.13. Sociocultural cleavages and disadvantaged minorities in comparative perspective

*Data Source:* Authors' computations using the World Political Cleavages and Inequality Database (see wpid.world).

*Note:* The figure represents the difference between the share of specific sociocultural minorities and the share of other voters voting for selected "pro-poor" parties in the last election available. The Turkish AKP corresponds to a "social-exclusive party": it is supported by low-income voters of the majority but not by the disadvantaged Kurdish minority. The Democratic Party in the United States is a "social-inclusive party," supported by both low-income voters and disadvantaged Black voters. Ethnic minorities correspond to non-Tswana groups in Botswana and speakers of Fulani/Serer/Mande languages in Senegal.

Western democracies, who are more likely to vote for left-wing parties, but this analysis can be extended to a number of other sociocultural groups and countries in our dataset.

When do minorities support the same coalitions as other low-income voters, and when do they not? Figure 1.13 represents the difference between the share of selected minorities and the share of other voters voting for the main low-income coalition in a number of countries in our dataset. At the right of the figure are "social-inclusive parties," which are supported by both low-income voters and minorities. The Black vote for the Democratic Party in the United States, the Māori vote for labor and green parties in New Zealand, and the Muslim vote for social democratic parties in Western democracies correspond today to such cases of *aligned* class and sociocultural cleavages. This is also the case of the Indian Na-

tional Congress and various left-wing (socialist, communist, or lower-caste) parties in India, supported by both Muslims and lower-caste Hindus, as well as the Workers' Party in Brazil, which has been more popular among Afro-Brazilians than among White voters in recent years.

At the left of the figure are "social-exclusive parties," which achieve high results among low-income voters of the majority but not among minorities. Recep Tayyip Erdoğan's AKP in Turkey is today a clear example of such cross-cutting sociocultural cleavage. Since 2015, the AKP has been very popular among low-income Turkish voters, but not among the disadvantaged Kurdish minority, whose social and cultural demands have faced increasing repression in the context of the Syrian war and the fight against terrorism. This cleavage emerged as the result of a complete reversal of the party's attitude toward the Kurds, whose cultural specificities had initially been recognized by the new government (see Chapter 19). A comparable divide is visible in Algeria, where the Arabic nationalism promoted by the National Liberation Front has been strongly resented by the Berber population in the past decades (also see Chapter 19). Comparable cross-cutting minority-majority cleavages are also visible in Mexico and Peru, where conservative and progressive candidates have competed for representation of the low-income electorate and the Indigenous in recent years (see Chapter 15).

At the middle of the figure, finally, are countries where ethnic or sociocultural minorities have been only slightly more or less likely to vote for the pro-poor coalition. These include Costa Rica and Colombia, where the politicization of racial issues has historically been weak (see Chapter 15), as well as Botswana and Senegal, where both ethnic inequalities and ethnic cleavages have remained relatively low in comparative perspective (see Chapter 17).

These simple comparisons suggest that the alignment between class cleavages and sociocultural cleavages varies substantially across countries and over time. There are party systems where these two dimensions are aligned, just as there are democracies where they are strongly cross-cutting, and yet others where minorities do not vote very differently from the rest of the electorate. Western democracies could soon become cases with such cross-cutting sociocultural cleavages if nativist movements were to succeed in uniting a sufficient share of low-income and lower-educated voters. In fact, this realignment clearly seems to be on its way in the United States, where the Republican Party has been attracting a growing proportion of the low-income White electorate (see Chapter 2).

It also seems to be taking place in India, where the Bharatiya Janata Party (BJP) has gained support from an increasing number of low-income and lower-caste Hindus in recent years (see Chapter 9). If conflicts over the integration of immigrants and ethnoreligious minorities were to continue deepening in many regions of the world, social-exclusive parties could well continue to gain prominence in contemporary democracies in the future.

HIGH-INCOME MINORITIES. In three countries of our dataset, Taiwan, Malaysia, and South Africa, a dominant minority has historically controlled a significant share of economic resources. In Taiwan, following the end of the Chinese Civil War in the late 1940s, the Kuomintang government quickly established an authoritarian regime on the island, which disproportionately favored the new immigrants from the mainland (see Chapter 13). In Malaysia, the Chinese held a substantial share of wealth and enterprises at the time of independence from British rule in 1957, while the Bumiputera majority remained concentrated at the bottom of the income distribution (see Chapter 12). In South Africa, it was White European settlers who dominated the economic and political life of the country throughout the twentieth century, until democratization put an end to the apartheid regime in the 1990s (see Chapter 16).

In all three countries, we observe strong and persistent cleavages between the previously dominant minority and the disprivileged majority (see Figure 1.14). Due to large differences in the magnitude of ethnic inequalities in these countries, however, there are major variations in the interactions between these divides and social inequalities. South Africa is the country where racial inequalities, racial cleavages, and class cleavages are the highest of all the democracies studied in this volume. Since 1994, Black voters, who remain overwhelmingly concentrated at the bottom of the income and wealth distributions, have had a higher probability of voting for the African National Congress by over 65 percentage points, leading racial cleavages to *structure* class divides. However, South Africa's party system may well be moving from "race-based" to "class-based" conflicts in the future, as declining support for the African National Congress has been concentrated among high-income Black voters (see Chapter 16).

As in South Africa, persistent Chinese-Bumiputera inequalities have given an important socioeconomic dimension to ethnic cleavages in Malaysia. By contrast, ethnic cleavages in Taiwan have been essentially

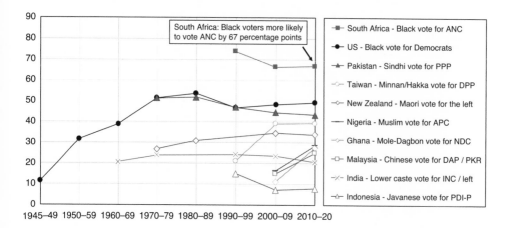

FIGURE 1.14. The strength and persistence of sociocultural cleavages in comparative perspective

*Data Source:* Authors' computations using the World Political Cleavages and Inequality Database (see wpid.world).

*Note:* The figure shows the difference between the share of a specific sociocultural group and the rest of the electorate voting for selected parties or groups of parties. In the United States in the 1940s, Black voters were more likely to vote for the Democratic Party by 12 percentage points, compared to 49 percentage points in the 2010s. Sociocultural cleavages have risen or remained stable at high levels in the majority of represented countries. They are highest in South Africa and lowest in Indonesia. For India, the gap corresponds to Scheduled Castes/Scheduled Tribes vs. Upper castes.

uncorrelated to economic status, as interethnic inequalities have declined significantly in the past decades to a relatively low level. This has made these divides cross-cutting identity-based cleavages, which remain driven primarily by diverging attitudes toward mainland China rather than by conflicts over economic resources (see Chapter 13). Differences in the link between ethnicity and inequality therefore explain in large part why class cleavages are today exceptionally strong in South Africa, strong in Malaysia, and weak in Taiwan (see Figure 1.7), despite similarities in the historical structure of ethnic conflicts in these three countries.

COUNTRIES WITH HIGH SOCIOCULTURAL DIVERSITY. In a third group of countries, finally, sociocultural diversity encompasses a larger set of groups of more or less significant sizes. Indonesia, Iraq, India, Pakistan, Nigeria, and Ghana clearly correspond to such cases. We also

observe significant variations in inequalities and electoral divides in these countries, as well as a general tendency of sociocultural conflicts to align with class. Nigeria, Ghana, and Pakistan, like South Africa and Malaysia, are countries characterized by what one could call *class-based sociocultural cleavages*, where both intergroup inequalities and cleavages are strong (see Figure 1.14). India is an intermediate case, where caste cleavages have an important socioeconomic dimension but are largely insufficient to account for the dynamics of class conflicts. In fact, class divides have declined in India in the past decades, while caste and especially religious cleavages have been increasingly restructuring political conflicts (see Chapter 9). In Indonesia, finally, we observe both weak ethnic inequalities and a low politicization of ethnic divides in national elections (see Chapter 12). These variations demonstrate that ethnic diversity is not tantamount to ethnic conflict. Political institutions and historical trajectories, by shaping both ethnic inequalities and ethnic identities, play a crucial role in determining the strength and persistence of sociocultural cleavages.

Furthermore, even in countries with strong ethnic cleavages, such as Nigeria, Ghana, and Pakistan, low-income parties never represent a specific group *exclusively*. Instead, they almost systematically capture the votes of both low-income sociocultural groups and poorer voters belonging to other groups. While we do observe significant evolutions over time in the tendency of parties to become more or less "ethnicized," this suggests that sociocultural identities can come to not only *structure* class cleavages, but also *trigger* class cleavages beyond these very identities. This is for instance the case with the All Progressives Congress in Nigeria, which has not only gradually become the party of Muslims concentrated in the poorer northern regions but also kept significant support from lower-educated Christian voters in the south (see Chapter 17).

## Spatial Identities, Regional Cleavages, and Separatism

Voters do not vote according to general ideological or national concerns only. In many cases, local interests, anchored in socioeconomic, sociocultural, and historical factors, form the basis of political parties' constituencies. In this section, we study how rural-urban and regional cleavages vary across countries and over time, paying special attention to how these cleavages interact with the structure of inequality and to the sources of the emergence or disappearance of separatist and regional movements, which have been on the rise in several democracies in the past decades.

### Rural-Urban and Center-Periphery Cleavages
### in Western Democracies

In the majority of countries of the world, big cities concentrate a substantial share of economic activity. Urban areas, thanks to better facilities, infrastructures, and economic opportunities, almost systematically give their residents better average standards of living than in the countryside.[65] Rural-urban and center-periphery cleavages therefore often have an important socioeconomic dimension.

In Figure 1.15, we reproduce a well-known result: rural areas have always been less likely to vote for socialist, social democratic, and communist parties than for conservative and Christian movements in Western democracies. This was a direct historical by-product of the industrial cleavage identified by Lipset and Rokkan. Left-wing movements arising from the Industrial Revolution were more popular among urban manual workers, while farmers remained more faithful to existing conservative forces. This inability of social democratic and affiliated parties to attract the low-income and lower-educated electorate beyond the working class was, to some observers, key to its limited success in Western democracies over the course of the twentieth century.[66] This also explains why class divides grew much stronger in countries where the stabilization of party systems occurred at the peak of industrialization (for instance, the United Kingdom and Sweden) than in countries where employment in the agricultural sector was still significant (for instance, Italy, Ireland, and Japan), where the rural-urban cleavage was thus strongly cross-cutting.

Figure 1.15 also suggests that rural-urban cleavages have remained remarkably stable in the past seventy years. Despite significant realignments in other dimensions of political conflicts, rural areas continue to be more likely to vote for the right, by 5 to 15 percentage points in most Western democracies. That being said, the fragmentation of the political space in multiparty systems has been associated with a reshuffling of rural-urban divides within left-right blocs: support for green parties tends to be particularly concentrated in big cities, while anti-immigration parties generally fare better in rural areas.[67] Today, countries where we

65. See appendix Figure C2, wpid.world, and A. Young, "Inequality, the Urban-Rural Gap, and Migration," *Quarterly Journal of Economics* 128, no. 4 (2013): 1727–1785.

66. A. Przeworski and J. Sprague, *Paper Stones. A History of Electoral Socialism* (University of Chicago Press, 1986).

67. See appendix Figures C3 and C4, wpid.world.

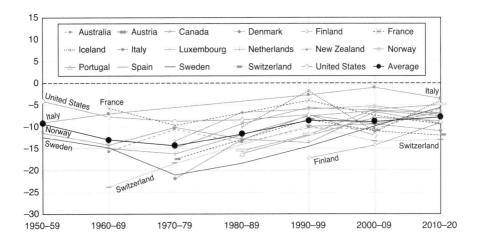

FIGURE 1.15. The rural-urban cleavage in Western democracies
*Data Source:* Authors' computations using the World Political Cleavages and Inequality Database (see wpid.world).
*Note:* The figure displays the difference between the share of rural areas and the share of urban areas voting for democratic/labor/social democratic/socialist/green parties. In all countries, rural areas have remained significantly less likely to vote for these parties than cities, with no clear trend over time. Estimates control for income, education, age, gender, employment status, and marital status (in country-years for which these variables are available).

observe the sharpest rural-urban divides (for instance, Switzerland, Austria, Denmark, Norway, and France) are also those where the vote shares of anti-immigration far-right parties are among the highest.

Finally, several Western democracies seem to have witnessed a significant transformation of center-periphery cleavages in recent years, as socialist, social democratic, and green parties have concentrated a growing share of the votes of capital cities.[68] If this transition were to continue, rural-urban cleavages could well intensify in the future, contributing to further blurring historical class cleavages.

### Rural-Urban Cleavages in Non-Western Democracies

Turning to non-Western democracies, we observe significant variations in the direction and strength of rural-urban cleavages, which we propose to summarize in four types (Figure 1.16).

68. See appendix Figures C8 and C9, wpid.world.

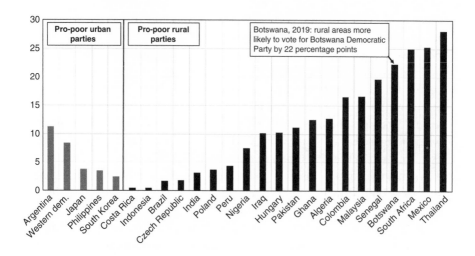

FIGURE 1.16. Rural-urban cleavages in comparative perspective
*Data Source:* Authors' computations using the World Political Cleavages and Inequality Database (see wpid.world).
*Note:* The figure displays the difference between the share of rural areas and the share of urban areas voting for the main pro-poor party in the last election available in the dataset. In the majority of countries, parties oriented toward low-income voters also tend to make significantly higher scores in rural areas than in cities. Western democracies: cross-country average over all countries with data.

In a first group of countries, we observe *cross-cutting rural-urban cleavages:* poorer rural areas are less likely than urban areas to vote for low-income parties. Strikingly, Western democracies and Argentina (due to the particular urban orientation of Peronism, see Chapter 15) are among the only countries where this is the case. In the majority of non-Western democracies covered in this volume, class and rural-urban cleavages are aligned.

In a second group of countries, we observe *weak rural-urban cleavages.* In these countries, rural-urban divides are either not politicized (for instance, in Japan, Brazil, and India) or politicized in a relatively complex way, with several pro-poor coalitions competing in both rural and urban areas (for instance, in Indonesia and Peru). Notice that this static view is far from sufficient. In Brazil, for instance, the Workers' Party was almost exclusively urban-based in the 1990s, but it gradually gained traction in the countryside as the social policies implemented by the governments of Lula da Silva and Dilma Rousseff largely benefited poor rural

63

households (see Chapter 14). Another particularly interesting case is Japan, where rural-urban cleavages used to be exceptionally pronounced but have gradually lost significance in the past decades (see Chapter 11).

In a third group of countries, rural areas have a higher likelihood of voting for low-income parties, but this is mainly because low-income ethnic groups are concentrated in rural areas. Such cases of *ethnic rural-urban cleavages* include South Africa, Malaysia, Ghana, and Pakistan, where ethnic cleavages are strong and where some ethnic groups are more concentrated in the cities than in the countryside. Rural-urban divides in Thailand, the highest observed in this volume, also have an equally strong socioeconomic dimension, but they are triggered by regional inequalities rather than by ethnicity (see below).

A fourth group of countries, finally, corresponds to one-party dominant systems. In countries such as Botswana and Senegal, we observe what one could call *incumbent rural-urban cleavages:* dominant parties are far more popular in the countryside than in the cities. As shown in their respective chapters and documented in existing comparative studies, one-party dominance is often tightly linked to the dynamics of clientelism and patronage.[69] In this context, dominant parties, thanks to clientelistic networks and other social transfers of various forms, tend to have a particularly strong grip on rural areas, especially in economically marginalized "captive constituencies."[70] Meanwhile, cities tend to concentrate a greater share of young, educated citizens, who often form the core of support for rising opposition movements. In Figure 1.17, we show that this phenomenon can be extended to a number of other historical cases of one-party dominance. The Indian National Congress in the 1960s, the Japanese Liberal Democratic Party in the same period, and the Botswana Democratic Party in recent years are all examples of dominant parties undergoing a period of decline. During these periods, peripheral regions tend to remain more faithful to the incumbent than do urban areas and especially capital cities, which concentrate the votes for opposition parties.

---

69. See, for instance, K. F. Greene, *Why Dominant Parties Lose: Mexico's Democratization in Comparative Perspective* (Cambridge University Press, 2007); E. Scheiner, *Democracy without Competition in Japan: Opposition Failure in a One-Party Dominant State* (Cambridge University Press, 2009); Kitschelt and Wilkinson, *Patrons, Clients and Policies.*

70. M. Wachman and C. Boone, "Captured Countryside? Stability and Change in Sub-national Support for African Incumbent Parties," *Comparative Politics* 50, no. 2 (2018): 189–208.

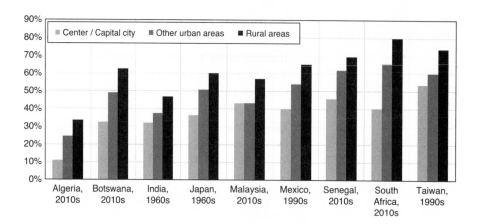

FIGURE 1.17. Rural-urban cleavages in one-party dominant systems: vote for dominant parties by geographical location

*Data Source:* Authors' computations using the World Political Cleavages and Inequality Database (see wpid.world).

*Note:* The figure represents the share of votes received by dominant parties by geographical location in a selected number of countries and time periods. In all these one-party dominant systems, dominant parties systematically receive greater support from rural areas than from cities. Dominant parties: FLN/RND (Algeria), BDP (Botswana), Congress (India), LDP (Japan), BN (Malaysia), PRI (Mexico), APR (Senegal), ANC (South Africa), Kuomintang (Taiwan). Centers correspond to Alger (Algeria), Gaborone (Botswana), Delhi (India), Wards (Japan), the Central region (Malaysia), the Center region (Mexico), the Western region (Senegal), Gauteng and Western Cape (South Africa), and the North region (Taiwan).

## Regional Cleavages

We now extend our analysis beyond the rural-urban dichotomy to study regional cleavages in a more general way. Where do we observe the strongest regional cleavages in contemporary democracies, and how do these cleavages interact with the structure of inequality? To answer these questions, one can start by ranking countries in our dataset according to a simple indicator: the share of variance in voting behaviors explained by regional divides. This indicator would be 0 in a country with no regional cleavage at all, and 100 percent in the extreme case where all regions vote for their own specific parties. As shown in Figure 1.18, it exceeds 5 percent in fifteen countries of our dataset.

The vast majority of these democracies share one point in common: they are countries with significant ethnic diversity and some form of

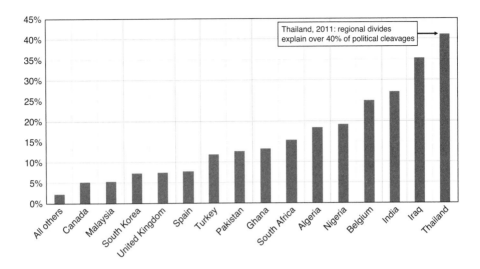

FIGURE 1.18. Regional cleavages in comparative perspective

*Data Source:* Authors' computations using the World Political Cleavages and Inequality Database (see wpid.world).

*Note:* The figure represents the share of variations in electoral behaviors that can be explained by regional divides in the last election available. Thailand, Iraq, India, and Belgium are the countries with the deepest regional cleavages, with over a quarter of political cleavages amounting to regional differences in vote choices. The indicator corresponds to McFadden's pseudo R-squared of a multinomial logistic regression of regional location on the full voting variable (including all parties). Notice that the interpretation is not strictly equivalent to the share of variance explained (values between 20% and 40% generally correspond to excellent fits).

clustering of ethnic groups by region. Iraq's unique sectarian system, explicitly set up to allocate political power between the various communities (principally Kurds, Shia Muslims, and Sunni Muslims), represents the most extreme case of such *ethnoregional cleavages* (see Chapter 19). Nigeria, South Africa, Ghana, and Pakistan are also clear examples of regionally structured party systems with a pronounced ethnic component. As shown in the previous section, these cleavages have a clear class dimension, as the regional division of ethnic groups coincides with significant sociospatial inequalities.

Thailand stands out as the country where regional voting has been pushed to its most extreme level, despite the absence of comparable ethnic fragmentation. Here, regional inequalities appear to have played the

greatest role. Extreme wealth disparities between Bangkok and the northern territories, fueled by decades of unequal economic growth, triggered the rise of class cleavages that are among the highest observed in this volume (see Figure 1.7 and Chapter 12). Four Western democracies, Belgium, Spain, the United Kingdom, and Canada, are included in this chart. They have all seen the emergence of powerful separatist movements in recent decades (see below). If we were to have data going back to the nineteenth century, we would likely observe comparably significant regional cleavages in other Western democracies (for instance, France).

Finally, our results reveal that far from monotonically decreasing with the passing of time, economic development, or democratization, regional cleavages seem to have significantly increased in a number of democracies (see Figure 1.19). In the Indian subcontinent, the decline of

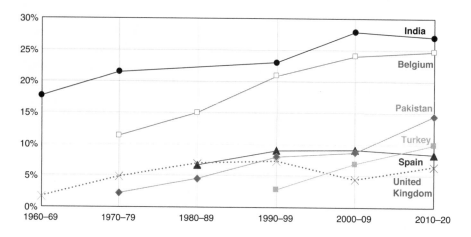

FIGURE 1.19. Regional cleavages in historical perspective

*Data Source:* Authors' computations using the World Political Cleavages and Inequality Database (see wpid.world).

*Note:* The figure represents the share of variations in electoral behaviors that can be explained by regional divides in a selected number of countries. Regional divides have grown significantly in India, Belgium, Pakistan, Turkey, Spain, and the United Kingdom in the past decades, driven by the regionalization of existing coalitions and the formation of new regionally based parties. The indicator corresponds to McFadden's pseudo R-squared of a multinomial logistic regression of regional location on the full voting variable (including all parties). Notice that the interpretation is not strictly equivalent to the share of variance explained (values between 20% and 40% generally correspond to excellent fits).

the once-dominant Indian National Congress coincided with an extraordinary regionalization of electoral politics, in such a way that India could be considered to have not one, but several state-specific party systems today (see Chapter 9). A similar trajectory is visible in Pakistan, where the Pakistan Peoples Party, once popular among the low-income and lower-educated electorate, beyond ethnic affiliations, has seen its support become increasingly limited to rural Sindh (see Chapter 10). Belgium, Spain, and the United Kingdom have all seen the emergence of regionalist parties, which we now consider in greater detail.

### Class and Sub-state Nationalism

Toward the end of the nineteenth century, leading thinkers argued that socioeconomic divisions stemming from the Industrial Revolution were going to gain more prominence at the expense of territory, culture, and nationality.[71] Sub-state nationalism was also left aside by scholars in the 1950s and 1960s, when modernization approaches to the state, politics, and development were most influential, and more recently in the 1990s, when many claimed that regional nationalism would fall victim to the forces of globalization.[72] Despite these predictions, sub-state nationalism has not disappeared; if anything, it has intensified. Flanders in Belgium, Catalonia in Spain, Québec in Canada, and Scotland in the United Kingdom all saw the rise of powerful separatist movements in recent decades.

While the causes underlying the emergence and strength of these movements are extremely complex, involving dimensions of sociocultural identity, collective mobilization, and historical specificities,[73] our dataset suggests that socioeconomic factors have also mattered in structuring regional divides. In Flanders and Catalonia, both rich regions within their respective countries, separatist movements have been more popular among high-income voters. In Scotland and Québec, two regions that share a

71. K. Marx and F. Engels, *The Communist Manifesto* (1848), trans. Samuel Moore (Penguin, 1967); É. Durkheim, *The Division of Labor in Society* (1893) (Free Press, 2014).

72. On the 1950s and 1960s, see K. Deutsch, *Nationalism and Social Communication: An Inquiry into the Formation of Nationality* (MIT Press, 1966). On the 1990s, see E. J. Hobsbawm, *Nations and Nationalism since 1780: Programme, Myth, Reality* (Cambridge University Press, 1992).

73. E. Gellner, *Nations and Nationalism* (Cornell University Press, 1983); A. Lecours, "Sub-state Nationalism in the Western World: Explaining Continued Appeal," *Ethnopolitics* 11, no. 3 (2012): 268–286.

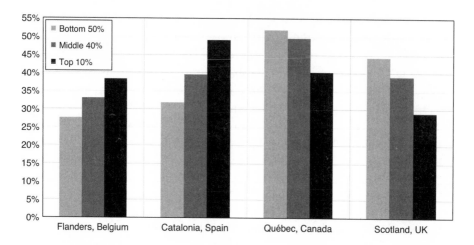

FIGURE 1.20. Class and regionalism: vote for independentist parties in Belgium, Spain, Canada, and the United Kingdom by income group
*Data Source:* Authors' computations using the World Political Cleavages and Inequality Database (see wpid.world)
*Note:* The figure displays the share of votes received by selected nationalist parties by income group in Flanders, Catalonia, Québec, and Scotland. Nationalist parties receive greater support from top-income voters in Flanders and Catalonia and from low-income voters in Québec and Scotland. Parties and time periods represented: VU/N-VA in Flanders in the 2010s, nationalist parties in Catalonia in the 2010s, Bloc Québécois in Québec in the 1990s, and Scottish National Party in Scotland in the 2010s.

history of lower economic development relative to their respective countries, nationalism has on the contrary found greater support among the low-income electorate (see Figure 1.20).

In Belgium, Flemish sub-state nationalism has its origins in opposition to the Francophone nature of the Belgian state after its creation in 1830. After the end of World War II and with Belgium's entry to the European Economic Community in 1957, economic disparities between the two regions worsened. Flanders became more prosperous by attracting foreign investment, leading some Flemish to be increasingly against subsidizing declining Walloon industries (see Chapter 7). Our results are therefore consistent with the idea that economic elites are more likely than low-income Flemish voters to oppose greater interregional fiscal redistribution.

In Spain, Catalan nationalism has its roots in the late nineteenth century with a bourgeoisie who felt Catalonia was held back in its development by the Spanish state. The traditional autonomist program of

Catalan nationalism was for the most part achieved during the redemocratization process in the late 1970s, but dissatisfaction with Spanish federalism started increasing again by the late 1990s. The Catalan government proposed to revise the Catalan Statute of Autonomy, but the Spanish Constitutional Court annulled much of the reform proposal in 2010. The nationalist movement then took a secessionist turn, exacerbated by the socioeconomic difficulties created by the 2008 financial crisis. As with Flanders, our analysis of Catalonia is thus consistent with high-income voters wanting their region to keep fiscal receipts for regional uses rather than to redistribute them to the rest of Spain (see Chapter 6).

In Scotland, nationalist sentiments date to the Treaty of Union of 1707, uniting England and Scotland to create the Kingdom of Great Britain, but it was only after the two World Wars that Scottish home rule gained important support. The neoliberal fiscal and social policies carried out during the governments of Thatcher (1979–1990) and Major (1990–1997) generated much opposition in Scotland and fed the Scottish mobilization in favor of home rule, attracting the electorate traditionally dominated by the Labour Party. The movement culminated with two referendums, in which a majority of Scottish voters supported devolution (1997) but rejected independence (2014). Supporters of home rule have defended the need for increased autonomy, not to keep fiscal receipts for their own region, but rather to limit the effect of future British neoliberal measures and to preserve the freedom to implement more progressive policies.[74]

In Canada, finally, the divergence of Canadian and Québécois interests dates to the settlement of North America in the 1700s, fueled by linguistic divisions and persisting inequalities between the English-speaking majority and the poorer French-speaking population.[75] Nonetheless, it was not until the mid-twentieth century that the Québécois government started to

74. D. Béland and A. Lecours, "Nationalism and the Politics of Austerity: Comparing Catalonia, Scotland, and Québec," *National Identities* 20, no. 4 (2019): 1–17; D. Béland and A. Lecours, *Nationalism and Social Policy: The Politics of Territorial Solidarity* (Oxford University Press, 2008); N. McEwen, *Nationalism and the State: Welfare and Identity in Scotland and Quebec* (Peter Lang, 2006); G. Mooney and C. Williams, "Forging New 'Ways of Life'? Social Policy and Nation Building in Devolved Scotland and Wales," *Critical Social Policy* 26, no. 3 (2006): 608–629.

75. P. Hossay, *Contentions of Nationhood: Nationalist Movements, Political Conflict, and Social Change in Flanders, Scotland, and French Canada* (Lexington Books, 2002).

demand that their province be seen as a distinct society with special status. A referendum was held in 1995, in which a majority of Québécois voters did not support independence. As in Scotland, the idea that the province has more egalitarian and progressive values than the rest of the country has been an important element of the Bloc Québécois' discourse.[76]

Taken together, these findings suggest that regional socioeconomic disparities can help to shed light on the relationship between class and sub-nationalism.

## Generational Cleavages

In this section, we briefly study the strength and evolution of age differences in party choice in our dataset and discuss possible drivers behind the observed dynamics. We document the link between generational divides and party system transformation, as well as conflicts over political integration and foreign policy. In Western democracies, we discuss the link between generational cleavages and the emergence of multi-elite party systems.

### Generational Cleavages and Party System Transformation

A body of social psychology has emphasized that conservatism rises with age due to changes in personality and cognition that occur naturally as people age (*within* cohort effects).[77] The political science literature has instead emphasized that opinions formed when young tend to be long-lasting, so differences in opinion that may appear to be caused by age are in fact often generational in origin (*across* cohort effects). In particular, according to the "silent revolution" theory first formulated by Ronald Inglehart, new generations born in the second half of the twentieth century in Western democracies would give greater importance to liberal "post-materialist" values, having been socialized in an era of unprecedented affluence.[78] Older generations, by contrast, would have remained more likely to continue upholding authoritarian and conservative

76. Béland and Lecours, *Nationalism and Social Policy*.

77. See, for instance, C. J. Soto, O. P. John, S. D. Gosling, and J. Potter, "Age Differences in Personality Traits from 10 to 65: Big Five Domains and Facets in a Large Cross-sectional Sample," *Journal of Personality and Social Psychology* 100, no. 2 (2011): 330–348.

78. Inglehart, *Silent Revolution*; R. Inglehart, *Culture Shift in Advanced Industrial Society* (Princeton University Press, 1990).

values. The replacement of old generations by new ones would thus lead to a progression in the share of social-liberal citizens and an ever-shrinking share of conservatives in Western societies. The emergence of populist authoritarian leaders in recent years would have accordingly represented a conservative response to this sociopolitical transformation, fueled by feelings of sociocultural anxiety and reinforced by growing material insecurity linked to globalization and rising inequality.[79]

We do not find any evidence that older generations have become more conservative than younger generations in Western democracies in the past decades. While there are fluctuations across countries and over time, the gap in the share of young and old voters supporting left-wing parties seems to have remained remarkably stable on average.[80] However, we do identify interesting variations in age differences in the case of specific parties. The share of votes received by green and new left-wing parties (such as Die Linke in Germany and Podemos in Spain) is clearly decreasing with age, consistent with the idea that new generations give greater weight to environmentalism and social-liberal values (see Figure 1.21). However, we find no evidence of an equally systematic generational divide when it comes to voting for anti-immigration parties. The share of votes received by anti-immigration parties is increasing in Denmark, Italy, Norway, New Zealand, Switzerland, and Sweden, but it is clearly decreasing in Austria, Spain, Finland, and France.

These findings call into question the notion of a backlash among older generations against current social change, common to all Western democracies: in a number of European countries, nativist parties have disproportionately attracted younger voters in the past decades. Although it is beyond the scope of this book to provide a thorough explanation for these differences across countries, the divergence may be due to country differences in how generations born between the two World Wars experienced the politicization of class cleavages and the rise of communism, how baby boomers socialized at a time of postwar economic growth, and how hard the new cohorts were hit by the 2008 economic recession.[81] These differences may also be linked to the different histories of anti-

---

79. Norris and Inglehart, *Cultural Backlash*.

80. See appendix Figures D1 to D4, wpid.world.

81. F. Gougou and N. Mayer, "The Class Basis of Extreme Right Voting in France: Generational Replacement and the Rise of New Cultural Issues (1984–2007)," in Rydgren, *Class Politics and the Radical Right*, 156–172; C. Miller-Idriss, "Youth and the Radical Right," in Rydgren, *Oxford Handbook of the Radical Right*, 348–365.

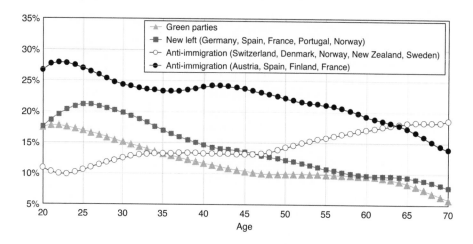

FIGURE 1.21. Generational cleavages and party system fragmentation in Western democracies

*Data Source:* Authors' computations using the World Political Cleavages and Inequality Database (see wpid.world).

*Note:* The figure represents the share of votes received by selected groups of parties in Western democracies by age in the last election available. Green parties and "New left" parties (Die Linke, Podemos, France Insoumise, Bloco de Esquerda, Norwegian Socialist Left Party) make much higher scores among the youth than among older generations. By contrast, there is no clear age profile in the case of far-right or anti-immigration parties. On the *x*-axis, 20 corresponds to voters aged 20 or younger; 70 corresponds to voters 70 or older.

immigration parties across Western democracies, as older generations may be less inclined to support anti-immigration parties with a particularly strong historical association with the extreme right (such as the Front National in France and the Freedom Party of Austria).

Also note that while the age gap in left-right voting has not displayed any clear trend, we do observe important generational divides between old and new parties in several countries. These divides were perhaps most clearly expressed in Spain in the past decade, when the emergence of challenger parties across the political spectrum (Podemos on the left, Ciudadanos at the center, and VOX on the right), all supported by younger voters, led to a profound reshuffling of political forces *within* each ideological bloc (see Chapter 6).

While differences in left-right voting behaviors *across* cohorts have not changed significantly in the past decades, political cleavages *within*

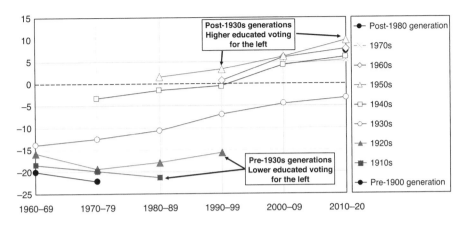

FIGURE 1.22. The reversal of educational divides in Western democracies: The role of generational replacement
*Data Source:* Authors' computations using the World Political Cleavages and Inequality Database (see wpid.world).
*Note:* The figure represents the difference between the share of higher-educated (top 10%) and lower-educated (bottom 90%) voters voting for democratic/labor/social democratic/socialist/green parties within specific cohorts. Between the 1960s and the 1990s, lower-educated voters born in the early decades of the twentieth century remained significantly more likely to vote for these parties than higher-educated voters born during the same period. In the last decade, on the contrary, young lower-educated voters were significantly less likely to vote for these parties than young higher-educated voters. Figures correspond to ten-year averages for Australia, Britain, Canada, Denmark, France, Germany, Italy, the Netherlands, Norway, Sweden, Switzerland, and the US.

cohorts do seem to have played an important role in reversing the educational cleavage in Western democracies. As shown in Figure 1.22, among the generations born after the 1940s, higher-educated voters have been more likely to vote for social democratic and affiliated parties than lower-educated voters, while the educational divide has remained negative among generations born before World War II. In other words, new generations have become increasingly divided along educational lines, with young higher-educated voters shifting toward social democrats and young lower-educated voters shifting toward conservatives. This suggests that the educational cleavage is likely to continue rising in the future, as old generations voting along historical class lines gradually disappear from the political scene. This finding is also consistent with the mechanism of educational expansion outlined above that pushes losers of the education

competition (young, lower-educated citizens) to move to the right. Note, however, that the reversal of the educational cleavage has also taken place within recent cohorts, which points to the role of other factors potentially related to political supply or ideological change.

In non-Western democracies, generational dynamics also play a role in times of party system transformation. In particular, they are highly relevant for understanding the decline of one-party dominant systems. Dominant parties are not supported only by rural and lower-educated voters, as we showed above. In many cases, they also fare significantly better among older generations (Figure 1.23). Note that many dominant parties arose from national independence movements, such as the National Liberation Front in Algeria, the Indian National Congress in India, and the Institutional Revolutionary Party in Mexico. The support for these parties from older generations therefore has a dimension of collective memory, which tends to be less vivid among the youth. Generational cleavages in

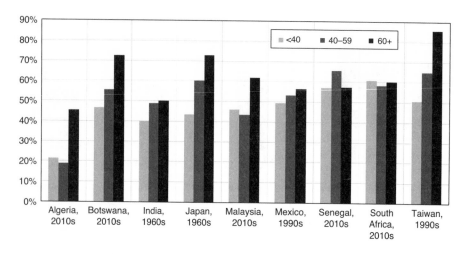

FIGURE 1.23. Generational cleavages in one-party dominant systems: vote for dominant party by age group

*Data Source:* Authors' computations using the World Political Cleavages and Inequality Database (see wpid.world).

*Note:* The figure represents the share of votes received by dominant parties by age group in a selected number of countries and time periods. In the majority of these one-party dominant systems, dominant parties receive greater support from older voters than from younger generations. Dominant parties: FLN/RND (Algeria), BDP (Botswana), Congress (India), LDP (Japan), BN (Malaysia), PRI (Mexico), APR (Senegal), ANC (South Africa), Kuomintang (Taiwan).

one-party dominant systems also have a socioeconomic dimension. Young, urban, and educated citizens, and in particular students, often form the backbone of rising opposition movements. As this new middle class often reaches higher standards of living than in the rural areas, age divides tend to enhance class cleavages in one-party dominant systems.

### Generational Cleavages and Political Integration

We also observe strong generational divides in countries with exceptionally divisive conflicts over issues related to political integration or national identity. In Figure 1.24, we represent four parties characterized by some of the most pronounced age divides observed in this volume: the Liberal Democratic Party in Japan in the 1960s, the pro-Beijing camp in Hong Kong in 2016, the Saenuri Party in South Korea in 2016, and the Conservative Party in the United Kingdom in 2017.

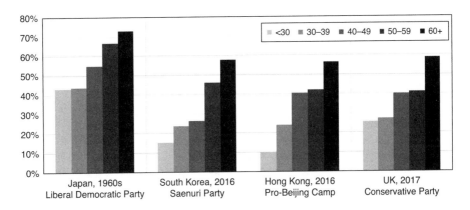

FIGURE 1.24. Generational cleavages, political integration, and foreign policy: Vote for selected parties by age group

*Data Source:* Authors' computations using the World Political Cleavages and Inequality Database (see wpid.world).

*Note:* The figure represents the share of votes received by the Liberal Democratic Party in Japan in the 1960s, the Saenuri Party in South Korea in 2016, the pro-Beijing camp in Hong Kong in 2016, and the Conservative Party in the United Kingdom in 2017 by age group. All these parties received significantly higher support among older generations than among the youth, which can be linked to the particular strength of cleavages over foreign policy and national integration in these party systems (war memory and remilitarization in Japan, attitudes toward the North Korean regime in South Korea, attitudes toward Mainland China in Hong Kong, and attitudes toward Brexit in the United Kingdom).

In postwar Japan, these divides expressed diverging attitudes toward war memory and military buildup. Left-wing parties, supported by the youth, were strongly opposed to remilitarization, while conservatives were more favorable to cooperation with the United States in the context of the Cold War (see Chapter 11). In Hong Kong, younger cohorts have been substantially more likely to relate to a sense of "Hongkonger" identity and to vote for the pro-democracy camp supporting greater autonomy from the mainland. In South Korea, younger generations show significantly lower support for unification with North Korea than older generations, but more strongly favor attempts to develop peaceful relations with the North Korean regime (see Chapter 13). In Britain, finally, the rise of generational cleavages is inseparable from the Brexit vote. Here, in contrast to the Hong Kong and South Korean cases, younger generations have been much more supportive of further political integration with Europe. This can in large part be explained by their higher level of education, which in turn determined their greater sense of European identity and their more progressive attitudes toward environmentalism and immigration.[82]

These four cleavages differ substantially in their causes and the issues they mobilize, but they are all inextricably tied to diverging attitudes toward supranational integration and international relations. Conflicts over political integration produce some of the deepest generational cleavages observed in contemporary democracies, because they inevitably question the very definition of national sovereignty and sociopolitical identities.

## Gender Cleavages

We conclude this chapter by studying gender differences in the voting preferences of the electorate, a recurrent theme in political science ever since the earliest systematic surveys of voting behavior. Studies carried out through the 1950s to 1970s found that women were more supportive of conservative parties and less likely to participate in politics than men

---

82. A. Zhang, "New Findings on Key Factors Influencing the UK's Referendum on Leaving the EU," *World Development* 102, no. 1 (2018): 304–314; B. Eichengreen, R. Mari, and G. Thwaites, "Will Brexit Age Well? Cohorts, Seasoning and the Age-Leave Gradient, Past, Present and Future" (NBER Working Paper No. 25219, 2018); K. Owen and C. Macfarland, *A Generation Apart: Were Younger People Left Behind by the EU Referendum?* (Covi, 2016).

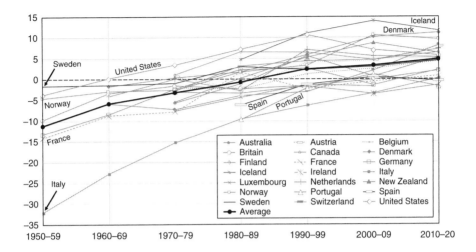

FIGURE 1.25. The reversal of gender cleavages in Western democracies
*Data Source:* Authors' computations using the World Political Cleavages and Inequality Database (see wpid.world).
*Note:* The figure displays the difference between the share of women and the share of men voting for democratic/labor/social democratic/socialist/green parties in Western democracies. In the majority of countries, women have gradually shifted from being significantly more conservative than men in the 1950s–1960s to being significantly more left-wing in the 2000s–2010s.

in Western democracies.[83] However, this "traditional gender cleavage" has disappeared since the 1980s and a "modern gender gap" has emerged, according to which women have become more likely to vote for social democratic and affiliated parties than men.[84] Figure 1.25 corroborates this fact by plotting the difference between the fraction of women and the fraction of men voting for left-wing parties in Western democracies. Whereas this difference was negative in all countries in the 1950s, it has become gradually positive, reaching 5 percentage points on average in the 2010s. Gender differences in voting behavior have thus progressively realigned in postindustrial societies.

83. M. Duverger, *The Political Role of Women* (UNESCO, 1955); S. M. Lipset, *Political Man: The Social Bases of Politics* (Doubleday, 1960).

84. R. Inglehart and P. Norris, "The Developmental Theory of the Gender Gap: Women's and Men's Voting Behavior in Global Perspective," *International Political Science Review* 21, no. 4 (2000): 441–463.

The traditional gender gap has been related to structural gender differences in religiosity and societal assignations, as well as to women having more conservative values.[85] Figure 1.25 indeed shows that the traditional gender cleavage was stronger in countries with a strong religious cleavage, such as France, Italy, and Spain. After controlling for religiosity or religious affiliation, the traditional gender cleavage shrinks from −32 percent to −11 percent in the 1950s in Italy and disappears completely in France in the 1960s.[86] In contrast, the gender cleavage barely changes after controls in countries with less important historical religious cleavages, such as Britain and Switzerland, or with strong class cleavages, such as Norway and Finland.

The dealignment of gender divides has been associated with the weakening of traditional social-party linkages, notably in terms of class and religion.[87] Nonetheless, the process of realignment of women toward social democratic and affiliated parties soon began. Most explanations emphasize sociostructural and cultural trends, which transformed the voting preferences of women and men, particularly among new generations.

Sociostructural and situational explanations relate to women's role and position in society and family life. Women's support for social democratic parties should increase in comparison to men's due to women's increased labor force participation and economic independence, as well as their greater exposure to labor market inequalities. Moreover, with the continuous changes in traditional gender stereotypes and family structures associated with greater instability (divorce, single parenting, and so on), women might be in favor of extending public welfare institutions.[88] In the United States and Western Europe, the decline of marriage, the rise of divorce, and the economic fragility of women have been shown to be important drivers behind the emergence of the modern

85. J. Blondel, *Votes, Parties and Leaders* (Penguin, 1970); M. Goot and E. Reid, "Women: If Not Apolitical, Then Conservative," in *Women and the Public Sphere*, ed. J. Siltanen and M. Stanworth (Hutchinson, 1984).

86. See appendix Figure E1, wpid.world.

87. Dalton et al., *Electoral Change in Advanced Industrial Democracies;* Franklin et al., *Electoral Change.*

88. S. Abendschön and S. Steinmetz, "The Gender Gap in Voting Revisited: Women's Party Preferences in a European Context," *Social Politics* 21, no. 2 (2014): 315–344.

gender gap.[89] In Northern Europe, the expansion of women's employment in the public sector also has been found to be an important factor in the increase in the vote for the left among women in recent decades.[90]

Cultural and attitudinal explanations are associated with the political attitudes and value orientations of women. Societal changes have come together with a decline in religiosity, which has affected more women than men due to closer religious ties among women, as well as the spread of "post-materialist" and feminist ideas.[91] Women have also been more engaged by environmental issues, which have spurred women's support for green parties, while anti-immigration parties have found greater support among men.[92] The recent gender alignment has thus mirrored the reversal of the education cleavage previously documented.

In non-Western democracies, while men and women do not systematically vote for different parties, we do observe a number of cases in which gender matters.[93] A first group of countries or elections corresponds to candidate effects: women are more likely to vote for women than for men.[94] This is the case in Brazil, for instance, where women were less likely to vote for Lula da Silva's Workers' Party in the 2000s, but then became significantly more likely to do so when Dilma Rousseff became the head of the party in 2010.[95] Another example is the 2011 Thai election, in which women were more likely than men to support the candidate of the Pheu Thai, Yingluck Shinawatra, by more than 15 percentage points, despite

89. L. Edlund and R. Pande, "Why Have Women Become Left-Wing? The Political Gender Gap and the Decline in Marriage," *Quarterly Journal of Economics* 117, no. 3 (2002): 917–961.

90. O. Knutsen, "Social Class, Sector Employment, and Gender as Party Cleavages in the Scandinavian Countries: A Comparative Longitudinal Study, 1970–95," *Scandinavian Political Studies* 24, no. 4 (2001): 311–350.

91. N. Giger, "Towards a Modern Gender Gap in Europe? A Comparative Analysis of Voting Behavior in 12 Countries," *Social Science Journal* 46, no. 3 (2009): 474–492.

92. T. E. Givens, "The Radical Right Gender Gap," *Comparative Political Studies* 37, no. 1 (2004): 30–54.

93. See appendix Figure E5, wpid.world.

94. C. L. Brians, "Women for Women? Gender and Party Bias in Voting for Female Candidates," *American Politics Research* 33, no. 3 (2005): 357–375; K. Dolan, *Voting for Women: How the Public Evaluates Women Candidates* (Routledge, 2018); R. L. Fox, *Gender Dynamics in Congressional Elections* (Sage, 1997); E. Plutzer and J. F. Zipp, "Identity Politics, Partisanship, and Voting for Women Candidates," *Public Opinion Quarterly* 60, no. 1 (1996): 30–57; M. Hinojosa, *Selecting Women, Electing Women: Political Representation and Candidate Selection in Latin America* (Temple University Press, 2012).

95. See appendix Figure A15, wpid.world.

not having been particularly supportive of her brother Thaksin ten years earlier.[96]

In a second group of countries, we observe gender divides that are more comparable to the traditional and modern gender divides visible in Western democracies, in the sense that they are more persistent and seem to be associated with parties or coalitions rather than with specific leaders or candidates. Israel is an example of a democracy with a modern gender cleavage, where women are slightly more likely to vote for progressive parties and less likely to support conservative forces (see Chapter 18). Colombia had a traditional gender gap that has gradually been closed since 2014, likely due to a gradual decline in religiosity and to the introduction of new social issues such as abortion and gender violence into the political agenda (see Chapter 15). Botswana presents one of the strongest and most persistent gender divides of non-Western democracies. The dominant Botswana Democratic Party, helped by its women's wing and the increased number of women assigned to top public positions, has indeed enjoyed higher support among women than among men since the early 2000s.[97]

Overall, these comparisons point to the lack of linear or determinist trajectories. There are highly developed and secular countries where no modern gender cleavage has emerged (for instance, Japan), just as there are middle-income countries where religion has a strong influence and yet where gender issues have been increasingly politicized (for instance, Colombia). "Modern" and "traditional" gender cleavages are arguably shaped by both religious and socioeconomic conditions, but political supply seems to also be playing a non-negligible role in shaping the representation of gender inequities.

## Toward a Typology of Socioeconomic Cleavage Structures

In this chapter, we have adopted a large historical and comparative perspective on how class cleavages vary across countries and how they interact with other dimensions of political conflict. Our analysis has revealed

96. See Chapter 12, appendix Figure AC7, wpid.world.

97. See Chapter 17, appendix Figure AC4, wpid.world; G. Nzongola-Ntalaja and M. C. Lee, eds. *The State and Democracy in Africa* (Africa World Press, 1998); B. Z. Osei-Hwedie, "The Political Opposition in Botswana: The Politics of Factionalism and Fragmentation," *Transformation* 45 (2001): 57–77.

substantial variations in the politicization of inequalities, mirroring the diversity of historical trajectories, socioeconomic structures, and lines of divisions in contemporary democracies.

Amid huge heterogeneity, we have identified interesting regularities. Class cleavages tend to be strong when cross-cutting cleavages related to religion or sociocultural values are weak. This relationship, however, is itself strongly conditioned by the link between identity and class. In countries where inequalities between "politically relevant identities" are high, class divides tend to be strong, because these identities come to embody significant socioeconomic disparities. In countries where these inequalities are weak, on the contrary, class divides do not align with dominant axes of political competition, leading to a weak politicization of inequality. Drawing on this simple distinction opens the way to reconsidering the link between inequality and political conflicts, in light of the processes by which inequalities are embodied by specific political actors. Accordingly, one may distinguish between simple ideal-typical forms of cleavage structures and party systems in contemporary democracies.

At one extreme are class-based party systems, characterized by strong and persistent socioeconomic divides whose influence on electoral behaviors is particularly pronounced. This was the case in the majority of postwar Western democracies, where the working class overwhelmingly supported left-wing parties. It is the case in some democracies such as Brazil or Argentina today, where economic status continues to play a major role in determining voter alignments. Countries where acute inequalities between ethnic or regional groups give a particularly pronounced economic dimension to sociocultural cleavages, such as South Africa, Nigeria, Ghana, Malaysia, and Thailand, also conform to this general pattern. One-party dominant systems often generate major differences in electoral behaviors across class lines too, because poorer, lower-educated voters in rural areas tend to remain more faithful to the incumbent. This is notably the case in Botswana and Senegal today, and it used to be the case in India, Japan, and Mexico when their dominant parties still wielded decisive political influence.

At another extreme are what we could call pure identity-based party systems, where socioeconomic divides are almost insignificant because other dimensions of political conflict, only weakly correlated to social inequalities, play the most determinant role. While this remains an ideal type, several examples of countries approaching this system are worth

mentioning. Iraq, with its political system explicitly encouraging the representation of voters' interests along ethnoreligious lines, was perhaps the closest contemporary democracies can get to this extreme until recently. South Korea and Taiwan, where issues of political integration and foreign policy have dominated party politics, and where attitudes toward these issues have been determined mostly by identities weakly correlated to class (age in South Korea, ethnicity in Taiwan), are also examples of a low politicization of inequalities. In many other democracies of the world, we see a comparable tendency of identity-based conflicts to assume growing importance and inhibit existing class divides, from the Muslim-Hindu cleavage in India to ethnic cleavages in Pakistan and nativist cleavages in Western democracies.

In between these two extremes are multidimensional or "multiconflictual" party systems, where socioeconomic divides do continue to structure electoral competition, but are blurred by the existence of a strong secondary dimension of political conflicts. Multi-elite party systems are the clearest example of such a configuration, where two dimensions of social class, income and education, determine electoral behaviors in opposite ways and have in some countries led to a growing fragmentation of multiparty systems. To some extent, nearly all democracies conform to this pattern in varying degrees, and multidimensional party systems should thus be seen as a middle way between pure class-based and pure identity-based party systems.

A last configuration, whose significance should not be understated, corresponds to depolarized or unstable party systems, where the representation of social divides is impeded by the lack of stable partisan affiliations. In such case scenarios, sociopolitical identities are only weakly linked to the socioeconomic structure. This could be said of several Latin American and Asian countries today, such as the Philippines, Indonesia, Peru, and Japan, where electoral instability, the proliferation of charismatic leaders, and a growing tendency toward the personalization of party politics have undermined the ability of party systems to represent social cleavages. To some extent, that could also be said of Western democracies today, where the weakening of traditional cleavages and the decline of political partisanship have been accompanied by the rise of electoral volatility and the growing importance of short-run factors.

These four ideal types, far from representing stable patterns across countries and over time, should be thought of as useful analytical tools

for revisiting the link between political cleavages and social inequalities. Many democracies have in the course of their histories transitioned from one type to another, sometimes following critical turning points, sometimes as the result of slow processes of realignment triggered by deep social transformations. Political cleavages do not derive from inevitable struggles between antagonistic groups. They are above all the result of the way political actors come to embody specific axes of social conflicts. Documenting as precisely as possible how these processes of representation have unfolded in the history of contemporary democracies is the objective of the case studies compiled in this volume.

## 2

# Brahmin Left versus Merchant Right

*Rising Inequality and the Changing Structure of Political Conflict in France, the United States, and the United Kingdom, 1948–2020*

## THOMAS PIKETTY

## Introduction

In this research I analyze the changing structure of political cleavages in France, Britain, and the United States. In order to do so, I exploit in a systematic manner the postelectoral surveys that were conducted after nearly every national election in these three countries over the 1948–2020 period. I construct homogenous long-run series on the changing structure of the electorate in these three countries—that is, who votes for which parties or coalitions depending on different dimensions of inequality (income, wealth, education, age, gender, religion, foreign or ethnic origins, and so on).

I document a striking long-run evolution. In the 1950s–1960s, the vote for "left-wing" (socialist-labor-democratic) parties was associated with lower-education and lower-income voters. This corresponds to what one might label a "class-based" party system: lower-class voters from the different dimensions (education, income, wealth) tend to vote for the same party or coalition, while upper- and middle-class voters from the different dimensions tend to vote for the other party or coalition. Since the 1970s–1980s, the "left-wing" vote has gradually become associated with higher-education voters, giving rise to what I propose to label a "multi-elite"

This is a short version of the working paper T. Piketty, "Brahmin Left vs Merchant Right: Rising Inequality and the Changing Structure of Political Conflict: Evidence from France, Britain and the US (1948–2017)" (WID.world Working Paper, 2018). This research is supplemented by a data appendix (including all computer codes) available online at piketty.pse.ens.fr/conflict.

85

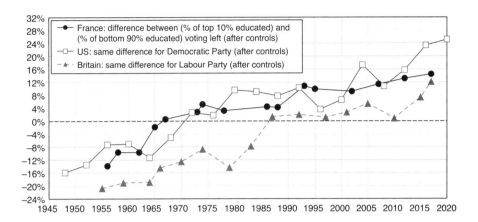

FIGURE 2.1. Voting for left-wing, democratic, and labour parties in France, the United States, and Britain, 1948–2020: From the worker party to the high-education party
*Data Source:* Author's computations using French, US, and British postelectoral surveys 1948–2020 (see wpid.world).
*Note:* In 1956, left-wing parties (socialists-communists-others) obtain a score that is 14 points lower among top 10% education voters than among bottom 90% education voters in France; in 2012, their score is 13 points higher among top 10% education voters (after controls for age, gender, income, wealth, father's occupation). The evolution is similar in the case of the Democratic vote in the US and the Labour vote in Britain. It also holds with no control.

party system in the 2000s–2010s: high-education elites now vote for the "left," while high-income/high-wealth elites still vote for the "right" (though less and less so). That is, the "left" has become the party of the intellectual elite (Brahmin left), while the "right" can be viewed as the party of the business elite (merchant right).[1] I show that the same transformation happened in France, the United States, and Britain (see Figure 2.1), despite the many differences in party systems and political histories between these three countries.

I argue that this structural evolution can contribute to explaining rising inequality and the lack of a democratic response to it, as well as the rise of "populism" (as low-education, low-income voters might feel

1. In India's traditional caste system, upper castes were divided into Brahmins (priests and intellectuals) and Kshatryas/Vaishyas (warriors, merchants, and tradesmen). To some extent, the modern political conflict seems to follow this division. For a broader comparative perspective on the long-run ideological transformation of "inequality regimes," see T. Piketty, *Capital and Ideology* (Harvard University Press, 2020).

abandoned).[2] I also discuss the origins of this transformation. I stress three main mechanisms: the rise of the identity cleavage; the process of educational expansion; and the shift in global ideology toward the market system and private property. The identity-based mechanism is often described as the central explanation behind the realignment of the US party system. Namely, following the civil rights movement in the 1960s and the pro–African American turn of the Democratic Party, a number of White lower-class voters gradually started to vote Republican, leading half a century later to a complete reversal of the social structure of the White vote vis-à-vis the two parties. One problem with this explanation is that there was no civil rights movement and no racial conflict in France or Britain (at least not in the 1950s–1960s), and that we observe the same evolution in the three countries. The rise of the conflict over migration (and more generally, over globalization) certainly played an important role in the European context, a role that is comparable in some ways to the racial conflict in the US context. However, the migration cleavage became salient relatively late in Europe (mostly since the 1980s and 1990s), while the shift in the socioeconomic composition of the party electorates seems to begin much earlier (namely, as early as the 1950s–1960s, like in the United States).

A second mechanism that could better help to explain the long-run evolution of the cleavage structure (and particularly the commonality of the observed evolutions across developed countries) is related to the process of educational expansion. At the time when only primary and secondary education was widely widespread, it was relatively straightforward to design an egalitarian educational platform. Parties seeking to reduce social inequalities could simply aim to bring the entirety of a generation to the completion of primary school, and then to the completion of secondary school. With the rise of tertiary education, things have become more complicated. Left parties, which used to be viewed as pro-poor, have

2. It is worth stressing that with regard to the massive increase in abstention that took place between the 1950s–1960s and the 2000s–2010s (particularly in France and Britain; in the United States abstention has always been relatively large in the postwar period as compared to Europe), it arose for the most part within the lower-education and lower-income groups. See T. Piketty, "Brahmin Left vs Merchant Right: Rising Inequality and the Changing Structure of Political Conflict: Evidence from France, Britain and the US (1948–2017)" (WID.world Working Paper, 2018), appendix Figures A1 and A2, wpid.world. A natural interpretation is that these voters do not feel well represented in the "multi-elite" party system.

increasingly been viewed as parties defending primarily the winners of the higher education game rather than the less well-off.[3] The important point is that the education-based mechanism could have delivered the observed evolution of political cleavages, even in the absence of the identity-based and migration-based mechanism.

Lastly, a third possible mechanism, arguably the most important of all, involves the shift in global ideology toward inequality and market forces and the changes in attitudes with respect to progressive taxation and private property that occurred following the conservative revolution of the 1980s and the fall of Soviet communism. If one believes that it is undesirable (and/or impossible) to reduce socioeconomic inequality and if one chooses to organize globalization accordingly (for example, by having free capital flows with no fiscal coordination), then it is not surprising that the political conflict focuses on other issues such as border control, immigration, and identity (including cultural conflicts between migrants/minorities and nonmigrants/majorities as well as between high-education, high-income, and high-wealth elites).

Finally, I also discuss the various possible evolutions of the party system: "multi-elite" stabilization; complete realignment of the party system along a "globalists" (high education, high income) versus "nativists" (low education, low income) cleavage; and return to class-based redistributive conflict (either from an internationalist or a nativist perspective). The elections held in the three countries in 2016–2020 suggest that several different evolutions are possible. France and the United States illustrate the possibility of a shift toward the "globalists" versus "nativists" cleavage structure, while Britain supports the "multi-elite" stabilization scenario (and possibly the return to class-based internationalism, though this seems less likely, at least in the short run).

Two general lessons emerge from this research. First, with multidimensional inequality (by income, education, wealth, ethnic or foreign origins, and so on), it is more complicated to build redistributive coalitions than in a simple one-dimensional world. With many dimensions of inequality and redistributive policies, multiple political equilibria and bifurcations can naturally occur. Globalization and educational expansion

---

3. In Piketty, "Brahmin Left," section 5, I present a simple model arguing that this might be related to the development of a new form of merit-based ideology among the highest educational achievers (similar in spirit to the standard merit-based ideology developed by the highest income and wealth achievers).

have created new dimensions of inequality and conflict, leading to the weakening of previous class-based redistributive coalitions and the gradual development of new cleavages. Next, without a strong egalitarian-internationalist platform, it is difficult to unite low-education, low-income voters from all origins within the same coalition and to deliver a reduction in inequality. Extreme historical circumstances can and did help to deliver such an encompassing platform, but there is no reason to believe that this is a necessary or a sufficient condition.[4]

The rest of this chapter is organized as follows: I first present my results on changing political cleavages in France, then proceed with the case of the United States and Britain, before offering concluding comments.

## Changing Political Cleavages in France

In this section, I analyze the changing structure of political cleavages in the case of France. I begin by briefly describing the evolution of the structure of political parties and the popular vote in France over the 1946–2017 period and the postelectoral surveys I will be using. I then present my main results on the reversal of the education, income, and wealth cleavages, and the shift to a "multi-elite" party system.[5] I finally present results on changing cleavages by religion and foreign origins and on the emergence of two-dimensional, four-quarter political cleavages in France.

### Changing Political Parties and Electoral Results in France, 1946–2017

The French multiparty system has always been substantially more complicated and diversified than the US and British two-party systems. This can be attributed to the differences in electoral systems (two-round versus one-round), though this itself could be endogenous, at least in part. In order to analyze changing voting patterns and political cleavages in France, I will examine both presidential and legislative elections.

Beginning in 1965, French voters have elected their president directly via universal suffrage. In most presidential elections since 1965, one

---

4. E.g., the Great Depression, World War II, and the rise of communism certainly made the social democratic New Deal platform more desirable, while unregulated globalization, the conservative revolution, and the fall of communism contributed to weaken it.

5. See Piketty, "Brahmin Left," figures 2.2a to 2.2g, wpid.world, for an analysis of gender and age cleavages.

observes in the second round a pretty tight race between a "left" or "center-left" candidate (usually supported by the Socialist Party, the Communist Party, and other left-wing parties) and a "right" or "center-right" candidate (usually supported by the Gaullist Party and other right-wing parties).[6]

I will also be using legislative elections outcomes, first because they cover longer historical periods (legislative elections have been conducted approximately every five years since the beginning of the Third Republic in 1871), and next because they provide a better testament to the complexity of French politics (though this is not my main focus here). If we look at the overall evolution of popular vote shares obtained by left-wing parties (combining center-left, left, and extreme-left parties) and right-wing parties (combining center-right, right, and extreme-right parties) in all legislative elections that were conducted in France from 1946 to 2017, we find that it is usually relatively close to fifty-fifty (Figure 2.2).[7]

I stress that this basic left-versus-right characterization of the French party system should be viewed as an enormous simplification of a much more complex landscape. The only reason for making this simplification is that I am primarily interested in making comparisons with the evolution of political cleavages observed in the United States and Britain (two countries with well-established two-party systems).

### Data Sources: French Postelectoral Surveys, 1958–2017

There is a long tradition of postelectoral surveys in France. Major surveys have been conducted after all national elections (legislative and presidential) since 1958. Most of these surveys were conducted by a consortium of academic organizations. The corresponding microfiles have been well preserved and documented and are easily accessible.[8]

These postelectoral surveys are reasonably large in size (typically about 4,000 observations, though the earlier surveys are somewhat smaller, around 2,000–2,500). This is sufficient to deliver significant results regarding long-run evolutions (though not necessarily for year-to-year variations). These surveys include detailed questionnaires involving dozens of variables on sociodemographic characteristics, including in particular

6. The electoral scores obtained by both contenders have generally been close to a perfect fifty-fifty split of the popular vote. See Piketty, "Brahmin Left," figure 2.1a.

7. See Piketty, "Brahmin Left," figures 2.1b to 2.1e. I use first-round legislative elections because they are more meaningful (many parties do not qualify for the second round in a large number of constituencies).

8. See Piketty, "Brahmin Left" and online data appendix for details.

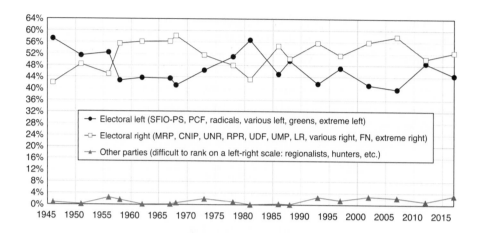

FIGURE 2.2. Legislative elections in France, 1946–2017

*Data Source:* Author's computations using official election results (see wpid.world).

*Note:* The scores obtained by left-wing parties (socialists, communists, radicals, greens, and other parties from the center left, left, and extreme left) and right-wing parties (all parties from the center right, right, and extreme right combined) have oscillated between 40% and 58% of the votes in the first rounds of legislative elections conducted in France over the 1946–2017 period. The score obtained by the LREM-MODEM coalition in 2017 (32% of votes) was divided 50–50 between center left and center right.

gender, age, family situation, education (including highest degree obtained), occupation, religion, and income (with a relatively large number of income brackets, typically about ten to fifteen). One of the particularities of the French postelectoral surveys is that they also include relatively detailed information on wealth and asset ownership, which turns out to be particularly interesting for our purposes. Recent surveys also include very useful information on foreign origins.

### The Reversal of the Education Cleavage

I now present my main results, namely, the complete reversal of the education cleavage. At the beginning of the period, in the 1950s–1960s, the more-educated voters systematically vote more for the right: the higher the education level, the higher the right-wing vote. At the end of the period, in the 2000s–2010s, the pattern I observe is the complete opposite: the higher the education level, the higher the left-wing vote. This complete reversal takes place in a gradual manner over more than half a century and appears to be extremely robust.

The simplest indicator one can use to visualize this long-term trend is the difference between the fraction of university graduates voting left and the fraction of non–university graduates voting left. This difference was large and negative in the 1950s and early 1960s, with a gap of about −20 percentage points; the gap gradually dropped in absolute value during the 1960s–1970s and was close to zero during the 1980s; and it became slightly positive in 1990s and strongly positive in the 2000s–2010s, with a gap of around +10 percentage points. The shift from the 1950s–1960s to the 2000s–2010s amounts to about 30 percentage points, which corresponds to a complete and massive change in the relationship between education and voting behavior.

Next, it is striking to see that when we look separately at voters with primary, secondary, and tertiary degrees, the relationship between education and left-wing vote used to be systematically and monotonically downward sloping and it has become systematically and monotonically upward sloping. In the 1950s–1960s, in election after election, voters with primary degrees vote more for the left than those with secondary degrees, who themselves vote more for the left than those with tertiary degrees (higher education). In the 2000s–2010s, it is exactly the opposite: in election after election, voters with primary degrees vote more for the right than those with secondary degrees, who vote more for the right than those with tertiary degrees (higher education). Looking at the patterns for all French elections from 1956 to 2017 gives a sense of how deep and far-reaching this transformation is (see Figures 2.3 and 2.4).

It is also striking to see that this holds within the set of university graduates. Back in the 1970s, voters with more advanced tertiary degrees (in particular the graduates of *grandes écoles*—that is, selective higher education, as opposed to shorter and/or less selective higher education tracks) vote more for the right than those with less advanced degrees do. In the 2000s–2010s, it is exactly the opposite: the more advanced the degrees, the stronger the vote for the left.[9]

Finally, the reversal of the education cleavage appears to be strongly significant from a statistical standpoint, and highly robust to the inclusion of control variables. Generally speaking, the inclusion of control variables affects the levels of our simple education-gradient indicator (the difference between the vote shares among university graduates and nongraduates), but does not affect the trend. For instance, including gender

9. See Piketty, "Brahmin Left," figure 2.3f.

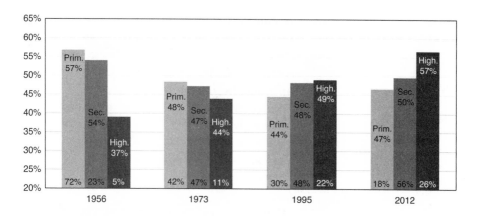

FIGURE 2.3. Educational expansion and left-wing vote by education in France, 1956–2012
*Data Source:* Author's computations using French postelectoral surveys 1956–2012 (see wpid.world).
*Note:* In 1956, left-wing parties (SFIO-PS, PCF, Rad., etc.) obtained 57% of the vote among voters with no degree (other than primary), 54% among voters with secondary degrees (Bac, Brevet, BEP, etc.), and 37% among university graduates (higher education). In 2012, the left-wing candidate (Hollande) obtained 47% of the vote among voters with no degree and 57% among university graduates.

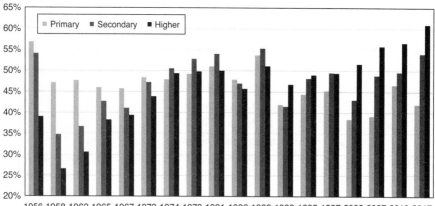

FIGURE 2.4. Left-wing vote by education in France, 1956–2017: Election by election
*Data Source:* Author's computations using French postelectoral surveys 1956–2017 (see wpid.world).
*Note:* In 1956, left-wing parties (SFIO-PS, PCF, Rad., etc.) obtain 57% of the vote among voters with no degree (other than primary), 54% among voters with secondary degrees (Bac, Brevet, BEP, etc.), and 37% among university graduates (higher education).

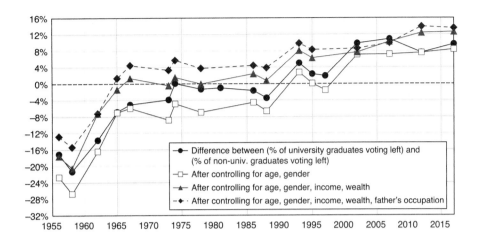

FIGURE 2.5. Left-wing vote in France, 1956–2017: From the worker party to the high-education party
*Data Source:* Author's computations using French postelectoral surveys 1956–2017 (see wpid.world).
*Note:* In 1956, left-wing parties obtained a score that was 17 points lower among university graduates than among non-university graduates; in 2012, their score was 8 points higher among university graduates. Including control variables does not affect the trend (only the level).

and age control variables pushes the education gradient downward; this is because young cohorts tend to be both more educated and more left-wing. However, this effect is moderate when compared to the total education gradient, and most importantly, the age effect has always been there (with volatile variations but no long-term trend, as we early noticed), so this does not affect the trend (see Figure 2.5).

Conversely, including income and wealth variables pushes the education gradient upward; this is because higher-income and/or higher-wealth individuals tend to be both more educated and more right-wing (see below). However, this effect is again moderate when compared to the total education gradient, and most importantly, it is approximately constant over time, so that controlling for income and wealth again leaves the trend unaffected. The same conclusion applies if one also controls for father's occupation. I also used other control variables, including father's and mother's education levels (when available), and this leaves the trend unaffected.

From an intergenerational perspective, it is worth stressing that the percentage of university graduates has increased enormously over the past

half-century. Back in 1956, 72 percent of the electorate held only primary school degrees, 23 percent held secondary degrees, and only 5 percent held tertiary degrees; by 2012, primary degree holders make up only 18 percent of the electorate, versus 56 percent for secondary degree holders and 26 percent with tertiary degrees (including 16 percent with advanced degrees) (see Figure 2.3). In other words, when we look at the parents and grandparents of individuals voting in the 2000s–2010s, almost everybody had parents or grandparents who were primary (or sometimes secondary) degree holders. But the point is that even after controlling for family origins, those who made it to higher degrees vote more for the left, and those who did not make it vote more for the right. In other words, the left has become the party of the winners of the higher education system.

To take into account the structural change in the distribution of educational attainment, I also estimated the evolution of the difference between the fraction of left vote among top 10 percent–education voters and the fraction of left vote among bottom 90 percent–education voters (education deciles are defined within a given year, and average decile-level vote shares are computed assuming a constant left score within each education-year cell). I find the same trend, both before controls and after controls.[10]

### Stability and Attenuation of Income/Wealth Cleavages

I now present results on income and wealth cleavages. One of the most simplistic—yet very widespread—ways of describing the left versus right cleavage involves the poor versus rich dimension: poor people would vote for the left, while rich people would vote for the right. As I highlight in this research, the empirical evidence is actually a lot more mixed and complex. If we look at the profile of left-wing vote by income percentile in France over the 1956–2017 period, we find that the curve is relatively flat within the bottom 90 percent of the income distribution; one needs to delve into the group of top 10 percent incomes (and especially the top 5 percent and top 1 percent incomes) to see a significantly lower vote share for the left (see Figure 2.6). In effect, several counterbalancing factors contribute to attenuate income effects within the bottom 90 percent. In particular, many self-employed workers—and especially independent small farmers, which have long been very numerous in France—have at the same time relatively

10. See Piketty, "Brahmin Left," figure 2.3k, as well as Figure 2.9 of this chapter. I also include controls for attitudes toward migration and find the same pattern. See Piketty, "Brahmin Left," figure 2.3l.

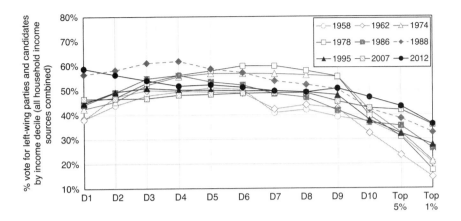

FIGURE 2.6. Left-wing vote by income decile in France, 1958–2012

*Data Source:* Author's computations using French postelectoral surveys 1958–2012 (see wpid.world).

*Note:* In 1978, left-wing parties (PS, PCF, Radicaux, etc.) obtained 46% of the vote among voters in the bottom 10% of the income distribution, 23% of the vote among voters in the top 10%, and 17% among the top 1%. Generally speaking, the profile of left-wing vote by income percentile is relatively flat within the bottom 90%, and strongly declining for the top 10%, especially at the beginning of the period.

low incomes and a weak propensity to vote for the socialist and communist left (which has long been associated with the defense of wage earners and the collectivization of the means of the production, something independent producers usually do not like much). This is another illustration of the multidimensionality of inequality and political cleavages.

If we look at the profile of the left-wing vote by wealth percentile (rather than by income percentile), then we find a much steeper curve: the percentage of left-wing vote is systematically much higher in lower-wealth deciles than among voters in the middle of the distribution, and much higher in the middle than among top 10 percent wealth holders (see Figure 2.7). This much steeper profile illustrates the fact that the political conflict about economic inequality has historically been much more about property than about income per se.[11] These findings also show how critical it is to have information about wealth and asset ownership (and not only

11. The property of the means of production does play a special role: as noted above, the self-employed workers and especially peasants systematically vote more to the right in French postelectoral surveys (controlling for other factors). But even for a given employment

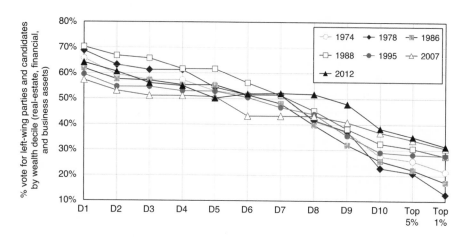

FIGURE 2.7. Left-wing vote by wealth decile in France, 1974–2012

*Data Source:* Author's computations using French postelectoral surveys 1974–2012 (see wpid.world).

*Note:* In 1978, left-wing parties (PS, PCF, Radicaux, etc.) obtained 69% of the vote among voters in the bottom 10% of the wealth distribution, 23% of the vote among voters in the top 10%, and 13% among top 1% wealth holders. Generally speaking, the profile of left-wing vote by wealth percentile is strongly declining all along the distribution, especially at the beginning of the period.

about income) in order to analyze political cleavages. The wealth variables available in post-1974 French postelectoral surveys are imperfect and probably underestimate the steepness of the profile, but they are sufficiently precise to demonstrate that wealth is a stronger determinant of voting attitude than income. To my knowledge, this simple fact has not been established in previous research.[12]

I now turn to the evolution over time of the income and wealth gradients. As one can already see from Figures 2.6 and 2.7, the steepness of the profile seems to be particularly strong at the beginning of the period (from the 1950s to the 1980s), especially at the top of the income and wealth distributions, and to decline over time. To further investigate this issue, it is useful to focus on a simple steepness indicator, namely the difference between the fraction voting left among top 10 percent income earners and the fraction voting left among bottom 90 percent

status (wage earner, self-employed, or not working), I find the same steep profile of vote by wealth percentile.

12. See Piketty, "Brahmin Left."

income earners (and the corresponding difference for top 10 percent and bottom 90 percent wealth holders). The main results that we obtain can be summarized as follows (see Figures 2.8 and 2.9).

First, in the absence of controls, the income gradient is clearly declining over time: the gap in left vote between top 10 percent and bottom 90 percent income earners used to be around −10 and −15 percentage points from the 1950s to the 1980s, and it is on the order of −5 points in the 2000s–2010s. However, the attenuation of the income gradient over time looks less strong after the introduction of controls, and especially education controls.[13] This is due to the reversal of the education gradient: high education and high income always tend to be positively correlated; at the beginning of the period, high education is associated with stronger right-wing vote, so controlling for education reduces the impact of high income on right-wing vote; conversely, at the end of the period, high education correlates to weaker right-wing vote, so controlling for education reinforces the income effect. After including controls, the gap in the left vote between top 10 percent and bottom 90 percent income groups is relatively close in 1958–1962 and in 2007–2012, around −10 points, so it is unclear whether we really see an attenuation of the gap at this stage.

Next, one should be careful about the interpretation of the results for 2017. Without controls, the income gap in the left vote becomes slightly positive in 2017, meaning that top 10 percent voters support the "left" more than bottom 90 percent income voters. However, the gap is back to zero (very slightly negative) after inclusion of controls. Most importantly, it is unclear at this stage whether the 2017 election should be viewed as an outlier or a new normal. In the results presented in Figure 2.8 for income cleavages in 2017 (as well as in the results that I presented in the previous subsection for education cleavages in 2017), I define the left versus right vote on the basis of the first round of the 2017 presidential elections: the "left" vote includes the votes for Mélenchon/Hamon (28 percent) and Macron (24 percent), a total of 52 percent; the "right" vote includes the votes for Fillon (22 percent) and Le Pen/Dupont-Aignan (26 percent), a total of 48 percent. This is not an entirely unreasonable definition of "left" versus "right," in the sense that it cuts the electorate into approximately two halves and that most voters (when asked to rank parties and candidates on a left-right scale) rank Macron to the left of Fillon/Le Pen/Dupont-Aignan. However, it is clear that such left versus

13. See Piketty, "Brahmin Left," figure 2.4c.

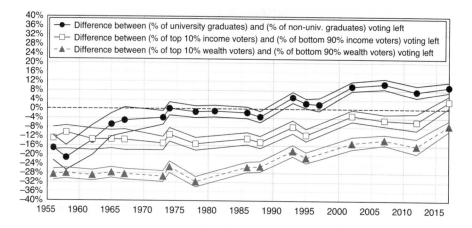

FIGURE 2.8. Political conflict in France, 1956–2017: Toward a multi-elite party system, or a great reversal?

*Data Source:* Author's computations using French postelectoral surveys 1956–2017 (see wpid.world).

*Note:* The left-wing vote used to be associated with lower-educated and low-income voters; it has gradually become associated with higher-educated voters, giving rise to a multi-elite party system (education vs. wealth); it might also become associated with high-income voters in the future, leading to a great reversal and complete realignment of the party system. Fine lines indicate 90% confidence intervals.

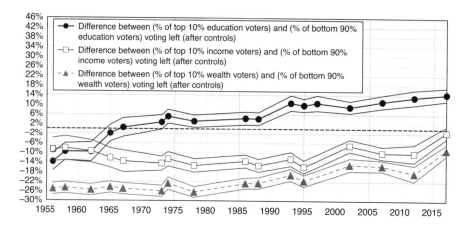

FIGURE 2.9. Political conflict in France, 1956–2017: Toward a multi-elite party system, or a great reversal? (after controls)

*Data Source:* Author's computations using French postelectoral surveys 1956–2017 (see wpid.world).

*Note:* The left-wing vote used to be associated with lower-educated and low-income voters; it has gradually become associated with higher-educated voters, giving rise to a multi-elite party system (education vs. wealth); it might also become associated with high-income voters in the future, leading to a great reversal and complete realignment of the party system. Fine lines indicate 90% confidence intervals.

right groupings are highly unsatisfactory and that the 2017 French election is better viewed as the archetype of a two-dimensional, four-quarter election (see Table 2.1 below). If we were to use solely the first-round Melenchon-Hamon presidential vote as the "left" vote (and/or the legislative left vote, excluding La République En Marche!/Modem), then the gap in the left vote between top 10 percent and bottom 90 percent income voters would be negative in 2017 (roughly the same level as in 2012: about −10 points before controls, −5 points after controls).[14] And if we were to look at the gap in the first-round Macron presidential vote (and/or in the legislative LRM/Modem vote) between top 10 percent and bottom 90 percent income voters, it would be strongly positive (about +15 points before controls and +10 points after controls).

Finally, if we look at the evolution of the wealth gradient, we also find an attenuation of the gap in left vote between top 10 percent and bottom 90 percent wealth voters, although the attenuation is again less clear once we introduce control variables.[15] The one stable fact is that the wealth gradient is systematically larger than the income gradient: after controls, and leaving aside 2017, the gap in left vote between top 10 percent and bottom 90 percent voters is usually between −15 and −20 points for wealth and about −10 points for income.[16] The difference between the two is always statistically significant, which shows that high wealth is a stronger determinant of right wing vote than high income.[17]

### Multi-elite Party System or Great Reversal?

By combining the results on changing cleavages by education and by income/wealth, I am now in a position to synthetize my main findings. I compare in Figure 2.8 the evolution of the gap in left vote between university graduates and non-university graduates and the gap in left vote between top 10 percent and bottom 90 percent income and wealth voters, before controls. I do the same in Figure 2.9 for the left vote gap between top 10 percent and bottom 90 percent education voters and between top

14. In contrast, the results on education cleavages are virtually unaffected if we move to this Mélenchon-Hamon definition of the left vote (rather than Mélenchon-Hamon-Macron).

15. See Piketty, "Brahmin Left," figure 2.4d.

16. The wealth gap drops in absolute value in 2017 (though it is still negative), but again, this entirely comes from the highly affluent profile of the Macron vote.

17. See for instance the confidence intervals in Figures 2.8 and 2.9.

10 percent and bottom 90 percent income and wealth voters, after controls, which is probably the most meaningful way to look at the data.[18]

The general conclusion is clear: we have gradually moved from a class-based party system to what I propose to call a "multi-elite" party system. Back in the 1950s–1960s, the party system was defined along class lines: the vote for left-wing parties was associated with both low-education and low-income voters, while the vote for right-wing parties was associated with both high-education and high-income voters. The left vote has gradually been associated with higher education voters, and in the 2000s–2010s we have a system where high-education voters support the "left" while high-income voters support the "right." For reasons explained above, the inclusion of control variables accentuates the separation between the education and the income and wealth dimensions. In effect, the most left-wing voters have become those with high education and relatively low income and wealth, while the most right-wing voters have become those with relatively low education and high income and wealth. This was not the case in the 1950s–1960s, when all dimensions were pushing in the same direction.

The difficult question—a question that I am unable to fully answer in the present research—is where does this structural transformation come from, and is this is a stable equilibrium or not? To the extent that high education commands high income in the long run, one might argue that a "multi-elite" party system is inherently unstable. That is, one might expect that the gap in the left vote between top 10 percent and bottom 90 percent income voters will also become structurally positive in the future, just like the gap in the left vote between top 10 percent and bottom 90 percent education voters. If this were to happen, it would correspond to a complete realignment of the party system: the former "left" (which used to be associated with low-income, low-education voters) would be associated with high-income, high-education voters; whereas the former "right" (which used to be associated with high-income, high-education voters) would be associated with low-income, low-education voters. In effect, such a party system would have little to do with the "left" versus "right" party system of the 1950s–1960s. Maybe it should better be described as an opposition between the "globalists" (high income, high education) and the "nativists" (low income, low education).

18. See Piketty, "Brahmin Left," figures 2.5a to 2.5d for all the other combinations.

It is unclear, however, at this stage whether this complete realignment will take place. One can also find some forces pushing for a stabilization of the "multi-elite" party system. One such force is the wealth effect. In effect, the education gap has become strongly positive (high-education voters now strongly support the "left") and the wealth gap has remained strongly negative (high-wealth voters maintain strong support for the "right"), while the income gap is in between the two and remains moderately negative. This reflects the fact that income is determined by a combination of education (human capital), wealth (nonhuman capital), and other factors. One could imagine a situation where some families and individuals specialize in the accumulation of education, and some others in the accumulation of wealth, so that the "multi-elite" party system persists.[19] Also, some members of the high-education elite might voluntarily make career choices that are financially less rewarding than those of the high-income and high-wealth elites. I will further discuss these issues when I present evidence on changing political cleavages in the United States and Britain.

### The Transformation of Religious and Origin-Based Cleavages

I now turn to the evolution of religious and origin-based political cleavages. The structure of the electorate by religion has changed substantially in France between 1967 (when questions on religious practice were first asked in postelectoral surveys) and 2017. The fraction of the electorate reporting to be "Catholic" declined from 91 percent to 55 percent, while the fraction reporting to have "no religion" rose from 6 percent to 35 percent and the fraction reporting "other religions" rose from 3 percent to 10 percent.[20] Among "Catholics," the fraction reporting to be "practicing Catholics" (which I define as those who report going to church at least once a month) declined from 25 percent to 6 percent, and the "nonpracticing Catholics" dropped from 66 percent to 49 percent. Among "other religions," Islam rose from less than 1 percent to 5 percent, while Protestantism/Judaism/Buddhism/other rose from 3 percent to 5 percent.

---

19. Note that the correlation structure between education, income, and wealth—as measured in postelectoral surveys—appears to be relatively stable over time, at least as a first approximation. That is, the raw correlation between income and education appears stable around 0.3–0.35 over the 1958–2017 period, while the income-wealth raw correlation is stable around 0.2–0.3 and the education-wealth correlation is stable around 0.1–0.15.

20. See Piketty, "Brahmin Left," figure 2.6a.

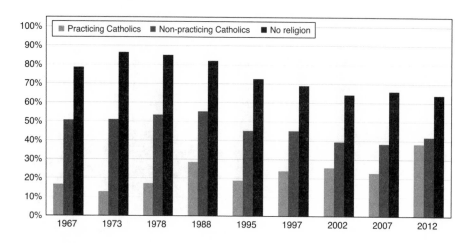

FIGURE 2.10. Left-wing vote by religion in France, 1967–2012

*Data Source:* Author's computations using French postelectoral surveys 1967–2012 (see wpid.world).

*Note:* In 2012, the left-wing candidate (Hollande) obtained 38% of the vote among voters reporting to be practicing Catholics (attending church at least once a month), 42% among nonpracticing Catholics, and 64% among voters reporting no religion.

While Muslim voters are still a very small minority, they have become a noticeable minority (comparable in size to practicing Catholics).

Regarding the Catholic voters versus no-religion voters, we observe a strong and persistent right versus left cleavage. The gap has reduced over time, but it is still very substantial and significant (see Figure 2.10). Catholic voters tend be older and to have higher income and wealth than voters with no religion, which partly explains their support for right-wing parties. But even after controlling for all observable characteristics, practicing Catholics vote a lot more for the right, while atheists (individuals who report no religion) vote a lot more for the left.[21] Although the magnitude of the difference has declined over time, it is still on the order of 10–20 points in recent years—that is, comparable or greater than the effects associated with education, income, or wealth.

I now turn to the effects associated with other religions, particularly Islam. Until 1988, Islam is not registered separately from other religions in postelectoral surveys. In 1988 and 1995, Muslim voters make up about

21. See Piketty, "Brahmin Left," figures 2.6c and 2.6d.

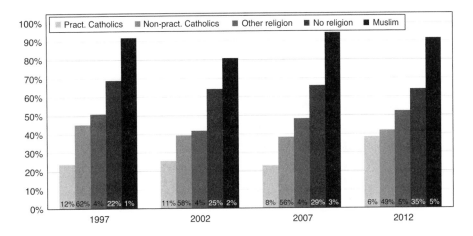

FIGURE 2.11. Left-wing vote by religion in France: The case of Islam
*Data Source:* Author's computations using French postelectoral surveys 1997–2012 (see wpid.world).
*Note:* In 2012, the left-wing candidate (Hollande) obtained 38% of the vote among practicing Catholics (attending church at least once a month), 42% among nonpracticing Catholics, 52% among voters reporting another religion (Protestantism, Judaism, Buddhism, etc., except Islam), 64% among voters with no religion, and 91% among Muslims.

1 percent of the electorate, and their reported vote is more left-wing than that of Catholic voters and comparable to that of voters with no religion. From 1997 to 2012, the fraction of (self-reported) Muslim voters in the electorate gradually rises from 1 percent to 5 percent, and the fraction of them voting for left-wing parties rises to even higher levels, typically in the 80–90 percent range (see Figure 2.11). Although the number of observations is limited, the fact that Muslim voters lean to the left is highly significant from a statistical standpoint, and more so over time.[22] Muslim voters tend to be younger and have lower income and wealth than other voters, which partly explains their left vote. However, all explanatory variables combined can explain only a relatively small part of the Muslim preference for the left; after taking into account all controls, the impact is systematically on the order of 30–40 percentage points, year after year (see Figure 2.12). This is substantially larger than all other effects we have studied so far (gender, age, education, income, or wealth). The strong left-wing preference of Muslim voters could seem surprising, espe-

22. See Piketty, "Brahmin Left," figure 2.6h.

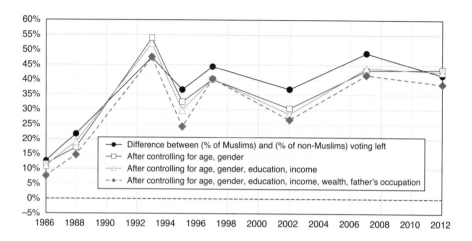

FIGURE 2.12. Political conflict in France, 1986–2012: Muslim vote leaning to the left
*Data Source:* Author's computations using French postelectoral surveys 1986–2012 (see wpid.world).
*Note:* In 2012, the left-wing candidate (Hollande) obtained a score among Muslim voters that was 42 points higher than among other voters; the gap falls to 38 points after controlling for age, gender, education, income, wealth, and father's occupation.

cially in light of the fact that the left vote historically has been strongly associated with atheists versus Catholics in France (and it still is), and given that the family values of Muslim voters (particularly with regard to women's role and homosexuality) are pretty far from those of lefty atheists. This suggests that there is something stronger going on in other dimensions of the political conflict; presumably this has to do with the fact that Muslim voters perceive a lot of hostility from right-wing parties.

Ideally, one would like to be able to distinguish between the effect on voting attitudes of reported Muslim religion and the effect of different foreign origins (which might well have an impact on perceived discrimination and racism). Unfortunately, detailed questions on family origins were not asked before the 2007 postelectoral survey, which limits how much one can say about this.

The results obtained with foreign origins in 2007–2012 are relatively straightforward and consistent with those obtained with religion.[23] As of 2012, 72 percent of the French electorate reports to have no foreign

23. See Piketty, "Brahmin Left," figure 2.6j.

grandparent, while 19 percent reports to have at least one foreign grandparent from another European country (in practice, mostly from Spain, Italy, or Portugal), and 9 percent reports to have at least one grandparent from an extra-European country (in practice, mostly from the Maghreb or Sub-Saharan Africa). Those with a European foreign origin vote exactly the same way as voters with no foreign origin (with left scores equal to 49 percent for both groups in 2012, versus 52 percent for the entire electorate), while those with an extra-European origin vote massively for the left (77 percent). If we combine all explanatory factors of the vote, both socioeconomic factors (gender, age, education, income, and wealth) and origins, we find that the pro-left attitude of Muslim voters is robust to the inclusion of foreign origins. More precisely, socioeconomic control variables reduce the Muslim left-wing preference from +42 points to +38 points in 2012, and adding foreign origins (including separate dummies for each region of origin) further reduces the effect to +26 points.[24] In other words, given gender, age, education, income, wealth, and region of origin (for instance, North Africa), there is still a sizable effect associating self-reported Muslim identity and the left-wing vote.

### Two-Dimensional, Four-Quarter Political Cleavages in France

We also have other direct survey evidence about the strength of the migration cleavage in French politics. Beginning in 1988, French postelectoral surveys systematically ask voters whether they believe there are too many immigrants. The proportion of voters responding that there are too many immigrants has declined over time: it used to be as large as 70–75 percent in the 1980s and until the mid-1990s (versus 25–30 percent believing that there are not too many immigrants), and it has declined to about 50 percent in 2007–2012, with a rebound a little above 55 percent in 2017.[25] However, the intensity of the right versus left cleavage on migration seems to have actually increased: the gap in the left vote between voters believing there are not too many immigrants and those believing the opposite has always been large and positive (about 30–40 points, bigger than any other effect except the Muslim effect), and if anything, it seems to have risen from the 1980s to the 2010s, both before and after controls, albeit in a relatively irregular manner.[26] In other words, the issue

24. See Piketty, "Brahmin Left," figure 2.6k.
25. See Piketty, "Brahmin Left," figure 2.6l.
26. See Piketty, "Brahmin Left," figure 2.6m.

of migration seems to have become more divisive over time; the population is split almost fifty-fifty on whether there are too many migrants (there is still a majority believing that there are too many migrants, but there is now a large minority—of almost equal size—believing the opposite), and the voting cleavage between the two quasi-halves is bigger than ever.

It is worth noting that when the French voters are asked whether social justice entails further redistribution from the rich to the poor, we again observe that the electorate is split into two halves of comparable size: the fraction of the electorate responding that we should reduce inequality was equal to 52 percent in 2017 (versus 55–60 percent in 2002–2012).[27] The interesting point, however, is that the pro-migrant/anti-migrant halves and the pro-poor/pro-rich halves are almost entirely uncorrelated, in the sense that by combining these two questions we obtain four quarters of comparable size, particularly in 2012–2017 (see Figure 2.13).[28]

The four quarters can be labeled Internationalists-Egalitarians (pro-migrant, pro-poor); Internationalists-Inegalitarians (pro-migrant, pro-rich); Nativists-Inegalitarians (anti-migrant, pro-rich); and Nativists-Egalitarians (anti-migrant, pro-poor). Back in 2002, the Internationalists-Inegalitarians made up much less than a quarter of the electorate (only 12 percent); this is the group that has been growing the most (up to 23 percent in 2017). Unfortunately, the rich-poor question was not asked in the same manner before 2002 (and the immigrant question was not asked at all before 1988), so it is impossible to do consistent longer-run analysis.

Finally, it is interesting to note that this four-quarter decomposition of the electorate fits very well with the results of the 2017 French presidential election, which looks like a perfect illustration of two-dimensional, four-quarter politics. That is, in the first round the electorate was split into four groups of almost exactly equal size (see Table 2.1): 28 percent of the vote for the "left" candidates Mélenchon/Hamon (these happen to be the most pro-migrant and pro-poor voters); 24 percent of the vote for the "centrist" candidate Macron (these voters are also pro-migrant,

27. The rich-poor question is deliberately phrased in a fairly aggressive manner, namely: "In order to achieve social justice we need to take from the rich and give to the poor. Do you agree or disagree?" As with the immigration questions ("There are too many immigrants in France. Do you agree or disagree?"), I grouped together the answers "completely agree"/"somewhat agree" and "completely disagree"/"somewhat disagree" and excluded the individuals who do not answer (less than 5 percent).

28. See Piketty, "Brahmin Left," figure 2.60.

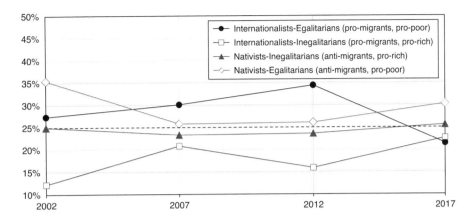

FIGURE 2.13. Two-dimensional political conflict and four-quarter electorate in France
*Data Source:* Author's computations using French postelectoral surveys 2002–2017
(see wpid.world).
*Note:* In 2017, 21% of voters are "internationalists-egalitarians" (they consider that
there are not too many migrants, and that we should reduce inequality between rich
and poor); 26% are "nativists-inegalitarians" (they consider that there are too many
migrants and that we should not reduce rich-poor gaps); 23% are "internationalists-
inegalitarians," and 30% are "nativists-egalitarians."

though a bit less so, and they are also pro-rich); 22 percent for the "right"
candidate Fillon (these are anti-migrant and pro-rich voters); and
26 percent for the "extreme-right" candidates Le Pen / Dupont-Aignan
(these are the most anti-migrant voters, and they are also pro-poor).

## Changing Political Cleavages in the United States

In this section, I present detailed results on the changing structure of political cleavages for the case of the United States. I begin by briefly describing the evolution of political parties and popular vote in the United
States over the 1948–2020 period and the postelectoral surveys I will be
using. I then present my main results on breakdowns by education, income, and wealth and the shift to a "multi-elite" party system. I finally
present results on breakdowns by ethnic and foreign origins.[29]

29. See Piketty, "Brahmin Left," figures 3.2a and 3.2b for an analysis of gender and
age cleavages.

*Table 2.1* Two-Dimensional Political Conflict in France 2017: An Electorate Divided into Four Quarters

| Presidential Election 2017 (1st Round) | All Voters | Mélenchon/Hamon ("Egalitarian Internationalist") | Macron ("Inegalitarian Internationalist") | Fillon ("Inegalitarian Nativist") | Le Pen/Dupont-Aignan ("Egalitarian Nativist") |
|---|---|---|---|---|---|
| | 100% | 28% | 24% | 22% | 26% |
| "There are too many immigrants in France" (% agree) | 56% | 32% | 39% | 62% | 91% |
| "In order to achieve social justice we need to take from the rich and give to the poor" (% agree) | 51% | 67% | 46% | 27% | 61% |
| University graduates (%) | 33% | 39% | 41% | 36% | 16% |
| Monthly income > €4,000 (%) | 15% | 9% | 20% | 26% | 8% |
| Home ownership (%) | 60% | 48% | 69% | 78% | 51% |

*Data Source:* Author's computations using French postelectoral survey 2017 (see wpid.world).

*Note:* In 2017, 28% of first-round voters voted for Mélenchon/Hamon, 32% of them believed that there were too many migrants in France (vs 56% among all voters), and 67% believed that we should take from the rich and give to the poor (vs 51% on average). This electorate can therefore be viewed as "egalitarian-internationalist" (pro-migrants, pro-poor), while the Macron electorate is "inegalitarian-internationalist" (pro-migrants, pro-rich), the Fillon electorate is "inegalitarian-nativist" (anti-migrants, pro-rich), and the Le Pen/Dupont-Aignan electorate is "inegalitarian-internationalist" (anti-migrants, pro-poor). The votes for Arthaud/Poutou (2%) and Asselineau/Cheminade/Lassalle (2%) were added to the votes for Mélenchon-Hamon and Fillon, respectively.

*Changing Political Parties and Electoral Results*
*in the United States, 1948–2020*

The US party system is the best existing example of a two-party system (Democrats versus Republicans). As such, it is much simpler than the French party system, and also much simpler than most party systems observed in Europe (including in Britain) and around the world. Although it is formally simple, the US party system is nevertheless relatively exotic and mysterious to many outside observers in Europe and elsewhere: How is it that the Democratic Party, which was the proslavery party in the nineteenth century, gradually became the New Deal party and the "progressive" party over the course of the twentieth century? One of the points I am trying to make in this research is that a better understanding of this historical trajectory might be highly relevant for analyzing the evolution of multidimensional political cleavages that might occur in Europe, North America, and elsewhere in the twenty-first century.

The apparent formal simplicity of the US party system should also not overshadow the fact that there has always been large ideological heterogeneity within each of the two main parties. These conflicts are not being addressed via the continuous creation of a multitude of new parties (as they are in a country like France), but this does not mean they do not exist: they rather take different forms and involve different institutional processes like factions and primaries in order to arbitrate them.

I will focus on voting attitudes in US presidential elections (rather than congressional elections) because they are usually more centered on national issues and involve the same candidates and policy platform for all voters (by construction).[30] The shares of the popular vote observed in US presidential elections 1948–2020 have usually been relatively close to fifty-fifty (Figure 2.14). In particular, the vote shares obtained by third-party candidates are usually very small (less than 10 percent of the vote for all third-party candidates combined), with the exception of Wallace in 1968 (14 percent) and Perot in 1992 and 1996 (20 percent and 10 percent, respectively). In what follows, I will exclude these candidates and focus on the Democrats versus Republicans voting patterns (excluding third-party voting), first because I am mostly interested in long-run evolutions (and third-party candidates are all unique in their own

---

30. I have also computed the same results for votes in congressional elections, and I find the same transformations. See online data appendix for computer codes and series.

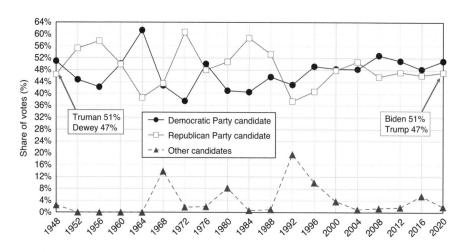

FIGURE 2.14. Presidential elections in the US, 1948–2020

*Data Source:* Author's computations using official election results (see wpid.world).

*Note:* The scores obtained by Democratic and Republican parties candidates in presidential elections conducted in the US between 1948 and 2016 have generally varied between 40% and 60% of the vote (popular vote, all states combined). The scores obtained by other candidates have generally been relatively small (less than 10% of the vote), with the exception of Wallace in 1968 (14%) and Perot in 1992 and 1996 (20% and 10%).

ways), and next because my main purpose is to make comparisons with left versus right voting patterns in France and Britain.

### Data Sources: US Postelectoral Surveys, 1948–2020

There exists a long tradition of postelectoral surveys in the United States. I will be using two main series of surveys: first the ANES series (American National Election Studies) and next the NEP series (National Exit Polls). Both series have strengths and drawbacks (which is why I choose to use both). The ANES surveys have been organized following every presidential election in the United States from 1948 to 2020 (and also after every midterm congressional election). They have been run by an academic consortium and the microfiles are easily accessible.[31]

In this research, I choose to rely primarily on ANES surveys because they provide the longest available consistent series. Their sample size was

31. ANES microfiles are available online at the ANES website (http://www.election studies.org). The academic consortium in charge of ANES has been based mostly at the University of Michigan (ICPSR/ISR).

relatively limited in early surveys (about 1,000–2,000 observations) but it has grown over time (up to 4,000–5,000 observations in recent surveys). ANES surveys include dozens of questions on gender, age, education, occupation, income, religion, race, and so on. Unfortunately, unlike the French postelectoral surveys, they do not include detailed questions on wealth and asset ownership.[32]

The NEP surveys have been organized following every US presidential election from 1972 to 2016 (and also after most congressional elections) by a consortium of media organizations (including CBS, CNN, NYT, and no on). They are less easily accessible than the ANES microfiles, they do not cover the pre-1972 period, and their questionnaire is more rudimentary and includes much fewer variables. Also, the income question asked in NEP usually includes much fewer income brackets than the corresponding ANES question (typically five to ten brackets in NEP instead of fifteen to twenty or more in ANES), so it contains less information.[33] NEP, like ANES, does not include wealth information. Given my purposes in this research, the only real advantage of NEP files is their bigger sample size (up to 20,000–25,000 observations in recent elections). I have therefore used NEP files mostly to perform robustness checks and to replicate ANES findings for the years and variables for which NEP data is available. In what follows I will focus on the ANES results.[34]

### The Reversal of the Education Cleavage

I now present my findings on the reversal of the education cleavage. Generally speaking, the results that I obtain for the United States regarding education cleavages are almost identical to those obtained for France. Given the enormous differences in party systems, socioeconomic structures, and political histories between the two countries, this is very striking.

Let me start with the simplest indicator of the education cleavage, the gap in Democratic vote between university graduates and non-university graduates. Back in the 1940s–1960s, the gap was large and negative,

32. We do have basic information on home ownership and self-employment status, which gives results similar to those for France. Unfortunately, we cannot compute wealth deciles.

33. See Piketty, "Brahmin Left," for additional details.

34. With the exception of the 2020 election, for which I have relied on preliminary results from NEP surveys. See online appendix.

around −15 points: university graduates voted a lot more for Republican candidates than other voters did. The gap gradually shrank over time, and by 2016 and 2020 it had become strongly positive, close to +15 points. Of course, there might be a special Trump effect in 2016 and 2020—an issue to which I will return below, and which appears to be particularly strong with respect to the income cleavage. Regarding education, however, what we see in 2016 and 2020 does not seem out of line with what we saw in previous years; it fits well in the continuity of a long-run evolution, in the same way that the education cleavage in France did for the 2017 election (see above).

The detailed results by highest degree are again very striking (see Figure 2.15). In the 1940s–1960s, we observe a monotonically decreasing relationship between education and Democratic support: the higher the education level, the lower the Democratic vote. For example, in the 1948 election, more than 60 percent of voters with primary or no degrees (that is, high school dropouts, 63 percent of the electorate at the time)

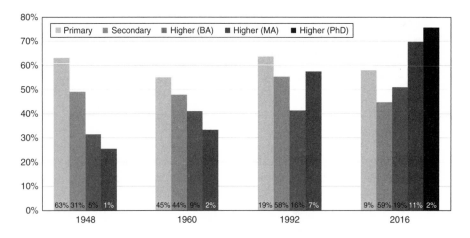

FIGURE 2.15. Vote for Democratic Party by education in the US, 1948–2016
*Data Source:* Author's computations using US postelectoral surveys 1948–2016 (ANES) (see wpid.world).
*Note:* In 2016, the Democratic Party candidate (Clinton) obtained 45% of the vote among high school graduates and 75% among PhDs. Primary: voters with no high school degree. Secondary: high school degree but not bachelor's degree. Higher (BA): bachelor's degree. Higher (MA): advanced degree (master's, law/medical school). Higher (PhD): doctoral degree.

supported the Democratic candidate, versus about 50 percent of voters with secondary degrees (high school graduates, 31 percent of the electorate) and only 20 percent of voters with university degrees (only 6 percent of the electorate). This monotonically decreasing relationship has changed gradually during the 1970s–1990s, and by 2000–2020 it has started to look more and more upward sloping at the top of the educational pyramid.

By 2016, the relation between education and Democratic vote is close to being monotonically increasing. The only exception (and the only difference in France) lies at the very bottom of the distribution: high school dropouts support the Democratic candidate more than high school graduates do. This is largely due to a minority effect (though not entirely). Above high school level, the relation between education and Democratic vote is strongly increasing. In particular, 70 percent of voters with master's degrees (11 percent of the electorate) supported the Democratic candidate. At the very top of the educational distribution, 76 percent of voters with PhD degrees (2 percent of the electorate) voted for Democrats. In contrast, only 51 percent of voters with bachelor's degrees (19 percent of the electorate) and 44 percent of high school graduates (59 percent of the electorate) did the same.

We now look at the evolution of the education voting gap before and after controls. The controls for gender and age have limited impact, while the controls for income and race have a significant upward effect on the levels. This is due to the fact that minority voters tend both to have much lower education levels and to vote massively more for Democrats. Controlling for race, the gap in Democratic vote between university graduates and non-university graduates is pushed upward and becomes marginally positive during the 1980s–1990s and strongly positive in 2000–2020 (well before the Trump election).

Given the magnitude of educational expansion over the 1948–2020 period, the most meaningful way to analyze changing political cleavages by education is probably to look at the gap in voting behavior between top 10 percent education voters and bottom 90 percent education voters (and more generally, to compare relative positions in the percentile distribution of education rather than absolute levels).

The results on the gap in the Democratic vote between top 10 percent and bottom 90 percent education voters are reported in Figure 2.16, both before and after controls. The complete reversal of the gap, from large and negative in the 1940s–1960s to large and positive in the 2000s–2010s,

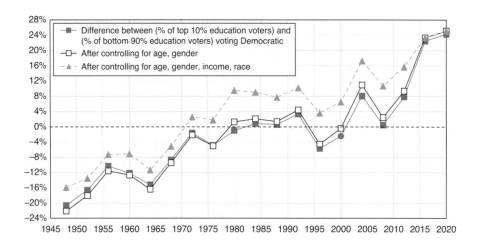

FIGURE 2.16. Voting for the Democratic Party in the US, 1948–2020: From the worker party to the high-education party

*Data Source:* Author's computations using US postelectoral surveys 1948–2020 (ANES) (see wpid.world).

*Note:* In 1948, the Democratic candidate obtained a score that was 21 points lower among top 10% education voters than among bottom 90%; in 2016, the score of the Democratic candidate was 23 points higher among top 10% education voters.

is even more spectacular than when we look at the gap between university graduates and non-university graduates, particularly in recent decades.[35] This is because the gradient within university graduates has become very large in the recent period (with holders of advanced degrees supporting Democratic candidates much more strongly than those with bachelor's degrees). It is also striking to see that the after-control top 10 percent versus bottom 90 percent education gradient observed in the 2016 and 2020 elections appears to be just a little bit higher than in previous elections, and very much in line with the long-run evolution. In this particular sense, the Clinton-Trump and Biden-Trump elections are not an anomaly.

Finally, and maybe most importantly, the reversal of the education gradient appears to be almost identical in timing and magnitude in the United States and in France. This is true whether we look at the gap in voting attitudes between university graduates and non-university graduates,

35. See Piketty, "Brahmin Left," figure 3.3a.

before or after controls, or between top 10 percent and bottom 90 percent education voters, before or after controls.[36]

### *Stability and Attenuation of Income/Wealth Cleavages*

I now turn to my findings on changing US political cleavages by income. I have computed the profiles of Democratic vote share by income percentiles for all presidential elections from 1948 to 2016, using the same estimation method as for France. The profile is generally downward sloping, particularly at the level of the top 10 percent (except in 2016). Within the bottom 90 percent, the profile appears to be more strongly downward sloping (that is, less flat) in the United States than in France, which seems to be related to the lesser historical importance of the "poor right-wing self-employed" (in particular, "poor right-wing farmer") in the United States as compared to France, at least in the post–World War II era. At the level of the top 10 percent, the profile is generally more strongly downward sloping in France than in the United States. But overall, the two countries display broadly similar income profiles.

If we now look at the profile observed during the 2016 US presidential election, we see something entirely new: for the first time, top 10 percent income voters support the Democratic candidate more than the Republican candidate, and more so than lower-income groups.[37] By computing the evolution of the gap in Democratic vote between top 10 percent and bottom 90 percent income voters, both before and after controls, one can see that this gap was approximately constant from the 1940s–1950s to the 1980s–1990s, increased slightly in the 2000s and early 2010s, and most importantly, rose sharply in 2016. This is the real innovation of the 2016 election: high-education voters had already turned Democratic many elections before, but for the first time, high-income voters turned Democratic as well. The same result is visible in 2020, though to a lesser degree.[38]

36. See Piketty, "Brahmin Left," figures 3.3d to 3.3g.
37. See Piketty, "Brahmin Left," figures 3.4a and 3.4b.
38. However, one should notice that the results are still preliminary at the time of writing this chapter. According to the National Exit Polls (NEP) 2020, updated on the websites of their main organizers (such as the *New York Times*), Biden and Trump seem to have obtained relatively similar results among voters with incomes above $250,000 (about 7 percent of the electorate). The ANES 2020 files are not yet available at the time of writing, which prevents us from studying this point in greater detail.

Regarding political cleavages by wealth, we unfortunately do not have the same kind of detailed wealth questionnaires in US postelectoral surveys as in French surveys. Note, however, that we do have some basic wealth variables for a number of elections (particularly regarding home ownership, and sometimes for other assets), and this data shows the same pattern that what we find for France (we also find the same profile for Britain, see below), namely that high wealth is an even stronger predictor of the vote for Republicans (or right-wing parties in the French context, or Conservatives in British context) than high income. We also have more detailed US wealth data for certain years (for instance, 2012), which again confirms this finding.[39] It seems likely that this conclusion also applies in earlier years and throughout the period 1948–2020, just like in France and Britain.[40]

### Multi-elite Party System or Great Reversal?

By combining our results on changing US political cleavages by education and by income, we obtain the following picture. Whether we measure education cleavages by comparing university graduates versus non-university graduates (before and after controls), or by comparing top 10 percent versus bottom 90 percent education voters (also before and after controls), which is probably most meaningful, we find the same broad evolution of the party system in the United States.[41] Moreover, the evolution is very similar to that observed in France. Back in the 1940s–1960s, the US party system could be characterized as a class-based system, in the sense that low-education and low-income voters supported the same party (the Democrats), while high-education and high-income voters supported the other party (the Republicans). The United States has gradually moved toward a "multi-elite" party system, whereby the high-education elite vote for Democrats and the high-income elite vote for the Republicans. We have also included in Figure 2.17 the results

39. The 2012 data comes from the US version of the CSES project (Comparative Study of Electoral Systems), an international consortium organizing homogenous postelectoral surveys in dozens of countries. All its data is available online (www.cses.org). The project includes four waves so far: module 1 (1996–2001), 2 (2001–2006), 3 (2006–2011), and 4 (2011–2016). Module 4 includes a special questionnaire on wealth (including categorical questions on ownership for several asset categories: home ownership, stocks, savings, and professional business assets).

40. See the discussion below on Britain.

41. See Piketty, "Brahmin Left," figures 3.5e to 3.5h.

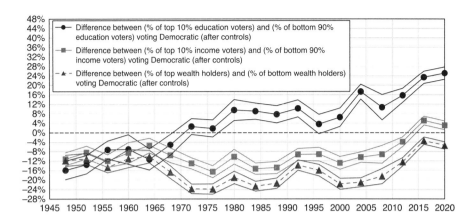

FIGURE 2.17. Political conflict in the US, 1948–2020: Toward a multi-elite party system, or a great reversal?

*Data Source:* Author's computations using US postelectoral surveys 1948–2020 (ANES, see wpid.world).

*Note:* The Democratic vote used to be associated with lower-educated and low-income voters; it has gradually become associated with higher-educated voters, giving rise to a multi-elite party system (education vs. income); it might also become associated with high-income voters in the future, leading to a great reversal and complete realignment of the party system. Fine lines indicate 90% confidence intervals.

obtained for the wealth cleavage by combining income information with the home ownership variable available in ANES surveys. This should be viewed as exploratory, given the lack of better wealth data.[42]

In the same way as for France, it is unclear at this stage whether this "multi-elite" party system will persist, or whether it will gradually evolve toward a complete realignment of the party system along "globalists" (high education, high income) versus "nativists" (low education, low income) lines. The 2016 and 2020 elections clearly seem to point in this direction: for the first time, the Democratic vote was associated with both high-education and high-income voters. It could be that this is largely due to a specific Trump factor, and that the high-income elite will return to Republicans in the near future (of course, this will depend on the choice of Republican and Democratic candidates). The important point, how-

42. Namely, we define a high-wealth index equal to 1 for individuals who are homeowners and members of the top 20 percent income group, and equal to 0 otherwise. See the discussion below for the case of Britain, where more asset variables are available.

ever, is that the unusual political events observed in the United States and France in 2016–2020 should also be viewed within the context of a long-run transformation of the party system. The latter is now facing different possible trajectories: stabilization of the "multi-elite" party system; "globalists" versus "nativists" realignment; or return to some form of class-based system.

### The Transformation of Racial and Origin-Based Cleavages

I now turn to the evolution of US racial and origin-based cleavages. Here the basic facts are relatively well known, and I would like to stress the differences and similarities with French evolutions (which are less well known), and most importantly, the interaction with the multi-elite transformation.

I report in Figure 2.18 the evolution of vote shares for the Democratic Party candidate by ethnic groups in US presidential elections from 1948 to 2020. The proportion of Blacks (African Americans) in the electorate has been relatively stable around 10–12 percent throughout the period, and the fraction voting Democratic has constantly been within the

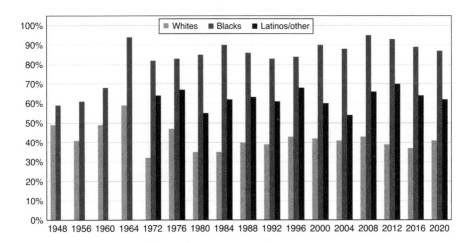

FIGURE 2.18. Vote for Democratic Party by ethnic origin in the US, 1948–2020
*Data Source:* Author's computations using US postelectoral surveys 1948–2020 (ANES) (see wpid.world).
*Note:* In 2016, the Democratic Party candidate (Clinton) obtained 37% of the vote among White voters, 89% of the vote among Black voters, and 64% of the vote among Latino and other voters.

80–95 percent range from 1964 (the beginning of the civil rights movement) until the present day. In previous elections (1948–1960), the Democratic vote share among Blacks was less overwhelming, though already very substantial (about 60–70 percent). The fact that Black voters already supported the Democrats before the party officially supported desegregation can be rationalized in a number of ways. First and foremost, from the 1930s onward, or even before, the Democratic New Deal–type policy platform was already benefiting low-income, low-education voters (and therefore the vast majority of Black voters, albeit indirectly). Next, northern Democrats were not segregationists (unlike southern Democrats), and their attitude on racial issues was not necessarily very different from that of Republicans.[43]

In any case, the point is that from 1964 onward, Black voters have always given overwhelming majorities (80–95 percent) to Democratic candidates, and this has become one of the most (if not the most) significant factors shaping the structure of US political conflict. In contrast, Whites have never given a majority to a Democratic candidate since 1964 (with a Whites-only voting system based on popular vote, all presidents would have been Republicans).

It is striking to see that the overwhelming Black vote for Democrats (80–95 percent) is quantitatively similar to the overwhelming Muslim vote for left-wing parties in France since the mid-1990s (80–95 percent;

---

43. The limited opinion survey evidence that we have from 1936 onward suggests that Blacks were already supporting Democratic candidates (i.e., Roosevelt) in the 1936–1944 presidential elections by a margin of about 70–30 (close to what we see in the 1948–1960 elections); party identification among Blacks moved more gradually (about 50–50 in 1936–1944, up to 70–30 in 1948–1960, and over 90–10 from 1964 onward), suggesting that it took more time for the Black electorate to acknowledge that Democrats had pro-Black candidates. See, e.g., C. Ladd and C. Hardley, *Transformations of the American Party System: Political Coalitions from the New Deal to the 1970s* (Norton, 1975), and D. Bositis, "Blacks and the 2012 Democratic National Convention" (Joint Center for Political and Economic Studies, 2012), table 1, for a compilation of early opinion polls (mostly from Gallup). Unfortunately, there is very little survey data available before 1936, and one needs to use local-level election data to recover individual-level cleavages. See also E. Schickler, *Racial Realignment: The Transformation of American Liberalism, 1932–1965* (Princeton University Press, 2016). Post-1860 Republicans were abolitionists and pro–free labor, but this obviously does not imply that they were strong supporters of the political and economic emancipation of African Americans. Democrats were able during the Reconstruction period to rebuild a winning coalition by portraying Republicans as captured by the northeast financial and manufacturing elite (a coalition which in many ways planted the seeds for the future New Deal Democratic coalition). See, e.g., N. Barreyre, *Gold and Freedom: The Political Economy of Reconstruction* (University of Virginia Press, 2015).

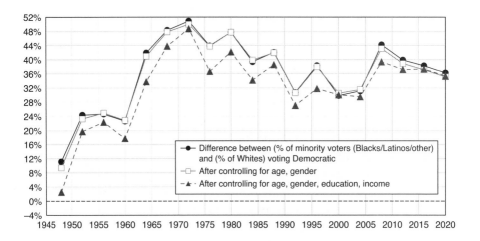

FIGURE 2.19. Minority vote in the US, 1948–2020: Before and after controls
*Data Source:* Author's computations using US postelectoral surveys 1948–2020
(ANES, see wpid.world).
*Note:* In 1948, the Democratic candidate obtained a score that was 11 points higher
among minority voters than among Whites; in 2016, the Democratic Party candidate
obtained a score that was 39 points higher among minority voters.

see Figure 2.11). Also, as with the Muslim vote in France, adding control
variables for education, income, wealth, and so on explains only a relatively small fraction of the Black vote for Democrats (see Figure 2.19, and
compare to Figure 2.12 for France). In the two countries, these voting
patterns can be accounted for by the fact that both minorities—the Black
racial minority in the United States and the Muslim ethnoreligious minority in France—perceive substantial hostility on the "right" side of the
political spectrum (Republicans in the United States, right-wing parties
in France) and more sympathy on the "left" side (Democrats in the United
States, left-wing parties in France). On the other side, a substantial portion of the White majority believes that the "left" unduly favors the minority, which in their view justifies their vote for the "right."

Although there are commonalities between the two situations, there
are also enormous differences, and in particular with respect to the
role of the Latino vote in the United States. Non-Black minorities accounted for a very small fraction of the US electorate during the 1940s–
1960s (less than 1 percent), but since the 1970s they have increased
enormously, up to almost 20 percent of the electorate in the late 2010s

(mostly Latinos).[44] Latinos and other non-Black minority voters have always given a strong majority to Democratic candidates: between 55 percent and 70 percent of their vote in all presidential elections from 1972 to 2016. Although this is less overwhelming than the Black Democratic vote, it is still a very strong majority; the gap with the White vote is strong and persistent, about 20 percentage points, and only moderately reduced by controls. This constitutes a very big difference with France (or more generally, with European countries). In France, about 10 percent of the electorate in the 2010s has extra-European foreign origins (mostly Maghreb and Sub-Saharan Africa), roughly the same fraction as the Black population in the United States, and about 20 percent of the electorate has European foreign origins (most from Spain, Portugal and Italy), roughly the same fraction as the Latino population in the United States. But the big difference is that the French Latinos are not Latinos, in the sense that they vote exactly the same way as the population with no foreign grandparent (see Figure 2.20).

In the case of the United States, it has long been argued that racism and anti-Black attitudes help to explain the smaller size of the welfare state and social transfers (as compared to Europe).[45] In particular, racial issues are the most common explanation for why the Democrats gradually lost a large part of the working-class White vote after the civil rights movement (especially in the South), thereby contributing to weakening and eventually dismantling the Democratic New Deal coalition. In effect, racial diversity and racial conflict have made it more complicated to keep poor Blacks and poor Whites in the same coalition. This helps to explain the transition away from the "class-based" party system of the 1950s–1960s and toward the "multi-elite" party system of the 2000s–2020s.

This certainly does not imply, however, that this is the only explanation. First, the extent of "racism" of certain White voters in the United States (or France or elsewhere) cannot simply be taken as given. At some level, it must be related to actual experience with race relations, and also to the ability (or failure) of certain social policies and institutions to unify the perception of identity and class solidarity. For example, French

44. Here we include non-Black, non-Latino minorities (less than 2 percent of the electorate in 2016) with Latino voters.

45. See, e.g., A. Alesina, E. Glaeser, and B. Sacerdote, "Why Doesn't the US Have a European-Style Welfare State?" (Brookings Papers on Economic Activity, 2001), and J. Roemer, D. Lee, and K. Van des Straeten, *Racism, Xenophobia, and Distribution: Multiissue Politics in Advanced Democracies* (Harvard University Press, 2007).

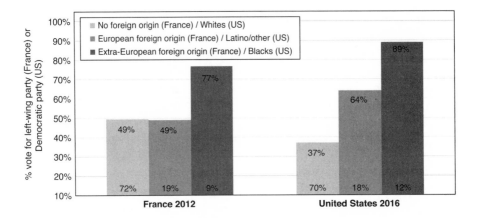

FIGURE 2.20. Political conflict and national-ethnic origins: France vs US
*Data Source:* Author's computations using US and French postelectoral surveys (see wpid.world).
*Note:* In 2012, the French left-wing candidate (Hollande) obtained 49% of the vote among voters with no foreign origin (no foreign grandparent), 49% of the vote among voters with European foreign origins (mostly Spain, Italy, Portugal, etc.), and 77% of the vote among voters with extra-European foreign origins (mostly Maghreb and sub-Saharan Africa). In 2016, the US Democratic Party candidate (Clinton) obtained 37% of the vote among Whites, 64% of the vote among Latinos/others, and 89% of the vote among Blacks.

Latinos are not seen and do not see themselves as Latinos, unlike US Latinos. The fact that social policies have been relatively segmented in the United States (that is, targeted toward specific groups) has arguably made it more difficult to develop a sense of common interest and to counteract racist perceptions and other prejudices.[46]

Next, even in the absence of any racial divide, one can find other reasons and mechanisms (for example, related to educational expansion per se) that may have contributed to the shift from a "class-based" to a "multi-elite" party system. In the case of the United States, I find the same

46. V. Ashok, I. Kuziemko, and E. Washington, "Support for Redistribution in an Age of Rising Inequality: New Stylized Facts and Some Tentative Explanations" (Brookings Papers on Economic Activity, 2015) analyzes other reasons explaining declining support for redistribution within specific groups in recent decades (in spite of rising inequality), e.g., among the elderly (who might fear losing Medicare benefits if social transfers are extended to other groups) and among African Americans (which might reflect the fact that "transfers" have been increasingly associated with race-based aid and negative perceptions).

transformation of the party system into a "multi-elite" pattern even if I exclude entirely the southern states. Maybe most importantly, in the case of France, I find that the gradual shift toward the "multi-elite" system started in the 1960s–1970s, before the cleavage about migration (and particularly about non-European migrants and Islam) really became salient—that is, in the 1980s–1990s. This points to the existence of a separate mechanism that can help to explain the transformation of the structure of political conflict, independently from the issue of migration and racial/ethnic/religious diversity (which of course does not mean that this issue did not contribute as well).

### Changing Political Cleavages in Britain

In this section, I present detailed results on the changing structure of political cleavages for the case of Britain. I begin by briefly describing the evolution of political parties and the popular vote in Britain over the period 1945–2017 and the main data sources (postelectoral surveys) that I will be using. I then present my main results on breakdowns by education, income/wealth, and the shift to "multi-elite" party system. I finally present results on breakdowns by religious and ethnic groups.[47]

*Changing Political Parties and Electoral*
*Results in Britain, 1945–2017*

Together with the US system, the British party system is the best example of a two-party system. The shares of popular vote obtained by the various parties competing in all British general elections that took place from 1945 to 2017 show that the top two parties over this seventy-two-year period have always been the Conservative Party and the Labour Party.[48] In the famous 1945 election, Attlee's Labour Party attracted 48 percent of the vote, versus 36 percent for Churchill's Conservative Party. This led

---

47. See Piketty, "Brahmin Left," figures 4.2a and 4.2b for an analysis of gender and age cleavages.

48. See Piketty, "Brahmin Left," figure 4.1a. Note that in the eighteenth and nineteenth centuries the two-party system comprised the Conservatives and the Liberals (or the Whigs). It took almost half a century, from 1900 to 1945, for the Labour Party to replace the Liberals as the second major party. In other words, the British system has always been a two-party system, but the identity of the two parties has changed, and transitions from one two-party system to the next one can take a very long time. Internal party transformations usually provide a simpler mechanism to shift the party system.

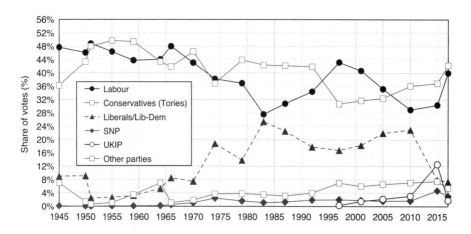

FIGURE 2.21. Legislative elections in Britain, 1945–2017
*Data Source:* Author's computations using official election results (see wpid.world).
*Note:* In the 1945 legislative elections, the Labour Party obtained 48% of the vote and
the Conservatives 36% of the vote (hence a total of 84% of the vote for the two main
parties). In the 2017 legislative elections, the Conservatives obtained 42% of the vote
and the Labour Party 40% of the vote (hence a total of 82%). Liberals/Lib-Dem:
Liberals, Liberal Democrats, SDP–Liberal Alliance. SNP: Scottish National Party.
UKIP: UK Independence Party. Other parties include green and regionalist parties.

in the following years to the creation of the National Health Service and
the modern British welfare state. In the 2017 election, May's Conservative Party obtained 42 percent of the vote, versus 40 percent for Corbyn's
Labour. Third parties usually obtain less than 10–15 percent of the vote,
except in 1987–1992 and 2005–2010, when the Lib Dems attracted over
20 percent of voters; by 2015–2017, they were back around 5–10 percent
(see Figure 2.21).[49]

The stability of the two major British parties (Conservative and
Labour) provides a striking contrast with the French political scene, where
both sides of the spectrum have a long history of permanently creating
new party names and acronyms. The contrast is usually attributed to the
different voting systems (one-round system in Britain, two-round in
France), but as I already noted, this might be endogenous, at least in part.
In the context of the present research, I will exclude other votes and

49. The Liberal Democrats (Lib Dems) are the modern incarnation of the Liberals.
During the 1980s they briefly formed the Liberals/SDP Alliance with a split from the
Labour Party.

concentrate on the Labour versus Conservative vote. The justification for excluding other votes is again that my main purpose in this research is to look at broad, long-run evolutions and to make comparisons with the two other countries.

### Data Sources: British Postelectoral Surveys, 1963–2017

There exists a relatively long tradition of postelectoral surveys in Britain. The most complete and longest series are the BES surveys (British Election Study). They are organized by a consortium of academic organizations and the microfiles are easily accessible.[50] The first BES survey was conducted in 1963 (including retrospective questions on voting attitudes in the general elections of 1959 and 1955), and subsequently BES surveys were conducted after all general elections since 1964.

Like the French and US equivalent surveys, BES surveys include dozens of questions on gender, age, education, occupation, income, wealth, religion, ethnic and foreign origins, and so on. Sample size is about 4,000 observations in recent surveys (but closer to 1,000–2,000 in early surveys). The wealth variables are less detailed than in the French surveys, but more detailed than in the United States (see below).

### The Reversal of the Education Cleavage

I now turn to the results on the education cleavage. I find the same basic result as in France and the United States. In particular, the gap in the Labour vote between university graduates and non-university graduates used to be large and negative in the 1950s–1960s (as large as −20 points or even −30 points), and it gradually dropped in absolute values during the 1970s–1990s, before becoming positive in the 2000s–2010s, both before and after controls. The same conclusion holds when I look at the gap in Labour vote between top 10 percent and bottom 90 percent education voters (both before and after controls), which is probably the most consistent way to look at this evolution (see Figure 2.22).[51]

It is worth noting that although the trend is virtually identical in the three countries, the level of the gap in left vote between high- and low-

---

50. The BES project has been based for the most part at the Universities of Manchester and Oxford. All files are accessible online (http://www.britishelectionstudy.com).

51. See also Piketty, "Brahmin Left," figures 4.3a to 4.3c for the alternative specifications.

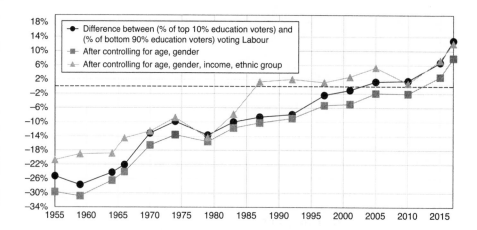

FIGURE 2.22. Voting for the Labour Party in Britain, 1955–2017: From the worker party to the high-education party

*Data Source:* Author's computations using British postelectoral surveys 1955–2017 (BES, see wpid.world).

*Note:* In 1955, the Labour Party obtained a score that was 25 points lower among top 10% education voters than among bottom 90% education voters (registered voters are ranked by highest degree); in 2017, the score of the Labour Party was 13 points higher among top 10% education voters. Controls alter levels but do not affect trends.

education voters has always been somewhat lower (that is, more negative, or less positive) in Britain than in France and the United States (see Figure 2.1 above). This holds whether we are comparing the left vote gap between university graduates and non–university graduates, both before and after controls, or the left vote gap between top 10 percent and bottom 90 percent education voters, both before and after controls, the latter variant being the most robust comparison.[52]

In other words, the British party system used to be even more "class-based" than the French and US systems; in the 1950s–1960s, it was very rare for educated individuals to vote for Labour rather than for the Conservative Party. It took a very long time for the educated elite to shift their vote from Conservative to Labour (as compared to France and the United States), and when they finally did shift, they did so less massively than in

52. See also Piketty, "Brahmin Left," figures 4.3d to 4.3g for the alternative specifications.

France and the United States. This is consistent with the ideological and political origins of the Labour versus Conservative divide in Britain, which are indeed more explicitly class-based (as the very name of the "Labour" Party indicates) than the cleavages that led to the development of the party systems in the other two countries.[53] The interesting point, however, is that at the end of the day, the long-run evolutions appear to be very similar, particularly in recent years, when university graduates and especially those with the highest degrees (the top 10 percent education group) have massively shifted to Labour.

### Multi-elite Party System or Great Reversal?

I now present the results on income and wealth cleavages. The profile of the Labour vote by income percentile has generally been relatively steep in Britain, both within the bottom 90 percent (typically steeper than in France) and at the level of the top 10 percent. The gap in Labour vote between top 10 percent and bottom 90 percent income voters has always been substantial in Britain, particularly at the beginning of the period, both before and after controls, with a slight attenuation over time.[54]

If we combine the findings on education, income, and wealth cleavages, we find that Britain has gradually moved from a "class-based" party system (with low-education, low-income, and low-wealth voters supporting Labour) to a "multi-elite" party system: high-education voters now strongly support Labour, while high-income and especially high-wealth voters strongly support the Conservative Party (see Figure 2.23).[55]

One interesting difference with France and the United States is that in Britain there is no sign that high-income voters could shift sides and support Labour in the near future. If anything, the "multiple elite" nature of the British party system was reinforced in the recent 2015–2017 elections: high-education voters have increased their support for the Labour Party,

---

53. In an interesting article ("Am I a Liberal?," published in 1925 in *The Nation and Athenaeum*, republished in his *Essays in Persuasion*, 1931), John Maynard Keynes—a perfect example of the educated elite—famously explained why he would never vote Labour: "I do not believe that the intellectual elements in the Labour Party will ever exercise adequate control; too much will always be decided by those who do not know *at all* what they are talking about. . . . I incline to believe that the Liberal Party is still the best instrument of future progress." Had he not died in 1946, he might have finally become a Labour Brahmin, but this certainly would have taken a long time.

54. See Piketty, "Brahmin Left," figures 4.4a to 4.4c.

55. See also Piketty, "Brahmin Left," figures 4.5a to 4.5h for the alternative specifications.

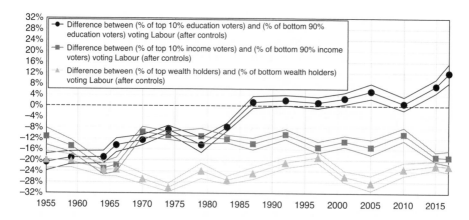

FIGURE 2.23. Political conflict in Britain, 1955–2017: Toward a multi-elite party system, or a great reversal?

*Data Source:* Author's computations using British postelectoral surveys 1955–2017 (BES, see wpid.world).

*Note:* The Labour Party vote used to be associated with lower-educated and low-income voters; it has gradually become associated with higher-educated voters, giving rise to a multi-elite party system (education vs. income); it might also become associated with high-income voters in the future, but at this stage this scenario seems less likely in Britain than in France or the US. Fine lines indicate 90% confidence intervals.

while high-income voters have increased their support for the Conservatives. This stands in clear contrast with the recent evolutions observed in France and the United States (see Figure 2.9 for France and Figure 2.17 for the United States), where high-income voters were moving in the direction of the "left-globalists" (Clinton-Macron), suggesting the possibility of a gradual shift toward a complete realignment of the party system along "globalists" (high education, high income) versus "nativists" (low education, low income) lines.

Despite its imperfections, available evidence on wealth cleavages in Britain also confirms the stabilization of the "multi-elite" system. High-wealth voters have always had a strong Conservative preference (even stronger than that of high-income voters), and this does not seem to be changing.[56] The fact that high-income and high-wealth voters show no

---

56. Here I define high-wealth as full home ownership (no mortgage). This information on mortgages is available on a consistent basis in BES surveys (unlike in the United States). I would get similar results by combining home ownership and income information, like in

tendency to shift to Labour can naturally be related to the relatively strong pro-redistribution stance taken by the party leadership (Corbyn). Of course, one could also imagine a different scenario for the future—for example one where post-Corbyn Labour takes an increasingly pro-EU stance (and the Conservative Party an increasingly protectionist stance), so that high-income and high-wealth voters join Labour on this basis; this could mean that Britain also moves toward a globalists versus nativists cleavage. But this does not seem to be the most likely evolution at this stage.

In any case, the point is that this comparison between Britain, France, and the United States illustrates that different evolutions are possible, including a stabilization of the "multi-elite" party system or a complete realignment (globalists versus nativists). A third possibility would be a return to a class-based party system. In principle, this could happen either from an internationalist or a nativist perspective. In the context of Britain and the Labour Party (a party that has long been associated with a pro-migrant stance, as compared to Conservatives), the internationalist perspective is more relevant. A return to a class-based system would correspond to a situation in which the Labour leadership would amplify its pro-redistribution platform. In order to regain the low-education vote, however, one would need to be very persuasive regarding the possibility of an internationalist egalitarian platform (for example, based on trans-national fiscal coordination to enforce a more progressive tax system) that would benefit them (more than the anti-migrant stance that many support). This is uncertain but not impossible. The general point is that with multidimensional inequality and cleavages, multiple equilibria and bifurcations are possible, depending on different party strategies, or small differences in tight election races.

### The Transformation of Religious and Origin-Based Cleavages

I now turn to the results on the transformation of religious and origin-based cleavages in Britain. Generally speaking, the results are very close to those obtained for France.

---

the United States. In the BES surveys of the 1980s–1990s, we also have information on ownership of newly privatized stock ownership, and this again is strongly associated with the Conservative vote. Unfortunately, we do not have enough consistent asset ownership variables to estimate wealth deciles in a reliable manner (as I do for France).

This is particularly striking with regard to the evolution of religious cleavages.[57] Just like in France, more than 90 percent of voters used to describe themselves as Christians—96 percent in 1964 (combining Anglicans, other Protestants, and Catholics). This proportion gradually fell to 43 percent in 2017. In the meantime, the proportion of voters reporting "no religion" rose from 3 percent in 1964 to 48 percent in 2017 (even more than in France). Just like in France, the Christians versus no-religion divide is strongly associated with the Conservatives versus Labour voting pattern (though the magnitude of the effect is somewhat smaller in Britain). Next, and most importantly, we observe exactly the same patterns with the Muslim vote. In Britain, like in France, Islam used to be nonexistent (it is still largely nonexistent in the United States). Before 1979 Islam was included with other religions in BES surveys, so we cannot look specifically at Muslim voters. When the question is first asked in the 1979 survey, less than 1 percent of voters describe themselves as Muslims. The proportion gradually rises in the following three decades, up to 5 percent of voters in 2017, exactly the same level as in France, albeit with different origins (British Muslims largely come from South Asia, while French Muslims mostly originate from North Africa, reflecting different colonial experiences). Even more strikingly, British Muslims have always voted massively for the Labour Party, typically around 80–95 percent, just like in France (see Figure 2.24, and compare to Figure 2.11 for France), and also like the Black Democratic vote in the United States. The magnitude of the effect seems to have increased somewhat over time, but it was already massive at the beginning of the period.

Unfortunately, the British surveys do not include questions about foreign grandparents and countries of origin, like in the recent French surveys, so we cannot fully compare the results between the two countries. In 1979, the British surveys started asking questions on self-designated ethnic groups. At that time, 98 percent of the voters described themselves as "White" (or "English," or "Scottish," and so on), while about 1 percent described themselves as "African-Caribbean" and about 1 percent as "Indian-Pakistani-Bangladeshi." By 2017, the proportion self-defined as "White" has declined to 89 percent, while "African-Caribbean" has increased to 3 percent, "Indian-Pakistani-Bangladeshi" to 6 percent, and other categories (mostly "Chinese" and "Arab") to 2 percent. As in France,

57. See also Piketty, "Brahmin Left," figure 4.6a.

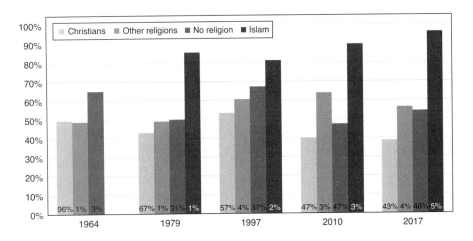

FIGURE 2.24. Labour vote by religion in Britain, 1964–2017
*Data Source:* Author's computations using British postelectoral surveys 1964–2017
(BES, see wpid.world).
*Note:* In 2017, the Labour Party obtained 39% of the vote among self-reported Christians
(including Anglicans, other Protestants, and Catholics), 56% among voters reporting
other religions (Judaism, Hinduism, etc., except Islam), 54% among voters reporting no
religion, and 96% among self-reported Muslims. Before 1979, Islam is included with
other religions.

voters in Britain with extra-European origins give strong support to the
Labour Party (see Figure 2.25). This holds independent of religion, but
there seems to be an additional effect associated with Islam as such (like
in France, though the data is imperfect).

The main reason Muslim and extra-European voters so overwhelmingly support the Labour Party in Britain throughout the 1979–2017 period is the same reason as in France: voters with extra-European origins
(and especially Muslims) perceive a lot of hostility from the Conservatives and more sympathy from the Labour Party. Also, in 1979, British
surveys start asking questions about whether there are too many immigrants in Britain (similar to the questions that appear in French surveys in
1988). It is striking to see that a vast majority of voters respond that there
are too many immigrants (over 75 percent in 1979), but Conservative and
Labour voters give very different responses on how to address the problem:
Conservative supporters believe that the only viable solution is to stop
immigration altogether, while Labour supporters believe that creating
more jobs and constructing more housing units in large cities could help

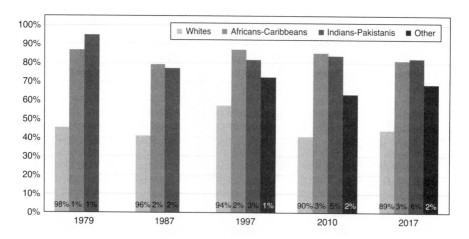

FIGURE 2.25. Labour vote by ethnic group in Britain, 1979–2017

*Data Source:* Author's computations using British postelectoral surveys 1979–2017 (BES) (see wpid.world).

*Note:* In 2017, the Labour Party obtained 41% of the vote among self-reported ethnic "Whites," 81% among "Africans-Caribbeans," 82% among "Indians-Pakistanis-Bangladeshis," and 69% among "Other" (including "Chinese," "Arabs," etc.). In 2017, 5% of voters refused to answer the ethnic identity question (and 77% of them voted Labour) (not shown here).

solve the problem (though a large proportion also favors a complete end to immigration). When asked which party is more likely to deliver a full stop to immigration, 96 percent say the Conservatives (and only 4 percent say Labour). In retrospect, the issue appears to have played a significant role in the 1979 election and the Conservative victory.[58]

It is tempting to relate this to the US research showing that racist White flight strongly contributed to the decline of the Democratic Party following the civil rights movement (see above), and in particular, contributed to the election of Nixon in 1968, and later to the 1980 Reagan and

58. It has also been argued that attitudes on migration already played a decisive role in the 1970 Conservative victory, following Enoch Powell's famous "Rivers of Blood" speech (April 20, 1968) against the Race Relations Bill promoted by the Labour government. According to Gallup polls conducted at the time, 73 percent of the British electorate supported Powell (and disapproved of the decision by Tory leader Heath to sack him from the shadow cabinet) and 84 percent supported a drastic reduction in immigration. Powell was sacked, but the episode helped to make the Labour versus Conservative conflict on migration more salient.

2016 Trump elections. This is interesting, especially because the Thatcher and Reagan victories are usually associated with the rise of neoliberalism; it is possible that the rise of ethnoreligious cleavages played a larger role than what is usually assumed. Also, this shows that major transformations of cleavage structures can take place within the same institutional party structure, without changing the names of the party or creating new parties. In the case of France, it is natural to associate the historical rise of the low-education right-wing vote with the development of the National Front (and the historical decline of low-education left-wing vote with the demise of the Communist Party).[59] However, the US and British cases show the same structural transformations can take place within the same two-party systems—that is, without a Communist Party and without a National Front. Of course, this is not to say that parties are unimportant. But this shows that it can be fruitful and reasonable to group parties into broad ideological coalitions (as we did for France) to compare the evolution of political cleavages in countries with very different party systems and political histories. Some of the most important evolutions might be taking place independent of the institutional party structure, and they appear to be better explained by the changing structure of underlying intellectual and substantial cleavages than by the specific institutional vehicles carrying these cleavages.

## Concluding Comments and Perspectives

In this research, I have used French, US, and British postelectoral surveys covering the 1948–2020 period to document a striking long-run evolution in the structure of political cleavages. In the 1950s–1960s, the vote for left-wing (socialist-communist-labour-democratic) parties was associated with lower-education and lower-income voters. It has gradually become associated with higher-education voters, giving rise to a "multi-elite" party system in the 2000s–2010s: high-education elites now vote for the "left," while high-income/high-wealth elites still vote for the "right" (though less and less so). I have argued that this can help to explain rising inequality and the lack of democratic response to it, as well

---

59. Detailed results by party show that the communist vote was indeed stronger among low-education voters in the 1950s–1960s (as compared to the socialist vote and center-left vote), and that the FN vote is also stronger among low-education voters in the 2000s–2010s (as compared to the votes for center-right and other right-wing parties).

as the rise of "populism." In effect, globalization and educational expansion have created new dimensions of inequality and conflict, leading to the weakening of previous class-based redistributive coalitions and the gradual breakdown of the postwar left-right party system.

It is clear, however, that we still face many limitations in our understanding of these issues. Two open questions stand out. First, to what extent could the transition to a "multi-elite" party system have happened without the rise of identity/migration cleavage? Next, can "multi-elite" party systems persist, or are they inherently unstable? I have stressed that educational expansion per se could generate multidimensional cleavages and a persistent conflict between the high-education elite and the high-income elite, even in the absence of an identity/migration cleavage. In order to go further, it would be interesting, for instance, to test whether "multi-elite" cleavages also develop in countries that have little exposure to migration. The body of comparative research presented in this book is an attempt to go in this direction.

## 3

# Electoral Cleavages and Socioeconomic Inequality in Germany, 1949–2017

FABIAN KOSSE AND THOMAS PIKETTY

### Introduction

This chapter draws on political attitudes surveys to study the changing relationships between party support, electoral cleavages, and socioeconomic inequality in Germany. The development of political cleavages in Germany is a particularly interesting case. On the one hand, the political system shows a high degree of stability and is strongly shaped by the interplay of two parties that have led all federal governments since 1949. On the other hand, the relation between left (social democratic and affiliated) voting and socioeconomic characteristics has changed by leaps and bounds, largely driven by the inception and establishment of new parties since 1980.

Our main finding is that the general evolution observed in Germany shares many similarities with the rise of the "multi-elite" cleavage structure (Brahmin left versus merchant right) that was documented in the case of France, the United States, and the United Kingdom. We also stress a number of specificities related to the German trajectory and discuss future prospects for party realignments.

### From the Weimar Republic to the *Kanzlerdemokratie*

We seek to analyze the electoral attitudes of voters in the Bundesrepublik Deutschland (Federal Republic of Germany) from 1949 to 2017. For the period from 1949 to 1989 we analyze data of West Germany, and from

We thank Clara Bohle, Larissa Fuchs, and Severin Süss for their outstanding research assistance.

1990 onward we analyze data of the unified Federal Republic of Germany. Regarding the political system, united Germany is considered to be the enlarged continuation of West Germany, and most former East German parties were absorbed by their West German counterparts.[1] Therefore, the West German political system experienced relatively small changes following reunification.

As a result of the past experiences of the fragility of democracy, the political system of Germany is characterized by an institutional design that aims to avoid the systemic shortcomings the Weimar Republic suffered from.[2] Among other factors, this shaped an electoral system combining the systems of majority voting and proportional representation (mixed-member proportional representation). While allowing smaller parties to retain their political influence, it reduces the risk of a parliamentary fragmentation.[3] The fear of unstable majorities is mirrored in the implementation of a 5 percent electoral threshold to limit the number of small parties included in the Bundestag (federal parliament). The role of the president within the political system has been significantly weakened since the Weimar Republic. Instead, there is a strong focus on the *Bundeskanzler* (federal chancellor) and the Bundestag. The *Bundeskanzler* plays a central role in steering everyday politics, which has led some observers to describe Germany's political system as a *Kanzlerdemokratie*.[4] The Bundestag elects the *Bundeskanzler* and is the leading legislative organ. Together with a strongly federal political system, power in the parliamentary democracy of Germany is much more decentralized than in presidential democracies such as the United States or France.[5] Given the decisive role of the Bundestag, we focus our empirical analysis on voting behavior in federal elections, which determine the composition of the Bundestag and are regularly held every four years.

1. O. Winkel, "Die deutsche Einheit als verfassungspolitischer Konflikt," *Zeitschrift für Parlamentsfragen* 28, no. 3 (1997): 475–501.

2. The term "Weimar Republic" refers to the period from 1918 to 1933 when Germany's first parliamentary democracy was in place. It started with the proclamation of the republic and ended with Hitler's *Machtergreifung* (seizure of power).

3. M. G. Schmidt, *Das politische System Deutschlands* (C. H. Beck, 2016), 45–46.

4. Schmidt, *Das politische System Deutschlands*, 172–180. For a more detailed evaluation across time, see K. Niclauß, ed., *Kanzlerdemokratie: Regierungsführung von Konrad Adenauer bis Angela Merkel* (Springer Fachmedien Wiesbaden, 2015).

5. Schmidt, *Das politische System Deutschlands*, 194–195.

## Classifying the Parties

To classify the parties within the German political system, one can rely on several methods essentially leading to the same results. One may, for instance, rely on the expert survey conducted by Benoit and Laver.[6] Academics specializing in political parties and electoral politics rated all major parties' locations on a left-right scale ranging from 1 to 20, where 1 stands for the hypothetical case of an ideal left party and 20 for the ideal right.[7] Assuming the left-right dimension to be symmetric on both ends, parties with attributed values lower than 10 are categorized as left, while those with values higher than 10 are categorized as right. As the expert survey was conducted in 2003, a categorization based on these ratings assumes a relative stability of parties' positions in the party system. The literature indicates that this assumption of stability across time is plausible for the German context.[8] This holds true especially in the case of a comparatively coarse left-right distinction. While a shift of a party's position within its assigned category is plausible, shifts across the left-right divide appear to be unlikely. Only the Free Democratic Party (FDP) appears to be potentially problematic, due to the varying influence of social- and left-liberal groups over time. For convenience, we consistently categorize the FDP with Christian democrats and other right-wing parties, as suggested by the results shown in Benoit and Laver.[9]

6. K. Benoit and M. Laver, "Estimating Party Policy Positions: Comparing Expert Surveys and Hand-Coded Content Analysis," *Electoral Studies* 26, no. 1 (2007): 90–107.

7. To categorize parties on the left-right dimension, experts were asked to "locate each party on a general left-right dimension, taking all aspects of party policy into account" (Benoit and Laver, "Estimating Party Policy Positions," 131).

8. S. Franzmann and A. Kaiser, "Locating Political Parties in Policy Space: A Reanalysis of Party Manifesto Data," *Party Politics* 12, no. 2 (2006): 163–188.

9. A categorization of (almost) all parties that have been in the Bundestag (1949–2017) is displayed in appendix Table A1, World Political Cleavages and Inequality Database, http://wpid.world. We did not categorize the SSW (South Schleswig Voters' Association), which is a small regional party. The SSW gained one mandate in 1949. We also did not categorize the Zentrum (Centre Party), for which the left-right categorization is ambiguous. The Zentrum gained a few mandates in 1949 (3.1 percent) and 1953 (0.8 percent). Since the expert survey from 2003 did not cover parties that previously lost their relevance (KPD, DP, GB/BHE, BP, WAV, DRP) or have emerged since then (AfD), we updated the list according to their categorization in the literature. See T. Däubler, "Links-Rechts und darüber hinaus—Eine Neuvermessung der Deutschen Parteienlandschaft mit einem auf die MARPOR/CMP-Daten angewandten IRT-Modell," in *Parteien unter Wettbewerbsdruck,* ed. S. Bukow and U. Jun (Springer Fachmedien Wiesbaden, 2017), 57–88. Parties that

## Historical Development of the Bundestag

The German political system shows a high level of stability with regard to the parties that are represented in the Bundestag. While the CDU/CSU (an alliance between the Christian Democratic Union of Germany and the Christian Social Union in Bavaria), the SPD (Social Democratic Party of Germany) and the FDP have (almost)[10] always been represented in the Bundestag, B90/Grüne (Alliance 90/the Greens) and Die Linke (the Left) have been represented continuously since first gaining seats in 1983 and 1990, respectively. Only the results of the first two elections, 1949 and 1953, slightly depart from this pattern of persistence of parties. In these elections, several exceptions allowed for a circumvention of the 5 percent electoral threshold, resulting in some mandates for several smaller parties.[11] Most of these parties were attributed to the conservative and right spectrum. Besides the SPD, the Communist Pary (KPD) was the only other left party to be elected in the Bundestag in the Bundesrepublik's early years. In 1949, the KPD gained 5.7 percent of votes but failed to reach the 5 percent electoral threshold in 1953 and was banned in 1956.

From 1949 to 1963 Konrad Adenauer (CDU/CSU), the first *Bundeskanzler* of the Bundesrepublik Deutschland, led conservative and right governing coalitions formed by the CDU/CSU, the FDP, and/or smaller right-wing parties. Figure 3.1 indicates that during the 1950s the smaller mostly right-wing parties lost votes and the CDU/CSU established itself as the leading party of the right spectrum of the political party system in Germany.[12] In 1957, CDU/CSU won the first and, to date, only absolute majority for a single German parliamentary group in a free election.

---

never gained a mandate for the Bundestag are not considered for this classification and the following analyses.

10. The FDP was not represented in the Bundestag from 2013 to 2017, as they just failed to reach the 5 percent threshold in the 2013 election.

11. In 1949 and in 1953, the 5 percent threshold was waived for parties that won at least one district. Since 1957, parties have needed to win at least three districts to waive the 5 percent threshold. Moreover, in 1949, the 5 percent threshold did not apply on the national level, only on the state level. In 1990 it was sufficient to reach 5 percent in parts of either former East Germany or former West Germany.

12. In Figure 3.1 and all other analyses, we consider the shares of votes, which determine the number of seats in the Bundestag. Since 1953, this has been known as the *Zweitstimme*. In 1949, there was only one vote.

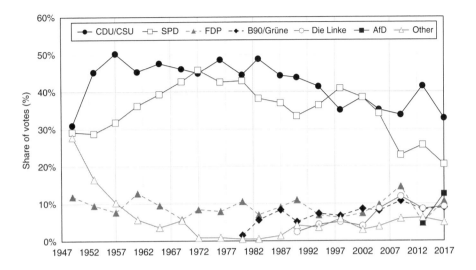

FIGURE 3.1. Federal election results in Germany, 1949–2017
*Data Source:* Authors' computations using official election results (see wpid.world).
*Note:* The figure shows the share of votes (*Zweitstimme*) received by selected German political parties in federal elections between 1949 and 2017.

Adenauer's successor, Ludwig Erhard (CDU/CSU), led a right governing coalition with the FDP from 1963 until 1966. One year after the election in 1965, the FDP left the coalition due to conflicts over economic policies. In the following years, from 1966 to 1969, CDU/CSU and SPD formed the first "grand coalition" led by Kurt Georg Kiesinger (CDU/CSU).

In the late 1950s, following the Godesberg Program of 1959, the SPD became more of a mainstream party, renouncing Marxist-inspired ideas and promoting a liberal socialism that aims to be democratic, pragmatic, and reformist. In the following years, the SPD gained votes and in 1969, Willy Brandt became the first *Bundeskanzler* of the SPD thanks to a coalition with the FDP. In the 1972 election the SPD gained its best-ever federal election result and, for the first time, won more seats than the CDU/CSU. Pursuing the coalition with the FDP, Brandt resigned in 1974 after a member of his staff was exposed as an agent of the East German secret service. Brandt's successor was Helmut Schmidt (SPD), who also led a coalition with the FDP. In 1982, the FDP left the coalition due to conflicts over economic and social policies and joined a coalition with

CDU/CSU. The new coalition was led by *Bundeskanzler* Helmut Kohl and lasted until 1998.

The federal election in 1983 marks the emergence of Die Grünen (later, B90/Grüne). It was the first time since 1957 that any other party than CDU/CSU, SPD, or FDP secured representation in the parliament. In the following elections, B90/Grüne were repeatedly elected into the Bundestag and established themselves at the federal level. As indicated in Figure 3.1, the early rise in votes received by the B90/Grüne was accompanied by a decline in votes received by the SPD.

The first election after the reunification of Germany was held in December 1990 and resulted in the appearance of a fifth party in the Bundestag, the PDS (Party of Democratic Socialism), which was the legal successor of the SED (Socialist Unity Party of Germany), the governing party of the German Democratic Republic (East Germany). In the 1990s, the PDS gained most of its votes in the eastern parts of Germany and struggled to establish itself at the federal level. The PDS was part of the merger that formed Die Linke in 2007.

After the federal election in 1998, the SPD and, for the first time, B90/Grüne formed the governing coalition led by *Bundeskanzler* Gerhard Schröder. While the coalition was confirmed in the 2002 election, parts of the SPD and the trade unions were dissatisfied with the government's social policies, especially the labor market reforms. In 2004, several left-wing protest movements against the policies of SPD–B90/Grüne merged and formed the WASG (Labour and Social Justice—the Electoral Alternative), which collaborated with the PDS early on and formally merged into Die Linke in 2007. As shown in Figure 3.1, the merged party nearly doubled the vote share of the PDS, which again was accompanied by a decline in votes received by the SPD.

Since 2005, *Bundeskanzlerin* Angela Merkel (CDU/CSU) has led coalitions with the SPD (2005–2009, 2013–2017, 2017–2021) and the FDP (2009–2013). Figure 3.1 shows that the SPD (in 2009 and 2017), as well as the FDP (2013), lost a significant share of votes in elections following governing coalitions led by *Bundeskanzlerin* Merkel.

In 2013, the AfD (Alternative for Germany) narrowly missed the 5 percent electoral threshold, but it gained 12.6 percent of votes in 2017, and thereby, for the first time since 1953, a new right party entered the Bundestag. Initially, the AfD was predominantly seen as a Eurosceptic and national-liberal party, but it later moved to the far right as a result of

intraparty conflicts. As of March 2020, parts of the AfD were classified as "verifiable right-wing extremist" by federal authorities and therefore were placed under intelligence surveillance.[13]

With the appearance of the AfD, for the first time since 1953, six parliamentary groups were represented in the parliament. Figure 3.1 indicates that CDU/CSU and SPD have lost significant vote shares since the days of a three-party parliament in the 1960s and 1970s. The first grand coalition of CDU/CSU and SPD in 1966 represented 86.9 percent of voters, while the current grand coalition of 2017 represents only 53.4 percent of voters.

Looking at the joint shares of left and right parties over time reveals an upward trend for the group of left parties and a downward trend for the group of right parties.[14] This trend peaked in the late 1990s and early 2000s and seems to have reversed since then. Looking at the SPD specifically indicates that the increase in the vote shares received by left parties in the 1960s and 1970s was entirely driven by the outreach of the SPD (the only left party in the parliament). However, since the emergence of Die Grünen (later, B90/Grüne) in the 1980s and Die Linke in the 1990s, the SPD nearly constantly lost votes, while the joint share of left parties increased slightly. This (inverse) U-shaped pattern since 1990 is much more pronounced in the regions of former East Germany, while the two parts of Germany did not differ with regard to the respective joint shares of left and right in 1990 and 2017.

## Analysis of Political Cleavages

To explore individual-level determinants of voting behavior, we rely on a series of postelection surveys. To do so, we built on the work of Arndt and Gattig, who collected a list of postelection surveys for the years 1949–2005, and we extended this list using the German Longitudinal Election Study (GLES), which covers the years 2009–2017.[15] Given the

13. Bundesamt für Verfassungsschutz, "Fachinformation: Einstufung des 'Flügel' als erwiesen extremistische Bestrebung," Der Verfassungsschutz, accessed July 11, 2020, https://www.verfassungsschutz.de/SharedDocs/Kurzmeldungen/DE/2020/fachinformation-einstufung-fluegel-als-extremistische-bestrebung.html.

14. See appendix Figures A1a and A1b, wpid.world, for election results by groups of parties.

15. C. Arndt and A. Gattig, *Dokumentation zur Erstellung eines Kumulierten Datensatzes aus den Studien der Bundestagswahlen 1949 bis 2005* (Jean Monnet Centre for

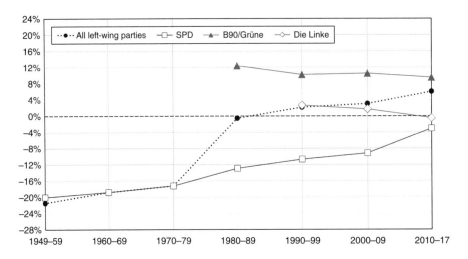

FIGURE 3.2. The reversal of the educational cleavage in Germany (left-wing parties), 1949–2017
*Data Source:* Authors' computations using German postelectoral surveys (see wpid.world).
*Note:* The figure shows the difference between the share of top 10% educated voters and the share of bottom 90% educated voters voting for selected left-wing parties. In the 1950s, left-wing parties (jointly) obtained a score that was 21 points lower among top 10% educated voters than among other voters; in the 2010s, their score was 6 points higher.

varying definitions and quality of available sociodemographic variables, we focus on a limited set of individual characteristics that could be harmonized across surveys.

In the first step of our analysis, we look at the relation between left voting and education. To account for the structural change in the distribution of educational attainment, we estimated the evolution of the difference between the fraction of left vote within top 10 percent educated voters and the fraction of left vote within bottom 90 percent educated voters. Figure 3.2 plots the difference in voting left between the top 10 percent educated voters and the rest, and it documents the same reversal of the education cleavage found in most other Western countries discussed in this book. A special feature of the German political system seems to be that much of this development is driven by a jump in the 1980s. The

European Studies, Universität Bremen, 2007). An overview of these data sources is provided in appendix Table A1, wpid.world.

inclusion of control variables moderately affects the levels of the education-gradient indicator but does not affect the trend.[16] Controlling for gender and age moves the education gradient downward (young cohorts tend to be both more educated and more likely to vote left, see below), while including income moves it upward (individuals with higher incomes tend to be both more educated and more likely to vote right, see below).

Focusing on the SPD indicates a continuous increase of the education gradient from the 1950s to the present, although this trend is relatively flat and the education gradient was still slightly negative in the most recent elections. The figure indicates that the jump of the education gradient when considering the set of left parties in the 1980s is strongly driven by the emergence of the B90/Grüne, as their education gradient has always been strongly positive. In contrast, the emergence of Die Linke in the 1990s had only a small impact on the joint left education gradient, as their specific gradient was constantly around zero. Separating former West Germany and East Germany reveals that while the gradients are, except for B90/Grüne, a bit bigger in East Germany, the patterns are similar in both regions.[17] Note that in former East Germany in the 1990s the PDS (later, Die Linke) shows a pronounced positive education gradient, which decreases in later elections. The literature suggests that many former East German elites supported the PDS in the 1990s, after they lost their privileges and positions following German reunification.[18]

Figure 3.3 repeats the analysis of the development of the education gradient for the right parties, jointly and separately. The development of the joint education gradient of the right parties mechanically mirrors the development of the left gradient: it is decreasing and shows a pronounced (downward) slump in the 1980s. The gradients of the CDU/CSU and FDP show a similar decreasing trend. While the gradient of the CDU/CSU

16. See appendix Figure A2, wpid.world, which displays the same relation but controls for age, gender, religion, and income. For the definition of controls, see Arndt and Gattig, *Dokumentation*. Controls are included as dummies for each category.

17. See appendix Figure A3, wpid.world. For a detailed discussion about East-West differences in voting behavior, see K. Arzheimer and J. Falter, "Goodbye Lenin? Bundes- und Landtagswahlen seit 1990: Eine Ost-West-Perspektive," in *Wahlen und Wähler: VS Verlag für Sozialwissenschaften*, ed. J. W. Falter, O. W. Gabriel, and B. Weßels (VS Verlag für Sozialwissenschaften, 2005), 244–283.

18. O. Niedermayer, "Die Wählerschaft der Linkspartei.PDS 2005: Sozialstruktureller Wandel bei gleich bleibender Politischer Positionierung," *Zeitschrift für Parlamentsfragen* 37, no. 3 (2006): 523–538.

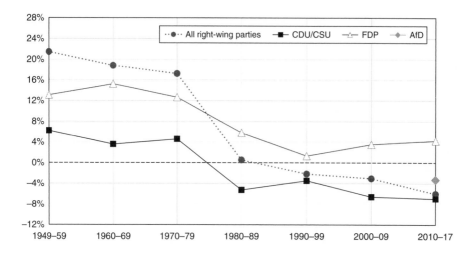

FIGURE 3.3. The reversal of the educational cleavage in Germany (right-wing parties), 1949–2017

*Data Source:* Authors' computations using German postelectoral surveys (see wpid.world). *Note:* The figure shows the difference between the share of top 10% educated voters and the share of bottom 90% educated voters voting for selected right-wing parties. In the 1950s, right-wing parties (jointly) obtained a score that was 21 points higher among top 10% educated voters than among other voters; in the 2010s, their score was 6 points lower.

switches signs in 1980, the gradient of the FDP has always been higher and has remained positive to the present. As the AfD emerged only in the 2010s, we cannot analyze the long-run development of their education gradient. However, comparing the 2013 and the 2017 elections indicates a strongly decreasing education gradient with the radicalization to the right (about +1 percentage point in 2013 as compared to −7 percentage points in 2017). Similar gradients can be found in the former West Germany and East Germany.[19]

In Figures 3.4 and 3.5, we analyze the gender and age cleavages in Germany. Figure 3.5 confirms the well-known result that female voters have become more left-wing over time (see Chapter 1). Starting at a relatively low level in the 1950s, the female gradient strongly increased in the 1960s and 1970s and has consistently been close to zero since the 1980s.

19. See appendix Figure A4, wpid.world.

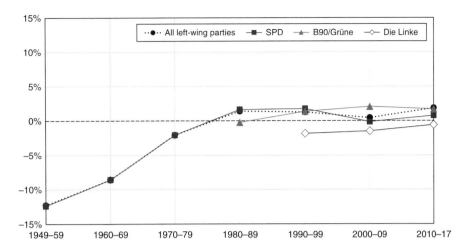

FIGURE 3.4. The reversal of the gender cleavage in Germany, 1949–2017
*Data Source:* Authors' computations using German postelectoral surveys (see wpid.world).
*Note:* The figure shows the difference between the share of women and the share of men voting for selected left-wing parties. In the 1950s, left-wing parties (jointly) obtained a score that was 12 points lower among women than among men; in the 2010s, their score was 2 points higher.

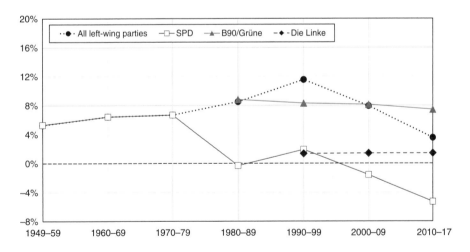

FIGURE 3.5. Left-wing voting and generational cleavages in Germany, 1949–2017
*Data Source:* Authors' computations using German postelectoral surveys (see wpid.world).
*Note:* The figure shows the difference between the share of voters aged below the median age and the share of median-aged voters voting for selected left-wing parties. In the 1950s, left-wing parties (jointly) obtained a score that was 5 points higher among young voters than among median-aged voters; in the 2010s, their score was 4 points higher.

This development is not driven by the entry of B90/Grüne or Die Linke; it is similar for all left parties.

Figure 3.5 shows that younger voters are more prone to left-wing voting than older voters (median split). The age gradient was largest in the 1990s and has decreased since then. The general pattern is in line with findings for other Western countries (see Chapter 1). Looking at the party-specific age gradients reveals a stable, strongly positive age gradient for the B90/Grüne and a pronounced drop in the gradient of the SPD in the 1980s when the B90/Grüne emerged, followed by a steady decline since then.

Analyzing divisions between rich and poor in the German context is possible only to a limited extent, as surveys nearly never include information about wealth. Nevertheless, we use the available information on income to explore the development of the income gradient in Germany. Figure 3.6 shows the evolution of the difference between the fraction of left vote within top 10 percent income voters and the fraction of left vote within bottom 90 percent income voters. As for several other Western

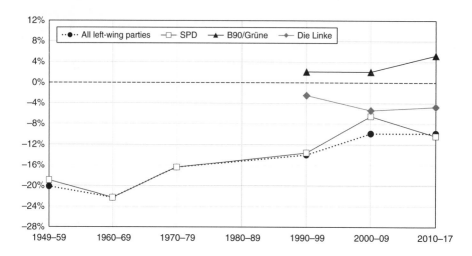

FIGURE 3.6. Left-wing voting and income in Germany, 1949–2017
*Data Source:* Authors' computations using German postelectoral surveys (see wpid.world).
*Note:* The figure shows the difference between the share of top 10% earners and the share of bottom 90% earners voting for selected left-wing parties. In the 1950s, left-wing parties (jointly) obtained a score that was 20 points lower among top 10% income voters than among other voters; in the 2010s, their score was 10 points lower.

countries, the income gradient has declined over time. This holds for the joint gradient of all left parties, as well as for the SPD-specific gradient. However, as opposed to countries like France or the United States, and more in line with the United Kingdom or Australia, the joint gradient has always remained negative at a sizable level (see Chapter 1). Only the B90/Grüne–specific gradient is consistently positive. There has also been a declining but always positive gradient for the right parties.[20] A notable exception is the AfD, which shows a negative income gradient of 3 percentage points in the 2010s.

Until 1990, almost all German voters were, in nearly equal shares, either Catholics or Protestants. The fraction of voters who were members of other churches was only about 1 percent and the fraction of voters who were members of no church was about 5 percent. Since the 1990s, the fraction of voters not a member of any church has strongly increased (36 percent in the 2010s). This rise was partly driven by German reunification, as a much lower share of voters from the former East Germany were members of a church. However, irrespective of the relative sizes of the religious groups, differences in electoral behaviors between these groups have remained significant up to the present: the share of the left vote has remained smaller among Catholics than among Protestants, and largest among voters belonging to other religions or to no religion. Only since 2017, the data contain information about Muslim voters. While they are only a small minority among voters (1–2 percent), Muslims were the group with the highest share of left vote (72 percent) in the 2017 election.[21]

## Concluding Remarks

The development of the education cleavage in Germany seems to have followed patterns similar to those in most other Western democracies. A phenomenon strongly influencing the German party system was the emergence and establishment of a green party in the form of Die Grünen, later B90/Grüne. This broadening of the left spectrum was associated with a slight increase in the joint share of left votes and was accompanied by a pronounced shift of the education cleavage in the 1980s. In line with France, the United States, and the United Kingdom, intellectual and economic elites seem to have drifted apart in Germany, with high-education

20. See appendix Figure A5, wpid.world.
21. See appendix Figure A6, wpid.world.

elites voting for the left and high-income elites voting for the right. As described in Chapter 2, this pattern is in line with the "multi-elite" stabilization scenario and is mirrored by the rise of the radical right, embodied in Germany by the emergence of the AfD, as low-education/low-income voters might feel neglected.

Understanding the coexistence of two parties with very different ideologies—the SPD and the AfD—both indicating negative education and income gradients, requires explicit models of multi-issue party positioning, which are far beyond the scope of this chapter. However, in the short term, the analysis of political attitudes toward redistribution and openness (pro-migration) in 2013 and 2017 indicates that in these domains the voters of the SPD (who are pro-redistribution and pro-openness) and the AfD (who are anti-redistribution and anti-openness) fundamentally differ, which suggests the disruption of previous class-based redistributive coalitions and the rise of new cleavages.[22]

Finally, regarding the possibility of a unification of intellectual and economic elites within the same party in the future (similar to what happened, to some extent, with the LRM vote in France and the Democratic vote in the United States), the prospects look very uncertain at this stage. A possible government coalition between B90/Grüne and CDU/CSU could represent an evolution in this direction. But the possibility and sustainability of such a realignment remains to be demonstrated.

22. See appendix Table A3, wpid.world.

# 4

# Changing Party Systems, Socioeconomic Cleavages, and Nationalism in Denmark, Finland, Iceland, Norway, and Sweden, 1956–2017

CLARA MARTÍNEZ-TOLEDANO AND ALICE SODANO

## Introduction

This chapter studies the changing relationship between party support and electoral socioeconomic cleavages in Northern Europe. How have political cleavages developed in some of the world's oldest and most egalitarian democracies? Have Nordic countries transitioned toward a multi-elite party system, like most Western democracies? How have deeply rooted, long-lasting nationalistic ideas changed the party system over the course of the century? We answer these questions using postelectoral surveys conducted in Norway, Denmark, Sweden, Finland, and Iceland from the mid-twentieth century until the present.

The Nordic countries have been described as having unusually stable and well-functioning multi-party systems.[1] The five countries also have strong historical, cultural, and political links with each other. Nonetheless, they do not have the same historic preconditions, economic resources, or foreign policy positions, and in recent decades their party systems have evolved differently. These differences have recently been found to largely

We are grateful to Amory Gethin and Thomas Piketty for their useful advice.

1. J. E. Lane, T. Martikainen, P. Svensson, G. Vogt, and H. Valen, "Scandinavian Exceptionalism Reconsidered," *Journal of Theoretical Politics* 5, no. 2 (1993): 195–230; P. Esaiasson and K. Heidar, eds., *Beyond Westminster and Congress: The Nordic Experience* (Ohio State University Press, 2000).

explain why Nordic countries are distinctly dissimilar in voter alignment and in their political systems.[2]

All Nordic countries except Iceland have been found to have stronger class-based party systems than most Western democracies. We confirm the existence of these strong class cleavages and document that their decline coincided with the emergence of a multi-elite cleavage structure comparable to that found in most Western democracies (see Chapter 1). In the 1950s–1960s, Nordic countries had a class-based system, as the left-wing vote (socialist, social democratic, and communist) was associated with the lowest-educated and lowest-income voters. Since the 1970s–1980s, it has gradually become associated with the highest-educated voters.

Nonetheless, the move toward a multi-elite party system has happened at different speeds in Northern Europe. It has been faster in Norway and Denmark, where the traditional left has lost the support of the lowest educated to the benefit of the right and the far right, while the New Left (green and new left-wing parties) has attracted the vote of the highest educated. In contrast, the reversal of the education cleavage has been less pronounced in Sweden and Finland, as the traditional left has managed to keep a larger share of its working-class electorate. In Sweden, the persistent hegemony of the Social Democratic Party has prevented the emergence of a clear multi-elite party system, despite strong support for the Left Party among the highest educated. This is also the case in Finland, where the Social Democratic Party continues to attract a significant share of the lower-educated electorate. The exception is Iceland, which did not develop a strong class-based party system and has had a very stable multi-elite party system since the late 1970s.

This structural evolution can help to explain the rise of populism and nationalism, as the lowest-educated and the lowest-income voters might feel left behind. In Norway and Denmark, the anti-immigration Progress Party emerged in the 1970s as an antitax party, in contrast to the True Finns, founded two decades later as successors of the Agrarian Party, who were in favor of greater progressive taxation. The Swedish exceptionalism myth vanished with the success of the far-right Sweden Democrats in the 2010s, whereas in Iceland the renewed political line of the Progressive Party prevented new nationalist parties from emerging. Increasing

---

2. Å. Bengtsson, K. Hansen, Ó. Þ. Harðarson, H. M. Narud, and H. Oscarsson, *The Nordic Voter: Myths of Exceptionalism* (ECPR Press, 2013).

migration to Northern Europe has also led to the implementation of tighter immigration policies that may have favored the emergence of a religious cleavage according to which Muslim voters are more left-wing, in line with what was found in most Western countries (see Chapter 1).

## Norway

### Party System and Election Results, 1945–2017

The Norwegian constitution signed in 1814 transformed Norway from an absolute into a constitutional monarchy. However, it was not until 1898 and 1913 that universal male and female suffrage, respectively, were established. The Norwegian multiparty system was long dominated by the Labour Party (Det norske Arbeiderparti, DNA), the largest party since 1927 in the parliament (the Storting). The DNA uninterruptedly led single-party majority governments from 1945 until 1961, followed by alternating coalitions and minority governments.

The Labour Party's strong support for joining the European Community (EC) weakened its hegemony: the electorate's rejection of membership in the 1972 referendum was followed by a decrease of about 11 percentage points in the party's vote share in the 1973 Storting election (Figure 4.1). That loss did not come with an increase in support for the right. The main winner in the Labour Party's defeat was an anti–European Community faction that separated from Labour during its pro-membership campaign and joined the Communists and the Socialist People's Party in the Socialist Electoral League. In the 1980s, in line with the "rightist wave" across Europe, the Norwegian electorate shifted toward the right.[3] The Conservative Party formed its own minority government in 1981 with 32 percent of the vote, and it took part in a coalition government with the Christian Democratic Party and the Center Party in 1983.

On the eve of the 1994 second EU-membership referendum, divergent ideological positions within the center-right coalition allowed Labour to return to power. At the same time, the new anti-immigration Progress Party was gaining support among the right-wing electorate, surpassing the Conservatives in the 1997, 2005, and 2009 parliamentary elections.

3. W. M. Lafferty, "The Political Transformation of a Social Democratic State: As the World Moves In, Norway Moves Right," *West European Politics* 13, no. 1 (1990): 79–100.

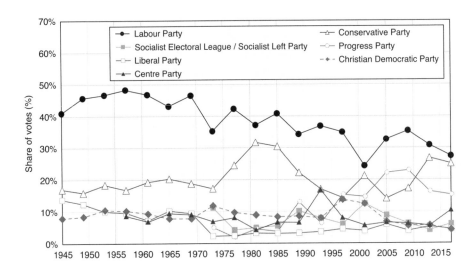

FIGURE 4.1. Election results in Norway, 1945–2017

*Data Source:* Authors' computations using official election results (see wpid.world).

*Note:* The figure shows the share of votes received by selected political parties or groups of parties in parliamentary elections held in Norway between 1945 and 2017. The Labour Party received 27% of the votes in 2017.

From 2005 to 2013, the country was governed by the Red-Green Coalition, an alliance of the Labour Party, the Center Party, and the Socialist Left Party, in which the agrarian Center Party represented the environmentalist ideology.

In what follows, we will study the changing relationship between party support and socioeconomic characteristics using Norwegian postelectoral surveys for all general elections from 1957 to 2017.[4] The Norwegian Labour Party and the Socialist Left Party are classified as left-wing parties, while right-wing parties include the Conservative Party, the Progress Party, and the Christian Democrats. Because of their centrist positions, the Liberal Party and the Center Party are not included in either the left or the right in our analysis.

4. See appendix Table AD1, World Political Cleavages and Inequality Database, http://wpid.world.

*The Decline of the Labour Party and the Emergence*
*of a Multi-elite Party System*

The transformation and the increasing fragmentation of the Norwegian political system have come together with a transformation of political attitudes. Whereas in 1957–1965 the difference between the share of tertiary-educated and non-tertiary-educated voters voting for socialist, social democratic, and communist parties fell by almost 30 percentage points, this difference has become positive, reaching more than 7 points in the 2010s.[5] In contrast, the difference between the share of top 10 percent and bottom 90 percent earners voting left remains negative over the entire period (Figure 4.2). The divergence between highest-educated voters and top-income earners reveals that Norway has moved toward a multi-elite party system, as has been documented for the majority of Western democracies (see Chapter 1).

To shed light on the drivers of this transformation, we can further decompose the electorate by educational attainment and consider specific parties. Between the 1960s and 1990s, the relationship between educational attainment and left vote was monotonically downward sloping. The reversal in the 2000s was mainly driven by the substantial reduction in the support for the Labour Party among the lowest-educated voters, exacerbated by a simultaneous increase in the share of tertiary-educated voters supporting it.[6] Despite this reduction, Labour is still supported by a larger share of primary-educated voters than university graduates, but it has increasingly competed with the Progress Party and the Conservative Party in the political representation of the primary educated since the 1990s, signaling a clear shift by the lowest educated to the right in recent decades. The Socialist Left Party has also contributed to the reversal of the education cleavage, as it has counted on the support of highest-educated voters since its debut in 1973 as the Socialist Electoral League. This finding is common to the majority of Western countries, where New Left parties have gained the support of the higher-educated segment of the electorate.

The transformation of the education cleavage has not come together with a reversal in the income cleavage. In particular, the share of the left-

5. See appendix Figure AB18, wpid.world, for the difference between the top 10 percent and the bottom 90 percent educated voting left.

6. See appendix Figures AB1, AC27, and AC28, wpid.world.

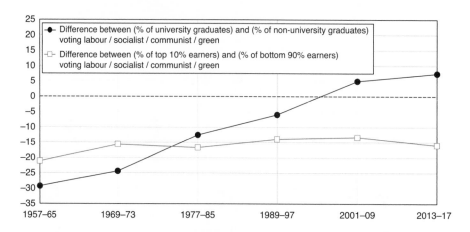

FIGURE 4.2. The emergence of a multi-elite party system in Norway, 1957–2017
*Data Source:* Authors' computations using Norwegian postelectoral surveys (see wpid.world).
*Note:* The figure shows the relative support of top-income and highest-educated voters for the Labour Party, the Socialist Left Party, and other affiliated parties. In the 1950s–1960s, top-income and highest-educated voters were less likely to vote labour/socialist/communist than low-income and lower-educated voters. The labour/socialist/communist/green vote has gradually become associated with higher-educated voters, giving rise to a multi-elite party system. Estimates control for income/education, gender, age, marital status, employment status, region, and union membership.

wing vote has remained quite flat across the income distribution up to the 90th percentile over the 1957–2017 period, above which the share of the left-wing vote sharply decreases. Considering specific right-wing parties reveals greater support for the Conservative Party among high-income voters, while the Progress Party has attracted a higher share of voters among low-income groups.[7]

### Declining Class Cleavages and the Emergence of Other Socioeconomic Cleavages

One of Norway's most important political cleavages relates to social class. From the 1950s until the 1990s, nearly 70 percent of voters identifying with the working class voted for the left, compared to 30 percent of other voters (Figure 4.3). Since the 2000s, this cleavage has weakened due to

7. See appendix Figures AB2, AB3, AC12, and AC16, wpid.world.

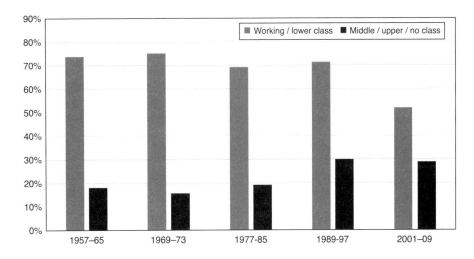

FIGURE 4.3. The decline of class voting in Norway, 1957–2009
*Data Source:* Authors' computations using Norwegian postelectoral surveys
(see wpid.world).
*Note:* The figure shows the share of votes received by the Labour Party, the Socialist
Left Party, and affiliated parties by subjective social class. In 1957–1965, 74% of voters
identifying with the "working class" or the "lower class" voted labour/socialist and
affiliated, compared to 52% in the 2000s. No data available in the 2010s.

the decrease in the support for social democratic and socialist parties
among the working class and the simultaneous increase in left votes
among the rest of the population.[8] The decline in class polarization is explained mainly by the weakening of class identity and the consequent
electoral mobility, which is stronger in Norway than in the rest of Nordic
countries.[9]

The decrease in the importance of the class cleavage has coincided with
the emergence of the Norwegian multi-elite party system. In fact, class was
so relevant in explaining party choice that it shifted the education gradient
up on average from −22 to −7 until the 1990s.[10] With the shrinking of

8. O. Knutsen, "Social Class, Sector Employment, and Gender as Party Cleavages in
the Scandinavian Countries: A Comparative Longitudinal Study, 1970–95," *Scandinavian
Political Studies* 24, no. 4 (2001): 311–350.

9. T. Worre, "Class Parties and Class Voting in the Scandinavian Countries," *Scandinavian Political Studies* 3, no. 4 (1980): 299–320.

10. See appendix Figure AB25, wpid.world.

class polarization from the 2000s, the sensitivity of the education gradient to the inclusion of class as a control has become negligible.

Over the 1980s, another interesting transformation characterized the Norwegian political scenario: the country experienced a strong reversal of the traditional gender cleavage, according to which women were more right-wing.[11] Women used to vote relatively more for the Christian People's Party, which defended religiosity and traditional moral values.[12] This reversal was mainly driven by the increasing share of women voting for the Socialist Left Party, which has been the left-wing political group closest to the feminist movements.[13] In addition, we find that the modern gender cleavage is largely explained by the expansion of women's employment in the public sector, confirming preexisting findings in the literature.[14] A gradual increase in the share of voters employed in the public sector has also occurred, together with a decline in private employees' support for the left and a slight increase in the share of left-wing public employees, leading to the emergence of a sectoral cleavage.[15]

### The Progress Party's Anti-immigration Platform and the New Religious Cleavage

The roots of Norwegian nationalism date back to its fight for the construction of a national identity during the nineteenth and early twentieth century, as Norway only achieved full independence from neighboring countries in 1905. However, immigration was not perceived to be an issue until the 1970s, when the number of immigrant workers started to increase.[16] The anti-immigration Progress Party, founded in 1973 as a no-tax party, gained the support of the lowest-educated and lowest-income voters. Although it captured only a limited share of votes in the 1970s, mainly attracting young voters from disadvantaged socioeconomic backgrounds, the 1987 election first and the elections of the 2000s later represented turning points in the party's electoral success.[17] Over time, the

11. See appendix Figures AB10 and AB21, wpid.world.

12. O. Listhaug, "The Gender Gap in Norwegian Voting Behaviour," *Scandinavian Political Studies* 8 (1985): 187–206.

13. See appendix Figures AC21and AC31, wpid.world, for the voting support by gender for the Christian Democrats and the main left-wing parties, respectively.

14. Knutsen, "Social Class, Sector Employment, and Gender."

15. See appendix Figures AB11 and AB24, wpid.world.

16. E. Bergmann, *Nordic Nationalism and Right-Wing Populist Politics: Imperial Relationships and National Sentiments* (Springer, 2016).

17. See appendix Figures AC15 to AC18, wpid.world.

focus of the party's platform has moved from labor immigration and the increasing number of foreign workers in the country to the threat of Muslim immigrants to Western culture and values.[18]

These positions have certainly played an important role in the determination of a religious cleavage leading Muslims to vote more for left-wing parties: Table 4.1 shows that 70 percent of Muslims voted for the main left-wing parties over the 2013–2017 period, and 59 percent of them supported the Labour Party.[19] In contrast, support for the Labour Party among Catholics, Protestants, or voters with no religion did not exceed 30 percent. As in a number of other Western democracies (see Chapter 1), a new religious cleavage therefore seems to have emerged in Norway.

## Denmark

### Denmark's Political System and Election Results, 1945–2019

Denmark's path toward democracy was marked by two pivotal events: the adoption of the Constitutional Act in 1849, which stipulated the end of the absolute monarchy, and the first election held under universal suffrage in 1915. The constitution's revision of 1953 introduced the unicameral Danish parliament (the Folketing) and a proportional representation system, which highly influenced the structure of the following governments, making it difficult for one party to obtain an absolute majority. Danish political history is thus characterized by the predominance of minority coalitions. The 1950s were a period of relative political stability, due to the balance of power between the three biggest parties, the Social Democratic Party, the Liberal Party (Venstre), and the Conservative People's Party, and the three smallest parties, the Social Liberals, the Communist Party, and the Justice Party.

The first deviation that led to left-right polarization happened in 1960, when the Justice Party lost all its seats, while the Socialist People's Party, founded by former members of the Communist Party, entered in the Folketing along with the Independent Party on the right-wing side of

---

18. K. Fangen and M. Vaage, "'The Immigration Problem' and Norwegian Right-Wing Politicians," *New Political Science* 40, no. 3 (2018): 459–476.

19. The Muslim vote is available only for the last decade (2013–2017). These results need to be interpreted with caution, as the percentage of Muslim voters in our sample is quite small.

Table 4.1 The Structure of Political Cleavages in Norway, 2013–2017

Share of Votes Received (%)

| | Socialist Left Party | Labour Party | Green Party | Liberal Party | Centre Party | Christian Democrats | Conservative Party | Progress Party |
|---|---|---|---|---|---|---|---|---|
| **Education** | | | | | | | | |
| Primary | 5% | 30% | 1% | 3% | 8% | 5% | 25% | 20% |
| Secondary | 4% | 27% | 3% | 4% | 9% | 5% | 29% | 16% |
| Tertiary | 8% | 27% | 4% | 8% | 5% | 5% | 30% | 8% |
| **Income** | | | | | | | | |
| Bottom 50% | 6% | 28% | 4% | 5% | 8% | 5% | 25% | 15% |
| Middle 40% | 6% | 30% | 3% | 5% | 7% | 3% | 30% | 11% |
| Top 10% | 4% | 20% | 1% | 8% | 5% | 1% | 46% | 11% |
| **Gender** | | | | | | | | |
| Women | 9% | 30% | 3% | 6% | 6% | 6% | 27% | 10% |
| Men | 4% | 25% | 3% | 5% | 8% | 4% | 31% | 10% |
| **Age** | | | | | | | | |
| 20–39 | 9% | 25% | 5% | 8% | 7% | 5% | 25% | 12% |
| 40–59 | 5% | 28% | 2% | 5% | 7% | 4% | 33% | 12% |
| 60+ | 4% | 30% | 1% | 4% | 8% | 8% | 27% | 15% |
| **Religion** | | | | | | | | |
| No religion | 16% | 30% | 7% | 7% | 3% | 3% | 18% | 7% |
| Catholic | 9% | 9% | 0% | 0% | 4% | 10% | 49% | 14% |
| Protestant | 4% | 27% | 2% | 5% | 8% | 5% | 31% | 14% |
| Muslim | 11% | 59% | 0% | 4% | 0% | 4% | 13% | 5% |
| Other | 6% | 15% | 9% | 9% | 2% | 25% | 17% | 6% |

*Data Source:* Authors' computations using Norwegian postelectoral surveys (see wpid.world).
*Note:* The table shows the average share of votes received by the main Norwegian parties by selected individual characteristics over the 2013–2017 period. The Labour Party was supported by 9% of Catholic voters, compared to 59% of Muslim voters, during this period.

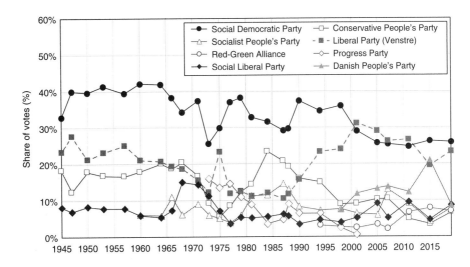

FIGURE 4.4. Election results in Denmark, 1945–2019
*Data Source:* Authors' computations using official election results (see wpid.world).
*Note:* The figure shows the share of votes received by selected political parties or groups
of parties in general elections held in Denmark between 1945 and 2019. The Social
Democratic Party received 26% of votes in 2019.

the political spectrum (Figure 4.4).[20] Until 1973, governments had been
mainly constituted by the Social Democratic Party, sometimes in coalition
with the Social Liberal Party on the left, and by the Venstre-Conservative
coalition on the right, also in some cases with the support of the Social Liberal Party.

The 1973 election has been defined as a landslide election that brought
upheaval to the Danish multiparty system.[21] The number of elected parties doubled, and the far-right Progress Party entered the parliament for
the first time, with 16 percent of votes, becoming the second party of the
country. With only 12 percent of votes, Venstre formed a minority coalition with the main right-wing parties (above all, the Conservative Party
and the Progress Party) and the Social Liberal Party. Although the majority of the traditional parties registered losses, the hardest hit from the

20. J. Stehouwer and O. Borre, "Four General Elections in Denmark, 1960–1968,"
*Scandinavian Political Studies* 4 (1969): 133–148.

21. C. Green-Pedersen, "Minority Governments and Party Politics: The Political and
Institutional Background to the 'Danish Miracle,'" *Journal of Public Policy* 21, no. 1 (2001):
53–70.

landslide election was the Social Democratic Party, whose vote share collapsed from 37 percent in 1971 to 26 percent in 1973. In 1975, they returned to government and remained in power until 1982. However, the Social Democrats' weakened position made it necessary to get support from the right-wing bloc in order to govern.

In 1978, the Social Democratic Party attempted cross-bloc cooperation with Venstre, which proved unsuccessful and came to an end only one year later.[22] The coalition had to deal with the consequences of a dramatic economic crisis triggered by the first oil shock in 1973, and with the difficulty of getting the proposed policies approved, since support from the nonsocialist coalition was essential. In 1982, a center-right minority government constituted by the Conservative People's Party and Venstre, along with the Center Democrats and the Christian People's Party, came to power and remained until 1988. From 1988 to 1990, the Conservative People's Party and Venstre formed another government coalition with the Social Liberal Party.

During the same period, the Social Democratic Party took positions closer to the center to attract centrist parties in a future coalition. In 1993, they succeeded and formed a coalition government with the Center Democrats, the Social Liberal Party, and the Christian Democrats. The Socialist People's Party, which used to present itself as an alternative to the left of the Social Democratic Party, also shifted its position toward the center, with the aim of eventually cooperating with the Social Democratic Party. This strategy cost the party a large loss of support during the 1990s, to the benefit of the Red-Green Alliance, the most left-wing party in the Folketing.[23] On the extreme right of the political spectrum, the 1990s also saw the gradual decline of the Progress Party and the birth of the anti-immigration Danish People's Party in 1995. In the 2015 election, the latter became the second-largest party in the country, supporting a Venstre minority government along with the Conservatives and the Liberal Alliance.

In what follows, we will study the changing relationship between party support and socioeconomic characteristics using Danish postelectoral surveys covering all general elections held from 1960 to 2015.[24] For the

22. Green-Pedersen, "Minority Governments."

23. B. Daiber, C. Hildebrandt, and A. Striethorst, *From Revolution to Coalition: Radical Left Parties in Europe* (Rosa Luxemburg Foundation, 2012), 27.

24. See appendix Table BD1, wpid.world.

sake of simplicity and following the existing literature, we have classified the Social Liberal Party as a left-wing party, despite its centrist orientation that led it to support both right-wing and left-wing governments.[25]

### Toward a Multi-elite Party System

The transformation of the political system in Denmark, as in Norway, has been associated with the emergence of a multi-elite party system. The difference in the share of the left vote among tertiary-educated voters and non-tertiary-educated voters after controls was equal to −15 percentage points in 1960–1968, after which it gradually increased until reaching +5 percentage points in the last decade. In contrast, the difference in left vote between the top 10 percent and bottom 90 percent earners has remained negative over the whole 1960–2015 period (Figure 4.5). While the Conservative Party has always been supported by the highest-income voters and the Danish People's Party by the lower socioeconomic classes, Venstre registered the majority of votes among bottom-income earners until the 1980s, before a reversal that aligned it with the conservative right.[26]

The analysis of the evolution of electoral support for specific education groups and left-wing parties provides interesting insights into the drivers of the reversal of the educational cleavage. The change in voting behavior was mainly driven by the joint influence of the Socialist People's Party and the Social Liberals on the higher educated, reinforced by the emergence of the Red-Green Alliance in the 1990s. The educational cleavage is less marked when we exclude the contribution of the Social Liberal Party in recent years, as this party has counted on the support of the highest educated since the 1960s. However, the reduction in the support for the Social Democratic Party among the lowest educated plays a minor role in the determination of the reversal: like the Norwegian Labour Party, the Danish Social Democrats still rely on a majority of primary-educated voters. While in 1990–1998 they had a vote share of 43 percent, this share fell to almost 30 percent in the following decades. The decline coincides with the rise in confidence in the Danish People's Party among the lowest-educated and lowest-income voters.[27] These

25. Bengtsson et al., *Nordic Voter.*
26. See appendix Figures BC17, BC22, and BC32, wpid.world.
27. See appendix Figures BC36 to BC38, wpid.world.

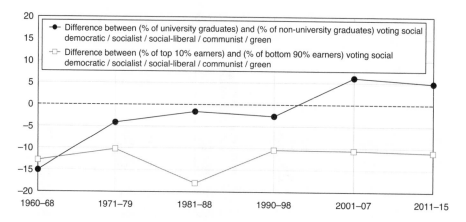

FIGURE 4.5. The emergence of a multi-elite party system in Denmark, 1960–2015
*Data Source:* Authors' computations using Danish postelectoral surveys (see wpid.world).
*Note:* The figure shows the relative support of top-income and highest-educated
voters for the Social Democratic Party, the Socialist People's Party, the Social Liberal
Party, the Red-Green Alliance, and affiliated parties. In the 1960s, top-income and
highest-educated voters were less likely to vote social democratic/socialist/social
liberal/communist than low-income and lower-educated voters. The social demo-
cratic/socialist/social liberal/communist/green vote has gradually become associated
with higher-educated voters, giving rise to a multi-elite party system. Estimates control
for income/education, gender, age, marital status, employment status, region, and
union membership.

results are in line with the findings of Rune Stubager, who classifies the
parties on a libertarian-authoritarian dimension and documents the existence of an educational cleavage in Denmark and the same party-specific
voting patterns we have described.[28]

### Class, Sector, and Other Socioeconomic Cleavages

Denmark is also characterized by strong class cleavages. From the 1960s
to the 1990s, the share of self-identified working-class voters supporting
social democratic, socialist, social liberal, and communist parties was
larger than 80 percent, compared to 40 percent of other voters. Over the
last decade, class polarization has almost vanished, in large part due to
a sharp decline in the vote for the left among the working class (Figure 4.6).

28. R. Stubager, "The Changing Basis of Party Competition: Education, Authoritarian-
Libertarian Values, and Voting," *Government and Opposition: An International Journal
of Comparative Politics* 3 (2013): 372–397.

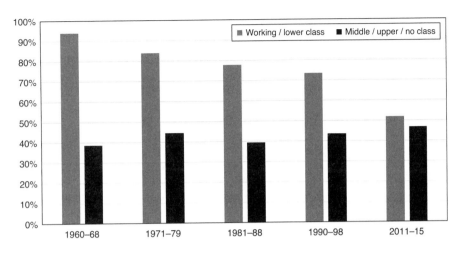

FIGURE 4.6. The decline of class voting in Denmark, 1960–2015
*Data Source:* Authors' computations using Danish postelectoral surveys (see wpid.world).
*Note:* The figure shows the share of votes received by the Social Democratic Party, the Socialist People's Party, the Social Liberal Party, the Red-Green Alliance, and affiliated parties by subjective social class. In the 1960s, 94% of voters identifying with the "working class" or the "lower class" voted for these parties, compared to 52% in the 2010s. No data available in the 2000s.

As in the case of Norway, the educational gradient is highly sensitive to the inclusion of perceived social class, confirming the importance of the class cleavage.[29]

In addition to having education, income, and class cleavages, Denmark stands out among the Nordic countries for having a particularly strong sectoral cleavage.[30] While during the 1960s and 1970s there were no significant differences in left vote between public-sector and private-sector employees, there has been a sharp decline in the share of private-sector employees voting for the left since the 1980s. This transformation coincided with the deterioration of private-sector confidence in the Social Democratic Party in dealing with the economic and political crisis of the 1980s. The Venstre-Conservative governments at the time attracted part of this lost vote share by openly promoting privatization of the

29. See appendix Figure BB24, wpid.world.
30. See appendix Figures BB9 and BB25, wpid.world.

public sector and the reduction of corporate taxes.[31] The employment sector also seems to play a crucial role to explaining the emergence of a modern gender cleavage, as its inclusion as a control in the regression of the difference between women and men voting left shifts the curve downward.[32]

### Attitudes toward Immigration and the Rise of the Danish People's Party

The success of the Danish People's Party from the mid-1990s reveals the importance of the immigration issue in Danish society. Anti-immigration rhetoric was first introduced in the parliament by the Progress Party in the 1970s, though at that time its main focus was the abolition of the income tax and the reduction of bureaucracy. With an increase in the number of asylum seekers, immigration started to become a heated topic in political debates. After the dissolution of the coalition with the Social Liberal Party in 1993, the Conservative Party and Venstre embraced the Progress Party's platform, tightening their positions on immigration.[33]

The anti-immigration stance was reinforced by the emergence of the Danish People's Party, which considered immigration to be a threat to national identity and burdensome for the Danish welfare state. In 1998, the year of the Danish People's Party's debut in the parliament, almost 60 percent of individuals interviewed believed that immigration was a topic of great or decisive importance, and 46 percent stated that too many public resources were invested in refugees' aid, according to the surveys used in this chapter. The terrorist attacks of 2001 eroded the distance between the anti-immigration party and the mainstream political parties, which until then had criticized the anti-Muslim positions of the Danish People's Party.[34] Over time, the attention of the public has also shifted toward Muslims and Islam. In 2007, while 34 percent of respondents saw general immigration as a menace, 47 percent expressed concern about the interaction between Muslims and Danish culture. As shown in Table 4.2, the Danish People's Party's electorate is aligned with

31. K.V. Andersen, C. Greve, and J. Torfing, "Reorganizing the Danish Welfare State, 1982–93: A Decade of Conservative Rule," *Scandinavian Studies* 68, no. 2 (1996): 161–187.
32. See appendix Figure BB23, wpid.world.
33. C. Green-Pedersen and P. Odmalm, "Going Different Ways? Right-Wing Parties and the Immigrant Issue in Denmark and Sweden," *Journal of European Public Policy* 15, no. 3 (2008): 367–381.
34. Bergmann, *Nordic Nationalism*.

Table 4.2  The Structure of Political Cleavages in Denmark, 2011–2015

|  | Share of Votes Received (%) | | | | | | |
|---|---|---|---|---|---|---|---|
|  | Red-Green Alliance | Socialist People's Party | Social Democratic Party | Social Liberal Party | Venstre | Conservative People's Party | Danish People's Party |
| **Education** | | | | | | | |
| Primary | 6% | 4% | 32% | 3% | 25% | 2% | 23% |
| Secondary | 9% | 7% | 32% | 8% | 24% | 4% | 13% |
| Tertiary | 9% | 8% | 32% | 12% | 22% | 6% | 7% |
| **Income** | | | | | | | |
| Bottom 50% | 11% | 7% | 32% | 7% | 19% | 3% | 17% |
| Middle 40% | 7% | 6% | 34% | 8% | 25% | 5% | 13% |
| Top 10% | 3% | 3% | 29% | 13% | 30% | 8% | 6% |
| **Gender** | | | | | | | |
| Women | 9% | 8% | 34% | 8% | 22% | 4% | 12% |
| Men | 7% | 5% | 29% | 7% | 25% | 4% | 17% |
| **Age** | | | | | | | |
| 20–39 | 11% | 7% | 28% | 11% | 21% | 4% | 12% |
| 40–59 | 7% | 7% | 34% | 8% | 24% | 5% | 14% |
| 60+ | 4% | 5% | 35% | 3% | 28% | 4% | 19% |
| **Sector** | | | | | | | |
| Private/Mixed | 4% | 5% | 30% | 10% | 36% | 5% | 9% |
| Public | 11% | 14% | 45% | 16% | 18% | 4% | 6% |
| **Location** | | | | | | | |
| Urban | 10% | 7% | 34% | 9% | 21% | 4% | 12% |
| Rural | 5% | 6% | 29% | 6% | 28% | 4% | 18% |

*Data Source:* Authors' computations using Danish postelectoral surveys (see wpid.world).

*Note:* The table shows the average share of votes received by the main Danish parties by selected individual characteristics over the 2011–2015 period. The Social Democratic Party was supported by 45% of public-sector employees, compared to 30% of other active voters.

that of other anti-immigration parties across Europe, in that it has mainly attracted voters from disadvantaged backgrounds.

## Sweden

### The Swedish Five-Party System and Election Results, 1948–2018

Sweden has been a parliamentary democracy since 1917, and universal suffrage was introduced soon after, in 1921. The Swedish political system has been considered a prototype of a five-party system. While in Norway and Denmark the first deviations from the model had happened during the 1970s and especially with the 1973 "earthquake" elections, the Swedish parliament (the Riksdag) alone hosted the five traditional parties until 1988.[35] These parties were grouped in two opposing blocs, the left-wing one led by the Social Democratic Party with the support of the Left Party, successor of the Communist Party of Sweden, and the bourgeois bloc constituted by the conservative Moderate Party, the Liberal People's Party, and the agrarian Center Party.

Over the course of the twentieth century, the Social Democratic Party has been the largest party in the Riksdag. In particular, it was in power for more than sixty years from 1932 to 2006, generally obtaining 40 to 50 percent of votes (Figure 4.7). Although most Swedish governments have been minority governments, as in Denmark, the political supremacy of the Social Democratic Party has led to less political instability. Until the 1970s, the Swedish "moderate pluralism" tended toward a one-party dominant system led by the Social Democratic Party. This was partly due to the uncertainty about the ability of the right-wing bloc to govern due to the evident disagreements among the three parties within the bloc (the Moderate Party, the Liberal People's Party, and the Center Party).[36]

The 1970s were a decade of significant institutional changes, such as the adoption of a unicameral parliament in 1970 and the promulgation of the 1974 constitution, which transferred full legislative power to the parliament. At the same time, it also saw the first setback in the Social Democrats' dominance. In 1976, the Center Party, the Liberal People's Party, and the Moderate Party formed the first coalition government in

35. J. Pierre, ed., *The Oxford Handbook of Swedish Politics* (Oxford University Press, 2016).

36. G. Sartori, *Parties and Party Systems* (Cambridge University Press, 1976).

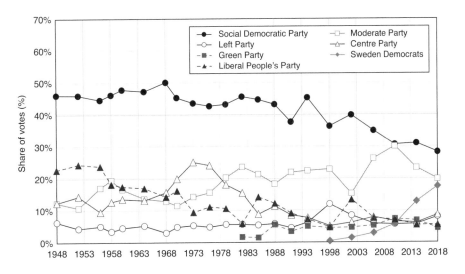

FIGURE 4.7. Election results in Sweden, 1948–2018
*Data Source:* Authors' computations using official election results (see wpid.world).
*Note:* The figure shows the share of votes received by selected political parties or groups
of parties in general elections held in Sweden between 1948 and 2018. The Social Democratic
Party received 28% of votes in 2018.

forty-four years, although the Social Democrats had won 43 percent of the
vote. The latter returned to power in 1982, after six years in opposition.
Moreover, the Moderate Party became the second-largest party in the parliament from 1979 onward, surpassing the Liberals and the Center Party.

This turmoil was a precursor of the transformation that the Swedish
political system was to experience. Until 1988, the stable five-party
model had persisted, mainly due to the 4 percent vote share threshold that
parties needed to gain seats in the Riksdag, but then the environmentalist
Green Party, founded after the 1980 nuclear power referendum and inspired by the subsequent antinuclear movements, entered the parliament.
The year 1991 also saw a minor "earthquake" election.[37] Two additional
parties managed to gain representation in the Riksdag, the Christian
Democrats and the right-wing New Democracy. Meanwhile, the old Social Democratic Party obtained its lowest result since 1928, receiving
only 38 percent of votes. The Moderate Party formed a minority govern-

37. N. Aylott, "Back to the Future: The 1994 Swedish Election," *Party Politics* 1, no. 3
(1995): 419–429.

ment with the support of the Liberal Party, the Center Party, and the Christian Democrats.

The new government had the difficult task of dealing with the financial crisis that hit the country at the beginning of the 1990s. The conservative government implemented liberal reforms, privatizing publicly owned firms, cutting corporate and capital taxes as well as public spending, and designing programs to reduce inflation and budget deficits. While in 1994 the Social Democrats regained the lost consensus, the same cannot be said for the next election four years later. The party lost more than 10 percentage points, whereas the Left Party experienced an impressive increase in support, becoming the third party in the parliament. This outcome was an expression of voters' dissatisfaction with the austerity policies implemented by the Social Democratic Party, but it was also linked to the Left Party's anti-EU position in the referendum of 1995, as well as its fight to defend the welfare state and its gradual detachment from the communist ideology. However, the Left Party's support of the Social Democrats cost them a loss of almost 6 percentage points in 2006.

The 2010 election represented a real turning point in Swedish political history. On the left-wing side, the Social Democrats, the Left Party, and the Greens created for the first time a red-green coalition. On the right-wing side, a far-right anti-immigration party, the Sweden Democrats, entered the Riksdag for the first time, with 5.7 percent of votes. The appearance of this party on the political scene can be considered the last piece in the demise of Swedish "exceptionalism." In what follows, we will analyze the evolution of the relationship between voting behavior and socioeconomic characteristics using Swedish pre- and postelectoral surveys covering all general elections from 1956 to 2014.[38]

### The Path toward a Multi-elite Party System

The long persistence of the traditional party system has undoubtedly affected the evolution of voting patterns in Sweden. The delay in the political upheavals with respect to Norway and Denmark are reflected, above all, in the analysis of the education cleavage. While the difference in left vote between the top 10 percent and the bottom 90 percent of earners is stable and negative as in the rest of Nordic countries, the same alignment does not occur for education (Figure 4.8). The negative gap in left vote between tertiary- and non-tertiary-educated voters presents an

38. See appendix table CD1, wpid.world.

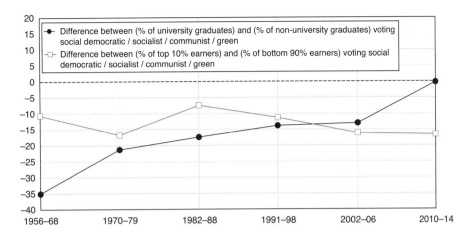

FIGURE 4.8. Toward a multi-elite party system in Sweden, 1956–2014
*Data Source:* Authors' computations using Swedish electoral surveys (see wpid.world).
*Note:* The figure shows the relative support of top-income and highest-educated voters
for the Social Democratic Party, the Left Party, the Green Party, and affiliated parties.
In the 1950s–1960s, highest-educated and top-income voters were less likely to vote
social democratic / socialist / communist than low-income and lower-educated voters.
The social democratic / socialist / communist / green vote has become increasingly
associated with higher-educated voters, leading Sweden closer to becoming a multi-elite
party system. Estimates control for income / education, gender, age, marital status,
employment status, union membership, and region.

upward trend but approaches zero only in the 2010–2014 elections. This
suggests that like Norway and Denmark, Sweden has experienced a transition to a multi-elite system, but at a lower speed.

The stability in the income cleavage between top-income and bottom-
income earners is largely due to the persistent support for the Moderate
Party and the Liberal People's Party from top earners and support for
the Sweden Democrats from the low-income segment of the electorate.[39]
Swedish surveys make it possible to further explore the "rich-poor" dimension, providing information about the assets held by voters in some
years. The evolution of the left vote by wealth group presents a downward
and monotonic trend, with the bottom 50 percent voting more for the
left, followed by the middle 40 and finally by the top 10 percent.[40]

39. See appendix Figures CC10, CC14, and CC22, wpid.world.
40. See appendix Figure CB6, wpid.world.

The delayed path toward the reversal of the educational cleavage can be better understood by analyzing voting patterns by party. The share of left-wing tertiary-educated voters has increased over time, yet the left has also managed to retain the majority of primary-educated voters over the entire period, as the share of primary-educated voters voting left used to be about 60 percent and has fallen only to 50 percent in the last decade.[41] Although the shift to the right among the lowest educated has been weaker than in Norway and Denmark, the decomposition of the vote by party also reveals many similarities that may contribute to closing this gap. Indeed, the Left Party first and the Green Party later have captured the support of the highest educated since their debuts in the political arena. On the right, the Liberal People's Party and the Moderate Party have relied on a majority of tertiary-educated voters, even though the Moderates have gained more support among lower-educated voters in the last decade. Moreover, in line with their twin parties around Europe, the far-right Sweden Democrats have exerted a strong pull on the lower socioeconomic classes who until the 2000s had favored the Social Democratic Party: the fraction of primary-educated voters voting for the Social Democrats fell by over 10 percentage points from 2002–2006 to 2010–2014, the decade of the far-right party's success. This competition between the Sweden Democrats and the Social Democratic Party to represent the most disadvantaged classes is extremely similar to the ones documented in the Norwegian and Danish contexts.[42] The recent dynamics suggest that if the Sweden Democrats continue to absorb the lowest-educated vote, the education gradient is likely to become positive over the next decade. Sweden would then be more aligned with the multi-elite party systems observed in most Western democracies.

### Social Class, Unionization, and Other Socioeconomic Cleavages

Class cleavages are of remarkable importance in the Swedish context. From the 1950s to the 1990s, 70 to 80 percent of voters identifying with the working class voted for social democratic, socialist, and communist parties, as opposed to 30 to 40 percent of the rest of the population. In the 2010s, the decrease in the share of working-class voters supporting the left has modestly undermined class polarization (Figure 4.9). The relevance of social class can be confirmed when analyzing its contribution

41. See appendix Figure CB1, wpid.world.
42. See appendix Figures CC25 to CC28, wpid.world.

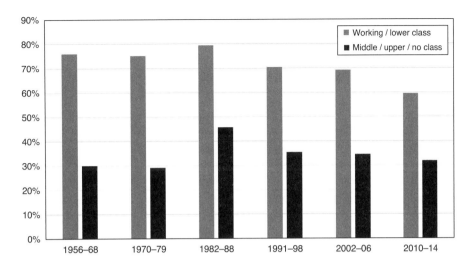

FIGURE 4.9. Class voting in Sweden, 1956–2014
*Data Source:* Authors' computations using Swedish electoral surveys (see wpid.world).
*Note:* The figure shows the share of votes received by the Social Democratic Party, the Left Party, the Green Party, and affiliated parties by subjective social class. In the 1950s–1960s, 76% of voters identifying with the "working class" or "lower class" voted for these parties, compared to 60% in the 2010s.

to the evolution of the educational cleavage. The inclusion of social class leads to an impressive upward shift of the education gradient that seems to disappear only in the last decade.[43] This persistence can be explained by the Swedish Social Democrats' primacy in attracting the working-class consensus until the early 2000s.

The strength of the Swedish class cleavage allows one to explore another interesting aspect, the strong connection between union membership and voting behavior. Union members' tendency to be more left-wing, also visible in other Nordic countries, is particularly pronounced in Sweden, and can be linked to the strong historical ties between the Swedish Trade Union Confederation and the Social Democratic Party.[44] Finally, we also document the emergence of a modern gender cleavage

43. See appendix Figure CB26, wpid.world.
44. See appendix Figures CB7 and CB23, wpid.world. M. Bengtsson, T. Berglund, and M. Oskarson, "Class and Ideological Orientations Revisited: An Exploration of Class-Based Mechanisms," *British Journal of Sociology* 64, no. 4 (2013): 691–716.

that can be entirely explained by the increasing share of women employed in the public sector.[45] The expansion of the welfare state has accentuated the public-private divide, with private employees voting less for the left, as observed in Norway and Denmark.[46]

### The Sweden Democrats and the End of Swedish "Exceptionalism"

The absence of an extreme right party at the end of the 1990s and the accommodating immigration policies have long led the public and academics to view Sweden as an exceptional model of refugee reception. This peculiar feature of the Swedish context used to clearly differentiate it from other Nordic countries, despite the similarities in their party systems. However, the surveys at our disposal suggest that by the 1980s and 1990s, respondents were concerned about the increasing number of asylum seekers: in 1994, 21 percent of interviewees believed that the phenomenon was highly worrying, and by 2002, 47 percent were in favor of stricter controls at the borders. In contrast to Denmark, in Sweden attitudes toward immigration at that time had not translated into political changes, as political parties had not brought this issue to the center of their political agendas.[47] Nonetheless, the Swedish exceptional model vanished with the rise of the Sweden Democrats in the 2010s. Even though they were founded in 1988, they did not enter the parliament until 2010, after renovating their reputation for having ties with neo-Nazi movements. With their anti-immigration rhetoric and rejection of a multicultural society, they have increasingly gained the support of young, low-income, and low-educated voters in recent years (Table 4.3).

### Finland

#### Finland's Multiparty System and Election Results, 1945–2019

Finnish independence was recognized in 1917, after five hundred years under Swedish rule and a century of Russian annexation. In 1918, Finland entered a civil war opposing the Bolshevik-leaning Red Guards, supported by the Russian Soviet Federative Socialist Republic, against the

---

45. See appendix Figure CB21, wpid.world.
46. See appendix Figures CB10 and CB25, wpid.world.
47. C. Green-Pedersen and J. Krogstrup, "Immigration as a Political Issue in Denmark and Sweden," *European Journal of Political Research* 47, no. 5 (2008): 610–634.

*Table 4.3*  The Structure of Political Cleavages in Sweden, 2010–2014

| | | | Share of Votes Received (%) | | |
|---|---|---|---|---|---|
| | Left Party | Green Party | Social Democrats | Alliance | Sweden Democrats |
| **Education** | | | | | |
| Primary | 5% | 4% | 38% | 37% | 12% |
| Secondary | 6% | 7% | 31% | 46% | 9% |
| Tertiary | 8% | 15% | 18% | 53% | 2% |
| **Income** | | | | | |
| Bottom 50% | 7% | 9% | 33% | 37% | 10% |
| Middle 40% | 5% | 8% | 28% | 51% | 6% |
| Top 10% | 5% | 6% | 16% | 67% | 4% |
| **Gender** | | | | | |
| Women | 6% | 11% | 28% | 47% | 5% |
| Men | 6% | 6% | 30% | 46% | 10% |
| **Age** | | | | | |
| 20–39 | 7% | 12% | 25% | 44% | 6% |
| 40–59 | 6% | 8% | 27% | 50% | 7% |
| 60+ | 6% | 6% | 34% | 44% | 9% |
| **Sector** | | | | | |
| Private/Mixed | 4% | 9% | 22% | 54% | 8% |
| Public | 10% | 12% | 30% | 42% | 4% |

*Data Source:* Authors' computations using Swedish electoral surveys (see wpid.world).
*Note:* The table shows the average share of votes received by the Social Democratic Party, the Left Party, the Green Party, the Alliance Coalition (Moderate Party, Centre Party, Christian Democrats, and Liberals), and the Sweden Democrats over the 2010–2014 period. The Social Democrats were supported by 38% of primary-educated voters, compared to 18% of university graduates.

White Guard, supported by the German Empire, leading to the eventual military victory of the latter. After a brief attempt to establish a kingdom, the country became a republic. Nevertheless, the construction of a democratic system had already started in 1906 with the establishment of universal suffrage.

In the aftermath of the Second World War, the Finnish parliament (the Eduskunta) was dominated by four big parties: the Social Democratic Party, the Agrarian League (rebranded as Center Party in 1965), the liberal-conservative National Coalition Party, and the Finnish People's

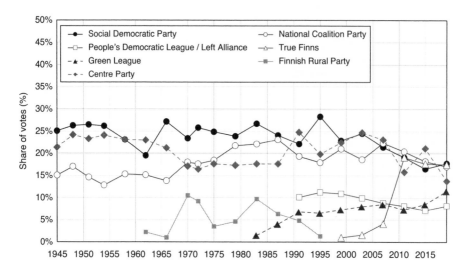

FIGURE 4.10. Election results in Finland, 1945–2019
*Data Source:* Authors' computations using official election results (see wpid.world).
*Note:* The figure shows the share of votes received by selected political parties or groups of parties in parliamentary elections held in Finland between 1945 and 2019. The Social Democratic Party received 18% of votes in 2019.

Democratic League reuniting the left-wing forces of the country under the lead of the Communist Party of Finland (Figure 4.10). The party system has always been highly fragmented and none of these parties has ever occupied a dominant position, contrary to what has been documented for Norway and Sweden. Thus, the biggest parties have surpassed the threshold of 25 percent of popular votes in parliamentary elections only a few times. The failure to achieve a majority of seats has certainly influenced government formation and its subsequent stability. From the late 1940s to the end of the 1960s, the country witnessed the succession of almost twenty different governments. Moreover, while other Nordic countries were mainly characterized by the alternation of opposite blocs, in Finland cross-bloc coalitions have been the most frequent solution. Another peculiarity of the Finnish political system was the influence exercised by the head of state during the process of government formation. This distinction remained in place until the adoption of the new Finnish Constitution in 2000, which practically excluded the president

from the process. For instance, in 1987 his influence culminated in the formation of a coalition between the Social Democrats and the National Coalition Party.[48]

The 1990s were marked by a sequence of important events that led to further political fragmentation. The country went through a severe financial crisis and the unemployment rate rose from 3 to 17 percent during the first half of the decade. In 1991, the Center Party, which had mediated between the left and the right since the postwar period, formed a center-right government with the National Coalition Party. They proposed austerity policies aimed at reducing public services and the provisions of the welfare state built during the 1960s by the Social Democrats and the left-wing parties.[49] The unpopularity of the center-right government benefited the Social Democratic Party, which took power in the following election in 1995 with 28 percent of votes, thanks to a five-party coalition with the National Coalition Party, the centrist Swedish People's Party, the Green League, and the Left Alliance, the successor of the Finnish People's Democratic League. Four years later, a constitutional reform limited the role of the head of the state in favor of the parliament, which has since then been entitled to elect the prime minister.[50]

Despite increasing political fragmentation, the Social Democratic Party, the Center Party, and the National Coalition Party continued to achieve the highest vote shares throughout the 2000s, with around 20 to 25 percent each, until the 2011 election, which represented a real turning point in Finnish political history. The far-right True Finns, founded in 1995, became the third party in the Eduskunta with 19 percent of votes. It then surpassed the Social Democratic Party in the following election, enabling it to take part in a center-right coalition government with the Center Party and the conservatives.

In what follows, we will analyze the changing relationship between party support and socioeconomic characteristics using Finnish postelectoral surveys covering all parliamentary elections held from 1972 to 2015.[51] The Social Democrats, the Left Alliance, and the Greens are categorized as

48. M. Mattila and T. Raunio, "Government Formation in the Nordic Countries: The Electoral Connection," *Scandinavian Political Studies* 25, no. 3 (2002): 259–280.

49. J. Kiander, "The Evolution of the Finnish Model in the 1990s: From Depression to High-Tech Boom" (Discussion Paper 344, VATT Institute for Economic Research, 2004), https://www.doria.fi/handle/10024/148330.

50. Kiander, "Evolution of the Finnish Model."

51. See appendix Table DC1, wpid.world.

left-wing parties, whereas the Finnish Rural Party, the National Coalition Party, and the True Finns are categorized as right-wing parties. The Center Party is excluded from these two categories.

### Toward a Multi-elite Party System?

The relationship between voting behaviors and education in Finland shares more similarities with the Swedish scenario than with the Norwegian and Danish contexts. While top-income earners are more right-wing over the whole period, the highest educated have gradually become more left-wing (Figure 4.11), but this increase has not been large enough to generate the same reversal in the education gradient as in the case of Norway or Denmark.

The replication of the analysis for the main left-wing parties reveals interesting insights into the underlying mechanisms. The Social Democratic Party has close ties with the largest union confederation and has counted on a majority of lower-educated voters since the late 1970s. In

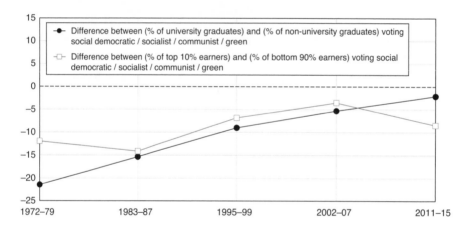

FIGURE 4.11. Toward a multi-elite party system in Finland, 1972–2015
*Data Source:* Authors' computations using Finnish electoral surveys (see wpid.world).
*Note:* The figure shows the relative support of top-income and highest-educated voters for the Social Democratic Party, the Finnish People's Democratic League/Left Alliance, the Green League, and affiliated parties. In the 1970s, top-income and highest-educated voters were less likely to vote social democratic/socialist/communist than low-income and lower-educated voters. The social democratic/socialist/communist/green vote has increasingly become associated with higher-educated voters, leading Finland to get closer to becoming a multi-elite party system. Estimates control for income/education, gender, age, employment status, union membership, and region.

contrast, the Greens, as in Sweden, have mainly been supported since their emergence in the 1980s by highest-educated voters. Support for the Left Alliance used to be stronger among lower-educated voters, but the composition of its electorate has profoundly changed in recent decades and now the party obtains slightly more support among the highest educated.[52] The Left Alliance defines itself as a red-green party, where green refers to environmental issues and red stands for the tradition of the workers' movement but also, in a broader sense, the demand for social justice.[53] However, its cooperation with the Social Democrats, as well as its rapprochement with the neoliberal wave in recent decades led to a loss of credibility and a decline in the support for the party, especially among the lower educated. Despite the loss of support among the lower educated of the Left Alliance and the strong support among the highest educated toward the Greens, the persisting large vote share and class-based nature of the Social Democrats explains why the transition toward a multi-elite party system has been late and is still incomplete.

On the right-wing side, the National Coalition Party has always obtained higher support among tertiary-educated and high-income voters, which was also documented for traditional conservative parties in Western Europe. In addition, the difference between tertiary- and non-tertiary-educated voters supporting the party has further increased over the last decade, which suggests that the True Finns have managed to capture a part of the already exiguous share of low-educated and low-income voters supporting the Conservatives.[54] If the True Finns continue absorbing the lowest-educated vote, the education gradient is likely to become positive over the next decade. Finland would then be more aligned with the multi-elite party systems of most Western democracies.

### The Importance of Class and Other Socioeconomic Cleavages

In line with Norway, Denmark, and Sweden, Finland also presents a persistent and strong class cleavage.[55] Finnish electoral surveys do not include questions on perceived social class in every election, so we have

---

52. See appendix Figure DC26, wpid.world.
53. Daiber, Hildebrandt, and Striethorst, "From Revolution to Coalition."
54. See appendix Figures DC10, DC14, and DC25 to DC28, wpid.world.
55. O. Knutsen, "The Regional Cleavage in Western Europe: Can Social Composition, Value Orientations, and Territorial Identities Explain the Impact of Region on Party Choice?," *West European Politics* 33, no. 3 (2010): 553–585.

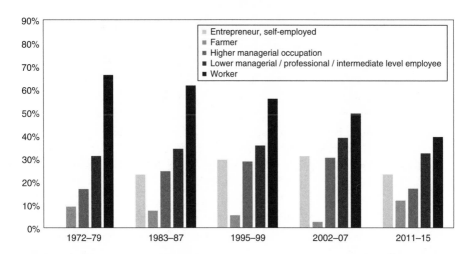

FIGURE 4.12. Vote for Social Democrats/Communists/Socialists/Greens by occupation in Finland, 1972–2015

*Data Source:* Authors' computations using Finnish electoral surveys (see wpid.world). *Note:* The figure shows the share of votes received by the Social Democratic Party, the Finnish People's Democratic League/Left Alliance, the Green League, and affiliated parties by occupation. In the 1970s, 66% of workers voted social democratic/communist/socialist, compared to 9% of farmers. The "Entrepreneur and self-employed" category is not reported separately from other categories for the 1972–1979 period.

used occupational class as a proxy. Figure 4.12 shows that workers are clearly more left-wing than any other occupational class throughout the whole period, but the share of workers voting for social democratic, socialist, communist, and green parties has declined from more than 65 to less than 40 percent from the 1970s to the 2010s.[56] The importance of occupational class is also demonstrated by the fact that it is the only control variable that strongly affects the education gradient, shifting the curve upward.[57]

56. Note that in this case, workers are all those employees who are not entrepreneurs or self-employed, managers, intermediate-level employees, or farmers. Figure DB10 in the appendix, wpid.world, reveals a strong Finnish subjective class cleavage in the available decades (1980s, 1990s, and 2000s).

57. See appendix Figure DB24, wpid.world.

Apart from education, income, and class, another important political divide in Finland relates to region of residence: voters in southern Finland have been disproportionately more left-wing than in central or northern Finland. The regional cleavage is strongly correlated with rural-urban and class cleavages, as most urban areas and workers are in southern Finland.[58] The country has also experienced the emergence of a modest "green" modern gender cleavage, in contrast to the rest of Nordic countries, where women have shifted their votes from the National Coalition and the Center Party only to the Greens and the Left Alliance, but not to the Social Democrats.[59]

### Finnish Nationalism and the Peculiar Profile of the True Finns

Finland is a homogeneous country with a low level of immigration, so right-wing nationalist politics were not prominent around the mid-twentieth century. Nonetheless, agrarian populism has been present in Finnish politics since the beginning of the 1960s. The Finnish Agrarian Party was founded in 1959 to defend the interests of the rural Finnish, who felt alienated in the fast-moving postwar society, against the urban elite.[60] The party obtained its greatest electoral support in the 1970s and early 1980s, when it won approximately one-tenth of the vote. It then started to have financial difficulties and it was succeeded in 1995 by a new nationalist party, the True Finns.

The True Finns managed to gain seats in the parliament as early as 1999, although the peak of its success was reached in the 2007 election. The party diverges from analogous political organizations in other Nordic countries in several respects. First, it has a more moderate profile and it did not originate from neo-Nazi movements, as the Sweden Democrats did. In addition to having a less aggressive narrative, the True Finns also differ from the Danish and Norwegian models in their view of the economy. The Danish and Norwegian Progress Parties were founded as no-tax parties, whereas the True Finns advocated for progressive taxation and the reintroduction of a wealth tax.[61] This position has created uncertainty about its location in the left-right political spectrum.

58. See appendix Figures DB7 and DB8, wpid.world.
59. See appendix Figure DC29, wpid.world.
60. D. Arter, "The Breakthrough of Another West European Populist Radical Right Party? The Case of the True Finns," *Government and Opposition* 45, no. 4 (2010): 484–504.
61. Arter, "Breakthrough."

However, when it comes to the immigration issue, the party aligns with other far-right anti-immigration parties across Europe, rejecting multiculturalism, asking for a reduction in the number of asylum seekers, and emphasizing the burden of migrants on the Finnish welfare state at the expense of the Finnish population. This alignment with far-right parties is corroborated by analysis of the characteristics of the party's supporters in the most recent decade: the True Finns have attracted mainly rural, lower-educated, and lower-income voters (Table 4.4).

*Table 4.4*    The Structure of Political Cleavages in Finland, 2011–2015

| | Share of Votes Received (%) | | | | | |
|---|---|---|---|---|---|---|
| | Left Alliance | Green League | Social Democrats | Centre Party | National Coalition Party | True Finns |
| **Education** | | | | | | |
| Primary | 5% | 3% | 28% | 19% | 10% | 24% |
| Secondary | 8% | 5% | 21% | 20% | 14% | 22% |
| Tertiary | 8% | 13% | 10% | 17% | 31% | 10% |
| **Income** | | | | | | |
| Bottom 50% | 9% | 8% | 20% | 21% | 12% | 20% |
| Middle 40% | 7% | 8% | 17% | 17% | 23% | 18% |
| Top 10% | 6% | 9% | 11% | 16% | 32% | 15% |
| **Age** | | | | | | |
| 20–39 | 15% | 17% | 12% | 17% | 4% | 9% |
| 40–59 | 7% | 15% | 17% | 20% | 4% | 8% |
| 60+ | 3% | 23% | 23% | 20% | 6% | 6% |
| **Gender** | | | | | | |
| Women | 9% | 10% | 17% | 18% | 18% | 16% |
| Men | 7% | 6% | 18% | 19% | 20% | 21% |
| **Location** | | | | | | |
| Urban | 8% | 9% | 18% | 15% | 22% | 17% |
| Rural | 6% | 4% | 16% | 28% | 13% | 22% |

*Data Source:* Authors' computations using Finnish electoral surveys (see wpid.world).
*Note:* The table shows the average share of votes received by the main Finnish parties by selected individual characteristics over the 2011–2015 period. The Social Democrats were supported by 28% of primary-educated voters, compared to 10% of university graduates.

## Iceland

### *Iceland's Party System and Election Results, 1946–2017*

After centuries of Danish rule, Iceland was recognized as a fully sovereign state in 1918 and joined Denmark in a personal union with the Danish king. While universal suffrage was achieved in 1920, it was only in 1944 that Iceland became an independent republic. The Icelandic political scenario has since then revolved around four political parties or coalitions: the center-left Social Democratic Alliance, which is the result of the merger between the existing left-wing parties in 2000 (the Social Democratic Party, the People's Alliance, the Women's List, and National Awakening); the left-wing socialist and Eurosceptic Left-Green Movement, founded in 1999 following disagreements over the formation of a broader left-wing alliance; the right-wing Independence Party, born in 1929 after the unification of the Conservative and Liberal Parties; and the Progressive Party, a center-right agrarian party founded in 1916 (Figure 4.13). The Independence Party has long been the largest party in the Icelandic parliament (the Althing), having consistently won the largest number of seats since 1942. Before 2009, left and center-left parties represented a weaker force in the parliament, with no party achieving a majority. Nevertheless, the Social Democrats and the People's Party took part in government cabinets led by the Independence Party and the Progressive Party.

The financial crisis of 2008 caused a political upheaval, leading to the end of the relative stability that had characterized the Icelandic political landscape over the twentieth century. In October 2008, the three major banks of Iceland went bankrupt and the financial system collapsed. The International Monetary Fund intervened with a $2.1 billion bailout program. Protests broke out shortly after that. From October 2008 to January 2009, Icelandic citizens took part in the largest protests in the history of the country, calling for the resignation of the Independence Party's government and forcing the government to hold early elections. In the elections of April 2009, the first left-wing coalition in the history of Iceland came into office with 52 percent of votes. The new coalition formed by the Social Democratic Alliance (SD) and the Left-Green Movement (L-G) had to deal with the daunting task of economic recovery. By 2013, the unemployment rate had fallen below 5 percent, but this was not enough to guarantee another victory for the left-wing coalition. The 2013 elections saw a huge defeat of the governing parties, with losses of 17 (SD) and 11 (L-G) percentage points. The center-right opposition bene-

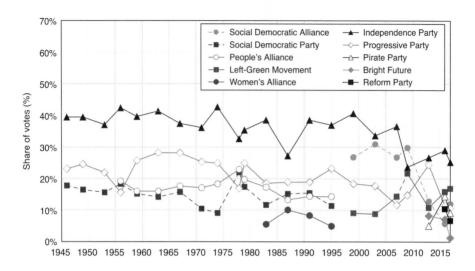

FIGURE 4.13. Election results in Iceland, 1946–2017
*Data Source:* Authors' computations using official election results (see wpid.world).
*Note:* The figure shows the share of votes received by selected political parties or
groups of parties in parliamentary elections held in Iceland between 1946 and 2017.
The Independence Party received 25% of votes in 2017.

fited from the unpopular austerity policies put in place by the government,
regaining the majority in the parliament. In the 2013 elections, there was
also a shift toward new political parties: in addition to the four traditional parties, six new political parties were represented for the first time
in the parliament.

In 2016, the Progressive Party's new prime minister, Sigmundur Davið
Gunnlaugsson, was forced to resign due to his involvement in the Panama
Papers scandal, and the Progressive Party was defeated in the anticipated
elections of October 2016 as the Independence Party became the largest
party. Moreover, three emerging parties, the Pirate Party, Bright Future,
and the Reform Party, obtained 32 percent of votes. The latter two joined
the Independentists in a coalition government that lasted less than one
year, due to a scandal related to Bright Future's leader. In the highly anticipated elections of October 2017, finally, the Independence Party, the
Left-Green Movement, and the Progressive Party obtained a majority of
votes. With the aim of restoring political stability, the three parties
formed a large left-right coalition led by the Left-Green's leader, Katrín
Jakobsdóttir.

In what follows, we will study the changing relationship between party support and socioeconomic characteristics using postelectoral surveys covering all parliamentary elections held in Iceland from 1978 to 2017.[62] The Left-Green Movement and the Social Democratic Alliance are classified as left-wing, while the Independence Party and the Progressive Party are classified as right-wing. The Pirate Party is excluded from the left-right classification, as it considers itself an antisystem political organization.

### The Stability of the Multi-elite Party System

Iceland has experienced the emergence of new parties in recent decades, in line with what we observed in other Western democracies. Nonetheless, the country is singular in that the income and education gradients have been very stable since the 1980s, moving in parallel trends but with opposite signs (Figure 4.14). While the difference between the share of top 10 percent and bottom 90 percent earners voting left has generally fluctuated between 0 and −10 percentage points, the gap in left vote between tertiary-educated and non-tertiary-educated voters has fluctuated between +5 and +10 points. Contrary to the rest of Nordic countries, therefore, the emergence of a multi-elite party system in Icelandic politics is not recent—it seems to have prevailed in the 1980s.

To better understand the stability of the education cleavage in Iceland, one can investigate variations by party. Whereas the socialists and social democrats have counted on the support of the lowest-educated voters in other Nordic countries, in Iceland they have been supported primarily by the highest educated since at least the 1980s. The education gradient has barely changed since the 1970s, given that the decline in the highest-educated vote for the Social Democratic Alliance during the 2000s has been largely captured by the Left-Green Movement since its debut in the mid-1990s. The Independence Party has also captured a fraction of the highest-educated vote from the Social Democratic Alliance since the 2000s, but to a much lower extent than the Left-Green Movement. Hence, the shift in the vote among the highest educated from the predecessors of the Social Democratic Alliance toward the Left-Green Movement is clearly behind the stability in the Icelandic education gradient.

The Progressive Party, in contrast, has relied on a majority of lowest-educated voters among its electorate since the 1980s. The Pirate Party also

62. See appendix Table ED1, wpid.world.

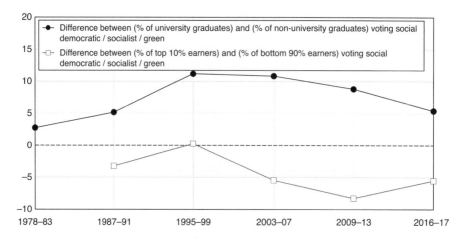

FIGURE 4.14. The persistence of a multi-elite party system in Iceland, 1978–2017
*Data Source:* Authors' computations using Icelandic postelectoral surveys (see wpid.world)
*Note:* The figure shows the relative support of top-income and highest-educated voters for the Social Democratic Alliance, the Left-Green movement, and affiliated parties. Since the 1970s–1980s, the social democratic/socialist/green vote has always been associated with higher-educated voters, while top-income voters have remained more likely to vote for right-wing parties. Iceland has thus been characterized by a multi-elite party system. Estimates control for income/education, gender, age, employment status, marital status, union membership, and region. The 1983 survey does not contain information on income.

attracted slightly more of the primary educated in 2013, but that advantage faded in 2017. Its success in the 2010s among different socioeconomic groups represents another major differentiation with respect to the other Northern European countries, where dissatisfaction with the political establishment among lower-educated and lower-income earners has benefited new far-right nationalist parties. The Pirate Party, in contrast, has been closer to the left-wing side of the political spectrum on social issues, promoting the enhancement of civil rights, direct democracy, and the right to privacy and to self-determination. Thus, the stability of the education gradient may be further explained by the influence that the Progressive Party (the formerly agrarian party) has retained in the rural and poorer areas of the country and by the absence of a strong far-right party capturing the vote of the lowest educated.[63]

63. See appendix Figure EC25, wpid.world.

To better understand the stability in the income cleavage in Iceland, it is also very useful to decompose the vote by income group and party. The Independence Party presents a strong and persistent positive income gradient, while other parties (except for the Left-Green Movement) do not have a clear gradient.[64] The few low-income voters who used to vote for the Socialists and Social Democrats until the 1990s have shifted their vote toward the Left-Green Movement, which has disproportionately attracted the vote of young low-income voters. Overall, these results are in line with those of Eva Önnudóttir and Ólafur Harðarson, who argue that the Icelandic political cleavage system has remained intact despite major changes in party-voter linkages.[65]

### The Weak Class Cleavage, the Persistence of the Rural-Urban Cleavage, and Other Socioeconomic Cleavages

The existence of an early multi-elite party system in Iceland might be due to the lack of a strong class cleavage and the absence of any party historically attracting both lower-educated and low-income voters. Icelandic electoral surveys do not include questions on perceived social class, so we have used occupational class as a proxy. Figure 4.15 shows that in stark contrast with the rest of Nordic countries, class cleavages are not very pronounced in Iceland, as workers are not substantially more left-wing than higher managerial employees or self-employed individuals.

Apart from the education and income cleavages, Iceland presents other important socioeconomic cleavages, in particular a strong and persistent rural-urban cleavage.[66] Voters and MPs in the peripheral areas in Iceland have in general been more favorable to economic support for agricultural areas and less willing to reduce the level of road and tunnel construction in rural areas.[67] Moreover, MPs from the periphery have been more willing to protect communities and municipalities in peripheral areas that

---

64. See appendix Figures EC2, EC6, EC10, EC14, and EC18, wpid.world.

65. E. H. Önnudóttir and Ó. Þ. Harðarson, "Political Cleavages, Party Voter Linkages, and the Impact of Voters' Socio-Economic Status on Vote-Choice in Iceland, 1983–2016/17," *Stjórnmál og Stjórnsýsla* 14, no. 1 (2018): 101–130.

66. Note that the rural-urban cleavage can also be seen as a center-periphery cleavage, considering as urban the capital area (about 63 percent of the population in 2016) and as rural the rest of the country, since this variable was the only one available throughout the whole period of analysis.

67. H. Valen, H. M. Narud, and Ó. T. Hardarson, "Geography and Political Representation," in Esaiasson and Heidar, *Beyond Westminster and Congress,* 107–131.

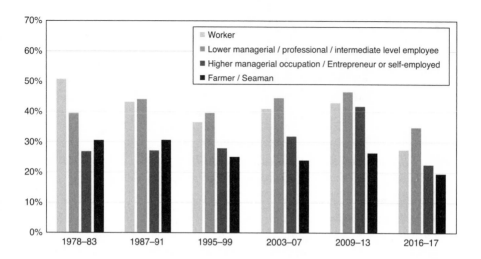

FIGURE 4.15. Vote for Social Democrats / Socialists / Greens by occupation in Iceland, 1978–2017

*Data Source:* Authors' computations using Icelandic postelectoral surveys (see wpid.world).
*Note:* The figure shows the share of votes received by the Social Democratic Alliance, the Left-Green movement, and affiliated parties by occupation. In the 1970s, 51% of workers voted social democratic / socialist / green, compared to 27% of voters employed in higher managerial occupations or who were entrepreneurs or self-employed.

are struggling to hold on to their industries and inhabitants.[68] The party that has better represented the interests of rural areas has been the agrarian Progressive Party, although its importance in the periphery has weakened over time. The importance of the Progressive Party largely explains why the difference between the shares of rural and urban left-wing voters has remained negative to the present.[69] As in the other Nordic countries, a strong and rising sectoral cleavage opposing public-sector and private-sector employees also seems to have developed in recent decades.[70]

Finally, we also observe the emergence of a modern gender cleavage since the 1980s.[71] Women's tendency to be more left-wing was driven mainly by the Social Democratic Alliance until the outbreak of the financial

68. G. H. Kristinsson, *Úr digrum sjóði: Fjárlagagerð á Íslandi* (Félagsvísindastofnun Háskóla Íslands, 1999)
69. See appendix Figure EB24, wpid.world.
70. See appendix Figure EB20, wpid.world.
71. See appendix Figure EB22, wpid.world.

crisis, after which declining confidence in the Social Democrats among women was offset by increasing support for the left-wing feminist and environmentalist Left-Green Movement. The gender gap arose at the end of the 1980s mainly due to women's strong support for the Women's Alliance fighting for gender equality and for women's representation in the political system, as the country was lagging behind the other Nordic countries in this aspect.[72]

### Icelandic Nationalism and the Role of the Progressive Party and the Pirate Party

Contrary to the rest of the Nordic countries, Iceland currently lacks a strong extreme-right-wing party. However, this peculiarity should not be interpreted as a manifestation of a weaker nationalist feeling, but as a deep rooting of postcolonial nationalism within the main traditional parties. Since gaining full independence in 1944, Icelanders have faced a dilemma: emphasizing self-rule and thus isolationism in foreign relations on the one hand, or participating in international relations to support its bid for recognition as a European partner on the other.[73] Hence, political parties, too, have split along these lines to attract either internationalists, represented by the Social Democratic Party and the Social Democratic Alliance, or isolationists, represented by the Progressive Party, the Independence Party, the People's Party, and the Left-Green Movement. In the 2016 and 2017 elections, 22 percent of pro-EU voters supported the Social Democratic Alliance, compared to only 3 percent of voters opposed to EU integration. In contrast, 40 percent and 16 percent of anti-European voters voted for the Independence Party and the Progressive Party, respectively, compared to 7 percent and 6 percent of pro-EU voters (Table 4.5).

After the onset of the financial crisis, a completely renewed political agenda was initiated by the traditional Progressive Party. The old agrarian party took a hard stance against foreign creditors and international institutions, and it introduced anti-Muslim rhetoric, which until then had been absent in the country, as there is no significant Muslim minority in Iceland. The Progressive Party thus moved closer to far-right parties in Western Europe. It was the first such party among the Nordic countries to head a government, forming a coalition with the Independence Party

---

72. See appendix Figures EC23 and EC26, wpid.world.
73. Bergmann, *Nordic Nationalism*.

Table 4.5  The Structure of Political Cleavages in Iceland, 2016–2017

Share of Votes Received (%)

| | Left-Green Movement | Social Democratic Alliance | Pirate Party | Bright Future | Reform Party | Progressive Party | Independence Party |
|---|---|---|---|---|---|---|---|
| **Education** | | | | | | | |
| Primary | 15% | 6% | 8% | 3% | 5% | 16% | 27% |
| Secondary | 16% | 9% | 9% | 3% | 7% | 12% | 30% |
| Tertiary | 20% | 12% | 8% | 6% | 13% | 7% | 24% |
| **Income** | | | | | | | |
| Bottom 50% | 21% | 9% | 10% | 3% | 6% | 13% | 23% |
| Middle 40% | 15% | 10% | 8% | 5% | 11% | 12% | 28% |
| Top 10% | 12% | 12% | 7% | 4% | 17% | 11% | 32% |
| **Gender** | | | | | | | |
| Women | 23% | 10% | 6% | 4% | 8% | 11% | 24% |
| Men | 12% | 9% | 10% | 3% | 10% | 12% | 30% |
| **Location** | | | | | | | |
| Urban | 18% | 9% | 9% | 5% | 12% | 7% | 27% |
| Rural | 16% | 9% | 7% | 2% | 4% | 18% | 28% |
| **Sector** | | | | | | | |
| Private/Mixed | 14% | 7% | 9% | 4% | 12% | 12% | 30% |
| Public | 26% | 13% | 7% | 5% | 8% | 11% | 19% |
| **EU Membership** | | | | | | | |
| Against | 13% | 3% | 6% | 2% | 5% | 16% | 40% |
| Pro | 18% | 22% | 16% | 8% | 17% | 6% | 7% |

*Data Source:* Authors' computations using Icelandic postelectoral surveys (see wpid.world).

*Note:* The table shows the average share of votes received by the main Icelandic parties by selected individual characteristics over the 2016–2017 period. The Social Democratic Alliance was supported by 22% of voters favorable to Iceland joining the European Union during this period, compared to 3% of voters opposed to Iceland joining the EU.

in 2013. Looking at the characteristics of its electorate reveals that the Progressive Party's main supporters are rural, low-income, and low-educated voters, which is much in line with the profiles of other new far-right parties across Europe. This suggests that the new political line followed by the Progressive Party has partly filled the gap occupied in other European countries by the far right, and it may explain why the two new far-right nationalist parties, the Iceland National Front, founded in 2016, and the Freedom Party, founded in 2017, have so far received very little support.

# 5

# Political Cleavages, Class Structures, and the Politics of Old and New Minorities in Australia, Canada, and New Zealand, 1963–2019

### AMORY GETHIN

## Introduction

This chapter combines existing postelectoral surveys conducted in Australia, Canada, and New Zealand since the 1960s to study the evolution of political cleavages in these three countries. The democratic politics of the old British dominions were shaped by differing patterns of religious, linguistic, and ethnic diversity inherited from the processes of settler colonialism that took place in the nineteenth century. Historical specificities in the course of colonialist expansion contributed to differentially structure their party systems, the legacies of which can still be observed in contemporary politics, notably in the form of the linguistic cleavage in Canada, the religious cleavage in Australia, and the Māori-European cleavage in New Zealand.

Historical legacies have also been associated with significant differences in the old dominions' party systems. In Australia and New Zealand, the strength of class politics in the postwar era clearly structured political conflicts on a left-right (labor versus conservative) axis. This was never the case in Canada, where the Liberal Party succeeded in aggregating a diverse and changing coalition as early as the 1960s. Yet, education has had a growing impact on electoral behaviors in all three countries, as higher-educated voters have increasingly tilted toward labor,

I thank Jennifer Curtin, Gary Marks, Clara Martínez-Toledano, and Thomas Piketty for their useful comments and advice. I also wish to thank the teams of the Australian Data Archive, the Australian Election Studies, the Canadian Election Studies, and the New Zealand Election Studies for making available the data used in this chapter.

green, and liberal parties. In Australia and New Zealand, this transformation was largely driven by the rise of green parties; in Canada, it came more decisively from transformations within the existing Liberal Party and New Democratic Party.

The study of political cleavages in Australia, Canada, and New Zealand can also be useful to understand the roots of political change in Western democracies. It has sometimes been argued, for instance, that the new educational divide in Western Europe could be accounted for by the growing importance of issues related to immigration, the integration of ethnoreligious minorities, or European integration. Understanding whether or not comparable changes are under way in the three countries studied in this chapter, where immigration and the integration of old and new minorities have arguably taken different forms, can shed light on the contributions and limitations of such narratives.

Four main findings emerge from the analysis developed in this chapter. First, in line with the existing literature, I document a long-run decline in class-based voting in Australia and New Zealand, but not in Canada, where it is well known that class cleavages never truly materialized and where class polarization may even have been growing since the 2000s. Second, I document a clear shift of higher-educated voters toward labor, social democratic, green, and liberal parties in these three countries. This has led to the emergence of "multi-elite" party systems, in which top-income voters continue to vote for conservative parties, while most educated voters now support labor, green, liberal, and affiliated parties.

Third, I investigate how the political representation of religious and ethnic minorities has intersected with the politics of class. In New Zealand, the overrepresentation of the Māori in low-income groups has reinforced class cleavages, as Māori voters have been disproportionately more likely to vote for the Labour Party, the Greens, and other left-wing parties. This is not the case in Australia and Canada, where Catholic minorities were not significantly poorer than the rest of the population, leading the religious cleavage to represent an independent dimension of political conflicts. One interesting difference between Canada and Australia is that religious groups have remained more spatially and culturally differentiated in the former than in the latter, which may explain why Catholic-Protestant cleavages have persisted in Canada, while they have been gradually replaced by a secular-religious divide in Australia.

Finally, I exploit available data on respondents' country of birth to capture the strength of a new "nativist" dimension of political conflicts. The main result that emerges from this analysis is that this dimension is much less pronounced in Australia, Canada, and New Zealand than in Western European countries.[1] In Australia and New Zealand, non-Western (mainly Asian) immigrants do not vote very differently from natives. One specificity of New Zealand, however, is the existence of the anti-immigration New Zealand First Party (NZF), which by receiving greater support from Māori voters has succeeded in "mobilizing" a minority against another. The NZF has joined coalitions with both the left and the right, which suggests that unlike what we observe in most European countries, immigration issues have not been absorbed into left-right divides in New Zealand. This is also true in Canada, where new Muslim and Sikh minorities have been more likely to vote for the Liberal Party than for the New Democratic Party.

## Australia

### *The Transformation of the Australian Party System*

Australia inherited its political system from the United Kingdom. A two-party system, opposing the Australian Labor Party (ALP) to the Liberal/National coalition (an alliance of the Liberal Party and the National Party, formerly Country Party), persisted throughout most of the twentieth century. While other small parties have generally managed to gather between 10 percent and 20 percent of popular votes, the ALP and the coalition have been the two main actors of Australian politics since the end of World War II (see Figure 5.1).

The long-run decline of the ALP, from 50 percent of votes in 1946 to 33 percent in 2019, has nonetheless coincided with the rise of new parties, such as the Democratic Labor Party (1955–1978) that originated as a Catholic, anticommunist faction of the ALP, or the Australian Democrats (1977–2016), a centrist party breaking away from the Liberal Party,

---

1. The exception to this conclusion is the vote of the Muslim, Sikh, and Hindu religious minorities, which are, as in most Western European countries, substantially more likely to vote for left-wing and liberal parties; see appendix Tables A3, B3, and C3, World Political Cleavages and Inequality Database, http://wpid.world. These minorities are, however, extremely small in the old dominions (typically, less than 1 percent of the adult population).

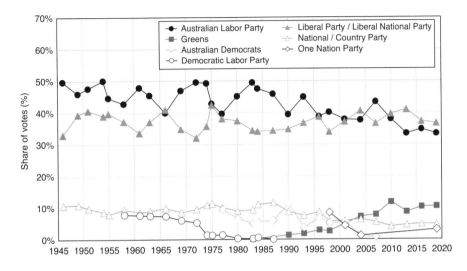

FIGURE 5.1. Election results in Australia, 1946–2019

*Data Source:* Author's computations using official election results (see wpid.world).

*Note:* The figure shows the share of votes received by selected political parties or groups of parties in federal elections held in Australia between 1946 and 2019. The Labor Party received 33% of votes in 2019.

founded on principles related to direct democracy and environmental awareness. Since 1990, the Australian Greens have gained increasing support, adopting ideological stances further on the left of the political spectrum. These trends are comparable to the decline of social democratic parties and the concomitant rise of green parties in a number of other Western democracies studied in this volume (see Chapter 1). The One Nation Party (ONP), created in 1997 by former liberal candidate Pauline Hanson, is usually located to the right of the Liberal/National coalition. It has found greater support among older men, working-class voters, and residents of Queensland, combining anti-immigration and anti-Aboriginal positions with a platform of economic protectionism and support for farmers and small businesses.[2] Finally, independent candidates have also

2. R. Gibson, I. McAllister, and T. Swenson, "The Politics of Race and Immigration in Australia: One Nation Voting in the 1998 Election," *Ethnic and Racial Studies* 25, no. 5 (2002): 823–844; B. Grant, T. Moore, and T. Lynch, eds., *The Rise of Right-Populism: Pauline Hanson's One Nation and Australian Politics* (Springer, 2019).

grown in importance in recent years, and have proved critical to government formation and the balance of power,[3] although the electoral system with single-member constituencies has mitigated the rise of small parties in the House of Representatives.

There have been significant changes in the policies proposed and implemented by the ALP in the past decades. Following the Chifley Labor government's attempt to nationalize the banks in the late 1940s and the party's failure to gain popular support in subsequent years, ALP leaders gradually reformed the party by limiting the influence of socialist and communist movements.[4] Gough Whitlam, elected in 1972, conducted a series of social reforms, increasing the wages of public-sector workers and introducing free university education and universal health care. However, Whitlam's mandate was also linked to a period of political polarization, and he was controversially dismissed during an institutional crisis in a context of inflation, rising unemployment, and government scandals.

This episode led to a further "moderation" of the ALP's policy proposals, which arose with the return of the party to power in 1983. The Labor governments of Bob Hawke (1983–1991) and Paul Keating (1991–1996) embraced a more economically liberal agenda, including free trade and the privatization of state-owned enterprises.[5] The evolution of income inequality in Australia during the past decades, as in most English-speaking countries, correlates with these shifts in ideological positions, declining significantly until the 1970s, before rising steadily from the mid-1980s onward.[6]

## The Decline of Class Divides

I now turn to the study of electoral behaviors in Australia by drawing on comprehensive postelectoral surveys regularly conducted in Australia

3. J. Curtin and J. Sheppard, "The Independents," in *Morrison's Miracle: The 2019 Australian Federal Election*, ed. A. Gauja, M. Sawer, and M. Simms (ANU Press, 2020), 359–373.

4. S. Scalmer, "The Affluent Worker or the Divided Party? Explaining the Transformation of the ALP in the 1950s," *Australian Journal of Political Science* 32, no. 3 (1997): 401–418.

5. G. N. Marks, "Accounting for the Declining Impact of Class on the Vote in Australia," in *Political Choice Matters: Explaining the Strength of Class and Religious Cleavages in Cross-national Perspective*, ed. G. Evans and N. D. Graaf (Oxford University Press, 2012), 247–261.

6. A. B. Atkinson, B. Anthony, and A. Leigh, "The Distribution of Top Incomes in Australia," *Economic Record* 83, no. 262 (2007): 247–261.

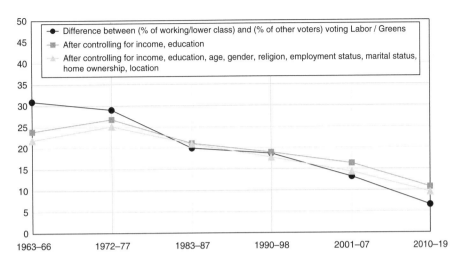

FIGURE 5.2. The decline of class voting in Australia, 1963–2019
*Data Source:* Author's computations using Australian electoral surveys (see wpid.world).
*Note:* The figure shows the difference between the share of voters identifying with the
"working class" or the "lower class" and the share of voters identifying with the "middle
class" or "no class" voting for the Labor Party or the Australian Greens, before and
after controls. Class voting has significantly declined in Australia in the past decades.

since 1987, the Australian Election Studies, as well as a number of other
surveys, which allow me to cover the majority of elections held in the
country between 1963 and 2019.[7] Nearly all surveys have directly asked
respondents about their perceived feeling of class affiliation, which provides a unique insight into the effect of subjective class identities on the
vote and its long-run evolution. This is shown in Figure 5.2, which plots
the difference between the share of individuals considering that they
belong to the "working class" or the "lower class" and the share of other
voters voting for the ALP or the Greens. In the 1960s and 1970s, self-
identified working-class voters were more likely to vote for the ALP by
about 30 percentage points. This gap gradually decreased in the following
decades, both before and after controls, until reaching 7 percentage points
in the 2010s.

This strong decline of class voting in Australia is consistent with the
findings of other studies using similar variables or occupational catego-

7. See appendix Table A1, wpid.world.

ries, and was found to have started even earlier than the 1960s.[8] Hence, in spite of the fact that subjective class affiliations do continue to be strongly correlated to income and education,[9] they have lost most of their relevance when it comes to explaining vote choices in federal elections. This is consistent with theories of political change emphasizing the supply side of electoral competition, that is the role played by political parties' strategies, partly independently from societal changes, in shaping political cleavages.[10] The rise of undecided voters and the declining effect of partisanship on the vote also arguably played an important role in explaining this dealignment process.[11]

### The Transformation of the Religious Cleavage

Another historical division of Australian society opposed Catholics to the Protestant majority. This cleavage was imported by the first settlers of the early nineteenth century, perpetuated with the immigration waves of Irish Catholics and English Anglicans associated with the gold rushes of the 1850s, and reinforced by the opposition between the nationalistic aspirations of the Irish in contrast to the loyalist positions of English and Scottish immigrants. These tensions then continued into the Australian party system, with Catholic organizations being closely tied to the ALP.

There has been a dramatic transformation of religious affiliations in Australia in the past decades, with the share of voters declaring no religion rising from less than 5 percent in the 1960s to nearly a third of the electorate in the 2010s. Almost all of this rise can be attributed to Protestants, whose share in the Australian population has declined from two thirds to one third of the voting age population, while the share of Catholics has remained stable at about 25 percent.[12]

---

8. I. McAllister, *The Australian Voter: 50 Years of Change* (University of New South Wales Press, 2011); A. Scott, *Fading Loyalties: The Australian Labor Party and the Working Class* (Pluto Press Australia, 1991); D. Aitkin, *Stability and Change in Australian Politics* (ANU Press, 1982).

9. See appendix Table A2, wpid.world, on the stability of working-class affiliations, and appendix Figures A67 and A68 on the composition of income groups by social class.

10. Marks, "Accounting for the Declining Impact of Class."

11. G. N. Marks, "Partisanship and the Vote in Australia: Changes over Time, 1967–1990," *Political Behaviour* 15, no. 2 (1993): 137–166; S. M. Cameron and I. McAllister, "Trends in Australian Political Opinion" (Australian Election Study, Australian National University, 2016).

12. See appendix Figure A4, wpid.world.

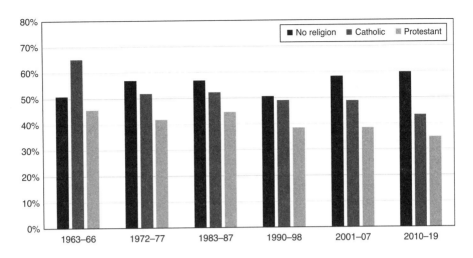

FIGURE 5.3. The religious cleavage in Australia. Vote for ALP / Greens by religious affiliation, 1963–2019
*Data Source:* Author's computations using Australian electoral surveys (see wpid.world).
*Note:* The figure shows the share of votes received by the Australian Labor Party and the Australian Greens by religious affiliation. Between the 1960s and the 2010s, support for these parties declined significantly among Catholic voters, while it increased slightly among nonreligious voters.

What have been the consequences of this transformation on the structure of Australian political cleavages? As shown in Figure 5.3, a growing cleavage between religious and nonreligious voters has emerged in parallel to the historical cleavage opposing Protestants and Catholics. The share of Catholics voting for the ALP (and later the Greens) has declined from 65 percent to 43 percent between the 1960s and the 2010s, while these two parties have become increasingly popular among voters declaring no religion.

This rising divide between religious and nonreligious voters is consistent with the growing political salience of new social issues, such as the right to abortion or same-sex marriage, which have created growing debates and tensions in recent years. In the 2019 federal election, for instance, the ALP's program included a requirement for public hospitals to offer abortion procedures, which led religious antiabortion groups such as the Australian Christian Lobby to campaign against the party.

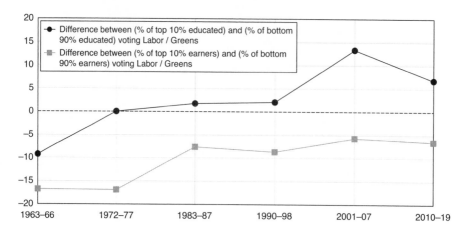

FIGURE 5.4. The emergence of a multi-elite party system in Australia, 1963–2019
*Data Source:* Author's computations using Australian electoral surveys (see wpid.world).
*Note:* The figure shows the relative support of top-income and highest-educated voters for the Labor Party and the Australian Greens. In the 1960s, top-income and highest-educated voters were less likely to vote Labor than low-income and lower-educated voters. The Labor/Green vote has gradually become associated with higher-educated voters, giving rise to a multi-elite party system. Estimates control for income/education, age, gender, religion, employment status, marital status, subjective class, home ownership, and location.

### The Emergence of a Multi-elite Party System

The transformation of Australia's party system, as in many Western democracies, has also been associated with the political divergence of highest-educated and top-income voters (see Chapter 1). As shown in Figure 5.4, the ALP received much greater support among low-income voters than among the top 10 percent in the 1960s and 1970s. This gap has declined since then, but it has remained negative and relatively stable since the 1980s. Meanwhile, highest-educated voters have gradually shifted to the left, and are now significantly more likely to vote for the Labor and the Greens than the lower educated.

### The Contemporary Structure of Australian Political Cleavages

Table 5.1 provides a more granular perspective on the structure of the vote in the past decade by decomposing the share of votes received by the ALP, the Australian Greens, the National Party, and the Liberal Party

*Table 5.1*  The Structure of Political Cleavages in Australia, 2010–2019

| | Share of Votes Received (%) | | | |
|---|---|---|---|---|
| | Labor | Greens | Liberal | National |
| **Education** | | | | |
| Primary | 36% | 7% | 44% | 5% |
| Secondary | 34% | 7% | 45% | 4% |
| Tertiary | 36% | 17% | 39% | 2% |
| Postgraduate | 36% | 16% | 38% | 2% |
| **Income** | | | | |
| Bottom 50% | 36% | 9% | 42% | 5% |
| Middle 40% | 36% | 13% | 41% | 3% |
| Top 10% | 30% | 12% | 53% | 1% |
| **Social Class** | | | | |
| Working/lower class | 42% | 7% | 37% | 5% |
| Middle/no class | 30% | 13% | 48% | 3% |
| **Country of Birth** | | | | |
| Australia | 34% | 11% | 42% | 4% |
| Europe-US-Canada | 35% | 10% | 44% | 2% |
| Non-Western countries | 40% | 8% | 45% | 1% |

*Data Source:* Author's computations using Australian electoral surveys (see wpid.world).
*Note:* The table shows the average share of votes received by the main Australian political parties by selected individual characteristics over the 2010–2019 period. During the past decade, the Australian Greens have received greater support from higher-educated voters, high-income voters, voters identifying with the middle class or with no class, and voters born in Australia.

by education, income, social class, and country of birth. A number of interesting results are visible. First, the Australian Greens' voting base is completely different from that of the ALP: tertiary-educated voters, middle- and high-income voters, and self-identified middle-class voters disproportionately support them. Second, while the Labor Party received higher support among working-class voters, education and income only had a weak effect on voting for the ALP. This suggests that "residual" class identities are today of greater importance than actual economic status in determining support for Labor. Third, the structure of the vote for the Liberal Party and the National Party shows similar diverging patterns: the Liberal Party receives more votes from lower-educated, high-income voters, while the National Party performs better among working-class, lower-educated, low-income voters.

This fragmentation of the political space in Australia is similar to that found in the majority of Western European countries (see Chapter 1). In Western Europe, however, the shift of lower-educated voters toward the right was associated with the rise of both green and far-right parties; in Australia, it was more decisively driven by the Australian Greens. That being said, it is important to stress that this transformation is not only due to the rise of the Greens: there have also been major changes in the structure of the vote for the Labor Party, which has become relatively less concentrated among low-income, lower-educated, and self-identified working-class voters in past decades.[13] This change may have been the result of strategic shifts in the positions and issue emphases of the Labor to avoid electoral leakage toward the Greens, but the long-run analysis also suggests that it started well before the Greens even existed. The electoral weakness of the extreme right in Australia might also explain why foreign-born individuals have only been marginally more likely to support left-wing parties in Australia, as shown in Table 5.1. This lower salience of the nativist cleavage is, as we shall see, common to the three old dominions.

## New Zealand

### New Zealand's Party System

The beginning of New Zealand's modern democracy goes back to the introduction of universal suffrage in 1893, which led to a first two-party system opposing the Liberal Party and the conservative Reform Party in the first elections of the twentieth century. The quick rise of the Labour Party, culminating in its victory in the 1935 general election, led to the amalgamation of liberal and conservative movements into the National Party in 1936.[14] This second two-party system, opposing the Labour Party to the National Party, persisted in the decades following the end of World War II (see Figure 5.5). Until the 1980s, the main minor party was the Social Credit, which scored between 10 percent and 20 percent of votes by drawing support from both National and Labour constituencies.[15]

13. See appendix Figures A40 and A42, wpid.world.

14. The Liberal Party of the late nineteenth century did, however, make coalitions with parts of the labor movement, visible in "Liberal-Labour" candidates, members of the Liberal Party who received endorsements from the labor movement or trade unions.

15. S. L. Dickson, "Social Credit and Class Voting," *Political Science* 21, no. 1 (1969): 31–41.

The 1990s announced the end of the postwar two-party system. Small parties had already started growing in the 1970s and 1980s, notably the Values Party (often considered to be the world's first environmentalist party of national significance), which polled 5 percent of the vote in 1975, as well as the libertarian New Zealand Party created by tycoon Bob Jones (12 percent of votes in 1984). However, it was the 1993 electoral reform that led to a decisive strengthening of new parties, with the adoption in 1996 of a mixed member proportional system in place of the first-past-the-post system operating since 1914.

In the proliferation of small parties that followed, only the Green Party and the New Zealand First (NZF) were able to emerge on a sustained basis. The Green Party traces its origin to the Values Party. After winning nearly 7 percent of votes in the 1990 elections, it cofounded the Alliance, a merger of other centrist and left-wing parties, which received 18 percent of votes in the 1993 elections. The Greens have run again independently since 1999, reaching 5 to 10 percent of votes in most elections (see Figure 5.5).

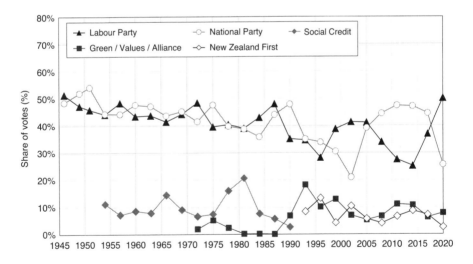

FIGURE 5.5. Election results in New Zealand, 1946–2020
*Data Source:* Author's computations using official election results (see wpid.world).
*Note:* The figure shows the share of votes received by selected political parties or groups of parties in general elections held in New Zealand between 1946 and 2020. The Labour Party received 50% of votes in 2020.

The NZF was founded in 1993 by former National Party politician Winston Peters, and has been supported by 5 to 10 percent of voters in most elections since then. It has taken centrist positions on economic issues, and more conservative and nationalist positions on social issues. The policy proposals of the NZF have included, for instance, an annual cap on immigration, buying back state-owned enterprises, lowering taxes, and lengthening judicial sentences. The NZF has formed governments with both the National Party (1996 and 1998) and the Labour Party (2005 and 2017).

As in Australia, there have been significant ideological shifts in the policies implemented by ruling parties in New Zealand.[16] Founded in 1916, the Labour Party has its origins in the trade union movement but was always on the moderate side of socialist reform, banning members of the Communist Party from joining the organization. After securing a majority in 1938, it implemented a number of reforms in health, education, and social security, until it was defeated by the National Party in 1949. In the 1980s, the deregulation, privatization, and free trade programs implemented by Labour governments yet led to lasting internal dissent and eventually to a historical defeat in the 1990 general election, with only 35 percent of votes. Similar reforms of state restructuring and labor market liberalization were then pursued by the National government. While the Labour Party succeeded in coming back to power in coalition with small parties in the following years, the 1990s and 2000s saw a further decline of its popularity overall, which culminated with its all-time low vote share of 25 percent in 2014. The comeback of the Labour in 2017, followed by Jacinda Ardern's crushing victory in the 2020 elections in the context of the COVID-19 pandemic, nonetheless seem to have announced a reversal of this medium-run trend.

### The Decline of Class Divides

I now turn to documenting the evolution of political cleavages in New Zealand by drawing on a set of electoral surveys covering elections held between 1972 and 2017.[17] As in the case of Australia, I focus on three key transformations: the evolution of class voting, the vote of minorities,

16. See, for instance, R. Mulgan, *Politics in New Zealand,* 3rd ed. (Auckland University Press, 2004), chapter 11.

17. See appendix Table B1, wpid.world.

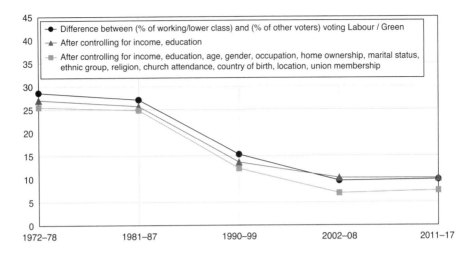

FIGURE 5.6. The decline of class voting in New Zealand, 1972–2017
*Data Source:* Author's computations using New Zealand electoral surveys (see wpid.world).
*Note:* The figure shows the difference between the share of voters identifying with the "working class" or the "lower class" and the share of voters identifying with the "middle class" or "no class" voting for the Labour Party / the Greens / other left-wing parties, before and after controls. Class voting has significantly declined in New Zealand in the past decades.

and the emergence of a multi-elite party system. I restrict the analysis to the determinants of the vote for the Labour Party, the Green Party, and a number of other minor center-left and left-wing parties.

Exactly as in Australia, there has been a sharp decline in class voting in New Zealand, both before and after controls: individuals identifying with the "working class" or the "lower class" were more likely to vote for the Labour by nearly 30 percentage points in the 1970s, compared to 10 percentage points in the past decade (Figure 5.6).

This transformation stands in contrast with the socioeconomic structure of subjective class affiliations, which has not changed significantly in the past decades: identification with the working class continues to strongly correlate with lower income levels.[18] This is consistent, as in the Australian case, with the idea that changes in class voting have been primarily due to a transformation in the political representation of class. As suggested by Figure 5.6, and as other studies have documented using mea-

18. See appendix Figures B73 and B74, wpid.world.

sures based on occupational categories, the decline of class-based voting was most pronounced at the end of the 1980s, when the Labour government implemented pro-market economic reforms, alienating many of its traditional working-class supporters.[19]

### Ethnic Cleavages and the Vote of Māori, Pacific, and Asian Minorities in New Zealand

Unlike Australian aboriginals, indigenous people and immigrants have represented sizable minorities in New Zealand. In the 2018 census, 70 percent of the population identified as Pākehā (or European), 16.5 percent as Māori, 15 percent as Asian, and 9 percent as Pacific. Asians are the population group whose size has grown most dramatically in recent years, from 6.6 percent in 2001 to 15 percent in 2018, as New Zealand experienced some of the highest per capita immigration flows among OECD countries. Among ethnic minorities, it is however the Māori who have most consistently cumulated social disadvantages in the past decades, including poorer health, lower life expectancy, and lower income levels, even if inequalities between Asians or Pacific people and Europeans are also significant and have persisted to the present.[20]

The indigenous status of the Māori in New Zealand has given them specific political rights, recognized by the three-article Treaty of Waitangi signed by representatives of the British Crown and Māori chiefs in 1840. The treaty both ceded complete government to the British Crown (article 1) and guaranteed that the Māori chiefs would retain their existing authority (article 2). Article 3 stated that the Māori people would be given full rights and protections as British subjects. Articles 2 and 3 were however soon forgotten, and colonial settlers deprived the Māori of a large share of their land in the second half of the nineteenth century through a combination of sales and confiscation. Furthermore, two versions of the treaty exist: one in Māori and one in English. The Māori

19. E. Haddon, "Class Identification in New Zealand: An Analysis of the Relationship between Class Position and Subjective Social Location," *Journal of Sociology* 51, no. 1 (2015): 737–754; Mulgan, *Politics in New Zealand,* chapter 12.

20. "Ethnicity," Stats NZ, accessed May 16, 2020, https://www.stats.govt.nz/topics /ethnicity; L. Marriott and D. Sim, "Indicators of Inequality for Māori and Pacific People" (Working Papers in Public Finance, Victoria University of Wellington, 2014), https://www .wgtn.ac.nz/cpf/publications/working-papers/working-paper-pdfs/WP09_2014 _Indicators-of-Inequality.pdf. The share of Māori in electoral surveys is much lower than in census data (see appendix Table B2, wpid.world), due to difficulties in sampling the Māori electorate.

version of article 1 did not cede sovereignty, but only governance, while the English version gave the queen the full right to power and sovereignty. These diverging interpretations have been a significant point of contest throughout New Zealand's contemporary history. It was only by the 1930s that the first Labour government would make a decisive move toward honoring the treaty by ending ethnic discrimination in access to welfare benefits.[21] In the 1970s, the second Labour government also set the Waitangi Tribunal to address renewed conflicts over land alienation, which led to further concessions and redistribution. Politically, Māori specificity was recognized though the Māori electorates, which have attributed reserved seats to Māori representatives since 1867 (7 of the 120 seats in the 2017 elections). People of Māori descent can choose to be on the Māori roll or on the general roll through the "Māori option" implemented in 1975 by the Labour government.[22]

The past decades have therefore witnessed persisting debates over the politics of Māori representation, the surge of a new Asian immigration, and the rise of new parties specifically representing Māori interests—such as the Mana Motuhake, the Māori Party, or the Mana Movement. As shown in figure 5.7, Māori and Pacific people have always been disproportionately more likely to vote for the Labour and other left-wing parties since the 1970s, while Asian voters have remained approximately as likely as Europeans to do so. The Māori-Pākehā cleavage in New Zealand is therefore very strong, comparable in size, for instance, to the bias of Muslims in France toward left-wing parties (see Chapter 1). By contrast, the emergence of a new Asian minority does not seem to have generated any form of new electoral divide.

### The Emergence of a Multi-elite Party System

As Figure 5.8 shows, a multi-elite party system comparable to that visible in Australia seems to have gradually emerged in New Zealand, as highest-educated voters have become increasingly likely to vote for the Labour Party, the Greens, and affiliated parties since the 1970s. Meanwhile, there has been no secular trend in support for left-wing parties among

21. Historical connections between the Labour Party and Māori voters go far back, and were formalized when the first Labour government of 1935 allied with representatives of the Rātana movement. The Rātana Church has since then been instrumental in allowing the Labour to hold Māori electorates.

22. J. Vowles, H. Coffé, and J. Curtin, *A Bark but No Bite: Inequality and the 2014 New Zealand General Election* (ANU Press, 2017), chapters 2 and 10.

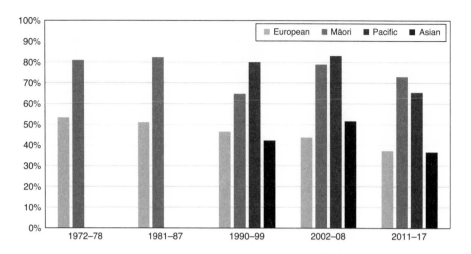

FIGURE 5.7. The ethnic cleavage in New Zealand, 1972–2017. Vote for Labour/
Green/Other left by ethnic group
*Data Source:* Author's computations using New Zealand electoral surveys (see wpid.world).
*Note:* The figure shows the share of votes received by the New Zealand Labour Party,
the Green Party, and other left-wing parties by ethnic group. Voters identifying as
"European" or "Asian" have remained significantly less likely to vote for these parties
than voters identifying as "Māori" or "Pacific."

top-income earners, whose tendency to vote conservative has stabilized
at about 10 percentage points higher than that of low-income voters. As
in Australia, the Green Party did play a significant role in this transformation by attracting a large share of higher-educated voters, but there
have also been changes in the structure of the vote for the Labour Party,
which used to receive greater support from lower-educated voters and
has now been attracting a higher share of the tertiary educated.[23] Therefore, while the fragmentation of New Zealand's party system may have
accelerated this transition, it cannot be held sole responsible for these
changes.

### The Contemporary Structure of Political Cleavages in New Zealand

The previous analysis has revealed three clearly identifiable dimensions
of political conflicts in New Zealand: a declining class dimension, an

23. See appendix Figures B43 and B44, wpid.world.

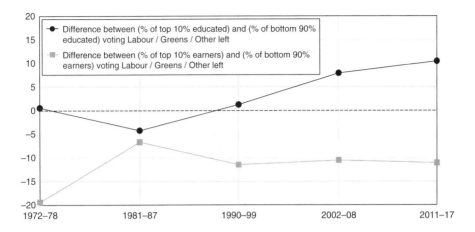

FIGURE 5.8. The emergence of a multi-elite party system in New Zealand, 1972–2017
*Data Source:* Author's computations using New Zealand electoral surveys (see wpid.world).
*Note:* The figure shows the relative support of top-income and highest-educated voters for the New Zealand Labour Party, the Green Party, and other left-wing parties. In the 1970s–1980s, top-income and highest-educated voters were less likely to vote for left-wing parties than low-income and lower-educated voters. The left-wing vote has gradually become associated with higher-educated voters, giving rise to a multi-elite party system. Estimates control for income/education, age, gender, occupation, home ownership, marital status, ethnic affiliation, religion, church attendance, country of birth, location, and union membership.

ethnic dimension, and, more recently, a growing educational cleavage. Table 5.2 reveals some particularly interesting intersections between them by showing the structure of the vote for New Zealand's four biggest parties in recent elections. The Labour Party appears to be a relatively hybrid entity today, still gaining votes from working-class and low-income voters—though less so than in previous decades—but also attracting as many postgraduates as primary-educated voters. This is also the case of the Greens who, as in the case of Australia, are supported by middle-class, middle-income, and higher-educated citizens.

The vote for the New Zealand First, by contrast, is characterized by relatively unique patterns in comparative perspective. The NZF receives more votes from lower-educated, low-income, working-class voters. Given that the party has been fighting for both limitations to Asian immigration and lower taxes, it therefore closely resembles far-right Western European parties in that respect (see Chapter 1). However, in contrast to

*Table 5.2*   The Structure of Political Cleavages in New Zealand, 2011–2017

| | Share of Votes Received (%) | | | |
|---|---|---|---|---|
| | Labour | Greens | National | NZF |
| **Education** | | | | |
| Primary | 35% | 4% | 43% | 11% |
| Secondary | 27% | 9% | 49% | 7% |
| Tertiary | 27% | 17% | 44% | 3% |
| Postgraduate | 36% | 15% | 33% | 5% |
| **Income** | | | | |
| Bottom 50% | 34% | 8% | 37% | 9% |
| Middle 40% | 25% | 10% | 51% | 5% |
| Top 10% | 18% | 9% | 63% | 4% |
| **Social Class** | | | | |
| Working/lower class | 34% | 7% | 32% | 14% |
| Middle/upper/no class | 21% | 11% | 48% | 6% |
| **Ethnicity** | | | | |
| European | 27% | 10% | 48% | 7% |
| Māori | 47% | 8% | 11% | 12% |
| Pacific | 64% | 0% | 23% | 11% |
| Asian | 29% | 5% | 57% | 0% |

*Data Source:* Author's computations using New Zealand electoral surveys (see wpid.world).

*Note:* The table shows the average share of votes received by the main New Zealand political parties by selected individual characteristics over the 2011–2017 period. During the past decade, the NZF has received greater support from lower-educated voters, low-income voters, and voters identifying as Māori.

these parties, the NZF has not been primarily supported by the ethnic majority: 7 percent of Europeans voted for the NZF in the last three elections, compared to 12 percent of Māori voters. Even more surprising is the fact that Asians have been actually slightly more likely to vote for the National Party than for the Labour Party. This contrasts sharply with the dynamics visible in Western European countries, where immigrants and new minorities tend to be clearly supportive of social democratic and affiliated parties, in the context of conservative parties' increasing opposition to immigration.

These results are consistent with the idea that with the exception of the NZF, ruling parties in New Zealand—as well as the majority of citizens—have been relatively favorable to Asian immigration, or at least

have not been sharply opposed to it.[24] In 2017, for instance, as much as 79 percent of New Zealanders answered "Strongly agree," "Agree," or "Neutral" when asked whether "Immigrants are generally good for New Zealand's economy." By contrast, the Māori were on average more opposed to immigration than Europeans: in 2017, 15 percent of Europeans strongly agreed to the above question, compared to 6 percent of self-identified Māori respondents.[25] The NZF therefore represents a unique case of a party successfully "mobilizing" an ethnic minority against another.[26] Unlike the majority of Western democracies studied in this volume, the politics of minorities in New Zealand have not been clearly integrated into the existing left-right axis, but seem to have represented a secondary, separated dimension of political conflict.

## Canada

### Canada's Two-and-a-Half Party System

Canada gained autonomy from British rule in the second half of the nineteenth century, when in 1867 the self-governing Dominion of Canada was formed, and the first federal election was won by the Conservative Party against the Liberal Party. Unlike in Australia and New Zealand, however, where the rise of the labor movement pushed toward the fusion of liberal and conservative forces, socialist movements never gained sufficient traction in Canada to significantly alter the old party system.[27] The Co-operative Commonwealth Federation, founded in 1932 by socialist and social democratic groups, did not exceed 16 percent of votes at its peak in 1945. It then merged with the Canadian Labour Congress to form the New Democratic Party (NDP) in 1961. The NDP has not done much

---

24. J. Vowles and J. Curtin, *A Populist Exception? The 2017 New Zealand General Election* (ANU Press, 2020).

25. Author's computations using National Election Study data. See also P. Spoonley, "Rising Asian Immigration Highlights New Zealand's Changing Demographics," The Conversation, February 12, 2014, https://theconversation.com/rising-asian-immigration -highlights-new-zealands-changing-demographics-23002.

26. Notice that part of the NZF's success among Māoris may be due to a leader effect, as Winston Peters is partly Māori. In fact, the NZF does not have particularly strong stances pushing for greater representation of Māori people, and it has shifted from holding all five Māori electorates in 1996 to officially rejecting the electorate system, campaigning in 2017 in favor of a referendum on abolishing Māori seats.

27. R. K. Carty, W. Cross, and L. Young, *Rebuilding Canadian Party Politics* (University of British Columbia Press, 2000), chapter 2.

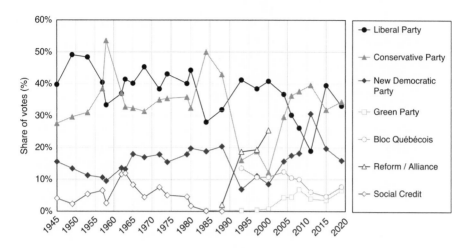

FIGURE 5.9. Election results in Canada, 1945–2019
*Data Source:* Author's computations using official election results (see wpid.world).
*Note:* The figure shows the share of votes received by selected political parties or groups of parties in federal elections held in Canada between 1945 and 2019. The Liberal Party received 33% of votes in 2019. The Conservative Party corresponds to the Progressive Conservative Party of Canada before 2002. The New Democratic Party corresponds to the Co-operative Commonwealth Federation before 1962.

better since then, never exceeding 20 percent of votes, with the exception of the 2011 election (see Figure 5.9). The inability of left-wing movements to gain a majority of support at the national level resulted in large part, it has been argued, from the regionalization of Canadian politics, and more importantly, from the inability of the NDP to connect with trade unions in Québec.[28] The two biggest parties in Canada have therefore remained the Conservative Party and the Liberal Party.

Several minor parties have nonetheless played a secondary role in Canadian politics since the end of World War II. The Social Credit Party, a social-conservative party promoting social credit theories of monetary reforms, obtained 5 to 10 percent of votes in the 1960s and 1970s. The Reform Party was a conservative party originally founded to give a voice to Western Canadians' interests at the end of the 1980s, in a context of

28. R. Johnston, "The Class Basis of Canadian Elections" (paper presented at the Annual Meeting of the Canadian Political Science Association, Edmonton, Alberta, June 2012), https://www.cpsa-acsp.ca/papers-2012/Johnston.pdf.

growing dissatisfaction toward the Conservative government elected in 1988. It dissolved in 2000 in favor of the Alliance, which itself joined the Conservative Party before the 2004 federal election. The Bloc Québécois has had a strong influence in Québec and has won the majority of seats in the province in most elections since 1993. It is both a social democratic and a separatist party, aiming to protect regional interests but also to defend social welfare programs. The Green Party of Canada, finally, founded in 1983, has grown from less than 1 percent of votes in 2000 to almost 7 percent in 2019, promoting environmentalism, social justice, and participatory democracy.

The evolution of parties' ideological positions in Canada shows a number of similarities with Australia and New Zealand. After World War II, the Liberals moved toward the left of the political spectrum on economic issues, especially during the Pierre Trudeau period (1968–1979 and 1980–1984). After the economic and political crises of the 1990s, however, Liberal governments (1993–2003 and 2003–2006) then started to defend more liberal economic positions, emphasizing the need to keep taxes low and a sustainable government debt. The Conservative party has also undergone significant changes since the 1960s. Originally, the party was generally considered to mainly represent English Canadians' interests, bringing together a large share of the Protestant electorate. At the beginning of the 1980s, Progressive Conservatives shifted to promoting the values of free-market economics, especially under the Mulroney administration (1984–1993). Rising discontent with the conservatives under Mulroney's second term—in particular the divisive Canada–United States Free Trade Agreement, the 1980s recession, and the implementation of the new Goods and Services Tax—led to the collapse of the Conservatives in the 1993 federal election, who received a mere 16 percent of votes. Finally, the New Democratic Party originally promoted a transition toward the end of capitalism and the establishment of a socialist society. It gradually moved toward the center of the political spectrum to become a social democratic party, promoting social welfare programs and liberal values. These two dimensions were directly visible in the NDP's platform at the 2015 federal election, which included increasing corporate tax rates and reducing poverty, but also promoting gender equality and the welcoming of Syrian refugees.[29]

29. R. Andersen, "The Class-Party Relationship in Canada, 1965–2004," in *Political Choice Matters: Explaining the Strength of Class and Religious Cleavages in Cross-national Perspective*, ed. G. Evans and N. D. Graaf (Oxford University Press, 2012), 165–182.

*Religious, Linguistic, and Regional Identities in Canada*

Region, language, and religion were found to be the strongest predictors of electoral behaviors in Canada throughout the country's democratic history.[30] The exceptional divide between French and English speakers, as well as the spread of the population on a large territory, were generally cited as factors accounting for the development of varieties of political cultures, party affiliations, and policy positions, which have persisted to the present.[31] These identities played a significant role in inhibiting the emergence of a stable class cleavage in the second half of the twentieth century. On the left of the political spectrum, the New Democratic Party was unable to unite union members of Québec and the Western provinces, thereby condemning the party to a role of secondary political actor.[32] In addition, the importance of religious, linguistic, and regional affiliations in determining support for Liberals, Conservatives, and the NDP left little space for other dimensions of political conflict to fully materialize.[33] While some authors have argued that class does matter in some regions, or that the lack of class cleavage is the result of parties' deliberate obliteration of class politics, there is a relative consensus that social class has remained a poor predictor of electoral behaviors overall.[34]

The Canadian electorate can be divided into four broad regions: Québec (about 26 percent of the voting age population), Ontario (38 percent), the Western Provinces (29 percent), and the Eastern Atlantic Provinces (7 percent). English speakers make up two thirds of the adult population, French speakers about 25 percent. Language, religion, and region have been tightly associated in Canada, though never perfectly. The majority of

30. C. D. Anderson and L. B. Stephenson, "The Puzzle of Elections and Voting in Canada," in *Voting Behaviour in Canada*, ed. C. D. Anderson and L. B. Stephenson (University of British Columbia Press, 2010), 1–39; Carty, Cross, and Young, *Rebuilding Canadian Party Politics*, chapter 2.

31. J. L. Guth and C. R. Fraser, "Religion and Partisanship in Canada," *Journal for the Scientific Study of Religion* 40, no. 1 (2001): 51–64; A. Henderson, "Political Cultures in Canada," *Canadian Journal of Political Science/Revue Canadienne de Science Politique* 37, no. 3 (2004): 595–615.

32. Johnston, "Class Basis of Canadian Elections."

33. R. R. Alford, *Party and Society* (Rand-McNally, 1963).

34. E. Gidengil, "Class and Region in Canadian Voting: A Dependency Interpretation," *Canadian Journal of Political Science/Revue Canadienne de Science Politique* 22, no. 3 (1989): 563–587; M. D. Ornstein, H. M. Stevenson, and A. P. Williams, "Region, Class and Political Culture in Canada," *Canadian Journal of Political Science/Revue Canadienne de Science Politique* 13, no. 2 (1980): 227–271.

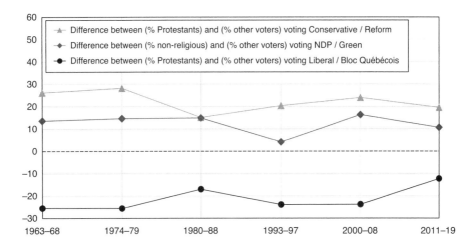

FIGURE 5.10. The religious cleavage in Canada, 1963–2019
*Data Source:* Author's computations using Canadian electoral surveys (see wpid.world).
*Note:* The figure shows the relative support of voters belonging to specific religious groups for the main Canadian political parties, after controlling for income, education, age, gender, employment status, marital status, country of birth, and union membership. Protestant voters have remained significantly more likely to vote conservative than non-Protestants, while nonreligious voters have remained more supportive of the New Democratic Party and the Green Party.

French speakers live in Québec and are Catholics, but about a third of Catholics are English speakers, and about a tenth of Québec residents are English speakers.[35] Québec residents were historically significantly overrepresented in lower-income groups, even though regional inequalities always remained limited in Canada in comparative perspective. These disparities have decreased significantly since then, but have not completely disappeared.[36]

Figure 5.10 reveals a remarkable persistence of religious cleavages in Canada by representing the relative support for the Conservatives, the NDP and the Greens, and the Liberal Party and the Bloc Québécois among specific religious affiliations. Putting the Liberal Party and the

35. See appendix Table C2, wpid.world.

36. See appendix Figures C80 to C87, wpid.world. Broad regional inequalities are low, but they are more significant when considering smaller geographical entities; see S. Breau, "Rising Inequality in Canada: A Regional Perspective," *Applied Geography* 61 (2015): 58–69.

Bloc Québécois together for this particular analysis can be justified by the fact that the decline of the Liberal Party in Québec in the 1990s can be in large part attributable to the rise of the Bloc Québécois. Nonreligious voters have always been supportive of the NDP, while the conservatives have always received much greater support from Protestants since the 1960s. The Liberal Party used to receive more votes from Catholics—many of which shifted to supporting the Bloc Québécois in the 1990s—and now attracts an important proportion of nonreligious voters and new religious minorities (see below).

The religious cleavage in Canada has therefore remained exceptionally strong. While in Australia, the Catholic-Protestant cleavage was gradually replaced by a religious-secular cleavage, religious divisions in Canada have always been split in three, with nonreligious voters voting for the NDP, Protestants voting for conservative parties, and Catholics (and more recently new religious minorities, see below) voting for the Liberals. The Australian Labour Party of the 1960s brought together the Catholic minority and the working class; the New Democratic Party, by contrast, never gained sufficient support in Québec and therefore remained more oriented toward nonreligious voters of Ontario and the western provinces, who represented only a small fraction of the population.[37]

### The Politicization of Inequality in Canada: A Persistent Lack of Class Cleavage?

As explained above, the existing literature on political cleavages in Canada failed to identify the existence of a stable class cleavage, whether using occupational categories or subjective measures of class affiliations. Figure 5.11 reproduces this finding by focusing on income, showing the relative support of top 10 percent income earners toward the three main Canadian parties. With the exception of the 1960s, top-income earners have always been less likely to vote for the NDP and more favorable to the Conservatives, with the Liberal Party standing in between. Interestingly, these results are similar to those found in other Western democracies, with comparable orders of magnitude, suggesting that socioeconomic divides in Canada are not exceptionally weak on that dimension (see Chapter 1).

---

37. See appendix Figures C29 to C35, wpid.world, for similar figures on region and language. See also Carty, Cross, and Young, *Rebuilding Canadian Party Politics*, chapter 2.

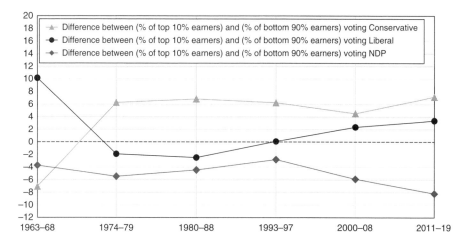

FIGURE 5.11. Political conflict and income in Canada, 1963–2019
*Data Source:* Author's computations using Canadian electoral surveys (see wpid.world).
*Note:* The figure shows the difference between the share of top 10% earners and the share of bottom 90% earners voting for the main Canadian political parties, after controlling for education, religion, age, gender, employment status, marital status, country of birth, and union membership. With the exception of the 1960s, the Conservative Party has always been more popular among high-income voters, while support for the New Democratic Party has become increasingly concentrated among low-income voters.

Furthermore, the Liberal Party seems to have become gradually more oriented toward high-income voters since the 1970s, while support for the NDP has become increasingly concentrated among low-income constituencies in recent years. These results suggest that the politicization of inequality in Canada has changed significantly since the 1970s. On the one hand, the NDP followed a major transformation from a mainly urban, English-speaking party supported by union members and middle-income voters to a more broad-based party supported by the poor.[38] On the other hand, the Liberal Party has now become more popular among economic elites, making its voting base resemble more closely that of the Conservative Party in that respect. These results resonate well with the fact that both Liberals and Conservatives have been moving to the right

38. On the full structure of the vote for the NDP, see appendix Figures C56 to C63, wpid.world.

of the political spectrum on economic matters in recent years, while the NDP has remained more left-wing.[39]

It is also worth noticing that this transition has coincided with a marked decline in electoral turnout since the 1990s, from 75 percent in 1988 to 66 percent in 2019, so that the Liberals' shift to the right may have been associated with a movement of low-income voters not only toward the NDP, but also toward abstention. Unfortunately, turnout cannot be studied consistently with the Canadian Election Studies data without some substantive methodological corrections, as postelectoral surveys have been unable to correctly sample nonvoters, especially in recent years.[40] This is left for future research.

### The Emergence of a Multi-elite Party System in Canada

Figure 5.12 suggests that as in Australia and New Zealand, there has been a growing educational divide opposing the Liberals, the NDP, and the Greens to the Conservative Party. This is especially visible in the relative support of higher-educated voters toward the Conservative Party, which was only marginally negative until the 1980s and declined substantially in the most recent elections.

Interestingly, in contrast to the majority of Western countries, the figure also reveals that lower-educated voters never were more inclined to vote for the NDP or the Liberal Party than for the Conservative party. This may perhaps be linked to the fact that class cleavages were never strong in Canada, so that no coalition was ever able to bring together the majority of the low-income, lower-educated electorate. Strikingly, the structure of the vote for the NDP in the 1960s was very similar to that of the Japan Socialist Party at the same period (see Chapter 11), being more concentrated among middle-income, urban, and higher-educated voters.[41]

### The Contemporary Structure of Political Cleavages in Canada

Table 5.3 decomposes the structure of the vote for the main Canadian political parties in the last three elections. Four interesting results stand

39. Andersen, "Class-Party Relationship in Canada."

40. C. H. Achen and T. Y. Wang, "Declining Voter Turnout in Taiwan: A Generational Effect?," *Electoral Studies* 58 (2019): 113–124. A preliminary attempt based on proportional reweighting of nonvoters can be found in A. Gethin, "Cleavage Structures and Distributive Politics" (master's thesis, Paris School of Economics, 2018), chapter 6.

41. See appendix Figures C56 to C63, wpid.world.

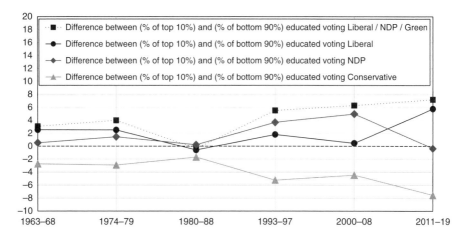

FIGURE 5.12. Educational divides in Canada, 1963–2019
*Data Source:* Author's computations using Canadian electoral surveys (see wpid.world).
*Note:* the figure shows the difference between the share of top 10% educated voters and
the share of bottom 90% educated voters voting for the main Canadian political
parties, after controlling for income, religion, age, gender, employment status, marital
status, country of birth, and union membership. The Liberal Party, the New Democratic Party, and the Green Party have always received greater support from higher-
educated voters, while the conservative vote has become increasingly concentrated
among the lower educated since the 1990s.

out. First, Canada's party system clearly appears to divide top-income
and highest-educated voters in the same way as it does in other Western
countries. Higher-educated voters are much less supportive of the
conservatives than the lower educated, while top-income earners are
more likely to vote for them. On the other side of the political spectrum,
the NDP and the Greens receive greater support from both low-income
and higher-educated voters. The Liberal Party has somehow managed to
bring together both types of elites, so that Canada's multi-elite party
system closely resembles that visible in France in 2017, where higher education tilted voters toward the left, higher income tilted voters toward
the right, and *En Marche!* united some voters from both groups at the
center of the political spectrum (see Chapter 2). In that sense, Canada's
recent political transformations do not appear particularly unique. Regionalization and linguistic identities may explain in part why class
politics in Canada differed significantly from most Western countries in
the early postwar decades, but this is not the case today.

*Table 5.3*   The Structure of Political Cleavages in Canada, 2011–2019

| | Share of Votes Received (%) | | | | |
|---|---|---|---|---|---|
| | New Democratic Party | Green Party | Liberal Party | Conservative Party | Bloc Québécois |
| **Education** | | | | | |
| Primary | 22% | 3% | 22% | 43% | 7% |
| Secondary | 23% | 5% | 27% | 37% | 7% |
| Tertiary | 25% | 4% | 34% | 32% | 5% |
| Postgraduate | 21% | 6% | 37% | 29% | 6% |
| **Income** | | | | | |
| Bottom 50% | 26% | 5% | 28% | 32% | 8% |
| Middle 40% | 23% | 4% | 30% | 36% | 6% |
| Top 10% | 15% | 3% | 34% | 43% | 4% |
| **Religion** | | | | | |
| None | 27% | 7% | 32% | 26% | 6% |
| Catholic | 25% | 3% | 27% | 31% | 13% |
| Other Christian | 18% | 4% | 25% | 51% | 1% |
| Jewish | 6% | 2% | 41% | 49% | 0% |
| Buddhist | 31% | 4% | 41% | 21% | 2% |
| Hindu | 33% | 2% | 38% | 27% | 0% |
| Muslim | 27% | 1% | 63% | 9% | 1% |
| Sikh | 26% | 1% | 54% | 19% | 0% |
| Other | 18% | 8% | 31% | 39% | 1% |
| **Country of Birth** | | | | | |
| Canada | 24% | 5% | 28% | 35% | 7% |
| Europe/US | 25% | 4% | 29% | 39% | 1% |
| Non-Western countries | 18% | 3% | 42% | 36% | 1% |

*Data Source:* Author's computations using Canadian electoral surveys (see wpid.world).
*Note:* The table shows the average share of votes received by the main Canadian political parties by selected individual characteristics over the 2011–2019 period. The Liberal Party received greater support from high-income, higher-educated, and Muslim voters.

That being said, language and religion do continue to strongly influ-ence electoral behaviors. The NDP and the Greens attract a higher share of nonreligious voters, while the Conservative Party gets the majority of protestant votes. The Liberal Party stands in between and finds stron-gest support among new Buddhist, Hindu, Muslim, and Sikh minorities. The Bloc Québécois has declined since the 1990s, but it still received

about a quarter of French votes in the past decade, and almost no votes from other linguistic groups. In contrast to Spain, where independentism has been supported by the elites (see Chapter 6 as well as the comparative analysis in Chapter 1), the Bloc Québécois seems to be slightly more successful among low-income and primary-educated voters.[42]

Finally, as in Australia and New Zealand, Canadian politics do not seem to display a particularly pronounced nativist dimension (also see Figure 1.11). In countries like France, the United States or Germany, new ethnic minorities have disproportionately supported social democratic, democratic, and socialist parties. In Canada, it is the Liberal Party that has been most successful among new religious minorities and citizens born in non-Western countries.

42. See appendix Figures C40 to C47, wpid.world.

## 6

# Historical Political Cleavages and Postcrisis Transformations in Italy, Spain, Portugal, and Ireland, 1953–2020

LUIS BAULUZ, AMORY GETHIN, CLARA MARTÍNEZ-TOLEDANO, AND MARC MORGAN

## Introduction

This chapter studies the changing relationship between party choice and socioeconomic conflicts in Italy, Spain, Portugal, and Ireland over the last decades. The focus on these four countries is particularly useful to understand the sources of political change in advanced democracies, as they all share a common history of late industrialization and were deeply hit by the 2008 global recession. The postcrisis austerity policies imposed by international organizations gave the impression that national elections had no room to change domestic policy and led to the emergence of challenger parties, which have profoundly transformed their party systems. Despite these similarities, socioeconomic cleavages have not followed the same patterns, depending on each country's specific political history.

Class cleavages have progressively disappeared in Italy and Spain. The emergence of new challenger parties (for example, Podemos in Spain and Movimento 5 Stelle in Italy), liberal parties (Ciudadanos in Spain), and nationalist anti-immigration parties (Lega in Italy and VOX in Spain) has led to a shift in the vote from traditional parties to these new parties among the young and a disproportionate increase in the vote share to the new left among the highest educated. In contrast, in Portugal class divisions deepened with the onset of the 2008 global financial crisis, when

We thank Kevin Cunningham, Federico Curci, Carmen Durrer, Javier Padilla, Thomas Piketty, Aidan Regan, and Paolo Santini for their useful comments.

the two mainstream parties (Partido Socialista and Partido Social Democrata) turned to more extreme positions. Ireland has also seen a rise in class divides after the recession with the rise in popularity of a "workers" party, Sinn Féin, focused on redistributive issues and public services, which has captured the vote of the underprivileged.

Many Western democracies have witnessed the emergence of "multi-elite party systems" in the past decades, in which highest-educated voters have become increasingly likely to vote for the historical "left" (the "Brahmin left"), while top-income voters have remained more faithful to the "right" (the "merchant right"). In Italy, the trends have been relatively similar, more so than in the three other countries studied here. The "merchant right" is, however, weaker in comparative perspective, due most likely to the exceptional strength of historical religious cleavages and to the salient decoupling of class and Catholicism, as voters might be drawn to the policy of one party on class lines, but resistant to that same party on religious lines. Spain is also approaching a multi-elite party system, but it has not fully reached it yet. This delay is likely due to its recent authoritarian past, which prevented the emergence of a strong far-right party capturing the vote from low-income and lower-educated voters. Instead, the only successful Spanish far-right formation, VOX, emerged in 2013 endorsing neoliberal policies and as a nationalist reaction to the Catalan independence movement, and thus not (at least not yet) on the back of lower-educated or low-income voters feeling left behind. The nationalist vote in the regions of Catalonia and the Basque Country has also weakened Spain's transition toward a multi-elite party system, as these parties tend to prioritize ethnolinguistic conflicts over social class issues, and left-wing nationalist parties disproportionately attract the highest-income and highest-educated voters.

Portugal and Ireland are singular in that they have not shown any sign of a transition to a "multi-elite party system." The Portuguese "exceptionalism" has been mainly driven by the absence of strong political conflicts over value-based issues; the weak party polarization among mainstream parties, which has helped the traditional left to keep a large share of the low-income and low-educated electorate and prevented the emergence of a strong far-right party; the persistent importance of the class-based communist vote; and the incapacity of the Left Bloc (Bloco de Esquerda, BE) to become strong enough among the highest educated to revert the educational cleavage. In Ireland, the persisting historical civil war cleavage and the strength of Catholicism largely explain why political

cleavages did not revolve around a clear left-right axis and the absence of a significant "Brahmin left" group. The recent electoral success of the pro-worker Sinn Féin has also prevented the emergence of a strong far-right party capturing the lower-educated and low-income vote, reinforcing the "single-elite party system."

## Italy

### Political Dynamics since the Second World War

Democracy was reestablished in Italy in 1946. Two years later the new constitution initiated the First Republic. Until the 1990s, the electoral system operated under proportional representation (PR), with very low thresholds. This formula resulted in a highly divided party system, yet it did not prevent one single party, the Christian Democrats (DC), from being in office during this period.[1] Since the 1990s, Italy has reformed its electoral system four consecutive times, more than any other Western European country.[2] These reforms have had a profound effect on the structure of party competition.

The first reform was approved by referendum in 1993, following numerous corruption scandals linked to the political establishment, which caused popular dissatisfaction with the political system and a growing demand for institutional changes. This initiated what has been popularly known as the "Second Republic," although the constitution was not modified. This reform changed the PR formula to one in which three-quarters of the Chamber of Deputies seats were based on a first-past-the-post system while the remaining quarter remained proportional. This reform incentivized pre-electoral alliances on the left and right of the political spectrum, consolidating a two-party system. Since 2005, three reforms have modified the balance between proportional and majoritarian formulas, but the strong incentive to reach pre-electoral coalitions remained in place. However, they have not prevented the emergence

1. O. Heath and P. Bellucci, "Class and Religious Voting in Italy," in *Political Choice Matters: Explaining the Strength of Class and Religious Cleavages in Cross-national Perspective*, ed. G. Evans and N. D. de Graaf (Oxford University Press, 2013), 309–336.

2. J. Karremans, G. Malet, and D. Morisi, "Italy–The End of Bipolarism: Restructuration in an Unstable Party System," in *European Party Politics in Times of Crisis*, ed. S. Hutter and H. Kriesi (Cambridge University Press, 2019), 118–138; A. Chiaramonte and R. D'Alimonte, "The New Italian Electoral System and Its Effects on Strategic Coordination and Disproportionality," *Italian Political Science* 13, no. 1 (2018): 8–18.

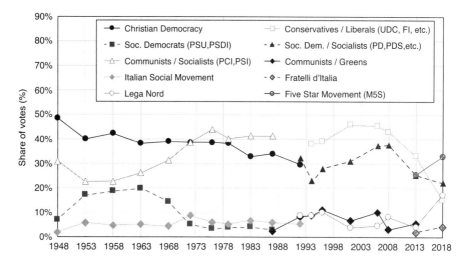

FIGURE 6.1. Election results in Italy, 1948–2018
*Data Source:* Authors' computations using official election results (see wpid.world).
*Note:* The figure shows the share of votes received by selected political parties or groups of parties in general elections held in Italy between 1948 and 2018. The Five Star Movement received 33% of votes in 2018.

of challenger parties, such as the Five Star Movement (M5S) in the last decade.

The history of the postwar Italian party system can thus be decomposed into three periods: 1946–1993, 1993–2013, and 2013–2020 (Figure 6.1). The first period lasts from the reestablishment of democracy in 1946 until the early 1990s. During this period, the main party on the right was Christian Democracy (Democrazia Cristiana, DC), while the main party on the left was the Italian Communist Party (Partito Comunista Italiano, PCI). Initially, the PCI was under the influence of the USSR, but during the 1970s it broke with Soviet orthodoxy, initiating what has been known as "Eurocommunism." Smaller parties coexisted on both the left and the right, such as the neofascist Italian Social Movement and the Italian Socialist Party.[3] The consolidation of the PCI as the main left-wing party largely shaped the establishment of two blocs following a communist-anticommunist logic. The consequence was that the DC led

3. G. Pasquino, "Political History in Italy," *Journal of Policy History* 21, no. 3 (2009): 282–297.

the government formation throughout the whole period, as smaller formations would ally with the DC to prevent a government of the PCI.[4]

The 1980s to the early 1990s were a transformative period. On the one hand, the PCI suffered a crisis of identity, especially upon the fall of the internationalist communist bloc between 1989 and 1991. On the other hand, numerous cases of corruption within the DC generated a crisis of political disaffection. The approval of the new electoral law in 1993 incentivized the establishment of a two-party system, with two main coalitions, one on the left and one on the right. The PCI split into the Democratic Party of the Left (Partito Democratico della Sinistra, PDS)—which became the main party in the center-left coalition, "The Olive Tree"—and the Communist Refoundation Party (Partito della Rifondazione Comunista, PRC). The PDS then progressively merged with smaller parties, which eventually led in 2007 to the creation of today's main left-wing party, the Democratic Party (Partito Democratico, PD), which still excludes the smaller PRC. The DC was dissolved in 1994. Some of its members who opposed the party's transformation into the liberal Italian People's Party (Partito Popolare Italiano, PPI) founded the Christian Democratic Centre (Centro Cristiano Democratico, CCD) in 1994 and the United Christian Democrats (Cristiani Democratici Uniti, CDU) in 1995. The latter two parties merged in 2001, and together with the newly founded European Democracy, formed the Union of Christian and Centre Democrats (Unione dei Democratici Cristiani e Democratici di Centro, UDC). Despite these evolutions, the main right-wing party after the DC has been Forza Italia (FI), founded in 1994 and led by media owner Silvio Berlusconi.

The 2010s led to another complete reconfiguration of the Italian party system. In a context of popular disaffection with the political class, partly influenced by the enduring economic impact of the Great Recession and the austerity measures adopted by Italy to escape the sovereign debt crisis, two challenger parties obtained important support in the 2013 general elections: the center-liberal formation Civic Choice (Scelta Civica, SC), with close to 11 percent of the popular vote, and the antiestablishment Five Star Movement (Movimento 5 Stelle, M5S), which obtained a 26 percent vote share. These two parties ran separately from the existing center-right and center-left coalitions. For the first time since 1993, the government

4. The PCI exceptionally supported the DC governments between 1976 and 1980, an agreement known as the "Historic Compromise."

was led by the PD, with the support of Berlusconi's party and other smaller formations (including SC), given the M5S's refusal to facilitate government formation.

The 2018 elections culminated the transformation of the Italian party system. The M5S won the elections with 33 percent of the popular vote. Meanwhile, the far-right regionalist Northern League (Lega Nord, LN) became the most supported party in the right-wing coalition, with 17 percent of the popular vote, surpassing Forza Italia. For the first time since the reestablishment of democracy, the government was not led by a mainstream party. Instead, an agreement was reached between the M5S and the LN. This alliance, however, proved unstable. After one year, tensions between the two parties led to the formation of a new government by the M5S and the PD.

### The Emergence of a Weak Multi-elite Party System

In what follows, we explore the changing relationship between socioeconomic characteristics and left-right voting behavior in Italy.[5] We start by analyzing the evolution of the income and education cleavages. Figure 6.2 shows that these two cleavages, and in particular income divides, have not been strong in Italy since the 1960s in comparison to other Western European countries (see Chapter 1). However, the trends reveal a pattern similar to that of other Western European countries.

The highest educated have become progressively more supportive of social democratic, socialist, and communist parties, while the income cleavage has remained essentially flat, with top-income earners voting slightly more for conservative and Christian democratic parties with the exception of the 1950s and the 2010s. The upward shift in the education gradient mainly happened between the 1970s and 1980s, which coincides with the period in which the relationship between the PCI and the Soviet Union gradually fell apart, as the party moved away from Soviet obedience and Marxist-Leninist orthodoxy toward Eurocommunism and the Socialist International on issues such as national sovereignty, socialist democracy, and the freedom of culture.[6] The exclusion of the M5S from

---

5. We group Italian parties into left-wing and right-wing blocs, following Heath and Bellucci, "Class and Religious Voting in Italy," for the period covering the First Republic, and Karremans, Malet, and Morisi, "Italy," for the years since 1993. For data sources, see appendix Table AD1, World Political Cleavages and Inequality Database, http://wpid.world.

6. V. Fouskas, *Italy, Europe, the Left: The Transformation of Italian Communism and the European Imperative* (Routledge, 2018).

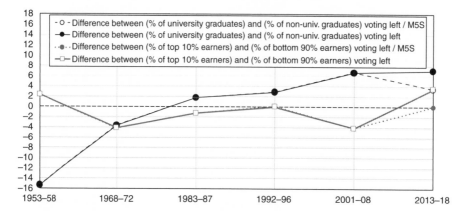

FIGURE 6.2. The emergence of a multi-elite party system in Italy, 1953–2018
*Data Source:* Authors' computations using Italian electoral surveys (see wpid.world).
*Note:* The figure shows the relative support of university graduates and top-income earners for social democratic/socialist/communist/green parties/the M5S. In the 1950s–1960s, highest-educated and top-income voters were less likely to vote for left-wing parties than low-income and lower-educated voters. The left-wing vote has gradually become associated with higher-educated voters, giving rise to a multi-elite party system. Estimates control for income/education, age, gender, religion, church attendance, employment status, marital status, union membership, location, and region.

the left exacerbates the relative difference in the left-wing vote among the highest educated, indicating that the new challenger party does not attract a disproportionate share of the highest educated.

The weak education and income gradients are largely related to the absence of a strong relationship between social class and partisanship, which is also common to the rest of Southern European countries.[7] In Italy, the weakness of this relationship is most likely reinforced by the decoupling of class and religion. Voters might be drawn to the policy of one party on class lines, but resistant to that same party on religious lines (for example, the case of working-class Catholics).[8] The religious cleavage

7. R. Günther and J. R. Montero, "The Anchors of Partisanship: A Comparative Analysis of Voting Behaviour in Four Southern European Countries," in *Parties, Politics, and Democracy in the New Southern Europe*, ed. P. Diamandouros and R. Günther (Johns Hopkins University Press, 2001), 83–152.

8. T. Mackie, M. Mannheimer, and G. Sani, "Italy," in *Electoral Change: Responses to Evolving Social and Attitudinal Structures in Western Countries*, ed. M. Franklin, T. Mackie, H. Valen, et al. (Cambridge University Press, 1992), 238–254.

is particularly strong in the Italian context. During the First Republic, the Christian Democrats, with direct links with the Catholic Church, obtained the majority of votes from practicing Catholics.[9] In fact, the religious cleavage also explains why the education and income cleavages were not very strong, as the DC competed with the Communists for the low-income and low-educated Catholic electorate.[10] The Second Republic entailed the disappearance of the DC and marked the beginning of the "Catholic diaspora"—that is, the decline in the association between practicing Catholicism and voting for the right.[11] The decline in the religious cleavage came together with the weakening of the class cleavage, due largely to the breakup of the PCI into separate parties. However, the association of Catholicism and religiosity with voting for the right is still positive and much stronger than class voting, which has weakened in recent years.[12]

### The 2010s: The Beginning of a New Era?

The 2013 and 2018 general elections heralded the definitive transformation of Italy's party system. Table 6.1 shows the structure of political cleavages in the 2018 elections. Socialists and social democrats have become the dominant parties among higher-educated individuals, while the traditional right and the LN obtain a more important share of votes from lower-educated voters. The M5S stands out in this context as a more hybrid party, absorbing a large share of the vote from traditional parties and making its best scores among both middle-educated and low-income voters.

The LN concentrates its votes within the lowest-educated and bottom-income electorate, a similar voter profile to most anti-immigration formations in Europe, which tend to obtain their largest support not only from lower-educated but also from low-income voters. Nonetheless, the LN also obtains a significant share of the vote among top income earners, in line with the vote profile of the far-right formation VOX in Spain. This distinct pattern might be related to its regionalist ideology and to its

---

9. See appendix Figures AB6 and AB7, wpid.world.
10. See appendix Figures AC21 and AC22, wpid.world.
11. Karremans, Malet, and Morisi, "Italy."
12. Heath and Bellucci, "Class and Religious Voting in Italy."

*Table 6.1*   The Structure of Political Cleavages in Italy, 2018

| | Share of Votes Received (%) | | | | |
|---|---|---|---|---|---|
| | Socialists/ Soc. Democrats | Five Star Movement | Conservatives/ Liberals | Lega | Fratelli d'Italia |
| **Education** | | | | | |
| Primary | 16% | 33% | 19% | 29% | 1% |
| Secondary | 24% | 38% | 7% | 22% | 5% |
| Tertiary | 34% | 30% | 10% | 14% | 7% |
| **Income** | | | | | |
| Bottom 50% | 21% | 38% | 9% | 22% | 6% |
| Middle 40% | 33% | 32% | 9% | 18% | 5% |
| Top 10% | 33% | 30% | 10% | 18% | 5% |
| **Age** | | | | | |
| 20–39 | 24% | 38% | 9% | 21% | 5% |
| 40–59 | 32% | 37% | 5% | 14% | 4% |
| 60+ | 26% | 37% | 8% | 19% | 5% |
| **Religion** | | | | | |
| No religion | 33% | 36% | 7% | 16% | 3% |
| Catholic | 23% | 34% | 8% | 25% | 8% |
| Other | 20% | 45% | 7% | 17% | 10% |
| **Region** | | | | | |
| North | 30% | 24% | 9% | 29% | 4% |
| Center | 28% | 33% | 9% | 18% | 7% |
| South | 23% | 51% | 8% | 8% | 6% |
| Islands | 22% | 51% | 11% | 8% | 6% |

*Data Source:* Authors' computations using Italian electoral surveys (see wpid.world).
*Note:* The table shows the share of votes received by the main Italian political parties by selected individual characteristics in 2018. Social democratic/socialist parties were supported by 16% of primary-educated voters, compared to 34% of tertiary-educated voters.

greater support within the richer northern regions of Italy. Meanwhile, the M5S became the most voted force in the south and the islands, both regions historically under the influence of traditional-right parties. Therefore, while regional divides do not seem to have altered the emergence of a multi-elite party system in Italy overall, the rise of new regionally based parties has given it a relatively unique shape in comparative perspective.

## Spain

### From Francoism to Democracy

The Spanish transition to democracy was triggered by the death of dictator Francisco Franco in 1975, which ended nearly four decades of dictatorship. The 1978 constitution defined Spain as a parliamentary monarchy with high levels of political decentralization. Due to the fragility of the previous democratic experience of 1930–1936, Spain's new institutional design was thought to provide stability, while attempting to accommodate the expected territorial conflict from regions that already had an autonomous status prior to dictatorship.[13]

The Spanish electoral system follows a PR formula. However, the small size of most constituencies acts as a corrective element favoring government formation, turning the formally proportional system into an almost majoritarian one.[14] The main beneficiaries of this system are mainstream national parties. Regional parties have generally acted as facilitators of government formation at the national level, whenever electoral results do not grant a majority in Congress to the national party with the most votes. Another important feature of the Spanish political system is its high level of decentralization. While Spain is not defined as a federal state, regional governments (the Autonomous Communities) exert in practice substantial prerogatives in terms of both legislation and competencies.[15]

The history of the Spanish political system since the end of the dictatorship can be decomposed into two periods (Figure 6.3). The first period is characterized by the formation of a two-party system and substantial government stability. The second period starts in 2014, following the aftermath of the Great Recession and the intensification of the independentist challenge in Catalonia, both of which led to a radical fragmentation and reconfiguration of the party system.

---

13. G. Vidal and I. Sánchez-Vítores, "Spain–Out with the Old: The Restructuring of Spanish Politics," in *European Party Politics in Times of Crisis*, ed. S. Hutter and H. Kriesi (Cambridge University Press, 2019), 75–94.

14. E. Del Pino and C. Colino, "National and Subnational Democracy in Spain: History, Models and Challenges" (Instituto de Politicas y Bienes Públicos Working Paper, 2010), http://ipp.csic.es/en/workpaper/national-subnational-democracy-spain-history-models-challenges.

15. L. Moreno, "Federalization and Ethnoterritorial Concurrence in Spain," *Publius: The Journal of Federalism* 27, no. 4 (1997): 65–84.

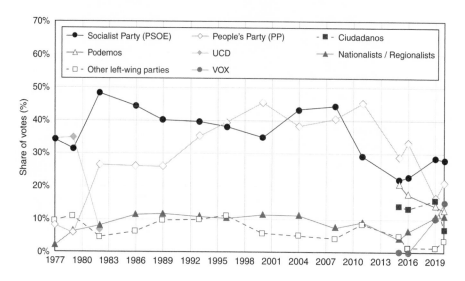

FIGURE 6.3. Election results in Spain, 1977–2019
*Data Source:* Authors' computations using official election results (see wpid.world).
*Note:* The figure shows the share of votes received by selected political parties or groups
of parties in general elections held in Spain between 1977 and 2019 (November 2019
elections represented as 2020). The Spanish Socialist Workers' Party (PSOE) received
28% of votes in the November 2019 elections.

The first two democratic elections (in 1977 and 1979) were dominated
by four main parties: the Socialist Party (Partido Socialista Obrero Es-
pañol, PSOE) and the Communist Party (Partido Comunista de España,
PCE) on the left, and the Union of the Democratic Centre (Unión de
Centro Democrático, UCD) and the People's Alliance (Alianza Popular,
AP) on the right. The Communist Party was the main opposition party
during Franco's regime, while the UCD incorporated opponents but also
reformist sectors from Francoism.[16] The PSOE progressively moderated
its political position, renouncing Marxist ideology in 1979, following its
underperformance in the elections of 1977 and 1979, which were won
by the UCD.

The 1982 elections redefined the political system in Spain. Following
a failed coup d'état led by Francoist military officials, the UCD collapsed
and was quickly replaced by the AP, later renamed the People's Party

16. J. Hopkin, *Party Formation and Democratic Transition in Spain: The Creation
and Collapse of the Union of the Democratic Centre* (Springer, 1999).

(Partido Popular, PP), as the main party on the right. The PSOE obtained the best results ever achieved by a single party during democracy, with close to 50 percent of the popular vote. The PSOE and PP have alternated in power since then. The PCE and its successor United Left (Izquierda Unida, IU) were relegated to a minor position, generally below 10 percent of the popular vote. Regionalist-nationalist parties consolidated a significant position in their constituencies, and often had a pivotal role facilitating the formation of governments and the approval of government budgets.

The financial crisis of 2008 and the subsequent European debt crisis led to a dramatic change in the party system.[17] Economic issues, together with corruption and political regeneration, gained prominence in the political debate. In addition, territorial tensions intensified in Catalonia, with an invigorated pro-independence movement. Since the 2014 European Parliament elections and the subsequent 2015 general elections, three new parties have consolidated a key position in Spanish politics. The first party to emerge was Podemos, a left-wing party focused on economic redistribution and political regeneration.[18] Ciudadanos, a center-liberal party originally from Catalonia, expanded in the rest of Spain by addressing demands for political renewal and defiance toward Catalan independentism.[19] In the general elections of April 2019, VOX, a far-right party of nationalist, conservative, and neoliberal ideology entered the Spanish parliament for the first time. The appearance of these three challenger parties has led to a multipolar system with fragile parliamentary majorities. After the inability to constitute a government forged new elections in November 2019, the PSOE and Podemos finally agreed to form the first coalition government since the end of the dictatorship.

17. Vidal and Sánchez-Vítores, "Spain"; M. Lisi, I. Llamazares, and M. Tsakatika, "Economic Crisis and the Variety of Populist Response: Evidence from Greece, Portugal and Spain," *West European Politics* 42, no. 6 (2019): 1284–1309; L. Orriols and G. Cordero, "The Breakdown of the Spanish Two-Party System: The Upsurge of Podemos and Ciudadanos in the 2015 General Election," *South European Society and Politics* 21, no. 4 (2016): 469–492.

18. Podemos has an alliance with several parties, including communists, greens, and several regional movements.

19. J. Rodríguez and A. Barrio, "Going National: Ciudadanos from Catalonia to Spain," *South European Society and Politics* 21, no. 4 (2016): 587–607.

### Class, Religion, and the Path toward
### a Multi-elite Party System

We explore the changing relationship between party choice and sociode-mographic characteristics using postelectoral surveys covering all general elections from 1979 to 2019.[20] In line with most Western democracies, right-wing parties tend to obtain significantly more votes from top-income earners across the whole period, with no strong trend (Figure 6.4). In contrast, while the 1980s saw the most-educated individuals voting more systematically for right-wing parties, today the bias toward the right still exists but it has been considerably reduced. Hence, Spain is approaching a multi-elite party system, but it has not fully reached it yet.

Spain's delay in reaching a multi-elite party system is likely linked to its tumultuous historical past. The Spanish Civil War (1936–1939) had been fought over socioeconomic cleavages, so these would inevitably be imprinted into partisanship. However, these political divisions were weakened during the redemocratization process for fear of democratic instability. The class vote intensified in 1982 as a consequence of the PSOE's breakthrough, as well as the displacement of the catchall UCD by the AP as the largest party on the center-right among middle- and upper-class voters. At the same time, the Communist Party lost much of its moderate middle-class electorate to a more homogeneous working-class constituency.[21] Nevertheless, class polarization weakened again from the 1990s, due to the success of the PP at broadening its electorate, as well as to the integration of the Communist Party into the IU electoral coalition, which transformed its base of support to include young, higher-educated voters, pushing the education gradient up.[22]

Similar to Italy, Spain upholds a strong religious cleavage. Catholic voters tend to vote less for left-wing parties, which are associated with the secular republican experience of the 1930s.[23] Religious polarization

20. See appendix Table BE1, wpid.world, for data sources.
21. Günther and Montero, "Anchors of Partisanship."
22. J. R. Montero and M. Torcal, "Value Change, Generational Replacement and Politics in Spain" (Centro de Estudios Avanzados en Ciencias Sociales Working Paper, 1994), https://epub.sub.uni-hamburg.de//epub/volltexte/2008/1920/pdf/1994_56.pdf. See also appendix Figure BB16, wpid.world.
23. M. Requena and D. de Revenga, "Religión y sociedad: La secularización de la sociedad española," in Tres décadas de cambio social en España, ed. M. Requena, D. de Revenga, and J. J. González Rodríguez (Alianza, 2005): 319–344. See also appendix Figure BB7, wpid.world.

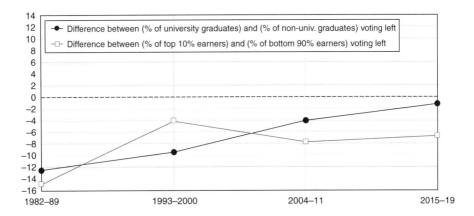

FIGURE 6.4. Toward a multi-elite party system in Spain, 1982–2019
*Data Source:* Authors' computations using Spanish electoral surveys (see wpid.world).
*Note:* The figure shows the relative support of university graduates and top-income earners for left-wing parties. In the 1980s, highest-educated and top-income voters were less likely to vote for left-wing parties than low-income and lower-educated voters. The left-wing vote has become increasingly associated with higher-educated voters, leading Spain to come closer to becoming a multi-elite party system. Estimates control for income/education, age, gender, employment status, marital status, religion, region, church attendance, sector of employment, type of employment, union membership, subjective social class, and location.

has weakened over time due to the increase in the number of voters with no religious affiliation, which rose from around 10 percent in the late 1970s to almost 30 percent in the late 2010s.[24] This secularization process is mainly the result of demographic changes: the younger generations have progressively become less religious.[25]

*Regional Identities and the Catalan Pro-independence Movement*
One of the most salient political conflicts in Spain revolves around regional identity. The Basque Country and Catalonia have been traditionally the regions in which nationalist tensions are most visible. Regional nationalist parties tend to prioritize ethnnolinguistic conflicts over so-

24. See appendix Table BE2, wpid.world.
25. L. Orriols, "Social Class, Religiosity, and Vote Choice in Spain, 1979–2008," in *Political Choice Matters: Explaining the Strength of Class and Religious Cleavages in Cross-national Perspective,* ed. G. Evans and N. D. de Graaf (Oxford University Press, 2013), 360–390.

cial class issues. Moreover, these regions have a higher income per capita than the Spanish average.[26] Hence, the left-wing nationalist vote is more represented among Spanish top-income earners than among middle- and low-income voters, so the income gradient at the national level becomes more negative when they are excluded from the analysis.[27] As the education gradient remains unchanged when including nationalists or not, their exclusion generates a larger distance between the income and education gradients, a pattern that is closer to the one observed in most Western democracies. The nationalist vote has thus hindered the development of a multi-elite party system in Spain.

Catalonia has been at the center of Spanish political conflict in recent years, due to the intensification of the pro-independence movement.[28] The peak in the regional conflict happened during the attempt in 2017 to hold a referendum on independence, which was not authorized by the Spanish Constitutional Court. The conflict not only increased the divisions inside Catalonia but also produced a strong backlash in the rest of Spain.

Figure 6.5 explores the difference in support for nationalist parties by income and education level in Catalonia. The nationalist vote is persistently associated with higher-income and more-educated voters, even after controlling for a large set of factors.[29] This tendency is consistent with the average high-income earner and higher-educated individual wanting their region to keep fiscal receipts for regional uses rather than redistribute them to the rest of Spain. Nonetheless, economic factors are

26. Instituto Nacional de Estadística, *Contabilidad regional de España* (INE, 2019).

27. See appendix Figure BC52, wpid.world.

28. The history of the Basque Country since the reestablishment of democracy has also been strongly influenced by the ethnoregionalist conflict, including the use of violence by the radical-left terrorist organization ETA in its attempt to obtain independence (the ETA ceased its armed activity in 2011 and dissolved permanently in 2018). See O. Strijbis and R. Leonisio, "Political Cleavages in the Basque Country: Meaning and Salience," *Regional and Federal Studies* 22, no. 5 (2012): 595–611.

29. The same income gradient is obtained using Catalan surveys from the Centre d'Estudis d'Opinió, even after controlling for family region of origin and region of birth. See G. Vidal and C. Gil, "La pela es la pela? Renta, clase social y secesionismo," *Agenda Pública*, December 22, 2019, http://agendapublica.elpais.com/la-pela-es-la-pela-renta-clase -social-y-secesionismo/. The nationalist income gradient in Catalonia is lower in the 2010s than the average of the 1980s–2000s, indicating that the recent pro-independence movement has also attracted the nationalist vote from other sectors of the population. See D. della Porta and M. Portos, "A Bourgeois Story? The Class Basis of Catalan Independentism," *Territory, Politics, Governance* (March 2020): 1–21.

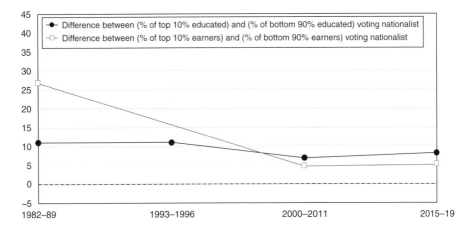

FIGURE 6.5. Nationalist vote, education, and income in Catalonia, Spain, 1982–2019
*Data Source:* Authors' computations using Spanish electoral surveys (see wpid.world).
*Note:* The figure shows the relative support of highest-educated and top-income voters for nationalist parties in Catalonia, after controlling for income/education, age, gender, employment status, marital status, religion, church attendance, type of employment, sector of employment, union membership, subjective social class, and location. During the 2015–2019 period, highest-educated voters were more likely to vote for nationalist parties by 8 percentage points on average.

not exclusive, and the cultural and identity channels seem to have also contributed to explaining the strong nationalist vote.[30] Age and rural-urban location are other important dimensions explaining the nationalist vote, with voters from rural areas and older generations showing higher support for nationalist parties.

### The Enlargement of the Party System

Following the Great Recession, the two-party system that existed since the reestablishment of democracy experienced a profound transformation. Nonetheless, the emergence of new parties has led to a shift in the vote from traditional parties (PP, PSOE, and IU) to new parties (VOX,

30. S. Ansolabehere and M. S. Puy, "Separatism and Identity: A Comparative Analysis of the Basque and Catalan Cases" (Málaga Economic Theory Research Center Working Paper, 2020), https://ideas.repec.org/p/mal/wpaper/2020-3.html; M. Clua i Fainé, "Identidad y política en Cataluña: El auge del independentismo en el nacionalismo catalán actual," *Quaderns-e de l'Institut Català d'Antropologia* 19, no. 2 (2014): 79–99.

*Table 6.2*  The Structure of Political Cleavages in Spain, 2019

| | Share of Votes Received (%) | | | | | |
|---|---|---|---|---|---|---|
| | Podemos | PSOE | Ciudadanos | PP | VOX | Nationalist parties |
| **Education** | | | | | | |
| Primary | 7% | 38% | 7% | 32% | 5% | 8% |
| Secondary | 16% | 27% | 11% | 16% | 16% | 10% |
| Tertiary | 20% | 22% | 15% | 17% | 9% | 12% |
| Postgraduate | 18% | 20% | 21% | 17% | 5% | 19% |
| **Income** | | | | | | |
| Bottom 50% | 13% | 35% | 9% | 23% | 11% | 6% |
| Middle 40% | 17% | 26% | 13% | 15% | 14% | 10% |
| Top 10% | 15% | 20% | 14% | 16% | 15% | 17% |
| **Age** | | | | | | |
| 20–39 | 23% | 21% | 14% | 11% | 17% | 8% |
| 40–59 | 15% | 28% | 13% | 16% | 13% | 11% |
| 60+ | 7% | 35% | 7% | 31% | 7% | 11% |
| **Location** | | | | | | |
| Urban areas | 15% | 28% | 12% | 18% | 13% | 10% |
| Rural areas | 6% | 30% | 8% | 28% | 10% | 13% |
| **Religion** | | | | | | |
| Catholic | 6% | 30% | 13% | 26% | 15% | 7% |
| Other | 17% | 39% | 9% | 10% | 9% | 11% |
| No religion | 35% | 24% | 8% | 4% | 7% | 17% |

*Data Source:* Authors' computations using Spanish electoral surveys (see wpid.world).
*Note:* The table shows the average share of votes received by the main Spanish political parties by selected individual characteristics during the two elections held in 2019. Podemos was supported by 7% of primary-educated voters, compared to 18% of voters with postgraduate degrees.

Ciudadanos, and Podemos) within each ideological bloc, not to a complete reconfiguration of voting preferences.[31]

Table 6.2 shows the composition of the Spanish party system along different socioeconomic dimensions in the last two elections held in 2019. Podemos and Ciudadanos have a relatively similar profile: they obtain

31. T. D. Lancaster, "The Spanish General Elections of 2015 and 2016: A New Stage in Democratic Politics?," *West European Politics* 40, no. 4 (2017): 919–937; P. Simón, "The Multiple Spanish Elections of April and May 2019: The Impact of Territorial and Left-Right Polarisation," *South European Society and Politics* 25, no. 1 (2020): 1–34.

their best results among higher-educated, higher-income, young, and urban voters. In contrast, VOX is overrepresented among voters with a secondary degree, and although it obtains important support from young top-income earners, it also collects a significant share of votes from bottom-income earners. This could signal its potential capacity to penetrate the least-favored groups in the future.

Overall, the new party system of Spain resembles that of other Western European countries, where traditional parties coexist with a consolidated radical left (Podemos), a center-liberal party (Ciudadanos), and a far-right party (VOX). The most notable difference is that VOX does not seem to have captured (at least as of yet) the vote from low-income and lower-educated voters. The difference might be due to the fact that the far right arose in Spain endorsing neoliberal policies and as a nationalist reaction to the Catalan independence movement, not on the back of the lower educated or low-income earners feeling left behind.[32] Furthermore, while Podemos fits particularly well the model of the "Brahmin left," the PSOE still maintains important support among the older low-income earners and the lowest educated. This has further delayed the emergence of a multi-elite party system in Spain.

## Portugal

### From Salazarism to Democracy

The Portuguese transition to democracy started in 1974 with a bloodless military coup that put an end to nearly five decades of dictatorship. In 1976, a new constitution was approved, defining Portugal as a semipresidential system with extensive powers for the president, which were later significantly reduced in the 1982 amendment of the constitution.[33] The Portuguese electoral system rests on a PR formula, whose exact configuration nonetheless limits the capacity of small parties to be elected, as it

32. See M. Grau Creus, "Checkmate to the Spanish Decentralization? The Decline of Public Support for Spain's Autonomous Communities," in *Identities, Trust, and Cohesion in Federal Systems: Public Perspectives,* ed. J. Jedwab and J. Kincaid (McGill–Queen's University Press, 2019), 57. The ideology of VOX is different from most European far-right political formations today. See M. Golder, "Far Right Parties in Europe," *Annual Review of Political Science* 19 (2016): 477–497.

33. M. Costa, A. Costa, and P. Magalhães, "The Political Institutions of Portuguese Democracies," in *Portugal in the Twenty-First Century,* ed. Sebastián Royo (Lexington Books, 2012), 23–48.

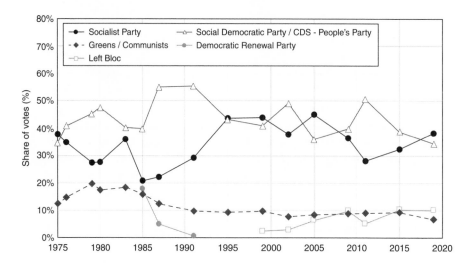

FIGURE 6.6. Election results in Portugal, 1975–2019
*Data Source:* Authors' computations using official election results (see wpid.world).
*Note:* The figure shows the share of votes received by selected political parties or groups of parties in legislative elections held in Portugal between 1975 and 2019. The Socialist Party received 38% of votes in 2019.

uses the closed-list D'Hondt method, which generates a strong bias in favor of large parties.

The history of the Portuguese party system since redemocratization can be decomposed into three periods: 1973–1987, 1987–2015, and 2015–2019 (Figure 6.6). In the first period, Portugal was characterized by a multiparty configuration and short-lived governments, with four parties obtaining significant support. The main political formations, with the exception of the Communist Party, were created right before or after the 1974 revolution.[34] On the right of the spectrum, two main parties emerged: the liberal Social Democratic Party (Partido Social Democrata, PSD) and the Christian democratic Center Democratic Party (Centro Democrático e Social, CDS).[35] On the left, two parties coexisted: the Socialist Party

34. The Portuguese Communist Party was created in 1921 and strongly opposed Salazar's dictatorship. Since the 1980s, the PCP has created alliances with the Greens and other small left-wing formations. See A. Freire, "Party System Change in Portugal, 1974–2005: The Role of Social, Political and Ideological Factors," *Portuguese Journal of Social Science* 4, no. 2 (2005): 81–100.
35. The CDS later evolved into the Social Democratic Centre–Popular Party (CDS–PP).

(Partido Socialista, PS) and the Portuguese Communist Party (Partido Comunista Português, PCP). The PS and the PSD became the two dominant parties. Both led government formations during this period, either from a minority position with external support in the parliament, or in coalitions.

The 1987 legislative elections initiated a second period in the party system of Portugal, which consolidated a two-party system. On the left, the PS became hegemonic, while the PCP lost electoral support, from a maximum of nearly 20 percent in the mid-1980s to below 10 percent in the early 1990s. On the right, the PSD consolidated as the predominant party on the right, while the CDS remained in a minor position, with less than 10 percent of the popular vote. From 1987 onward, government formation was more stable than in the preceding years, with most governments lasting the full four-year mandate stipulated by the constitution. In the absence of single-party majorities in the parliament, the PSD found its natural ally in the CDS. The PS drew on the support of the center-right when forming minority governments. Hence, this period was marked by a cordon sanitaire to the radical left and a tendency for mainstream parties to compete for the political center.[36] During this period a new party also emerged, the Left Bloc, which was formed by the merger of old radical-left parties. The new party progressively augmented its electoral support until reaching 10 percent of the popular vote in 2015.

The third period in the Portuguese party system started in 2015. It did not involve a rupture with the preceding two-party system, but rather a reconfiguration of the positioning of the two main parties, the PS and the PSD, both of which turned to more extreme positions regarding the postrecession austerity measures brought about by the "troika" (the European Central Bank, the European Commission, and the International Monetary Fund).[37] The PSD proposed to go beyond the troika and reduce the role of the state in society by revisiting the welfare model. The PS instead focused on alleviating the impact of the troika-sponsored measures, while keeping a pro-European orientation complying with the

36. F. Ferreira da Silva and M. S. Mendes, "Portugal: A Tale of Apparent Stability and Surreptitious Transformation," in *European Party Politics in Times of Crisis,* ed. S. Hutter and H. Kriesi (Cambridge University Press, 2019), 139–164.

37. Ferreira da Silva and Mendes, "Portugal."

EU's fiscal rules.[38] This experience is different from the one observed in other Southern European countries like Spain and Italy, where the emergence of challenger parties since the Great Recession has led to a new multiparty system. The absence of such a political transformation in Portugal could potentially be related to the fact that its economic situation was already delicate in the pre-2008 period and voters were familiarized with the austerity measures that had already been implemented by the two mainstream parties.[39]

The shift of the PS toward the left culminated in the two new scenarios following the elections of 2015 and 2019, where the PS governed in minority with external support, for the first time, from the two main radical-left formations—the Left Bloc and the Communists. This alliance put an end to the historical position of the two mainstream parties, which had always excluded the radical left from any government agreement, as in Spain until 2019.

### A Stable Single-Elite Party System

We analyze the sociodemographic characteristics of left-wing and right-wing voters using postelectoral surveys covering all Portuguese legislative elections from 1975 to 2019.[40] In contrast to Italy and Spain, Portugal is characterized by a relatively stable "single-elite party system": both highest-educated and top-income voters have shown much higher support for right-wing parties (Figure 6.7).[41] This makes Portugal quite exceptional in the Western European political landscape, where there has been a profound transformation of the educational cleavage, with more-educated individuals becoming more supportive of left-wing political parties.

This singular evolution of the education gradient in Portugal—following a decreasing trend since 1990—can be attributed to four main factors. First, the two mainstream parties, the PS and the PSD, did not emerge out of grassroots class-based cleavages, and they were created right before

---

38. J. M. Fernandes, "The Seeds for Party System Change? The 2015 Portuguese General Election," *West European Politics* 39, no. 4 (2016): 890–900.

39. Ferreira da Silva and Mendes, "Portugal."

40. See appendix Table CC1, wpid.world, for data sources.

41. However, the education and income gradients are less negative before controls. See appendix Figures CB18 and CB19, wpid.world.

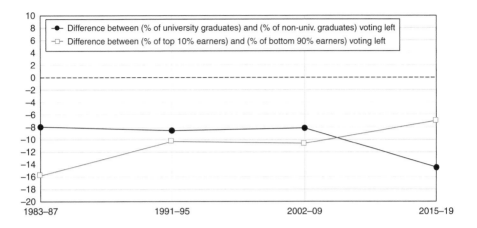

FIGURE 6.7. The absence of a multi-elite party system in Portugal, 1983–2019
*Data Source:* Authors' computations using Portuguese electoral surveys (see wpid.world).
*Note:* The figure shows the relative support of university graduates and top-income voters for socialists/communists/greens/the Left Bloc. Both highest-educated and top-income voters have remained significantly less likely to vote for left-wing parties throughout the period considered. In contrast to the majority of Western democracies, Portugal has therefore not become a multi-elite party system. Estimates control for income/education, age, gender, religion, church attendance, employment status, subjective social class, union membership, region, and location.

or after the 1974 revolution.[42] As they did not fear the emergence of a strong conservative party after the experience of the dictatorship, they opted to follow a "catchall strategy" and lacked well-defined ideological positions to broaden their electorates.[43] This explains why Portugal's education gradient became stronger in recent years, when the two mainstream parties turned to more extreme positions.

Second, although party polarization was very weak among the two mainstream parties until the 2000s, the Communist Party did adopt a mass-based model based on a pronounced class cleavage and articulated through institutionalized ties to the largest labor union.[44] It was the only

42. A. Alexandre, S. Zartaloudis, and Y. Papadopoulos, "How Party Linkages Shape Austerity Politics: Clientelism and Fiscal Adjustment in Greece and Portugal during the Eurozone Crisis," *Journal of European Public Policy* 22, no. 3 (2015): 315–334.

43. Ferreira da Silva and Mendes, "Portugal."

44. Ferreira da Silva and Mendes, "Portugal."

party with a well-defined left-wing ideology that showed significant levels of organization. Hence, thanks to its alliance with green movements, it managed to keep a significant vote share, with ample support from working-class voters, which contributed to the stability of the education and income gradients.[45] This contrasts with communist parties in the majority of Western democracies, which have lost importance over time or have transformed into more moderate and cross-class formations.

Third, Portugal does not completely escape the trends in income and education cleavages observed in other Western European countries. The predominance of the left among the lowest-educated and low-income earners is mostly the result of the popularity of the traditional left (the socialists and communists) within these groups of voters. In contrast, the Left Bloc seems to attract highest-educated voters and top-income earners, in line with the voting profile of Podemos in Spain. However, the difference is that this "Brahmin left" is still far from attracting a sufficient vote share, even from the highest-educated cohorts, to generate a realignment of voting preferences similar to that observed in other European countries.

Finally, political conflicts over sociocultural values have remained weak.[46] The country has no center-periphery tensions, immigration is not a salient issue, and Eurosceptic sentiments are also not widespread. Hence, the stability of the income and education gradient is also related to the fact that the main important recent division has been around the economic recession.

### Class, Religion, and Other Socioeconomic Cleavages

Consistent with a weak party polarization among mainstream parties until the 1990s and their turn toward more extreme positions since the mid-2000s, "subjective" class cleavages (measured from individuals' identification to specific social classes) seem to have risen in recent years after a period of decline (Figure 6.8). Notice that this rise is however not robust to controls for income and education, revealing that it is precisely the growing impact of these two variables on the vote that explains the comeback of class voting. The strength of the traditional left among the low-educated and low-income electorate is also related to age, region, and

45. See appendix Figures CC11 and CC12, wpid.world.
46. A. Gethin, "Cleavage Structures and Distributive Politics" (master's thesis, Paris School of Economics, 2018), chapter 8.

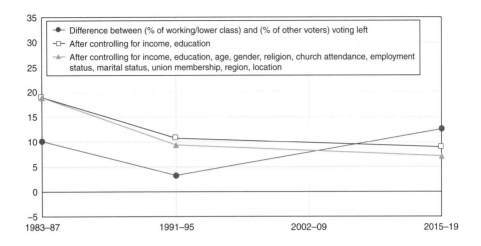

FIGURE 6.8. Class voting in Portugal, 1983–2019
*Data Source:* Authors' computations using Portuguese electoral surveys (see wpid.world).
*Note:* The figure shows the difference between the share of voters identifying with the
"working class" or the "lower class" and the share of voters identifying with the
"middle class" or with "no class" voting for socialists/communists/greens/the Left
Bloc, before and after controls. During the 2015–2019 period, self-identified working-
class voters were more likely to vote for left-wing parties by 13 percentage points.

the nativist cleavage. The young initially voted more for the left, but this
has changed in the last two elections (Table 6.3).[47] This reversal is different
from what we find in other Southern European countries, where the young
have consistently shown higher support for left-wing formations.

Table 6.3 shows that Portugal, unlike Italy and Spain, does not have
a strong regional conflict, although some regional differences exist.
The most notable is the high support for the left in urban locations (as
in other Western European countries, see Chapter 1) and a concentration of the left vote in the capital city of Lisbon and the traditional left
vote in the Alentejo region.[48] The latter is a highly industrialized area
with high degrees of worker mobilization around left parties. Moreover, the support for the traditional left is also very high among voters
from ex-colonies, with nearly 60 percent of voters born in Brazil supporting the PS.

47. See also appendix Figure CB15, CC5, and CC14, wpid.world.
48. See also appendix Figure CB9, wpid.world.

*Table 6.3*   The Structure of Political Cleavages in Portugal, 2015–2019

| | | Share of Votes Received (%) | | |
| | Left Bloc | Socialist Party | Greens/ Communists | Social Democratic Party/Social Democratic Center-People's Party |
|---|---|---|---|---|
| **Education** | | | | |
| Primary | 5% | 43% | 11% | 39% |
| Secondary | 13% | 37% | 9% | 37% |
| Tertiary | 14% | 24% | 6% | 52% |
| **Income** | | | | |
| Bottom 50% | 8% | 43% | 10% | 37% |
| Middle 40% | 9% | 35% | 10% | 41% |
| Top 10% | 15% | 24% | 6% | 54% |
| **Religion** | | | | |
| No religion | 24% | 32% | 17% | 23% |
| Catholic | 9% | 37% | 9% | 42% |
| Other | 15% | 42% | 7% | 34% |
| **Age** | | | | |
| 20–39 | 15% | 31% | 6% | 43% |
| 49–59 | 12% | 35% | 10% | 39% |
| 60+ | 6% | 43% | 11% | 39% |
| **Country of Birth** | | | | |
| Portugal | 10% | 37% | 10% | 40% |
| Brazil | 10% | 59% | 0% | 30% |
| Other ex-colony | 9% | 31% | 12% | 48% |
| **Region** | | | | |
| North | 10% | 38% | 5% | 42% |
| Center | 8% | 29% | 5% | 57% |
| Lisbon | 12% | 40% | 16% | 29% |
| Alentejo | 7% | 54% | 23% | 12% |
| Algarve | 15% | 36% | 11% | 36% |

*Data Source:* Authors' computations using Portuguese electoral surveys (see wpid.world).
*Note:* The table shows the average share of votes received by the main Portuguese political parties by selected individual characteristics over the 2015–2019 period. During this period, 43% of primary-educated voters voted for the Socialist Party, compared to 24% of university graduates.

## Ireland

### *The Irish Party System since Independence*

The Irish political landscape owes its particular shape and color to the struggle for independence from the United Kingdom and to its late but rapid socioeconomic development. The struggle for independence had its strongest expression in Sinn Féin—Ireland's oldest existing political party, founded in 1905. The Labour Party, marshaling the trade union movement, opted for a more pragmatic approach to the model of state when it was founded in 1912 in a context more favorable to "Home Rule" (self-government within the United Kingdom of Great Britain and Ireland). The First World War, and especially the Easter Rising rebellion of 1916, marked a turning point for Irish radical republicanism. This was expressed in Sinn Féin's sweeping 1918 general election victory, followed by its declaration of the republic and formation of a sovereign parliament in Dublin. This state of affairs provoked a series of seismic events including the Irish War of Independence (1919–1921) and the signing of the Anglo-Irish Treaty (1921), which established the Irish Free State and led to the Irish Civil War (1922–1923) and the partition of Ireland into North and South.[49]

The civil war thus became the foundational political cleavage in twentieth-century Ireland, which saw a pro-Anglo-Irish Treaty faction (the Labour Party and some Sinn Féin members of parliament, or MPs) fighting an anti-Treaty faction (the other members and supporters of Sinn Féin). The anti-Treaty side of Sinn Féin was itself split between abstentionists (elected MPs refusing to take their seats in Parliament) and non-abstentionists. After the war ended in victory for the pro-Treaty government, the pro-Treaty Sinn Féin MPs went on to form a new party in 1923, which eventually became Fine Gael in 1933. The nonabstentionist faction of Sinn Féin broke away from the party to form Fianna Fáil in 1926. The remaining Sinn Féin maintained the policy of abstentionism up until the 1987 general election; thus, for most of the twentieth century, the party effectively excluded itself from Irish electoral politics (see Figure 6.9), preferring to fight for a united Ireland (north and south) outside the consti-

---

49. D. Ferriter, *The Transformation of Ireland 1900–2000* (Profile Books, 2004).

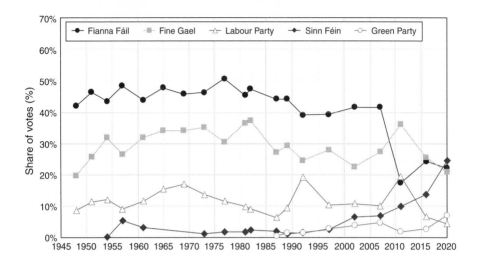

FIGURE 6.9. Election results in Ireland, 1948–2020
*Data Source:* Authors' computations using official election results (see wpid.world).
*Note:* The figure shows the share of votes received by selected political parties or groups of parties in general elections held in Ireland between 1948 and 2020. Sinn Féin received 25% of votes in 2020.

tutional fold. It was only in 2002 that Sinn Féin's parliamentary pragmatism began to bear fruit.[50]

At the 1932 election, Fianna Fáil became the largest party in Ireland, followed by Fine Gael's predecessor, the pro-Treaty Cumann na nGaedheal, which had dominated government during the previous decade. From 1932 to 2011, Fianna Fáil topped every election without interruption, often forming minority governments with parliamentary support of either the Labour Party or independent deputies, and later forming coalition governments with the liberal Progressive Democrats (PDs)—formed in 1985, mainly by politicians from Fianna Fáil, but also some from Fine Gael, and dissolved in 2009—and the Green Party (formed in 1981). Since 2011, Fine Gael has shared government twice, once with the Labour Party and once with independent MPs in a minority government. The 2020 election proved to be historic, as it led to the first-ever governmental

50. S. Whiting, "Mainstream Revolutionaries: Sinn Féin as a 'Normal' Political Party?," *Terrorism and Political Violence* 28, no. 3 (2016): 541–560.

coalition between Fianna Fáil and Fine Gael (along with the Greens), after the rise of Sinn Féin produced a hung parliament.

Ideological differences between parties in Ireland have been relatively narrow as compared to other countries, explaining the wide consensus on many issues.[51] This can be partly attributed to the legacy of the civil war on degrees of nationalism, and to the role of religion. Fine Gael originated as the pro-Commonwealth, conservative-Protestant, Home Rule party, favoring free market policies. Fianna Fáil is often ascribed the "catchall" label, highly pragmatic and overtly ambiguous. It was initially anti-Commonwealth, more constitutionally republican and conservative-Catholic, supporting industrial protectionism, social housing, and more ample social benefits. Consensus has also been facilitated by Ireland's unique proportional representation single-transferable vote (PR-STV) system, which allows voters to rank candidates in their constituency in order of preference on the ballot. These preferences then determine vote transfers between candidates vying for a seat, which encourages candidate-based voting, as well as cross-party preference voting, facilitating bipartisan parliamentary agreements for government.[52]

The policy differences between Fianna Fáil and Fine Gael were reduced over time to distinctions over degrees of nationalism and social liberties, with Fianna Fáil leading on the former and Fine Gael leading on the latter. In the economic sphere, there has been less variation between them, especially since the 1990s, with Fianna Fáil favoring slightly more active government and leaning on its historical proximity to the working class, particularly among the rural and elderly populations. This convergence facilitated the 2020 coalition deal between the two historically hegemonic parties.[53]

Sinn Féin's recent growth on the left of the political spectrum contrasts with their decades-long time spent on the fringes of parliamentary politics. They have sought to fill the void left by Fianna Fáil's drift to the

51. P. Mair, "Explaining the Absence of Class Politics in Ireland," in *The Development of Industrial Society in Ireland*, ed. J. H. Goldthorpe and C. T. Whelan (Oxford University Press, 1992), 383–410.

52. M. Gallagher, "Ireland: The Discreet Charm of PR-STV," in *The Politics of Electoral Systems*, ed. M. Gallagher and P. Mitchell (Oxford University Press, 2005), 511–532.

53. Today, expert survey respondents and electoral survey respondents coincide in placing Fianna Fáil and Fine Gael on the right of the political spectrum, with Fine Gael being a few points more to the right. See S. Müller and A. Regan, "Aidan Regan: Greens Must Avoid Falling into Deficit Trap," *Business Post*, June 7, 2020, https://www.businesspost.ie /columnists/aidan-regan-greens-must-avoid-falling-into-deficit-trap-87a3571a.

center-right, focusing on economic issues and attracting many protest votes, especially after the financial crisis of 2008 laid bare the management errors of previous Fianna Fáil governments, and the austerity drive of the subsequent Fine Gael–Labour government.[54] Their growing popularity has been facilitated partly by their self-exclusion from Irish parliamentary politics for sixty years and their blank historical record in government, as well as by the younger generations' lack of historical memory of the party's past associations with republican violence. One can contrast this experience with Ireland's second-oldest party and principal parliamentary force on the left, the Labour Party. By eschewing from the outset the nationalist debate dividing Fianna Fáil and Fine Gael, the Labour Party remained a compromise party for much of its existence, supporting coalitions with each of the main parties.[55]

An important factor explaining the Labour Party's (and more generally, the left's) difficulty in occupying a significant space in Irish parliamentary politics was the influence of religion, and particularly the Catholic Church. Ireland's population is overwhelmingly Catholic: by the 1990s Catholics still comprised 90 percent of the population. Secularization happened late, but then very quickly: the share of voters attending church once a month or more declined from 80 percent in the 1990s to 28 percent by 2020.[56] Centuries of English colonial rule had brought about a Catholic-Protestant cleavage, which tilted in favor of Catholicism after Irish independence. The Catholic Church supported Home Rule, the Anglo-Irish Treaty, and subsequently, with the rise of Fianna Fáil, a form of nationalism that did not disrupt existing distributions of wealth or traditional family values. Secular republicanism, especially from a socialist (or social democratic) perspective, had little chance of gaining ground. Therefore, a clear left-right partisan split, coupling economic and social issues, could not be observed with the same clarity in Ireland as compared to other countries, at least until very recently. The divisions hinged on varying degrees of social conservativism and economic protectionism.[57]

54. M. Marsh, D. M. Farrell, and T. Reidy, eds., *The Post-crisis Irish Voter: Voting Behaviour in the Irish 2016 General Election* (Manchester University Press, 2018).
55. Ferriter, *Transformation of Ireland.*
56. See appendix Table DA2, wpid.world. This shift was fueled by revelations in the 1990s related to the church's handling of child sex abuse claims and its management of publicly funded services in health and education.
57. Ferriter, *Transformation of Ireland.*

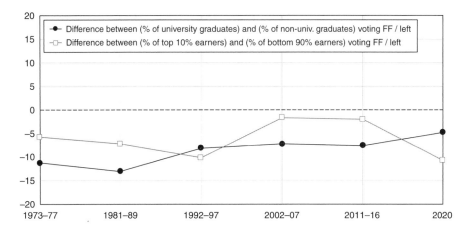

FIGURE 6.10. The absence of a multi-elite party system in Ireland, 1973–2020
*Data Source:* Authors' computations using Irish political attitudes surveys (see wpid.world).
*Note:* The figure shows the relative support of university graduates and top-income voters for Fianna Fáil (FF) and left-wing parties (Labour/Green/Other left). Both highest-educated and top-income voters have remained significantly less likely to vote FF/left throughout the period considered. In contrast to the majority of Western democracies, Ireland has therefore not become a multi-elite party system. Estimates control for income/education, age, gender, employment status, marital status, religion, and church attendance.

## The Absence of a Multi-elite Party System in Ireland

We now analyze long-term electoral dynamics in Ireland by combining a number of political attitudes surveys conducted since 1973.[58] Figure 6.10 depicts the relative votes for Fianna Fáil, Sinn Féin, the Labour Party, the Greens, and other left groupings among the highest-educated and top-income voters since the 1970s. High-income voters are not less likely to vote for Fine Gael and other right-wing parties today than they were in the past. There was some convergence in the voting patterns of these voters in the early 2000s, but the 2020 election returned the trend: top-income voters were biased against Fianna Fáil and the left by 11 percentage points, the highest it has ever been. This stands in contrast to what we observe in most of the Western countries studied in this book (see Chapter 1), in which the income gradient has remained stable or has decreased in the long run. Even more distinct from the trends in other

58. See appendix Table DA1, wpid.world, for data sources.

democracies has been the lack of a complete reversal in the education cleavage in Ireland: while highest-educated voters have become relatively more likely to vote for Fianna Fáil and the left over time, the gradient has remained significantly negative. Most importantly, while in other countries new parties on the left have attracted high-education voters, in Ireland we see the reverse phenomenon: the emergence of a new left party, Sinn Féin, forging a clear left-right class cleavage that was not present historically.

The reason why we place Fianna Fáil alongside the left is mainly practical, as left-wing parties do not otherwise make up enough votes to constitute a critical bloc, especially before the Great Recession. If we place Fianna Fáil alongside the right, class-based cleavages shrink, with the exception of the income cleavage in 2020, owing to the rise of Sinn Féin.[59] This is because Fianna Fáil was historically dominant among the lower-educated and lower-income electorates. The magnitude of Sinn Féin's appeal to these classes in 2020 is comparable to Fianna Fáil's in prior years.[60] The Labour vote is ironically the least determined by socioeconomic class.[61] Moreover, previous research has found that voters from both Fianna Fáil and Sinn Féin share relatively similar "populist" attitudes toward elites and national identity.[62]

Thus, Irish politics has not fully transformed into a multi-elite party system. Class has recently become more important for left-right voting; what has changed in 2020 is who is uniting the disadvantaged classes, compared to previous elections. Table 6.4 puts the spotlight on the historic 2020 election. Sinn Féin polled higher among primary-educated and poor voters, while Fianna Fáil captured more of the middle groups in both categories. Labour, and especially the Greens, seemed to be tilted more heavily toward the middle and upper classes in these respects. If anything, the "Brahmin left" is present in these parties, most notably in the Green Party, but it is marginal in the aggregate. Religion and age seem to distinguish left and right somewhat better: parties to the left of Fianna Fáil

---

59. See appendix Figure DC15, wpid.world.

60. See appendix Figures DD36 and DD37, wpid.world.

61. In appendix Figures DD1 to DD34, wpid.world, we present the detailed structure of the vote for Fianna Fáil, Fine Gael, Sinn Féin, and the Labour Party.

62. T. Reidy and J. Suiter, "Who Is the Populist Irish Voter?," *Journal of the Statistical and Social Inquiry Society of Ireland* 56, no. 1 (2017): 117–131.

*Table 6.4*　The Structure of Political Cleavages in Ireland, 2020

| | Share of Votes Received (%) | | | | |
|---|---|---|---|---|---|
| | Sinn Féin | Labour Party | Green Party | Fianna Fáil | Fine Gael |
| **Education** | | | | | |
| Primary | 43% | 4% | 1% | 23% | 13% |
| Secondary | 27% | 4% | 7% | 24% | 19% |
| Tertiary | 20% | 5% | 8% | 21% | 24% |
| **Income** | | | | | |
| Bottom 50% | 30% | 4% | 5% | 21% | 17% |
| Middle 40% | 20% | 5% | 8% | 25% | 22% |
| Top 10% | 16% | 4% | 8% | 22% | 33% |
| **Religion** | | | | | |
| No religion | 29% | 5% | 16% | 12% | 15% |
| Catholic | 23% | 4% | 3% | 28% | 22% |
| Protestant | 16% | 8% | 7% | 13% | 40% |
| **Age** | | | | | |
| 20–39 | 27% | 5% | 14% | 16% | 18% |
| 40–59 | 26% | 4% | 5% | 21% | 20% |
| 60+ | 20% | 5% | 4% | 30% | 24% |

*Data Source:* Authors' computations using Irish political attitudes surveys (see wpid.world).

*Note:* The table shows the share of votes received by the main Irish political parties by selected individual characteristics in 2020. Sinn Féin was supported by 43% of primary-educated voters during this election, compared to 20% of university graduates.

are supported more by nonreligious and relatively younger cohorts.[63] Fine Gael voters have been historically more rural than urban, with Fianna Fáil's voters only slightly more rural, and Labour having a very large urban bias.[64] We also find evidence that Sinn Féin appeared to be urban biased, but they increased their support relatively more in rural areas from 2002 to 2016, as they captured votes from the mainstream parties.[65]

63. The magnitude of the religious division has waned over time for the different parties. See appendix Figure DC13, wpid.world.

64. See appendix Figures DD9, DD18, and DD27, wpid.world.

65. Authors' computations using Comparative Study of Electoral Systems data.

The emergence of a "workers'" party in Ireland (Sinn Féin), along with the severe effects of the financial crisis and postcrisis austerity on its economic model, may explain why much of the underprivileged population has increasingly leaned toward the left. Income growth (after redistribution) has overwhelmingly benefited the top of the distribution a decade on since the economic crisis.[66] The novel focus of Sinn Féin on redistributive issues and public services may also explain the absence of an extreme-right party in Ireland, compared to other countries.[67]

66. See appendix Figure DD35, wpid.world.
67. E. O'Malley, "Why Is There No Radical Right Party in Ireland?," *West European Politics* 31, no. 5 (2008): 960–977.

# Party System Transformation and the Structure of Political Cleavages in Austria, Belgium, the Netherlands, and Switzerland, 1967–2019

CARMEN DURRER DE LA SOTA, AMORY GETHIN,
AND CLARA MARTÍNEZ-TOLEDANO

## Introduction

How has the emergence of new movements and ideologies transformed socioeconomic conflicts in Western Europe in the past fifty years? This chapter approaches this question by documenting the evolution of political cleavages in Belgium, the Netherlands, Switzerland, and Austria. These four countries provide interesting case studies to understand sources of political change in advanced democracies, as their party systems have undergone an exceptionally deep process of realignment and fragmentation. Having been torn apart by linguistic, regional, and religious conflicts, they share a common history of consensus decision-making, and they are often considered to be archetypical examples of consociational democracies, where the interests of antagonistic "pillars" were mediated by power-sharing agreements between the different parties. This cooperative dimension of democratic politics has remained a common feature of these four democracies, but the weakening of historical cleavages, the emergence of new political streams, and the rise of new divides have significantly transformed their party systems.[1]

We are grateful to Gabriel Gazeau and Thomas Piketty for their useful advice.

1. B. O'Leary, "Consociation in the Present," *Swiss Political Science Review* 25, no. 4 (2020): 556–574.

The 1980s and subsequent decades saw the proliferation of new political parties and a remarkable complexification of the political landscape. Green parties on the left and anti-immigration parties on the right, in particular, have increasingly challenged traditional Christian democratic, conservative, liberal, social democratic, and socialist forces. This evolution was most radical in Switzerland, where the far right (the Swiss People's Party) and the greens (the Green Party and the Green Liberal Party) now top the polls. While this is not yet the case in Belgium, the Netherlands, and Austria, a comparable disintegration of historical party systems has taken place, and a similar scenario could well arise in the future.

One of the most striking transformations of political cleavages in Western democracies has been the reversal of the educational cleavage and the emergence of "multi-elite party systems": while conservative and affiliated parties continue to be supported by top-income voters, highest-educated voters have gradually shifted from the "right" toward the "left" (see Chapters 2 to 6). The main finding of this chapter is to show that the exact same reversal took place in Belgium, the Netherlands, Switzerland, and Austria, though with interesting variations. In two-party systems such as the United States and the United Kingdom (see Chapter 2), this shift has essentially taken place within the main parties. In the four countries studied in this chapter, by contrast, the decline of traditional parties and the rise of new parties allows us to contrast new and old forces, and hence to shed light on the emergence of multi-elite party systems. Our results show that it was not only the rise of new green and anti-immigration parties, but in many cases also changes within old parties, that drove the shift of higher-educated voters toward left-wing parties.

Belgium's historical regionalization of politics has persisted to the present and there are strong differences in support for traditional parties between Flanders and Wallonia. The socialists are mainly supported in Wallonia, whereas the liberals and the Christian democrats are more popular in Flanders. Despite these regional divides, we still observe the same transition toward a multi-elite party system as in other Western countries. New actors have played the most decisive role in this process: green parties have become increasingly popular among university graduates, while Flemish nationalists have received growing support from lower-educated voters. The reversal of the education cleavage, however, does not seem to have fully occurred yet, which could be explained by

the ability of far-left and socialist parties to still gather an important share of the lower educated, while at the same time having succeeded at preventing the emergence of the far right in Wallonia thus far.

In the Netherlands, too, the emergence of a multi-elite party system has been associated with the rise of new liberal (D66), environmentalist (GroenLinks), and anti-immigration (the Pim Fortuyn List and the Party for Freedom) forces. This transformation has led to an exceptional fragmentation of the Dutch party system as well as to an early reversal of the educational cleavage, with higher-educated voters becoming more likely to vote for left-wing and liberal parties as early as the 1980s. Socialists and social democrats continue to attract some sections of their traditional constituencies, but they have seen their vote shares collapse and are now competing with the Party for Freedom in the representation of the low-income and lower-educated electorate. In addition to the sociocultural and environmentalist issues promoted by the liberals and the greens, a new nativist cleavage has emerged, mirrored by the massive support of Muslim voters for the left (or against the right), which has contributed to the blurring of traditional class and religious (Catholic versus Protestant) cleavages in recent years.

Switzerland is the country where the shift of the higher educated toward the left has been the most dramatic. This can be explained by the surge of the greens and the far right, but also by the transformation of historical parties. The Swiss People's Party, now the most successful anti-immigration force in Europe, has proved to be exceptionally popular among lower-educated voters in rural areas, while the greens have captured a growing share of the higher-educated vote in urban areas. Socialists and communists have nonetheless undergone a profound transformation too, and now achieve their best results among the higher educated. Unlike in Belgium, language divisions have played a rather small role in Swiss federal elections and have weakened over time, as the Swiss People's Party, historically tied to German-speaking Switzerland, has gained increasing support in the French- and Italian-speaking regions.

Finally, in Austria, we find that the emergence of a multi-elite party system has been driven in part by the emergence of the greens in the 1980s, disproportionately supported by university graduates in urban areas, as well as by the decreasing support for the Social Democratic Party among lower-educated voters. However, it has been the remarkable transformation and growing success of the Freedom Party, from a German

nationalist party to a powerful anti-immigration party, which has decisively led lower-educated voters to move toward the right. As in the Netherlands, this evolution has been accompanied by the advent of a new nativist cleavage, with Muslim voters being substantially more likely to vote for left-wing and liberal parties.

## Belgium

### The Democratization Process after the Revolution

The origins of modern-day Belgium date to the end of the Napoleonic era. After the fall of the French Empire in 1815, the Low Countries found themselves briefly reunited under Dutch rule. However, in 1830, the Belgian Revolution led to the secession of the southern provinces from the rest of the Netherlands and the creation of an independent Kingdom of Belgium. The unrest that sparked the revolution was mainly instigated by the French-speaking Catholic bourgeoisie, which rejected the preeminence of the Dutch language and of Calvinism associated with Dutch rule, and was also supported by the Catholic Flemish lower bourgeoisie.[2]

The revolution was a success and Belgium became a French-speaking parliamentary monarchy through the 1831 constitution. The two main parliamentary groups at the time were the liberals and the Catholics. Over the course of the nineteenth century, a progressive middle-class movement began contesting the dominance of the upper classes and established links with a fast-growing socialist movement, which gave rise to the Socialist Party in 1885. The proletarian movement and the bourgeoisie found a compromise with the introduction of male universal suffrage in 1894.[3] During the same period, a Flemish emancipation movement emerged, seeking equal status for Dutch speakers in the Belgian state. As a result, new Flemish nationalist parties were formed by liberals and Christian democrats.

After the end of World War II, the Communist Party grew considerably, and took part in coalition governments from 1944 to 1947. However, its growth was short-lived due mainly to the anticommunist reflex

---

2. J. Beaufays, "Belgium: A Dualist Political System?," *Publius: The Journal of Federalism* 18, no. 2 (1988): 63–73.

3. E. Witte, J. Craeybeckx, and A. Meynen, *Political History of Belgium: From 1830 Onwards* (Asp/Vubpress/Upa, 2009).

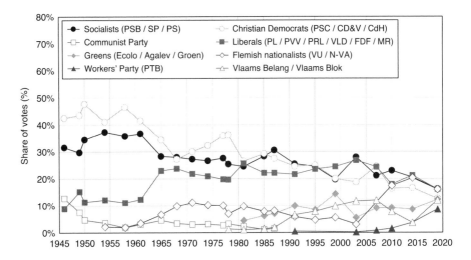

FIGURE 7.1. Election results in Belgium, 1946–2019
*Data Source:* Authors' computations using official election results (see wpid.world).
*Note:* The figure shows the share of votes received by selected political parties or groups of parties in federal elections held in Belgium between 1946 and 2019. Flemish nationalists received 16% of votes in 2019.

during the Cold War.[4] The composition of the government thus continued to fluctuate between the Christian democrats, the liberals, and the socialists, although from the 1950s onward the Christian democrats maintained a continuous presence, often in coalition with the socialists (Figure 7.1). Moreover, the Flemish movement gained renewed importance and a new nationalist Flemish party, the People's Union (Volksunie, VU), was founded in 1954.

With the entrance in the European Economic Community in 1957, the country entered a period of economic growth with an enlargement of the market for Belgian products and the launch of an ambitious plan for regional economic development in 1959. While Flanders attracted increasing foreign investment on a large scale, Wallonia's heavy industry was kept alive with large state subsidies. Economic disparities between the two regions worsened, which intensified their dissatisfaction with the

4. L. D. Winter and P. Dumont, "Belgium: Party System(s) on the Eve of Disintegration?," in *Changing Party Systems in Western Europe,* ed. D. Broughton and M. Donovan (Pinter, 1999), 183–206.

centralized state system. Some Flemish were against subsidizing a weak regional economy with a decadent industry, while some Walloons feared that the more populous and prosperous Flanders would soon dominate the state.[5]

Following massive strikes, a linguistic border was established in 1962 that split the country into zones of exclusive language use and a new special arrangement was introduced for the bilingual area around Brussels. The slow process of federalization continued with the parliament's approval of cultural autonomy for the regions of Flanders and Wallonia in 1971. It culminated with the St. Michael's Agreement in 1992, after which the establishment of the federal state was embraced in the new constitution of 1994.[6] The acceptance of federalism in place of separatism by the VU in the late 1970s was disapproved by a right-wing faction of the party, who formed the Vlaams Blok (dissolved and recreated as Vlaams Belang in 2004). This nationalist anti-immigrant political party gained increasing support during the 1990s, a period during which Belgium's immigrant population significantly grew.[7]

Together with the new nationalist parties, the party system was broadened between the 1960s and 1980s with the split of the three traditional parties—the Christian Social Party, the Liberal Party, and the Socialist Party—along linguistic lines. Moreover, the two environmental parties, Ecolo in Wallonia and Agalev (now Groen) in Flanders, were founded in 1980 and 1982, respectively. Hence, the only major political party that has operated since then as a single Belgian party is the left-wing Workers' Party (Parti du Travail de Belgique, PTB, in French, Partij van de Arbeid van België, PVDA, in Flemish), founded in 1979, which deemed the politics of the existing Communist Party of Belgium to have become too social democratic. In 2001, another Flemish nationalist party, the New Flemish Alliance (Nieuw-Vlaamse Alliantie, N-VA), was formed by members of the right-leaning faction of the VU.

In 2007, the Flemish Christian democrats won the parliamentary elections but failed to form a governing coalition. After six months of political deadlock, a new coalition government made up by Walloon and

5. K. Deprez and L. Vos, *Nationalism in Belgium: Shifting Identities, 1780–1995* (Springer, 2016).

6. K. Deschouwer, *The Politics of Belgium* (Palgrave Macmillan, 2012).

7. N. Rink, K. Phalet, and M. Swyngedouw, "The Effects of Immigrant Population Size, Unemployment, and Individual Characteristics on Voting for the Vlaams Blok in Flanders, 1991–1999," *European Sociological Review* 25, no. 4 (2009): 411–424.

Flemish parties finally took power in 2008. Following the withdrawal of the Flemish liberals and democrats, however, anticipated elections were held in 2010. The big winners were the separatist New Flemish Alliance and the French-speaking socialists, but they were unable to come to an agreement to form a coalition.

In 2011, a big coalition of Christian democrats, liberals, and socialists was eventually formed, and Elio Di Rupo became Belgium's first socialist prime minister since 1974 and the first Francophone prime minister in more than three decades. The country then entered a period of relative political stability, but the tension between the country's north and south remained. In the 2014 election, a Flanders-focused center-right coalition was formed that excluded the socialists from the government for the first time in more than two decades. In the 2018 election, traditional parties suffered losses in both regions. The Vlaams Belang resurged in Flanders, and with the N-VA, both Flemish separatist and nationalist parties, obtained nearly half of the total vote in Flanders. Meanwhile, the far-left PVDA/PTB and Ecolo rose in Wallonia.

### The Emergence of a Multi-elite Party System and the Regional Divide

How has the transformation of Belgium's party system after federalization shaped the reversal of the educational cleavage and the emergence of a multi-elite party system? In what follows, we analyze the evolution of the vote along these socioeconomic dimensions using political attitude surveys covering all federal elections held in Belgium from 1971 to 2014.[8]

Figure 7.2 shows the relative support for the socialists and environmentalists, who together have received 30 to 40 percent of votes in most elections since 1945, among highest-educated and top-income voters since 1971. While highest-educated voters were less likely to vote for the left by 11 percentage points in the 1970s, in the last two elections they were not more or less likely to do so. In contrast, top-income voters have remained more likely to support the right over the whole period. Hence, Belgium seems to have been moving toward a multi-elite party system, but this transformation has not fully taken shape: the gap in left vote between higher-educated and lower-educated voters seems to have stabi-

---

8. For data sources, see appendix Table AA1, World Political Cleavages and Inequality Database, http://wpid.world.

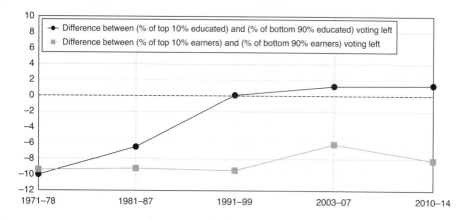

FIGURE 7.2. Toward a multi-elite party system in Belgium, 1971–2014
*Data Source:* Authors' computations using Belgian political attitudes surveys (see wpid.world).
*Note:* The figure shows the relative support of highest-educated and top-income voters for left-wing parties (PS/SP/Ecolo/Agalev/PTB). In the 1970s, highest-educated and top-income voters were less likely to vote for left-wing parties than low-income and lower-educated voters. The left-wing vote has become increasingly associated with higher-educated voters, leading Belgium to come closer to becoming a multi-elite party system. Estimates control for income/education, age, gender, employment status, marital status, religion, church attendance, region, and language.

lized around zero, in comparison to the other countries studied in this chapter where it has become strongly positive (see below).

To understand the drivers of the education and income gradients, it is useful to replicate the previous analysis for each of the main left-wing and right-wing parties or coalitions. Four parallel dynamics appear to have driven these changes.[9] First, the emergence of the environmental parties in the 1980s, supported by young university graduates in urban areas, strongly contributed to pushing toward the reversal of the educational cleavage. Second, the traditional left has, however, remained relatively more supported by lowest-educated voters throughout the whole period, which explains why this reversal has not been fully completed. Third, the rise of the Vlaams Blok, mainly supported by the lower educated, has absorbed the decline in the lowest-educated vote for the Christian democrats. Fourth, the stability of the income gradient is largely due to the persistence

9. See appendix Figure AC16, wpid.world.

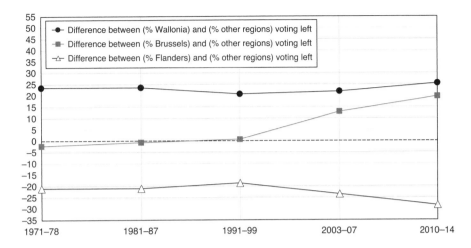

FIGURE 7.3. The regional cleavage in Belgium, 1971–2014
*Data Source:* Authors' computations using Belgian political attitudes surveys (see wpid.world).
*Note:* The figure shows the relative support of the main Belgian regions for left-wing parties (PS/SP/Ecolo/Agalev/PTB), after controlling for income, education, age, gender, employment status, marital status, religion, and church attendance. Wallonia has remained significantly more likely to vote for left-wing parties than Flanders throughout the past decades, while Brussels has become increasingly supportive of left-wing parties.

of the vote for the liberals among top-income earners and for the socialists among low-income earners.

Belgium has long been considered a clear example of consociational democracy, in which linguistic, regional, and religious interests have been mediated through power-sharing agreements between the different parties.[10] These historical divides have persisted and there is a strong stratification in the vote for traditional parties between Flanders and Wallonia. The socialists are mainly supported in Wallonia, whereas the liberals and the Christian democrats are more popular in Flanders. All three traditional parties used to be strong in Brussels, but since the 2000s, support for the socialists has grown considerably in the capital city, leading to a strong reversal in the left-right cleavage (Figure 7.3). The vote for envi-

10. K. Deschouwer, "And the Peace Goes On? Consociational Democracy and Belgian Politics in the Twenty-First Century," *West European Politics* 29, no. 5 (2006): 895–911.

ronmental parties is less regionally concentrated, as they are popular among higher-educated voters across all Belgium. Belgium's strong regional stratification of the vote is unique in comparative perspective, in that even the historically unitary traditional parties are split along linguistic lines, contrary to what is observed in other Western countries with regional nationalist parties such as Canada or Spain (see Chapters 5 and 6).

A strong differentiation of the vote is also prevalent along religious lines (Table 7.1). The Protestant minority is more inclined to vote for the socialists, whereas Catholics are more supportive of the Christian democrats. Green parties attract more votes among nonreligious voters. In line with what we observe in other Western democracies, Muslims vote massively for the left (see Chapter 1).

Overall, despite Belgium's extraordinary regionalization of politics, we still observe the same transition toward a multi-elite party system as in other Western countries. The regional dimension does still play a role, however, as the lowest-educated extreme right is concentrated in Flanders. The absence of a strong extreme-right party in Wallonia has been related to the creation of a successful cordon sanitaire by mainstream parties and the media, which did not happen in Flanders.[11] This has arguably contributed to the persistence of a powerful lower-educated left in Wallonia, whose strength has acted as a counteracting force preventing the complete reversal of the education cleavage.

## Netherlands

### The Emergence of the Dutch Political System

The history of the Netherlands as a sovereign state begins in 1648, when the seven northern provinces of the Low Countries were granted independence after defeating the Spanish in the Eighty Years' War. However, the country remained in practice no more than an alliance of widely autonomous provinces until the French Revolution. In 1795, with the widespread support of the local population, the French transformed the confederacy into a highly centralized, democratic republic. Several coups d'état ensued until Napoleon decided to appoint his brother Louis as king in 1806, thus transforming the country for the first time in its history into a kingdom.

---

11. L. de Jonge, "The Curious Case of Belgium: Why Is There no Right-Wing Populism in Wallonia?," *Government and Opposition* (2020): 1–17.

Table 7.1  The Structure of Political Cleavages in Belgium, 2011–2014

| | Share of Votes Received (%) | | | | | |
|---|---|---|---|---|---|---|
| | PS/SP/PTB | Ecolo/Groen | VLD/MR | CD&V/CdH | N-VA | Vlaams Belang |
| **Education** | | | | | | |
| Primary | 34% | 3% | 14% | 20% | 20% | 4% |
| Secondary | 27% | 6% | 18% | 20% | 20% | 4% |
| Tertiary | 16% | 16% | 25% | 20% | 18% | 1% |
| **Income** | | | | | | |
| Bottom 50% | 30% | 7% | 17% | 22% | 16% | 3% |
| Middle 40% | 22% | 11% | 21% | 18% | 21% | 3% |
| Top 10% | 13% | 11% | 28% | 17% | 26% | 2% |
| **Religion** | | | | | | |
| No religion | 25% | 12% | 20% | 12% | 22% | 4% |
| Catholic | 17% | 5% | 21% | 34% | 17% | 2% |
| Protestant | 30% | 9% | 12% | 24% | 18% | 2% |
| Muslim | 65% | 7% | 8% | 13% | 4% | 0% |
| **Region** | | | | | | |
| Brussels | 35% | 16% | 26% | 13% | 2% | 1% |
| Flanders | 15% | 8% | 15% | 24% | 31% | 5% |
| Wallonia | 41% | 10% | 29% | 14% | 0% | 0% |
| **Language** | | | | | | |
| Dutch | 12% | 10% | 15% | 27% | 32% | 4% |
| French | 36% | 12% | 34% | 13% | 1% | 0% |
| Other | 65% | 4% | 10% | 13% | 3% | 5% |

*Data Source:* Authors' computations using Belgian political attitudes surveys (see wpid.world).

*Note:* The table shows the average share of votes received by the main Belgian political parties by selected individual characteristics during the 2011 and 2014 elections. The PS, SP, and PTB received greater support from lower-educated voters, low-income voters, and Muslim voters. Total vote shares correspond to those reported in surveys and may not match exactly official election results.

After the fall of Napoleon in 1815, both centralism and monarchy, foreign to Dutch tradition, were preserved.

The wave of liberal revolutions that swept Europe in 1848 prompted a preemptive reform of the constitution, which is considered to mark the beginning of modern Dutch democracy. A system of parliamentary monarchy was adopted, although suffrage remained censitary. In 1917, the right to vote was finally extended to all men and two years later to women as well. The Pacification of 1917, as it became known, also introduced the single district proportional rule, an idiosyncratic characteristic of the modern Dutch electoral system. Since then, the entire country has been considered as a single constituency, with no electoral threshold to enter the parliament, which has enabled the emergence and survival of small parties.

With the advent of democracy, the political system came to reflect the deep cleavages of Dutch society. Since its independence from the Spanish Empire, the country faced a major internal religious division. The Reformation had been enormously successful across the Dutch provinces, but the Spanish presence in the southeastern parts of the territory during the Eighty Years' War assured the survival of Catholic bastions within the country. In addition, the Dutch Reformed Church experienced several splits over the nineteenth century, leaving a society widely fragmented on the basis of religion. At the time of the industrialization of the country in the 1870s and 1880s, the religious divide hampered the development of a strong working-class movement, yet a class cleavage still emerged among the secular segments of the population.[12]

The social groups defined by the religious divides and, to a lesser extent, by the class cleavage, were significantly isolated from one another. Catholics in particular had a separate school system, a labor union, media outlets, and even a health care network. The strength of these divisions led to consider these social groups as full right subcultures, called "pillars" (*zuilen*).

Scholars distinguished three to five pillars: on the religious dimension, a Catholic one and one or two Protestant ones; on the class dimension, a socialist one and, "only by default,"[13] a liberal one. The degree of integration varied widely across pillars, with the Catholics constituting by

---

12. R. B. Andeweg and G. A. Irwin, *Governance and Politics of the Netherlands* (Palgrave Macmillan, 2005), chapters 1 and 2.

13. Andeweg and Irwin, *Governance and Politics of the Netherlands*, 27.

far the most homogeneous group, and the liberals the most diverse.[14] Yet, to each pillar corresponded a party or group of parties: the majority of Catholics voted for the predecessor of the Catholic People's Party (Katholieke Volkspartij, KVP), the Protestants for either the Anti-Revolutionary Party (Anti-Revolutionaire Partij, ARP) or the Christian Historical Union (Christelijk-Historische Unie, CHU), and the secular working class for the predecessors of the Labor Party (Partij van de Arbeid, PvdA) and to a lesser degree for the Communist Party (Communistische Partij Nederland, CPN). The liberal vote remained quite split until the formation of the People's Party for Freedom and Democracy (Volkspartij voor Vrijheid en Democratie, VVD) at the end of the Second World War.[15] Voters, of course, did not always vote according to their pillar, and vote shares still fluctuated. Fragmentation was high, and it was, overall, clear to all political forces that they would remain a minority. This contributed to the emergence of a culture of consensual politics and to the establishment of a consociational democracy.

### The Decline of Traditional Cleavages and the Rise of Anti-immigration Parties

The height of pillarization and political stability came at the end of the Second World War.[16] For over two decades, electoral volatility was very low despite the large number of parties. However, by the end of the 1960s, wide societal changes and the rise of new values quickly transformed the political scene (see Figure 7.4). A process of *depillarization* unfolded, primarily attributed to the increasing secularization of Dutch society.[17]

New parties emerged, embodying social liberal and so-called New Left values, most notably Democrats 66 (Democraten 66, D66) and the Political Party of Radicals (Politieke Partij Radikalen, PRR).[18] The latter would merge in 1990 with the Communist Party and other small left-wing parties to form GreenLeft (GroenLinks, GL). The process of secu-

14. A. Lijphart, *The Politics of Accommodation: Pluralism and Democracy in the Netherlands* (University of California Press, 1975).

15. Andeweg and Irwin, *Governance and Politics of the Netherlands,* chapters 2 and 3.

16. Lijphart, *Politics of Accommodation.*

17. H. Kriesi, "New Social Movements and the New Class in the Netherlands," *American Journal of Sociology* 94, no. 5 (1989): 1078–1116.

18. S. Bornschier, "The New Cultural Divide and the Two-Dimensional Political Space in Western Europe," *West European Politics* 33, no. 3 (2010): 419–444; H. Kriesi, "Restructuration of Partisan Politics and the Emergence of a New Cleavage Based on Values," *West European Politics* 33, no. 3 (2010): 673–685.

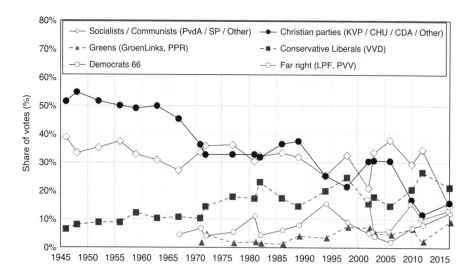

FIGURE 7.4. Election results in the Netherlands, 1946–2017
*Data Source:* Authors' computations using official election results (see wpid.world).
*Note:* The figure shows the share of votes received by selected political parties or
groups of parties in general elections held in the Netherlands between 1946 and 2017.
Conservative-liberal parties received 21% of votes in 2017.

larization severely weakened the Christian parties, which until the 1967
election had continuously held a majority of seats in the parliament. As a
means to regain some strength, the three main Christian parties, the KVP,
the ARP, and the CHU, formed an alliance in 1973 and eventually merged
into the Christian Democratic Appeal (Christen-Democratisch Appèl,
CDA) in 1980. The party's core appeal became its attachment to traditional values and its opposition to core liberal demands, in particular the
legalization of euthanasia, abortion, and the rights of sexual minorities.

Despite the arrival of new parties parliament, consensual politics remained a key feature of the Dutch system.[19] Over the next decades, all
major parties eventually shared a coalition government. The configurations of the alliances were highly variable, depending more on the key
polarizing issues and the electoral performance of the different parties
in each election than on long-lasting agreements. As in many other

19. A. Lijphart, "From the Politics of Accommodation to Adversarial Politics in the
Netherlands: A Reassessment," *West European Politics* 12, no. 1 (1989): 139–153.

Western democracies, sociocultural issues progressively gained prominence, to the detriment of economic concerns. This culminated in the formation in 1994 of a grand coalition purple government uniting the social democratic PvdA and the conservative-liberal VVD, which had historically held opposite views on economic issues, together with the smaller D66. The coalition, led by the PvdA Prime Minister Wim Kok, was returned in 1998 and made the Netherlands the first country to legalize euthanasia and gay marriage.[20]

However, under the image of consensus and stability, discontent with the grand coalition was growing and anti-immigration sentiments were gaining in popularity among the electorate. The unrest that had been building up finally broke into the political system in the "long year 2002" with the arrival of a new political figure, Pim Fortuyn. He embodied the idea that immigration had gone too far in the Netherlands and that the political elite had neglected the needs of the Dutch.[21] A few days before the election, he was assassinated by an animal rights activist, which was the first political murder in the country in 330 years. His party, the Pim Fortuyn List (LPF), nonetheless had unprecedented success for a new party in the Netherlands, gathering 17 percent of the votes. The LPF was included in the governing coalition, but without its leader, it quickly started disintegrating and lost most of its support in the 2003 elections.[22]

After this brief recess, anti-immigration forces resurged with the founding of the Party for Freedom (Partij voor de Vrijheid, PVV) by Geert Wilders, former member of the VVD, in 2004. A "one-man party," the PVV quickly gained electoral support, nourished by the same discontent with Dutch multiculturalism that had propelled the LPF's success.[23] Interestingly, however, anti-immigration, anti-Islamic, and anti-EU stances are possibly the only common traits between the PVV and the LPF and their European counterparts, as these two parties have simultaneously held progressive stances on social matters.[24] In defending a "national

20. Andeweg and Irwin, *Governance and Politics of the Netherlands,* chapter 5.

21. K. Aarts and J. Thomassen, "Dutch Voters and the Changing Party Space, 1989–2006," *Acta Politica* 43, no. 2–3 (2008): 203–234.

22. Andeweg and Irwin, *Governance and Politics of the Netherlands,* chapter 11.

23. K. Vossen, *The Power of Populism: Geert Wilders and the Party for Freedom in the Netherlands* (Routledge, 2016): 1.

24. J. J. M. van Holsteyn, "The Radical Right in Belgium and the Netherlands," in *The Oxford Handbook of the Radical Right,* ed. J. Rydgren (Oxford University Press, 2018), chapter 24.

culture," they have set to defend abortion rights, the rights of sexual minorities (Pim Fortuyn was indeed openly gay), and the legalization of euthanasia. However, it is important to note that these issues are no longer a relevant point of political competition in the Netherlands, due to their widespread acceptance.[25]

In parallel to the rise of anti-immigration forces, the 2000s also witnessed the growth of the Socialist Party (Socialistische Partij, SP), a small party to the left of the PvdA, which reached 16.6 percent of the vote in 2006, thus becoming temporarily the third-largest force in parliament. However, the party has since lost much of its earlier gains, obtaining only 9 percent of the vote in the last elections. Simultaneously, the ideologically close GreenLeft has seen moderate progress, reaching a similar level of support.

### The Emergence of a Multi-elite Party System and the Decline of Old Divides

How did these radical changes in the Dutch party system translate into electoral choices? Using available postelectoral surveys, we are able to track electoral behaviors in the Netherlands in all federal elections held from 1967 to 2017.[26]

As in most Western democracies, the Netherlands has transitioned to a multi-elite party system in the past fifty years (Figure 7.5). In the 1960s and 1970s, highest-educated voters were not more or less likely to vote for the left any more than other voters. By the 2010s, they had become 10 percentage points more likely to support the social democrats, D66, the SP, and the greens, after controlling for other socioeconomic factors. Meanwhile, top-income voters have remained consistently more likely to vote for the VVD, with no clear trend. The shift of highest-educated voters toward socialist, social democratic, liberal, and green parties is, however, smaller than in other countries addressed in this chapter, partly due to the fact that D66, notorious for its success among higher-educated voters, had already entered the political arena in 1966. The Netherlands thus represents a case of a relatively early transition to a multi-elite party system. Nevertheless, the reversal of the education cleavage has not yet completely reached the PvdA and SP, which still find greater support among primary-educated voters than among university graduates, aside

25. Aarts and Thomassen, "Dutch Voters and the Changing Party Space."
26. See appendix Table BA1, wpid.world, for data sources.

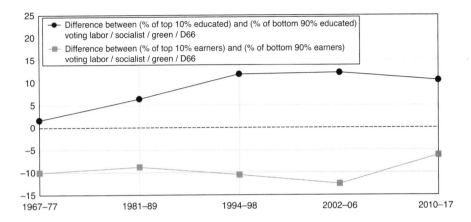

FIGURE 7.5. The emergence of a multi-elite party system in the Netherlands, 1967–2017
*Data Source:* Authors' computations using Dutch electoral surveys (see wpid.world).
*Note:* The figure shows the relative support of highest-educated and top-income voters for
left-wing and liberal parties (PvdA/SP/GroenLinks/D66/Other left). The left-wing/liberal
vote has become increasingly associated with highest-educated voters, while top-income
voters have remained more likely to vote for right-wing parties, giving rise to a multi-elite
party system. Estimates control for income/education, age, gender, employment status,
marital status, religion, church attendance, region, location, union membership, and
subjective social class.

from an exceptional period during the 2000s. The emergence of a multi-
elite party system has thus been strongly driven by new parties, with the
GL and D66 achieving better results among university graduates and the
PVV being substantially more popular among primary-educated voters.[27]

Besides collecting data on income and education, Dutch postelectoral surveys are unique in having consistently asked respondents to self-identify
on a comparable, detailed social class scale since the 1960s, which allows
us to have a particularly granular perspective on the link between voters'
self-perceived social class and their partisan affiliations. These data reveal a sharp decline in class cleavages: self-identified working-class voters
were more likely to vote for left-wing and centrist parties by nearly
25 percentage points in the 1960s and 1970s, while they are now only
marginally more likely to do so (Figure 7.6). This shift has been largely

27. See appendix Figure BC17, wpid.world.

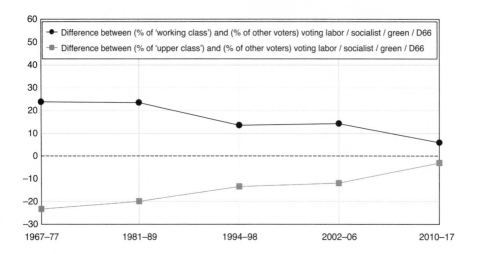

FIGURE 7.6. The decline of class voting in the Netherlands, 1967–2017
*Data Source:* Authors' computations using Dutch electoral surveys (see wpid.world).
*Note:* The figure shows the relative support of voters identifying with the "working class" and of voters identifying with the "upper class" for left-wing/liberal parties (PvdA/SP/GroenLinks/D66/Other left). Class voting has declined significantly in the Netherlands in the past decades. Estimates control for income, education, age, gender, employment status, marital status, religion, church attendance, region, location, and union membership.

driven by new parties, as the class profile of most parties has proved to be highly resilient over time.[28]

The transformation of political cleavages in the Netherlands has thus been facilitated by the extraordinary fragmentation of its party system, a fragmentation arguably enabled and encouraged by its system of proportional representation. In this context, the Dutch case turns out to be particularly interesting for understanding sources of political change in Western democracies, as it enables us to distinguish precisely the electorates of political movements that often unite under the banner of single parties or coalitions in less fragmented systems.

Table 7.2 addresses this question by showing the decomposition of the vote from 2010 to 2017 for all major parties by income, education, self-perceived social class, rural-urban location, and religion. Together, these five socioeconomic dimensions appear to differentiate very clearly the

28. See appendix Figure BC19, wpid.world.

*Table 7.2*  The Structure of Political Cleavages in the Netherlands, 2010–2017

| | Share of Votes Received (%) | | | | | | |
|---|---|---|---|---|---|---|---|
| | SP | PvdA | GL | D66 | CDA | VVD | PVV |
| **Education** | | | | | | | |
| Primary | 13% | 21% | 3% | 3% | 17% | 13% | 20% |
| Secondary | 11% | 15% | 4% | 7% | 13% | 26% | 11% |
| Tertiary | 5% | 16% | 10% | 17% | 9% | 28% | 3% |
| **Income** | | | | | | | |
| Bottom 50% | 12% | 18% | 6% | 7% | 13% | 18% | 13% |
| Middle 40% | 7% | 16% | 7% | 12% | 11% | 28% | 8% |
| Top 10% | 3% | 12% | 6% | 15% | 12% | 39% | 6% |
| **Social Class** | | | | | | | |
| Working | 16% | 22% | 5% | 3% | 10% | 9% | 24% |
| Upper working | 14% | 22% | 4% | 4% | 12% | 17% | 13% |
| Middle | 9% | 15% | 6% | 10% | 14% | 25% | 9% |
| Upper middle | 3% | 13% | 9% | 17% | 9% | 36% | 4% |
| Upper | 3% | 9% | 4% | 23% | 8% | 45% | 2% |
| **Location** | | | | | | | |
| Very rural | 9% | 16% | 4% | 7% | 20% | 24% | 9% |
| Rural | 9% | 14% | 4% | 9% | 17% | 25% | 10% |
| Medium | 8% | 15% | 5% | 8% | 12% | 29% | 11% |
| Urban | 10% | 16% | 7% | 10% | 10% | 23% | 11% |
| Very urban | 8% | 21% | 10% | 14% | 6% | 21% | 10% |
| **Religion** | | | | | | | |
| No religion | 11% | 18% | 7% | 12% | 5% | 27% | 12% |
| Catholic | 10% | 14% | 3% | 7% | 24% | 25% | 12% |
| Protestant | 4% | 8% | 5% | 5% | 27% | 19% | 5% |
| Muslim | 4% | 48% | 7% | 6% | 3% | 14% | 0% |

*Data Source:* Authors' computations using Dutch electoral surveys (see wpid.world).
*Note:* The table shows the average share of votes received by the main Dutch political parties by selected individual characteristics over the 2010–2017 period. The SP and PVV both received greater support from low-income and lower-educated voters. Total vote shares correspond to those reported in surveys and may not match exactly official election results.

electorates of political parties in the Netherlands. The Socialists (SP) and the Social Democrats (PvdA) embody the legacy of old class cleavages and achieve better results among low-income, lower-educated, and self-identified working-class voters. Meanwhile, the conservative-liberal VVD and the social-liberal D66 are largely supported by high-income, higher-

educated, upper-class voters, with D66 drawing an even larger share of its support from urban, secular elites. The CDA, the third big descendant of the postwar party system, has a primarily rural and religious electoral base, appealing in particular to Catholic and Protestant voters in the countryside. Education and location appear to be the strongest predictors of support for GreenLeft, which, like D66, also fares better among the higher educated in highly urbanized areas. The main difference between their electorates is the relatively flat income profile of Green-Left voters and, interestingly, their self-identification with the "upper-middle" class (but not the "upper" class).

Finally, the PVV is closer to the PvdA and the SP than to any other parties in socioeconomic terms: it is disproportionately supported by low-income, lower-educated, working-class voters, even if the overrepresentation of the lower educated is strongest among the PVV's electorate. What appears to distinguish these two groups most, however, is their support among religious minorities. In the past decade, nearly half of all Muslim voters voted for the PvdA, while not a single one declared having supported the PVV in the postelectoral surveys used in this section. A new nativist cleavage, in addition to the sociocultural and environmental issues embodied by the GL and D66, therefore seems to have contributed to the blurring of traditional class and religious cleavages in the Netherlands in recent years.

## Switzerland

### The Emergence of the Swiss Political System

The modern Swiss state was born in 1848, at the end of a brief and almost bloodless civil war between the minority Catholic cantons and their Protestant counterparts. For centuries, Switzerland had existed as a rather loose confederacy of allied states and subject territories, whose primary function was to protect its members' independence from foreign powers. Following the Reformation, only some of the cantons converted to Protestantism, causing a long-lasting divide within the Confederacy that would lead to several internal conflicts and hamper any attempts to establish a more centralized state.

It was not until Napoleon's invasion in 1798 and the subsequent creation of the Helvetic Republic that Switzerland was first unified under a central government. The wildly unpopular republic lasted less than five years, but it prompted the emergence of the two political movements that

would shape Swiss politics throughout the nineteenth century. On the one hand, the radicals (liberals) supported a tighter union between the cantons, the protection of individual rights, and the separation of church and state. On the other hand, the Catholic conservatives set to defend cantonal autonomy and the overall status quo. The two movements would later transform into political parties at the turn of the twentieth century, with the creation of the Free Democratic Party in 1894 and the Christian Democratic Party in 1912. In the decades that followed the fall of Napoleon, the radicals rapidly gained support across the Protestant cantons, spurring fear among the Catholic minority. In 1847, the tensions finally burst into a civil war. The Catholics were defeated within a few weeks, and shortly after, a new constitution was adopted, transforming Switzerland into a federal state. The constitution established a bicameral parliament elected by universal male suffrage, composed of a chamber representing the people and one representing the cantons, both with equal power. The executive power was given to the Federal Council, a council of seven members elected by the parliament and ruling in collegiality, and a first form of direct democracy was introduced at the federal level.

In addition to the religious divisions, Switzerland was shaped also by a long-lasting cleavage between the cities and the countryside. Multiple rural revolts had already erupted against the urban elites during the time of the Confederacy. As support for the liberals slowly started to fade among the popular classes in the second half of the nineteenth century, two new political forces emerged. In the cities, the labor movement gained strength, and the Swiss Social Democratic Party was founded in 1888. In the countryside, farmers parties grew, although they would not unite in a federal party, the Party of Farmers, Traders, and Independents, until 1936.

Until the rise of green parties during the last two decades, these four political forces dominated Switzerland's political arena (see Figure 7.7). After World War I, the Free Democratic Party lost its uncontested majority and in the late 1920s, the Social Democrats became the biggest party in parliament. For almost fifty years, vote shares remained quite stable albeit also quite split, with no party gathering more than 30 percent of the vote. In 1959 the Federal Council, too, achieved stability, with the adoption of the "Magic Formula." Its seven seats were allocated according to a fixed yet unwritten rule that gave two seats each to the Social Democrats, the Free Democratic Party, and the Christian Democrats, and one to the Farmers' Party. This uncommon permanent grand coalition of left-

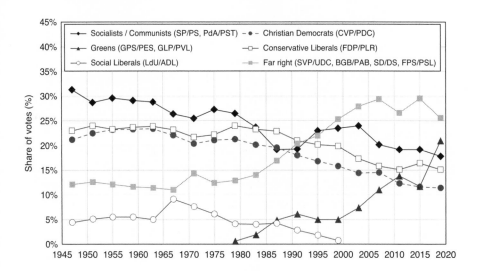

FIGURE 7.7. Election results in Switzerland, 1947–2019

*Data Source:* Authors' computations using official election results (see wpid.world).

*Note:* The figure shows the share of votes received by selected political parties or groups of parties in federal elections held in Switzerland between 1947 and 2019. Far-right parties received 26% of votes in 2019.

and right-wing parties made Switzerland the paradigmatic example of a consensual democracy.[29]

### *The Rise of the Swiss People's Party and the Polarization of Swiss Politics*

In the late 1960s, the Western world saw the rise of a new ideological conflict, with opposing "libertarian-universalistic" and "traditionalist-communitarian" poles.[30] The Social Democrats were particularly quick in adopting the universalistic ideas of the New Left, which included the defense of equal rights for women and sexual minorities and the protection of the environment. Simultaneously, local environmentalist parties started appearing across Switzerland, and the Green Party was finally founded at the federal level in 1983. The Swiss left progressively concentrated around

29. H. Kriesi and A. H. Trechsel, *The Politics of Switzerland: Continuity and Change in a Consensus Democracy* (Cambridge University Press, 2008).

30. D. Oesch and L. Rennwald, "The Class Basis of Switzerland's Cleavage between the New Left and the Populist Right," *Swiss Political Science Review* 16, no. 3 (2010): 343–371.

these two parties, constituting "an exceptionally strong universalistic pole."[31] The traditionalist pole, however, was not yet represented in the political system.

In 1971, the old Farmers' Party became the Swiss People's Party after merging with a small centrist party. Until that point, it had played a secondary role in the country's politics. After the rise of Christoph Blocher to the head of the Zurich branch in 1977, however, the party experienced a deep structural and ideological transformation. A successful industrialist and a fierce opponent of Swiss integration into the international community, Blocher transformed the Swiss People's Party from a moderate, centrist organization of farmers and small business owners into a radical, anti-immigration, anti-European party with a fiercely liberal economic agenda. The new Swiss People's Party came to represent the rejection of the universalist ideas adopted by the New Left, already latent in large sectors of Swiss society.[32] The ideological shift and the aggressive campaigning strategies introduced by Blocher proved very effective, propelling the party from a modest 15 percent of the vote in 1995 to a staggering 29 percent in 2007, and turning it into one of the most successful far-right parties in Western Europe.[33] These dynamics have led to a significant polarization of Swiss politics. The apparent immobility of the Swiss political system thus came to an end in the 1990s. In 2003, the Magic Formula was broken for the first time, as the Swiss People's Party, which had become the biggest party in parliament, took a second seat in the Federal Council at the expense of the Christian Democrats.[34]

### The Emergence of a Multi-elite Party System and the Persistence of Old Divides

How did the dramatic transformation of the Swiss party system affect electoral choices? Using existing postelectoral surveys, we are able to

---

31. H. Kriesi, "Conclusion: The Political Consequences of the Polarization of Swiss Politics," *Swiss Political Science Review* 21, no. 4 (2015): 725.

32. S. Bornschier, "The New Cultural Conflict, Polarization, and Representation in the Swiss Party System, 1975–2011," *Swiss Political Science Review* 21, no. 4 (2015): 680–701.

33. A. Afonso and Y. Papadopoulos, "How the Populist Radical Right Transformed Swiss Welfare Politics: From Compromises to Polarization," *Swiss Political Science Review* 21, no. 4 (2015): 617–635.

34. H. Kriesi, R. Lachat, P. Selb, S. Bornschier, and M. Helbling, *Der Aufstieg der SVP: Acht Kantone im Vergleich* (Verlag Neue Zürcher Zeitung, 2005).

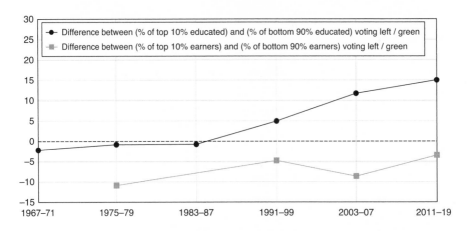

FIGURE 7.8. The emergence of a multi-elite party system in Switzerland, 1967–2019
*Data Source:* Authors' computations using Swiss electoral surveys (see wpid.world).
*Note:* The figure shows the relative support of highest-educated and top-income voters for left-wing and green parties (SP/PS, GPS/PES, GLP/PVL, Other left). In the 1960s–1970s, highest-educated and top-income voters were less likely to vote for left-wing parties than low-income and lower-educated voters. The left-wing/green vote has gradually become associated with higher-educated voters, giving rise to a multi-elite party system. Estimates control for income/education, age, gender, employment status, marital status, religion, region, home ownership, and union membership.

track changes in the composition of the electorate of Swiss political parties in federal elections from 1967 to 2015.[35]

As in many Western democracies, the last fifty years have been marked by the reversal of the educational cleavage. Figure 7.8 shows the support for the Social Democrats, the Green Party, the Green Liberals, the Alliance of Independents, and other small centrist and left-leaning parties among highest-educated and top-income voters since 1967. This group of parties, while heterogeneous, shares similar views on immigration, European integration, and environmental protection issues, which stand at the center of the political debate in Switzerland.[36] While in the late 1960s and early 1970s, highest-educated voters were slightly less likely to vote for these parties than the rest of voters, by the 2010s they had become more likely to do so, by over 15 percentage points, after controlling for other socioeconomic factors.

35. See appendix Table CA1, wpid.world, for data sources.
36. Bornschier, "New Cultural Conflict."

This major shift is explained not only by the rise of new parties, but also by a reversal in the link between education and support for the traditional left. Indeed, the Social Democrats have attracted a larger share of university graduates than primary-educated voters since the 1990s, coinciding with the rise of the Swiss People's Party.[37] The reversal is also clear when looking at voting by occupation. The Social Democrats and Communists lost the support of clerks and manual workers in the 1990s, as the Swiss People's Party became the new party of the working class.[38] Social and cultural specialists, a broad category including workers involved in "medical services, teaching, social work, arts, and journalism," among others, have become the new stronghold of the left across many Western democracies, but the phenomenon is particularly strong in Switzerland.[39] This development is consistent with the idea of the primacy of cultural and identity issues over economic concerns. As a result of these shifts, Switzerland now has one of the strongest educational cleavages among the Western democracies studied in this book (see Chapter 1).

The importance of the cultural dimension of politics can also be seen in the exceptional weakness of income in accounting for divisions between left and right (Figure 7.8). Income matters only when it comes to the division between the moderate and the radical right, and the overall party choice within the moderate right bloc. The center-right Free Democratic Party remains the party of the elite, attracting both top-income and higher-educated voters, though it now competes for the latter with the left. Both the moderate Christian Democrats and the far-right Swiss People's Party fare better among low-income, lower-educated voters, but in the case of the Swiss People's Party, the cleavage is much more substantial (see Table 7.3).

In addition to the educational and income cleavages, the historical rural-urban divide remains very significant in Switzerland. Despite changes in its political platform, the Swiss People's Party—heir of the Farmers' Party—still fares significantly better in rural areas. Conversely, both the Social Democrats and the two green parties receive much of their support

37. See appendix Figures CD1 to CD36, wpid.world, for detailed results by party.

38. See appendix Figure CB14, wpid.world. See also L. Rennwald, "Class (Non)Voting in Switzerland 1971–2011: Ruptures and Continuities in a Changing Political Landscape," *Swiss Political Science Review* 20, no. 4 (2014): 550–572.

39. Kriesi, "New Social Movements."

*Table 7.3*   The Structure of Political Cleavages in Switzerland, 2011–2019

| | Share of Votes Received (%) | | | | |
|---|---|---|---|---|---|
| | **Left Wing** SP/PS PdA/PST | **Christ. Democrats** CVP/PDC | **Conserv. Liberals** FDP/PRD | **Greens** GPS/PES GLP/PVL | **Far Right** SVP/UDC FPS/PSL SD/DS |
| **Education** | | | | | |
| Primary | 17% | 19% | 12% | 8% | 33% |
| Secondary | 18% | 11% | 16% | 13% | 29% |
| Tertiary | 26% | 11% | 20% | 23% | 10% |
| **Income** | | | | | |
| Bottom 50% | 20% | 12% | 12% | 12% | 30% |
| Middle 40% | 21% | 11% | 18% | 16% | 21% |
| Top 10% | 15% | 12% | 26% | 21% | 19% |
| **Region** | | | | | |
| German | 19% | 11% | 15% | 15% | 27% |
| French | 25% | 13% | 22% | 15% | 18% |
| Italian | 18% | 19% | 25% | 7% | 14% |
| **Location** | | | | | |
| Urban | 25% | 9% | 17% | 19% | 19% |
| Rural | 16% | 13% | 17% | 12% | 29% |

*Data Source:* Authors' computations using Swiss electoral surveys (see wpid.world).

*Note:* The table shows the average share of votes received by the main Swiss political parties by selected individual characteristics over the 2011–2019 period. Far-right parties received greater support from low-income and lower-educated voters, as well as in German-speaking regions and in rural areas. Total vote shares correspond to those reported in surveys and may not match exactly official election results.

from urban voters.[40] Given the growth of the center-left bloc in recent elections, and the strong territorial bias of the Swiss People's Party's electorate, the rural-urban cleavage will likely remain a key feature of Swiss politics and may even gain more influence in the near future.

In contrast to the Belgian experience, language divisions have played a rather small role in Swiss federal elections, which speaks perhaps to the successful construction of Swiss national identity as a "unity in diversity."[41]

40. See appendix Figures CB7 and CC14, wpid.world.
41. Kriesi and Trechsel, *Politics of Switzerland*, 9.

The Swiss People's Party, historically tied to German-speaking Switzerland, is the only party that has consistently concentrated most of its electorate in a given linguistic region. However, after peaking in the 1990s, the language gap has reduced significantly, as support for the party grew in the French- and Italian-speaking regions.[42] Language divisions have, nevertheless, been quite strong in referendums concerning Swiss relations with the EU, as Italian and German speakers have shown much stronger opposition to further integration.[43]

Overall, the emergence of a new cultural divide and the subsequent polarization of Swiss politics have led to the emergence of a multi-elite party system, where the Social Democrats and the green parties are increasingly supported by higher-educated voters in urban areas, while the far-right Swiss People's Party concentrates the rural, lower-educated, and low-income vote. The electorates of the historical center-right parties, the Free Democratic Party and the Christian Democrats, have not changed much in composition, though they have experienced a significant decline in size. These two parties thus stand as vestiges of the historical political cleavages that once structured Swiss politics.

## Austria

### The Transformation of the Austrian Party System

Austria took a first step toward democracy in 1873, when a meager 6 percent of the adult male population elected for the first time the Imperial Assembly of Cisleithania, but it was only by 1919 that the enfranchisement of women paved the way for universal suffrage. Two main political forces had materialized during the second half of the nineteenth century. On the left were the social democrats, who appealed to class struggle, the nationalization of big corporations, and the taxation of elites. On the right were the Christian socialists, supported by the Catholic Church and appealing to farmers, artisans, and the bourgeoisie. German nationalists consisted a third movement, and they received nearly 6 percent of the votes in the 1919 elections. The dominant themes of their campaigns were the unification of Austria and Germany (Anschluss),

---

42. See appendix Figure CD35, wpid.world.
43. Kriesi and Trechsel, *Politics of Switzerland,* 14.

anticlericalism, and antisemitism. The majority of their members would join Hitler's Nazi Party after the German annexation of Austria in 1938.[44]

The organizations that emerged in the Second Republic were the direct continuation of prewar political movements. The Austrian People's Party (Österreichische Volkspartei, ÖVP), created in 1945, replaced the Christian Social Party dissolved in 1934, and it secured a majority of votes and seats in the 1945 election (see Figure 7.9). Given the task of reconstruction and the memory of the war, the ÖVP again formed a coalition with the Socialist Party (Sozialistische Partei Österreichs, SPÖ) and included a communist minister in the cabinet. This was part of a historical tradition of consensual democracy, originated in the First Republic (1919–1934), which aimed at buffering the antagonistic "pillars" of Austrian society by incorporating members of all major parties in the cabinet.[45] It took full shape after 1945 under the *proporz* system of proportional allocation of posts by party in the public sector and in the administration.[46] Coalition governments hence became the norm in Austria, leading to alliances that would appear politically infeasible in other Western countries. Among the most surprising of these was the coalition reached between the Greens and Sebastian Kurz's ÖVP in January 2020 in spite of their diametrically opposite views on immigration policy.[47]

Austria's party system was particularly stable from 1945 to the mid-1980s. After a period of alternation between the ÖVP and the SPÖ, the SPÖ became the dominant party from 1970 to 1983. The Federation of Independents (Verband der Unabhängigen, VdU), rebranded as the Freedom Party of Austria (Freiheitliche Partei Österreichs, FPÖ) in 1956, represented the remnants of German nationalism, but it shifted to office-seeking strategies from the late 1960s. Under Norbert Steger (1980–1986), in particular, the FPÖ attempted to reshape itself into a centrist liberal

---

44. O. Rathkolb, "The Austrian Voter in Historical Perspective," in *The Changing Austrian Voter,* ed. G. Bischof and F. Plasser (Transaction Publishers, 2008), chapter 1.

45. Rathkolb, "Austrian Voter."

46. K. R. Luther, "Dimensions of Party System Change: The Case of Austria," *West European Politics* 12, no. 4 (1989): 3–27.

47. M. Janik, "Austria's New ÖVP-Green Coalition is Unlikely to Alter the Country's Conservative Course," London School of Economics European Politics and Policy blog, January 10, 2020, https://blogs.lse.ac.uk/europpblog/2020/01/10/austrias-new-ovp-green -coalition-is-unlikely-to-alter-the-countrys-conservative-course/.

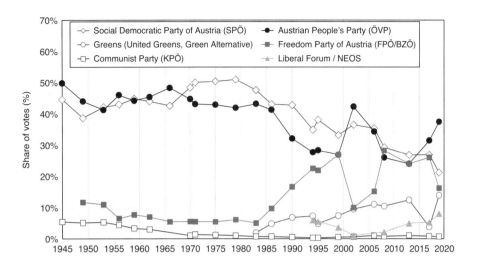

FIGURE 7.9. Election results in Austria, 1945–2019
*Data Source:* Authors' computations using official election results (see wpid.world).
*Note:* The figure shows the share of votes received by selected political parties or groups of parties in general elections held in Austria between 1945 and 2019. The Social Democratic Party received 21% of votes in 2019.

party promoting antistatism and free markets.[48] The Communist Party, already weak in 1945, lost significance in the 1950s and 1960s.

In 1986, Jörg Haider took over the leadership of the FPÖ and transformed it into a radical antiestablishment party. Key to its growing success were its opposition to the *proporz* system and coalition governments (which it accused of being undemocratic and corrupt), opposition to immigration, a hardline stance on crime, and EU skepticism. This strategy yielded benefits in 1999, when the FPÖ narrowly overtook the ÖVP and became the second-largest party in Austria for the first time in the FPÖ's history. Importantly, the FPÖ was able to capture constituencies from both the ÖVP and the SPÖ with a program mixing elements from the right and the left, including anti-immigration policies, market liberalization, and social policies appealing to blue-collar workers. Internal conflicts and dissatisfaction with the coalition ÖVP-FPÖ government formed after the 1999 elections nonetheless led to the collapse of the FPÖ in the

48. K. R. Luther, "Electoral Strategies and Performance of Austrian Right-Wing Populism, 1986–2006," in Bischof and Plasser, *Changing Austrian Voter*, chapter 5.

2002 election, followed by the creation of the splinter Alliance for the Future of Austria (Bündnis Zukunft Österreich, BZÖ) by Haider in 2005.[49] Yet, the party reclaimed success in the elections of 2008, 2013, and 2017, emphasizing the need for stricter immigration controls.[50] In 2019, support for the FPÖ plummeted again in the context of the Ibiza affair, which involved a discussion between Vice Chancellor Heinz-Christian Strache and a woman posing as a niece of a Russian oligarch over an exchange of news coverage against government contracts.

The decline of traditional parties has also coincided with the rise of the greens and the liberals (Figure 7.9). The Green Alternative (Die Grünen; Die Grüne Alternative since 1993) has grown significantly since the mid-1980s, from less than 5 percent of votes to 14 percent in the 2019 elections. At the center of the political spectrum, the Liberal Forum, founded in 1993 by liberal members of the FPÖ, was successful in the mid-1990s, promoting liberalism and free-market policies, but quickly lost support. It merged in 2014 with NEOS to create NEOS—The New Austria and Liberal Forum, which has been growing since then and reached 8 percent of votes in 2019.

The existing literature on political cleavages in Austria has revealed long-run trends comparable to those visible in other Western democracies. In the 1950s and 1960s, three main cleavages divided the Austrian electorate: a religious cleavage between Catholics and nonbelievers, a welfare state cleavage opposing white collars and blue collars, and a cleavage between citizens with Austrian and German identities. The existence of distinct political cultures underlying party support, or *Lager* (camps), then ensured a stable basis of support for the three main parties.[51] The SPÖ and the ÖVP represented the first two cleavages, while the national cleavage, at first represented by the FPÖ, disappeared as German identities dwindled and new voters replaced the prewar generations. This cleavage structure underwent further changes in the past decades, including the decline

49. J. Aichholder, S. Kritzinger, M. Wagner, and E. Zeglovits, "How Has Radical Right Support Transformed Established Political Conflicts? The Case of Austria," *West European Politics* 37, no. 1 (2014): 113–137.

50. C. Plescia, S. Kritzinger, and P. Oberluggauer, "Austria 2017: Conflict Mobilization in a Reconstructing Political Landscape," in *The Year of Challengers? Issues, Public Opinion, and Elections in Western Europe in 2017*, ed. L. De Sio and A. Paparo (Centro Italiano Studi Elettorali, 2018), 189–191.

51. K. R. Luther and W. C. Müller, "Consociationalism and the Austrian Political System," *West European Politics* 15, no. 1 (1992): 1–15.

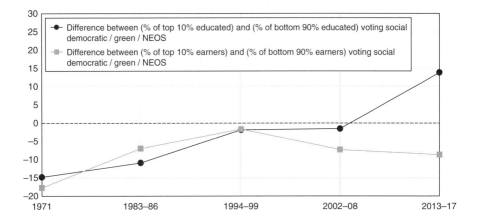

FIGURE 7.10. The emergence of a multi-elite party system in Austria, 1971–2017
*Data Source:* Authors' computations using Austrian political attitudes surveys
(see wpid.world).
*Note:* The figure shows the relative support of highest-educated and top-income voters
for left-wing, green, and social-liberal parties (SPÖ/KPÖ/Greens/NEOS). In the
1970s, highest-educated and top-income voters were less likely to vote for these parties
than low-income and lower-educated voters. The left-wing/green/social-liberal vote
has gradually become associated with higher-educated voters, giving rise to a multi-elite
party system. Estimates control for income/education, age, gender, employment status,
marital status, religion, and location.

of party identification, the growth of "late deciders," the decrease in electoral turnout, and the near disappearance of class voting.[52] These changes
happened later in Austria than in most Western democracies, but at a
faster pace: they mainly took place in the 1980s and 1990s, which points
to the role of the FPÖ in destabilizing traditional partisan affiliations.[53]

### The Emergence of a Multi-elite Party System in Austria

How has the transformation of Austria's party system shaped the reversal
of the educational cleavage and the emergence of a multi-elite party
system? Figure 7.10 shows the relative support for the SPÖ, the KPÖ, the
Greens, the Liberal Forum, and NEOS among highest-educated and top-

52. F. Plasser and P. A. Ulram, "Electoral Change in Austria," in Bischof and Plasser,
*Changing Austrian Voter,* chapter 2.
53. F. Plasser and G. Seeber, "Austrian Electoral Behavior in International Comparison," in Bischof and Plasser, *Changing Austrian Voter,* chapter 7.

*Table 7.4*  The Structure of Political Cleavages in Austria, 2013–2017

| | Share of Votes Received (%) | | | | |
|---|---|---|---|---|---|
| | SPÖ/KPÖ | Greens | NEOS | ÖVP | FPÖ/BZÖ |
| **Education** | | | | | |
| Primary | 33% | 5% | 4% | 31% | 25% |
| Secondary | 29% | 7% | 5% | 31% | 26% |
| Tertiary | 26% | 21% | 11% | 34% | 5% |
| **Income** | | | | | |
| Bottom 50% | 35% | 6% | 5% | 27% | 23% |
| Middle 40% | 27% | 11% | 6% | 32% | 22% |
| Top 10% | 20% | 12% | 8% | 43% | 14% |
| **Location** | | | | | |
| Urban | 33% | 11% | 7% | 26% | 20% |
| Rural | 25% | 7% | 4% | 37% | 25% |
| **Religion** | | | | | |
| No religion | 38% | 14% | 8% | 13% | 21% |
| Catholic | 24% | 8% | 5% | 39% | 23% |
| Protestant | 35% | 10% | 7% | 25% | 23% |
| Muslim | 66% | 2% | 18% | 10% | 4% |

*Data Source:* Authors' computations using Austrian political attitudes surveys (see wpid.world).

*Note:* The table shows the average share of votes received by the main Austrian political parties by selected individual characteristics over the 2013–2017 period. Left-wing parties (SPÖ/KPÖ) received greater support from low-income and lower-educated voters, as well as in urban areas. Total vote shares correspond to those reported in surveys and may not match exactly official election results.

income voters since 1971. Highest-educated voters were less likely to vote for the left by 15 percentage points in 1971; in the last two elections, they had become more likely to do so by 14 points. Top-income voters have also converged in their voting patterns, but continue to support the right. Austria has therefore clearly transitioned to a multi-elite party system.

Three parallel dynamics drove these changes. First, the FPÖ grew, and its voting base went through a radical transformation: while in 1971 it was more successful among highest-educated and top-income voters, it gradually became the party of low-income, lower-educated voters. This is consistent with the three phases of FPÖ ideology, from a centrist liberal party in the 1970s to a catchall antiestablishment party in the 1980s, and finally to an anti-immigration radical right party. Second, the rise of

the Greens and NEOS, both disproportionately supported by university graduates in urban areas, reinforced the reversal of the educational cleavage. Third, the SPÖ's electorate has also become more diverse, first in terms of income in the 1970s and 1980s, and then in terms of education in the most recent elections.[54]

Table 7.4 provides a synthetic picture of the structure of political cleavages in Austria in the past decade. Both the SPÖ and the FPÖ appear to be stronger among primary-educated and low-income voters, but university graduates are more strongly biased against the FPÖ. The SPÖ's lesser emphasis on new liberal cultural issues could explain why it still achieves better results among the lower educated, especially in comparison to its counterparts in Switzerland, where we have seen that historical left-wing parties are now disproportionately supported by the higher educated.[55] Rural-urban locations distinguish left from right more clearly: the SPÖ, the KPÖ, the Greens, and NEOS are all stronger in cities. Religion also clearly distinguishes the left from the right: more than 85 percent of Muslims (about 1.5 percent of the electorate in 2017) and 60 percent of nonbelievers (20 percent of the electorate) voted for socialist and liberal parties in 2013–2017.

# 8

# Political Conflict, Social Inequality, and Electoral Cleavages in the Czech Republic, Hungary, and Poland, 1990–2018

ATTILA LINDNER, FILIP NOVOKMET, THOMAS PIKETTY, AND TOMASZ ZAWISZA

## Introduction

The legacy of the communist regime and the rapid transition from a central planning economy to a market-based economy had a profound impact on access to economic opportunities, challenged social identities, and shaped party politics in all Central European countries. This chapter focuses on three of them—the Czech Republic, Hungary, and Poland—to provide insights on the changing relationship between economic inequality and party support in the aftermath of the Cold War.

Combining and harmonizing survey data on electoral behavior since the first free national elections in 1990/1991, this chapter aims to shed light on the drivers behind the political changes observed over the last thirty years. In all three countries, the left (social democratic, socialist, and affiliated parties) has seen a decline in support since the fall of the Iron Curtain. Populist and nativist political movements, on the other hand, have emerged and increased their popularity ever since. The conformity of these political developments suggests that the transition from communism to democracy had important implications for the evolution of electoral cleavages. This chapter therefore studies the role of

We are grateful to Anna Becker for the outstanding research assistance, to Gábor Tóka for his help with obtaining survey data on Hungary, and to Lukáš Linek for helping with obtaining the data on the 2017 Czech elections. We would also like to thank Ferenc Szűcs, who provided invaluable insights.

postcommunist legacies, democratization, economic growth, and rising income inequality in explaining the left's decline. It further aims to understand the social and ideological coalitions underlying subsequent party dynamics and in particular how populist and nativist parties could become a dominant force in the Czech Republic, Hungary, and Poland.

## From Communism to Democracy

The three Central European countries studied here share a common legacy of communist systems. In the aftermath of the Second World War, they fell under the influence of the Soviet Union. Nevertheless, Czechoslovak, Hungarian, and Polish communist parties could to some extent develop their own form of communism within their own countries. This autonomy was however limited, which became apparent from the Soviet interventions in response to the Hungarian Revolution of 1956 as well as the Prague Spring in 1968.

The transition of political institutions from communism to democracy took place in just two years, from 1989 to 1991. The transition from a centrally planned to a market-based economy, however, was longer and more painful. The experience with democracy during the initial years was accompanied by rising unemployment and a dramatic deterioration in living conditions for many. Rising average incomes right after the immediate shock of transition were soon followed by a rapid growth in income inequality. All three countries experienced a sharp rise in the top 1 percent income share. Poland's top 1 percent share, which was at 10 percent by 1995, was slightly higher than the top 1 percent income share in Hungary and the Czech Republic, where it stood at around 7 percent at the time. At the peak of the economic boom and prior to the Great Recession, the top 1 percent share reached 15 percent in Poland and 10 percent in Hungary and the Czech Republic.[1]

The opening up of the public sphere revealed deep cultural and ideological cleavages, which were suppressed for many years by controlled discourse and compressed economic inequality in the communist era.

1. P. Bukowski and F. Novokmet, "Between Communism and Capitalism: Long-Term Inequality in Poland, 1892–2015" (WID.world Working Paper, 2019); F. Novokmet, "The Long-Run Evolution of Inequality in the Czech Lands, 1898–2015" (WID.world Working Paper, 2018); D. Mavridis and P. Mosberger, "Income Inequality and Incentives: The Quasi-Natural Experiment of Hungary, 1914–2008" (WID.world Working Paper, 2017).

Nevertheless, the commonly shared desire to join key Western and transatlantic institutions such as NATO and the European Union alleviated the political consequences of these deeply rooted cleavages in the initial years. The three countries became members of NATO in 1999 and members of the European Union in the 2004 enlargement. By mid-2000 all three countries had joined the key multilateral institutions meant to ensure prosperity and peace in Europe.

## Party Systems since Democratization

We start our analysis by describing the evolution of the party system in the three central European countries under study.

CZECH REPUBLIC. The first democratic elections in Czechoslovakia took place in June 1990. The absolute winner was the Civic Forum (Občanské fórum, OF),[2] a political movement springing from the anticommunist demonstrations organized during the Velvet Revolution. Right-wing parties together obtained 75 percent of the votes in the 1990 elections (Figure 8.1a), and 50 percent of the total votes were cast for the Civic Forum alone.[3] The Civic Forum united dissident groups from the broad anticommunist platform. Herbert Kitschelt and his coauthors justify the movement's success by pointing out that in the absence of "pre-existing proto-parties on the scene after the sudden collapse of the communist regime, political support initially congealed around broad anti-communist electoral alliances that emphasized civil rights and democratic reforms."[4]

The following elections saw parties' programs differentiated more clearly, especially on economic-distributive issues. The right continued to dominate elections in 1992 and 1996, obtaining close to 60 percent of votes (Figure 8.1a). The respective governments were led by the Civic Democratic Party (Občanská demokratická strana, ODS), a pro-market center-right party and the strongest party to emanate from the Civic Forum after its dissolution. The Civic Democratic Party, under its leader

---

2. Public against Violence (VPN) was its counterpart in Slovakia.

3. We put Civic Forum on the right of the political spectrum due to its dominantly liberal leadership and due to the fact that the right-wing liberal Civic Democratic Party (ODS) was formed from it.

4. H. Kitschelt, Z. Mansfeldova, R. Markowski, and G. Tóka, *Post-Communist Party Systems: Competition, Representation, and Inter-party Cooperation* (Cambridge University Press, 1999).

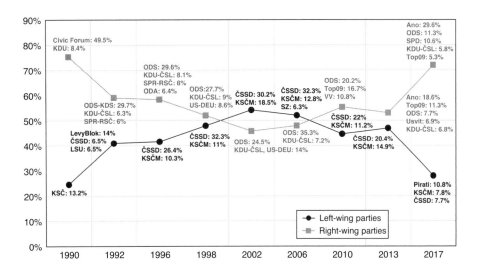

FIGURE 8.1 *(a)*. Election results in the Czech Republic, 1990–2017
*Data Source:* Authors' computations using official election results (see wpid.world).
*Note:* Labels show parties that received more than 5% of total votes.

Vaclav Klaus, was the main architect of the reforms conducted following the transition in the Czech Republic.[5]

The widespread disillusionment that followed the shattering of the "Czech transitional miracle," accompanied by the perceived failure of voucher privatization and corruption scandals, led to a strong rise of the left in the mid-1990s, and a major political and financial crisis in 1997 resulted in the fall of the ODS government. However, in contrast to Poland and Hungary, in the Czech Republic the largest party on the left, the center-left Czech Social Democratic Party (Česká strana sociálně demokratická, ČSSD), was not a direct successor of the former ruling communist party. Instead, the successor party was the Communist Party of Bohemia and Moravia (Komunistická strana Čech a Moravy, KSČM), which assumed a more unreformed position and thus chose not to follow its Hungarian and Polish counterparts, who transformed themselves into social democratic parties to appeal to a broader electorate.[6] As seen in

5. S. Hanley, *The New Right in the New Europe: Czech Transformation and Right-Wing Politics, 1989–2006* (Routledge, 2007).

6. A. M. Grzymala-Busse, *Redeeming the Communist Past: The Regeneration of Communist Parties in East Central Europe* (Cambridge University Press, 2002).

Figure 8.1a, Czech electoral competition from 1998 to 2013 was characterized by close races between the left and the right, with both of their vote shares close to 50 percent. The governments in this period were led either by the ODS or by the ČSSD. The entire period was generally marked by a notable stability in party competition (in stark contrast to the right-wing parties in Poland, for instance), with the two main parties on the left and on the right alternating at the top, followed by relatively stable vote shares of the KSČM and the Christian Democratic Union (Křesťanská a demokratická unie—Československá strana lidová, KDU-ČSL).[7]

The implosion of the two "mainstream" parties—first the ODS in 2013, following a corruption scandal, and then the ČSSD in 2017—resulted in a profound realignment of the Czech political scene. On the right, new parties emerged such as the conservative Tradition Responsibility Prosperity 09 (Tradice Odpovědnost Prosperita, TOP 09), Mayors and Independents (Starostové a nezávislí, STAN), and most importantly, the "technocratic populist" ANO 2011 of the billionaire Andrej Babiš, which became the winner of the 2017 elections. Furthermore, the support for the populist radical right party Freedom and Direct Democracy (Svoboda a přímá demokracie, SPD) increased. At the opposite end of the political spectrum, a prominent entrant was the antiestablishment cosmopolitan-liberal Pirate Party, which came third in the 2017 elections. What most of the newcomer parties have in common is their programmatic focus on the fight against corruption (while enduring corruption scandals are an important reason for the decline of mainstream parties). Meanwhile, as Figure 8.1a shows, the vote share obtained by left parties collapsed dramatically in the 2017 election. As the traditional supporters of the center-left ČSSD switched support to ANO 2011, the left parties obtained less than one-third of all votes.[8]

HUNGARY. The first election in Hungary resulted in a fragmented party system with eleven parties receiving more than 1 percent of votes. This fragmented system articulated a number of cross-cutting and weakly

---

7. T. Haughton and K. Deegan-Krause, "In with the New (Again): Populist Appeals and Party System Volatility from Macro and Micro Perspectives" (paper presented at the Annual Meeting of the American Political Science Association, Washington, DC, September 2010).

8. The center-left party lost some supporters from areas they were traditionally strong in, such as the industrialized regions of Ústí nad Labem and Ostrava. At the same time, the Czech Pirate Party became the most important party on the left.

correlated political cleavages.[9] Notable political cleavages were present between the former communist parties, represented by the Hungarian Socialist Party (Magyar Szocialista Párt, MSZP) and the parties formed from the opposition movements of the 1980s. A further cleavage could be drawn among the communist-era dissidents between the pro-market, liberal parties embodied by the Alliance of Free Democrats (Szabad Demokraták Szövetsége, SZDSZ) and Fidesz, and the right-wing Christian national parties represented by the Hungarian Democratic Forum (Magyar Demokrata Fórum, MDF), the Christian Democratic People's Party (Kereszténydemokrata Néppárt, KDNP), and the Independent Smallholders' Party (Független Kisgazdapárt, FKgP).[10] The latter group received around 60 percent of the votes and so the first democratically elected government in Hungary after the communist era was formed by right-wing parties.

Nevertheless, the economic hardship caused by the transition took its toll, and the support for governing right-wing parties soon decreased dramatically. People's nostalgia for the socialist regime and the perceived incompetence and factionalism of the right-wing government put into power the formal communist party (MSZP) in the second Hungarian elections in 1994. Although the MSZP had a majority in the parliament and could therefore have governed alone, they opted to form a coalition with the largest liberal party, the SZDSZ, to improve the international reputation of their government and show their commitment to the market system and democracy. The government formed from this peculiar coalition between former communists and dissidents implemented a radical reform agenda that involved a series of austerity measures and pro-market policies.

Meanwhile, the other liberal party, Fidesz, became increasingly conservative and rose to become the leading force of the center right.[11] By the next election in 1998, Fidesz was the dominant party on the right,

9. G. Tóka and S. Popa, "Hungary," in *Handbook of Political Change in Eastern Europe*, ed. S. Berglund, J. Ekman, K. Deegan-Krause, and O. Knutsen (Edgar Elgar, 2013), 291–338.

10. We assign Fidesz to the left-liberal parties in the 1990 election. In the early 1990s, Fidesz was a center-liberal party and its closest ideological ally was the SZDSZ. However, the 1993 party congress changed Fidesz's political position from liberal to civic-centrist, and after the 1994 elections the party moved to the conservative right.

11. K. Gergely and G. Tóka, "The Electorate, 1990–1998," in *Hungary: Government and Politics 1848–2000*, ed. M. Ormos and B. K. Király (Social Science Monographs, 2001), 495–518.

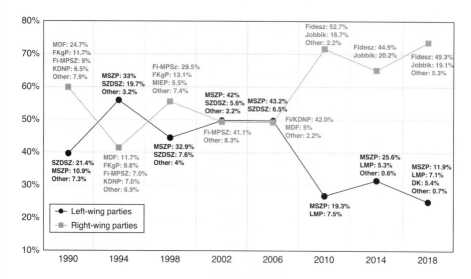

FIGURE 8.1 *(b)*. Election results in Hungary, 1990-2018
*Data Source:* Authors' computations using official election results (see wpid.world).
*Note:* List votes are reported. After 2006 votes for Fidesz include votes for KDNP.

and this electoral success put them into power. A right-wing coalition government was formed by Fidesz and the FKgP, a populist agrarian party.

The alliance of the SZDSZ with the MSZP and Fidesz's shift to the right eliminated the independent liberal pole in the Hungarian party system and led to the emergence of a major political cleavage between the left-liberal parties and right-wing Christian national parties. In Figure 8.1b, we plot vote shares by this political cleavage starting with the first democratic election in 1990. The vote shares of left-liberal and right-wing parties were each close to 50 percent until 2010. Governments formed from right-wing parties (1998–2002) and from left-liberal parties (2002–2010) were alternating in power. In this period, something very close to a two-party system emerged and the different cleavages were absorbed in the opposition between the two poles.[12]

In 2010 a significant realignment of the party system took place. Support for the left parties that were in power from 2002 to 2010 collapsed. Their electoral base dropped to 25 percent as a result of the economic hardship ignited by the Great Recession and the perceived failure of their

12. Tóka and Popa, "Hungary."

293

austerity-driven "reform" agenda. Meanwhile, the Fidesz party led by Viktor Orbán received more than 50 percent of the votes.

Furthermore, two new political forces emerged in the 2010 election. Jobbik (Jobbik Magyarországért Mozgalom, The Movement for a Better Hungary) built up support from far-right voters and dissatisfied voters who had lost faith in "traditional" left- and right-wing parties, while LMP (Lehet más a politika, Politics Can Be Different) was formed around green issues. While these new parties opposed vehemently the policies implemented by Fidesz, they also kept equal distance from the left-wing parties that were in power from 2002 to 2010. As a result, the party system that had resembled a two-party system became again more fragmented in 2010. In this political landscape, the winner-take-all aspect of the Hungarian electoral system, which was further strengthened in the new constitution passed in 2011, worked in favor of Fidesz.[13] The party could translate 45 to 50 percent of votes into a supermajority representation in the Hungarian parliament in the subsequent elections in 2014 and 2018.

This unprecedented electoral mandate allowed Orbán to reshape and take over key economic and political institutions. The government adopted a new constitution and passed a new media law that made the public broadcaster an outlet of Fidesz. Public procurement contracts were won by a small group of entrepreneurs loyal to the prime minister. Meanwhile, Fidesz adopted increasingly Eurosceptic and populist elements in its rhetoric and its policies. For instance, before the 2014 election the government's flagship policy was *rezsicsökkentés,* which compelled utility suppliers, which were predominantly owned by multinational companies, to cut utility prices. The party also introduced strong anti-immigration and antirefugee rhetoric in response to the refugee crisis in 2015 and developed nativist tendencies.

In response to the third consecutive supermajority for Fidesz (2010, 2014, 2018), political cleavages between the opposition parties started to vanish. They were replaced by one dominant cleavage defined in relation to Viktor Orbán's regime.

POLAND. The history of the Polish party system after 1989 can be structured around two key periods: a period of consensus on transition to

---

13. G. Tóka, "Constitutional Principles and Electoral Democracy Constitution Building," in *Consolidated Democracies: A New Beginning or Decay of a Political System?*, ed. E. Bos and K. Pócza (Nomos Verlag, 2014), 311–328.

a market economy (1989–2005), and the liberal-nativist divide (2005 onward). In the former period, the cleavage between the parties of the former regime and those from the opposition movement was dominant. The latter period saw the emergence of an economic-distributive cleavage and a liberal-nativist one. In the 1989 Polish legislative elections, in which one-third of the lower-house seats were contested by representatives of the Solidarity opposition movement, Solidarity campaigned on a pro-democracy platform, with immense success. A coalition government composed of Solidarity and breakaway satellites of the Communist Party led to a non-communist government that formed and enacted the Balcerowicz plan. This set the tone for Poland's economic transition: a free-market economy through price liberalization, a tight monetary policy, and privatization of state-owned enterprises.

The first fully free parliamentary elections, in 1991, were won by the right on a platform of ridding politics of elements of the communist regime. However, it was marked by a severe splintering of groupings formerly under the Solidarity banner, along economic, sociocultural, and anticommunist dimensions. From 1991 to 2005, the two dominant political cleavages related to the pace and shape of economic reform on the one hand, and parties' relationships with the former communist regime on the other. Figure 8.1c shows the vote shares for the left and right in Poland since 1991. As shown, the period 1991–2005 was characterized by alternating right-wing and left-wing governments. Underlying this was significant initial fragmentation and volatility in the composition of parties on the right of the political spectrum,[14] while the left continued to be dominated by the postcommunist Democratic Left Alliance (Sojusz Lewicy Demokratycznej, SLD) and the agrarian Polish People's Party (Polskie Stronnictwo Ludowe, PSL).

The left-wing electoral victories in this period, in 1993 and 2001, were a product of fatigue with economic reforms pursued by preceding right-wing governments, their internal divisions, and their perceived incompetence. Nonetheless, under the two left-wing SLD-PSL governments, the

---

14. In 1991, there were eight right-wing parties that received more than 2 percent of the vote, although none received more than 12 percent in an election without an electoral threshold. Only three right-wing parties crossed the 5 percent threshold in the 1993 elections, leading most of these right-wing parties to unify under the AWS coalition for the 1997 election.

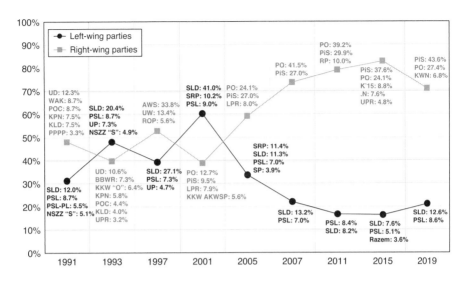

FIGURE 8.1 *(c)*. Election results in Poland, 1991–2019
*Data Source:* Authors' computations using official election results (see wpid.world).
*Note:* Labels show parties that obtained more than 3% of total votes.

overall direction of reform was maintained. They pursued fiscally conservative policies and sustained efforts toward Poland's accession to international organizations such as NATO and the EU.

Meanwhile, on the right, there was an absence of programmatic clarity
on economic issues, with the notable exception of the Democratic Union
(Unia Demokratyczna, UD), later the Freedom Union (Unia Wolności,
UW). This was the only party with a consistent market-liberal platform.
For the other parties on the right, the sociocultural cleavage and the
cleavage with ex-communists were central.[15] There were groupings on
both the right and left that opposed aspects of the economic transformation, but pro-reform wings tended to dominate economic policy when in
government. The right-wing government formed after the 1997 elections,
led by Solidarity Electoral Action (Akcja Wyborcza Solidarność, AWS),
opted for a series of reforms in coalition with the market-liberal UW, with
Balcerowicz again as minister of finance. As an illustration of the continuity of economic policy between the left- and right-wing governments

15. Kitschelt et al., *Post-Communist Party Systems.*

of the time, Balcerowicz admitted that "the SLD's economic policies and goals [were] virtually indistinguishable from those of UW."[16]

Austerity under the 2001–2005 left-wing government led to the collapse of the left in the 2005 election. Since then, electoral competition in Poland has been dominated by two major parties on the right, namely Civic Platform (Platforma Obywatelska, PO) and Law and Justice (Prawo i Sprawiedliwość, PiS). This period is marked by a decline in the importance of the cleavage between former dissident groups and former communist parties, and a rise in the prominence of an economic-redistributive cleavage. PO can be seen as being in the tradition of the market-liberal Freedom Union, while the latter inherited the socially conservative outlook of some of the right-wing parties of the early 1990s.[17] PO primarily emphasized the need for infrastructure development and further integration into the EU, while PiS reached out to groups who did not share the gains of the transition and developed a conservative social platform, a rejection of the post-1989 consensus,[18] and a weeding out of corruption. Several smaller parties also emerged on both right and left, but were often short-lived. In 2005, the first coalition government involving PiS emerged, but it collapsed in 2007 after a corruption scandal involving the minor coalition partners, ushering in a period of two consecutive PO-dominated governments from 2007 to 2015. In the 2015 election, PiS managed to obtain a majority of seats in parliament and form a government without a coalition partner. This election saw no left-wing party gain seats in parliament for the first time since 1991, after a left-wing coalition led by the SLD failed to cross the 8 percent threshold. The 2019 election saw PiS maintain its number of seats from 2015, with PO continuing to dominate the opposition benches, and with a return of left-wing seats to parliament.

In all three Central European countries, we find that the support for traditional left parties collapsed toward the end of the period we study here. In many cases, this collapse in support was driven by the fact that

16. *Financial Times,* March 27, 1997.

17. In fact, Law and Justice can be seen as a direct descendant of the conservative Center Agreement Party (Porozumienie Centrum, PC), founded in 1990 by Jarosław Kaczyński, which did well in the 1991 elections with a staunchly anticommunist platform, receiving 8.7 percent of the vote. This party then joined the AWS umbrella group in 1997, and members of PC made up the core of Law and Justice after it was formed by Lech and Jarosław Kaczyński for the 2001 elections.

18. For instance, in 2005 Law and Justice argued for the creation of a new "Fourth Polish Republic" rejecting the corrupt norms of public life that characterized the Third Polish Republic (the official name of the Polish state post-1989).

left-wing parties in the region often pursued conservative economic policies, and fiscal austerity in particular.[19] Furthermore, the slower than anticipated economic catch-up to Western European living standards, accompanied by the economic impact of the Great Recession, shook the political and economic institutions in Central Europe. In each country, nativist and populist parties attained power starting with Viktor Orbán's Fidesz in 2010, Law and Justice in 2015, and ANO in 2017.[20] We will describe below what drives these tendencies.

## Inequality and Political Cleavages

### *Income*

We first look at the evolution of income-based electoral cleavages in the three countries since the early 1990s. As in the other chapters in this volume, we present the evolution of income gradients as summarized by a simple steepness indicator, namely the difference between the fraction voting left (or right) among top 10 percent income earners and the fraction voting left (or right) among bottom 90 percent income earners.

CZECH REPUBLIC. Figure 8.2a shows the evolution of the income gradient from the top 10 percent to the bottom 90 percent in the Czech Republic. The figure provides clear evidence of "class voting" in the Czech Republic and confirms the claim that economic-redistributive divides have been a major political cleavage. Specifically, voters in the top 10 percent of income in the Czech Republic always vote more for the right (ODS-Top09) than voters in the bottom 90 percent of income.[21] In contrast, the left (ČSSD-KSČM) exhibits a negative income gradient that mirrors that of

19. M. Tavits and N. Letki, "When Left Is Right: Party Ideology and Policy in Post-communist Europe," *American Political Science Review* 103, no. 4 (2009): 555–569.

20. R. Wike, J. Poushter, L. Silver, K. Devlin, J. Fetterolf, A. Castillo, and C. Huang, "European Public Opinion Three Decades after the Fall of Communism," Pew Research Center, October 15, 2019. https://www.pewresearch.org/global/2019/10/15/european-public-opinion-three-decades-after-the-fall-of-communism/. The term "populist" has been contentious, and we choose to use it in the way it has been developed by Cas Mudde, namely as a thin-centered ideology that considers society to be ultimately separated into two homogenous and antagonistic groups, 'the pure people' and 'the corrupt elite,' and argues that politics should be an expression of the general will of the people. See C. Mudde, "The Populist Zeitgeist," *Government and Opposition* 39, no. 4 (2004): 541–563.

21. Appendix Figures A3a and A4a, World Political Cleavages and Inequality Database, http://wpid.world, show a steeply rising profile of voting for right-wing parties (and a declining profile of voting for left-wing parties), with almost 70 percent of vote within the top 10 percent income group voting for the right.

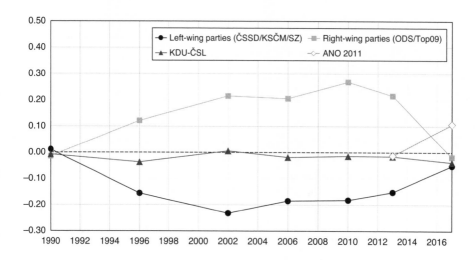

FIGURE 8.2 *(a)*. Vote and income in the Czech Republic, 1990–2017
*Data Source:* Authors' computations using postelectoral surveys (see wpid.world).
*Note:* The figure shows the difference between the share of top 10% earners and the share
of bottom 90% earners voting for the main Czech parties or groups of parties, after
controlling for age, gender, and education. In 1996, left-wing parties obtained a score
that was 16 points lower among top 10% earners than among the bottom 90%; in 2017,
their score was 5 points lower. The right includes Civic Forum in 1990 and STAN in 2017.

the right. The income gradient of the Christian democrats (KDU-ČSL)
has been consistently around zero, in line with its centrist positioning.

It is interesting to note that the importance of class voting has come
full circle from the first democratic elections in 1990 to the most recent
elections in 2017. The 1990 elections, as discussed above, could better
be seen as the democratic plebiscite. By the mid-1990s, programmatic left-
right competition on economic issues had already crystallized in the Czech
Republic, epitomized by competition between the liberal-conservative
Civic Democratic Party (ODS) on the right side of the spectrum and
the Czech Social Democratic Party (ČSSD) on the left. Indeed, the Czech
Social Democratic Party has programmatically positioned itself on economic (and social policy) issues and has also refused to play the card of
"cultural liberalism."[22] In addition, the left in the Czech Republic includes

22. M. Perrotino and M. Polašek, "Czech Republic," in F. Escalona, M. Vieira, and
J. M. De Waele, eds., *The Palgrave Handbook of Social Democracy in the European
Union* (Palgrave Macmillan, 2013), 438.

the electorally relatively strong Communist Party (KSČM), which has consistently promoted an anti-market position and disproportionally attracted the support of low-income voters.

Looking at the results of the 2017 elections, the question of whether these results suggest a structural decline of class voting in the Czech Republic naturally arises. The income gradient of the left shows a declining trend since the early 2000s, with an even more notable decline in 2017.[23] On the other hand, the drop in the gradient of the established right (principally of ODS) in 2017 is still more precipitous, and it is only partly compensated by the rising income gradient of ANO 2011.

Overall, the "cultural" discourse has undoubtedly become more important in Czech elections. The erosion of two mainstream parties, firmly positioned at the opposite poles of the traditional left-right axis, and the victory of the populist ANO 2011 with a (deliberately) less divisive programmatic profile (the party principally ran on an anticorruption platform), may suggest that identity-based politics is on rise and the Czech political arena has started to assume contours observed in Hungary and Poland.

HUNGARY. Figure 8.2b highlights that unlike in the Czech Republic, "class" voting aspects have played a rather limited role in understanding political cleavages in Hungary, except in the 2018 election. In fact, the relationship between income and the vote appears to be quite the opposite of what we would expect based on traditional "class voting" in 1998 (and also in 2014), when left-wing parties (social democrats and affiliated) won a larger fraction of top 10 percent voters than right-wing parties did. Overall, the income gradient in party support remains quite flat until the 2018 election.

The missing income gradient in explaining the support for social democratic parties can be attributed in part to the cooperation between liberal and left parties since 1994. Since the major left party in Hungary (MSZP) was the successor of former communist parties, it sought to establish credibility regarding its commitment to a market economy. To demonstrate a decisive break with the past, the left-wing parties often pursued conservative economic policies, in particular fiscal austerity,[24] and sought an alliance with the market-liberal SZDSZ.

---

23. Note that although the income gradient of ČSSD becomes insignificant in 2017, the income gradient of the Communist Party remains consistently negative.

24. Tavits and Letki, "When Left Is Right."

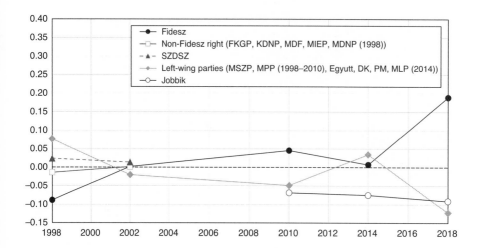

FIGURE 8.2 *(b)*. Vote and income in Hungary, 1998–2018
*Data Source:* Authors' computations using postelection surveys for 1998 and 2002,
ESS for all other years (see wpid.world).
*Note:* The figure shows the difference between the share of top 10% earners and the
share of bottom 90% earners voting for the main Hungarian parties or groups of
parties, after controlling for age, gender, and education. In 1998, top 10% earners
were less likely to vote Fidesz by 9 percentage points, while they were more likely to
do so by 19 percentage points in 2018. No data on income in 2006.

The liberal-left coalition implemented a series of austerity measures from
2006 to 2010. These measures eroded the party's support in low-income
groups, but were somewhat popular among the top 10 percent voters
who saw these policies as a step in the right direction in reforming the
country.[25]

Interestingly, in the 2018 election we see a voting pattern that is consistent with class voting. The right-wing Fidesz gets disproportionately
more votes from the rich than from the poor, while left-wing parties attracted the opposite type of voters. Nevertheless, it is unclear yet whether
these results suggest a structural emergence of class voting in Hungary
or this voting pattern constitutes an outlier. The 2018 election was

25. Survey data from Hungarian Election Studies in 2009 showed that the MSZP's
left-wing identity was questioned by many: around 62 percent of voters thought that the
MSZP was the party of the elite and only 25 percent agreed that the socialists represented
the workers and the poor. See A. Bíró-Nagy, "Hungary," in Escalona, Vieira, and Waele,
*Palgrave Handbook of Social Democracy,* 454.

uniquely centered around the issue of immigration, a topic that only recently became relevant in the context of the 2015 refugee crisis. In contrast, in the 2014 election Fidesz attracted a larger fraction of the voters from the bottom 90 percent than left-wing parties did, thanks largely to the *rezsicsökkentés* (see above), which was highly popular among low-income voters.

Figure 8.2b also shows the income gradients for other right-wing parties. In 1998 and 2002 the voting gradient of the non-Fidesz right is similar to that of Fidesz. After 2010, the voting gradient for Jobbik, the far-right radical nationalist party, diverges from Fidesz's as a larger fraction of its electoral base is drawn from voters among the bottom 90 percent. By the end of the period, Jobbik's income gradient looks more similar to that of the left-wing parties than that of Fidesz.

POLAND. With the notable exception of the vote for UD/UW, the main liberal party in the 1990s, as in Hungary, in Poland we initially find little evidence of "class" voting, until the emergence of political competition between Law and Justice and Civic Platform from 2005 (Figure 8.2c). For the three elections from 1991 to 1997, we present the income gradients for three parties. The first is the SLD on the left. The second, on the right, is the post-Solidarity NSZZ "Solidarność" (in 1991 and 1993), which became the core of AWS in 1997. This latter group continues the tradition of the Solidarity trade union as a political party. Additionally, we show the income gradient for the Democratic Union (UD), which later transformed into the Freedom Union (UW) and represented a both economically and socially liberal electoral platform.

In the first fully free elections after the transition, in 1991, we see evidence of an income gradient only for the liberal UD party. In 1993 and 1997, voters from the bottom 90 percent tended to be slightly more likely than the top 10 percent to vote for the main left-wing party, the SLD, but this was reversed in the 2001 and 2005 elections. This weak income gradient reflects a similar trend found in Hungary in this period and is likely to demonstrate the constraints faced by postcommunist parties.[26] The main party inheriting the Solidarity tradition, NSZZ Solidarność, tended to have a small negative income gradient in 1991 and 1993, and in this period could claim to be a working-class party with more justification than the SLD. However, after NSZZ Solidarność established AWS

26. Tavits and Letki, "When Left Is Right."

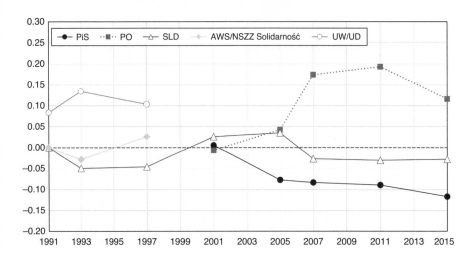

FIGURE 8.2 *(c)*. Vote and income in Poland, 1991–2015

*Data Source:* Authors' computations using POLPAN (1991–1997), CSES (2001, 2005), and ESS (2007–2015) (see wpid.world).

*Note:* The figure shows the difference between the share of top 10% earners and the share of bottom 90% earners voting for the main Polish parties or groups of parties, after controlling for age, gender, and education. During the 2007–2015 period, top 10% earners were less likely to vote PiS by between 8 and 12 percentage points, while they were more likely to vote for the Civic Platform by 12 to 19 percentage points.

in the 1997 elections, in which AWS won the largest share of the vote, the party seems to have had increased its relative appeal to the top 10 percent.

While in the 1990s we did not observe a stark gradient in income for the SLD, or for AWS in 1997, a very sharp positive gradient emerged for Civic Platform from 2005, and a sharp negative gradient emerged for PiS in the same period. Interestingly, in 2001, we do not see a relationship between belonging to the top 10 percent and a vote for either Civic Platform or PiS. By 2005, however, we see a distinct separation between these two parties along the income dimension, with PiS capturing a larger share of the vote from the bottom 90 percent than from the top 10 percent, while the top 10 percent was more likely to vote for Civic Platform. In 2007, voters in the top 10 percent were more likely than voters in the bottom 90 percent to vote for Civic Platform, by 17 percentage points, while voters in the top 10 percent were 8 percent less likely to vote for PiS, after controls for education, age, and gender. The negative income gradient for PiS was a feature of Polish elections in all subsequent elections,

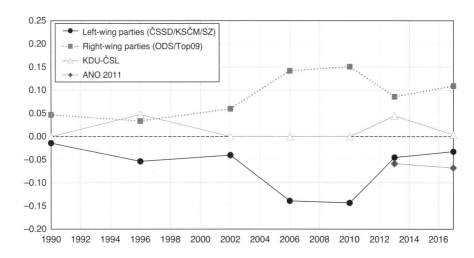

FIGURE 8.3 *(a)*. The educational cleavage in the Czech Republic, 1990–2017
*Data Source:* Authors' computations using postelectoral surveys (see wpid.world).
*Note:* The figure shows the difference between the share of university graduates and the
share of non-university graduates voting for the main Czech parties or groups of parties,
after controlling for age, gender, and income. In 1996, university graduates were more
likely to vote for right-wing parties by 3 percentage points, compared to 11 points in 2017.

although the positive income gradient for Civic Platform became less
strong in the 2015 election. The latter phenomenon is likely a reflection of
Civic Platform's trend toward being more of a catchall party, which is also
borne out by the success of the pro-market and socially liberal party
Modern in the 2015 election. If anything, belonging to the bottom
90 percent made it more likely that an individual would vote PiS in 2015.

## Education

Chapter 2 shows that left-wing parties (socialists, labor, democrats) in
France, the United Kingdom, and the United States have profoundly
transformed themselves from parties of low-educated to high-educated
voters (see also Chapter 1). It further argues that this reversal of the education cleavage may be seen as one of the most important political realignments in recent decades. Looking at the education gradient in Figures 8.3a, 8.3b, and 8.3c—expressed as the difference between the fraction
of university graduates voting left (right) and the fraction of non–university

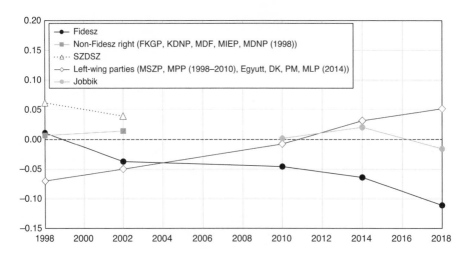

FIGURE 8.3 *(b)*. The educational cleavage in Hungary, 1998–2018

*Data Source:* Authors' computations using postelection surveys for 1998 and 2002, ESS for all other years (see wpid.world).

*Note:* The figure shows the difference between the share of university graduates and the share of non-university graduates voting for the main Hungarian parties or groups of parties, after controlling for age, gender, and income. In 1998, university graduates were more likely to vote Fidesz by 1 percentage point, while they were less likely to do so by 11 points in 2018. No data on income in 2006.

graduates voting left (right)—reveals that these tendencies are observed only in Hungary and not in the Czech Republic or Poland.

CZECH REPUBLIC. Figure 8.3a shows the evolution of the education gradient in the Czech Republic. Broadly in line with income, voting for the right (left) is associated with higher (lower) education. It can be seen that college-educated voters have always tended to vote more for the right. The gap has consistently been large and positive, suggesting a difference of 5 to 15 percentage points between voters with a university degree and those with lower education. The left, on the other hand, has disproportionally attracted lower-educated voters. The education gradient of the ČSSD displays a more irregular pattern (negative most of the time, but around zero in 2002 and 2017). Overall, the observed patterns do not suggest a clear trend and there is no indication that the educational cleavage has been reversed, as observed in Western Europe.

HUNGARY. Figure 8.3b shows that in Hungary education is more important than income in explaining voting behavior. In the 1998 elections

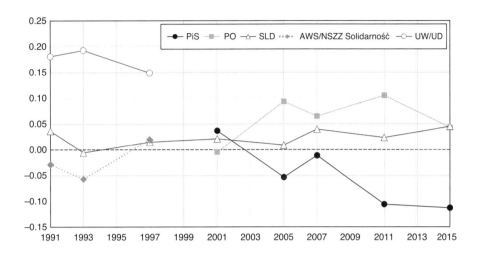

FIGURE 8.3 *(c)*. The educational cleavage in Poland, 1991–2015
*Data Source:* Authors' computations using POLPAN (1991–1997), CSES (2001, 2005), and ESS (2007–2015) (see wpid.world).
*Note:* The figure shows the difference between the share of university graduates and the share of non-university graduates voting for the main Polish parties or groups of parties, after controlling for age, gender, and income. During the 2007–2015 period, university graduates were less likely to vote PiS by 1 to 11 percentage points, while they were more likely to vote for the Civic Platform by 5 to 11 percentage points.

left parties (MSZP, MPP) were more popular among low-educated voters, while the liberal party, SZDSZ, was more popular among higher-educated voters. We do not observe a stark gradient in education for Fidesz and other right-wing parties. Thereafter, the left-wing parties increasingly attracted highly educated, urban voters, while Fidesz became more popular among lower-educated, rural voters. These differences become especially apparent in the most recent elections in 2018. By then, the left had become the party of the intellectual elite (Brahmin left), while the right seemed to attract voters from the business elite (merchant right)—a pattern that is also observed in most Western European countries (see Chapter 1).

POLAND. In Figure 8.3c, we plot the education gradient in Polish elections over the 1991–2015 period. Analogous to the pattern for income, in 1991 it does not appear that the lower educated are more likely than the more highly educated to vote for the SLD. If anything, the contrary seems to be true, and this persists for the entire period. Combined with weak evidence of an income gradient, which was only occasionally and

slightly negative for the SLD in 1993–1997 and 2007–2015, the SLD is the strongest candidate for a "Brahmin left" party in the specific context of posttransition Poland. It would appear that NSZZ Solidarność had a small but noticeable negative gradient in education in 1991–1993, although this disappears in 1997 after this party founded the AWS coalition.[27] Finally, a very strong positive education gradient exists for the UD/UW party in 1991–1997.

As was the case for income, there is no education gradient for both Civic Platform and PiS in 2001. However, by 2005 a separation has occurred between the two parties, with a gap opening up between voters with college education and those below. From this point on, voters with higher education were more likely to vote for Civic Platform, while those with below college education were more likely to vote for PiS. However, as for income, the education gradient for Civic Platform declined somewhat in 2015. The negative gradient in voting for PiS remained strong in both 2011 and 2015.

### Conclusion

Politics in Central European countries have been turbulent in the last thirty years, and this was accompanied by changing political cleavages. Nevertheless, there are notable similarities among the three countries studied here.

One of the most salient cleavages for the three countries we study appears to be education, with liberal free-market parties dominating the high-education vote immediately after the transition from communism: ODS in the Czech Republic, SZDSZ in Hungary, and UW/UD in Poland. To a large extent, this education cleavage was mirrored by a cleavage in income in the Czech Republic and in Poland, but not in Hungary. In each country, these political parties had an overwhelmingly important influence on the nature of economic reforms, in Poland and the Czech Republic as key members of right-wing governing coalitions, and in Hungary as a partner in a coalition with the ex-communist MSZP.

The key differences between the three countries can be seen when we compare the emergence and success of parties catering to a low-income and low-education electorate. It is particularly insightful to compare the

27. AWS was comprised of a multitude of other right-wing groupings, though NSZZ Solidarność was its initiator and largest constituent.

experiences of Hungary and Poland on the one hand with that of the Czech Republic on the other. In Poland, neither the postcommunist SLD on the left nor the myriad of right-wing parties that emerged out of the Solidarity movement established themselves as either low-income or low-education parties. In Hungary, the ex-communist MSZP was initially a party with an electoral base of lower-educated voters, but this was eroded over time because MSZP was implementing pro-market policies when in power. Meanwhile, in the Czech Republic, both the ex-communist KSČM and the social democratic ČSSD established themselves as low-income and low-education parties.

Why did left-wing (social democratic and affiliated) parties in Poland and Hungary not take up that role by pursuing more egalitarian policies, for example? An important factor is that the main left parties in both countries were the successors of the ruling parties under the previous socialist regimes. The desire to break with the communist past hindered these parties from pursuing a distributional agenda and filling the traditional position of left-wing parties. We can find a notable example of this phenomenon in Hungary. When the former communist party MSZP won the elections in 1994 and obtained a majority representation in the parliament, it decided to join forces with the pro-market liberal SZDSZ to form the government rather than pushing for more redistribution single-handedly.

By the 2000s, the left-wing parties in Hungary and Poland were not viable alternatives for lower-education or lower-income voters. This had profound implications for political competition in these countries. After the initial transition period, corruption scandals and austerity had a critical influence on the public's disillusionment with governments dominated by the ex-communist left. Starting in 2005, PiS in Poland managed to attract lower-income and lower-education voters who had not benefited from the fruits of the transition, while at the same time putting forward a conservative and nativist political platform. The formerly market-liberal Fidesz rode a wave of anger at the MSZP government in 2010 and ultimately adopted a nativist platform in a similar way. Fidesz's electoral base, however, differed from that of PiS, as it received considerable support from high-income voters and became a high-income party in the 2018 elections. The opposition to PiS in Poland was centered around the market-liberal Civic Platform. In Hungary, opposition to Fidesz was centered around the MSZP, which has become more economically egalitarian in recent years.

In contrast, the collapse of support for the left in the Czech Republic was not matched by the rise of a nativist political alternative, as in Poland and Hungary. Rather, the rise of ANO may best be explained by their focus on a "centrist populism." While it rejects establishment politicians as the corrupt elite, this party is close to the center of the electorate in terms of attitudes on redistribution and the EU, and it does not exhibit a strong gradient in either income or education. We posit that the type of right-wing populism found in Poland and Hungary was simply not viable as an electoral strategy in the Czech Republic, as the main parties had already dominated the polar positions on the economic-redistributive and nativist parts of the political spectrum.

Importantly, the present-day cleavages found in Central Europe have started to resemble those found in Western European countries. Both the nativist-globalist conflict and the pro- and antiredistribution cleavage manifest in the electoral competition observed in Poland, Hungary, and in the Czech Republic. Interestingly, however, the pro-EU vote is associated with the market-liberal parties in Poland and the Czech Republic and with egalitarian left-wing parties in Hungary.

What can explain these observed differences? Both Fidesz in Hungary and PiS in Poland positioned themselves to take advantage of the vacuum created by the disappearance of the left-wing parties. However, Fidesz's market-liberal roots made it opt for a different stance on redistribution than PiS, which consciously headlines redistributive policies. Furthermore, Fidesz took power in 2010 after the collapse of the left, which can be attributed to their perceived incompetence at governing through and handling the Great Recession. As a result, these parties could not be a viable alternative for low-income voters, and so Fidesz did not need to implement redistributive policies to attract these voters. Instead, Fidesz achieved a large electoral coalition premised on a rejection of the left-wing incumbent parties. On the other hand, PiS came into power in 2015 after its main competitor, Civic Platform, handled the Great Recession relatively successfully. In that context, PiS managed to persuade low-income voters by implementing pro-redistribution policies.

Finally, there are also considerable differences in the nature of populism across the three countries studied here. To a certain extent, the populist parties have responded to an increase in demand for protection from economic insecurity and from the radical change in cultural values. A mixture of conservative identity politics and economic redistributive

policies of populist parties such as Law and Justice in Poland and Fidesz in Hungary has fallen on fertile ground. This has coalesced into the broader "social-nativist" agenda.[28] However, we see in both of these countries that no redistributive-economic political cleavage between the left and right was shaping political competition during the first phase of transition, which could explain why the populists could later fill this gap. In the Czech Republic, where such a cleavage was salient and had long existed, the populist entry did not have a strong redistributive dimension.[29]

Social democratic and affiliated parties in Hungary and in Poland therefore seem to have relied on a relatively highly educated electorate with low income. This has potentially opened up space for nativist populism in Hungary and Poland. Between these two countries, however, there are important differences. In Poland, the emergent nativism is more egalitarian. In Hungary, the picture is more nuanced as the electoral coalition sustaining Fidesz is different, and populism therefore is more inegalitarian. In the Czech Republic, however, where the left has been representing low-income and low-education individuals from the beginning, populism has taken a centrist, and less nativist, stance.

28. T. Piketty, *Capital and Ideology* (Harvard University Press, 2020).

29. This is apparent in appendix Figures A10a, A10b, and A10c, wpid.world, which show the evolution of the political preferences by party of each country's voters along two key dimensions: openness, as measured by pro-EU sentiment, and redistributive preferences.

# 9

# Caste, Class, and the Changing Political Representation of Social Inequalities in India, 1962–2019

ABHIJIT BANERJEE, AMORY GETHIN, AND THOMAS PIKETTY

## Introduction

What governs the choice of who to vote for in India? How has it changed over time? And to what extent has Indian democracy and its now 900 million voters succeeded in aggregating political conflicts associated with caste, class, religion, ethnolinguistic diversity, and rising inequality? To answer these questions, this chapter makes use of postelectoral surveys conducted from 1962 to 2016, covering both national elections and state elections.[1] In India, the political representation of inequality has largely been determined by the caste system. Caste has always been tightly linked to occupation and wealth, but it has never been the sole determinant of socioeconomic inequalities. Understanding how caste, religion, and class interact, and to what extent political parties have relied on mobilizations based on one or the other, is one of the objectives of this chapter. Our findings reveal three main patterns.

First, the transformation of India's party system since independence has come with the rise of caste and religious cleavages. In the 1960s and 1970s, the hegemony of the Indian National Congress relied on a broad coalition bringing together Muslims, lower castes, and upper-caste Brahmins. This had changed by the 1990s, as challenges from growing Hindu

We thank Nitin Bharti, Christophe Jaffrelot, Yajna Govind, Jules Naudet, and Clara Martínez-Toledano for their useful comments. This chapter draws on A. Banerjee, A. Gethin, and T. Piketty, "Growing Cleavages in India? Evidence from the Changing Structure of Electorates, 1962–2014" (WID.world Working Paper 2019/05).

1. For the full list of surveys used in this chapter, see appendix Table A4, World Political Cleavages and Inequality Database, http://wpid.world.

nationalist movements (in particular the Bharatiya Janata Party, BJP) but also from center-left and caste-based parties gradually ate into its support base, with the result that it lost most of its support from social groups other than lower castes and Muslims.

Second, we find that rising income and wealth inequalities since the 1990s have not led to growing class divides. If anything, highest-educated and upper-class voters were slightly more likely to vote for the BJP in the early 1990s, but this difference has boiled down to zero in recent years. Class cleavages thus exist in India, but they have decreased and remain almost entirely intermediated by caste and religious identities. However, it is worth stressing that lower-class voters from the majority religion (Hinduism) and minority religion (Islam) do continue to vote for the same parties and coalitions, in contrast to what we increasingly observe in Western democracies. To some extent, this can be accounted for by the construction of a common political interest via the system of quotas and reservations.

Third, we go beyond national politics and study voting patterns in state elections. We find that our main results apply to the state level, but with interesting variations across states. Upper castes tend to favor the BJP and affiliated parties in general, while there is no clear link between socioeconomic status and the vote once the effect of caste is accounted for. We find much lower caste polarization in Tamil Nadu and West Bengal, two states with strong regional parties and where the BJP has remained weak to the present.

This chapter adopts a resolutely long-run historical perspective, which allows us to go beyond contingent factors and contextualize the recent rise of the BJP within the frame of broader socioeconomic and political transformations. Our approach is also fundamentally comparative in the way we analyze the development of political cleavages in India, their interactions with underlying social structures, and how these interactions compare to those found in other contemporary democracies. In doing so, we hope to contribute to the social sciences literature departing from the Orientalist myth of "Indian exceptionalism," to instead considering caste as a "category of 'status' and 'power,' quite like 'race,' or in some other contexts, ethnicity."[2]

2. S. S. Jodhka, "Ascriptive Hierarchies: Caste and Its Reproduction in Contemporary India," *Current Sociology* 64, no. 2 (2016): 228–243.

The chapter is organized as follows. First, we provide a brief overview of the caste system and how it structures social inequalities in India. Second, we describe the transformation of India's party system from the dominance of the Indian National Congress to the rise of both regional parties and the BJP. Third, we show that this transformation has been associated with growing caste and religious cleavages, but declining class cleavages. Finally, we reproduce our analysis of caste and class divides at the state level.

## Religion, Caste, and the Changing Structure of Inequality

Since at least the late nineteenth century, Hinduism and Islam have been the two dominant religions of the Indian subcontinent, comprising approximately 95 percent of the population, with the remainder being divided between Sikhs, Buddhists, Christians, and more recently, individuals declaring no religion. Representing almost a quarter of the Indian population just before independence, the share of Muslims had dropped to only 10 percent by 1951, due to both the separation of Pakistan from India and the mass population transfers between the two countries that ensued. It has rebounded slightly since then, increasing from about 10 percent in 1952 to 14 percent in 2011.[3]

The Indian caste system can be traced back to at least the Vedic period (1500 BCE–500 BCE). The Manusmṛiti (Law of Manu) formalizes the separation of society into four large *varnas,* or functional social classes: Brahmins (priests and scholars), Kshatriyas (warriors and rulers), Vaishyas (merchants), and Shudras (laborers serving the other *varnas*). In practice, however, this text was more normative than descriptive, and Indian society never strictly conformed to these separations. In fact, the relevant unit of observation has instead been the *jati,* which defines the elementary social unit composing local communities, clans, and tribes. The extraordinary diversity of regional specificities, languages, religions, and cultural practices, as well as individual occupations and historical traditions, have come with thousands of *jati.* The inclusion of the *jatis* into the four *varnas* was never clearly defined before British colonization.[4] The 1901 census, by labeling the population based on caste and assigning all *jatis* to specific *varnas,* contributed to a rigidification of the

---

3. T. Piketty, *Capital and Ideology* (Harvard University Press, 2020), chapter 8.
4. Piketty, *Capital and Ideology,* chapter 8.

caste system.[5] It is also important to stress that caste is not a rigid or even perfectly defined category: it remains a flexible label structured at the local level. It is precisely this malleability and adaptability of caste that explains its persistence to the present day.[6]

Independent India inherited this division of society and initiated a systematic policy of positive discrimination directed toward the "weaker sections of society," the "Scheduled Castes" (SCs) and the "Scheduled Tribes" (STs), which included reservations in educational institutions, public-sector employment, and electoral constituencies. SCs correspond to the lowest strata of the caste hierarchy, being theoretically outside of the caste system according to Hindu orthodoxy and considered "untouchable" by the other castes, while STs refer to specific tribal communities or Indigenous people. Together, these two groups represented 20 to 25 percent of the population at the time of independence.[7] Throughout the second half of the twentieth century, reservations were then gradually extended to the highly heterogeneous group of "Other Backward Classes" (OBCs), first locally, and then at the federal level in 1989. Debates over reservations contributed to the growing politicization of caste, from violent upper-caste protests to the emergence of caste-based parties.[8]

Contemporary analyses converge in emphasizing the multidimensionality of caste and its close ties to social, economic, and political life. Following Jules Naudet and Surinder Jodhka, one may define caste as an "ascription-based structure of hierarchy and inequality" establishing social boundaries in five dimensions. First, caste has a religious dimension in Hinduism, where notions of purity and pollution condition cultural values and interactions between caste groups. Second, caste has a "power" dimension beyond religious values: caste networks and caste influence can be used strategically, notably in democratic politics. Third, caste is related to the state system, as the classification of castes by the state, in

5. N. Dirks, *Castes of Mind: Colonialism and the Making of Modern India* (Princeton University Press, 2001); G. Cassan, "Identity-Based Policies and Identity Manipulation: Evidence from Colonial Punjab," *American Economic Journal: Economic Policy* 7, no. 4 (2015): 103–131.

6. D. Mosse, "Caste and Development: Contemporary Perspectives on a Structure of Discrimination and Advantage," *World Development* 110, no. 1 (2018): 422–436.

7. Piketty, *Capital and Ideology,* chapter 8.

8. On the political rise of the lower castes and the emergence of caste-based parties, see, in particular, C. Jaffrelot, *India's Silent Revolution: The Rise of the Lower Castes in North India* (Columbia University Press, 2003).

particular in the context of affirmative action programs, contributes to reifying caste identities. Fourth, caste has an important economic dimension, contributing to the segmentation of labor markets, cooptation, discriminatory practices, and endogamy. Finally, caste also encompasses aspects of living culture, including communitarian pride, spatial segregation, caste associations, and even culinary traditions.[9]

Summing up, if one focuses on the adult population, broad caste and religious groups in the twenty-first century can be divided into four large groupings in the surveys at our disposal: Muslims (about 12 percent of respondents), SCs and STs (30 percent), OBCs (33 percent), Brahmins (5 percent), and other upper castes and other groups (20 percent).[10] As explained above, these groups do not correspond to precisely defined identities, and it is the *jati* that should ultimately be the relevant unit of observation. Unfortunately, however, *jatis* cannot be tracked over time since the 1960s. The operationalization of more precise measures of caste is a subject of considerable complexity, which we leave for future research.[11]

Available evidence points to caste being moderately correlated with economic status when put into comparative perspective. In 2014, the average income of SCs and STs was about 26 percent lower than that of the rest of the population, down from 45 percent in 1951. This difference was lower than the current Black-White income gap in the United States (55 percent), and much lower than the Black-White income gap in South Africa (80 percent).[12]

At the same time, overall income and wealth inequalities have grown substantially in India: the top 1 percent income share rose from 7 percent in 1980 to 21 percent in 2015, and the top 1 percent wealth share from

9. S. Jodhka and J. Naudet, introduction to *Handbook of Caste,* ed. S. Jodhka and J. Naudet (Oxford University Press, forthcoming).

10. See appendix Figure A2, wpid.world. Fluctuations over time in the shares of religious and caste groups are due to low sample sizes and measurement error of surveys, as well as difficulties in making some categories perfectly comparable over the period. Notice that the caste system is not limited to the Hindu population: there are also caste groups among Christians, Sikhs, and Muslims—even if there are also individuals belonging to these religions who declare that they belong to no caste. We separate Muslims as a whole from other caste groups. The caste proportions cited above therefore correspond to caste groups among non-Muslims.

11. For a promising attempt combining open-ended questions with network analysis, see M. Ferry, "Caste Links: Quantifying Social Identities Using Open-Ended Questions" (OSC Papers No. 2019–1, 2019), https://www.sciencespo.fr/osc/sites/sciencespo.fr.osc/files /OP_2019-1-EN-def.pdf.

12. Piketty, *Capital and Ideology,* figure 8.6.

12 percent in 1960 to 31 percent in 2012.[13] Caste has thus become less and less significant in explaining differences in standards of living in India, at the same time as caste groups have become increasingly differentiated in socioeconomic terms. This is especially true of upper castes, many of which have become polarized between a wealthy elite and a large fraction of lagging-behind individuals, fostering strong resentment of reservations among low-income upper castes, many of which are today poorer than OBCs or even SCs.[14]

The surveys at our disposal, though imperfect, depict similar trends. From 1967 to 2014, for instance, the share of Brahmins with university degrees increased from 23 percent to 29 percent, while the share of tertiary-educated SCs and STs was multiplied by eight, from 1 percent to 8 percent. Educational inequalities between castes therefore remain very significant, but they are slowly decreasing. Comparable inequalities are also visible in terms of social class: in 2014, about 20 percent of SCs and STs belonged to the upper class, compared to 50 percent of Brahmins.[15]

### The Decline of the Congress and the Fragmentation of India's Party System since 1947

The structure of democratic competition in India changed dramatically in the past seventy years. In 1947, at the time of independence from British rule, the Indian National Congress (INC) led by Mahatma Gandhi and Jawaharlal Nehru was by far the dominant political movement. Founded in 1885, the organization had guided the country toward independence with an ideology rooted in a secular vision of the nation. In practice, however, the Congress relied on a very heterogeneous and unstable "coalition

13. L. Chancel and T. Piketty, "Indian Income Inequality, 1922–2015: From British Raj to Billionaire Raj?," *Review of Income and Wealth* 65, no. 1 (2019): 33–62; N. Bharti, "Wealth Inequality, Class, and Caste in India, 1961–2012" (WID.world Working Paper 2018/14); C. Jaffrelot, *Inde, l'envers de la puissance: Inégalités et révoltes* (CNRS Éditions, 2012).

14. C. Jaffrelot and A. Kalaiyarasan, "Dominant Castes, from Bullock Capitalists to OBCs?," in *Interpreting Politics: Situated Knowledge, India, and the Rudolph Legacy*, ed. J. Echeverri-Gent and K. Sadiq (Oxford University Press, 2020), 111–154.

15. See appendix Figures A5 to A11, wpid.world. Our social class scheme is based on P. Chakrabarti, "One Nation, Many Worlds: Varieties of Developmental Regimes in India" (International Growth Centre Working Paper, 2017), https://papers.ssrn.com/sol3/papers.cfm?abstract_id=3492136.

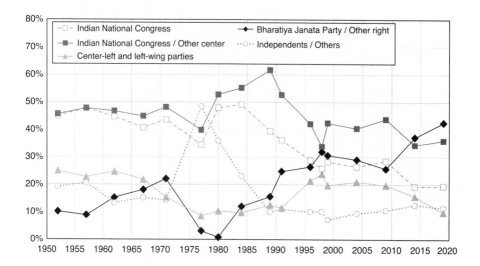

FIGURE 9.1. Election results in India, 1952–2019

*Data Source:* Authors' computations using official election results (see wpid.world).
*Note:* The figure shows the share of votes received by the main Indian political parties or groups of parties in Lok Sabha elections between 1952 and 2019.

of extremes"[16] comprising Muslims, Dalits, and Brahmins. This tension was visible in the leadership of the INC itself: Nehru, the first prime minister of India, came from a Kashmiri upper-caste background, while B. R. Ambedkar, the first minister of law and justice, was an untouchable. Internal divisions within the INC during the drafting of the constitution eventually led Ambedkar to resign from the cabinet and run as an independent candidate.[17]

In the first direct election held in independent India, in 1951–1952, the INC won by a landslide, receiving 45 percent of votes and 364 of the 489 seats of the lower house of parliament, the Lok Sabha (Figure 9.1). Left-wing parties, including the Communist Party of India (CPI) and the Praja Socialist Party, were supported by almost a quarter of voters, and they have continued to secure between 10 percent and 25 percent of votes

16. P. R. Brass, "The Politicization of the Peasantry in a North Indian State: II," *Journal of Peasant Studies* 8, no. 1 (1980): 3–36.

17. R. Guha, *India after Gandhi: The History of the World's Largest Democracy* (HarperCollins, 2007), chapters 6 and 7.

in most elections since then.[18] On the other side of the political spectrum were political parties promoting Hindu nationalism against the secular vision of the INC, in particular the Bharatiya Jana Sangh (BJS), the political arm of the Rashtriya Swayamsevak Sangh (RSS), a nationalist paramilitary volunteer organization.[19] The BJS and other right-wing parties received 10 percent of votes in 1951–1952 and as much as 22 percent of votes in 1971.

Three major changes in party politics came in the decades that followed, leading to the decline of the Congress and a gradual fragmentation of India's party system. The first one was the rise of regional parties, which led to an increasing divergence of state party systems. This was first visible in Kerala, where the communists won against the Congress in the 1957 Kerala assembly elections, as well as in the state of Madras (now Tamil Nadu), where the Dravida Munnetra Kazhagam (DMK) arose to power in 1967. In both of these states, the INC lost its status of dominant party as early as the 1960s.[20]

A second change in India's party system, associated with the rise of lower-caste parties, came at the turn of the 1990s. These notably included the Bahujan Samaj Party (BSP; literally, people in majority), founded in 1984, which aimed to represent SCs, STs, OBCs, and religious minorities. It soon became one of the strongest parties in the country, in particular in the most populous state of India, Uttar Pradesh.[21]

The third, most substantial change in India's party system was the rise of the Bharatiya Janata Party (BJP, or Indian People's Party). In 1977, following the state of emergency declared by Prime Minister Indira Gandhi, a two-year period of suspension of elections and civil liberties, a number of parties across the political spectrum from communists to Hindu nationalists formed a large coalition, the Janata Party, to defeat the Congress. This led the INC to lose control of the Lok Sabha for the first time, but the coalition quickly broke apart due to inevitable internal divisions, and Indira Gandhi was reelected in 1980. After these elections, the BJP, founded in 1980 as the successor of the BJS, grew stronger until in 1996 it became the largest party at the Lok Sabha for the first time, with 161

18. Our groupings of political parties are based on both manual coding and expert classifications, which are reported in appendix Tables A1, A2, and A3, wpid.world.

19. C. Jaffrelot, *The Hindu Nationalist Movement in India* (Columbia University Press, 1998).

20. Guha, *India after Gandhi*.

21. See Jaffrelot, *India's Silent Revolution*.

of the 545 seats (against 140 for the INC). This rise closely coincided with the decline of the INC (Figure 9.1). After a stabilization phase in the 2000s, during which the INC and the BJP each received 25 to 30 percent of votes, the BJP grew again in 2014 and 2019, thus becoming the new dominant party at the national level.[22] However, as we shall discuss below, regionalization has implied that the BJP has not yet been able to penetrate states where regional parties completely replaced the Congress in the early postindependence decades.

## Caste Coalitions, Religious Divides, and the Rise of Hindu Nationalism

We now turn to the analysis of caste and religious cleavages in India, focusing on three main groups of parties. The first group includes the Congress and other centrist parties traditionally allied to the INC in the Lok Sabha, such as the Nationalist Congress Party and the DMK. The second group corresponds to the BJS, the BJP, and other "right-wing" parties close to Hindu nationalists such as the Shiv Sena. The third group brings together low-caste, center-left, and left-wing parties such as the BSP, the CPI (communists), and the Samajwadi Party (socialists). Despite inevitable limitations in their internal consistency, these groupings do reveal interesting dynamics, and our main conclusions are unchanged when considering the Congress or the BJS/BJP alone.[23]

Figure 9.2 plots the share of votes received by the Congress and other center parties by caste and religion. The INC has always found greater support among Muslims and lower castes than among upper castes, but this cleavage has grown significantly over time. In 1962, differences in support for the INC among caste and religious groups were in fact not particularly strong: about 50 to 55 percent of Muslims, SCs/STs, and Brahmins voted for the Congress, compared to between 40 and 45 percent of OBCs and other Forward Castes (FCs). Caste differences in support for the INC had become much stronger by 2014: about 45 percent of Muslims voted for the Congress and other center parties, compared to 19 percent of Brahmins.

---

22. See appendix Figure A1, wpid.world, for vote shares received by the INC and the BJS/BJP since 1951–1952.

23. All results for the Congress and the BJP can be found in extended appendix B, wpid.world.

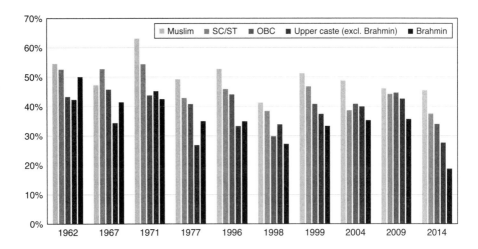

FIGURE 9.2. The Congress vote by caste and religion in India, 1962–2014
*Data Source:* Authors' computations using Indian electoral surveys (see wpid.world).
*Note:* The figure shows the share of votes received by the Indian National Congress
and other centrist parties by caste and religion. In 2014, 45% of Muslim voters voted
Congress/center, compared to 37% of Scheduled Castes and Scheduled Tribes (SC/ST),
34% of Other Backward Classes (OBC), 28% of upper castes (excluding Brahmins), and
19% of Brahmins.

This transformation was driven by the shift of upper castes and, more
recently, of OBCs and SCs/STs toward the BJP and other right-wing parties (see Figure 9.3). The BJS and the BJP have always received greater
support among upper castes, but they used to be small parties. The rise
of the BJP has been spread across all non-Muslim groups in similar proportions, leading to a sharper division of the Indian electorate across caste
and especially religious groups. In 2014, only 10 percent of Muslims supported the BJP and affiliated parties, compared to 31 percent of SCs and
STs and 61 percent of Brahmins. The structure of the vote for left-wing
parties (socialist, communist, and lower-caste parties), by contrast, has
remained generally associated with Muslims and lower castes, with ups
and downs but no sign of long-term change.[24]

Figure 9.4 details the evolution of the relative support of upper castes
for the BJP and affiliated parties, before and after controls.[25] Upper castes

24. See appendix Figure B37, wpid.world.
25. Comparable figures can be found for other groups of parties in the appendix,
wpid.world.

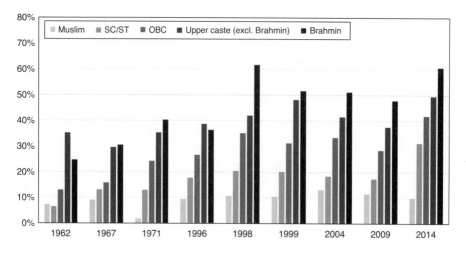

FIGURE 9.3. The BJP vote by caste and religion in India, 1962–2014
*Data Source:* Authors' computations using Indian electoral surveys (see wpid.world).
*Note:* The figure shows the share of votes received by the Bharatiya Janata Party (BJP)
and affiliated parties by caste and religion. In 2014, 10% of Muslim voters voted BJP
and affiliated, compared to 31% of Scheduled Castes and Scheduled Tribes (SC/ST),
42% of Other Backward Classes (OBC), 52% of upper castes (excluding Brahmins),
and 61% of Brahmins.

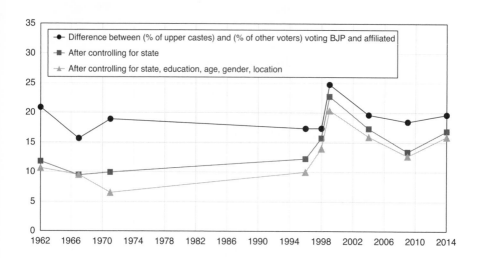

FIGURE 9.4. Caste cleavages in India, 1962–2014
*Data Source:* Authors' computations using Indian electoral surveys (see wpid.world).
*Note:* The figure shows the difference between the share of upper castes and the share
of other voters voting for the Bharatiya Janata Party (BJP) and affiliated parties, before
and after controls. Upper castes have always been more likely than other voters to vote for
the BJP (as well as for its predecessor, the BJS) and other affiliated parties since the 1960s.

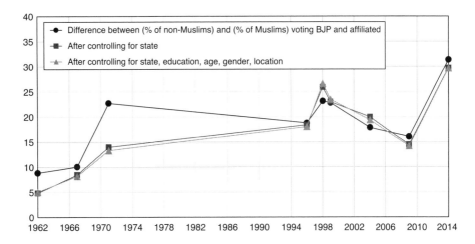

FIGURE 9.5. The religious cleavage in India, 1962–2014
*Data Source:* Authors' computations using Indian electoral surveys (see wpid.world).
*Note:* The figure shows the difference between the share of non-Muslims and the share of Muslims voting for the Bharatiya Janata Party (BJP) and affiliated parties, before and after controls. Muslim voters have always been much less likely than non-Muslims to vote for the BJP (as well as for its predecessor the BJS) and other affiliated parties since the 1960s, but this gap has grown dramatically, from 9 percentage points in 1962 to 32 points in 2014.

appear to have always been more likely to vote for right-wing parties, by about 20 percentage points on average. Controlling for state of residence, education, age, gender, and rural-urban location reduces this gap, but it suggests that caste cleavages have risen over time: all things being equal, upper castes were more likely to support right-wing parties by 5 to 10 percentage points in the 1960s and 1970s, compared to 12 to 16 points in recent years. Accordingly, Muslim voters have become increasingly inclined to vote for centrist and left-wing parties, relative to non-Muslims. In the early 1960s, non-Muslims were more likely to vote for the BJS and other right-wing parties by 5 percentage points; in 2014, they had become more likely to do so by 30 percentage points, revealing an extreme and growing religious polarization of the Indian electorate (see Figure 9.5).

Together, these results point to India becoming an increasingly fractured democracy, with the majority of upper castes voting for the BJP and

affiliated parties and the majority of lower castes and especially Muslims voting for other parties. This contrasts with the early postindependence decades, during which the Congress was supported by a large coalition of Muslims, lower castes, and Brahmins, while right-wing and left-wing parties were no more than minor political forces capturing votes from small fractions of both ends of the caste hierarchy.

In comparative perspective, the collapse of India's dominant party system shares interesting similarities and differences with that of Japan, South Africa, and Malaysia. Just like the INC, the Liberal Democratic Party of Japan (LDP) remained in power for several decades by receiving mass support from both the upper levels (business elites) and the lower levels (small farmers) of society. Unlike the Congress, however, its decline came with a dealignment of class divides and a remarkable diversification of its voting base, which was key to its renewed success in recent decades (see Chapter 11). The evolution of the Congress is in that respect more comparable to the recent electoral dynamics visible in Malaysia (see Chapter 12) and South Africa (see Chapter 16). In these two countries, as in India, previously dominant parties have now become the parties of more narrowly defined underprivileged social groups: Muslims and lower-class voters in the case of Malaysia's National Coalition, and low- and middle-income Africans in the case of South Africa's African National Congress. However, as we shall see, caste and religion remain more important than social class in India, in contrast to what we observe in these two countries, where socioeconomic status is becoming an increasingly relevant determinant of electoral behaviors.

At this point, let us stress again that our objective is not to understand the microfoundations of the vote in India. As mentioned earlier, it is the *jati*, not the *varna*, which is the relevant unit of observation when it comes to explaining Indian voters' political attitudes.[26] Our figures therefore likely underestimate the strength of caste and religious conflicts, whose intensity and nature vary within local communities, states, and specific political parties. Our broad perspective mainly informs on caste and religious divides at the national level, and how these divides have changed in the long run.

26. See, for instance, C. Jaffrelot, "The Caste-Based Mosaic of Indian Politics," *Seminar* 633 (2012): 49–53; C. Jaffrelot, "Lok Sabha Election Special: Do Indians Vote Their Caste?," *India Today*, April 19, 2020.

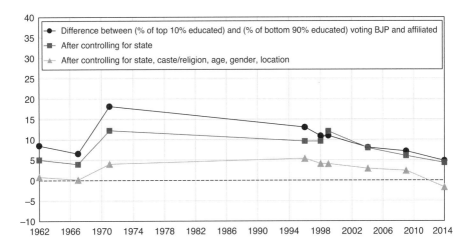

FIGURE 9.6. The educational cleavage in India, 1962–2014

*Data Source:* Authors' computations using Indian electoral surveys (see wpid.world).

*Note:* The figure shows the difference between the share of top 10% educated voters and the share of bottom 90% educated voters voting for the Bharatiya Janata Party (BJP) and affiliated parties, before and after controls. Higher-educated voters have always been more likely than other voters to vote for the BJP (as well as for its predecessor the BJS) and other affiliated parties since the 1960s, but this gap has gradually decreased since the 1990s.

## Class Cleavages and Their Interaction with Caste and Religious Inequalities

Besides their conditioning by caste affiliations, to what extent have electoral cleavages been structured by socioeconomic divides in India? Figure 9.6 provides a first answer to this question by showing the relative support of highest-educated voters for the BJP and affiliated parties since the 1960s. While higher-educated voters have always been more likely to vote for these parties, this gap seems to have significantly decreased since the 1990s, until boiling down to zero in recent years after controls. Lower-educated voters have therefore become more and more favorable to the BJP over time, even when holding geographical location, caste, and other socioeconomic characteristics constant.[27]

27. We find comparable results in the case of income. See appendix Figure B63, wpid. world.

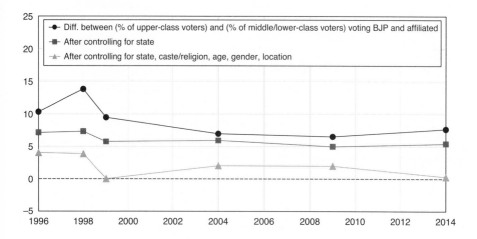

FIGURE 9.7. Class cleavages in India, 1996–2014
*Data Source:* Authors' computations using Indian electoral surveys (see wpid.world).
*Note:* The figure shows the difference between the share of upper-class voters and the share of middle- and lower-class voters voting for the Bharatiya Janata Party (BJP) and affiliated parties, before and after controls. Upper-class voters have always been more likely than other voters to vote for the BJP since 1996, but this gap becomes statistically nonsignificant after controls, so that upper classes are not more or less likely to vote BJP at a given caste and other characteristics.

The same result holds in terms of social class since 1996 (Figure 9.7). Upper-class voters—defined here as comprising occupations such as mid- to high-level civil servants, business owners, and large landowners—have been more likely to vote for the BJP and affiliated parties by about 5 to 15 percentage points since 1996. However, this effect is entirely driven by the fact that upper castes are more likely to belong to the upper class: all things being equal, the link between social class and support for the BJP is nonsignificant.

Such absence of any independent class cleavage suggests that the Indian party system has primarily aggregated socioeconomic divides through their interaction with caste and religious mobilizations, which have remained the strongest predictors of electoral behaviors, and all the more so in recent elections. As caste, religion, and class have become less and less intertwined, furthermore, the political representation of economic inequalities in India has accordingly weakened.

Social class does, nonetheless, distinguish voting patterns among *jatis,* in particular among those that are strongly differentiated in socioeconomic

terms.[28] Strikingly, the effects of caste and class went in opposite directions in the 2019 elections. Poorer non-Yadav OBCs, for instance, largely because of their resentment of Yadavs' domination of OBCs reservations, voted massively for the BJP. The BJP was also more successful among poorer upper castes, who tend to perceive quota politics as a growing threat to their historical status.[29] This may be key to explaining why class did not seem to have a unidirectional effect on the vote overall. Social class is not a variable that linearly structures national political cleavages in India. It does so in a more complex way, partly through caste and religion, and partly through subtler interactions in local contexts. This pattern notably differs from what we observe in a number of other countries with strong sociocultural cleavages such as South Africa and Malaysia, where class has been playing a much clearer role, beyond racial and ethnic affiliations, in recent years.

### The Dynamics of State Politics: Toward BJP Hegemony or State Divergence?

We conclude this chapter with a short analysis of voting behaviors in state elections. The separation of powers between the central government and state governments in India is based on the principle of "cooperative federalism." The national parliament has exclusive power to legislate over the items of the "Union List," comprising policy areas such as defense, foreign trade, and the income tax, while the state legislature decides on matters listed in the "State List," such as police forces, health care, and transport. In addition to these two lists, the "Concurrent List" includes powers to be considered by both levels of government, such as education and criminal law. In practice, cooperative federalism implies that state governments hold considerable power in shaping economic policies and providing public services and social transfers.

The twenty-eight states and eight union territories of India (compared to fourteen states in 1956) are the outcome of a unique decentralization process, which some observers described as crucial to the survival of Indian democracy to the present. This process notably differed from the

---

28. Jaffrelot, "Lok Sabha Election Special." On the rising importance of class cleavages in Delhi, see S. Kumar, *Changing Electoral Politics in Delhi: From Caste to Class* (Sage Publications, 2013).

29. C. Jaffrelot, "Class and Caste in the 2019 Indian Election–Why Have So Many Poor Started Voting for Modi?," *Studies in Indian Politics* 7, no. 2 (2019): 149–160.

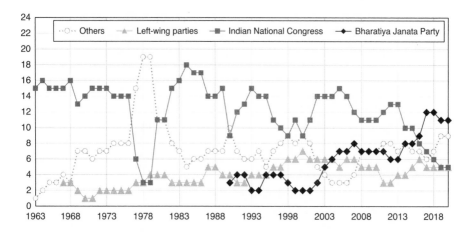

FIGURE 9.8. State elections and the transformation of Indian party systems, 1963–2020
*Data Source:* Authors' computations combining data from F. R. Jensenius, "Competing Inequalities? On the Intersection of Gender and Ethnicity in Candidate Nominations in Indian Elections," *Government and Opposition* 51, no. 3 (2016): 440–463 before 2015, and hand coded data after 2015 (see wpid.world).
*Note:* The figure shows the number of Indian states ruled by selected parties or groups of parties between 1963 and 2020. Excludes union territories and states where no elections have been held. The number of states ruled by the Bharatiya Janata Party grew from three states in 1990 to eleven states in 2020 (October).

trajectory of neighboring Pakistan (see Chapter 10), where excessive centralization was a repetitive factor of political instability and involvement of the military in national politics.[30] Indian states are therefore particularly interesting units of analysis for studying variations in the structure of political cleavages in India and their relationship to the representation of social inequalities.

State election results from 1963 to 2020 show interesting common points and differences with Lok Sabha election results (Figure 9.8).[31] While the BJP was able to form a national government as early as the 1990s, it was only in 2016 that it succeeded in ruling a majority of states. This discrepancy is due to the fact that support for the BJP at first grew faster

30. C. Jaffrelot, *The Pakistan Paradox: Instability and Resilience* (Hurst Publishers, 2015); Guha, *India after Gandhi.*
31. We are grateful to Francesca Jensenius for making available constituency-level electoral results from 1962 to 2015. See "Indian Election Data," Francesca Jensenius (personal website), accessed March 20, 2021, https://www.francesca.no/data-2.

in many of the more populous states of the Hindi Belt—the region encompassing most of northern India, where Hindi is widely spoken—but it was only in recent years that it managed to decisively win elections in the majority of these states.

Furthermore, the growing success of the BJP has mostly come at the expense of the INC, while the share of states ruled by left-wing and regional parties has remained approximately stable since the 1990s. This pattern suggests that when it comes to local politics, the BJP is still far from being as dominant as the INC was in the years that followed independence. The multiplication of states, the rise of regional parties, and the persistence of powerful left-wing coalitions in a number of states— such as Kerala and West Bengal—have, to the present, put a limit on the spread of Hindu nationalism.

The long-run decline of the Congress, the rise of the BJP in the Hindi Belt, and the regionalization of party politics have been three powerful forces driving the divergence of Indian party systems. This divergence has implied large variations across states in the relative vote shares received by regional parties, Congress, and the BJP. In this context, at least three varieties in Indian state party systems can be identified today. First, in some states such as Gujarat and Rajasthan, Congress hegemony was gradually replaced by a two-party system with the INC opposing the BJP. In a second type of state, both Congress and the BJP have had to build coalitions with smaller parties: in Maharashtra, for instance, a coalition between the BJP and the Shiv Sena has been competing with a coalition between the Congress and the Nationalist Congress Party (NCP). In a third type of state, finally, the Congress has almost completely disappeared and has been replaced by regional parties. In Tamil Nadu, for instance, two regional parties, the All India Anna Dravida Munnetra Kazhagam (AIADMK) and the DMK, have more or less alternated in power since the beginning of the 1970s. A comparable regionalization of electoral politics is visible in West Bengal, where the Left Front dominated the political landscape from the mid-1970s until the victory of the center-left All India Trinamool Congress (AITC), in coalition with the Congress, in the 2011 and 2016 elections, despite growing support for the BJP in recent years.

What have been the consequences of this remarkable diversification of state party systems for caste and class cleavages? Figure 9.9 represents the share of votes received by selected political parties by caste and religion over the 1996–2016 period in states for which we have dedicated

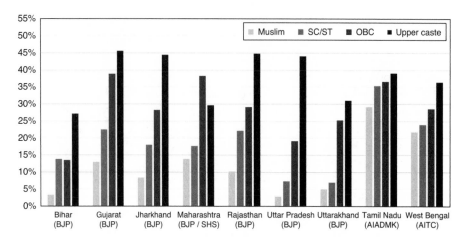

FIGURE 9.9. Caste and religious cleavages in state elections in India
*Data Source:* Authors' computations using Indian electoral surveys (see wpid.world).
*Note:* The figure shows the share of votes received by selected political parties by caste and religion in state elections for selected Indian states. The BJP has systematically received greater support from upper castes than from lower castes and Muslims. Caste and religious cleavages are lower in Tamil Nadu and West Bengal. Figures are aggregated over the period available for each state (see appendix Table A3, wpid. world). BJP: Bharatiya Janata Party; SHS: Shiv Sena; AIADMK: All India Anna Dravida Munnetra Kazhagam; AITC: All India Trinamool Congress.

surveys.[32] Caste strongly differentiates support for the BJP: in all states, upper castes are substantially more likely to vote BJP than SCs/STs or Muslims. The OBCs' voting behaviors are more variable. In states with strong left-wing parties (Bihar and Uttar Pradesh) they tend to be less supportive of the BJP, while their political preferences align more closely with those of the upper castes in states where the BJP opposes centrist parties (Gujarat, Maharashtra, and Rajasthan).

Looking at the two states where the BJP is not a significant contender, Tamil Nadu and West Bengal, we find much lower levels of caste polarization. In Tamil Nadu, over the 2001–2016 period covered by our data, the AIADMK received greater support from upper castes than from lower

32. See appendix Table A4, wpid.world, for the full list of surveys available. Results of multivariate regressions of determinants of support for selected parties in all states and all elections, as well as additional figures on state elections, can be found in appendix C of this chapter.

castes and Muslims, but differences between these groups were relatively low. The same result holds when considering the structure of the vote for the AITC in West Bengal. In both states, the BJP has remained relatively weak, capturing 3 percent of votes in Tamil Nadu and 10 percent of votes in West Bengal in the 2016 state elections. Interestingly, furthermore, even if available data do not allow us to conclude with certainty, social class seems to play a greater role in these two states than in states where the BJP is strong. In 2016, for instance, upper-class voters were more likely to vote for the AIADMK by 16 percentage points, after controlling for caste and other sociodemographic variables.[33]

These findings suggest that it is specifically the rise of the BJP that has been associated with growing caste and religious cleavages in India. In a number of states of the Hindi Belt, a party system with the BJP opposing the INC, characterized by extreme caste and religious polarization, superseded the domination of the INC of the 1950s and 1960s. In contrast, in states where strong left-wing or regionalist movements preceded the rise of Hindu nationalism of the 1980s, such as Tamil Nadu and West Bengal, caste and religious cleavages have remained more moderate, and at the time of writing the BJP has so far failed to become a relevant competitor.

Such persistence of regional forces could suggest that the rise of the BJP in the 2014 and 2019 elections may soon be reaching its upper limit. The party of Narendra Modi may become even stronger in states where it has already established itself at the expense of the Congress, but conquering states where local parties have been ruling for several decades will be yet another challenge. Regional diversification, along with the increasing centralization of executive power in the hands of the prime minister, could therefore lead not only to the growing marginalization of the Muslim community, but also to greater linguistic and regional divides in the future.

## Conclusion

India's party system seems to have developed mostly along the lines of caste and religious conflicts. The Bharatiya Janata Party disproportionally attracts voters from upper castes. The Indian National Congress and centrist parties are more successful among lower-caste Hindus and especially Muslims. Left-wing parties find greater support among SCs, STs, and OBCs. This fragmented and polarized party system stands in sharp

---

33. See appendix Tables C2 to C12, wpid.world.

contrast to the situation in the early decades of Indian democracy, when the Congress accommodated a diversity of interests across caste and religious groups. Socioeconomic inequalities continue to have a significant influence on political cleavages in India, but this influence has been weakening and continues to be almost entirely conditioned by its interaction with caste and religious mobilizations.

According to Pradeep Chhibber and Rahul Verma, two ideological lines of division have structured Indian politics since independence: one opposing political movements on whether the state should regulate the economy and redistribute property (the *politics of statism*), and one opposing them on whether the state should protect marginalized groups from assertive majoritarian tendencies (the *politics of recognition*). The politics of statism would accordingly divide citizens with different education levels, while opinions on the politics of recognition would vary more across caste and religious groups.[34] The decline of class cleavages documented in this chapter, together with the rise of caste and religious cleavages, suggests that the politics of recognition could well end up prevailing completely over the politics of statism in the near future.

Our results may also provide insights into why the Indian state has not been under more pressure to improve the delivery of social services or to carry out the reforms necessary for improving the environment or the employment landscape. The politics of recognition have played a key role in correcting the legacies of caste discrimination and could even contribute to explaining the remarkable persistence of democratic norms in India to the present.[35] However, the amount of redistribution delivered through the quota system remains limited, simply because there are not so many government jobs and high-quality educational institutions. It remains an open question whether the dramatic rise of inequalities in India could eventually move political debates more decisively toward class-based divides over the access of lower and middle classes to high-quality public services (irrespective of caste or religious identities), progressive taxation, and the reduction of income and wealth disparities.

34. P. K. Chhibber and R. Verma, *Ideology and Identity: The Changing Party Systems of India* (Oxford University Press, 2018), chapter 2.

35. S. Ruparelia, "How the Politics of Recognition Enabled India's Democratic Exceptionalism," *International Journal of Politics, Culture, and Society* 21, no. 1 (2008): 39–56; F. Jensenius, *Social Justice through Inclusion: The Consequences of Electoral Quotas in India* (Oxford University Press, 2017); J. Naudet, "'Paying Back to Society': Upward Social Mobility among Dalits," *Contributions to Indian Sociology* 42, no. 3 (2008): 413–441.

# 10

## Social Inequality and the Dynamics of Political and Ethnolinguistic Divides in Pakistan, 1970–2018

AMORY GETHIN, SULTAN MEHMOOD, AND THOMAS PIKETTY

### Introduction

This chapter studies the changing structure of political cleavages in Pakistan, the second-most populated Muslim-majority country in the world, by making use of a unique set of exit polls covering every direct election from 1970 to 2018. Our analysis reveals at least three key dimensions of Pakistani political conflicts since 1970. The first one has to do with a primarily economic "class-based" division with the Pakistan Peoples Party (PPP) opposing the more procapitalist, elite-supported Muslim League parties. This cleavage has interacted with ethnicity and language, which have remained the strongest predictors of electoral behaviors since 1970. We also show that oppositions between political parties have been characterized by a third, enduring division between secular and religious visions of the nation, which is manifested in the strong support for the PPP among Shia Muslims and other religious minorities, as well as in the persistence of significant vote shares accruing to Islamic parties.

Finally, we discuss the long-run transformation of the political space from "popular left-wing politics" to "right-wing Islamic policies" by emphasizing the role played by General Zia-ul-Haq's military regime from 1977 to 1988. We also explain the recent rise of Imran Khan's Pakistan Tehreek-e-Insaf (PTI), a party with broad support across former PPP voters as well as Islamic ideological voters, through a successful political coalition facilitated by the military and landed political and industrial elites.

We are grateful to Christophe Jaffrelot, Saad Gulzar, Bakhtawar Ali, Clara Martínez-Toledano, and Juliet-Nil Uraz for their useful suggestions, as well as to Gallup Pakistan for providing us with the polling data used in this chapter.

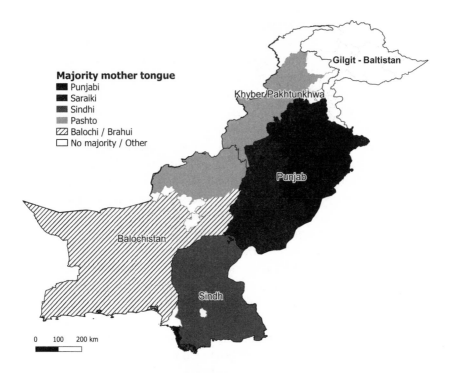

FIGURE 10.1. Geographical distribution of major ethnic groups in Pakistan
*Data Source:* Authors' elaboration using 1998 census data.
*Note:* This map provides a simple description of the spatial distribution of major ethnic groups in Pakistan. Pashtuns mainly live in the Northwest of the country, Punjabis in the Northeast, Sindhis in the Southeast, and Baloch people in the Southwest.

## Independence, Military Dictatorship, and Electoral Contests: The Making of Pakistani Democracy

The history of Pakistan as an independent state began in 1947, when the partition of India led to the creation of a country primarily defined by its religion: Islam. Aside from this defining trait of the new political community, the state of Pakistan was and has remained a highly heterogeneous and fractured nation, divided across regional and ethnolinguistic identities, and in particular consisting of two discontinuous east-west territories (today, Pakistan and Bangladesh), separated by India with a Hindu majority. The confrontation between this persistent diversity, the concentration of power in West Pakistan, and the obsession of political

elites to impose a centralized nation-state led to deep-seated conflicts and lasting institutional instability.[1] This instability culminated in the Bangladesh War of Independence of 1971 and in the separation of East and West Pakistan, following the refusal of the central government to accept the electoral victory of the Awami League, an East Pakistan political party, after years of political and economic tensions between the two territories crystallized in the first direct election in 1970.

After the division of the subcontinent, elections took place in Pakistan, one in 1954 and another in 1962, but they were indirect and highly controversial since they were not based on adult franchise and the latter was held under direct military rule.[2] We therefore exclude them from our analysis. The first direct elections based on adult franchise took place in 1970 as a compromise accepted by the military regime in the face of protest. These elections led to the victory of the opposition. The Awami League, led by Sheikh Mujib from East Pakistan, obtained a large majority with about 40 percent of the popular vote, followed by 20 percent of the votes for the West Pakistani PPP (63 percent of the vote in West Pakistan).[3]

The Pakistan Peoples Party and president General Yahya Khan did not want a Bengali ethnic "minority" party from East Pakistan to form the government, and the assembly was never invited by the president to form the government, as per the constitutional requirement. This caused great unrest in what was formerly East Pakistan, which escalated into a civil war and eventually led, after Indian intervention, to the independence of East Pakistan, which became the state of Bangladesh in 1971. Following this defeat, President Yahya Khan and the military leadership resigned, and the PPP's founding leader, Zulfiqar Ali Bhutto, took over as the first civilian chief martial law administrator and president. It was during Zulfiqar Ali Bhutto's tenure that the new constitution of Pakistan was

1. C. Jaffrelot, *The Pakistan Paradox: Instability and Resilience* (Hurst Publishers, 2015).

2. S. Bose and A. Jalal, *Modern South Asia: History, Culture, Political Economy* (Routledge, 2017).

3. See appendix Table A1, World Political Cleavages and Inequality Database, http://wpid.world, for figures on the share of seats received by groups of parties in the 1970 provincial elections, which were held ten days after the general elections. The Awami League won 288 of 300 seats in East Pakistan and no seat in West Pakistan. West Pakistani provinces were more divided across parties.

passed and ratified by all provinces in 1973. This led Bhutto to relinquish the presidency, as he was elected prime minister by the legislature. Bhutto's legacy also included the implementation of socialist policies, including land reforms and the nationalization of industries.

Bhutto was removed through a military coup by General Zia-ul-Haq in 1977, convicted of planning the assassination of a political rival, and executed following a controversial decision by Pakistan's Supreme Court during Zia's military regime in 1979. Zia then built a relatively stable political coalition with Islamists, conservative political parties, and religious leaders and managed to stay in power for eleven years (the longest-serving head of state in Pakistan) without being elected. His rule is widely considered to have been a time of political repression and Islamization reforms.[4] Zia died in a plane crash on August 17, 1988, and Benazir Bhutto, the daughter of Zulfiqar Ali Bhutto, rose to power after winning the election that ensued.

The 1990s were a period of political tussle between two parties, the center-left Pakistan Peoples Party led by Benazir Bhutto and the center-right Pakistan Muslim League led by Nawaz Sharif. These two parties and individuals alternated in power until October 1999, when General Pervez Musharraf seized power through a military coup. Pakistan thus came once again under direct military rule, with General Musharraf winning a controversial referendum in 2002 that gave him five years in office. However, conflict with the judiciary and a mass political movement led by lawyers against him weakened his grasp on power. The December 2007 assassination of Benazir Bhutto under Musharraf's watch was the final nail in his political coffin, and he resigned a day before impeachment proceedings were to start against him in 2008. There has been no direct military rule in Pakistan since then. Nevertheless, the 2018 elections brought to power what many commentators believe to be a military establishment–backed political party, the Pakistan Tehreek-e-Insaf.[5]

4. S. Mehmood and A. Seror, "Religious Leaders and Rule of Law" (NES Working Paper 280, 2021), https://www.nes.ru/files/Preprints-resh/WP280.pdf.

5. See, for instance, A. Shah, "Pakistan in 2018: Theft of an Election," *Asian Survey* 59, no. 1 (2019): 98–107; A. D. Behera, "Pakistan General Elections 2018: Clear Signs of a Guided Democracy," *International Studies* 55, no. 3 (2018): 238–252; S. O. Wolf, "44d 2020—False start for Democracy in Pakistan" (South Asia Democratic Forum, 2020), https://www.sadf.eu/wp-content/uploads/2020/01/COMMENT-165.pdf.

## The Evolution of Pakistan's Party System, 1970–2018

Three groups of parties have historically received the highest shares of popular votes in Pakistan: the Pakistan Muslim League (PML), the Pakistan Peoples Party (PPP), and, in 2018, the Pakistan Tehreek-e-Insaf (see Figure 10.2).[6] The Muslim League, as was originally known, was the successor of the All-India Muslim League led by Muhammad Ali Jinnah, which spearheaded the movement to establish Pakistan.[7] Even if its programmatic foundations can be broadly described as socially conservative and economically procapitalist, the PML has espoused different ideologies over time, which is apparent from the various splits and new parties that emerged from the original independence movement. After the declaration of martial law by Ayub Khan in 1958, the Muslim League was dissolved, but its promilitary faction, the Convention Muslim League, continued to support the new military regime.

Reformed in 1962, the Pakistan Muslim League was still unable to unite in the 1970 elections that followed Khan's resignation, and three factions contested the election against each other: the Convention Muslim League, the Council Muslim League, and the Muslim League faction of Abdul Qayyum Khan. In the 1977 election, Muslim League parties again did not contest as a single block; instead, they joined the Pakistan National Alliance, a heteroclite coalition of nine Islamic and conservative parties representing the opposition to Bhutto's government. A new Pakistan Muslim League party was then founded in 1985 by Muhammad Khan Junejo with politicians supporting the new government of General Zia-ul-Haq, but it split again in 1988 into two factions, one led by Junejo (the PML-J) and one led by businessman Nawaz Sharif (the PML-N).

The PML-N soon became the dominant conservative party, first by leading the Islamic Democratic Alliance (Islami Jamhoori Ittehad, IJI) in the general elections of 1988 and 1990, and then as an independent party in 1993 and 1997. The party divided yet again in 1997, with the new Pakistan Muslim League (Q) supporting the military coup staged by Pervez

6. The results presented in 1970 correspond to West Pakistan only. We also exclude the 1985 election, which was contested on a nonparty basis. The figures associate in one group the parties of the Muslim League (PML) with the coalitions in which they participated (PNA in 1977 and IJI in 1988).

7. See, for instance, the autobiography of Ayub Khan: M. A. Khan, "Friends Not Masters. A Political Autobiography," *VRÜ Verfassung und Recht in Übersee* 1, no. 3 (1970): 368–369.

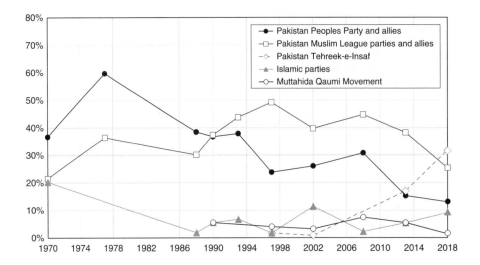

FIGURE 10.2. Election results in Pakistan, 1970–2018
*Data Source:* Authors' computations using official election results (see wpid.world).
*Note:* The figure shows the share of votes received by selected political parties or groups of parties in general elections held in Pakistan between 1970 and 2018. Figures for 1970 correspond to West Pakistan only.

Musharraf. The PML-N and PML-Q contested the 2002 and 2008 elections separately, but the PML-N eventually became the predominant Muslim League party again in the elections of 2013 and 2018, with respectively 33 percent and 24 percent of the popular votes.

The Pakistan Peoples Party was created in 1967 by Zulfiqar Ali Bhutto in Lahore, with a platform promising to provide *"roti, kapra,* and *makan"* (food, clothing, and housing) to all Pakistanis.[8] It became the single biggest party in West Pakistan in 1970, with 37 percent of votes as compared to 21 percent for all Muslim League parties combined. Nevertheless, it failed to win the election in the country as a whole due to the overwhelming success of the Awami Party in East Pakistan. It was only in 1973, following the Bangladesh War of Independence and the resignation of General Yahya Khan, that Bhutto eventually became prime

8. M. Lodhi, "Bhutto, the Pakistan Peoples Party, and Political Development in Pakistan: 1967–1977" (PhD diss., London School of Economics and Political Science, 1980). Notice that in spite of these redistributive appeals, the PPP was not particularly "socialist." In fact, Bhutto gradually eliminated from the party's leadership those who believed in socialism.

minister of the new nation. Bhutto was reelected in 1977 as the PPP achieved a landslide victory with 60 percent of votes, in part thanks to vote rigging. These elections were followed by Zia's coup. The PPP then lost its dominant position completely during the 1990s, and it was only thanks to divisions within the PML that it won the elections of 1988, 1993, and 2008.

The Pakistan Tehreek-e-Insaf was founded in 1996 by former cricket player Imran Khan on a platform of development and the fight against corruption. Its agenda included investments in education and health care, anticorruption measures, and trade liberalization. The PTI won the general election of 2018, putting an end to thirty-eight years of alternation between the Muslim League and the PPP in the electoral arena. The popularity of its anticorruption platform, as well as the tacit support of the military establishment behind the scenes, were the key distinguishing factors enabling the PTI's rise to power.[9] The progression of the PTI from less than 1 percent of votes in 1997 to 32 percent in 2018 coincided with the decline of both the PPP and the PML, revealing the party's success among voters traditionally supporting one or the other of these two movements.

At least two other groups of parties are key to understanding the structure of political competition in Pakistan: Islamic parties and the Muttahida Qaumi Movement. Islamic parties reject both capitalism and communism and have aimed at transforming the country into an Islamic state governed by Sharia law. Their platform notably promotes changes in the constitution, in the criminal system, and in economic and financial practices. Their electoral success since 1970 has fluctuated, in part because they have joined several coalitions with other conservative and Muslim League parties, which makes it hard to trace their importance as an independent ideological bloc. From 20 percent of votes in 1970, their importance has since declined, but has not vanished. Islamic parties had renewed success in 2002 by contesting the general election as a single coalition, the Muttahida Majlis-e-Amal (United Council of Action), obtaining 11 percent of votes, which some argue was with the help of Pakistan's military establishment.[10] Likewise, the Muttahida Majlis-e-Amal and other Islamic parties received 9 percent of votes in 2018.

---

9. A. Shah, "Pakistan: Voting under Military Tutelage," *Journal of Democracy* 30, no. 1 (2019): 128–142.

10. Bose and Jalal, *Modern South Asia*.

The Muttahida Qaumi Movement (MQM), finally, is a secular party founded in 1984 by Altaf Hussain. Its original objective was to represent the interests of the Muhajirs, Urdu-speaking Muslims who emigrated from India to Pakistan following the political division of the subcontinent in 1947; a large majority of them settled in Karachi. Its best result was a fourth place in the elections of 2008, with 7.4 percent of votes.

In summary, Pakistan's party system historically set the PPP against a changing coalition of conservative parties more or less supportive of democracy, Islamization, and military intervention, with the latter group receiving 35 percent to 55 percent of votes from 1970 to 2013. The rise of the PTI in 2013 and its victory in 2018 put an end to this binary structure. It accelerated the long-run decline of the PPP, which was supported by only 13 percent of voters in 2018 as compared to 31 percent in 2008. It also came at the expense of the conservatives, whose total share of votes fell from 47 percent in 2008 to 34 percent in 2018.[11]

## Language, Geography, and Inequality in Pakistan

How have Pakistani political parties represented different forms of inequalities and social identities in democratic elections? We provide new insights into this research question by bringing together a unique dataset of exit polls conducted at the time of general elections by Gallup Pakistan, from 1988 to 2018. Gallup Pakistan surveyed between 3,000 and 5,000 voters exiting the voting booths, allowing us to study the structure of Pakistani political parties' supporters and the interactions between ethnolinguistic, regional, and social identities in most general elections since 1970.[12]

Pakistan is divided into four provinces: Punjab (54 percent of the population in 2018), Sindh (28 percent), Khyber Pakhtunkhwa (formerly

11. The importance of independent candidates and small parties should also not be underestimated, as each of these two groups received 2 to 20 percent of votes since 1970 (see appendix Figure A1, wpid.world).

12. The 1988 election surveyed respondents on their previous voting behaviors in the general elections of 1977 and 1970, so we use this retrospective question to approximate voting patterns for these years. Other important data limitations are worth mentioning. Women were not surveyed before 2002. No weighting was designed by surveyors, so we use linear calibration to make the survey representative in terms of region and election results by party. Also notice that by definition, exit polls do not address turnout, since they survey individuals coming out of voting stations. This is a substantial limitation in a country where electoral turnout has regularly been below 50 percent.

*Table 10.1*   Composition of the Pakistani Population, 1988–2018

|  | 1988 | 2002 | 2018 |
|---|---|---|---|
| **Provinces** | | | |
| Punjab | 58% | 57% | 54% |
| Sindh | 24% | 24% | 28% |
| Khyber Pakhtunkhwa | 14% | 14% | 12% |
| Baluchistan | 5% | 5% | 6% |
| **Languages** | | | |
| Punjabi | 44% | 44% | 44% |
| Saraiki | 11% | 10% | 10% |
| Sindhi | 12% | 15% | 16% |
| Urdu | 8% | 8% | 8% |
| Pashto | 15% | 15% | 15% |
| Balochi | 4% | 4% | 4% |
| Others | 7% | 4% | 3% |

*Data Source:* Authors' computations using census statistics covering the entire Pakistani population (see wpid.world).

*Note:* In 2018, Punjab concentrated 54% of the Pakistani population.

known as the North-West Frontier Province, NWFP, 12 percent), and Baluchistan (6 percent). Regional boundaries are closely linked to linguistic specificities (see Figure 10.1). Punjabi and Saraiki speakers (44 percent and 10 percent of the population in 2018, respectively) are in large majority located in the Punjab, with Saraiki speakers being more prevalent in rural areas. Meanwhile, the Sindh province is linguistically divided into Sindhi speakers (16 percent of the population), who constitute the majority of the rural population, and Urdu speakers who are the descendants of Muhajir migrants from India and are concentrated in urban areas (especially in Karachi). Pashto speakers amount to 15 percent of the population and over 80 percent of residents of Khyber Pakhtunkhwa. Finally, nearly all Balochi speakers live in Baluchistan.[13]

This ethnolinguistic and geographic diversity comes with significant socioeconomic inequalities. Sindhi and Saraiki speakers are significantly poorer than the rest of the population, representing 39 percent of the bottom 50 percent but only 17 percent of the top decile. Pashtuns are

13. See appendix Figure A3, wpid.world, for the complete linguistic composition of voters by region.

slightly richer than other ethnolinguistic groups, while the Punjabi cut across all social classes.[14] Ethnic inequalities are therefore closely tied to the rural-urban divide. That being said, language and geography remain only moderately correlated to social class overall, opening up the possibility of class cleavages cross-cutting ethnic identities, or conversely, of ethnolinguistic cleavages cross-cutting socioeconomic divides.

## The Changing Structure of Ethnolinguistic Divides

We start our analysis by focusing on changes in the ethnolinguistic dimension of electoral divides. Figure 10.3 plots the share of votes received by the PPP by language from 1970 to 2018.[15] In the first direct election of 1970, as much as 95 percent of Sindhis voted for Zulfiqar Ali Bhuto's Pakistan Peoples Party, compared to less than 40 percent of other ethnolinguistic groups. This support was in large part rooted in the fact that Bhutto, as a large landowner from Larkana in the center of Sindh, had the resources for patronage politics in rural constituencies, as well as ethnic legitimacy, which allowed him to galvanize support in the province.[16] In the past forty years, the decline of the PPP has not been concentrated in a specific region or language; it has happened among all groups, so that the gap between Sindhi speakers and other groups has remained very stable. As Figure 10.4 shows, furthermore, the massive relative support received by the PPP among the Sindhis cannot be accounted for by differences in income or education levels across ethnic groups. Both before and after accounting for the independent effects of education, income, and other socioeconomic characteristics, Sindhi speakers have always been more likely to support the PPP by 30 to 60 percentage points.

The transition from the overwhelming victory of Bhutto in 1977 to the rise of the PTI did, however, mark a progressive ethnicization of the Pakistan Peoples Party's supporters. In the 1970s and 1980s, the PPP was able to win elections by receiving significant support from non-Sindhi ethnic groups, and in particular from the heavily populated Punjab province. This was not the case anymore in 2018, when the PPP only obtained a majority among Sindhis as compared to less than 10 percent

---

14. See appendix Figures A4 and A5, wpid.world.

15. We exclude the Baloch in our analyses of language, given that they represent less than 4 percent of the population, leading to very low sample sizes and unreliable estimates.

16. S. Das, *Kashmir and Sindh: Nation-Building, Ethnicity, and Regional Politics in South Asia* (Anthem Press, 2001).

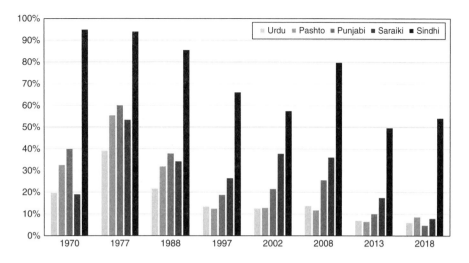

FIGURE 10.3. The PPP vote by language, 1970–2018
*Data Source:* Authors' computations using Pakistani polls (see wpid.world).
*Note:* The figure shows the share of votes received by the Pakistan Peoples Party (PPP) by linguistic group. Sindhi speakers have always been more likely to vote PPP than the rest of the electorate. This cleavage has been reinforced over time, as the PPP vote has become increasingly restricted to Sindhis.

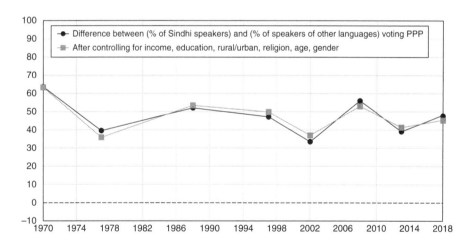

FIGURE 10.4. Ethnolinguistic cleavages and the PPP vote in Pakistan, 1970–2018
*Data Source:* Authors' computations using Pakistani polls (see wpid.world).
*Note:* The figure shows the difference between the share of Sindhi speakers and the share of speakers of other languages voting for the Pakistan Peoples Party (PPP), before and after controls. Sindhi voters have always been more likely to vote PPP since 1970, a pattern that is barely affected by the introduction of controls.

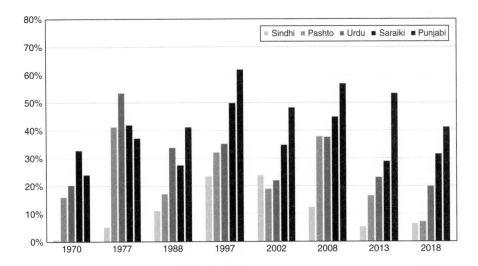

FIGURE 10.5. The PML/IJI/PNA vote by language, 1970–2018
*Data Source:* Authors' computations using Pakistani polls (see wpid.world).
*Note:* The figure shows the share of votes received by Pakistan Muslim League (PML) parties or the associated alliances (IJI/PNA) by linguistic group. Pakistan Muslim League parties have seen their electorate become increasingly restricted to Saraiki and Punjabi speakers in the past decades.

of votes among all other groups, which explains why its nationwide vote share did not exceed 13 percent. This transition, from a dominant party with a diversified electoral base to an exclusive party relying on a single minority group, is comparable to the decline of the Indian National Congress and its shift toward Muslims and lower castes in the past seventy years—although caste and religion, rather than ethnicity, played a greater role in the latter transformation (see Chapter 9). This transformation highlights how dominant parties are always forced to rely on unstable coalitions, whose erosion often comes with a focus on increasingly specific social identities. However, this result should not be exaggerated in the case of Pakistan: the decline of the PPP was the outcome of a chaotic process of democratic contests, repression, and military intervention, rather than solely the result of dissatisfaction with a single ruling party.

The evolution of Muslim League parties and their coalitions reveals comparable transitions. PML parties have always received greater support in the Punjab (see Figure 10.5), yet they always had to rely on support from

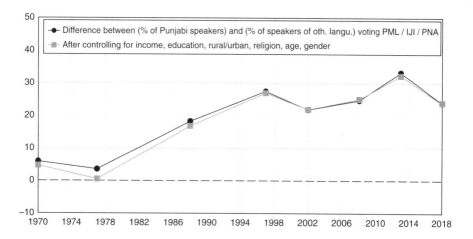

FIGURE 10.6. Ethnolinguistic cleavages and the PML/IJI/PNA vote in Pakistan, 1970–2018

*Data Source:* Authors' computations using Pakistani polls (see wpid.world).

*Note:* The figure shows the difference between the share of Punjabi speakers and the share of speakers of other languages voting for Pakistan Muslim League (PML) parties or the associated alliances (IJI/PNA), before and after controls. This difference has grown over time, from 6 percentage points in 1970 to 24 percentage points in 2018.

other regions to win elections. However, while in the 1990s the electorate of the PML-N was broader than that of the PPP, it has become increasingly limited to the Punjabi electorate (Figure 10.6). This increase mirrors the progressive fragmentation of conservative forces in Pakistan, from the PNA coalition in 1977 and the IJI coalition in 1988 to 1990 to the PML-N running as a single party from 1993 onward. As in the case of the PPP, the premium received by right-wing parties in the Punjab is robust to controlling for the effect of other sociodemographic variables.

How has the emergence of the PTI affected these cleavages? Table 10.2 shows the share of votes received by parties or groups of parties by language in the 2018 general election. Two main conclusions can be drawn from these figures. First, the structure of Pakistan's party system into five broad groups of parties is highly correlated to linguistic divisions. The PPP is supported mainly by Sindhis, the PML by Punjabi and Saraiki speakers, and the MQM by Mujahirs. Second, the PTI stands out as the only party receiving substantial vote shares among all ethnic groups, even

*Table 10.2*   Ethnolinguistic Cleavages in Pakistan, 2018

| Language/Party | PPP | PML | PTI | Islamic | MQM | Others |
|---|---|---|---|---|---|---|
| Balochi | 7% | 7% | 15% | 18% | 0% | 52% |
| Pashto | 8% | 7% | 54% | 15% | 0% | 15% |
| Punjabi | 5% | 41% | 31% | 7% | 0% | 17% |
| Saraiki | 8% | 32% | 34% | 5% | 1% | 20% |
| Sindhi | 54% | 7% | 21% | 8% | 1% | 9% |
| Urdu | 6% | 20% | 30% | 11% | 18% | 16% |

*Data Source:* Authors' computations using Pakistani polls (see wpid.world).

*Note:* The table shows the share of votes received by the main Pakistani political parties by linguistic group in 2018. PPP: Pakistan Peoples Party; PML: Pakistan Muslim League parties; PTI: Pakistan Tehreek-e-Insaf; Islamic parties include the Muttahida Majlis-e-Amal and the Tehreek-e-Labbaik Pakistan; MQM: Muttahida Qaumi Movement; Others mainly includes independent candidates. In 2018, 54% of Sindhi speakers voted PPP, compared to only 5% of Punjabi speakers.

though more than half of Pashtuns voted for the PTI in 2018, which can be explained by Khan's Pashtun origin as well as by the party's historical success in the Pashtun region.

## The Political Unification of the Pakistani Elite and the Rise of the PTI

Independently from ethnoregional affiliations, economic divides have been a key dimension of political conflicts in Pakistan since independence. Originally, the PPP was formed by an alliance of socialists favoring labor unions and poor farmers. In 1972, Bhutto announced the nationalization of key industries, engaged in a land reform redistributing acres to landless peasants, and nationalized health and education. In the 1970s, party politics in Pakistan therefore had a strong socioeconomic dimension. The PPP's success in West Pakistan in the 1970 elections, in particular, drew on its efforts to pit socialist "workers" against large landowning and feudal politicians (despite the fact that many of the latter were to be found in the party's ranks, including Bhutto himself). Following the end of General Zia-ul-Haq's martial law, however, Benazir Bhutto's government was relatively more market oriented and did not renationalize the industries, though it did start a large transfer program, the Benazir Income Support Program. Similarly, the PML-N evolved from being fervently backed by Islamic conservative alliances and the military establishment to having its own center-right policies and agenda, and even

exerting some degree of independence from the military, which many argue led to its eventual downfall.[17]

The PTI, however, may have seen the largest swing in both its ideology and electoral success. Support for the PTI, originally limited to the urban middle class until 2013, grew dramatically as the party changed its anti–status quo, antimilitary establishment and reformist agenda, broadening its support base to Islamists and gaining support from large industrialists and from the feudal politicians dominating rural Punjab. This was facilitated by Pakistan's strong military establishment. That being said, the PTI did manage to keep the support base it had in 2013 even as it pandered to Islamic voters using religious rhetoric and support for the blasphemy law in its election campaigns.[18] In this sense, only the PPP in the 1970 elections was able to win the rural areas with a popular agenda and promise of reform, while earlier PML-N candidates and more recently the PTI were able to win only through a successful coalition with large landowners, industrial elites, and the military establishment that dominates electoral politics in rural Pakistan.[19]

Figure 10.7 shows the share of votes received by the PPP by income group from 1970 to 2018. Low-income voters have been more likely than richer individuals to support the PPP in all elections since 1970. Comparable patterns are visible when looking at education.[20] To what extent can this success among low-income earners be explained by the lower income levels of Sindhis? Figure 10.8 shows the difference between the share of top 10 percent earners and the share of bottom 90 percent earners voting for the PPP, before and after controlling for other sociodemographic characteristics of the electorate. From 1970 to 2018, high-income earners have been less likely to support the PPP, by about 10 percentage points on average. After controlling for region and language, the difference gets closer to zero, but remains negative at about 5 percentage points on average. Hence, the lower income levels of Sindhis did partly explain the suc-

---

17. Bose and Jalal, *Modern South Asia*.

18. M. J. Nelson, "Islamist Politics in South Asia after the Arab Spring: Parties and Their Proxies Working with—and against—the State" (Brookings Institution, 2015), https://www.brookings.edu/wp-content/uploads/2016/07/Pakistan_Nelson-FINALE.pdf; J. M. Dorsey, "Pakistan and Its Militants: Who Is Mainstreaming Whom?" (RSIS Working Paper, 2018), https://www.researchgate.net/publication/328450636_Pakistan_and_Its_Militants_Who_is_Mainstreaming_Whom.

19. Shah, "Pakistan."

20. See appendix Figures A13 to A16, wpid.world.

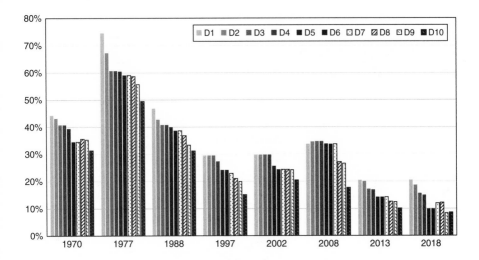

FIGURE 10.7. The PPP vote by income decile in Pakistan, 1970–2018
*Data Source:* Authors' computations using Pakistani polls (see wpid.world).
*Note:* The figure shows the share of voters supporting the Pakistan Peoples Party (PPP) by income decile. In 2018, 20% of bottom 10% income earners (D1) voted PPP, compared to 9% of top 10% income earners (D10).

cess of the PPP among the poor, but not entirely; low-income earners from other regions, and in particular in the Punjab, were key to explaining the party's electoral victories. This independent income effect, however, seemed to have completely disappeared in 2013 and 2018, which reflects the restriction of the PPP's voting base to Sindhis.

Economic status therefore does seem to have played a significant role in determining electoral divides in Pakistan beyond ethnic and regional affiliations. Support for PML parties shows more fluctuating patterns, with no clear persisting income or education gradient. Similarly, Islamic parties have historically been slightly more popular among higher-income and higher-educated voters, but this is partly explained by their relatively high vote shares among the Urdu-speaking population and Pashtuns.[21]

Turning to Imran Khan's party, we find that both higher-income and higher-educated voters have been significantly more likely to vote for the

21. See appendix Figures A10 to A20, wpid.world.

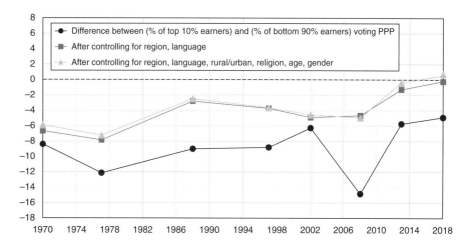

FIGURE 10.8. The PPP vote and income in Pakistan, 1970–2018
*Data Source:* Authors' computations using Pakistani polls (see wpid.world).
*Note:* The figure shows the difference between the share of top 10% earners and the share of bottom 90% earners voting for the Pakistan Peoples Party (PPP), before and after controls. The PPP has always received greater support from bottom-income earners since 1970, but this difference has declined over time, from 8 percentage points in 1970 to 5 percentage points in 2018 before controls, and from 7 points to 0 after controlling for region and ethnolinguistic affiliation.

PTI in the last two Pakistani elections (Figure 10.9).[22] Moreover, the effects of income and education are only moderately reduced when controlling for region, language, and other variables. This shows that middle- and upper-class voters, and especially the higher educated, have been more likely to vote for the PTI, independent of regional or ethnolinguistic affiliations.

The recent success of the PTI has therefore announced a historical change in the structure of political cleavages in Pakistan. The party system of the 1970s and 1980s mainly set low-income PPP voters located in the Sindh and other rural areas against a broad coalition of conservative parties with diverse ideologies and voting bases. The decline of the PPP has been associated with the fragmentation of class affiliations, the ethnicization of traditional parties' constituencies, and the unification by the PTI of a new elite cutting across linguistic identities.

22. See appendix Figures A12, A15, and A20, wpid.world, on the vote share received by the PTI by income and education levels.

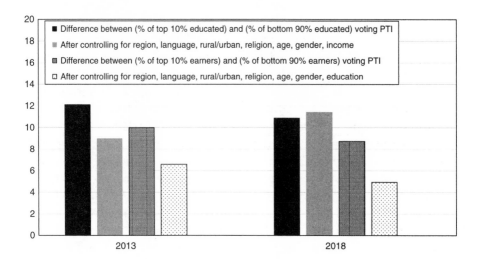

FIGURE 10.9. The PTI vote by income and education in Pakistan, 2013–2018
*Data Source:* Authors' computations using Pakistani polls (see wpid.world).
*Note:* The figure shows the relative support of top-income and highest-educated voters for the Pakistan Tehreek-e-Insaf (PTI) in the general elections of 2013 and 2018, before and after controls. The PTI received greater support from top-income and highest-educated voters in these two elections. This difference is maintained after controls.

## Islamization and the Politics of Minorities

The country of Pakistan was explicitly created to welcome the Muslim population of the Indian subcontinent. From 1988 to 2018, more than 97 percent of voters declared being Muslim in all exit polls at our disposal (see Table 10.1). The majority of Pakistani Muslims declared being Sunni, as compared to an estimated 5 percent to 20 percent declared as Shia. The true share of Shia Muslims in the Pakistani population remains very difficult to estimate, given Pakistan's contemporary history of Islamization and repression of religious minorities, which implies that underreporting of Shia identity may be significant.[23]

This repression was notably visible during the rule of General Zia-ul-Haq. Soon after coming to power in the military coup of 1977, General Zia consolidated his power through a wave of Islamization policies.

23. M. Kalin and N. Siddiqui, *Religious Authority and the Promotion of Sectarian Tolerance in Pakistan* (US Institute of Peace, 2014).

Building on a coalition of anti-Bhutto Islamists, he set out a series of policies that adversely impacted minorities. A key casualty was the Shia community, which organized large protests against Zia's interpretation of (Sunni) Islam and his implementation of its requirements on them. Following mass protests, he revised his proposed uniform enforcement of zakat (compulsory charity) on every Muslim citizen in Pakistan to apply only to Sunni Muslims. Yet, Zia tried to reduce the influence of Shia political and militant organizations by fanning the flames of extremism and giving Sunni extremist organizations license to persecute the Shia population with impunity.[24] Perhaps the most lasting symbol of his legacy is the infamous addition of Section 295C to the Pakistan Penal Code, which stipulated the death penalty for blasphemy. No one has ever been convicted and executed under this law, but it has given rise to a large number of cases against minorities and spurred acts of vigilantism and violence against Christian and Hindu minorities.

The PPP has always received substantially greater support among religious minorities than among the majority Sunni voting population (see Figure 10.10). This support for the PPP has been even stronger among non-Muslims: in the 2018 general election, the PPP was backed by an all-time low 11 percent of Sunnis, but by 29 percent of Shia and as much as 46 percent of non-Muslims. This result is consistent with the PPP's historical secular socialist ideology, as compared to the more conservative and Islamic policies proposed and implemented by the Pakistan Muslim League parties and by military regimes. This result remains significant after controls.[25]

The vote of minorities therefore appears to have represented a third independent dimension of Pakistani electoral politics, alongside ethnolinguistic and class divides. Such persistent and strong support from historically disadvantaged minorities for the PPP is comparable to that found in many other countries, from the Muslim vote for the Congress in India (see Chapter 9) to the vote of non-Muslim religious minorities for the Indonesian Democratic Party of Struggle (see Chapter 13).

24. F. Ispahani, "Cleansing Pakistan of Minorities," Hudson Institute, July 31, 2013, https://www.hudson.org/research/9781-cleansing-pakistan-of-minorities.

25. See appendix Figure A24, wpid.world.

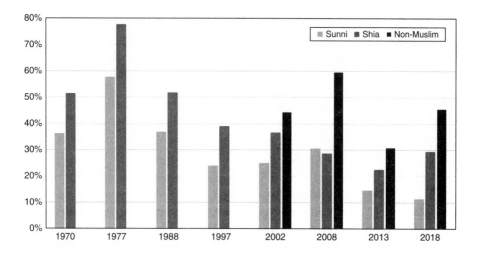

FIGURE 10.10. The religious cleavage in Pakistan, 1970–2018. The PPP vote by religious affiliation

*Data Source:* Authors' computations using Pakistani polls (see wpid.world).

*Note:* The figure shows the share of voters supporting the Pakistan Peoples Party (PPP) by religious affiliation. In 2018, the PPP was supported by 11% of Sunni Muslims, 29% of Shia Muslims, and 46% of non-Muslim voters.

## The Effect of Zia's Islamization Policies

We conclude this chapter by emphasizing the crucial role of General Zia-ul-Haq's policies in explaining the transformation of Pakistan's party system from the electoral domination of the mass-based PPP of the 1970s to the success of the PTI supported by elites and the military in 2018.[26] There are two key policy changes that are attributed to General Zia. The first one is the decentralization reform of 1979. The military regime of General Zia used the strategy of "divide and rule" by creating a new class of "collaborative" local political elites that were beholden to the military regime.[27] This political elite consisted of religious leaders, Islamist and

26. S. K. Burki, "The Politics of Misogyny: General Zia-ul-Haq's Islamization of Pakistan's Legal System," *Contemporary Justice Review* 19, no. 1 (2016): 103–119; M. M. Tariq, "The Rise and Impact of Islamic Fundamentalism in Pakistan after the Soviet Invasion in Afghanistan, with Special Reference to KPK and Baluchistan," *Balochistan Review* 24, no. 1 (2011).

27. A. Jalal, *Democracy and Authoritarianism in South Asia: A Comparative and Historical Perspective,* vol. 1 (Cambridge University Press, 1995).

conservative politicians as well as disgruntled members of the PPP. The local government system introduced by Zia enabled him to consolidate his power since he free rode on the local legitimacy of religious and political leaders.

Second, a critical policy change attributed to General Zia's regime is the Islamization policies known under the broad slogan "Nizam-e-Mustafa" (The System of the Prophet Muhammad). These included the constitution of a separate judicial branch, the Shariat Courts, to judge legal cases under Islamic doctrine. Likewise, new criminal offenses were added in Pakistani penal courts, with adultery, fornication, and blasphemy becoming criminal offenses punishable under Pakistani law. Furthermore, the banking system forbade the payment of interest to lenders and instead substituted it with profit and loss payments.[28]

There was also an effort to "cleanse" school textbooks and libraries of "un-Islamic material" and change the school curriculum. Arabic was introduced as a second language in schools. Religious practice was strongly encouraged, and national television was used for confessional propaganda purposes. Overall, General Zia's policies aimed to build a political coalition of Islamists and conservative politicians that supported him and his conservative policies and tried to create a population receptive to these ideas through use of propaganda and repression of dissent.

Therefore, the active indoctrination of a whole generation via Islamist propaganda and promotion of conservative ideas and policies may have given rise to an educated political class adverse to secular and socialist ideals. This may account for the decline of the PPP documented in this chapter and help to explain the consolidation of conservative political views we see in other available surveys.[29]

28. G. Kepel, *Jihad: The Trail of Political Islam* (Harvard University Press, 2002).

29. A. Siddiqa, "Red Hot Chilli Peppers Islam: Is the Youth in Elite Universities in Pakistan Radical?" (Foreign-Security Policy paper, Heinrich Böll Stiftung, 2010), https://issuu.com/cjiqbal/docs/red_hot_chilli_peppers_islam_-_complete_study_repo.

## 11

# Political Cleavages and the Representation of Social Inequalities in Japan, 1953–2017

**AMORY GETHIN**

## Introduction

This chapter studies the evolution of the structure of political cleavages in Japan from 1953 to 2017. Party identifications in Japan are partly the legacy of its unique democratic transition, which took place under US occupation from 1945 to 1951. This transition, by imposing the renunciation of military buildup and the establishment of US military bases throughout the archipelago, gave to foreign policy and the question of remilitarization an exceptional importance.

The party system that emerged in the 1950s, with conservative parties opposing socialists and communists, therefore differed significantly from the class-based party systems visible during the same period in Western Europe. While the mobilization of the working class was far from insignificant, it came with marked rifts between urban educated elites and people in poorer rural areas, as well as divides between generations expressing deep ideological differences in attitudes toward war memory and the colonization of Southeast Asia from 1920 to 1945. In this context, the Liberal Democratic Party (LDP) succeeded in becoming the single dominant party during the entire 1955–1993 period by aggregating a diverse electorate consisting of low-income rural households, lower-educated voters, and business elites.

I wish to thank Kentaro Asai, David Chiavacci, Sébastien Lechevalier, Thanasak Jenmana, Clara Martínez-Toledano, Thomas Piketty, Carmen Schmidt, and Yoshida Toru for their comments and advices. I am also grateful to the teams of the Social Science Japan Data Archive, the Japanese Election Studies, the Comparative Study of Electoral Systems, and the Inter-University Consortium for Political and Social Research for making the data used in this chapter available.

The political and economic turmoil associated with the "lost decade" of the 1990s coincided with the end of the LDP's hegemony and a lasting transformation of the party system. Yet, as the analysis of voting behaviors will show, it was in the long run that the structure of Japanese political cleavages changed profoundly. While education has remained a significant determinant of party identification, this is not the case with income, union membership, age, or rural-urban location, which have gradually lost most of their explanatory power. This form of "depolarization" of Japan's political space is paradoxical, given the context of growth slowdown, rising inequalities, and job insecurity that has characterized the recent decades. It both reveals and contributes to sustaining the growing dissatisfaction of citizens toward political parties, as evidenced by the decline in electoral turnout visible since the beginning of the 1990s.

I first discuss the transformation of party politics in Japan from the dominance of the LDP to the fragmentation of the party system since the 1990s. I then document how urbanization, industrialization, and tertiarization have transformed the structure of social inequalities in Japan. I conclude the chapter by showing how the decline of the LDP has been associated with the gradual alteration of the class, rural-urban, and generational cleavages that had structured the Japanese party system in the early postwar decades.

## Democratization and the Fragmentation of Japan's Party System

In their seminal study of political attitudes in Japan in 1976, Scott Flanagan and his coauthors document the evolution of cleavage politics in the country since the end of World War II.[1] One of the specificities of Japanese democratization, they argue, is that a variety of factors hindered the development of a class cleavage. When the foundations of contemporary Japanese democracy were laid down at the end of World War II under US occupation, it was not Japan's first experience with democracy. A first step toward a democratic system can be traced back to the Meiji era (1868–1912), when the country introduced a parliamentary system based on property qualification, comparable to those existing in Europe during the nineteenth century. The 1890 legislative elections had thereby

1. S. C. Flanagan, S. Kohei, I. Miyake, B. Richardson, and J. Watanuki, *The Japanese Voter* (Yale University Press, 1991).

allowed slightly more than 1 percent of the population to elect representatives to the National Diet,[2] a proportion that increased following
waves of democratization, until the adoption of universal male suffrage
in 1925.

Overall, in the first four decades of the twentieth century, the political
mobilization of the masses was limited by the maintenance of a two-party
system featuring two catchall parties, which both aggregated the interests of landowners, business elites, and bureaucrats. The alternation of
these two parties in power, as well as the suppression of communist parties and the minority position of industrial workers, helped to inhibit class
divides.[3]

The military defeat in 1945 and the US occupation that followed laid
the foundations for democratic competition in the country for several decades. During the occupation, a number of major reforms were made,
including the promulgation of a new constitution, substantial land redistribution, recognition of labor unions, and guarantees of freedom of
speech. Among other factors, the land reforms conducted from 1946 to
1950 succeeded in reallocating agricultural land to many small independent farmers, eroding class sentiments in rural areas. Large landowners
received assets that paid a fixed nominal return as compensation, but
their value rapidly declined with postwar inflation. The US administration also restructured the big business conglomerates (*zaibatsu*) that had
controlled a significant part of the Japanese economy since the Meiji period. Finally, Japan's late industrialization also played an important role
in limiting the strength of socialist and communist movements. In 1950,
still 50 percent of the labor force was engaged in the primary sector, compared to 25 percent in West Germany, for instance. This gave greater
salience to the industrial-agrarian cleavage and limited the power of the
working class, whose electoral strength would never reach the levels

2. E. O. Reischauer, *Histoire du Japon et des Japonais* (Seuil, 1997), chapter 9. The
National Diet is the bicameral legislature of Japan, created in 1889 following the adoption
of the Meiji Constitution. It is composed of the House of Representatives and the House
of Councillors. The two houses have been directly elected since the adoption of the 1947
postwar constitution.

3. Notice, however, that the Minseito and its predecessor the Kenseikai were more
liberal and more labor oriented than the Seiyukai. The Minseito was also stronger in urban
constituencies than the Seiyukai, so the rural-urban cleavage that dominated postwar
Japanese politics was already apparent in the Meiji era. See, for instance, J. M. Ramseyer
and F. M. Rosenbluth, *Japan's Political Marketplace* (Harvard University Press, 1993).

observed in Western democracies in the 1950s and 1960s.[4] The newly created Japan Socialist Party and Japan Communist Party thus failed to defeat the conservative forces that were in large part inherited from the prewar era.

While class cleavages were not as significant as in Western democracies, the first twenty years of the postwar democracy were characterized by strong divides over social values. In that respect, Japan's structure of political competition was quite different from that observed in Western democracies at the same period: "In this confrontation between the conservatives and the leftists, the issue was neither capitalism nor socialism; nor was the underlying cleavage determined by class. Rather, the differences arose from a conflict between the traditional values of emperor worship, emphasis on hierarchy and harmony, and belief in a militarily strong nation—all of which were strongly supported in the prewar era—and the 'modern' values of the postwar era of individualism, equality, and fear of military build-up and war."[5] This explains why both analysts and voters in Japan have generally preferred to differentiate parties along a "progressive-conservative" rather than a "left-right" scale.[6] In the economic dimension, finally, by defending the interests of farmers and fishers, building ties with agricultural cooperatives, and actively redistributing the fruits of economic growth to rural areas, the Liberal Democratic Party was quick to establish its dominance in the countryside.[7]

One of the remarkable achievements of the LDP, however, was to remain in power despite the major structural changes Japan underwent. In particular, industrialization and urbanization eroded the party's traditional electoral base, as the share of farmers in the overall population decreased rapidly throughout the second half of the twentieth century. Economic growth played an important role in explaining the party's adaptation to these transformations. Conservatives were able to avoid political confrontation with socialist and communist parties by emphasizing

4. C. Schmidt, "Social Cleavages, Voter Alignment, and Dealignment in Japan," *Hitotsubashi Journal of Social Studies* 35, no. 2 (2003): 63–77.

5. J. Watanuki, "Social Structure and Voting Behaviour," in Flanagan et al., *Japanese Voter*, 49–82.

6. W. Jou and M. Endo, *Generational Gap in Japanese Politics: A Longitudinal Study of Political Attitudes and Behavior* (Palgrave Macmillan, 2016), chapter 2.

7. D. Chiavacci, "Divided Society Model and Social Cleavages in Japanese Politics: No Alignment by Social Class, but Dealignment of Rural-Urban Division," *Contemporary Japan* 22, no. 1 (2010): 47–74.

policies focusing on the economy. Under the "Yoshida Doctrine" promulgated by Prime Minister Shigeru Yoshida (1946–1947 and 1948–1954), the government focused on postwar reconstruction and modernization. This emphasis on economic development was then pursued under Hayato Ikeda's (1960–1964) "income-doubling plan" aiming to double personal incomes within ten years, an objective that was reached in only seven. Japan's exceptional economic growth until the 1990s, together with low income inequality, were important factors enabling the continuation of conservative forces' success.[8]

At the end of the 1980s, the golden age of economic growth came to an end with the burst of speculative bubbles in real estate and stock markets, which were followed by the "lost decade" of the 1990s, a period of economic stagnation. The economic crisis, together with the multiplication of bribery scandals involving high-ranked LDP politicians, led to the formation of new parties calling for political reforms, such as the Japan Renewal Party (JRP) and the Japan New Party (JNP), both founded by former members of the LDP. The LDP's domination of Japanese politics ended in 1993, when an eight-party coalition government was formed, headed by JNP leader Hosokawa Morihiro. However, the coalition broke apart as soon as April 1994. What followed was a period of political chaos, with continuous creations, mergings, and fragmentations of new progressive and conservative parties. At the beginning of the 2000s, Japanese politics finally seemed to be moving more decisively toward a two-party system, as the Democratic Party of Japan (DPJ) managed to bring together a growing number of politicians from the center-right and the center-left, including former LDP members such as Ichirō Ozawa and Yukio Hatoyama.[9]

In 2009, the DPJ eventually won a majority of seats, based on a program primarily focused on putting an end to LDP dominance and pushing for political processes, rather than bureaucrats, to play a greater role in policy making.[10] However, public dissatisfaction with its inability to fight the economic crisis and to implement the policies it had promised, together

---

8. I. Kabashima, "Supportive Participation with Economic Growth: The Case of Japan," *World Politics* 36, no. 3 (1984): 309–338.

9. W. Jou, "Electoral Reform and Party System Development in Japan and Taiwan: A Comparative Study," *Asian Survey* 49, no. 5 (2009): 759–785.

10. T. Yoshida, "L'alternance de 2009 au Japon: La mutation d'un régime de parti dominant?," in *Politiques de l'alternance: Sociologie des changements de politiques*, ed. P. Aldrin, L. Bargel, N. Bue, and C. Pina (Éditions du Croquant, 2016), 137–161.

with perceived mismanagement of the Fukushima nuclear disaster,[11] quickly sent the party back into opposition in 2012. The return of the Liberal Democratic Party's dominance was confirmed in the 2017 general election. Taking advantage of the context of the North Korea missile threat, Shinzo Abe (LDP) called a snap election, and the Democratic Party of Japan separated into two factions that would in turn undergo further splits and mergers: the Constitutional Democratic Party of Japan, which joined other center-left parties, and the more liberal Party of Hope, which joined the new Democrat Party for the People in 2018. Therefore, the rise of the DPJ in the 2000s did not lead to the stabilization of a two-party system, and opposition to the LDP still seems to be largely unstable and unconsolidated at the time of writing.

Three important differences separating the first party system of the 1955–1993 period from Japan's "second postwar party system" are also worth mentioning.[12] First, the 1994 reform of the voting system has changed the rules of the electoral game. Under the old single nontransferable vote (SNTV) system, each constituency elected multiple members of the parliament, which encouraged candidate-centered elections and contributed to factionalism as multiple candidates from the same party had to compete in the same district. The reform replaced it with a mixed electoral system with single-member districts, in which about two-thirds of seats are allocated on a first-past-the-post basis (289 in 2017), and about one-third of seats are allocated using proportional representation (176 in 2017). This change has encouraged a shift from clientelistic redistribution to programmatic platforms, but the persisting lack of partisan identities in Japan has resulted in weaker linkages between voters and parties and have contributed to make the new party system more volatile.[13]

Second, all governments since 1993 have been coalition governments. In 2009, for instance, the DPJ allied with the SDP and three other small

11. K. E. Kushida, "The Fukushima Nuclear Disaster and the DPJ: Leadership, Structures, and Information Challenges during the Crisis," *Japanese Political Economy* 40, no. 1 (2014): 29–68.

12. R. J. Hrebenar, "The Second Postwar Party System and the Future of Japanese Politics," in *Party Politics in Japan*, ed. R. J. Hrebenar and A. Nakamura (Routledge, 2015), 189–200.

13. K. M. McElwain, "Party System Institutionalization in Japan," in *Party System Institutionalization in Asia: Democracies, Autocracies, and the Shadows of the Past*, ed. A. Hicken and E. M. Kuhonta (Cambridge University Press, 2015), 74–107.

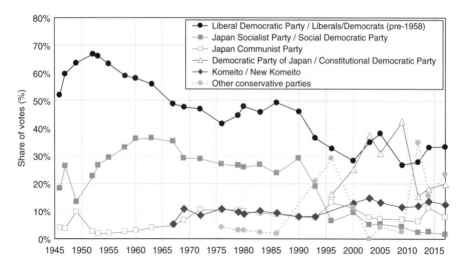

Figure 11.1. Election results in Japan, 1946–2017
*Data Source:* Author's computations using official election results (see wpid.world).
*Note:* The figure shows the share of votes received by selected political parties or groups of parties in general elections held in Japan between 1946 and 2017. The Liberal Democratic Party received 33% of votes in 2017.

parties, while the LDP has ruled in coalition with the Kōmeitō since 1999. The Kōmeitō, founded in 1964 to promote the interests of the Soka Gakkai Buddhist religious movement, has received a stable 10 to 15 percent of votes in most elections since then (see Figure 11.1). The LDP and Kōmeitō hold vastly different positions on key issues and were harsh opponents from the 1960s to the 1990s. In particular, while the LDP has championed increased defense spending and attempts to revise the Article 9 "peace clause" of the constitution, the Kōmeitō's core principles have on the contrary always been pacifism and social welfare. The LDP-Kōmeitō alliance is based on electoral complementarity rather than policy views: by coordinating nominations in single-member districts, the LDP has been able to gain sufficient seats to form governments, and the Kōmeitō has been able to send members to the Diet in the new electoral system.[14]

14. A. P. Liff and K. Maeda, "Electoral Incentives, Policy Compromise, and Coalition Durability: Japan's LDP–Kōmeitō Government in a Mixed Electoral System," *Japanese Journal of Political Science* 20, no. 1 (2019): 53–73.

Third, the second postwar party system has brought with it a surge of floating voters, making political outcomes more uncertain and partisan affiliations even more unclear. The share of nonpartisans, who do not identify themselves as either conservative or progressive, increased from 16 percent in 1966 to 60 percent in the early 2000s.[15] In addition to this, parties themselves have converged in some dimensions of their programs. Just before the 2009 elections, for instance, as much as 69 percent of voters believed that there was no big difference in the policies proposed by the DPJ and LDP.[16] Concomitantly, electoral turnout has decreased significantly since the 1990s, and voters have remained highly disconnected from the political process. In 2012, for instance, opinion polls revealed that half of the Japanese electorate were not interested in the political campaign.[17]

## Japan's Changing Electorate and the Transformation of Inequality

I now turn to the analysis of political behaviors in Japan, using a set of surveys conducted from 1953 to 2017 that allows me to track the link between voting decisions and the main characteristics of individuals over time.[18] Given limitations in data quality and comparability, I choose to focus on decade-to-decade changes. Another difficulty has to do with changes in the party system itself, as the decline of the LDP after 1993 is partly attributable to the multiplication of LDP splinter parties. I account for these changes by grouping together a larger set of conservative parties, including the LDP, the Kōmeitō after 1999, the JNP, the Shinseitō, the New Frontier Party, and the Your Party in the analysis.[19]

As shown in Table 11.1, there have been substantial transformations in the structure of Japan's electorate since the end of World War II, with a massive expansion of education, a significant aging of the population,

15. C. Schmidt, "Japan's New Party System: Characteristics and Future Perspectives," in *Germany and Japan after 1989. Reform Pressures and Political System Dynamics*, ed. R. Czada and K. Hirashima (Institute of Social Science, University of Tokyo, 2008), 1–22.

16. Yoshida, "L'alternance de 2009," 151.

17. R. J. Hrebenar and A. Nakamura, *Party Politics in Japan* (Routledge, 2015).

18. See appendix Table A1, World Political Cleavages and Inequality Database, http://wpid.world.

19. See appendix Figure A1, wpid.world. An exception is the 1953 election, for which the LDP did not yet exist, so I group together the Liberal Party (Jiyutō), the Reformist Party (Kaishintō), and independent candidates in opposition to the socialist and communist parties.

*Table 11.1*    Composition of the Japanese Electorate, 1953–2017

|  | 1953 | 1963–67 | 1976 | 1990–96 | 2003–09 | 2012–17 |
|---|---|---|---|---|---|---|
| **Education** | | | | | | |
| Primary | 69% | 63% | 45% | 25% | 17% | 14% |
| Secondary | 29% | 27% | 41% | 57% | 63% | 61% |
| Tertiary | 2% | 9% | 14% | 18% | 20% | 25% |
| **Location** | | | | | | |
| Towns and villages | | 34% | 27% | 23% | 18% | 10% |
| Medium-sized cities | | 48% | 54% | 55% | 60% | 57% |
| Big cities | | 18% | 19% | 21% | 22% | 33% |
| **Age** | | | | | | |
| 20–39 | 56% | 48% | 44% | 30% | 23% | 21% |
| 40–59 | 33% | 37% | 42% | 47% | 38% | 35% |
| 60+ | 11% | 15% | 14% | 24% | 39% | 44% |

*Data Source:* Author's computations using Japanese political attitudes surveys (see wpid.world).

*Note:* The table shows the evolution of the structure of the Japanese electorate between 1953 and 2017. This period has been marked by a strong increase in the general level of education, urbanization, and the aging of the population. In 2012–2017, 33% of voters lived in big cities and 25% had a university degree.

and a gradual migration of people from rural areas to the cities. The share of the electorate holding university degrees rose from 2 percent in 1953 to 25 percent in the last decade,[20] while the share of adults living in towns and villages has decreased from more than one-third in the 1960s to only one-tenth of the population in the 2010s. Importantly, urbanization also led to a decline in rural-urban inequalities, which as we will show below used to play an important role in structuring political divides.[21] Economic development has boosted life expectancy, which combined with low fertility has transformed Japan into one of the countries in the world with the highest share of elderly citizens.

There have also been substantial changes in overall economic inequalities in Japan. In the 1950s and 1960s, Japan was seen as a highly equal society: thanks to the policies implemented during the occupation and to

20. The definition of tertiary education excludes technical colleges, and the analysis focuses on the voting-age population, which explains why the share of university graduates may be lower than the figures provided by international sources such as the OECD.

21. See appendix Figures A5 and A6, wpid.world.

the social movements that flourished in the 1950s, the "Japanese compromise" of the 1955–1973 period relied on a generally fair distribution of economic prosperity. In this context, Japan was often depicted as embodying a new ideological model, a society freed from the class antagonisms that structured political conflicts in other industrialized countries. This view was in large part constructed and reinforced by the media and the political establishment,[22] but it did resonate to some extent with the everyday experiences of Japanese citizens.

Since the economic crisis of the 1990s, important changes in the Japanese model have instigated new dynamics. In the context of the crisis, political circles started to question Japan's social institutions, emphasizing the need to focus on economic recovery rather than on equality of outcomes and opportunities.[23] More generally, Japan went through a longer-run process of liberalization of its coordinated economy, from the financial liberalization and privatization reforms of Yasuhiro Nakasone (1982–1987) to the flexibilization of the labor market conducted under prime ministers Hashimoto (1996–1998), Obuchi (1998–2000), and Koizumi (2001–2006).[24] Available evidence points to a rise in income inequality coinciding with these changes: the share of income received by the top 10 percent rose from 33 percent in 1980 to 42 percent in 2010, so inequality in Japan is still lower than in the United States but higher than in Europe.[25]

The exact causes of rising inequality in Japan are still debated, but a number of stylized facts have been identified by existing studies. Unlike in the United States, in Japan we do not observe a massive enrichment of top incomes, but rather a strong rise in poverty. This increase had multiple interrelated causes, including rising unemployment, an increase in the number of single-headed households, the aging of the population, a growing number of nonregular workers, a resegmentation of the Japanese labor market driven by globalization and deindustrialization, lower tax progressivity, and the absence of correcting mechanisms such as social

22. D. Chiavacci, "From Class Struggle to General Middle-Class Society to Divided Society: Societal Models of Inequality in Postwar Japan," *Social Science Japan Journal* 11, no. 1 (2008): 5–27.

23. Chiavacci, "Divided Society Model."

24. S. Lechevalier, *The Great Transformation of Japanese Capitalism* (Routledge, 2016).

25. T. Piketty, *Capital and Ideology* (Harvard University Press, 2020), figure 1.6.

welfare or redistribution.[26] In any case, it is clear that Japan has become an increasingly divided society.

## Education, an Early and Stable Marker of Diverging Values

Let us start by documenting the link between education and party choice. As shown in Figures 11.2 and 11.3, education appears to be a strong and persistent determinant of the vote. In 1953, more than 70 percent of primary-educated voters supported the conservatives, compared to less than 50 percent of university graduates. In the 2010s, this gap had slightly decreased but was still significant. Accounting for the effect of other characteristics does reduce this difference and makes the trend slightly flatter in recent decades, mainly because younger and urban citizens tend to be both more educated and more likely to vote against the conservatives (see below). However, education does still have a significant independent effect during the entire period.[27]

It is therefore remarkable that in contrast to most Western democracies, where lower-educated voters formed the core electorate of social democratic, socialist, and communist parties in the postwar decades and have now shifted to voting for conservative parties (see Chapter 1), higher-educated voters in Japan consistently supported the progressive opposition to the LDP as early as the 1950s. The very particular process of postwar Japanese democratization can potentially explain this unique pattern. In Europe and the United States, the progression of the welfare state was in large part the outcome of the extraordinary mobilization of the working class; in Japan, social and economic equality was imposed from outside by the United States and reinforced by war destruction. In this particular context, divisions between political parties focused on the question of remilitarization, Article 9 of the constitution, and the role of the emperor, with socialist and communist parties advocating unconditional pacifism and the maintenance of the new democratic order. Such

26. L. Lechevalier, "The 'Re-segmentation' of the Japanese Labour Market: Investigating the Impact of Industrial Dynamics," in *Social Inequality in Post-growth Japan: Transformation during Economic and Demographic Stagnation*, ed. D. Chiavacci and C. Hommerich (Routledge, 2017), 57–72; T. Tashibanaki, "Inequality and Poverty in Japan," *Japanese Economic Review* 57, no. 1 (2006): 1–27.

27. See also appendix Figures FA9 and FA20, wpid.world, which focus on the top 10 percent of voters in terms of education.

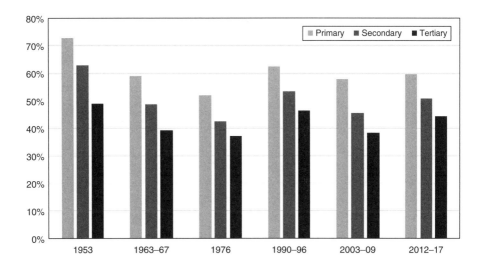

FIGURE 11.2. The conservative vote by education in Japan, 1953–2017
*Data Source:* Author's computations using Japanese political attitudes surveys (see wpid.world).
*Note:* The figure shows the share of votes received by the Liberal Democratic Party (LDP) and other conservative parties by education level. The conservative vote has been concentrated among primary-educated voters since the 1950s, a cleavage that has persisted until the 2010s.

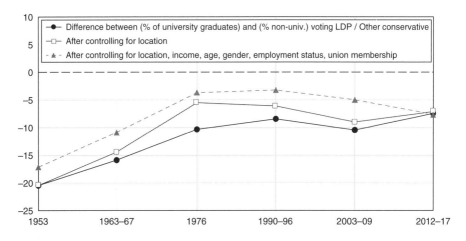

FIGURE 11.3. The educational cleavage in Japan, 1953–2017: Between decline and persistence
*Data Source:* Author's computations using Japanese political attitudes surveys (see wpid.world).
*Note:* The figure shows the difference between the share of university graduates and the share of non-university graduates voting for the Liberal Democratic Party (LDP) and other conservative parties, before and after controls. In 1953, university graduates were 20 percentage points less likely to vote conservative, compared to 8 percentage points over the 2012–2017 period.

values were at the time much more widespread in cities and among university graduates.

Foreign policy and war memory not only have been core foundations of Japanese democracy, they also have remained a key dimension of contemporary political conflicts. This was notably evident from the controversies surrounding the visits of conservative prime ministers to the Shinto shrine of Yasukuni, where over a thousand individuals designated as war criminals by the International Military Tribunal for the Far East at the end of World War II are enshrined. Partisan identities therefore remain in part determined by symbolic, memorial, and diplomatic issues today, with opposition parties being more supportive of an official recognition of the war crimes committed by Japan in the 1930s and 1940s, as well as of limitations to military spending or overseas interventions. Prime Minister Shinzo Abe repeatedly acknowledged that rewriting Article 9 was one of his most important lifetime political goals, a revision that the Kōmeitō and opposition parties have successfully blocked so far.[28]

### The Persistence and Transformation of Rural-Urban Divides

Highly populated rural areas were at the heart of conservative domination of Japanese politics in the postwar decades. As shown in Figures 11.4 and 11.5, the rural-urban cleavage used to be as strong as the educational divide, and greater than that observed for the same period in most Western countries (see Chapter 1).

However, this divide seems to have gradually faded as a result of the demographic transition and the ability of the LDP to adapt and diversify its support base accordingly. In the postwar period, rural support for the conservatives was based on tight relationships with agricultural cooperatives, as well as patronage networks redistributing the fruits of economic growth from the cities to rural areas, the *kōenkai*.[29] As urbanization inevitably eroded its voting base, the LDP needed to adapt its policies and political priorities toward the new urban majority if it was to remain in power. This rupture was visible in the reforms implemented in the 1990s and 2000s, notably those led by Junichirō Koizumi, which put an end to the economic privileges of rural districts and reduced public spending. These reforms hurt the rural areas but were popular among

28. Liff and Maeda, "Electoral Incentives, Policy Compromise."
29. McElwain, "Party System Institutionalization in Japan."

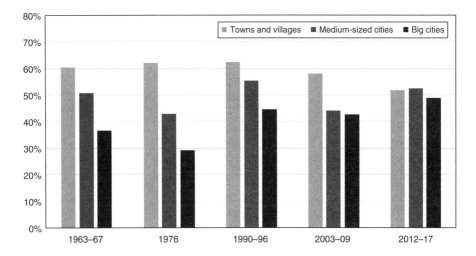

FIGURE 11.4. The conservative vote by degree of urbanization in Japan, 1963–2017
*Data Source:* Author's computations using Japanese political attitudes surveys (see wpid.world).
*Note:* The figure shows the share of votes received by the Liberal Democratic Party (LDP) and other conservative parties by rural-urban location. In 1963–1967, the LDP received 60% of votes in rural areas, compared to 37% in big cities. The difference in conservative votes between cities and rural areas has declined over time.

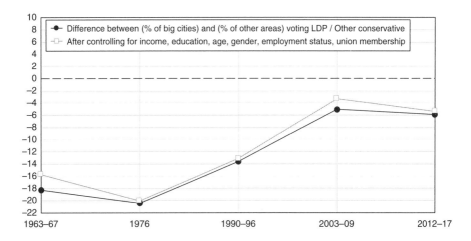

FIGURE 11.5. The decline of the rural-urban cleavage in Japan, 1963–2017
*Data Source:* Author's computations using Japanese political attitudes surveys (see wpid.world).
*Note:* the figure shows the difference between the share of big cities and the share of other cities and rural areas voting for the Liberal Democratic Party (LDP) and other conservative parties, before and after controls. The vote share received by conservative parties in big cities was 18 percentage points lower than in other cities and rural areas in the 1960s, compared to 6 percentage points in the 2010s.

the urban youth.[30] It was this remarkable ability of the LDP to reinvent itself, and gain support among the growing metropolitan areas, which enabled the party to keep winning elections to the present.

## The Declining Representation of Economic Inequalities

The conservatives' strength was thus historically driven by mass support in rural areas and among the primary educated, who were significantly poorer than the rest of the population, especially in the early postwar decades. Overall, however, the relationship between income and vote choice in Japan was clearly nonlinear in the 1960s and 1970s, being highest among low-income and top-income voters, and lowest among middle-income groups (Figure 11.6). This pattern directly reflects the very specific structure of Japanese political conflicts crystallized in the postwar era. The LDP was, on the one hand, highly successful at obtaining large majorities in rural areas, which at the time included the majority of the poor. On the other hand, it was also supported by business elites in a context of sustained growth driven by a symbiosis between the state, the bureaucracy, and large corporations. Socialist and communist parties, meanwhile, received stronger support from the urban educated middle class.

This relationship clearly appears to have vanished at the end of the twentieth century. Since the 1990s, the link between income and support for conservative parties has not shown any consistent pattern. As shown in Figure 11.7, the fall in the relative support of top-income voters for the LDP is robust to controlling for other available individual characteristics. While significant declines in the effect of income on party support are visible in other developed countries (see Chapter 1), such a complete disappearance of any link between income and the vote is rare in comparative perspective.

This remarkable depolarization of class divides is also visible when considering other available measures of socioeconomic status. Union members, for instance, were less likely to support the LDP by over 40 percentage points in 1960s, compared to only 10 percentage points in the 2010s (see Figure 11.8).[31] The same trend emerges when considering

---

30. Chiavacci, "Divided Society Model." See also J. Kingston, *Contemporary Japan: History, Politics, and Social Change since the 1980s* (Wiley-Blackwell, 2012), 110–111.

31. See also appendix Figure A14, wpid.world. Union membership has declined substantially, from about 50 percent in the early 1950s to less than 17 percent in 2019. See

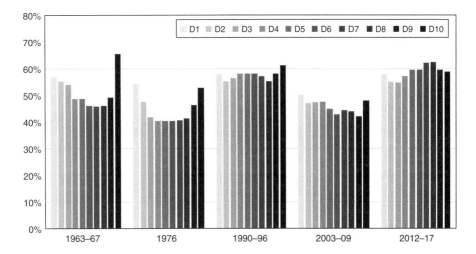

FIGURE 11.6. The conservative vote by income in Japan, 1963–2017

*Data Source:* Author's computations using Japanese political attitudes surveys (see wpid.world).

*Note:* The figure shows the share of votes received by the Liberal Democratic Party (LDP) and other conservative parties by income decile. In the 1960s, the LDP was supported by 57% of bottom 10% income earners (D1) and 65% of top 10% income earners (D10).

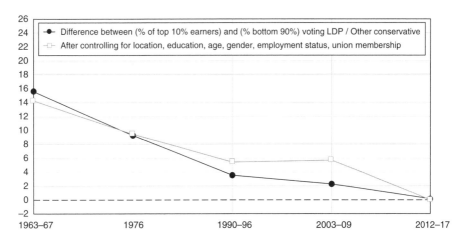

FIGURE 11.7. The conservative vote among top-income earners in Japan, 1963–2017

*Data Source:* Author's computations using Japanese political attitudes surveys (see wpid.world).

*Note:* The figure shows the difference between the share of top 10% earners and the share of bottom 90% earners voting for the Liberal Democratic Party (LDP) and other conservative parties, before and after controls. In the 1960s, top 10% earners were 16 percentage points more likely to vote conservative, compared to 0 percentage points in the 2010s.

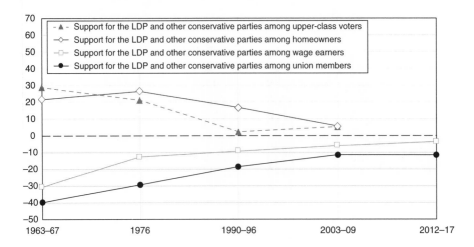

FIGURE 11.8. The depoliticization of inequality in Japan, 1963–2017
*Data Source:* Author's computations using Japanese political attitudes surveys (see wpid.world).
*Note:* The figure shows the difference in the vote share received by the Liberal Democratic Party (LDP) and other conservative parties between specific categories of voters (upper-class voters, homeowners, wage earners, and union members) and other voters. In the 1960s, upper-class voters were 29 percentage points more likely to vote conservative than the rest of the electorate, compared to 5 percentage points in the 2010s. Upper classes are defined as the top 10% of social classes, based on survey questions on the self-perceived position of respondents on the social ladder.

support for the LDP among wage earners, homeowners (the only, albeit highly imperfect, measure of wealth available), and individuals self-identifying as belonging to the "upper classes" of society.[32] Voting differences across occupational categories similarly seem to have diminished over the past decades: in 1963, for instance, 35 percent of blue collars, 62 percent of the self-employed, and 74 percent of farmers voted for the LDP; in 2014 and 2017, farmers were still strongly supportive of the LDP

---

Japan Institute for Labour Policy and Training, "Labor Union Organization Rate, Number of Union Members," accessed June 15, 2020, https://www.jil.go.jp/kokunai/statistics/timeseries/html/g0701_01.html.

32. A number of surveys have asked respondents to locate their position in the economic hierarchy from "lower" or "working" class to "upper" or "higher" class, so I combine these scales to derive a simple measure of voters belonging to the "top 10 percent" in terms of subjective class.

and other conservative parties, but differences across all other occupational categories were almost completely insignificant.[33]

These results provide clear evidence that the political representation of inequality in Japan has changed profoundly. Several mechanisms may explain this phenomenon. On the one hand, existing progressive parties broadened their electorates by moderating their platforms. An example of such moderation was the transformation of the Japan Socialist Party into the Social Democratic Party in 1996, which coincided with the end of the Cold War. On the other hand, new parties created in the 1990s, including the DPJ formed in 1998, arguably took advantage of the 1990s and 2008 economic crises—as well as the charges of corruption within the LDP and general discontent toward neoliberal policies—to benefit from their status as new parties and attract the LDP's traditional electoral base. Dealignment was therefore at least partly the result of the DPJ competing with the LDP on equal grounds by defending similar views on economic and social policy.

### From Meiji to Millennials: The Decline of Generational Divides

I conclude this chapter by looking at the evolution of generational differences in support for the conservatives. Japan's early postwar party system was strongly structured by conflicts over traditional and modern values, attitudes toward the war and colonization of Asia, and support for peace and democratization. These conflicts had a particularly strong generational component: as much as 90 percent of those aged sixty or above supported the conservatives in 1953.[34] Key to these divides were the diverging social experiences the different generations had lived through. Individuals aged fifty or above in 1953 had been brought up during the Meiji era and had witnessed the expansion of the Japanese Empire and the success of the first years of the war. In contrast, younger generations had primarily lived through the traumatic experiences of military obsession, atomic bombing, and surrender.

As shown in Figure 11.9, this cleavage seems to have very gradually disappeared. The long-run transition of Japan's democracy from a dominant-party system to a fragmented party system was therefore not

33. See appendix Tables A3 and A4, wpid.world.
34. See appendix Figure A16, wpid.world.

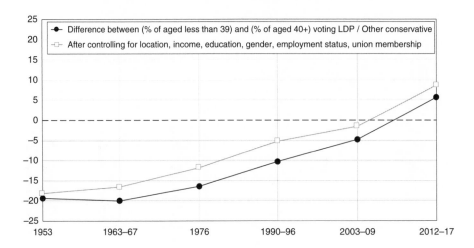

FIGURE 11.9. The reversal of the generational cleavage in Japan, 1953–2017
*Data Source:* Author's computations using Japanese political attitudes surveys
(see wpid.world).
*Note:* The figure shows the difference between the share of voters younger than 39 and
the share of voters older than 40 voting for the Liberal Democratic Party (LDP) and
other conservative parties, before and after controls. In 1953, voters younger than 39
were 19 percentage points less likely to vote conservative. In the 2010s, they had
become 5 percentage points more likely to do so.

the result of urbanization and educational expansion only. It was also
driven by the aging and eventual disappearance of the supporters of the
old imperial and military order. Arguably, the transformation of the generational cleavage also helped to reinforce the decline of other cleavages,
as dealignment happened more quickly among new cohorts.

Figure 11.10 depicts this transition from another angle, by plotting
the share of votes received by the conservatives by *generation* (by decade
of birth) from 1953 to 2017. In all elections, a very strong and persistent
divide separated voters enfranchised during the Meiji period from those
who started voting in the postwar era. This generational effect, however,
has followed a very clear *reversal:* the 1970s, 1980s, and 1990s generations have been much more likely than those born in the 1940s and 1950s
to vote for conservative parties.

At least two complementary factors may explain this transformation.
First, age divides in Japan were never only about values: they also always

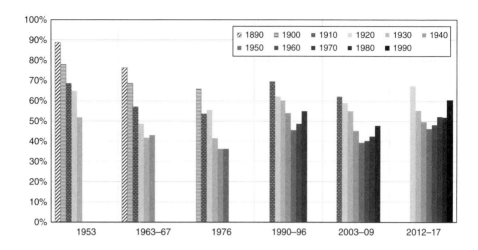

FIGURE 11.10. The conservative vote and generational renewal in Japan, 1953–2017
*Data Source:* Author's computations using Japanese political attitudes surveys (see wpid.world).
*Note:* The figure shows the share of votes received by the Liberal Democratic Party (LDP) and other conservative parties by decade of voters' birth. In 1953, 89% of voters born in the 1890s voted conservative, compared to 52% of those born in the 1930s. In the 2010s, by contrast, new generations had become more likely to vote conservative than the postwar generations, with 60% of voters born in the 1990s supporting the LDP and other conservative parties.

had a socioeconomic component, linked in particular to the generosity of the Japanese social system to retirees. As pension reforms eroded redistribution mechanisms from the younger cohorts to the elderly from the 1980s onward, new generations accordingly may have become less opposed to the LDP on economic matters.[35] Second, the new generations seem to perceive the party system very differently, notably in terms of reformism rather than progressivism, and thus may be voting for parties based on their ability to instigate changes rather than on their ideological positions on foreign policy or economic issues.[36]

35. D. P. Aldrich and R. Kage, "Japanese Liberal Democratic Party Support and the Gender Gap: A New Approach," *British Journal of Political Science* 41, no. 4 (2011): 713–733.

36. W. Jou and M. Endo, *Generational Gap in Japanese Politics*, chapter 3.

## Conclusion: The Dealignment and Growing Uncertainty of Japanese Politics

This chapter documented the factors underlying the long-run transformation of Japan's political cleavages. Demographic changes were a key driver of the transition from the dominant-party system led by the Liberal Democratic Party to an unstable party system with the LDP, the Democratic Party of Japan, and a number of satellite opportunistic parties competing for access to political power. Urbanization, educational expansion, and the aging of the population were powerful transformations driving the decline in LDP support. Yet, the party was able to remain in power throughout most of this period by broadening its appeal to younger voters, urban voters, and the middle class. The unavoidable implication of this conversion was a dealignment of traditional divides.

This declining representation of economic and social identities in Japan is paradoxical, given the rise in job precariousness and inequalities since the beginning of the lost decade of the 1990s. It is all the more puzzling because popular support for redistribution in Japan is high in comparative perspective, and is much higher among low-income individuals, two facts that suggest that a clear class-based social cleavage exists.[37] Surprisingly, this social cleavage does not seem to have been politicized. Quite the contrary: even if the Democratic Party of Japan in part based its appeal on bringing back the "Japanese model" of shared prosperity, its policies were in practice not very different from those of the LDP. In contrast with the Japanese Socialist Party, which was clearly located on the left of the political spectrum, the DPJ was composed of heterogeneous conservative and progressive elements from both the LDP and former opposition parties.

Changes in Japan's political space and rising income inequality since the 1990s also coincided with a significant decrease in political participation: turnout in the general elections of 2014 was the lowest in contemporary Japanese history, reaching 53 percent, and it did not exceed 54 percent in 2017. This is consistent with the hypothesis that ideological depolarization and the declining representation of social cleavages in

37. R. Kambayashi, S. Lechevalier, and T. Jenmana, "Decomposing Preference for Redistribution beyond the Trans-Atlantic Perspective" (Hitotsubashi University Institute of Economic Research Discussion Paper no. 707, 2020), https://halshs.archives-ouvertes.fr /halshs-02497274/document; see also A. Gethin, "Cleavage Structures and Distributive Politics" (master's thesis, Paris School of Economics, 2018), figure 1.1.

Japanese politics have led a growing number of voters to lose interest in the democratic process. Will the volatility of Japan's "second postwar party system" be sustainable? Given the LDP's capacity to gain back popular support in recent years, whether cleavage structures will come back to what they were until the end of the 1980s or Japan's transition to a "divided society model" will eventually lead to new class-based divides remains an open question.

# 12

# Democratization and the Construction of Class Cleavages in Thailand, the Philippines, Malaysia, and Indonesia, 1992–2019

AMORY GETHIN AND THANASAK JENMANA

## Introduction

What determines the emergence of class cleavages and the political representation of social inequalities in new democracies? This chapter approaches this question by using existing political attitudes surveys to document the determinants of voting behaviors in four recent Southeast Asian democracies: Thailand, the Philippines, Malaysia, and Indonesia. In Thailand and Indonesia, mounting opposition and economic distress in the 1990s put an end to military rule and led to the organization of freer and fairer elections. In the Philippines, the People Power Revolution of 1986 triggered the collapse of the Marcos authoritarian regime and the restoration of democracy. In Malaysia, the gradual consolidation of the opposition starting at the end of the twentieth century led to the decline of the ruling National Front coalition and eventually to the victory of the Alliance of Hope in 2018.

The emergence and stabilization of new political forces nonetheless followed very different trajectories in these four countries. In Thailand, democratization was associated with the rise of Thaksin Shinawatra's Thai Rak Thai Party, which was strongly supported by low-income voters and especially by the poorer northern regions of the country. In Malaysia, where regular elections have been held since

We are grateful to Clara Martínez-Toledano, Thomas Piketty, Dirk Tomsa, and Andreas Ufen for their useful comments.

1959, opposition to the dominant National Front coalition mainly came from two sides, Islamic parties and secular parties supported by ethnic minorities. The political systems of Indonesia and the Philippines, in contrast, have displayed growing instability, with political parties increasingly serving as vehicles providing electoral resources to charismatic leaders.

These diverging dynamics resulted in significant variations in the link between socioeconomic status and the vote, and thus in the political representation of inequality. While class cleavages clearly materialized in Thailand and Malaysia, they have been more variable in the Philippines and have dwindled in Indonesia. We argue that these differences in class polarization can be better understood in light of the strength of other cleavages (in particular ethnic, religious, and regional cleavages) and the extent to which these cleavages have interacted with socioeconomic concerns, consistent with what we observe in many other democracies studied in this volume, such as in Pakistan (Chapter 10) and countries in East Asia (Chapter 13) and Sub-Saharan Africa (Chapter 17).

This mechanism appears to be particularly relevant in explaining the trajectories of Thailand and Malaysia. In Thailand, extreme regional inequalities, among the highest observed in this volume, have fostered the emergence of a center-periphery cleavage with an exceptionally pronounced class dimension, which crystallized political identities and proved to be critical to Thaksin's success. In Malaysia, it was persisting ethnic inequalities between the Chinese elites and the Bumiputera majority that partly aligned ethnic and class conflicts. Regional identities in Thailand and ethnic identities in Malaysia therefore proved to be powerful catalyzers for the emergence of what could become class-based party systems in the future, if democratization were to be achieved and political organizations were to become more institutionalized in these two countries.

Ethnoregional identities and inequalities in Indonesia and the Philippines, by contrast, have not encouraged the movement toward class-based party systems. This can partly be explained by the fact that ethnic and regional inequalities were never as strong and as binary in these two countries as they were in Malaysia and Thailand. The weakness of these cleavages can also be traced back to the history of colonial rule and independence movements, which delegitimized political parties

and deliberately downplayed ethnic conflicts. While the lower classes did find a voice in the electoral arena since democratization, and social class has in practice been a significant determinant of electoral behaviors, this association has been driven primarily by specific candidates rather than by political parties. In Indonesia, the rise of opportunistic leaders has led to a remarkable dealignment of existing political cleavages. In the Philippines' exceptionally unstable party system, low-income voters have been more supportive of "pro-poor candidates," but this has not translated into the formation of stable party-voter linkages. Furthermore, center-periphery and class divides have represented cross-cutting dimensions of political conflicts, a separation that culminated in Rodrigo Duterte's success at securing the votes of both peripheral regions and the urban middle class. In summary, the diverging trajectories of Thai, Filipino, Malaysian, and Indonesian political cleavages lie at the intersection of the structure of social inequalities, the legacy of colonial and postcolonial history, and the making of democratic electoral systems.

## Thailand

Among Southeast Asian countries, Thailand is unique both in the ethnic and religious homogeneity of its population—with over 95 percent of the electorate following Theravada Buddhism and speaking Thai—and in the distinctive regional structure of its inequalities. In this section, we argue that these two factors played a key role in generating a strong polarization of the electorate along class lines during the democratization era of the 2000s. These dynamics were driven by political supply, with the redistributive policies implemented by Thaksin Shinawatra leading to the mass mobilization of the poor; they trumped other dimensions of political conflict and had a strong regional component; and they led to a democratic backlash, with the middle and upper classes uniting to support military-inspired political leadership.

### Democratization and Inequality in Thailand

Thailand engaged in a process of democratization at the turn of the twenty-first century. The military governments of the postwar era, supported by the monarchy, with the help of export-led industrialization, US financial aid, and foreign direct investment, had been highly successful

at continuously fueling economic growth since the 1960s.[1] However, much of this prosperity was shared by only a small proportion of the population; the majority of the working population remained employed in agriculture, while much of the fruits of development accrued to those involved in large enterprises, export industries, and the banking sector.[2] The 1997 Asian financial crisis marked a new era for Thailand. The public discontent that arose from economic shocks, along with a general dissatisfaction with military rule, which had been growing since the beginning of the 1990s, fueled a growing demand for political and economic reforms. The 1997 constitution thus introduced a number of innovations in the democratic process, strengthening the executive, allowing the upper house to be fully elected, and improving the separation between executive and legislative bodies.

What followed was the era of Thaksin Shinawatra, the leader of the Thai Rak Thai Party (TRT), who was elected to office in 2001 with more than 40 percent of popular votes (see Figure 12.1). At first, Thaksin mainly presented himself and the party as the ones who would restore economic growth, but the accumulation of political scandals and the elites' associated discontent led the TRT to shift to more redistributive appeals. Among many of the policies implemented during his mandate were the universal health care plan, farmers' debt rescheduling, affordable social housing, and major village microcredit schemes.

The years that followed were characterized by relative political instability. A 2006 coup d'état sent Thaksin into exile. His sister Yingluck Shinawatra, running for the newly created Pheu Thai Party (PTP), nonetheless won the 2011 elections with a program promising to pursue his policies—notably, increasing substantially the minimum wage. On May 22, 2014, however, Royal Army General Prayut Chan-o-cha launched another coup d'état, the twelfth in Thailand's contemporary history.[3] The new 2017 constitution drafted under the junta finally gave the military decisive advantages, including allowing it to make appointments to the Senate and permitting the bicameral legislature to elect a nonmember to be prime minister.

1. A. Satitniramai, *The Rise and Fall of the Bankers' Capitalism: 60 Years of the Thai Political Economy* [in Thai] (SameSkybooks, 2013).

2. T. Jenmana, "Democratisation and the Emergence of Class Conflicts: Income Inequality in Thailand, 2001–2016" (WID.world Working Paper, 2018).

3. C. J. Baker and P. Phongpaichit, *A History of Thailand* (Cambridge University Press, 2014).

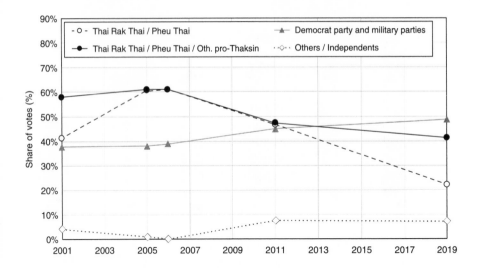

FIGURE 12.1. Election results in Thailand, 2001–2019

*Data Source:* Authors' computations using official election results (see wpid.world).

*Note:* The figure shows the share of votes received by selected political parties or groups of parties in general elections held in Thailand between 2001 and 2019.

This allowed Prayut to become prime minister in 2019, following elections widely perceived as unfree and unfair.[4]

## Social Inequalities in Thailand and the Strength of Regional Divides

Thailand's inequalities are not particularly well known, yet they appear to be among the highest in the world, and the highest among Southeast Asian countries.[5] The specificity of Thailand's inequalities lies in the extreme concentration of regional economic resources: since the 1960s, Thailand's richest provinces have always earned over six times the average income of the poorest provinces, while corresponding figures do not exceed four in Brazil, India, and Europe.[6] This inequality is tightly

---

4. Given the lack of data on these elections, the following analysis is limited to the evolution of electoral behaviors from 2001 to 2011.

5. Jenmana, "Democratisation."

6. See appendix Figures AA5 and AA6, World Political Cleavages and Inequality Database, http://wpid.world, as well as T. Jenmana and A. Gethin, "Extreme Inequality, Democratisation and Class Struggles in Thailand" (WID.world Issue Brief, 2019).

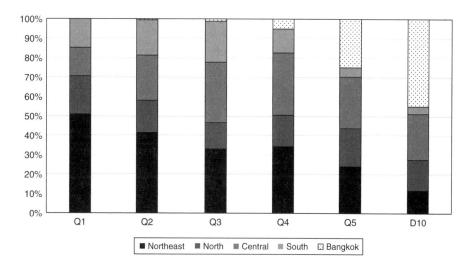

FIGURE 12.2. Regional inequalities in Thailand
*Data Source:* Authors' computations using Thai political attitudes surveys (see wpid.world).
*Note:* The figure shows the composition of income groups (quintiles Q1 to Q5 and the top decile D10) by region in 2011. In 2011, 45% of top 10% income earners lived in Bangkok, compared to only 12% in the Northeast. More than half of bottom 20% income earners were concentrated in the Northeast.

linked to the division between the center and the periphery, which has been at the heart of the Thai developmental state since the end of World War II, as the policies implemented by successive military regimes disproportionately benefited Bangkok.[7]

This spatial structure of the Thai economy is represented in Figure 12.2, which shows a simple composition of income groups by region in 2011. Bangkok residents represent about 45 percent of top 10 percent income earners in Thailand, compared to nearly 0 percent of the poorest quintile of the population. Meanwhile, the northeast region accounted for more than half of the poorest 20 percent but only 10 percent of the top decile. This is one of the strongest center-periphery divides documented in this volume.

7. P. Ouyyanont, *A Regional Economic History of Thailand* (ISEAS–Yusof Ishak Institute, 2018).

## Regionalization and the Rise of Class Cleavages

To what extent have Thailand's extreme inequality legacy and its regional component contributed to the emergence of class divides? In 2001, consistent with Thaksin's catchall platform emphasizing economic recovery, there were no clear differences between voters in terms of income or education (Figure 12.3). Following the TRT's turn toward pro-poor policies, however, which the elites largely opposed, the term "populism" emerged for the first time in Thai politics. By 2006, it had become self-evident that there was a rising class cleavage in Thailand, which culminated in protests that pitted "red-shirts" backing Thaksin against "yellow-shirts" supporting the ousting of Thaksin by the military. In 2011, even after controlling for all available sociodemographic variables except region, lower-educated and rural voters had become more likely to support the PTP by 15 and 20 percentage points, respectively (Figures 12.3 and 12.4). This support among the poor for the TRT and then the PTP can be directly linked to the social policies implemented by the Thaksin

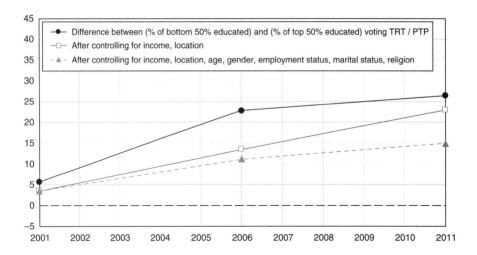

FIGURE 12.3. The educational cleavage in Thailand, 2001–2011

*Data Source:* Authors' computations using Thai political attitudes surveys (see wpid.world).
*Note:* The figure shows the difference between the share of bottom 50% educated voters and the share of top 50% educated voters voting for the Thai Rak Thai, the Pheu Thai, and other pro-Thaksin parties, before and after controls. In 2001, bottom 50% educated voters were 6 percentage points more likely to vote for these parties, compared to 26 percentage points in 2011.

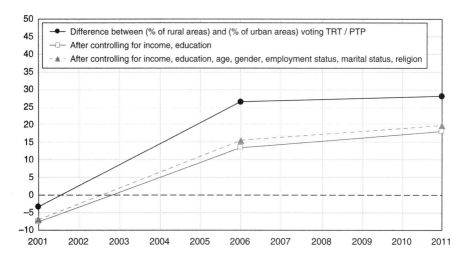

FIGURE 12.4. The rural-urban cleavage in Thailand, 2001–2011
*Data Source:* Authors' computations using Thai political attitudes surveys (see wpid.world).
*Note:* The figure shows the difference between the share of voters living in rural areas
and the share of voters living in urban areas voting for the Thai Rak Thai, the Pheu
Thai, and other pro-Thaksin parties, before and after controls. In 2001, the vote share
of these parties was 3 percentage points lower in rural areas than in urban areas; by
2011, it had become 28 percentage points higher.

government. The process of politicization of inequality in Thailand was
therefore very comparable to the case of Brazil, where growing support
among low-income citizens for Lula da Silva's Workers' Party was triggered by the implementation of redistributive policies during Lula's first
mandate (see Chapter 14).

The difference between Thailand and Brazil, however, is that in Thailand, regional and rural-urban inequalities explain almost entirely these
divides. In 2011, lower-educated and low-income voters were indeed
much more likely than other voters to support the PTP, but this gap drops
substantially and becomes statistically nonsignificant after controlling for
region of residence.[8] The rise of class cleavages in Thailand thus appears
to have been driven by exceptional regional divides, which provided a
solid foundation for the mobilization of the masses. This mobilization
allowed Thaksin and Yingluck Shinawatra to achieve important electoral
victories, as policies such as the introduction of a minimum wage and

8. See appendix Figure A5, wpid.world.

interventions on agricultural prices played a key role in increasing the incomes of the populated poorer regions, which turned out to benefit the lower classes as a whole, in a country where center-periphery inequalities are among the highest in the world.

## The Philippines

In comparison to Indonesia, Malaysia, and Thailand, the Philippines' party system has been exceptionally chaotic since the country's transition to democracy in 1986. In this section, we study how the interactions between ethnicity, class, and regional structures have shaped the political representation of social inequalities in the new democracy. Three main findings emerge from our analysis. First, we document that ethnic and regional specificities are only moderately linked to inequality—more than in Indonesia, but less than in Thailand—with Luzon and in particular the National Capital Region being overrepresented in top-income groups. Second, we show that while regional inequalities have contributed to consolidating class cleavages in Thailand, this is not the case in the Philippines, where educational and regional divides have represented cross-cutting dimensions of political conflict. Third, we show that the 2016 presidential election led for the first time to the complete separation of these two dimensions: support for Rodrigo Duterte in the 2016 presidential election was unique in bringing together both urban middle-class voters and voters in poorer peripheral regions.

### Elections and Political Parties in the Philippines since 1986

No other country in Southeast Asia has such a long experience of democracy as the Philippines, yet Filipino party systems never translated social cleavages into the political representation of interest groups. Instead, Filipino parties have always been opportunistic organizations building support through patron-client relationships, with the objective of securing the benefits of office and getting access to state resources.[9] This persisting feature of Filipino politics has its roots in the process of state building that occurred during the twentieth century. As the US colonial administration

9. J. C. Teehankee, "Clientelism and Party Politics in the Philippines," in *Party Politics in Southeast Asia: Clientelism and Electoral Competition in Indonesia, Thailand and the Philippines*, ed. D. Tomsa and A. Ufen (Routledge, 2013), 186–214.

gradually introduced elections at the beginning of the twentieth century, parties came to articulate the interests of local clans, or *principalia,* rather than to develop cleavages along social lines. While the rise of left-wing movements such as the peasant organization Hukbalahap could have enabled the mobilization of counterelites, these were altogether excluded from the democratic arena through harsh repression.[10] During the Third Republic (1946–1965), electoral competition hence pitted the Nacionalista Party against the Liberal Party, two virtually identical entities in terms of policy proposals and ideological affiliations.

After over twenty years of military rule under Ferdinand Marcos (1965–1986), the "People Power Revolution" of 1986 enabled the return of democracy, but the clientelistic nature of Filipino parties was left untouched. The lack of stable party loyalties among legislators, the presidential form of government, and the one-round first-past-the-post system adopted for presidential elections have since then been powerful incentives pushing individuals to launch new parties and run for the presidency.[11]

Five presidential elections have been held in the Philippines since the People Power Revolution of 1986. In 1992, General Fidel Ramos was elected with less than 24 percent of votes, against six other candidates. The 1992 election showed little variation in the determinants of support for candidates across social classes, and only regional and ethnolinguistic affiliations were significantly associated with candidate choices.[12] This changed in 1998, however, when movie star Joseph Estrada won the presidency with nearly 40 percent of popular votes, a large share of which came from the lower classes. The 1998 election marked a rupture in that Estrada had not used existing patronage networks as his first resource, but had instead directly appealed to the poor through a "dialectic of recognition and appropriation," promising to help the common people against the elites with his slogan "Erap [Estrada's nickname] for the Poor."[13] However, while Thaksin Shinawatra's pro-poor campaign had been followed by concrete redistributive policies in Thailand, this was not the

10. K. Nadeau, *The History of the Philippines* (Greenwood, 2008), chapter 5.

11. Y. Kasuya, *Presidential Bandwagons: Parties and Party Systems in the Philippines* (Anvil Publishing, 2009).

12. C. H. Landé, *Post-Marcos Politics: A Geographical and Statistical Analysis of the 1992 Presidential Election* (Institute of Southeast Asian Studies, 1996).

13. E. E. Hedman, "The Spectre of Populism in Philippine Politics and Society: Artista, Masa, Eruption!," *South East Asia Research* 9, no. 1 (2001): 5–44.

case with Estrada, who in fact largely continued the liberal economic agenda that his predecessors had initiated before him.[14]

What followed was a period of political polarization, which culminated in the "Second EDSA Revolution," a mass mobilization of mostly reformist elites amid corruption scandals, and in the resignation of Estrada, who was replaced by Gloria Macapagal-Arroyo in 2001. In the 2004 elections, Estrada's close associate Fernando Poe ran for the presidency against Arroyo but was defeated. Estrada ran again for president in 2010 and lost against the Liberal Party candidate Benigno Aquino.

The 2016 presidential election marked another turning point in Filipino politics. Rodrigo Duterte, former mayor of Davao City on the island of Mindanao, was elected president with 39 percent of votes. His platform focused on the "war on drugs" and on his explicit support for the extrajudicial killings of drug users and criminals. This was key to his success among the "angry new middle class," who were afraid that growing insecurity would wipe out the benefits they had gained from recent economic growth.[15] Four other candidates ran for the presidency: Mar Roxas and Miriam Defensor Santiago represented the continuity of the reformist Aquino government, while Grace Poe (the adopted daughter of Fernando Poe) and Jejomar Binay campaigned with pro-poor appeals comparable to those of Estrada and Fernando Poe from 1998 to 2010.[16]

Figure 12.5 gives a sense of these transformations by distinguishing three groups of candidates. The first group includes candidates of the traditional "reformist" or "liberal" elites running under the banners of the Lakas-CMD, the Liberal Party, or the Aksyon Party. The second group includes "pro-poor" candidates: Joseph Estrada in 1998 and 2010, Fernando Poe in 2004, and Grace Poe and Jejomar Binay in 2016. Finally, we treat Rodrigo Duterte separately as a third group. We stress that these classifications are highly artificial. However, they do represent distinguishable "perceptions" or "appeals" which, as we will now show, have indeed led to sharp electoral divides.

14. M. R. Thompson, "Class, Charisma, and Clientelism in Thai and Philippines Populist Parties," in Tomsa and Ufen, *Party Politics in Southeast Asia*, 62–79.

15. M. R. Thompson and J. C. Teehankee, "Duterte Victory: A Repudiation of Aquino," *Nikkei Asian Review*, May 12, 2016; J. C. Teehankee and M. R. Thompson, "Duterte and the Politics of Anger in the Philippines," *East Asia Forum*, May 8, 2016.

16. J. C. Teehankee and M. R. Thompson, "The Vote in the Philippines: Electing a Strongman," *Journal of Democracy* 27, no. 4 (2016): 125–134.

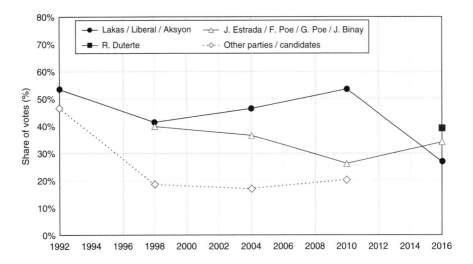

FIGURE 12.5. Election results in the Philippines, 1992–2016
*Data Source:* Authors' computations using official election results (see wpid.world).
*Note:* The figure shows the share of votes received in the first round of presidential elections by selected parties, groups of parties, or candidates in the Philippines. The candidate Rodrigo Duterte received 39% of votes in the 2016 election.

## Regional Inequalities in the Philippines

The Philippines can be divided into three regions: the northern island of Luzon (about 60 percent of the electorate, of which 14 percent live in the capital Manila), the southern island of Mindanao (about 20 percent), and the Visayas islands between Luzon and Mindanao (about 20 percent). More than 170 ethnolinguistic groups, the largest being the Visayas (about 25 percent) and the Tagalog (about 25 percent), populate these islands.[17] Despite this diversity, ethnic antagonism has been relatively rare in the history of the Philippines.[18] The exception is Mindanao, where migration from Luzon after World War II led to repeated conflicts in Muslim areas with the armed forces fighting separatist movements.

Regional inequalities in the Philippines are significant, though not as large as in Thailand. The National Capital Region has concentrated a

17. See appendix Table BA2, wpid.world.
18. A. A. Arugay and D. Slater, "Polarization without Poles: Machiavellian Conflicts and the Philippines' Lost Decade of Democracy, 2000–2010," *Annals of the American Academy of Political and Social Science* 681, no. 1 (2018): 122–136.

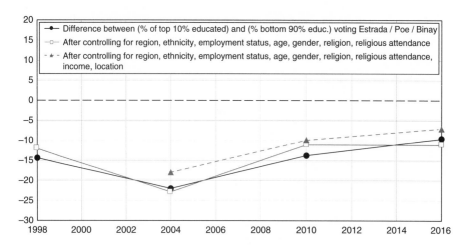

FIGURE 12.6. The educational cleavage in the Philippines, 1998–2016
*Data Source:* Authors' computations using Filipino electoral surveys (see wpid.world).
*Note:* The figure shows the difference between the share of top 10% educated voters and the share of bottom 90% educated voters voting for Joseph Estrada (1998, 2010), Fernando Poe (2004), Grace Poe (2016), and Jejomar Binay (2016) in the first round of presidential elections, before and after controls. These candidates all received higher support among the least educated. In 2004, higher-educated voters were less likely to vote for Joseph Estrada by 22 percentage points.

greater share of higher-income citizens compared to Mindanao and Visayas.[19] Regional specificities and inequalities thus pave the way for the emergence of a center-periphery cleavage, but the class dimension of this cleavage is not as strong as in Thailand and therefore it could represent a separate political cleavage.

### The Persistence of Class Polarization

As we discussed above, Filipino politics since 1998 have seen the emergence of "pro-poor" presidential candidates emphasizing their proximity with the masses, albeit in a more rhetorical than programmatic way. Figure 12.6 shows that grouping Joseph Estrada, Fernando Poe, Grace Poe, and Jejomar Binay together reveals the persistence of remarkably strong cleavages: university graduates have been less likely to vote for

19. See appendix Figures BA9 and BA10, wpid.world.

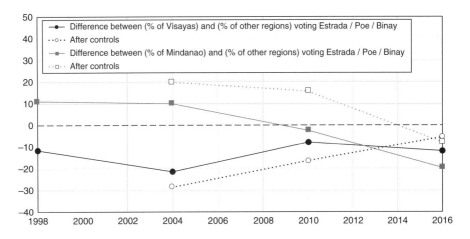

FIGURE 12.7. The regional cleavage in the Philippines, 1998–2016
*Data Source:* Authors' computations using Filipino electoral surveys (see wpid.world).
*Note:* The figure shows the difference between the share of voters living in the Visayas geographical zone and the share of voters living in other regions of the Philippines voting for the candidates Joseph Estrada (1998, 2010), Fernando Poe (2004), Grace Poe (2016), and Jejomar Binay (2016) in the first round of presidential elections, as well as the same difference between Mindanao and the rest of the country, before and after controlling for education, employment status, age, gender, religion, religious attendance, income, and rural-urban location. In 2016, the vote share of Grace Poe and Jejomar Binay was 20 percentage points lower in Mindanao than in other regions.

pro-poor candidates by 10 to 22 percentage points. This gap only marginally decreases after controls.

Such divisions are large in comparative perspective, and as large as what we observed in Thailand. Class cleavages therefore do not seem to have been a purely temporary feature of Filipino politics. The main difference between the Philippines and Thailand is that in the Philippines this dimension has been manifested in "moral" appeals rather than in competing economic programs or grassroots organizations.[20]

Have class cleavages been reinforced by, or coupled with, center-periphery cleavages? Figure 12.7 shows that support for pro-poor candidates has generally been lower in Visayas than in Mindanao and Luzon, so they have attracted voters from both the poorer periphery (Mindanao) and the center (the National Capital Region). The 2016 elections, how-

20. M. R. Thompson, "Class, Charisma, and Clientelism."

ever, signaled a change in this pattern: Grace Poe and Jejomar Binay obtained better results in Luzon than in Visayas and Mindanao. This, we will show below, is due to Rodrigo Duterte's success at capturing votes in the periphery. Regional differences therefore seem to have represented a clearly independent dimension of electoral behaviors in the Philippines, unlike in Thailand.

### The Structure of Political Cleavages in the 2016 Presidential Election

Table 12.1 provides a detailed description of the structure of the vote for each candidate in the 2016 presidential election. Two key results are visible. First, while class polarization appeared to be lower than in 2004, it was still significant in the case of Grace Poe and Jejomar Binay, who

*Table 12.1*   Structure of the Vote in the 2016 Filipino Presidential Election

| | Rodrigo Duterte PDP-Laban | Mar Roxas Liberal Party | Grace Poe Independent | Jejomar Binay UNA |
|---|---|---|---|---|
| **Education** | | | | |
| Primary | 42% | 24% | 19% | 13% |
| Secondary | 35% | 24% | 24% | 12% |
| Tertiary | 43% | 21% | 21% | 12% |
| **Region** | | | | |
| National Capital Region | 33% | 16% | 27% | 19% |
| Luzon | 29% | 26% | 27% | 16% |
| Visayas | 39% | 31% | 17% | 8% |
| Mindanao | 62% | 16% | 12% | 7% |
| **Religion** | | | | |
| Catholic | 37% | 25% | 22% | 12% |
| Protestant | 31% | 21% | 30% | 18% |
| Muslim | 75% | 5% | 3% | 13% |
| **Location** | | | | |
| Urban areas | 43% | 15% | 21% | 15% |
| Rural areas | 36% | 30% | 22% | 11% |

*Data Source:* Authors' computations using Filipino electoral surveys.

*Notes:* The table shows the share of votes received by the main Filipino presidential candidates by selected individual characteristics in 2016. Rodrigo Duterte received his highest vote share in Mindanao (62%) and in urban areas (43%).

achieved better results among lower-educated voters. Second, center-periphery divides were more clearly materialized in the 2016 election than before, but went in a direction opposite to that of class cleavages. Poe and Binay were the candidates of the poor, but they were also the candidates of the center. Duterte, on the contrary, was the candidate of the urban middle class, but also of the periphery and of the Muslim minority, with over 60 percent of voters from Mindanao supporting him.

These two facts largely explain why Duterte's voting base was so socially diverse. On the one hand, the candidate's radical proposal of a war on drugs was successful among the new, younger, educated middle class, who valued his emphasis on law and order. On the other hand, Duterte's stronghold in Mindanao enabled him to gain votes from poorer regions, and he reinforced that support with his proposal to move toward a federal form of government.[21]

## Malaysia

Postcolonial Malaysia, inheriting a large and ethnically diverse territory, established itself as a federal constitutional monarchy in 1963. A one-party dominant system soon emerged, as the National Front coalition (Barisan Nasional, BN) succeeded in amalgamating the interests of the majority of Malay, Chinese, and Indian elites. The 1997 Asian financial crisis shook the foundations of this regime and initiated a period of consolidation of the opposition, which culminated in the victory of the Alliance of Hope and the first handover in the country's history in 2018. In this section, we show that the decline of the BN has been associated with growing ethnic and class cleavages, as not only Chinese voters but also top-income and highest-educated voters from other ethnic groups have gradually shifted toward the opposition.

### Democratization and the Erosion of
### the One-Party Dominant System

After over a century of British rule, Malaysia became an independent nation in 1957. The new country brought together heterogeneous popula-

---

21. J. C. Teehankee, "Regional Dimensions of the 2016 General Elections in the Philippines: Emerging Contours of Federalism," *Regional and Federal Studies* 28, no. 3 (2018): 383–394.

tions. The Bumiputeras, divided into Muslim Malays and Indigenous peoples, represented and still represent the majority of the population (about 70 percent in 2020).[22] They coexisted with significant Chinese and Indian minorities (about 23 and 7 percent in 2020, respectively), most of whom were descended from workers brought by the colonial power throughout the nineteenth century. Unlike other major independence movements such as those in Senegal, Botswana, and India (see Chapters 9 and 17), Malaysia's political movements soon took on a strong ethnic dimension. While the Young Malays Union, founded in 1938 in Kuala Lumpur, advocated for the union of British Malaya and the Dutch East Indies regardless of ethnic origin, it never managed to achieve mass support. Similarly, the Malayan Communist Party called for an independent state with equality for all the races, but it remained primarily a Chinese organization until it was eventually crushed by the British during the Malayan Emergency (1948–1960).

The 1955 elections (see Figure 12.8), held under colonial rule, resulted in the landslide victory of the Alliance Party (which would become the National Front in 1973), a unique coalition between three parties representing the major ethnic groups: the United Malays National Organisation (UMNO, 59 percent of votes), the Malayan Chinese Association (MCA, 20 percent), and the Malayan Indian Congress (MIC, 3 percent). Malaysia's model of consociationalism was born. While political representation would remain shaped by ethnic identities, conflicts would be limited by the cooperation between the elites of the different groups. At the heart of this association lay a fragile agreement: the Malay majority would be given political supremacy, while protection of economic property, religion, and civil rights would be granted to Chinese and Indian communities.

Until the late twentieth century, the BN remained unchallenged by its two irreconcilable opponents, the Malaysian Islamic Party (Parti Islam Se-Malaysia, PAS), advocating for an Islamic state and Malay supremacy, and the Democratic Action Party (DAP), promoting the establishment of a secular, multiracial democracy. As in many other one-party dominant

---

22. Department of Statistics Malaysia, "Current Population Estimates, Malaysia, 2020," July 15 2020, https://www.dosm.gov.my/v1/index.php?r=column/cthemeByCat&cat =155&bul_id=OVByWjg5YkQ3MWFZRTN5bDJiaEVhZz09&menu_id=LopheU43NWJ wRWVSZklWdzQ4TlhUUT09.

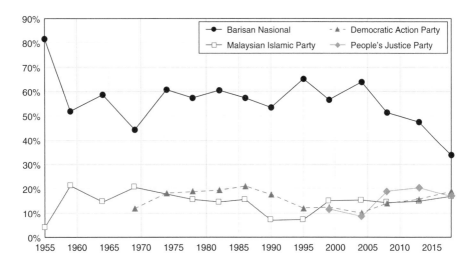

FIGURE 12.8. Election results in Malaysia, 1955–2018
*Data Source:* Authors' computations using official election results (see wpid.world).
*Note:* The figure shows the share of votes received by the main Malaysian parties in general elections held between 1955 and 2018. The National Front coalition (Barisan Nasional, BN) received 34% of the vote in 2018.

systems, electoral malapportionment in favor of rural areas, patronage networks, and other incumbency advantages hugely benefited the ruling party in a system often referred to as a "competitive authoritarianism."[23]

Yet, the Asian financial crisis triggered the rise of opposition movements in a context of internal struggles within UMNO.[24] As divisions between Prime Minister Mahathir bin Mohamad and Deputy Prime Minister Anwar Ibrahim grew in 1998 over economic policy, in particular, Anwar was fired, expelled from UMNO, and arrested on charges of corruption and sodomy that many perceived as illegitimate. This trig-

23. A. Croissant, "Malaysia: Competitive Authoritarianism in a Plural Society," in *Comparative Politics of Southeast Asia,* ed. A. Croissant and P. Lorenz (Springer International, 2018), 141–176; M. L. Weiss, "The Antidemocratic Potential of Party System Institutionalization: Malaysia as Morality Tale?," in *Party System Institutionalization in Asia: Democracies, Autocracies, and the Shadows of the Past,* ed. A. Hicken and E. M. Kuhonta (Cambridge University Press, 2015), 25–48.

24. A. L. Freedman, *Political Change and Consolidation: Democracy's Rocky Road in Thailand, Indonesia, South Korea, and Malaysia* (Palgrave Macmillan, 2006).

gered the emergence of the *reformasi* movement calling for democratic reforms, and the formation in 1999 of the National Justice Party, which became the People's Justice Party (Parti Keadilan Rakyat, PKR) in 2003 and won over 20 percent of the popular vote at its peak in 2013. After several alliances failed to coalesce sufficient support to defeat the incumbent, the 2018 elections finally enabled the first handover in the country's history, as the progressive and reformist Alliance of Hope (Pakatan Harapan, PH), bringing together the PKR, the DAP, and two other small parties, received 46 percent of the popular vote against 34 percent for the BN. This victory was possible thanks to the consolidation of a more coherent and comprehensive coalition emphasizing political reforms, anti-corruption measures, and enhanced liberties, as well as unprecedented mobilization through online social media.[25]

### Ethnic Inequalities in Malaysia

At the time of independence, colonial legacy had left high inequalities with an important ethnic component: the Bumiputera majority were substantially poorer than the Chinese, who held the lion's share of wealth thanks to their overrepresentation in industry and in the banking and insurance sectors.[26] During that period, Malaysia's socioeconomic structure was therefore very comparable to those of Taiwan and South Africa, two other countries where ethnic minorities have historically dominated the control of economic resources (see Chapters 13 and 16). As ethnic riots broke in 1969 in Kuala Lumpur, the government was prompted to put these inequalities at the center of its policy agenda. This led to the implementation of the New Economic Policy (NEP) in 1971 and the multiplication of positive discrimination policies in the decades that followed, which enabled the Bumiputera to be favored in many dimensions such as access to education, public-sector employment, housing, and corporate share ownership.

In part as the result of these measures, ethnic inequalities have declined, though they remain significant to the present. In 2014, the Chinese represented 16 percent of the poorest half of the population but

25. A. Ufen, "Opposition in Transition: Pre-electoral Coalitions and the 2018 Electoral Breakthrough in Malaysia," *Democratization* 27, no. 2 (2020): 167–184.

26. M. Ravallion, "Ethnic Inequality and Poverty in Malaysia since 1969" (NBER Working Paper No. w25640, 2019), https://papers.ssrn.com/sol3/papers.cfm?abstract_id=3350409.

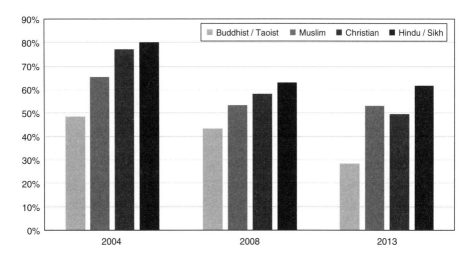

FIGURE 12.9. The ethnoreligious cleavage in Malaysia, 2004–2013. The Barisan Nasional vote by religious affiliation
*Data Source:* Authors' computations using Asian Barometer surveys (see wpid.world).
*Note:* The figure shows the share of votes received by the Barisan Nasional (BN) by religious affiliation. In 2013, 29% of Buddhist and Taoist voters voted BN, compared to 53% of Muslim voters and 62% of Hindu and Sikh voters.

60 percent of the top 1 percent.[27] Ethnic income gaps in Malaysia therefore appear to be lower than in South Africa but higher than in Taiwan, where the mainlander-native income gap has today almost completely disappeared.

### Ethnic Divides and Cross-ethnic Class Cleavages

How has the push for democratization, the subsequent decline of the BN, and the dynamics of inequality affected political cleavages in Malaysia? As shown in Figure 12.9, ethnic divides have risen in the past two decades. While variables on ethnic identities unfortunately are not available in the surveys used in this chapter, Buddhists and Taoists (most of whom are Chinese) have become much less supportive of the BN than Muslims (most of whom are Bumiputera). This is a well-known fact, and

27. M. Khalid and L. Yang, "Income Inequality and Ethnic Cleavages in Malaysia: Evidence from Distributional National Accounts (1984–2014)" (WID.world Working Paper, 2019).

it led BN politicians and state-controlled media to speak of an electoral "Chinese tsunami" and to accuse the Chinese of being ungrateful after the publication of election results in 2013.[28] Survey data on the most recent election was not available at the time of writing, but this dynamic seems to have continued in 2018, when according to existing polls, an estimated 95 percent of Chinese voted for the PH, compared to about two-thirds of Indians and one-third of Malays.[29]

The erosion of Malaysia's one-party system, or rather its "one-coalition system," has therefore led to the rise of ethnic voting. However, support for the BN has declined among all ethnic groups, not only the Chinese minority, and the BN remains a multi-ethnic coalition. Strikingly, socio-economic differentiation within ethnic groups appeared to be a major and rising factor distinguishing the BN from the opposition. In 2013, top-income voters were more likely to vote against the BN by 17 percentage points, a gap that remains significant after controlling for religion and other factors (Figure 12.10). This suggests that class has become increasingly relevant for understanding voting behaviors in Malaysia. Furthermore, at least until 2013, the BN appeared to be relatively more supported not only by poorer Muslims, but also by poorer voters belonging to other ethnic groups. In the 2013 elections, 35 percent of the poorest half of non-Muslims supported the BN, compared to 7 percent of the top decile (Figure 12.11).

The BN has thus remained much more popular among the poor, together with voters in rural areas and older voters, arguably thanks to patronage networks and lower access to political information among these social groups, but also thanks to its remarkable achievements in reducing poverty in the second half of the twentieth century.[30] Indeed, according to existing evidence, economic development in recent years seems to have benefited not only the Bumiputeras but also low-income Chinese and Indians, who have enjoyed significant above-average income growth.[31] On the contrary, urban, highest-educated elites have had greater access to political information and have been more concerned about corruption,

28. Ufen, "Opposition in Transition."
29. H. Hassan, "Malaysia Election: 3-Way Split in Malay Vote, Most Chinese Voted PH," *The New Paper,* June 14, 2018, https://www.tnp.sg/news/world/malaysia-election-3-way-split-malay-vote-most-chinese-voted-ph.
30. See appendix Figures CB5, CB6, CC6, and CC7, wpid.world.
31. See Khalid and Yang, "Income Inequality," figure 4.19.

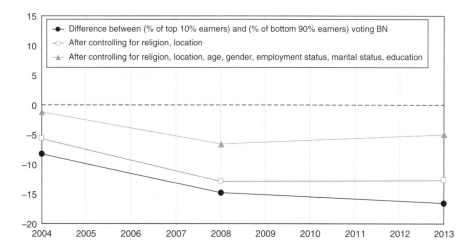

FIGURE 12.10. Vote and income in Malaysia, 2004–2013
*Data Source:* Authors' computations using Asian Barometer surveys (see wpid.world).
*Note:* The figure shows the difference between the share of top 10% earners and the share of bottom 90% earners voting for the Barisan Nasional (BN), before and after controls. In 2013, bottom 50% income earners were 17 percentage points less likely to vote BN. After controls (all other things being equal), this difference is reduced to 5 percentage points.

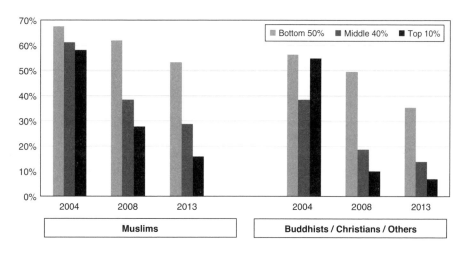

FIGURE 12.11. Ethnoreligious cleavages and class cleavages in Malaysia, 2004–2013
*Data Source:* Authors' computations using Asian Barometer surveys (see wpid.world).
*Note:* The figure shows the share of votes received by the Barisan Nasional (BN) by income group among Muslims and non-Muslims. The BN has been most strongly supported among bottom 50% income earners within these two groups. In 2013, among Muslims, 53% of bottom 50% income earners voted BN, compared to 16% of top 10% income earners.

democratization, and civil liberties, topics that the growing opposition has sought to embody.

Together, these results suggest that two parallel dynamics may shape Malaysian politics in the future. On the one hand, UMNO's history of favoring Malay interests, as well as uncertain political outcomes, may convince non-Malay voters to continue to increasingly support opposition parties. On the other hand, the BN could succeed in reinventing itself to regain some votes from minorities and become the coalition of the most disadvantaged citizens regardless of ethnicity.

## Indonesia

After three decades of authoritarian rule, Indonesia held in 1999 its first free election since 1955. In this section, we show that political cleavages in the world's largest Muslim-majority country have followed a very different trajectory from those in Thailand, the Philippines, and Malaysia. Instead of undergoing a process of polarization, Indonesia's party system seems to have been characterized by increasing dealignment. As a result, while religion, income, and other factors do continue to play a role, the rise of catchall parties has weakened the political representation of social inequalities in the new democracy.

### The Making of Indonesian Democracy

After four years of resistance against the Dutch, who had sought to recover their colony from the Japanese at the end of World War II, Indonesia was recognized as an independent nation by the Netherlands in 1949. At that time, unlike in Malaysia, the political movements that had flourished in the archipelago since the beginning of the twentieth century were not communal. The key point of tension was, instead, between Islam and Marxism. On one side were the Masyumi Party and the Nahdlatul Ulama, which represented respectively modernist and traditionalist Islamic movements. On the other side was the Indonesian Communist Party (Partai Komunis Indonesia, PKI) promoting a strongly secular vision of the new nation. In between, the Indonesian National Party (Partai Nasional Indonesia, PNI), associated with founding father Sukarno, emphasized secular nationalism and state centralism. Each of these parties received between 16 and 22 percent of votes in the legislative elections of 1955.[32]

32. C. Brown, *A Short History of Indonesia* (Allen & Unwin, 2003).

As tensions and political instability grew, Indonesian democracy soon deteriorated, until President Sukarno proclaimed the transition to a "guided democracy" in 1957, in which the key poles of the nation—the military, communists, and some Muslim movements—would be allowed to participate in a cooperative government. A coup attempt, followed by a countercoup organized by General Suharto, nonetheless led to the dissolution of the regime in 1965–1966. The PKI was blamed for having organized the coup, and the massive anticommunist purge that followed left between 500,000 and one million dead, effectively annihilating the left-wing pole of Indonesian politics. These series of events, together with Sukarno's and Suharto's general delegitimization of political parties as divisive and corrupted, had long-lasting effects on Indonesian democracy and on the personalization of political power.[33]

Under Suharto's New Order (1965–1998), Islamic movements were forced to unite in the United Development Party (Partai Persatuan Pembangunan, PPP), while nationalist and Christian parties were compelled to unite in the Indonesian Democratic Party (Partai Demokrasi Indonesia, PDI). Meanwhile, the Party of Functional Groups (Partai Golongan Karya, Golkar) was set up as the government's electoral vehicle, and it garnered a majority of votes in elections employed mainly to back the authoritarian regime. While divisions were downplayed and efforts were made to depoliticize the population, opposition to the regime was stronger in Java and urban areas. Golkar, on the contrary, achieved greater support in the peripheral regions of the country and in rural areas, a cleavage that persists to the present day.[34]

After decades of exceptional economic development, the Asian financial crisis put a sudden end to the regime, and Suharto stepped down in 1998. The post-Suharto era began with the reestablishment of democracy and the organization of legislative elections in 1999. Strikingly, with the exception of the missing communist element, the emerging party system seemed to reproduce many of the cleavages that had characterized the 1955 election.[35] The secular-nationalist and pro-poor Indonesian Democratic Party of Struggle (Partai Demokrasi Indonesia Perjuangan,

33. P. J. Tan, "Explaining Party System Institutionalization in Indonesia," in Hicken and Kuhonta, *Party System Institutionalization in Asia,* 236–259.

34. A. Ufen, "Lipset and Rokkan in Southeast Asia: Indonesia in Comparative Perspective," in Tomsa and Ufen, *Party Politics in Southeast Asia,* 40–61.

35. D. King, *Half-Hearted Reform: Electoral Institutions and the Struggle for Democracy in Indonesia* (Praeger, 2003).

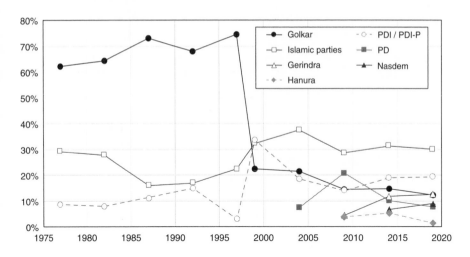

FIGURE 12.12. Election results in Indonesia, 1977–2019
*Data Source:* Authors' computations using official election results (see wpid.world).
*Note:* The figure shows the share of votes received by selected Indonesian political parties or groups of parties in legislative elections between 1977 and 2019. The PDI-P received 19% of votes in 2019. PD: Democratic Party; PDI: Indonesian Democratic Party; PDI-P: Indonesian Democratic Party of Struggle; NasDem: National Democratic Party; Islamic parties: PAN, PBB, PBR, PKB, PKNU, PKS, and PPP.

PDI-P), led by Sukarno's daughter Megawati Sukarnoputri, came first with 34 percent of votes, followed by Golkar with 22 percent (Figure 12.12). A variety of Islam-based parties came next; all together they received in total about one-third of the popular vote. The most important of these parties were the traditionalist National Awakening Party (Partai Kebang-kitan Bangsa, PKB), the PPP, and the modernist National Mandate Party (Partai Amanat Nasional, PAN).

This party system was soon beset by growing personalization and in-stability. In 2001, the catchall Democratic Party (Partai Demokrat, PD) was formed to support former general Susilo Bambang Yudhoyono. Yud-hoyono won the 2004 and 2009 presidential elections and the PD came first in the 2009 legislative elections with 21 percent of votes, but its suc-cess was short-lived: only 8 percent of voters supported the PD in the 2019 legislative elections. Similarly, the Great Indonesia Movement Party (Partai Gerakan Indonesia Raya, Gerindra) has mainly served as the po-litical platform of former general Prabowo Subianto, who lost against PDI-P candidate Joko Widodo in the 2014 and 2019 presidential races.

Other new parties include the Nasdem Party and Hanura, both splits from Golkar. As shown in Figure 12.12, the results achieved by the PDI-P and especially by Golkar, Indonesia's most institutionalized party,[36] never again reached their 1999 peaks after these new political forces emerged.

The Indonesian party system has therefore been characterized by extraordinary fragmentation in recent years, with no party securing more than 20 percent of votes in 2014 and 2019. Rather than reflecting a complexification of social divides, this process seems to have been driven by opportunistic actors and "presidentialized parties" often avoiding ideology and aiming to transcend cleavages.[37] While historical divides that materialized in the 1955 election do still seem to play a role, manifested by the persistence of traditional parties, they have become increasingly blurred.

### Political Cleavages and Socioeconomic Divides

To what extent has the Indonesian party system represented socioeconomic inequalities since democratization? Unlike in Malaysia, the major pre-independence political movements were not limited to specific ethnic groups in Indonesia, and ethnic inequalities and ethnic conflicts have remained limited in comparative perspective.[38] Ethnicity has accordingly never been a strong determinant of the vote: the PDI-P has been more popular in Java and Golkar in peripheral regions, but all parties have relied on large cross-ethnic and cross-regional coalitions since 1999.[39] This lack of cleavage has been reinforced by the electoral system, as only parties with sufficient national scope have been allowed to participate in elections.[40] Thus, since 2011, only parties present in all provinces, in 75 percent of the municipalities of each of these provinces, and in 50 percent of the subdistricts of each of these municipalities have been allowed to

36. D. Tomsa, *Party Politics and Democratization in Indonesia: Golkar in the Post-Suharto Era* (Routledge, 2008).

37. A. Ufen, "From *Aliran* to Dealignment: Political Parties in Post-Suharto Indonesia," *South East Asia Research* 16, no. 1 (2008): 5–41.

38. E. Aspinall, "Democratization and Ethnic Politics in Indonesia: Nine Theses," *Journal of East Asian Studies* 11, no. 2 (2011): 289–319. See also appendix Figures DA13 to DA16, wpid.world.

39. See appendix Figures DB11, DC11, and DH11, wpid.world, and S. Mujani, R. W. Liddle, and K. Ambardi, *Voting Behavior in Indonesia since Democratization: Critical Democrats* (Cambridge University Press, 2018), chapter 4. The exception is the PKB, whose base of support has been almost exclusively located in Java.

40. A. Ufen, "The Evolution of Cleavages in the Indonesian Party System" (GIGA Working Paper No. 74, 2008), https://papers.ssrn.com/sol3/papers.cfm?abstract_id=1123942.

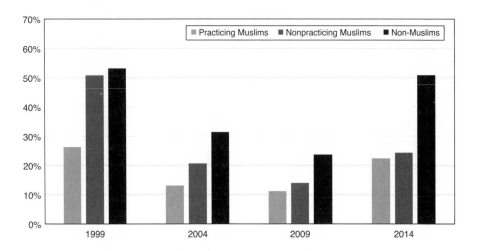

FIGURE 12.13. The PDI-P/NasDem vote by religious affiliation in Indonesia, 1999–2014
*Data Source:* Authors' computations using Indonesian electoral surveys (see wpid.world).
*Note:* The figure shows the share of votes received by the Indonesian Democratic Party of Struggle (PDI-P) and the National Democratic Party (NasDem) by religious affiliation. In 2014, 51% of non-Muslims supported these two parties, compared to 22% of practicing Muslims (Muslims reporting participating "Often" or "Very often/Always" in collective prayers).

contest national elections.[41] As a result of these various factors, regional and ethnic identities have not been major drivers of electoral and socio-economic differentiation in contemporary Indonesia, in contrast to the Thai and Malaysian cases.

Religion has proved to be a much stronger determinant of partisan affiliations. As shown in Figures 12.13 and 12.14, Muslims participating "often" or "always" in collective prayers have been much more likely to support Islamic parties, while the PDI-P and Nasdem have been more popular among nonpracticing Muslims and especially among religious minorities (mostly Christians and Hindus, about 10 percent of the electorate since 1999[42]). Golkar, Gerindra, and Hanura fall in between,

41. International Foundation for Electoral Systems, "Elections in Indonesia: 2019 Concurrent Presidential and Legislative Elections," April 9, 2019, https://www.ifes.org /faqs/elections-indonesia-2019-concurrent-presidential-and-legislative-elections.

42. See appendix Table AD2, wpid.world.

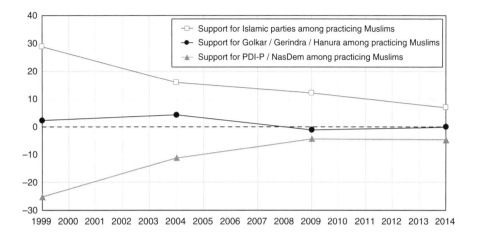

FIGURE 12.14. The religious cleavage in Indonesia, 1999–2014
*Data Source:* Authors' computations using Indonesian electoral surveys (see wpid.world).
*Note:* The figure shows the difference between the share of practicing Muslims voting for Islamic parties and the share of nonpracticing Muslims and non-Muslims voting for Islamic parties, and the same difference for Golkar/Gerindra/Hanura and PDI-P/NasDem, after controlling for income, education, rural-urban location, employment status, age, and gender. Religious cleavages have weakened in Indonesia in the past decades: practicing Muslims were 25 percentage points less likely to vote PDI-P/NasDem in 1999, compared to 5 percentage points in 2014.

with vote shares varying little across religious groups, which is consistent with Golkar's historical ability to amalgamate elites from various streams.[43] Pluralism, secularism, and attitudes toward minorities therefore appear to have represented an important dimension of Indonesian politics, a divide that has also been visible in party members' diverging attitudes toward these issues.[44]

This cleavage, however, lost much of its electoral significance from 1999 to 2014, especially with respect to practicing and nonpracticing Muslims, who differed only marginally in their voting behaviors in 2014.

43. We group Nasdem with the PDI-P here given the more secular and pro-poor orientation of Nasdem, but all our results are strongly robust to considering the PDI-P alone; see appendix Figures DI1 to DI12, wpid.world.
44. D. Fossati and E. Warburton, "Indonesia's Political Parties and Minorities," *ISEAS Perspective* 37 (2018): 1–13.

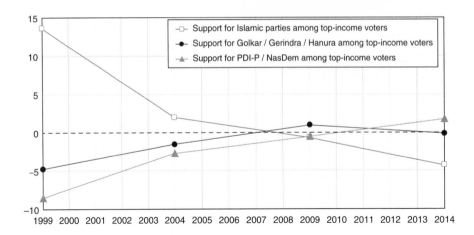

FIGURE 12.15. Vote and income in Indonesia, 1999–2014

*Data Source:* Authors' computations using Indonesian electoral surveys (see wpid.world).

*Note:* The figure shows the difference between the share of top 10% earners and the share of bottom 90% earners voting for Islamic parties, and the same difference for Golkar/Gerindra/Hanura and PDI-P/Nasdem, after controlling for religion, education, rural-urban location, employment status, age, and gender. The link between income and the vote has weakened in Indonesia in the past decades: top 10% earners were 9 percentage points less likely to vote PDI-P/NasDem in 1999, while they were 2 percentage points more likely to do so in 2014.

This is consistent with the fact that conflicts between Indonesian parties over religious matters have weakened, as historically secular parties have had to govern in large coalitions, often with Islamic parties.[45] Furthermore, the religious-secular cleavage, like the ethnic cleavage, has had only a weak socioeconomic component (in contrast to what we observe in Malaysia), as overall inequalities between Muslims and non-Muslims are low in Indonesia.[46] That being said, while this evolution holds when looking at the country as a whole, ethnoreligious divides did have a greater and rising influence on local politics in recent years. For instance, the 2016–2017 Islamic mobilization against the Chinese and Christian governor of Jakarta Basuki Tjahaja Purnama, who was accused by the protestors of committing blasphemy, incorporated not only religious

45. Ufen, "Lipset and Rokkan."
46. See appendix Figure DA8, wpid.world.

but also socioeconomic grievances directed against the non-Muslim Jakartan elite.[47]

Finally, we find that the PDI-P and Golkar used to be relatively more popular among low-income voters, while Islamic parties had better results among top-income voters in 1999 (Figure 12.15). This is consistent with the fact that the PDI-P has sought to embody Sukarno's secular-nationalist legacy, while Islamic parties and in particular the PAN have historically fared better among educated voters in urban areas.[48] This cleavage, however, appears to have disappeared or even reverted in recent years.

In summary, Indonesian political cleavages seem to have gradually declined since 1999 as the result of a combination of factors including personalization, party system fragmentation, and the rise of swing voters.[49] While this could help to lower political polarization, it could also contribute to further delegitimizing democracy and especially political parties, which already are very unpopular in Indonesia.[50] Whether the trend toward monopolization of political resources in the hands of charismatic individuals will continue, or new class-based parties and political coalitions could eventually counteract these tendencies, remains an open question.

47. M. Mietzner, B. Muhtadi, and R. Halida, "Entrepreneurs of Grievance: Drivers and Effects of Indonesia's Islamist Mobilization," *Bijdragen tot de taal-, land- en volkenkunde/Journal of the Humanities and Social Sciences of Southeast Asia* 174, no. 2–3 (2018): 159–187; E. Warbuton and L. Gammon, "Class Dismissed? Economic Fairness and Identity Politics in Indonesia," *New Mandala*, May 5, 2017, https://www.newmandala.org /economic-injustice-identity-politics-indonesia/.

48. Mujani, Liddle, and Ambardi, *Voting Behavior*. The exception is the PKB, which fares better in rural areas.

49. Ufen, "Lipset and Rokkan."

50. A. A. Yani, "The Dynamic of Indonesian Political Trust in the Beginning of Reform Era," *Politik* 12, no. 1 (2015): 55–68.

# 13

## Inequality, Identity, and the Structure of Political Cleavages in South Korea, Taiwan, and Hong Kong, 1996–2016

CARMEN DURRER DE LA SOTA AND AMORY GETHIN

### Introduction

South Korea, Hong Kong, and Taiwan have witnessed dramatic political transformations since the 1980s, including institutional reforms and the holding of elections on a regular basis. In South Korea, the presidential elections of 1987 announced the advent of democracy after almost three decades of military rule. In Taiwan, direct legislative elections in 1992 allowed opposition forces to run against the ruling Kuomintang for the first time. In Hong Kong, direct elections have been held since 1991, first by the British and then by the Chinese government since the handover of 1997.

In all three territories, the past decades have been associated with greater participation by the population in the making of the polity and with the formation of clear partisan divides. In Taiwan and Hong Kong, parties quickly organized into two camps: those opposing greater integration with mainland China, and those in favor of it. Foreign policy has also been at the heart of political conflicts in South Korea, as the institutionalization of the conservative-liberal opposition materialized diverging attitudes toward North Korea, although unlike in Taiwan and Hong Kong, the conflict has not concerned whether to seek unification, but how to interact with the northern regime in the meantime. Democratic reform, economic

We are grateful to Joel Campbell, Eui-Young Jung, Karl Ho, Wai-Man Lam, Sidney Michelini, Clara Martínez-Toledano, Thomas Piketty, and Sebastian Veg for their useful advice. We also thank the teams of the Comparative Study of Electoral Systems and the Hong Kong Election Study for making the datasets used in this chapter available for research.

issues, and cultural concerns have interacted with this integration/disintegration dimension of political conflict in these three territories.

South Korea, Taiwan, and Hong Kong also have gone through deep economic transitions. After several decades of sustained economic development, East Asian economies were hit hard by the Asian financial crisis of 1997 and have been unable to return to the exceptional rates of growth they had achieved from the 1960s to the mid-1990s. Income inequality has risen significantly, driven by a conjunction of changes on the labor market, soaring housing prices in big cities, and the failure of governments to implement policies protecting those most vulnerable to economic shocks.[1] These transformations have arguably affected existing boundaries of political mobilization, created new demands, and generated new divides. In this chapter, we use existing electoral surveys conducted in South Korea, Taiwan, and Hong Kong since the late 1990s to document how political cleavages have responded to these different transitions. Our results bring us to two main findings.

First, we document that relations to the "other"—mainland China for Hong Kong and Taiwan, and North Korea for South Korea—have remained at the heart of politics, trumping other dimensions of social conflicts and continuously shaping political cleavages. "National" or "local" identity feelings have risen in all three territories over the past decades, in particular among younger cohorts. In addition to preexisting historical regional divides, in South Korea electoral behaviors have been increasingly linked to age and education, as older, lower-educated voters display a greater rejection of engagement with the North Korean regime, despite their stronger hopes for unification. In Taiwan, identity has interacted with ethnicity, as mainlanders—immigrants who came from the mainland at the end of the Chinese civil war and their descendants—continue to display stronger attachment to China and to the hope of eventual unification. In Hong Kong, too, age and education are the strongest predictors of vote choice, as mounting polarization between pro-democrats and pro-Beijing forces have driven increasing student mobilization.

Second, while economic concerns do matter significantly in fostering mass mobilizations, we find only limited evidence of independent class

1. See the longer discussion below and C. Y. C. Chu, "Top Incomes in Taiwan, 1977–2013" (WID.world Working Paper 2015); C. T. Hung, "Income Inequality in Hong Kong and Singapore" (master's thesis, Paris School of Economics, 2018), http://piketty.pse.ens.fr /files/Hung2018.pdf.

cleavages in these three territories. In Hong Kong, rising housing prices and decreasing perceived social mobility have been important factors in the student protests, while in Taiwan, fears that greater trade integration with the mainland would worsen regional inequalities may also have helped to reinforce preexisting north-south divides. In South Korea, promises of action against rising economic polarization have become omnipresent in political campaigns, and income could be starting to play a role in independently influencing vote choices. That being said, we find that class cleavages remain determined primarily by their interactions with the integration/disintegration cleavage and its economic, social, and historical dimensions. In South Korea, a large share of the poor are elderly citizens, who favor a hard stance against North Korea and are consequently more supportive of conservative parties. In Taiwan, ethnicity is only weakly correlated to income; the mainlander-native cleavage is thus today one of "historical identities" rather than conflicting economic interests. In Hong Kong, low-income voters are more supportive of the pro-Beijing camp, but this is mainly because they tend to be older and are more likely to be immigrants, two groups with lower average incomes. All these factors suggest that the political representation of economic inequalities in these three territories remains in large part framed, and sometimes hindered, by divides over relations to the "other." Given mainland China's growing economic power and renewed expansionist attitude, as well as the growing threat of North Korean nuclearization, these divides are likely to persist and to play an increasing role in both domestic and foreign politics.

## South Korea

Contemporary South Korean politics has been inevitably shaped by the country's unique history. South Korea's borders were set in the arbitrary partition of the Korean peninsula by the United States and the Soviet Union at the end of World War II. The division of the Korean nation and the hostility of the North Korean regime have been defining features of South Korea's history and political system ever since.[2]

In this section, we show that South Korean political cleavages are changing quite significantly. While regionalism persists, its importance

2. H. Keum and J. R. Campbell, "Perils of Transition: Korea and Taiwan Democratization Compared," *Korean Journal of International Studies* 16, no. 1 (2018): 29–55.

has substantially decreased since democratization. A rising generational cleavage, as in Hong Kong, has determined much of the vote in recent elections, driven by diverging attitudes toward North Korea but also by the elderly poverty crisis. In addition, the economic polarization suffered since the 1997 crisis has brought redistributive issues to the center of the political discourse, and a modest class cleavage may be emerging, with low-income voters showing less support for the conservatives than the middle class, but only after accounting for age composition effects. University graduates have in parallel decreased their support for the conservatives, producing a unique configuration of low-income and higher-educated voters simultaneously favoring progressive parties.

### Democratization and the Transformation
### of South Korea's Party System

Before the partition, the Korean peninsula had continuously been a single political entity since 936, when it was unified under the Goryeo dynasty. After falling under Japanese domination in 1905, it officially became a Japanese colony in 1910 until the surrender of Japan in 1945, at which time the United States and the Soviet Union divided the peninsula into two occupation zones along the 38th parallel. In 1950, the attempt by North Korea to unify the peninsula under communist rule triggered the start of the Korean War, which reached a stalemate in 1953 after immense human and material losses.

In 1948, Syngman Rhee founded the Republic of Korea in the US zone of occupation. A series of anticommunist, US-backed authoritarian regimes ensued until 1987.[3] Rhee was ousted by a pro-democratic revolution in 1960, but only a year later, General Park Chung-hee placed the country under a military dictatorship. With the support of the United States, Park-Chung Hee led the country through a period of rapid economic growth while enabling the emergence of a crucial nucleus of power in South Korean politics, the chaebols, or big business conglomerates. He was, however, assassinated in 1979 by one of his friends at the head of the South Korean secret service, and Chun Doo-hwan, in charge of the investigation of Park's murder, took over the regime. By the late 1980s, rising public protests and international pressures facilitated the opening of the

---

3. With the exception of a short period of parliamentarism between the 1960 April Revolution and the military coup in May.

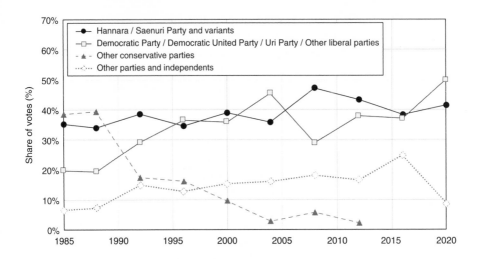

FIGURE 13.1. Election results in South Korea, 1985–2020
*Data Source:* Authors' computations using official election results (see wpid.world).
*Note:* The figure shows the share of votes received by selected groups of South Korean political parties in legislative elections between 1985 and 2020. The results correspond to those of single-member constituencies. Other names of the Hannara Party include United Future, Saenuri, Democratic Justice, Democratic Liberal, New Korea, and Liberty Korea. The conservatives (United Future) received 41% of votes in 2020.

South Korean regime, which culminated in the 1987 presidential election and the election of the first opposition president, Kim Dae-jung, in 1997.[4]

Due to South Korea's legacy of bureaucratic authoritarianism and "imperial presidency,"[5] party institutionalization has remained rather weak, with major parties often changing their names under each new leader. Two underlying coalitions can nonetheless be distinguished across elections: the conservative coalition, descending directly from the authoritarian regimes, and the progressive coalition that grew out of the democratic opposition. As shown in Figure 13.1, South Korea has progressively evolved into a two-party system, even though smaller parties have remained significant.[6]

4. O. Hellmann, *Political Parties and Electoral Strategy: The Development of Party Organization in East Asia* (Palgrave Macmillan, 2011), chapter 2.

5. Hellmann, *Political Parties*, chapter 2.

6. These results correspond to votes by constituency, which allocate 253 of the 300 seats, the remaining being allocated through proportional party lists.

Another major challenge facing South Korean democracy is endemic corruption, often linked to the tight grip of the chaebols on the country's economy and politics, and to the importance of patronage networks. Six out of seven presidents since the democratic transition have either been convicted of corruption or been part of a corruption scandal involving family members. Despite its challenges, democracy is still supported by a large majority of the South Korean population, a hopeful sign for its consolidation.[7]

### Social Inequalities in South Korea

The extraordinary economic development experienced by South Korea since the 1960s was internationally praised as an example of "growth with equity."[8] However, in the aftermath of the 1997 Asian financial crisis, South Korea's balanced growth came to an end and inequality rose substantially, driven by neoliberal economic reforms and the high concentration of the market under the chaebols.[9] One specificity of the South Korean trajectory is that this rise in inequality has disproportionately affected the older generation. South Korea's poverty rate among those over sixty-five has reached an alarming 44 percent in 2019, the highest among OECD countries, as the gradual distancing of the youth from familial values coupled with the aging of the population has left many elderly reliant on an underdeveloped public pension system.[10]

Rising inequalities have been a major cause of recent changes in the political discourse in South Korea, bringing more attention to redistributive issues across the political spectrum and fueling discontent with the chaebols' concentration of power. These changes are well reflected in the generalization of the motto "Democratize the economy" in recent po-

7. S. Denyer and M. J. Kim, "Another Former South Korea President Jailed for Corruption," *Washington Post*, October 5, 2018, https://www.washingtonpost.com/world /asia_pacific/another-former-south-korea-president-jailed-for-corruption/2018/10/05 /7e216cc6-c866-11e8-9158-09630a6d8725_story.html.

8. J. Stiglitz and B. Pleskovic, *Annual World Bank Conference on Development Economics 1997* (World Bank, 1998).

9. Y. Kim, "Hell Joseon: Polarization and Social Contention in a Neo-liberal Age," in *Korea's Quest for Economic Democratization,* ed. Y. Kim (Palgrave Macmillan, 2018), 1–20.

10. OECD, "Poverty Rate (Indicator)," OECD.org, accessed June 15, 2020, https:// data.oecd.org/inequality/poverty-rate.htm; see also appendix Figures A8, A17, and A18, World Political Cleavages and Inequality Database, http://wpid.world. OECD, *Pensions at a Glance 2015: OECD and G20 Indicators* (OECD Publishing, 2015).

litical campaigns. Former president Park Geun-hye, despite being a conservative, centered much of her 2012 campaign on social policies, and in 2017, Democratic candidate Moon Jae-in won the presidential election after running a campaign full of promises to expand the state's redistributive efforts and tackle the excessive power of the chaebols. While foreign policy and corruption still receive much of the attention, economic inequalities are becoming an increasingly relevant topic in the political arena. However, as we will further analyze, this has not necessarily led to rising class cleavages, as other dimensions of political conflict remain more determinant.[11]

## The North Korea Cleavage and the Intensification of Generational Divides

The Korean peninsula had been unified for over a thousand years at the time of its division in 1945, and Koreans shared a common language, culture, and national identity. It is therefore not surprising that the North Korean issue has remained at the forefront of politics to the present day. The hard stance on North Korea of the pre-democratic authoritarian regimes was adopted by the Grand National Party and its successors, while the Democratic Party historically advocated for a more pragmatic policy of engagement. President Kim Dae-jung's "Sunshine Policy" of the early 2000s was the concrete articulation of the Democratic vision, promoting cultural and economic exchanges with North Korea with the final goal of reaching de facto unification.[12] Despite easing tensions with the North, the policy also increased internal polarization, as conservatives accused the progressive government of serving the interests of the North Korean regime. Thus, the conservatives' return to power in 2007 to 2017 entailed a reversion to a more rigid approach. Since 2017, progressive president Moon Jae-in's North Korean policy has marked a return to the spirit of the Sunshine Policy, culminating in three inter-Korean summits

---

11. J. J. Yang, *The Political Economy of the Small Welfare State in South Korea* (Cambridge University Press, 2017); W. Kim, "Does Class Matter? Social Cleavages in South Korea's Electoral Politics in the Era of Neoliberalism," *Review of Political Economy* 22, no. 4 (2010): 589–616.

12. B. C. Koh, "The Foreign and Unification Policies of the Republic of Korea," in *Understanding Korean Politics: An Introduction*, ed. S. H. Kil and C. Moon (State University of New York Press, 2001), 231–268.

during 2018 and 2019. However, progress on the key issue of denuclearization has been rather limited so far.[13]

The North Korea cleavage is primarily structured along generational lines. Elderly voters tend to oppose the Democratic Party's engagement policy, yet they are significantly more supportive of unification and have a stronger sense of North Korea as being part of the same nation. The South Korean youth, as in Hong Kong and Taiwan, seem on the contrary to have begun to develop a sense of South Korean identity and to increasingly perceive North Korea as a stranger or enemy, even if they are more favorable to conciliatory diplomatic relations. While apparently contradictory, this configuration of opinions is easily understood in light of the historical events that marked each generation. While older voters, particularly those who witnessed the partition, tend to have stronger emotional ties to the North, the memory of the Korean War and decades living under anticommunist regimes have also fed their animosity toward the North Korean regime. The younger generations, in contrast, may not feel as close to North Koreans, but they keep a pragmatic perspective on inter-Korean relations, particularly centered on security concerns.[14]

This strong cleavage also mirrors diverging generational experiences from an economic perspective. Those aged over sixty in 2016 witnessed South Korea's spectacular economic development during the Park Chung-hee era, but have faced increasingly difficult material conditions as pensioners in recent years. The conservatives thus may have benefited from their historical ties to the Park regime, which may explain why the generational gap widened in 2012, when Park's daughter Park Geun-hye was the conservative leader.

Reflecting these divides, age has become a very strong predictor of voting behavior in recent years, with older people showing higher support for the conservatives than younger generations (Figure 13.2).[15] The

13. R. Pacheco Pardo, "Moon on a Mission: South Korea's New Approach to the North," *The Diplomat*, March 14, 2018, https://thediplomat.com/2018/03/moon-on-a-mission-south-koreas-new-approach-to-the-north/.

14. E. L. G. Campbell, *Uri Nara, Our Nation: Unification, Identity, and the Emergence of a New Nationalism amongst South Korean Young People* (Australian National University, 2011); K. Jiyoon, K. Kim, and K. Chungku, "South Korean Youths' Perceptions of North Korea and Unification" (Asan Institute for Policy Studies Issue Brief 2018–03, 2018), http://en.asaninst.org/contents/43527/.

15. The 2008 elections were rather exceptional, with a very low participation rate (46.1 percent) and a significant division of the conservatives into three parties, which may

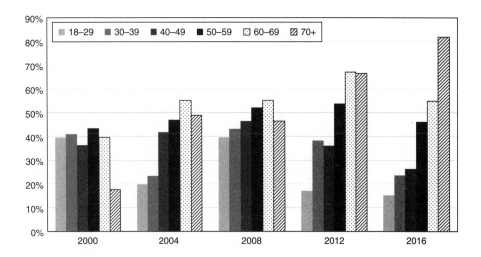

FIGURE 13.2. The generational cleavage in South Korea, 2000–2016. The conservative vote by age group
*Data Source:* Authors' computations using South Korean electoral surveys (see wpid.world).
*Note:* The figure shows the share of votes received by the Hannara/Saenuri Party by age group. Generational cleavages rose considerably in South Korea between 2000 and 2016. In 2016, 82% of voters aged over 70 voted for the Saenuri Party, compared to only 15% of voters aged 18 to 29.

gap is reduced after controlling for education, mainly due to a rising interaction between education and age and to the fact that tertiary graduates have been increasingly less likely to vote for the conservatives, but the divide remains significant after controls.[16]

### The Decline of the Regional Cleavage
Regional divides have famously been particularly strong in South Korea. The most salient divide, between the southwestern region of Honam and the southeastern region of Gyeongsang, dates to the pre-democratic era.

---

help to explain the discontinuity in 2008. See also Y. Kim and S. Park, "Emerging Cleavages in Korean Society: Region, Generation, Ideology, and Class," in Kim, *Korea's Quest for Economic Democratization,* 63–88.
   16. See appendix Figures A23 and A24, wpid.world.

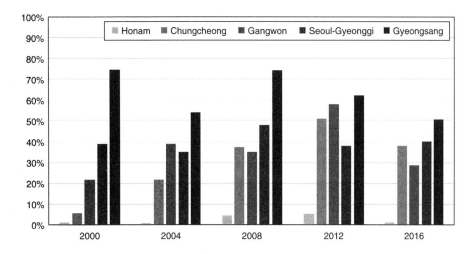

FIGURE 13.3. The regional cleavage in South Korea, 2000–2016: The conservative vote by region
*Data Source:* Authors' computations using South Korean electoral surveys (see wpid.world).
*Note:* The figure shows the share of votes received by the Hannara/Saenuri Party by region. In 2016, the conservatives received 51% of the vote in Gyeongsang, while they only received 1% in Honam. In 2016, Honam represented approximately 10% of the electorate, Chungcheong 10%, Gangwon 4%, Seoul-Gyeonggi 50%, and Gyeongsang 26%.

Park Chung-hee's native Gyeongsang province was privileged under his rule. Meanwhile, the Honam region, a stronghold of the democratic opposition, was marginalized.[17] After democratization, the "era of the three Kims" in the 1990s was also marked by strong regional voting, with each candidate receiving large majorities in his home region.[18]

However, regional voting seems to have gradually decreased in recent years (Figure 13.3), a change often linked to the electoral reforms introduced by the Kim Dae-jung administration and to the nomination of Roh Moo-hyun, a Gyeongsang native, as the new Democratic leader in 2002. Notice that regional cleavages are barely affected by the introduc-

17. A. L. Freedman, *Political Change and Consolidation: Democracy's Rocky Road in Thailand, Indonesia, South Korea, and Malaysia* (Palgrave Macmillan, 2006), chapter 2.
18. The "Three Kims" were Kim Jong-pil, from the Chungcheong province, Kim Young-sam from Gyeongsang, and Kim Dae-jung from Honam.

tion of control variables, which shows that residual regional identities, rather than their social structure, explain regional divides in South Korea.

### Toward Class Cleavages?

Class cleavages in South Korean politics have rarely been discussed, as the consensus used to be that they were absent due to the dominance of regional voting and the North Korea cleavage.[19] However, in recent years, economic polarization and the increased salience of redistributive issues in the political debate have reopened the question of class voting. One of the problems with analyzing class voting in South Korea is the very strong overlap between age and income.[20] The strong conservatism and the high rates of poverty among the elderly have led much of the literature to talk about "reverse-class voting."[21]

Indeed, if we look at voting results across income groups, the support for the conservatives appears to have grown among low-income voters.[22] However, once age is controlled for, or once voters older than sixty are removed from the sample, the conservative vote becomes very slightly lower among the bottom 50 percent income earners compared to the middle 40 percent (Figure 13.4). While it may be too early to claim that class cleavages are emerging in South Korea, given the short time span and the relatively low magnitude of the phenomenon, a change seems to have been taking place, which suggests that income could be playing an increasing role in the future.

Interestingly, low-income voters' support for liberal parties seems to have been rising at the same time as that of tertiary graduates (see Figure 13.5). South Korea therefore seems to be developing a unique set of political cleavages, in which university graduates vote with low-income voters. If this continues over time, it could mean the return of the students-workers coalition whose demonstrations greatly contributed to ending the authoritarian rule and precipitated the advent of democracy.

19. Hellmann, *Political Parties,* chapter 2.

20. Y. Lee and J. S. You, "Is Class Voting Emergent in Korea?," *Journal of East Asian Studies* 19, no. 2 (2019): 197–213.

21. W. J. Kang, "Income and Voting Behavior in Korean Politics: Why Do the Poor Support Conservative Political Parties?," *Journal of International and Area Studies* 24, no. 2 (2017): 15–33.

22. See appendix Figure A28, wpid.world.

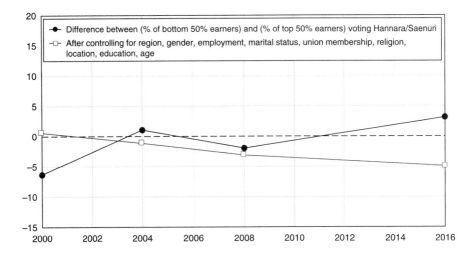

FIGURE 13.4. Vote and income in South Korea, 2000–2016
*Data Source:* Authors' computations using South Korean electoral surveys (see wpid.world).
*Note:* the figure shows the difference between the share of bottom 50% earners and the share of top 50% earners voting for the Hannara/Saenuri Party, before and after controls. Bottom 50% income earners were 6 percentage points less likely to vote conservative in 2000, while they were 3 percentage points more likely to do so in 2016.

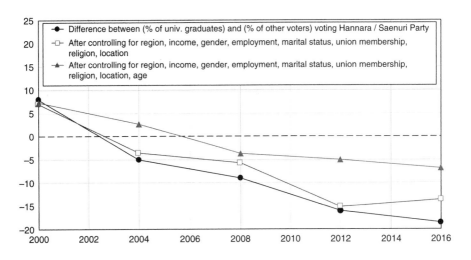

FIGURE 13.5. The educational cleavage in South Korea, 2000–2016
*Data Source:* Authors' computations using South Korean electoral surveys (see wpid.world).
*Note:* The figure shows the difference between the share of university graduates and the share of non-university graduates voting for the Hannara/Saenuri Party, before and after controls. The educational cleavage has significantly increased over time. In 2016, university graduates were less likely to vote conservative by 19 percentage points.

## Taiwan

As in Hong Kong, contemporary Taiwanese politics have been structured by the country's relations to mainland China. In this section, we show that democratization in Taiwan has led to the emergence of three main cleavages, which primarily materialize diverging political and socioeconomic attitudes toward the mainland: a strong ethnic cleavage between mainlanders and natives, a moderate regional cleavage between the richer north and the poorer south, and a moderate cleavage with lower-income and lower-educated voters against higher-income and higher-educated voters.

### Democratization and the Transformation of Taiwan's Party System

Taiwan and mainland China have a long common history. A series of immigration waves in the seventeenth century led Han Chinese to constitute most of the island's population and facilitated its incorporation into the Qing Chinese empire. Taiwan was later ceded to Japan in 1895, but was given back to China at the end of World War II. The defeat of Chiang Kai-shek's Republic of China (ROC) against the Communist Party of China in the Chinese Civil War finally led to the retreat of Chiang and two million of his followers to Taiwan in 1949.

When the Kuomintang (KMT) government moved to Taiwan, it quickly established an authoritarian regime, prohibiting political parties, repressing dissident opinions, and controlling mass media. Local elections were nevertheless implemented under the one-party regime and allowed independent candidates to run, leading non-KMT forces to gradually unify under the Tangwai movement (literally, outside the party), which grew in the 1980s as the strongest force pushing for democratization.[23] The majority of independents joined the new Democratic Progressive Party in 1986, and after a relaxation of legal constraints on the media and political parties, the KMT government organized the first direct legislative elections in 1992 and the first presidential elections in 1996.

As shown in Figure 13.6, Taiwan has since then gradually stabilized into a two-party system as support for the DPP grew in the 1990s and 2000s. Other candidates since democratization have mostly been KMT dissidents, such as former Taiwan governor James Soong, who started

23. C. Yu, "Parties, Partisans, and Independents in Taiwan," in *The Taiwan Voter*, ed. C. H. Achen and T. Y. Wang (University of Michigan Press, 2017), 71.

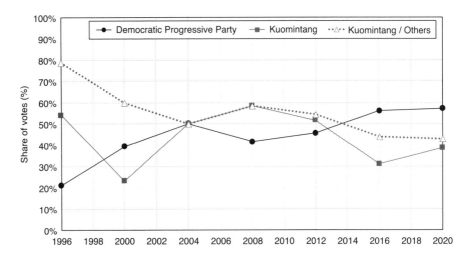

FIGURE 13.6. Presidential election results in Taiwan, 1996–2020
*Data Source:* Authors' computations using official election results (see wpid.world).
*Note:* the figure shows the share of votes received by selected parties or groups of
parties in presidential elections held in Taiwan between 1996 and 2020. The vote share
of the Democratic Progressive Party increased from 21% in 1996 to 57% in 2020.

running as an independent candidate after failing to gain the Kuomintang's nomination in 2000. Legislative elections have given greater space
to small parties, but the Legislative Yuan has also been divided into two
main blocs, the KMT-led Pan-Blue Coalition and the DPP-led Pan-Green
Coalition, with most elected representatives joining one or the other of
these coalitions.[24]

### Social Inequalities, Identity, and Ethnic Cleavages in Taiwan

The existing literature has shown ethnicity to be a strong determinant of
political attitudes, shaping opinions on reunification and relations to the
mainland. Ethnolinguistic groups in Taiwan can be divided into four
broad categories. The Minnans (about 72 percent of the electorate) and
Hakkas (14 percent) are residents whose ancestors migrated between the
seventeenth century and the first half of the twentieth century from
regions in China where the Minnan and Hakka dialects are spoken. The

24. See appendix Figures B6 and B7, wpid.world.

mainlanders (12 percent) are the descendants of the approximately two million people who emigrated from China at the end of the 1940s. The Aboriginal people (less than 2 percent) are Austronesian Indigenous people who lived on the island before the Han immigration waves—given low sample sizes, we exclude them from our analysis.[25]

When the KMT imposed military rule and a one-party state in the 1950s, it disproportionately favored the mainlanders, who were overrepresented in party membership and the civil service. Taiwan's social structure was therefore very comparable to that found in Malaysia (see Chapter 12) and South Africa (see Chapter 16), where a dominant ethnic minority (the Chinese minority in Malaysia, the White minority in South Africa) controlled a large share of economic resources. However, unlike in Malaysia and South Africa, where ethnic inequalities remained substantial throughout the twentieth century, in Taiwan the KMT initiated a large process of indigenization of the state bureaucracy in the 1970s after twenty years of mainlander domination.[26] This gradual incorporation of Minnans and Hakkas into the state elite, as well as the emergence of an export-led private sector and growing intermarriage between mainlanders and native Taiwanese, contributed to strongly reduce ethnic inequalities in Taiwan. Today, ethnicity and economic status are almost completely uncorrelated, especially when put in comparative perspective.[27] While ethnic cleavages could be the precursor of class cleavages in ethnically structured economies like South Africa and Malaysia, this was therefore not the case in Taiwan, where ethnicity was almost entirely disconnected from social class at the time of democratization.

In line with existing studies, Figures 13.7 and 13.8 show that the rise of the DPP since 1996 has coincided with the materialization of a strong ethnic cleavage, between the natives voting mostly for the DPP and the mainlanders preferring the KMT. This cleavage has remained very stable

---

25. See appendix Figure B11, wpid.world.

26. C. Yun-han and J. Lin, "Political Development in 20th-Century Taiwan: State-Building, Regime Transformation and the Construction of National Identity," *The China Quarterly* 165 (2001): 102–129.

27. See appendix Figures B17 and B18, wpid.world; J. Jao and M. McKeever, "Ethnic Inequalities and Educational Attainment in Taiwan," *Sociology of Education* 79, no. 2 (2006): 131–152; Y. Hao, "Converging Mainlander and Native Taiwanese, 1949–2012," *Australian Economic History Review* 57, no. 1 (2017): 84–107.

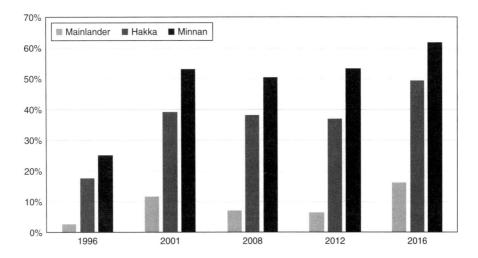

FIGURE 13.7. The DPP vote by ethnic group in Taiwan, 1996–2016

*Data Source:* Authors' computations using Taiwanese electoral surveys (see wpid.world).
*Note:* The figure shows the share of votes received by the Democratic Progressive Party (DPP) by ethnic group. In 2016, the DPP was supported by 62% of Minnan voters, compared to only 16% of Mainlanders.

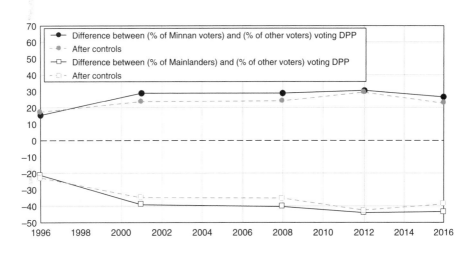

FIGURE 13.8. The ethnic cleavage in Taiwan, 1996–2016

*Data Source:* Authors' computations using Taiwanese electoral surveys (see wpid.world).
*Note:* The figure shows the relative support for the Democratic Progressive Party (DPP) among Minnan voters and Mainlanders, before and after controlling for income, education, age, gender, employment, marital status, union membership, religion, and region of residence. In 2016, Minnan voters were 27 percentage points more likely than other voters to vote DPP, while Mainlanders were 43 percentage points less likely to do so.

since 1996 and is highly robust to controlling for other sociodemographic variables.[28]

### Regional Cleavages and Spatial Inequalities

The Chinese growth and economic cooperation agreements have intensified exchanges between the two sides of the Taiwan Strait.[29] This trade liberalization has opened a potential for a new division between the "winners" and the "losers" of globalization, which could lead to a realignment of vulnerable workers toward the DPP, which is generally less favorable to strengthening relations with the mainland.[30] Democratization in Taiwan has indeed led to the emergence of a regional cleavage: as shown in Figure 13.9, the southern region has always been more likely to vote for the DPP. This gap peaked in 2008 and seems to have declined since then. Controlling for other sociodemographic variables, and in particular ethnicity, reduces this gap significantly—mainly because there are more mainlanders in the northern and middle regions—but not completely: residual regional identities thus appear to also matter in determining vote choice.

While ethnicity is a poor proxy for economic resources, regional income inequalities in Taiwan are strong and have risen since the 1990s, with the southern and central regions lagging behind the north, a divergence that has been attributed to the rise of the ICT sector and to increasing cross-strait economic integration.[31] Therefore, spatial differences in voting behaviors do seem to have represented a parallel political cleavage, partly based on historical ethnic locations, but also potentially rooted in economic inequality and interacting with attitudes toward trade with mainland China.

28. These results focus on presidential elections, with the exception of 2001, which covers legislative elections. See appendix Table B2, wpid.world, for data sources.

29. A. C. Tan and K. Ho, "Cross-Strait Relations and the Taiwan Voter," in Achen and Wang, *Taiwan Voter,* 158.

30. Y. Wu, "From Identity to Distribution: Paradigm Shift in Taiwan Politics: A First Cut" (paper presented at the Annual Conference of the American Association for Chinese Studies, New Brunswick, NJ, October 2013), https://aacs.ccny.cuny.edu/2013conference/Papers/Yu-Shan%20Wu.pdf.

31. See appendix Figures B19 and B20, wpid.world. M. Anderson and M. Klinthäll, "The Opening of the North-South Divide: Cumulative Causation, Household Income Disparity, and the Regional Bonus in Taiwan 1976–2005," *Structural Change and Economic Dynamics* 23, no. 2 (2012): 170–179.

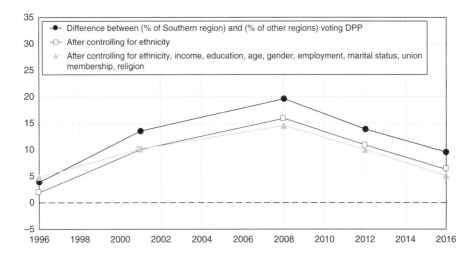

FIGURE 13.9. The regional cleavage in Taiwan, 1996–2016
*Data Source:* Authors' computations using Taiwanese electoral surveys (see wpid.world).
*Note:* The figure shows the difference between the share of Southern region residents and the share of residents of other regions voting for the Democratic Progressive Party (DPP), before and after controls. In 2016, the vote share of the DPP was 10 percentage points higher in the Southern region than in the rest of the country.

## *Toward Class Cleavages?*

Have economic conflicts and inequality only been represented through their interaction with the China question in Taiwan, or has an independent class cleavage also emerged in recent years? This has been a debated question. Some studies have argued that parties have increasingly focused on the economy independent of the question of relations with continental China, while others have shown evidence that voters' opinions on economic issues have been entirely mediated by their vision of independence/unification.[32]

Figure 13.10 shows that with the exception of 1996, poorer and less-educated voters have been more likely to vote for the DPP by 5 to 10 percentage points, with a peak in the mid-2000s, as in the case of regional divides. This peak could be linked to the rise of the radically pro-independence Taiwan Solidarity Union in 2001, which led the DPP to

---

32. Wu, "From Identity to Distribution"; C. H. Achen and T. Y. Wang, "Conclusion: The Power of Identity in Taiwan," in Achen and Wang, 273.

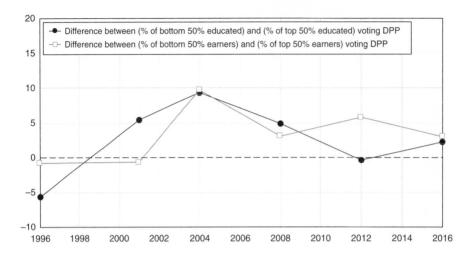

FIGURE 13.10. Vote, income, and education in Taiwan, 1996–2016

*Data Source:* Authors' computations using Taiwanese electoral surveys (see wpid.world).

*Note:* The figure shows the relative support for the Democratic Progressive Party (DPP) among low-income and lower-educated voters, after controlling for income / education, ethnicity, age, gender, occupation, marital status, union membership, religion, and region. In 2016, bottom 50% income earners were 3 percentage points more likely to vote DPP.

strategically shift to a more pro-independence stance before the 2004 election, thus contributing to greater divides on the independence issue. Meanwhile, there is no evidence that the electorate was more polarized in 2004 and 2008 on economic or welfare issues, which arguably became more salient in the postcrisis period. These results suggest that it is the independence-reunification cleavage that has most polarized voters' choices along class lines, consistent with recent evidence showing a similar inverted U-shaped trend in voter polarization on the independence-unification issue.[33]

In summary, lower-educated, low-income, and southern voters have been significantly more likely to vote for the DPP since the early 2000s, and this was even more the case in elections where partisan divides on the independence / unification issue were stronger. These findings are completely the opposite of what we find in Hong Kong, where pro-democracy

33. A. H. Wang, "The Myth of Polarization among Taiwanese Voters: The Missing Middle," *Journal of East Asian Studies* 19, no. 3 (2019): 275–287.

votes have been higher among higher-income and higher-educated voters (see below). This difference arguably is due to the fact that the China question has interacted with other dimensions of political conflict in very different ways in the two territories. While in Hong Kong, pro-Beijing forces have been more popular among older generations and immigrants, two groups on average poorer than the rest of the population, in Taiwan, on the contrary, the Kuomintang was historically the party of the mainlander elite, a divide that the DPP seems to have carried into the present day by representing not only formerly oppressed ethnic groups, but also disadvantaged voters and poorer regions. Additionally, while economic patronage from Beijing in Hong Kong may have made integration more appealing to low-income voters, increasing competition from mainland China's industries have on the contrary been negatively perceived by industrial workers in Taiwan, in a way comparable to the rise of antiglobalization sentiments among the working class in Western democracies.

Interestingly, age does not seem to have played a key role in Taiwan, and there is in fact evidence that a sizable share of the new generations has turned to abstention rather than to greater political mobilization as in Hong Kong.[34] However, this may be gradually changing in recent years, as students were notably omnipresent in the 2014 Sunflower student movement against the passing of the Cross-Strait Service Trade Agreement with Beijing.

## Hong Kong

Hong Kong was handed over to the People's Republic of China (PRC) by the United Kingdom in 1997, in application of the Sino-British Joint Declaration of 1984. The Hong Kong Special Administrative Region (HKSAR) was to fall under the principle of "one country, two systems": the city's capitalist system would remain unchanged for a period of fifty years, existing civil rights and freedoms would be guaranteed, and the government of the HKSAR would be composed of local inhabitants and elected

---

34. C. H. Achen and T. Y. Wang, "Declining Voter Turnout in Taiwan: A Generational Effect?," *Electoral Studies* 58 (2019): 113–124. There is, however, evidence that the rise of pro-independence views has been driven partly by the replacement of older cohorts by new cohorts of voters, who tend to be more in favor of independence. See C. Huang, "Generation Effects? Evolution of Independence-Unification Views in Taiwan, 1996–2016," *Electoral Studies* 58 (2019): 103–112.

democratically.[35] The PRC's refusal to respond to democratic aspirations, as well as the rise of a Hong Kong identity increasingly viewed by new generations as excluding rather than complementing Chinese identity, initiated a process of political polarization, which culminated in the mobilizations of June 2019 as millions took to the streets.[36]

In this section, we document extreme and rising generational divides—among the highest observed in this volume—which trump the effects of most other factors. The generational divide in Hong Kong has been mostly about identity, but not only that: key actors in the protests were in particular what the journalist Paul Mason called the "graduate[s] with no future," students disillusioned with their economic prospects in a city characterized by soaring housing prices and widening income disparities.[37] Second, we show that individuals born on the mainland are significantly more supportive of the pro-Beijing camp, but this effect is not as strong as one might expect. Finally, we find that integration with the PRC, Hong Konger identity, and democratization are the most divisive issues across generations, which suggests that cleavages related to institutions and sovereignty are more pronounced than distributional or immigration issues.

### Unachieved Democratization and the Transformation of Hong Kong's Party System

After more than 150 years of colonization by the British, with the exception of a brief period of Japanese occupation in the 1940s, Hong Kong reintegrated China in 1997. Democratization and the formation of political organizations had nevertheless already started in the 1980s, as the Sino-British negotiations of 1982–1984 politicized the Hong Kong population, before the first direct elections of the Legislative Council (LegCo), the unicameral legislature of the HKSAR, in 1991 (see Figure 13.11).[38]

---

35. N. Ma, "From Political Acquiescence to Civil Disobedience: Hong Kong's Road to Civil Disobedience," in *The Umbrella Movement: Civil Resistance and Contentious Space in Hong Kong*, ed. N. Ma and E. W. Cheng (Amsterdam University Press, 2020), 27–50.

36. BBC, "Hong Kong Protest: 'Nearly Two Million' Join Demonstration," BBC News, June 17, 2019, https://www.bbc.com/news/world-asia-china-48656471.

37. P. Mason, *Why It's Kicking Off Everywhere: The New Global Revolutions* (Verso, 2012), cited in L. Cooper and W. Lam, introduction to *Citizenship, Identity and Social Movements in the New Hong Kong*, ed. W. Lam and L. Cooper (Routledge, 2018), 1–12.

38. N. Ma, "Political Parties and Elections," in *Contemporary Hong Kong Politics*, ed. L. Wai-man, P. Luen-tim Lui, W. Wong, and I. Holliday (Hong Kong University Press, 2007), 117–134.

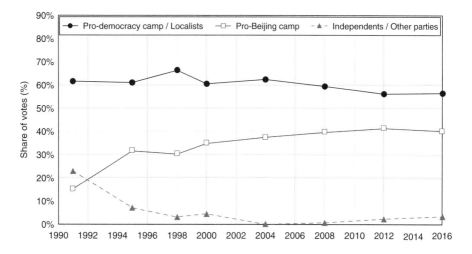

FIGURE 13.11. Election results in Hong Kong, 1991–2016
*Data Source:* Authors' computations using official election results (see wpid.world).
*Note:* The figure shows the share of votes received by selected groups of political parties in geographical constituencies in Legislative Council elections held in Hong Kong between 1991 and 2016. The Pro-Beijing camp received 40% of votes in the 2016 elections.

Pro-democracy parties have since then always received more than 55 percent of votes, while the pro-Beijing camp has grown from 15 percent in 1991 to 40 percent in 2016 thanks to the decline of independent candidates.

However, the pro-Beijing forces have always managed to retain control over political power. Hong Kong's electoral system has indeed disproportionally benefited the pro-Beijing camp and has contributed to dividing the opposition: half of the members of the LegCo are elected through functional constituencies representing specific interest groups, which are generally more supportive of the pro-Beijing camp.[39] Second, the chief executive, the head of government, is elected from a pool of pro-Beijing candidates by a 1,200-member electoral college, which has allowed the executive branch to be completely controlled by Beijing. Third, Beijing has been able to mobilize growing electoral resources by devel-

39. See, for instance, L. Pang-kwong, "Comparative Study of Electoral Systems Module 5: Macro Report," CSES, September 14, 2016, https://cses.org/wp-content/uploads/2019/05/cses5_MacroReport.pdf.

oping local networks providing material benefits and social services, co-ordinating candidate nominations in constituencies, and securing support from the growing number of immigrants from the mainland.[40]

The key issues discussed in Hong Kong politics have changed significantly in the past three decades. In the 1991 and 1995 LegCo elections, attitudes toward the Chinese government, the Tiananmen crackdown, and democratization were the main electoral issues. Democratization then became an even more important issue in the context of the 2003 protests against the security bill.[41] The China factor changed again after 2008 following widespread coverage of rights abuse and corruption, and anti-China sentiments grew; new movements of "progressive localism" reasserted demands for self-determination, while movements of "anti-China localism" born after the 2014 Umbrella protests went further, questioning for the first time the "one country, two systems" principle and even proposing the sovereign independence of Hong Kong as a new nation.[42] A "localist" camp emerged in the LegCo in the 2016 legislative election, receiving 19 percent of votes and winning six seats. Politics in Hong Kong have therefore been characterized by growing polarization, as claims are gradually shifting from autonomy and democracy to cultural exclusivism and even national sovereignty.[43]

### The Rise of Generational Cleavages

We now turn to the analysis of electoral behaviors in Hong Kong, using political attitudes surveys covering the LegCo elections of 1998, 2000, 2004, 2012, and 2016.[44] The most striking result that emerges from this analysis is the presence of extreme and growing generational cleavages

---

40. N. Ma, "The China Factor in Hong Kong Elections: 1991 to 2016," *China Perspectives,* no. 2017/3 (2017): 17–26; S. H. Wong, N. Ma, and W. Lam, "Immigrants as Voters in Electoral Autocracies: The Case of Mainland Chinese Immigrants in Hong Kong," *Journal of East Asian Studies* 18, no. 1 (2018): 67–95.

41. Ma, "From Political Acquiescence to Civil Disobedience."

42. Y. Chen and M. M. Szeto, "The Forgotten Road of Progressive Localism: New Preservation Movement in Hong Kong," *Inter-Asia Cultural Studies* 16, no. 3 (2015): 436–453.

43. M. P. Kaeding, "The Rise of 'Localism' in Hong Kong," *Journal of Democracy* 28, no. 1 (2017): 157–171; S. Ortmann, "The Development of Hong Kong Identity: From Local to National Identity," in Lam and Cooper, *Citizenship, Identity, and Social Movements,* 114–131.

44. See appendix Table C1, wpid.world.

since 1998: support for pro-democracy forces among voters born in the 1940s to 1960s has decreased steadily, while nearly 90 percent of voters born in the 1990s voted pro-democracy in 2016 (Figure 13.12). Controlling for education reduces this gap, as younger voters are much more educated than older voters, but age does have a substantial and growing independent effect on vote choice (Figure 13.13).

These results show that the core electorate of the pro-democracy movement lies in younger generations, who are much more likely to feel "Hong Kongese" and tend to be more supportive of democracy. This generational divide appears to be exceptionally strong and persistent in comparative perspective: such differences are visible in only a handful of cases, such as in South Korea since the 2000s (see above) and in Japan in the early postwar decades (see Chapter 11). Generational divides are generally found to be associated with center/periphery or integration/disintegration cleavages, two dimensions of political conflict that clearly have an exceptionally acute and rising importance in Hong Kong politics.

### Immigration and the Mainlander-Native Cleavage

Immigration from mainland China to Hong Kong since 1997 has been substantial and has been the subject of intense political debates.[45] Under the "one-way permit" policy, mainland Chinese who want to migrate to Hong Kong must apply through mainland authorities, and they usually obtain permanent residence status and the right to vote after seven years in the city. In 2016, about one in seven of the city's residents was an immigrant who arrived from the mainland after 1997, and over a quarter of the electorate in total was born in mainland China.[46]

Immigrants face numerous difficulties when arriving in Hong Kong, from social prejudice to discrimination. They are on average less educated, older, poorer, and overrepresented in low-skilled jobs in the service sector.[47] Growing immigration and the rise of anti-China sentiments have generated strong resentment among natives, who increasingly

45. S. H. Wong, K. Lee, K. Ho, and H. D. Clarke, "Immigrant Influx and Generational Politics: A Comparative Case Study of Hong Kong and Taiwan," *Electoral Studies* 58 (2019): 84–93.

46. J. F. Downes, "Mainland Chinese Immigration in Hong Kong: Analysing Anti-immigrant Sentiment," in Lam and Cooper, *Citizenship, Identity and Social Movements*, 51–71; appendix Table C2, wpid.world.

47. See appendix Table C5, wpid.world.

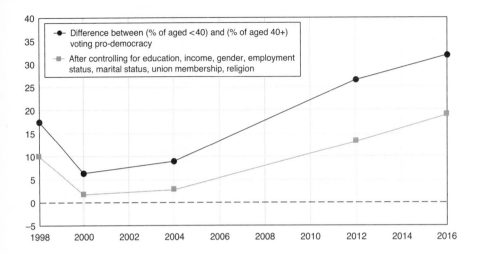

FIGURE 13.12. The generational cleavage in Hong Kong, 1998–2016
*Data Source:* Authors' computations using Hong Kong electoral surveys (see wpid.world).
*Note:* The figure shows the difference between the share of voters aged under 40 and
the share of voters aged 40 or more voting for the pro-democracy camp, before and
after controls. Generational cleavages have risen considerably in Hong Kong. In 2016,
voters younger than 40 were 32 percentage points more likely to vote for the pro-
democracy camp.

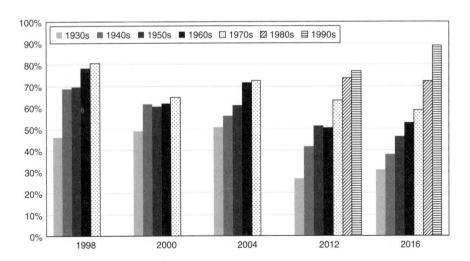

FIGURE 13.13. The generational cleavage in Hong Kong, 1998–2016: The pro-
democracy vote by decade of birth
*Data Source:* Authors' computations using Hong Kong electoral surveys (see wpid.world).
*Note:* The figure shows the share of votes received by the pro-democracy camp by
voters' decade of birth. In 2016, 89% of voters born in the 1990s voted for the
pro-democracy camp, compared to only 31% of those born in the 1930s.

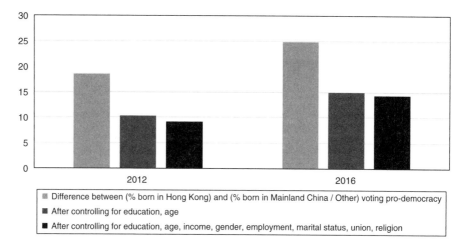

FIGURE 13.14. The native-mainlander cleavage in Hong Kong, 2012–2016
*Data Source:* Authors' computations using Hong Kong electoral surveys (see wpid.world).
*Note:* The figure shows the relative support for the pro-democracy camp among voters born in Hong Kong, before and after controls. In 2016, natives were 25 percentage points more likely to vote for the pro-democracy camp. This difference is reduced to 15 percentage points after controlling for education and age (at a given education level and age, natives are 15 points more likely to vote for the pro-democracy camp). Voters born outside of Hong Kong are mostly Mainlanders (born in continental China).

view new immigrants as foreigners supporting the Beijing establishment while benefiting from the city's economic opportunities.

How strong is the mainlander/native cleavage in Hong Kong? Natives were more likely to support pro-democracy parties by 25 percentage points in 2016 and by 15 points after controlling for age and education, mainly because immigrants are on average older than natives (Figure 13.14).[48] The immigration cleavage in Hong Kong, while significant, is therefore lower than the mainlander-native cleavage in Taiwan (see above) or the cleavage related to Muslim minorities in Western Europe (see Chapter 1).

Furthermore, this gap hides huge heterogeneity within generations: in 2016, as much as 80 percent of immigrants from the mainland aged below twenty-nine voted pro-democracy, compared to 28 percent of those aged

48. See also appendix Figure C13, wpid.world.

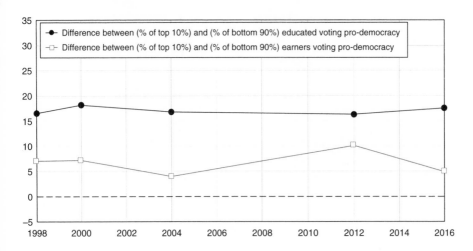

FIGURE 13.15. The pro-democracy vote by income and education in Hong Kong, 1998–2016
*Data Source:* Authors' computations using Hong Kong electoral surveys (see wpid.world).
*Note:* The figure shows the relative support for the pro-democracy camp among highest-educated and top-income voters. In 2016, top 10% educated voters and top 10% income earners were, respectively, 18 and 5 percentage points more likely to vote for the pro-democracy camp.

seventy or above.[49] This points to the greater strength of generational cleavages and to the key role of processes of socialization. It also shows that the mainlander-native cleavage cannot be fully explained by economic competition, as young natives and young immigrants show comparable levels of support for the pro-democracy camp.

### Generations, Immigrants, and the Political Representation of Class

Younger voters and natives are on average more educated and richer than older cohorts and immigrants, respectively. As the pro-democracy camp heavily relies on support from the youth and natives, it is therefore not surprising to see that higher-income earners, and especially higher-educated voters, have been significantly more likely to vote pro-democracy (Figure 13.15). These two gaps can however be almost entirely explained

49. See appendix Figure C29, wpid.world.

by these two compositional effects, even if higher-educated voters remain slightly more likely to vote pro-democracy after controls.[50]

Therefore, while economic concerns about rising housing prices and economic insecurity did play an important role in explaining pro-democracy support and protest participation among young natives, there is only limited evidence that economic status influences electoral behaviors beyond its interaction with age and origin, and there is even less evidence that poorer or less-educated voters have been shifting toward the pro-democracy camp.[51] This is a striking result, given that the youth are on average more concerned about income inequality (see below) and that the pro-Beijing camp is generally depicted as representing the elites (which are, it is true, numerically small and may not be adequately captured in our data). This points again to the dominance of the generational cleavage and the immigration cleavage in structuring political conflicts in Hong Kong.

### The Sociological Foundations of Generational Divides

We conclude with a simple analysis of the relationship between generational divides and political attitudes. Interestingly, generations of voters appear to diverge on many cultural, social, and economic issues (Figure 13.16). Younger voters are more likely to disagree or strongly disagree that closer integration with mainland China will benefit Hong Kong. They are more likely to think themselves as only "Hong Konger," rather than "Chinese," "Chinese Hong Konger," or "Hong Kong Chinese." They are more likely to disagree or strongly disagree that Hong Kong has a democratic political system, more likely to agree or strongly agree that Hong Kong has too many immigrants coming from China, and more likely to cite income inequality as one of the three most important problems facing Hong Kong at the present time. Identity and political integration, however, appear to have been the most divisive issues across generations: more than 70 percent of adults younger than twenty-five oppose integration with the mainland compared to 40 percent of those older than fifty-five, and similar gaps separate generations when it comes to associations with "Hong Konger" identity.

---

50. See, in particular, appendix Table C3, wpid.world, which shows that the effect of income on the vote falls to almost zero and is not significant after controls.

51. Notice, however, that the peak in housing prices may have created a divide between homeowners and tenants. See S. H. Wong and K. M. Wan, "The Housing Boom and the Rise of Localism in Hong Kong: Evidence from the Legislative Council Election in 2016," *China Perspectives* 3 (2018): 31–40.

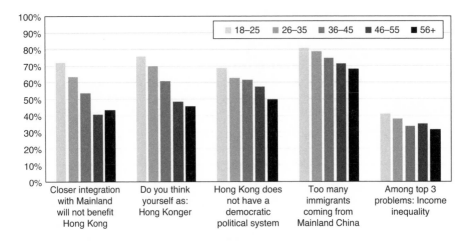

FIGURE 13.16. Attitudes toward Hong Kong identity, immigration, and integration with China by age, 2015

*Data Source:* Authors' computations using the Hong Kong Election Study 2015 (see wpid.world).

*Note:* This figure decomposes by age group the share of voters who (1) think that closer integration with Mainland China would not be beneficial for Hong Kong, (2) consider themselves more Hong Konger than Chinese, Hong Konger-Chinese, Chinese-Hong Konger, or Other, (3) believe that Hong Kong does not have a democratic political system, (4) think that there are too many immigrants coming from Mainland China, and (5) consider that income inequality is among the three most important problems in Hong Kong today. In 2015, 72% of voters aged 18 to 25 thought that closer integration with Mainland China would not benefit Hong Kong, compared to 43% of voters older than 56.

Therefore, political integration, cultural differentiation, and democratization seem to be the most divisive issues in Hong Kong, structuring political cleavages along generational lines. Support for the pro-democracy camp has grown tremendously since the 2015 survey used in this section was conducted, which was notably visible in the results of the 2019 local elections, in which the pro-democrats achieved their biggest success in Hong Kong's history. This success was in large part driven by a surge in turnout among younger voters,[52] which suggests that the generational cleavage could further deepen in the future.

52. K. Chung, "Hong Kong District Council Election Data Reveals Turnout Now Highest among Young People, Driven to the Ballot Box by Anti-government Protests," *South China Morning Post*, April 4, 2020, https://www.scmp.com/news/hong-kong/politics/article/3078401/hong-kong-district-council-election-data-reveals-turnout.

# Democracy and the Politicization of Inequality in Brazil, 1989–2018

AMORY GETHIN AND MARC MORGAN

## Introduction

How have political cleavages developed over the course of redemocratization in Brazil, one of the world's largest and most unequal countries? This is what we analyze in this chapter. The legacies of economic, educational, racial, and geographic inequalities in Brazil have left fertile ground for political polarization along social dimensions. Since the end of the military dictatorship in 1985 and the dawn of the New Republic in 1988, Brazilian party politics has been defined by the electoral strategies of the hegemonic party on the left, the Workers' Party (Partido dos Trabalhadores, PT). The rise of *petismo* in Brazil is interesting in a comparative perspective, as it shows how the consolidation of new divisions between social groups coincides with the concrete implementation of policies and the transformation of ideological affiliations. How has the electoral basis of the PT changed since 1989, and what are the implications of these changes in terms of the political salience of different forms of inequality? How can we explain the slow decline of the PT in the 2010s and the victory of Jair Bolsonaro, from the conservative Social Liberal Party (Partido Social Liberal, PSL), in 2018?

To answer these questions, we analyze electoral behaviors in Brazil since 1989 by combining a set of polls conducted by the Datafolha Institute just before the second round of all presidential elections.[1] In brief,

We thank Gedeão Locks, Clara Martínez-Toledano, Thomas Piketty, and Thiago Scarelli for their helpful comments on this chapter.

1. See appendix Table A2, World Political Cleavages and Inequality Database, http://wpid.world. The focus on presidential elections is limited by the data, but they are an

we find that the PT underwent an exceptional political metamorphosis, from a party of the young, highly educated, high-income elites to a party of the poor, increasingly located outside of the party's foundational locus in the south, particularly in the historically conservative northeast. We argue that key to understanding both this evolution and the party's subsequent fall to Bolsonaro in 2018 are contextual policy-driven factors and programmatic alliances. Importantly, we highlight how the extreme class polarization that emerged in Brazil over the 2000s is linked to how economic growth was distributed among the population by a party balancing policy priorities and feasibility.

## Brazilian Democratization in the Long Run of History

### A Legacy of Extreme Electoral Inequality

It was only thirty years ago that Brazil definitively adopted the democratic principle of "one adult person, one vote." Prior to 1989, social distinction and economic inequality dominated Brazil's history, at least since the settlement of Europeans around the turn of the sixteenth century. After its independence from Portugal in 1822, only domestically born, literate, rich male Catholics aged twenty-five and over could vote. An electoral law of 1881 extended suffrage to non-Catholics and naturalized citizens, but it still officially excluded poor literates, women, slaves, and the illiterate, which in total made up at least 85 percent of the voting-age population.[2] Brazil became the last country in the Western hemisphere to abolish slavery, in 1888, three years before the new republican constitution. Yet, Afro-Brazilians continued to be politically discriminated against thereafter due to their low level of education and limited access to land. While income and gender requirements for voting were abolished in 1891 and 1934, respectively, the political exclusion of the most underprivileged members of society was maintained for another century, until the 1988 constitution removed the literacy requirement, at a time when approximately 20 percent of the voting-age population were still illiterate (see Figure 14.1).

Given the early restrictions on participation, it is not surprising that such a limited proportion of the age-eligible population voted. In the final

---

important indicator of political affinities due to the outsized role assigned to the president in Brazil's federal system.

2. See appendix Table A1, wpid.world.

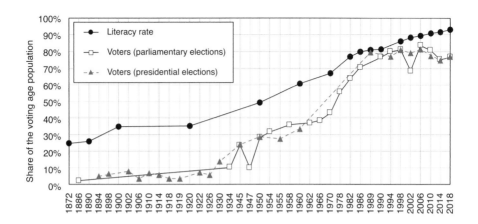

FIGURE 14.1. Literacy and political participation in Brazil, 1872–2018

*Data Source:* Literacy rates from Ipeadata, except 1950 and 1960, which are from the Censo Demográfico 1960 (IBGE). The estimates for 1872–1890 are imputed from the literacy rates of the total population. Estimates for 1900–2018 are imputed from the literacy rates of the population aged fifteen and over. Voter data is from the IBGE censuses and J. L. Love, "Political Participation in Brazil, 1881–1969," *Luso-Brazilian Review* 7, no. 2 (1970): 3–24, for 1886–1930, and from the International IDEA Voter Turnout Database for 1945–2018 (see wpid.world).

*Note:* The literacy rate refers to the proportion of the voting age population who can read and write. Voters are the people who actually voted in presidential and parliamentary elections as a share of the voting age population. Between 1886 and 1934 no data was found for parliamentary elections. Between 1960 and 1989 no direct elections for the president were held.

parliamentary elections of the empire (1822–1889) in 1886, this proportion was only 2 percent (see Figure 14.1). Inspired by the British system, parliamentary majorities alternated between liberals and conservatives under the auspices of the emperor.[3] Then, during the period known as the "Old Republic" (1891–1930), voters made up 5–6 percent of the voting-age population,[4] barely changing throughout the three decades. During this time, Brazilian politics was dominated by state-level factions of the conservative Republican Party, especially those of the rich states of São Paulo and Minas Gerais. This elite democracy was interrupted during Getúlio Vargas's 1930 Liberal Alliance revolution and his "popu-

3. J. L. Love, "Political Participation in Brazil, 1881–1969," *Luso-Brazilian Review* 7, no. 2 (1970): 3–24.

4. Presidential elections of the first Republic in 1894 and 1898.

list" reign until 1945. In particular, from 1937 to 1945, he established a dictatorship (*Estado Novo*) in which he appointed state governors, who in turn named municipal prefects.

The ballot of 1945 and the constitution of 1946, which established the Second Republic, brought free and more contested elections for almost twenty years until the military coup d'état of 1964. A marked increase in voter participation, following the continued expansion of literacy, can be observed during this era. However, despite the democratic progress, the proportion of voters remained comparatively low. For example, the 1960 presidential election in Brazil mobilized only 18 percent of the total population, compared to 44 percent in Argentina's 1958 presidential election.[5]

Therefore, for at least the first half of the twentieth century Brazil seemed to be in a vicious cycle whereby the political voice of the masses was limited by literacy requirements on voting, which mainly favored urban inhabitants. This made executive power much more dependent on urban Brazil. Parliamentary representation, on the other hand, was anchored to the total population of voting constituencies, and given that the majority of the country's population still lived in rural areas during this period, an important urban-rural political cleavage emerged.[6] Since illiteracy was greater in rural areas, the traditional rural landed class maintained control of Congress. The cleavage between the urban-oriented "populist" executive and the rural-dominated "patriarchal" legislature was at the origin of much of the political instability in the early 1960s, which fed into the 1964 military coup that deposed the Labor Party executive of João Goulart.[7]

The military dictatorship (1964–1985) abolished elections for the president of the republic and state governors for most of its reign, and banned all previously existing parties. Direct elections could be held only for federal and state deputies and municipal councilors and only with permissible candidates, either from the military's National Renewal Alliance (ARENA) or from the artificial "catchall" opposition, the Brazilian Democratic Movement (MDB). The 1979 reforms saw the military

5. Love, "Political Participation."

6. C. Furtado, "Political Obstacles to Economic Growth in Brazil," *International Affairs* 41, no. 2 (1965): 252–266.

7. M. Morgan and P. Souza, "Distributing Growth during Late-Development: New Evidence on Long-Run Inequality in Brazil" (working paper, 2021).

government abandon this two-party system in order to split the opposition, which was gaining electoral ground. ARENA was dissolved and replaced by the Democratic Social Party (Partido Democrático Social, PDS), while the MDB rebranded as the Brazilian Democratic Movement Party (Partido do Movimento Democrático Brasileiro, PMDB). New parties were formed, including the left-wing Workers' Party (Partido dos Trabalhadores, PT) and the center-right Brazilian Social Democracy Party (Partido da Social Democracia Brasileira, PSDB). Literacy had increased dramatically before the new republican constitution ended the literacy requirement for voting. Since then, the share of voters has stabilized at around 75–80 percent of adults.[8] The importance of income and education for electoral participation was further attenuated by other equally important policies, such as holding elections on Sundays, free media access to electoral campaigns, and electronic voting.[9]

### Redemocratization and the Rise of Petismo

Brazil held its first universal presidential election in 1989, following the promulgation of the new constitution of 1988. The election marked a new era of political activity. It included as much as twenty-two candidates in the first round, representing a diversity of ideological affiliations. Fernando Collor de Mello, from the conservative PRN (Partido da Reconstrução Nacional), received over 30 percent of votes in the first round, and was elected president of Brazil in the second round with 53 percent of popular votes against PT candidate Lula da Silva (see Figure 14.2). Collor's presidency was marked by the implementation of a neoliberal program aimed primarily at curbing hyperinflation, which involved the privatization of public companies, opening to free trade, and cuts in public spending. In 1994, Fernando Henrique Cardoso of the PSDB, whose policies as minister of finance had been efficient at fighting inflation, won the presidential election directly in the first round with 54.3 percent of

8. In theory, this proportion should be close to 100 percent given compulsory voting for persons aged eighteen and over. The 20 percent gap may be due to the fact that voting is still voluntary for illiterates (between 7 and 20 percent of the adult population during this period), for citizens above seventy years of age, for those who are sick on polling day, and for those not in their constituency due to state service on voting day. Literate adults aged between eighteen and seventy who miss three consecutive elections without a justification are subject to a fine of 3 to 10 percent of the minimum wage. If the fine is not paid, they risk becoming ineligible for civil servant positions, among other penalties.

9. M. Arretche, ed., *Paths of Inequality in Brazil* (Springer, 2019).

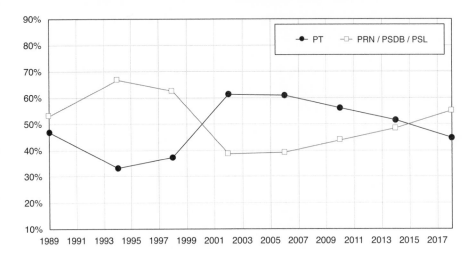

FIGURE 14.2. Presidential election results in Brazil, 1989–2018
*Data Source:* Authors' computations using official election results (see wpid.world).
*Note:* The figure shows the share of votes received by Brazilian political parties in the second round of presidential elections between 1989 and 2018. In 2018, the PT (Fernando Haddad) received 45% of votes. PT: Partido dos Trabalhadores; PRN: Partido da Reconstrução Nacional; PSDB: Partido da Social Democracia Brasileira; PSL: Partido Social Liberal.

votes (Lula received only 27 percent), and he was reelected in 1998 with 51.1 percent of popular support (against 31.7 percent for Lula). Cardoso continued Collor's privatization programs, but he was also the first president to implement large-scale social policies, such as the 2001 *Bolsa Escola,* a program of transfers dedicated to stimulate school participation, and the *Auxílio Gás,* which subsidized cooking gas for poor families.

Following Brazil's currency crisis, which started just after Cardoso's reelection, slower growth and rising unemployment eroded popular support for the leader of the PSDB. In 2002, Lula, demanding a new brand of politics, won the election in the second round with 61.3 percent of votes. Due to great uncertainty in financial markets prior to the election, he had penned the *Carta ao povo brasileiro,* a text in which he promised not to maintain the financial-monetary policy of Brazil if he won. His two terms (2002–2006 and 2006–2010) were marked by the implementation of vast public welfare and investment policies, but also by vote-buying scandals. A year before the 2006 election, the PT entered into a

tacit alliance with the established PMDB after the *Mensalão* corruption case threatened to bring down the president. As the direct heir of the only opposition party during most of the dictatorship, the PMDB was a decisive parliamentary force in the subsequent decades, and often the largest single party in the congress.[10] Prior to this alliance, the PT relied on punctual parliamentary support to implement its program. This support was arithmetically unstable, given the large and growing number of parties in the congress and the emergence of corruption cases in the PT.[11]

In 2010, Dilma Rousseff was elected president on a platform of extending Lula's achievements. She was reelected by a tight margin in 2014 against the PSDB candidate Aécio Neves, with 51.64 percent of votes. In 2016, during the sharpest recession the country had experienced since the early 1980s, allegations of accounting manipulations in the budget led to the initiation of an impeachment process against Rousseff, which saw Vice President Michel Temer (PMDB) take over her role. The process was preceded by the termination of the PT-PMDB alliance, which exploded with the ongoing revelations of the *Lava Jato* bribery investigations. The 2018 election occurred in a context of exceptional political and ideological polarization. Lula, then in prison on corruption charges, was barred from running as the PT's candidate and was replaced by his running mate, the former mayor of São Paulo Fernando Haddad. Jair Bolsonaro—a former military captain, and a congressman for twenty-seven years—of the far-right Social Liberal Party (PSL) topped the first round of the presidential election with 46 percent of votes against only 29 percent for Haddad and 12 percent for Ciro Gomes of the PDT. Bolsonaro was elected president with 55 percent of votes in the second round, promoting an economically liberal (pro-market) and socially conservative agenda (strongly opposing same-sex marriage, abortion, and secularism), with a strong stance against the political elite (especially the PT and its left-wing partners).

### From Collor de Mello to Bolsonaro: Political Transitions and Economic Change

As documented above, political change in Brazil since redemocratization can be defined by the rise and fall of the PT. These changes coincided with the improved macroeconomic conditions of the 2000s, the sharp recession

---

10. See appendix Figure A2, wpid.world.

11. In 2002, nineteen parties obtained seats in the parliament. This steadily increased to thirty by 2018.

of the mid-2010s, and the growing salience of corruption scandals. The victory of Bolsonaro in 2018 can be attributed in large part to unique contextual factors. That being said, there is more to party politics in Brazil than the limited role of charismatic leaders and short-term material gains.

In spite of a political system characterized by high party fragmentation and vote-seeking strategies, the PT emerged in the 1980s as a radical left-wing party with a strong ideological and organizational basis.[12] The party originally mobilized large networks of highly educated, middle-class urban populations who believed in the viability of socialism and in the party's redistributive stance. During the 1990s, however, popular support for Cardoso's *Plano Real* "suggested that the PT's promises to combat deep structural causes of poverty and inequality (for example, land distribution) were much less attractive to poor voters than immediate albeit limited improvements."[13] The PT's victory in 2002 was largely the result of a strategic shift to the center-left, though some fundamental ideologies were still represented, which ensured the support of unions and the urban middle class.[14] Even if Lula's welfare programs should be thought of in continuity with previous governments, there is extensive evidence that minimum wage increases and welfare programs during his first mandate, and in particular the *Bolsa Família*, led to a dramatic change in the Workers' Party's voting base, as poor voters with low levels of economic security, especially those concentrated in the historically deprived states of the northeast, massively turned toward the PT.[15] Since then, the PT's core principles and policy proposals have remained in line with the ideological underpinnings set during this period.

The second Lula government, a period often referred to as the *Milagrinho* (Mini miracle), was marked by higher economic growth than the preceding term. This shift was spurred mainly from the domestic expenditure side, as federal investments expanded at around 28 percent per

12. B. Ames, *The Deadlock of Democracy in Brazil* (University of Michigan Press, 2001); L. Secco, *História do PT 1978–2010* (Ateliê Editorial, 2011).

13. W. Hunter, "The Normalization of an Anomaly: The Workers' Party in Brazil," *World Politics* 59, no. 3 (2007): 459.

14. Hunter, "Normalization." See also D. Samuels, "From Socialism to Social Democracy: Party Organization and the Transformation of the Workers' Party in Brazil," *Comparative Political Studies* 37, no. 9 (2004): 999–1024.

15. C. Zucco and T. J. Power, "Bolsa Família and the Shift in Lula's Electoral Base, 2002–2006: A Reply to Bohn," *Latin American Research Review* 48, no. 2 (2013): 3–24; W. Hunter and T. J. Power, "Rewarding Lula: Executive Power, Social Policy, and the Brazilian Elections of 2006," *Latin American Politics and Society* 49, no. 1 (2007): 1–30.

year. Household consumption doubled its growth from the preceding period, while the real value of the minimum wage and social assistance transfers continued to rise.[16] These injections made Brazil quite robust to the global financial crisis, allowing Lula to leave office with high approval ratings. Yet, these indicators began to slow down during Dilma's first term. The price of commodities fell over the period, depressing the value of exports, while the government cut back on spending and increasingly turned to supply-side policies (tax and credit policy) to steer the economy, which precipitated a domestic recession during the PT's final two years in power.

### The Politicization of Inequality: Income, Education, and the New Welfare State

The structure of income inequality in Brazil is unique in the concentration observed at the very top of the distribution, where 150,000 people accumulate close to 15 percent of the country's national income.[17] It has also always been characterized by a tight relationship between low intergenerational mobility and a strong education gradient. Since the 1988 constitution, the general level of education has expanded significantly, with the share of individuals who attended university rising from 8 percent to 24 percent, while the share of illiterate or primary-educated individuals decreased from 70 percent to 26 percent between 1989 and 2018.[18] That being said, educational inequalities remain very significant: as much as 10 percent of the voting-age population in 2018 declared having never completed primary education.

How have these inequalities translated into different forms of political representation since 1989? Figure 14.3 represents the share of votes received by the PT among three broad groups: the poorest 50 percent, the next 40 percent, and the richest 10 percent of earners.[19] A complete reversal

16. L. Carvalho, *Valsa brasileira: Do boom ao caos econômico* (Editora Todavia, 2018).

17. L. Assouad, L. Chancel, and M. Morgan, "Extreme Inequality: Evidence from Brazil, India, the Middle East, and South Africa," *American Economic Association: Papers and Proceedings* 108 (2018): 119–123.

18. See appendix Table A3, wpid.world.

19. We focus on the determinants of support for the PT in the second round of presidential elections. This has the advantage of showing how voters have been divided into two broad coalitions representing different ideological affiliations.

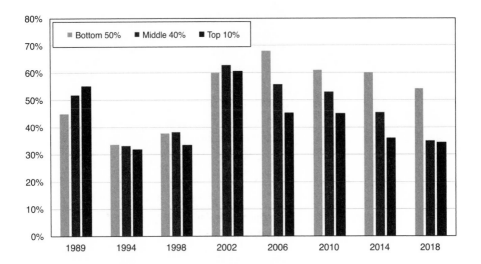

FIGURE 14.3. The PT vote by income in Brazil, 1989–2018
*Data Source:* Authors' computations using Brazilian electoral surveys (see wpid.world).
*Note:* The figure shows the share of votes received by the Workers' Party (Partido dos Trabalhadores, PT) in the second round of presidential elections by household income group. In 2018, 54% of bottom 50% income earners voted PT, compared to 34% of top 10% income earners.

of the link between income and support for the PT has gradually occurred in the past thirty years. In 1989, support for the PT was highest in the top decile; in 2018, low-income voters had become substantially more likely than the rest of the electorate to vote PT. Two separate phases can be identified. In the elections of 1994, 1998, and 2002, income was not significantly associated with vote choice in the second round of presidential elections. This corresponds to the period of widespread support for Cardoso's macroeconomic policies, which were not particularly targeted at specific groups, as well as Lula's landslide victory in 2002. This election was followed by a clear rupture in 2006: the share of top 10 percent voters supporting Lula dropped by 15 percentage points, while the share of bottom 50 percent voters supporting him increased significantly. This is in line with the electoral impact of new social investment policies, in particular the *Bolsa Família,* the minimum wage, and the expansion of public services outside of cities.

Higher support for the PT among poorer earners continued in the elections of 2010, 2014, and 2018, even though the PT did receive decreasing vote shares among all income groups. A particularly interesting evolution was the unprecedented convergence of the middle class and the elites in the last election: while the middle 40 percent were less likely to vote against the PT than the top 10 percent in 2006, 2010, and 2014, they became approximately as likely to do so in 2018. The 2018 election, therefore, divided the electorate into two groups: the poor, who voted in majority for Fernando Haddad, and the rest of the population, which was more biased against the PT than in any other election.[20]

The same reversal is visible when looking at education (Figure 14.4). In 1989, about 62 percent of tertiary-educated voters voted for Lula, compared to only 42 percent of illiterates or voters with only primary education; in 2018, it was almost the exact opposite. An interesting difference with the income gradient is that the PT was consistently supported by higher-educated voters in 1994 and 1998, while top-income earners were not more or less likely to vote for Lula in these two elections. This is consistent with the existing literature pointing to the educated "middle class" as being the original supporters of the PT.

Figure 14.5 plots the difference between the share of poorest 50 percent earners voting PT and the share of the top 50 percent voting PT from 1989 to 2018, before and after controlling for other individual variables. There has been a complete reversal in the relative support for the PT among the poor, who used to be more supportive of conservative parties and have gradually become much more favorable to the Workers' Party than the rest of the electorate. Controlling for education, age, gender, region, and rural-urban location does reduce the effect of income on the vote. This is because higher support for the PT among low-income voters is in part due to increasing votes coming from lower-educated voters, rural voters, and poorer regions—in particular the northeast (see the following section). After accounting for the independent effects of all these variables, income appears to be nonsignificant in 1989: all things being equal, poorer voters were not more or less likely to vote for Lula. How-

20. Unfortunately, the income variable available from Datafolha surveys does not allow further decompositions of votes within the bottom 50 percent. Evidence from the Comparative Study of Electoral Systems, however, does suggest that support for the PT also decreases with income within the bottom 50 percent of income earners. See appendix Figure C2, wpid.world.

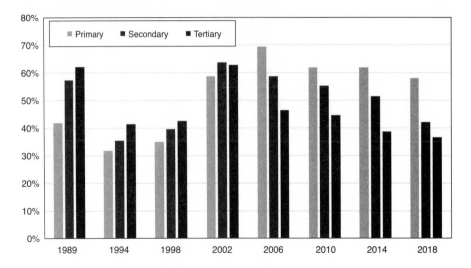

FIGURE 14.4. The PT vote by education level in Brazil, 1989–2018

*Data Source:* Authors' computations using Brazilian electoral surveys (see wpid.world).

*Note:* The figure shows the share of votes received by the Workers' Party (Partido dos Trabalhadores, PT) in the second round of presidential elections by education level. In 2018, 58% of primary-educated voters (or illiterates) voted PT, compared to 37% of university graduates.

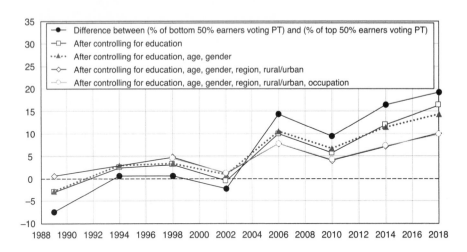

FIGURE 14.5. Political conflict and income in Brazil, 1989–2018

*Data Source:* Authors' computations using Brazilian electoral surveys (see wpid.world).

*Note:* The figure shows the difference between the share of bottom 50% earners and the share of top 50% earners voting for the Partido dos Trabalhadores (PT) in the second round of presidential elections, before and after controls. Support for the PT has become increasingly concentrated among low-income earners since 1989. In 2018, low-income voters were 19 percentage points more likely than high-income voters to vote PT.

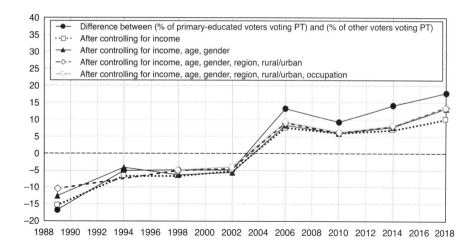

FIGURE 14.6. The educational cleavage in Brazil, 1989–2018
*Data Source:* Authors' computations using Brazilian electoral surveys (see wpid.world).
*Note:* The figure shows the difference between the share of primary-educated voters (or illiterates) and the share of other voters voting for the Partido dos Trabalhadores (PT) in the second round of presidential elections, before and after controls. Support for the PT has become increasingly concentrated among lower-educated voters since 1989. In 2018, primary-educated voters were 18 percentage points more likely than other voters to vote PT.

ever, the overall trend is robust to the consideration of other covariates, and in 2018 the bottom 50 percent were still more likely to support the PT by about 10 percentage points.

A similar evolution is visible when comparing popular votes for the PT from illiterate and primary-educated voters with those from voters with a higher level of education (Figure 14.6). An important difference with income, however, is that education remained significant at the beginning of the period after accounting for the effects of other individual variables: lower-educated voters were less likely to vote for the PT by 10 percentage points in 1989. Thus, income and education should not be seen as synonymous. This education gradient was also associated with significant differences in voting behaviors across age groups: until the early 2000s, younger cohorts corresponding to the new, higher-educated generations were more likely to support Lula than Collor or Cardoso.[21]

21. See appendix Figures A5 and A6, wpid.world.

In summary, the analysis of electoral behaviors in Brazil points to a unique case of a policy-driven shift to new class cleavages. The political system of the 1990s seems to have involved the PT's limited core of higher-educated, urban voters, next to a sparse coalition of volatile voters supporting the candidate considered to be most credible at fighting inflation and promoting growth. The social policies implemented during the early 2000s, and their relative success at reducing multidimensional poverty and labor income inequalities at the bottom of the distribution, coincided with the emergence of new class allegiances. In comparative perspective, this convergence of economic and intellectual elites toward the right of the political spectrum stands in contrast with the dynamics visible in other Western democracies. In Europe and the United States, university graduates have become increasingly supportive of social democratic, socialist, and green parties since the early 1970s, while top-income earners have remained more likely to vote for conservative parties, leading to the emergence of "multi-elite party systems" (see Chapter 1). In Brazil, by contrast, it was higher-educated voters (*alongside* higher-income voters) who were relatively more inclined toward Bolsonaro, with over 63 percent of them voting for the PSL candidate in the second round of the presidential election (Figure 14.4).

## The Regionalization of Political Conflicts

Brazil has always been characterized by an important regional divide. Demographically, about 45 percent of the voting-age population has been concentrated in the richer southeastern region since 1989, as compared to about 25 percent in the northeast, 15 percent in the south, and 15 percent in the north and center of the country.[22] In tandem with the evolution of the income and educational cleavages, the spatial distribution of PT voters has also undergone a notable shift. In the 1989 runoff, about 52 percent of residents from the richer southeastern and southern regions opted for Lula, compared to 43 percent of voters in the northeast (Figure 14.7). Lula thus captured the relatively more well-off, more educated, and younger voters residing in urban places: 60 percent of urban dwellers voted for the PT candidate in 1989.[23] Over time, as the PT vote share grew, the gap between the "urban south" and the "rural north"

22. See appendix Table A3, wpid.world.
23. See appendix Figure A7, wpid.world.

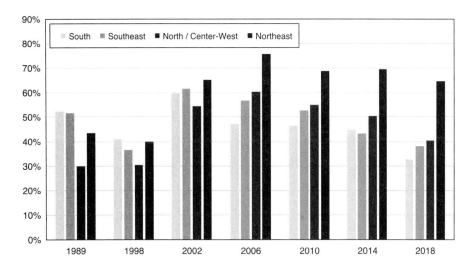

FIGURE 14.7. The PT vote by region in Brazil, 1989–2018
*Data Source:* Authors' computations using Brazilian electoral surveys (see wpid.world).
*Note:* The figure shows the share of votes received by the Workers' Party (Partido dos Trabalhadores, PT) in the second round of presidential elections by region. In 2018, 65% of voters of the Northeast Region voted PT, compared to 33% of voters of the South Region.

closed, and eventually reversed in favor of the northeast from 2002 onward. The PT claimed 76 percent of the northeastern electorate in 2006—a share that would fall over time, but never significantly below 65 percent. By contrast, in the south and southeast the PT vote faced a secular decline since 2002, falling from 60 percent to about 35 percent.

By the end of the 2010s, in terms of magnitude, the strongest predictor of the PT presidential vote had become being a resident of the northeast—historically the most deprived region in the country.[24] The difference between the share of voters living in the northeast region voting PT and the share of voters living in other regions voting PT reached over 25 percentage points in 2018, after having been −5 percentage points in 1989 (Figure 14.8). Even after controlling for income, education, and other sociodemographic

24. M. Arretche, "The Geography of Access to Basic Services in Brazil," in *Paths of Inequality in Brazil: A Half-Century of Changes,* ed. M. Arretche (Springer, 2018), 137–161.

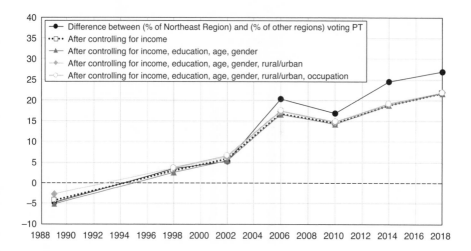

FIGURE 14.8. The regional cleavage in Brazil, 1989–2018
*Data Source:* Authors' computations using Brazilian electoral surveys (see wpid.world).
*Note:* The figure shows the difference between the share of voters living in the Northeast
Region and the share of voters living in other regions voting for the Partido dos
Trabalhadores (PT) in the second round of presidential elections, before and after
controls. Support for the PT has become increasingly concentrated in the Northeast
Region, where the PT's vote share was 27 percentage points higher than in the rest of
Brazil in 2018.

characteristics, similar magnitudes remain. The dramatic change again
seems to have taken place during Lula's first presidential term (2002–2006),
as transfers and infrastructural investment benefited the most disadvantaged families in Brazil, which are overwhelmingly located in the northeastern states. With a program heavily tilted toward poverty eradication
and material upgrading, the urban-biased vote that the PT used to get has
also gradually disappeared (Figure 14.9).

While it is true that the PT's support in the northeast has waned since
2006, it has done so proportionately less than in the other regions—
falling by 10 percentage points by 2018, rather than 20 points in the
case of the southeast (Figure 14.7). Whether the PT will be able to maintain its dominance of the northeast since it has lost the presidency will
be a test of time. This will likely depend on whether the party has truly
transformed the region's historic elite-voter linkages and built sustainable programmatic electoral allegiances.

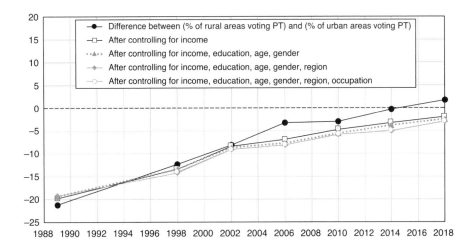

FIGURE 14.9. The rural-urban cleavage in Brazil, 1989–2018
*Data Source:* Authors' computations using Brazilian electoral surveys (see wpid.world).
*Note:* The figure shows the difference between the share of voters living in rural areas and the share of voters living in cities voting for the Partido dos Trabalhadores (PT) in the second round of presidential elections, before and after controls. The vote share obtained by the PT in rural areas was 21 percentage points lower than in urban areas in 1989, compared to 2 percentage points higher in 2018.

## Other Sociological Determinants of Electoral Behavior in Brazil

We conclude our analysis by looking more specifically at other forms of political divides. Race was at the heart of the country's political and economic history (see the first section). Inequalities between racial groups have remained significant to the present, with a larger share of slave descendants still living in the poorer northeast region and achieving lower average income and education levels.[25] In 2018, over 40 percent of Brazilians identified themselves as *Pardos* or *Morenos*, more or less corresponding to a "mixed" identity, while 39 percent self-identified as Whites (*Brancos*), 15 percent as Blacks (*Pretos*), and 5 percent as belonging to other groups.[26] The large share of individuals in the "multiracial" category speaks to Brazil's unique history of racial mixing and relative depo-

25. On the causal effect of racial affiliations on education opportunities, see L. Marteleto and M. Dondero, "Racial Inequality in Education in Brazil: A Twins Fixed-Effect Approach," *Demography* 53, no. 4 (2016): 1185–1205.
26. See appendix Table A3, wpid.world.

liticization of racial identities. In contrast to other colonial states like South Africa, where political unification and democratization at the turn of the twentieth century were restricted to the White population and based on an ideology of White unity (see Chapter 16), Brazil's 1891 constitution did not contain any reference to race that would formally exclude former slaves from political participation. Such exclusion did effectively take place in the following decades through literacy requirements, but it was not explicitly based on race. In South Africa, the search for White unity would lead to racial categories becoming increasingly rigid, and their institutional codifications would have long-term consequences for the representation of political and social inequalities. Almost the exact opposite happened in Brazil, where governments of the early twentieth century instead pushed for a process of incorporation dedicated to "Whitening" the populations of Indian or African blood. This would contribute to putting other dimensions of political conflict (in particular regional affiliations), instead of racial identities, at the heart of party politics.[27]

Available data does not allow us to track the evolution of the link between racial identities and political affiliations since redemocratization, but recent evidence points to significant differences in vote choices across racial groups. In 2018, 34 percent of Whites voted for the PT, as compared to 50 percent of *Pardos/Morenos* and 57 percent of Blacks.[28] This is consistent with the history of the PT, which has given more attention to Afro-Brazilian activists as it broadened its appeal beyond the southern White working class to encompass all occupational categories over time.[29] Two interesting facts are however important to stress. First, these differences are moderate in comparative perspective. In France, for example, differences in support for social democratic, socialist, and communist parties between Muslims and non-Muslims have reached levels higher than 30 percentage points in recent years, a figure comparable to that observed in the case of the African American vote for the Democratic Party in the United States (see Chapter 2). Sociocultural cleavages are even more extreme in South Africa, where democratization has come

27. E. S. Lieberman, *Race and Regionalism in the Politics of Taxation in Brazil and South Africa* (Cambridge University Press, 2003).

28. See appendix Figure A8, wpid.world.

29. L. A. Warner, "The Workers' Party and the Elimination of Racial Inequality: A New Stage in the Politicization of Race in Brazil" (working paper, Carleton College, 2005) https://acad.carleton.edu/curricular/POSC/faculty/montero/Lesley%20Warner.pdf.

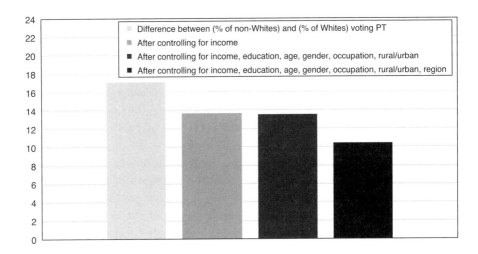

FIGURE 14.10. The racial cleavage in Brazil, 2018
*Data Source:* Authors' computations using Brazilian electoral surveys (see wpid.world).
*Note:* The figure shows the difference between the share of self-declared non-White voters and the share of White voters voting for the Partido dos Trabalhadores (PT) in the second round of presidential elections, before and after controls. In 2018, non-White voters were 17 percentage points more likely to vote PT before controls and 10 percentage points more likely to do so after controls (all other things being equal).

with a party system structured almost entirely along racial lines (see Chapter 16). Second, racial differences in vote choice in Brazil are driven partly by the other forms of political cleavages identified in the rest of this chapter. The difference between the share of non-Whites and the share of Whites voting for the PT was about 17 percentage points in 2018, but this difference drops to 14 percentage points when controlling for income and to 10 percentage points when controlling for education, age, gender, occupation, rural/urban location, and region (see Figure 14.10). Race therefore does have an independent effect on support for the PT, but this effect is relatively weak. Evidence based on other surveys suggests comparable patterns since 2002: if anything, relative support for the PT among non-Whites was slightly higher in 2014 than in 2018, and was lowest in 2002.[30]

30. See appendix Figure C6, wpid.world.

The findings on occupation are in line with the conclusion that income, education, and geography are at the heart of changing political identifications in Brazil. In most developed countries, self-employed workers and farmers have always been significantly more likely than wage earners to support conservative parties. This is not the case in Brazil, where differences across occupational categories have remained weak and are mostly explained by differences in earnings, education levels, and location.[31]

Two interesting changes, which are orthogonal to socioeconomic status, are however worth mentioning. The first one is what seems to be the growing importance of religious identities in the last election. From 2014 to 2018, the gap in support for the PT between Protestants and other religious groups grew significantly, from about 5 percentage points to 17 percentage points, and this change is robust to controlling for other individual characteristics (see Figure 14.11). This is consistent with Bolsonaro's particular appeal among Evangelicals. Again, it is nonetheless important to stress that such gaps are significantly lower than those found in many other developed and developing countries (for example, India; see Chapter 9). The voting behaviors of women have also followed patterns that are at odds with the long-run trends visible in other dimensions. At first strongly biased against the PT, in particular in 2002, women became much more supportive of the party in recent years: in 2018, they were more likely to support Haddad than Bolsonaro by 10 percentage points.[32] Such changes could well be due to candidate effects rather than to more profound differences in policy or ideological positions.

### Understanding the Rise of Bolsonaro: Growth, Inequality, and the Squeezed Middle Class

Exactly one year prior to the 2018 election, Brazilian voters were asked about the issues that would be most decisive in determining their vote. Contrary to what one might except, corruption was not the most important problem for a majority of Brazilians at the time: 32 percent of survey respondents chose health, 16 percent selected education, and 14 percent insisted on job creation as the policy areas that would primarily influence their candidate choices. "Fighting against corruption" was chosen by only

31. See appendix Figures A9, A10, and A11, wpid.world.
32. See appendix Figures A14 and A15, wpid.world.

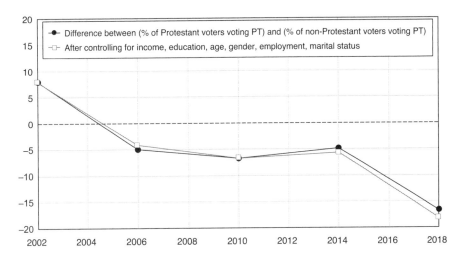

FIGURE 14.11. The religious cleavage in Brazil, 2002–2018
*Data Source:* Authors' computations using electoral (CSES) surveys (see wpid.world).
*Note:* The figure shows the difference between the share of Protestants and the share of
Catholics, nonbelievers, and other voters voting for the Partido dos Trabalhadores (PT)
in the second round of presidential elections, before and after controls. In 2018,
Protestant voters were less likely to vote PT by 17 percentage points.

18 percent of individuals. Strikingly, however, the intersection of issue relevance with personal socioeconomic characteristics appears to be fundamental in explaining the polarization of the Brazilian electorate.

Figure 14.12 decomposes the most important issues reported by survey respondents by the income group to which they belong. Poorer voters appear to be significantly more likely to emphasize health and employment matters, while richer citizens tend to attach greater importance to corruption and public security. It is striking to note that while the poor have been the group most affected by homicides in Brazil, they seem to give more weight to improvements in their material conditions, especially if violence is seen as a symptom of poverty.

The rise of Bolsonaro can thus be explained by his ability to appeal to voters on both types of issues. By positioning himself against the corruption and the violence "tolerated" by the current democratic system and by the incumbent government, he attracted a large portion of the middle and upper classes. And by blaming the post-2014 recession and

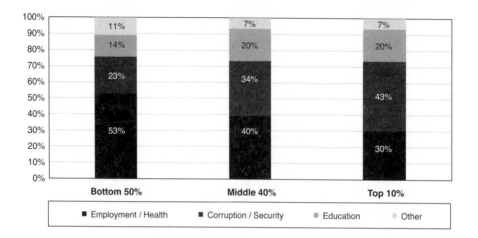

FIGURE 14.12. Reasons determining candidate choice in the 2018 presidential election by income group in Brazil

*Data Source:* Authors' computations using a survey conducted by the Datafolha Institute in October 2017 (see wpid.world).

*Note:* The figure decomposes answers to the question of the issue that would be most decisive in respondents' vote choice in the 2018 election by income group. In 2017, 53% of bottom 50% income earners considered employment and health to be the key issues determining their vote, compared to 30% of top 10% income earners.

unemployment rise on the PT, by supporting cuts to taxes and public spending as well as further privatization programs, he appeased a broad group comprised of poorer voters and many middle-class citizens and business elites. Amid the "crisis of representation," the fact that Bolsonaro was a political "outsider" facilitated his popularity.[33] The geography of the 2018 election supports this conclusion: only the northeastern region gave a majority to the PT's candidate, Fernando Haddad. These were voters who remained loyal to the party that they associated with vastly improving their economic opportunities, independent of the recent economic downturn, and who perceived that they had a lot to lose from the consequences of Bolsonaro's economic program.

33. J. A. Alves, "Transformation or Substitution? The Workers' Party and the Right in Northeast Brazil," *Journal of Politics in Latin America* 10, no. 1 (2018): 99–132.

While issues such as corruption, security, and even religion played a role in bringing Bolsonaro to power, economic-class divisions tied to geography appear to be the strongest cleavage in Brazilian society today. But these did not form overnight. The distribution of economic growth during the expansionary part of the PT's time in office (2002–2014) is a key metric by which to judge subsequent political developments. While average national income per adult grew by 18 percent over the period, the majority of the gains were split between two distant groups—the poorest half of the population and the very richest part. Most families in the bottom 50 percent (concentrating households from the northeast) saw their incomes grow by nearly twice the national average.[34] Growth was lowest for individuals between the 70th and 99th percentiles in the distribution.[35] This "squeezed middle class" can be seen as Brazil's "left-behind." Above them, significant income growth was captured by the Brazilian elite over the period due to a mix of favorable external conditions (commodity prices, exchange rates) and favorable internal conditions (large public investments, rising household consumption, industrial credit subsidies, and stable tax rates). Notably, these were the groups less likely to vote for the party that oversaw their prosperity.

Thus, the middle classes were pitted against the least privileged groups in society for their share of national income, which would become increasingly scarce after the economic slowdown from 2014. Furthermore, with prices beginning to rise from 2013, following rising labor costs—including for services routinely used by the upper-middle class (for example, domestic service)—this cohort would increasingly lose faith in a Workers' Party that was perceived to be only directly concerned for the poor and indirectly benefiting the very rich. On top of this, the subsequent economic decline, increased violence, and the multiplication of corruption charges against high-profile politicians across the political spectrum, but especially in the PT, along with the return of an invigorated Lula to the electoral process, made elites increasingly hostile to further PT-led executives.

34. On the regional composition of income groups, see appendix Figures B3 and B4, wpid.world.
35. See appendix Figure A16, wpid.world.

## Conclusion

Brazil has a long history of political divisions and social inequality. More than thirty years since the adoption of universal suffrage, Brazilian redemocratization can largely be characterized by the rise and fall of the Workers' Party, from its early roots among the White, highly educated young wage earners of southern states to its metamorphosis into a national multiclass party in the early 2000s and progressively into a party of the poor and marginalized citizenry from 2006 onward. The PT's fall may not be as definitive as the trend is suggesting, given its stranglehold of the populous northeast region. Compared to other countries analyzed in this book, the evolution of political cleavages in Brazil has been marked by important temporal shifts. But the singularity of Brazil is that voting patterns have taken a course inverse to those in more advanced countries. Rather than moving the country toward a multi-elite party system, Brazilian political cleavages—as expressed in presidential elections—have increasingly come to be defined on unidimensional class lines, with high-education and high-income voters converging in their rejection of the "traditional" center-left party.

PT's gradual process of consolidating mass support after the implementation of social investment policies is remarkably similar to the dynamics visible in Thailand in about the same period, when Thaksin Shinawatra's agricultural subsidies and minimum wage increases contributed to a new polarization of the political space along class lines (see Chapter 12). In both cases, it was redistributive policies during periods of strong economic growth that drove new divisions between the "rich" and the "poor." It would be wrong to posit that such political mobilization can be attributed solely to the "populist" rhetoric of a charismatic leader. Both in Thailand and Brazil, this mobilization also came with new, persistent party identifications. The emergence of class cleavages in Brazil therefore goes beyond short-term appeals and can be understood as rooted in a broader process of mass polarization brought about by how the fruits of economic growth were distributed. The rise of a political outsider like Bolsonaro in 2018 should equally be understood as a product of decisions made by the incumbent party and the contextual factors that allowed the PT to sow the seeds of its declining popularity.

# 15

# Social Inequalities, Identity, and the Structure of Political Cleavages in Argentina, Chile, Costa Rica, Colombia, Mexico, and Peru, 1952–2019

OSCAR BARRERA, ANA LEIVA, CLARA MARTÍNEZ-TOLEDANO, AND ÁLVARO ZÚÑIGA-CORDERO

## Introduction

This chapter exploits existing electoral surveys to analyze the political representation of social inequalities since the mid-twentieth century in six Latin American countries: Argentina, Chile, Costa Rica, Colombia, Mexico, and Peru. With the end of Spanish rule, nearly all Latin American countries were divided by the same liberal-conservative cleavage.[1] The liberals' ideological principles were anticlericalism, federalism, and free trade, while conservatives defended the church and favored centralization and protectionism. Despite this common point of departure in the nineteenth century, contemporary Latin American party systems are very diverse and no longer reflect this traditional cleavage.

Among the six countries we have analyzed, Colombia is the only one in which the traditional cleavage survived into the twentieth century. Prolonged and intense interparty fighting forged strong identification with the two traditional parties, so that the two-party system collapsed only after the adoption of electoral reforms in the early 2000s. The absence

We are grateful to Lavih Abraham, Ronald Alfaro-Redondo, María Julia Blanco, Francesco Bogliacino, Nicolás Dvoskin, Ignacio Flores, Gustavo García, Amory Gethin, Kyong Mazaro, and Thomas Piketty for their useful advice.

1. M. Coppedge, "The Evolution of Latin American Party Systems," in *Politics, Society, and Democracy: Latin America,* ed. S. Mainwaring and A. Valenzuela (Perseus, 1999), 171–206.

of political opportunities for outsiders contributed to the formation of left-leaning guerrilla movements in the early 1960s, among which the most powerful was the Armed Revolutionary Forces of Colombia (Fuerzas Armadas Revolucionarias de Colombia, FARC).

With the beginning of the twenty-first century, Colombia's political landscape experienced a profound transformation. The two traditional parties lost part of their hegemony to the benefit of left-leaning political groups, and the independent Álvaro Uribe consolidated a new right-wing political ideology. Positions on the FARC conflict have created class cleavages since the beginning of Uribism that have persisted to the present. The country's main problem has remained corruption, especially for high-income and high-educated anti-Uribist voters, while for low-income and low-educated Uribist voters the armed conflict is seen as more important, as they live in rural areas and have been more exposed to the violence.

Class cleavages are also prominent in Argentina and Chile. In Argentina, the hegemony of Peronism, which has governed the country for almost four decades since the 1940s, has created a sharp division of the electorate between Peronists and anti-Peronists. Although Peronism is well represented across all classes and sectors of Argentinian society, the low-income and low-educated are persistently more prone to vote for Peronist candidates.

The predictatorship political structure in Chile was characterized by the existence of three historical cleavages: Catholic-secular, class, and urban-rural. Since the end of Pinochet's dictatorship in 1990, a fourth cleavage emerged, splitting voters according to their support or opposition to the dictatorship and dominating the previous historical conflicts. The last decade has been a period of social unrest, due mainly to rising income disparities, market-oriented education, and dissatisfaction with the governing coalitions' responses to social demands. Political polarization has consequently increased, exacerbating class cleavages.

Costa Rica and Mexico have transitioned from, respectively, two-party and one-party dominant systems to more fractionalized multiparty systems. The 1948 revolution was the last violent political episode in the history of Costa Rica. The winning side established the National Liberation Party (Partido Liberación Nacional, PLN), of center-left social democratic orientation, which would become the hegemonic political party. The losing side reconstituted into a number of political parties and coalitions of center-right Christian democratic orientation that won the

elections three times before its political heirs established the Social Christian Unity Party (Partido Unidad Social Cristiana, PUSC) in 1983. The main political cleavage during the period was thus between the PLN's supporters and its adversaries. Dissatisfaction with corruption scandals, the deterioration of the welfare state during the economic recession of the 1980s, and the neoliberal turn of the PLN from sociodemocratic to neoliberal policies led to an increase in political dissatisfaction with traditional parties, the rise of abstention, a large shift of voters toward new parties, and the emergence of competing pro-poor (PLN and PRN) and pro-rich parties (PUSC and PAC) since the 2000s.

Mexico's democratic transition during the twentieth century has been a series of iterations of electoral fraud, opposition protest, and electoral reform, which have leveled the political playing field and opened new opportunities for electoral competition. The Institutional Revolutionary Party (Partido Revolucionario Institucional, PRI), the hegemonic party inspired by the ideals of the Mexican Revolution, has declined to the benefit of new left-leaning parties and the conservative National Action Party (Partido Acción Nacional, PAN). Nonetheless, as low-income, low-educated PRI voters have moved toward both PAN and the left, the country has maintained during this process a reasonably stable multi-elite party system, according to which higher education attainment is associated with a higher vote for the left, and higher income is associated with a higher vote for the PAN.

Peru had until the mid-twentieth century multiclass electoral constituencies mobilized by oligarchic leaders using clientelist networks. Strong class divisions in voting patterns did not emerge until the 1980s, after the rise of labor unions and urban social organizations in the 1970s. The strength of popular organizations had eroded by the end of the 1980s, however, in a context of deep economic crisis and political violence. This process made room for a new type of personalist leadership, initiated by Alberto Fujimori, which has continued to the present. Peru thus has presented volatile income and education cleavages since the mid-1990s. Indigenous issues have been gradually incorporated into the political process. They were initiated in the 1990s by Fujimori, who is of Japanese descent, and continued in the 2000s during the presidential campaigns of Alejandro Toledo and Ollanta Humala, who have Indigenous origins. Ethnic cleavages have thus blurred class cleavages in the last three decades.

## Argentina

### Peronism and the Making of Argentina's Party System

With the declaration of independence in 1816 and the military defeat of the Spanish Empire in 1824, a prolonged period of civil wars led to the formation of the federal republic of Argentina. From 1869 to 1914, the population grew by about 338 percent,[2] due in part to a great migratory wave coming mainly from Italy and Spain. During the European wars of the first half of the twentieth century, Argentina also became an important supplier of meat and grains to the belligerent countries, which enabled it to attain high levels of wealth and education and a relatively egalitarian social structure. However, tensions rose due to workers' poor social conditions.

Before 1930, the leader Hipólito Yrigoyen from the Radical Civic Union (Unión Cívica Radical, UCR) governed the country. Employing anti-oligarchy rhetoric, he gained support from the middle class in urban and rural areas, and a share of the urban working class. In the 1930s, a conservative elite governed the country under controverted charges of fraud and corruption. In 1943, Colonel Juan Domingo Perón participated in the military coup that overthrew the conservative government of Ramón Castillo, and he took control of the Ministry of Labor. Perón embraced the pro-social and anti-oligarchy principles of Yrigoyen, while arguing that the UCR lacked legitimacy to defend the interests of workers.[3] In 1946, Perón won the elections with the newly created Labor Party, a political organization formed with the support of labor unions, the military, and the Catholic Church. In response, an anti-Peronist block was formed with the support of the United States. The electoral alliance La Unión Democrática (UD) was composed of the UCR, the Socialist Party, the Progressive Democratic Party, the Communist Party, the Rural Society, and the Industrial Union. The UD accused Perón of being antidemocratic, which was the basis of the anti-Peronist rhetoric during his regime and after his fall.

2. Authors' estimation based on the 1869 and 1914 population censuses published by INDEC (Instituto Nacional de Estadística y Censos de la República de Argentina), https://www.indec.gob.ar/.

3. D. James, *Resistance and Integration: Peronism and the Argentine Working Class, 1946–1976* (Cambridge University Press, 1993).

Whereas from the Ministry of Labor Perón implemented generous social policies that strongly benefited workers, from the presidency he created a broad public health and education system, institutionalized the rights of workers and peasants, and encouraged the emergence of a class consciousness pushing workers to fight for their rights.[4] In 1947, to run for the 1952 presidential election, he founded the Justicialist Party (Partido Justicialista, PJ), which replaced the Labor Party. However, his separation from the church in 1954 led to political tensions that ended in a new violent military coup. Perón was forced into exile for about twenty years and Peronism was banned. This allowed the UCR and its political faction Integration and Development Movement (Movimiento de Integracion y Desarrollo, MID) to govern the country during the democratic periods (1958–1662 and 1963–1966). From exile, Perón organized the resistance, which jointly with political repression and the formation of guerrilla groups led to a violent era that reached its peak (el Cordobazo) in 1969. During this political crisis, in 1971 General Alejandro Lanusse restored democracy and allowed the reestablishment of political parties, including Peronism. Perón returned to office in 1973, in the middle of a dramatic right-left ideological rift within the party, which triggered the Ezeiza massacre.[5]

In 1976, two years after Perón's death, the country experienced another military coup, during which numerous left-wing activists from different parties (including Peronist) were tortured, killed, or expelled from the country.[6] The new military government adopted liberalization policies that caused a flood of imports and opened access to foreign loans, triggering a financial crisis.

The Falklands War accelerated the fall of the dictatorship and the country returned to a democratic regime in 1983. The anti-Peronist party UCR, directed by Raúl Alfonsín, won the elections. The new president refused to implement the austerity and liberalization policies advocated by multilateral institutions, but his at first heterodox policy attempts failed and resulted in hyperinflation.[7] In 1989, Carlos Menem became the

4. Coppedge, "Evolution of Latin American Party Systems."

5. In 1973, at Peron's reception at the airport, the right-wing Peronists open fire on the left-wing Peronists.

6. CONADEP, Nunca Más: Informe de la Comisión Nacional sobre la Desaparición de Personas (Eudeba, 1984).

7. E. Huber and J. D. Stephens, Democracy and the Left: Social Policy and Inequality in Latin America (University of Chicago Press, 2012).

first Peronist president after the dictatorship. During the 1990s, elections and civil liberties were institutionalized and macroeconomic stability was achieved for the first time in decades.[8]

In 1995, Menem was elected for a second term. As fears of hyperinflation faded, new issues, such as corruption and public accountability, became increasingly salient. A group of Peronists who were against Menem founded the center-left political coalition the Front for a Country in Solidarity (Frente País Solidario, FREPASO), which captured 30 percent of votes in the 1995 presidential election. FREPASO and the UCR undertook two strategic changes after 1995. First, they incorporated core elements of the neoliberal economic model, including fiscal balance, privatization, trade openness, and convertibility. Second, in 1997, both movements formed the Alliance for Work, Justice, and Education, which won the presidential elections in 1999 with Fernando de la Rúa.

Two years after the victory of Fernando de la Rúa, the Argentinian economy fell into a deep debt crisis. The unprecedented economic collapse, the successive resignation of two presidents, and a massive rebellion against the entire political elite led to the return of political instability. In 2003, the Peronist Néstor Kirchner was elected president. The "Kirchners" led the country for three consecutive terms: Néstor in 2003–2007, and his wife Cristina Fernández in 2007–2011 and 2011–2015. Political turmoil nonetheless gave rise to Let's Change (Cambiemos), a center-right force headed by Mauricio Macri, who became the president of Argentina in 2015 with the support of several unions.[9] He was defeated by the Justicialist Party's candidate, Alberto Fernández, in 2019.

### The Persistence of Class Cleavages in Argentina

Most Argentinians are loyal to one of two main political tendencies, either anti-Peronism or Peronism. In what follows, we study the relationship between several socioeconomic factors and the Peronist vote for all presidential elections from 1995 to 2019 (Figure 15.1).[10]

---

8. E. Calvo and M. V. Murillo, "Argentina: The Persistence of Peronism," *Journal of Democracy* 23, no. 2 (2012): 148–161.

9. I. Carrera, N. F. Fernández, and M. C. Cotarelo, "Trade Union Movement and the Attack from Financial Oligarchy: Argentine, 2016–2019," *Tempo Social* 32, no. 1 (2020): 75–98.

10. For data sources, see appendix Table AB1, World Political Cleavages and Inequality Database, http://wpid.world.

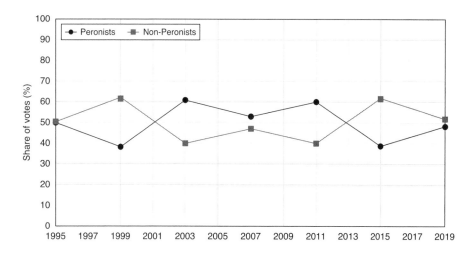

FIGURE 15.1. Election results in Argentina, 1995–2019
*Data Source:* Authors' computations using official election results (see wpid.world).
*Note:* The figure shows the share of votes received by selected groups of Argentinian political parties in general elections between 1995 and 2019. Peronist parties received 48% of votes in the 2019 election. Anti-Peronist parties are the Radical Civic Union (UCR), the Front for a Country in Solidarity (FREPASO), Acción por la Republica, Coalición Cívica ARI, Cambiemos, Frente de Izquierda, and Recrear.

The characterization of the socioeconomic structure of Peronism varies across scholars. Some have described Peronism as a movement representing working-class concerns, while others have characterized it as a multiclass movement that brings together different class interests.[11]

We find that the Peronist vote is more concentrated among lowest-educated and lowest-income voters, but with interesting variations over time (Figure 15.2). During the 1990s, in particular, Peronism received less support from low-income and lower-educated voters, driven partly by the antipopular policies adopted during Menemism (1995–1999) and by the well-structured anti-Peronist alliance between UCR and FREPASO.

Radicals attained the Argentinian presidency in 1999 but resigned two years later after a dramatic economic crisis. The Peronists' challenge was thus to recover popular support. In this context, the interim Peronist pres-

---

11. N. Lupu and S. C. Stokes, "The Social Bases of Political Parties in Argentina, 1912–2003," *Latin American Research Review* (2009): 58–87.

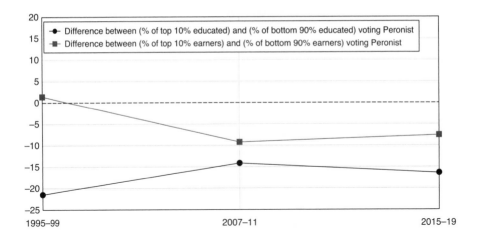

FIGURE 15.2. The Peronist vote by income and education in Argentina, 1995–2019
*Data Source:* Authors' computations using Argentinian postelectoral and political attitudes surveys (see wpid.world).
*Note:* The figure shows the relative support of highest-educated and top-income voters for Peronists, after controlling for age, gender, religious affiliation, religiosity, employment status, marital status, occupation, rural-urban location, region, ethnicity, and perceived social class. In 2015–2019, top 10% income earners were 8 percentage points less likely to vote for Peronists.

ident, Eduardo Duhalde, created an emergency conditional cash transfer and food program targeted to the poorest 20 percent citizens.[12]

The Kirchnerism terms of the 2000s came with a reduction in income inequalities. The Argentinian economy was performing well and the Peronist government extended social transfers, increased pension benefits, pushed up social benefits linked to the minimum wage, and increased the progressiveness of other social benefits. The government also strengthened unions and their bargaining power.[13] As a result, Peronism gained back popularity. The peak was reached in the 2000s, when nearly 70 percent of the poorest half of voters and primary-educated voters voted for the Kirchners.[14]

12. Huber and Stephens, *Democracy and the Left.*
13. R. Vuolo, "Asignación por Hijo" (Ciepp, 2009), https://www.ciepp.org.ar/images /N%C2%BA_21_-_Lo_Vuolo_-_Noviembre_2009.pdf.
14. See appendix Figures AA2 and AA3, wpid.world.

Political stability ended in 2015 with the onset of an economic crisis triggered by the fall in commodity prices and the breaking of relations with the Peronist central union federation.[15] As a result, popular support for the Peronists faded out, especially among lowest-educated voters, and Mauricio Macri, backed by an important share of unions, became president in 2015. In 2019, Peronists managed to gain back the support of low-income earners, due in part to a new economic crisis that disproportionately affected the most vulnerable groups in society. Despite these fluctuations, Peronism has clearly received enduring support from lowest-educated and low-income voters since the 1990s, which has contributed to the persistence of strong class cleavages in Argentina.

### Peronism and Other Socioeconomic Cleavages

Although, as we have shown, education, income, and class are important socioeconomic variables determining party choice in Argentina, the Peronist vote is also divided along other lines. Public-sector workers, self-employed individuals, and unpaid workers have been more prone to vote Peronist than private-sector workers and entrepreneurs, in line with what we observe in Colombia, Costa Rica, and Mexico, where civil servants tend to vote more for progressive parties. The Peronist vote is also stronger in urban areas, which reflects its large historical working-class electoral base since the pro-worker policies of Perón (Table 15.1). Nonetheless, the increase in Peronist votes in rural areas, northern regions, and La Pampa explained the massive support for Peronists during the 2000s, while Peronist vote shares remained relatively constant in the capital, in Cuyo, and in Patagonia.[16] After 2018, following the abortion debate, Peronism lost an important share of votes in the north, where the population is largely conservative and Catholic.[17]

Our analysis, however, does not show significant variations in the Peronist vote in terms of age or gender.[18] Religion does not seem to be an important dividing variable either, even during times when Peronist candidates such as Cristina Kirchner advertised their faith as a distinctive

---

15. S. Lazar, "Notions of Work, Patrimony, and Production," *Journal of Latin American and Caribbean Anthropology* 21, no. 2 (2016): 231–253.

16. See appendix Figures AA12 and AA13, wpid.world.

17. F. Mallimaci, V. Giménez Béliveau, and J. Esquivel, "Segunda encuesta nacional sobre creencias y actitudes religiosas en Argentina" (CONICET, 2019), http://www.ceil-conicet.gov.ar/wp-content/uploads/2019/11/ii25-2encuestacreencias.pdf.

18. See appendix Table BA3, wpid.world.

*Table 15.1*    The Structure of Political Cleavages in Argentina, 2015–2019

|  | Share of Votes Received (%) | |
|---|---|---|
|  | Peronists | Non-Peronists |
| **Education** | | |
| Primary | 55% | 45% |
| Secondary | 51% | 49% |
| Tertiary | 38% | 62% |
| **Income** | | |
| Bottom 50% | 55% | 45% |
| Middle 40% | 44% | 56% |
| Top 10% | 34% | 66% |
| **Occupation** | | |
| Public worker | 39% | 61% |
| Private worker | 34% | 66% |
| Entrepreneur | 27% | 73% |
| Self-employed | 38% | 62% |
| **Subjective Social Class** | | |
| Working class | 57% | 43% |
| Upper/Middle class | 32% | 68% |
| **Location** | | |
| Urban area | 47% | 53% |
| Rural area | 40% | 60% |

*Data Source:* Authors' computations using Argentinian political attitudes surveys (see wpid.world).

*Note:* The table shows the average share of votes received by Peronists and non-Peronists by selected individual characteristics in 2015–2019. Peronists were supported by 55% of primary-educated voters in this period, compared to only 38% of university graduates.

feature of their reliability and good values.[19] Hence, education, income, and class are the most important socioeconomic variables explaining the structure of the Peronist vote in Argentina.

## Chile

### *The Process of Redemocratization*

Chile broke from Spanish rule in 1818 and sealed its political stability with the signature of the Constitution of 1833. Over the nineteenth

19. See appendix Figure AA15, wpid.world.

century, the conservatives and liberals alternated in power and the economic elites had an important influence on the different governments. With the beginning of the twentieth century, several left movements appeared and for the first time a modern center-left alliance rose to power in 1938. In 1964, the centrist Christian Democratic Party (Partido Demócrata Cristiano, PDC, or DC), founded in 1957, formed a new government with the support of right-wing parties. This new party remained in power until 1970, after which Salvador Allende became the first president from the Socialist Party. Allende's government, marked by a deep economic crisis and hard negotiations with the opposition, ended in 1973 with a military coup instating Augusto Pinochet as military and political leader.[20]

The dictatorship lasted nearly two decades and was characterized by the repression of left-wing organizations and trade unions, as well as economic reforms with a free-market profile. Toward the end of the dictatorship, economic and political demands united several social actors. In 1988, a national plebiscite took place and the Chilean population denied Pinochet a new mandate, opening the way for the reestablishment of democracy in 1990.[21]

The regime left behind a fragile democratic system. In particular, the electoral system was binomial until 2013.[22] This implied that only two coalitions could realistically aspire to participate in the National Congress.[23] The by-product was a system of consensus politics and a two-

20. S. Collier and W. F. Sater, *A History of Chile, 1808–2002* (Cambridge University Press, 2004).

21. R. Bresnahan, "Chile since 1990: The Contradictions of Neoliberal Democratization," *Latin American Perspectives* 30, no. 5 (2003): 3–15. R. Ffrench-Davis, *Economic Reforms in Chile: From Dictatorship to Democracy* (Palgrave Macmillan, 2002).

22. Under this system, parties and independent candidates group themselves into lists or coalitions. Each list can propose up to two candidates per electoral region, province, or other geographical unit. Votes are counted by list, and unless the list with the majority of votes doubles the voting of the second majority, the candidates who got the most votes on each of the top two lists are elected into office. Hence, the first and the second majority get equal representation whenever the first majority does not double the second. See J. P. Luna and R. Mardones, "Chile: Are the Parties Over?," *Journal of Democracy* 21, no. 3 (2010): 107–121.

23. F. Riquelme, P. González-Cantergiani, and G. Godoy, "Voting Power of Political Parties in the Senate of Chile during the Whole Binomial System Period: 1990–2017" (arXiv Working Paper 1808.07854, 2018), https://www.researchgate.net/publication/327199719_Voting_power_of_political_parties_in_the_Senate_of_Chile_during_the_whole_binomial_system_period_1990-2017.

bloc party structure: the center-left bloc Coalition of Parties for Democracy (Concertación) had supported the "no" position in the referendum, while the right-wing bloc, Democracy and Progress (Democracia y Progreso), supported the continuation of Pinochet in office for another mandate.[24] The main parties in the center-left coalition were the Christian Democrats, the Socialists, and the Party for Democracy, founded in 1987.[25] The right-wing alliance consisted of the Independent Democrat Union (Unión Demócrata Independiente, UDI), founded in 1983, the heir to Pinochet, and National Renewal (Renovación Nacional, RN), founded in 1987, a more moderate right-wing party.[26]

The center-left alliance nominated a consensus Christian Democratic candidate, Patricio Aylwin, who won the 1989 election. During the 1990s and early 2000s, all presidents were from Concertación, including the Socialist Party's Michelle Bachelet. However, structural reforms were not implemented to combat high levels of economic inequality,[27] leading to social dissatisfaction, a decline in turnout, and the consequent loss of absolute majority by Concertación. Bachelet's government faced its first major social conflict, the Penguins' Revolution, led by high school students demanding higher equality in the educational system.[28]

In 2009, Chileans chose the first right-wing democratically elected government since 1958, led by Sebastián Piñera (RN). His government was also marked by protests by university students, followed by secondary students criticizing inequality in the educational system and its for-profit character.[29] The social discontent, together with the replacement in 2012 of the voting system of voluntary registry with compulsory voting with

24. M. B. Saavedra, *Sociedad civil en dictadura: Relaciones transnacionales, organizaciones y socialización política en Chile* (Ediciones Universidad Alberto Hurtado, 2013).

25. Collier and Sater, *History of Chile.*

26. C. Huneeus, "La derecha en el Chile después de Pinochet: El caso de la Unión Demócrata Independiente" (Kellogg Institute for International Studies Working Paper No. 285, 2001), https://kellogg.nd.edu/documents/1602; F. Agüero, "Chile: Unfinished Transition and Increased Political Competition," in *Constructing Democratic Governance in Latin America*, ed. J. I. Domínguez and M. Shifter (Johns Hopkins University Press, 2003), 292–320.

27. I. Flores, C. Sanhueza, J. Atria, and R. Mayer, "Top Incomes in Chile: A Historical Perspective on Income Inequality, 1964–2017" (WID.world Working Paper, 2018).

28. D. M. Chovanec and A. Benitez, "The Penguin Revolution in Chile: Exploring Intergenerational Learning in Social Movements," *Journal of Contemporary Issues in Education* 3, no. 1 (2008): 39–57.

29. C. Guzmán-Concha, "The Students' Rebellion in Chile: Occupy Protest or Classic Social Movement?," *Social Movement Studies,* 11, no. 3–4 (2012): 408–415.

a system of automatic registration but voluntary voting, led to a large fall in turnout.[30] In 2013, the center-left alliance moved further to the left by incorporating the Communist Party, and Bachelet returned to power.[31] She introduced important constitutional, educational, and fiscal reforms to deal with the social critics, but they were not sufficient for some factions on the left.[32] The end of the binomial system in 2015 paved the way for the alliance's final breakup in the last electoral process in 2017.[33] The new coalition Broad Front (Frente Amplio) emerged to the left of the Force of the Majority (La Fuerza de la Mayoría), a continuation of Concertación, leading to a more polarized political structure.

Piñera won again in the elections in 2017 and his government faced an even more salient unrest known as the Social Outbreak. Students' protests started in October 2019, triggered by the increase in subway fares, and the movement rapidly spread to the rest of society, leading to an agreement to change the constitution. The result from the October 2020 referendum was overwhelming support (almost 80 percent) for rewriting the constitution by an entirely popular elected body.

### Social Unrest and Political Cleavages during Redemocratization

In what follows, we analyze the changing relationship between party support and socioeconomic characteristics during the recent redemocratization process, using electoral surveys from 1989 until 2019.[34] Figure 15.3 summarizes the election results by the most important parties during our period of analysis. On the left of the political spectrum is Concertación, representing the center-left, the Communist Party, the

30. G. Contreras-Aguirre and M. Morales-Quiroga, "Jóvenes y participación electoral en Chile 1989–2013: Analizando el efecto del voto voluntario," *Revista Latinoamericana de Ciencias Sociales, Niñez y Juventud* 12, no. 2 (2014): 597–615; K. Bunker, "The 2013 Presidential and Legislative Election in Chile," *Electoral Studies,* 33, no. 4 (2014): 346–348.

31. M. von Bülow and G. B. Ponte, "It Takes Two to Tango: Students, Political Parties, and Protest in Chile (2005–2013)," in *Handbook of Social Movements across Latin America,* ed. P. Almeida and C. Ulate (Springer, 2015), 179–194.

32. S. Álvarez and A. Benitt, "Cronología del movimiento feminista en Chile 2006–2016," *Revista Estudos Feministas* 27, no. 3 (2019): 1–15.

33. K. Bunker, "La elección de 2017 y el fraccionamiento del sistema de partidos en Chile," *Revista Chilena de Derecho y Ciencia Política* 9, no. 2 (2018): 204–229.

34. See appendix Table BC1, wpid.world, for data sources.

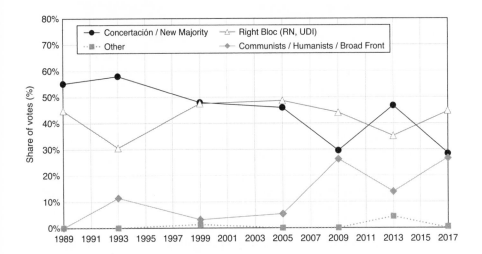

FIGURE 15.3. Election results in Chile, 1989–2017

*Data Source:* Authors' computations using official election results (see wpid.world).
*Note:* The figure shows the share of votes received by selected groups of Chilean political parties in presidential elections between 1989 and 2017. The Communists are included inside the Concertación in 2013 and 2017 because they ran together in the election, and the Christian Democratic Party (DC) is included inside the Concertación in 2017, even though they ran separately for the first time in that election. The right bloc received 45% of the vote in 2017.

Humanist Party, and since 2017, the Broad Front.[35] On the right is the alliance between RN and UDI (Figure 15.3).[36]

The predictatorship political structure in Chile was characterized by the existence of three main historical cleavages, which created the so-called three-thirds structure (left, right, and center) in the political system until 1973.[37] The first cleavage was defined by the religious conflict initiated in the second half of the nineteenth century that split political support

35. The Humanist Party participated in the Concertación until 1993, and the Communist Party in 2013 and 2017.

36. To classify the parties, for the 1989–2012 period we use the coding proposed by E. Huber and J. D. Stephens, "Latin America and the Caribbean Political Dataset, 1945–2012" (University of North Carolina, 2012), https://huberandstephens.web.unc.edu/common-works/data/, and for the most recent period, Bunker, "2013 Presidential and Legislative Election in Chile," and Bunker, "La elección de 2017."

37. T. R. Scully, "Reappraising the Role of the Center: The Case of the Chilean Party System" (Kellogg Institute Working Paper No. 143, September 1990), https://kellogg.nd.edu/documents/1337.

into a clerical bloc and an anticlerical bloc. At the beginning of the twentieth century, urbanization and industrialization fueled a clear class cleavage, which led to the emergence of left-wing parties and divided the political system along a left-right axis. Finally, from 1950 to 1970 the class cleavage extended to the countryside, where the Christian Democratic Party solidified the political center.[38]

Recent studies have challenged Lipset and Rokkan's "freezing hypothesis" that would imply that predictatorship cleavages would be preserved.[39] They have proposed instead a fourth democratic-authoritarian cleavage that splits voters into camps of critics or apologists of the military regime, which dominates the previous historical conflicts. The critics argued that the objective of the authoritarian regime to achieve political and economic stability did not justify the human rights violations and the suspension of democratic politics. The apologists instead believed that the neoliberal economic model developed during authoritarian rule deserved political protection.[40] Other researchers document that there was a general process of dealignment from the 1990s to the 2000s, marked by the decreasing association between political preferences on the one hand, and class, religion, and regime preferences on the other.[41]

In line with these results, we do not find a strong division along the left-right axis by income or education group after the dictatorship. Top-income earners have been slightly more likely to vote for the right, and this pattern has intensified in the last two elections. Meanwhile, university graduates were somewhat more left-wing relative to the rest of voters in the 1990s, but have progressively become less left-wing since the early 2000s (Figure 15.4).

While the stratification of the vote by income or education is not very strong along the left-right axis, it becomes more evident when decomposing the center-left bloc. Whereas the Concertación (excluding DC) is more popular among low-income earners, the Christian Democrats and

38. T. R. Scully, *Rethinking the Center: Party Politics in Nineteenth- and Twentieth-Century Chile* (Stanford University Press, 1992).

39. S. M. Lipset and S. Rokkan, *Party Systems and Voter Alignments: Cross-national Perspectives* (Free Press, 1967).

40. C. A. Bonilla, R. E. Carlin, G. J. Love, and E. S. Méndez, "Social or Political Cleavages? A Spatial Analysis of the Party System in Post-authoritarian Chile," *Public Choice* 146, no. 1–2 (2011): 9–21.

41. M. Bargsted and N. M. Somma, "Social Cleavages and Political Dealignment in Contemporary Chile, 1995–2009," *Party Politics* 22, no. 1 (2016): 105–124.

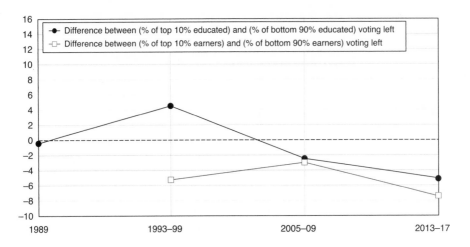

FIGURE 15.4. The left-wing vote by income and education in Chile, 1989–2017
*Data Source:* Authors' computations using Chilean political attitudes surveys (see wpid.world).
*Note:* The figure shows the relative support of top-income and highest-educated voters for center-left and left-wing parties, after controlling for age, gender, religious affiliation, religiosity, employment status, marital status, union membership, ethnicity, and region. In 2013–2017, top 10% income earners were 7 percentage points less likely to vote for the left. The left is defined as Concertación minus the Christian Democratic Party (DC) plus other left-wing parties that do not belong to the center-left alliance.

the left outside Concertación are equally supported by the income-poor and the income-rich (Figure 15.5).

The education gradient among political groups has fluctuated more than the income gradient and seems to be a product of the transfer of votes within the center-left coalition (Figure 15.6). In the last decade, the right bloc and the DC have lost support among the primary educated to the benefit of the Communists and Humanists and the other parties within the Concertación.[42]

The twenty-first century witnessed increasing unrest in Chilean society, spurred by rising income concentration, market-oriented education, and failures in the pension system. As the governing coalitions were

42. These results align with the exacerbation of the working-class cleavage in the 2010s (see appendix Figure BA24, wpid.world).

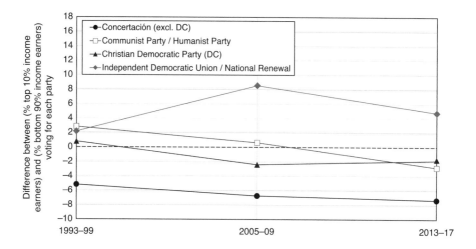

FIGURE 15.5. Vote and income in Chile, 1993–2017

*Data Source:* Authors' computations using Chilean political attitudes surveys (see wpid.world).

*Note:* The figure shows the difference between the share of top 10% earners and the share of bottom 90% earners voting for the main Chilean parties or groups of parties. In 2013–2017, top 10% income earners were 5 percentage points more likely to vote for the Independent Democratic Union and National Renewal.

unresponsive to social demands, political polarization increased.[43] Intermittent protests were staged throughout the period, culminating in the nationwide conflict in October 2019. This united the population around issues of social and economic inequality, exacerbating the class cleavage and thus aligning the vote by income and education, as shown in Figure 15.4.

The increase in polarization is also linked to the large fall in support for the DC. The weakening of Christian religious beliefs and the rapid process of urbanization have led voters to become less identified with the center ideology promoted by the DC and historically attached to Christianity and rural origins.[44] The religious cleavage has thus been reduced,

43. J. Fábrega, J. González, and J. Lindh, "Polarization and Electoral Incentives: The End of the Chilean Consensus Democracy, 1990–2014," *Latin American Politics and Society* 60, no. 4 (2018): 49–68.

44. M. Herrera, M. Morales, and G. Rayo, "Las bases sociales del Partido Demócrata Cristiano Chileno," *European Review of Latin American and Caribbean Studies/Revista Europea de Estudios Latinoamericanos y del Caribe* 107, no. 1 (2019): 55–74.

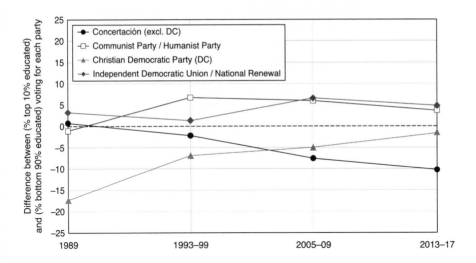

FIGURE 15.6. Vote and education in Chile, 1989–2017
*Data Source:* Authors' computations using Chilean political attitudes surveys (see wpid.world).
*Note:* The figure shows the difference between the share of top 10% educated voters and the share of bottom 90% educated voters voting for the main Chilean political parties or groups of parties. In 2013–2017, top 10% educated voters were 10 percentage points less likely to vote for Concertación.

and the support for the left comes from a wide base of believers and nonbelievers.[45]

The recent political polarization is most pronounced among the youth and those living in the center of the country (Table 15.2). The fall of around 30 percentage points in youth votes for the DC has been mostly divided between the two ends of the ideological spectrum—the left outside of Concertación and the right bloc. Left-wing parties within Concertación have also received a share of the youth vote, but they still fare better among middle-aged and older voters. Historically, the north and the south have been associated with higher support for the left and the right, respectively. Support for the left has nonetheless considerably increased in the last decade in the center of the country, the area that has seen the largest social unrest.

45. See appendix Figure BA21, wpid.world.

*Table 15.2*   The Structure of Political Cleavages in Chile, 2017

| | Share of Votes Received (%) | | | |
|---|---|---|---|---|
| | Communist Party / Humanist Party/ Broad Front/ Other left | The Force of the Majority (excl. Communists) | Christian Democratic Party | Independent Democratic Union/ National Renewal |
| **Education Level** | | | | |
| Primary | 19% | 27% | 6% | 48% |
| Secondary | 27% | 23% | 5% | 45% |
| Tertiary | 24% | 29% | 4% | 43% |
| **Income Group** | | | | |
| Bottom 50% | 26% | 24% | 5% | 45% |
| Middle 40% | 21% | 26% | 6% | 47% |
| Top 10% | 16% | 31% | 3% | 51% |
| **Region** | | | | |
| North | 25% | 26% | 2% | 47% |
| Center | 26% | 27% | 5% | 42% |
| South | 21% | 25% | 4% | 51% |
| **Age** | | | | |
| 20–39 | 33% | 19% | 2% | 47% |
| 40–59 | 21% | 29% | 5% | 44% |
| +60 | 16% | 34% | 9% | 42% |

*Data Source:* Authors' computations using Chilean political attitudes surveys (see wpid.world).
*Note:* The table presents the share of votes received by the main Chilean political groups in the 2017 election, by selected individual characteristics. In 2017, 48% of primary-educated voters voted for the Independent Democratic Union or National Renewal, compared to 43% of university graduates.

## Costa Rica

The modern political history of Costa Rica starts in the aftermath of the 1948 civil war, triggered by the annulling of the elections results of February 1948. A group of rebels led by José Figueres Ferrer formed the National Liberation Army and successfully toppled the government of Teodoro Picado (1944–1948).[46] Among the social and political achieve-

46. I. Molina, *Democracia y elecciones en Costa Rica: Dos contribuciones polémicas* (FLACSO, 2001).

ments of this period were the establishment of the Supreme Electoral Court of Costa Rica, the abolishment of the army, the end of racial segregation, and women's suffrage. The outcomes of the war also included exile for the losers and a ban on communist parties taking part in elections (revoked in 1974).

The two sides of the civil war were at the source of the dichotomous political environment that dominated Costa Rican politics for the next five decades. The winning side, led by Figueres Ferrer, established the National Liberation Party (Partido Liberación Nacional, PLN), of center-left social democratic orientation, which would become the dominant political party. The losing side, led by Rafael Ángel Calderón Guardia, reconstituted into a number of political parties and coalitions of center-right Christian democratic orientation that won the presidential elections three times before establishing the Social Christian Unity Party (Partido Unidad Social Cristiana, PUSC) in 1983. The successful transfer of control to the center-right in 1958 marked the beginning of a tradition of alternation of power that crystallized in the following decades (Figure 15.7).[47]

While we can only strictly define a two-party system from 1983 onward, the alliances on the right constituted after the civil war and the weakness of socialist parties contributed to the predominance of a bipolar party system since 1948.[48] Interestingly, no political party has won the elections more than twice in a row, not even in the most dominant years of the PLN during the 1970s and 1980s. Hence, some have interpreted the political history of Costa Rica as an affair of a dominant party versus everyone else.[49]

This institutional model, however, had already started to deteriorate in the late 1970s, due to a combination of economic factors (high levels of public debt, inflation, capital flight, and so on) and political violence in Central America. After Calderón Fournier from the PUSC and his successor from the PLN Figueres Olsen made a political pact in 1995 that was intended to continue the process of adjustment and reform of the state that had started in the 1980s, social discontent mounted, fracturing

47. M. A. Solís, *La institucionalidad ajena: Los años cuarenta y el final de siglo* (Editorial de la Universidad de Costa Rica, 2006).

48. F. Sánchez, "Cambio en la dinámica electoral en Costa Rica: Un caso de desalineamiento," *América Latina Hoy* 35 (2003): 115–146.

49. R. Alfaro-Redondo, *Divide y votarás* (PEN, 2019).

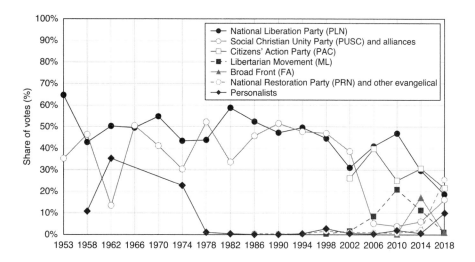

FIGURE 15.7. Election results in Costa Rica, 1953–2018
*Data Source:* Authors' computations using official election results (see wpid.world).
*Note:* The figure shows the share of votes received by selected Costa Rican political parties and groups of parties in presidential elections between 1953 and 2018. The National Restoration Party received 26% of the vote in 2018.

the base that had supported the PLN in the construction of the welfare state (1950–1978).[50]

The erosion of the 1990s revealed growing dissatisfaction with the political system as a whole, which translated first into an increase in electoral abstention in 1998, and later, with the emergence of the Citizens' Action Party (Partido Acción Ciudadana, PAC) in 2002, into a process often called "partisan dealignment."[51] As traditional parties converged toward the center in the 1980s and 1990s, the once center-left PLN suffered the most.[52] In this context, the PAC took the social democratic baton and attracted many intellectuals and prominent figures from the PLN and other parties. After two PLN governments, the PAC won the election for

50. R. Alfaro-Redondo and F. Alpízar, ed., *Elecciones 2018 en Costa Rica: Retrato de una democracia amenazada* (CONARE–PEN, 2020), 22–23.
51. Sánchez, "Cambio en la dinámica electoral."
52. C. Raventós-Vorst, M. V. Fournier Facio, O. Ramírez Moreira, A. L. Gutiérrez Espeleta, and J. R. García Fernández, *Abstencionistas en Costa Rica: Quiénes son y por qué no votan?* (Editorial de la Universidad de Costa Rica, 2005).

the first time in history, as the PLN collapsed in the second round in 2014.[53] Finally, the PLN finished third for the first time in 2018, when the PAC defeated the evangelical Christian National Restoration Party (Partido Restauración Nacional, PRN), founded in 2005.

### A Multiclass Party Cleavage

In what follows, we study political cleavages in Costa Rica from the 1970s to the present by classifying parties as left-wing (PLN, PAC, Broad Front) or right-wing (PUSC, PRN, Libertarian Movement, and other center-right parties). While the PLN has been a member of the Socialist International since the 1960s, it is arguable whether it still remains a center-left party, especially after 2006, when Óscar Arias, usually associated with the so-called neoliberal forces within the PLN, was reelected president for the second time.[54] In the interest of historical consistency, we have classified the PLN as a left-wing party, but we show that our results are unchanged whether the PLN is considered a left-wing party or not.[55]

The leaders of the 1940s polarized the population into two major political forces. Hence, the bipolar system from the 1950s to the 1970s was motivated by the tension between the PLN and "anti-PLN" (*antiliberacionismo*).[56] However, great fragmentation within the anti-PLN camp prevented the development of a two-party system from the beginning. The socialist left could not take part in elections before 1974, which made the process not strictly competitive.[57] Therefore, the principal political cleavage of Costa Rica from 1948 through 2000 was between the PLN's supporters and its adversaries.[58]

53. R. Alfaro-Redondo, M. Seligson, and E. Zechmeister, *Cultura política de la democracia en Costa Rica y en las Américas, 2014: Gobernabilidad democrática a través de 10 años del barómetro de las Américas* (PEN, 2015).

54. E. Arias, "Estado, neoliberalismo y empresarios en Costa Rica: La coyuntura del TLC," *Revista de Ciencias Sociales* 164 (2019): 69–86; J. Martínez and D. Sánchez-Ancochea, "How Did Costa Rica Achieve Social and Market Incorporation?," *CEPAL Review* 121 (2017): 123–137; B. M. Wilson, "When Social Democrats Choose Neoliberal Economic Policies: The Case of Costa Rica," *Comparative Politics* 26, no. 2 (1994): 149–168.

55. M. Coppedge, "A Classification of Latin American Political Parties" (Kellogg Institute Working Paper No. 244, November 1997), https://kellogg.nd.edu/documents/1539; Huber and Stephens, "Latin America and the Caribbean Political Dataset."

56. Sánchez, "Cambio en la dinámica electoral."

57. Alfaro-Redondo and Alpízar, *Elecciones 2018 en Costa Rica.*

58. Coppedge, "Evolution of Latin American Party Systems."

The hegemony of the PLN until the 1970s was partly due to a growing middle class of urban professionals and small coffee producers who relied on the state to support their production activities, strengthen the bureaucracy and expand public employment, and manage conflicts in the rural sector and between capital and labor.[59] This explains to a large extent why the party was slightly more supported by highest-income earners until the 1990s, while lower-income voters who did not benefit as much from these policies gave more support to the PUSC (Figure 15.8).

Frustration with the deterioration of the welfare state during the economic recession of the 1980s, the neoliberal turn of the PLN from social democratic to neoliberal policies, and corruption scandals led to an increase in political dissatisfaction with traditional parties, the rise of abstention (mainly among lower-income earners[60]), and a large shift of voters toward new parties such as the Libertarian Movement and the PAC among highest-income earners, the PRN among lower-income earners, and the Broad Front among all classes, as shown in Figure 15.8. The enlargement of the multiparty system thus resulted in a reconfiguration of the socioeconomic structure of the electorate with different competing pro-poor (PLN and PRN) and pro-rich parties (PUSC and PAC) since the 2000s.[61] The same findings are obtained when looking at the voting patterns by education.[62]

The reconfiguration of the political landscape in the last two decades has also changed the dynamics of the vote along occupational, regional, and religious lines. Left-wing education and economic elites vote strongly for the PAC and are mostly composed of professionals, wage earners, and public-sector workers, many of whom used to vote for the PLN (Table 15.3). Moreover, the PAC vote is clearly urban; since its first election in 2002 the party has never won in any of the peripheral provinces in the first round of presidential elections, not even in 2014 or 2018, when it went on to win the presidency.[63] The PLN, on the other hand, has per-

59. J. Martínez and D. Sánchez-Ancochea, *Good Jobs and Social Services: How Costa Rica Achieved the Elusive Double Incorporation* (Palgrave Macmillan, 2013).

60. Raventós-Vorst et al., *Abstencionistas en Costa Rica*.

61. Note that some of these parties, in particular the PLN, have historically had multiclass electorates. We refer to them as pro-poor and pro-rich, as since the 2000s they have had a larger share of bottom- and top-income earners, respectively.

62. See appendix Figure CC53, wpid.world.

63. Tribunal Supremo de Elecciones (TSE), "Elecciones en cifras 1953–2018: Recurso en línea" (TSE, 2018), https://www.tse.go.cr/estadisticas_elecciones.htm.

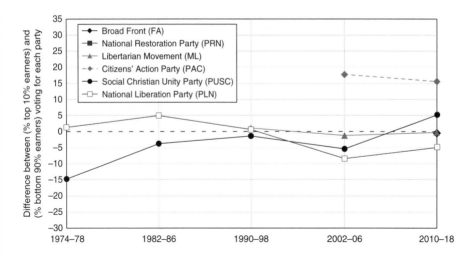

FIGURE 15.8. Vote and income in Costa Rica, 1974–2018

*Data Source:* Authors' computations using Costa Rican political attitudes surveys (see wpid.world).

*Note:* The figure shows the difference between the share of top 10% earners and the share of bottom 90% earners voting for the main Costa Rican political parties. In 2010–2018, top 10% income earners were 16 percentage points more likely to vote for the Citizens' Action Party.

sistently had better results in rural areas and in the lowlands, but a large share of its vote and that of PUSC was captured by the conservative PRN in the 2018 election (Table 15.3).

A Protestant cleavage became very salient in the 2018 presidential election. After a nonbinding sentence by the Inter-American Court of Human Rights that recommended that Costa Rica approve same-sex marriage, the evangelical Christian PRN managed to finish first in the first round, obtaining 73 percent of the Protestant vote.[64] In contrast to the situations in Peru and Mexico, the politicization of ethnicity has been weak in Costa Rica and thus there are no strong ethnic divisions in voting patterns (Table 15.3).

This analysis tells the story of two Costa Ricas: a prosperous, educated, and modern one in urban areas of the center of the country, which

64. Programa Estado de la Nación en Desarrollo Humano Sostenible, *Informe estado de la nación 2018* (PEN-CONARE, 2018), 204. On the election results, see appendix Figure CC52, wpid.world.

*Table 15.3*   The Structure of Political Cleavages in Costa Rica, 2010–2018

| | Share of Votes (%) | | | | | |
|---|---|---|---|---|---|---|
| | FA | PAC | PLN | ML | PUSC | PRN |
| **Education** | | | | | | |
| Primary | 4% | 27% | 40% | 4% | 5% | 15% |
| Secondary | 6% | 34% | 26% | 4% | 6% | 17% |
| Tertiary | 8% | 40% | 20% | 4% | 14% | 9% |
| Postgraduate | 5% | 46% | 25% | 3% | 10% | 7% |
| **Income** | | | | | | |
| Bottom 50% | 6% | 28% | 32% | 3% | 6% | 20% |
| Middle 40% | 5% | 34% | 27% | 5% | 8% | 15% |
| Top 10% | 5% | 47% | 25% | 4% | 12% | 5% |
| **Region** | | | | | | |
| Metropolitan area of San José | 7% | 33% | 27% | 2% | 10% | 13% |
| Central-urban | 5% | 42% | 29% | 4% | 6% | 8% |
| Central-rural | 3% | 31% | 34% | 6% | 6% | 14% |
| Lowlands-urban | 6% | 27% | 33% | 5% | 7% | 19% |
| Lowlands-rural | 5% | 28% | 33% | 3% | 5% | 21% |
| **Worker Type** | | | | | | |
| Business owner/partner | 6% | 37% | 21% | 4% | 10% | 14% |
| Wage earner | 7% | 34% | 28% | 4% | 8% | 13% |
| Self-employed | 4% | 33% | 29% | 5% | 7% | 15% |
| **Sector of Employment** | | | | | | |
| Private/mixed sector | 6% | 34% | 28% | 4% | 7% | 15% |
| Public | 8% | 37% | 28% | 5% | 10% | 9% |
| **Ethnicity** | | | | | | |
| White | 6% | 31% | 33% | 4% | 7% | 13% |
| Mestizo | 5% | 35% | 29% | 4% | 8% | 14% |
| Indigenous | 7% | 34% | 31% | 2% | 6% | 11% |
| Black/Mulatto | 5% | 38% | 25% | 2% | 5% | 18% |
| Other | 5% | 35% | 25% | 3% | 4% | 26% |

*Data Source:* Authors' computations using Costa Rican political attitudes surveys (see wpid.world).

*Note:* The table shows the average share of votes received by the main Costa Rican political parties by selected individual characteristics over the period 2010–2018. The PLN was supported by 40% of primary-educated voters during this period, compared to 25% of postgraduates.

mainly supports PAC, and a low-educated and poor one on the coasts and along the borders, which supports the old center-left (PLN) and conservative parties (for example, PRN).

## Colombia

### Colombia's Historical Two-Party System

Colombia became independent from Spain in 1810, obtaining full separation from colonial rule after the Battle of Boyacá in 1819. After the *Libertador* Simon Bolívar died in 1830, the country put in place a two-party system (Conservative-Liberal) that lasted for more than 150 years.[65] The Liberals' ideals were anticlericalism, federalism, and free trade, while Conservatives defended the church and favored centralization and protectionism.

Rural guerrillas aligned with the Liberal and the Conservative (los chulavitas) Parties were formed and interparty violence was widespread during the nineteenth and twentieth centuries, reaching its peak from 1948 to 1953, a period known as *La Violencia*. To pacify the country, the Conservative and Liberal parties agreed to the National Front (Frente Nacional, FN) deal, under which the presidency alternated every four years from 1958 to 1974, and parity in party representation across all government bodies was ensured. The FN deal excluded radical civil sectors, peasants, workers, and all those ideologically aligned with the left, and some of their most important demands, in particular land reform.[66] Traditional parties represented the interests of the landed elites, who were ideologically closer to the right.[67] The prolonged and intense fighting forged the public's strong identification with the two traditional parties, so bipartisan dominance only collapsed in the early 2000s, after the adoption of the electoral reforms included in the 1991 constitution.

The absence of political opportunities for outsiders, combined with the lack of state presence in the Colombian periphery, the survival of liberal rural guerrillas from *La Violencia,* and the inspiration from the Cold War, led to the formation of left-leaning guerrilla movements in the

---

65. D. Bushnell, *The Making of Modern Colombia: A Nation in Spite of Itself* (University of California Press, 1993).

66. M. Palacios and F. Safford, *Colombia: Fragmented Land, Divided Society* (Oxford University Press, 2002).

67. A. Dávila and F. Leal-Buitrago, *Clientelismo: El sistema político y su expresión regional* (Universidad de los Andes, 1990).

early 1960s. The most powerful was the Armed Revolutionary Forces of Colombia (Fuerzas Armadas Revolucionarias de Colombia, FARC).[68] The guerrillas were backed by the Colombian Communist Party, which approved the thesis of the combination of all forms of struggle, establishing that armed conflict is inevitable and necessary as a factor in the Colombian revolution.[69]

In the 1980s, the government was forced to negotiate with insurgents due to increasing violence in rural areas and repression of left-leaning supporters. As part of the peace talks, a faction of the guerrillas formed a left-wing political movement, the Patriotic Union (La Unión Patriótica, UP), to provide outsiders with a platform to participate in politics. The 1991 constitution further consolidated the opening of the political system by allowing historically excluded groups (such as left-wing or religious movements, peasants, Indigenous people, and union workers) to participate in elections.

### A New Political Dichotomy:
### Uribism versus Anti-Uribism

With the beginning of the twenty-first century, Colombia's political landscape experienced a profound transformation. The two traditional parties lost part of their hegemony, to the benefit of left-leaning political groups. In 2002, the independent Álvaro Uribe became president of the republic by offering a new right-wing populism and economic liberalism and promoting a military confrontation to resolve the conflict against the FARC; this program became known as "Uribism." His main contenders were the Liberal Party's Horacio Serpa and the candidate of an emerging party, the Alternative Democratic Pole (Polo Democrático Alternativo, PDA), which represented the left-wing ideology and came third. Álvaro Uribe was reelected in the first round in 2006, beating the intellectual left-wing candidate Carlos Gaviria (PDA), who won 22 percent of the votes, the highest share of votes obtained by a left-wing party in Colombian history.

---

68. C. Ayala, *Nacionalismo y populismo: Anapo y el discurso político de la oposición en Colombia: 1960–1966* (Universidad Nacional de Colombia, 1995).

69. J. Giraldo, *Aportes sobre el origen del conflicto armado en Colombia, su persistencia y sus impactos* (Comisión de Paz, 2015).

In 2010, Juan Manuel Santos, Uribe's former minister of defense and candidate of the Party of the Union (Partido de la Unidad Nacional, or Party of the U), was elected president with Uribe's support, against the intellectual progressive Antanas Mockus from the Green Party (Partido Verde). Santos differed from Uribe in his ideological approach to the conflict; he was not in favor of a military intervention and so made a third peaceful attempt to negotiate with the FARC. The negotiation prompted Uribe to form a new right-wing movement, the Democratic Center (Centro Democrático, CD), which became the main opposition party to the Santos government. Santos ran in 2014 for a second consecutive term, winning against Óscar Iván Zuluaga (CD), the Uribist candidate, and the left-wing candidate Clara López (PDA). In 2016, President Santos signed a historic peace agreement with the FARC ending about 60 years of military confrontations.

In 2018, Iván Duque, the Uribist candidate from the CD, was elected president after defeating the left-wing candidate of the new party Colombia Humana, Gustavo Petro, a dissident from the PDA. His victory resulted from divisions between anti-Uribist candidates, who failed to agree on the runoff despite their higher cumulated scores in the first round.

### Uribisim, Class Cleavages, and the Peace Process

In what follows, we analyze the link between electoral behaviors and socioeconomic factors in Colombia, using postelectoral surveys covering all presidential elections from 2002 to 2018.[70] To do so, we classify Colombian parties as right-wing if Álvaro Uribe was a member, or if the party was openly allied with an Uribist party, and as left-wing if they are openly anti-Uribist or if their programs included open support for the peace negotiation with the FARC (see Figure 15.9). The Party of the U is considered to be Uribist when it was supported by Uribe and anti-Uribist after 2014.[71]

Our results show that in every year except 2014, the anti-Uribist vote has been more pronounced among highest-educated and top-income voters (Figure 15.10). Uribe's popular support was indeed largely driven by his social agenda aimed at tackling poverty. During his term, Uribe

70. See appendix Table DC1, wpid.world, for data sources.
71. We use the right- and left-wing labels to facilitate comparative analysis. However, these categories are not precise in the Colombian context as left/right is usually associated with criminal left/right groups.

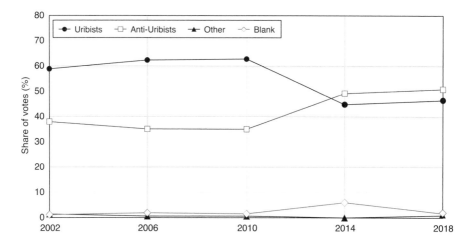

FIGURE 15.9. Election results in Colombia, 2002–2018
*Data Source:* Authors' computations using official election results (see wpid.world).
*Note:* The figure shows the share of votes received by selected groups of Colombian political parties in general elections between 2002 and 2018. Right-wing parties (Uribists): Partido de la U (2010), Partido Conservador, Cambio Radical, Primero Colombia, Movimiento Si Colombia, and Centro Democrático. Left-wing parties (anti-Uribists): Polo Democrático, Partido de la U (2014), Partido Liberal, Alianza Social Independiente, Partido Verde, Colombia Humana, and Compromiso Ciudadano. Left-wing parties received 51% of the vote in 2018.

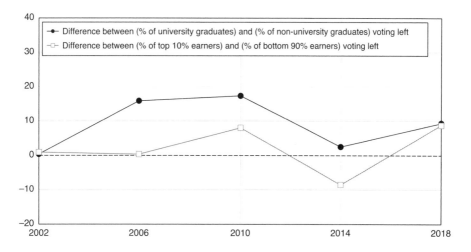

FIGURE 15.10. The anti-Uribist vote by income and education in Colombia, 2002–2018
*Data Source:* Authors' computations using Colombian postelectoral and political attitudes surveys (see wpid.world).
*Note:* The figure shows the relative support of tertiary-educated and top-income voters for left-wing (anti-Uribist) parties, after controlling for age, gender, region, rural-urban location, employment status, marital status, sector of employment, ethnicity, and religious affiliation. In 2018, university graduates were 9 percentage points more likely to vote for anti-Uribists.

massively extended social programs, such as the conditional cash-transfer scheme *Familias en Acción,* and held frequent public meetings with citizens throughout the country.[72]

The reversal in the education and income gradients in 2014 was mainly due to the dramatic shift of the lowest-educated and low-income voters toward the Party of the U.[73] This strong support for Santos among the lower classes can be explained by his new progressive pro-peace ideology, as well as by the social programs that were implemented during the previous presidency when he was an Uribist. Indeed, the popular support received by Uribe for his reelection in 2006 matches Santos's popular support in 2014. The education and income gradients returned to their 2011 levels in 2018, as Santos could not run for office for a third time, and as a consequence, lower classes shifted back to Uribism.

To what extent have positions toward the conflict represented class cleavages since the beginning of Uribism? The armed conflict was more salient for anti-Uribist voters, as they are strongly represented in rural areas where the guerrilla presence was greatest. In Uribe's view, the guerrillas were terrorist groups and the primary source of Colombia's problems. Hence, more than 70 percent of those who said that violence was the main problem in Colombia voted for Uribists from 2002 to 2010. However, that group began to believe that Santos's negotiation could succeed and voted for him in 2014. In contrast, for anti-Uribists, corruption was the main problem of the country.[74]

Class divisions and position on the conflict are also aligned with generational, rural-urban, and sectoral cleavages. The anti-Uribist vote is highest among young, urban voters working in the public sector (Figure 15.11). In line with the voting patterns by income and education levels, the dramatic drop in the difference in the left-wing vote between urban and rural areas in 2014 may be associated with both rural areas' interest in supporting the peace process and the large share of rural beneficiaries of social assistance policies. Generational and sectoral cleavages also reverted in 2014, as a large share of old and non-public-sector voters shifted toward the left and voted for Santos. The rural-urban cleavage is

72. Inter-Regional Inequality Facility, "Policy Brief 2" (Overseas Development Institute, February 2006), https://assets.publishing.service.gov.uk/media/57a08c2a40f0b652ddoo1162/IRIFPolicyBrief2.pdf.

73. See appendix Figures DA2 and DA3, wpid.world.

74. See appendix Figures DA18 and DB10, wpid.world.

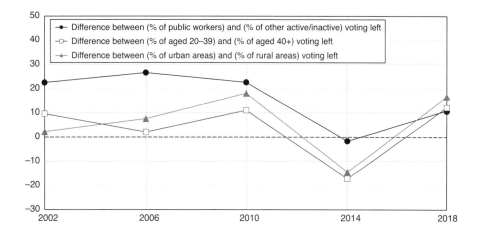

FIGURE 15.11. The anti-Uribist vote in Colombia, 2002–2018: Public workers, new generations, and urban areas
*Data Source:* Authors' computations using Colombian postelectoral and political attitudes surveys (see wpid.world).
*Note:* The figure shows the relative support of public workers, young voters, and urban areas for left-wing (anti-Uribist) parties, after controlling for income, education, gender, region, employment status, marital status, ethnicity, and religious affiliation. In 2018, voters aged 20 to 39 were 12 percentage points more likely to vote for anti-Uribists.

not a recent phenomenon, as Colombian cities have historically been the strongholds of the independent vote outside of the Liberal-Conservative tradition.[75]

Religion has also historically been an important dividing variable. The Conservative Party was allied with the Catholic Church in controlling the education system and privileging Conservative areas. Given literacy restrictions on the right to vote, which were lifted only in 1936, the uneven spread of literacy along partisan lines also unevenly broadened the electorate, thereby helping the Conservative Party in its pursuit of political hegemony.[76] This pattern reverted as education became more secular and anti-Conservative voters gradually turned more educated. The

75. H. F. Kline, *Colombia: Portrait of Unity and Diversity* (Westview Press, 1983).
76. M. Sánchez, *States Divided: History, Conflict, and State Formation in Mexico and Colombia* (Cornell University Press, 2017).

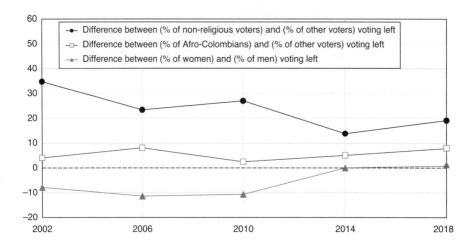

FIGURE 15.12. The anti-Uribist vote in Colombia, 2002–2018: Nonreligious voters, Afro-Colombians, and women

*Data Source:* Authors' computations using Colombian postelectoral and political attitudes surveys (see wpid.world).

*Note:* The figure shows the relative support of nonreligious voters, Afro-Colombians, and women for left-wing (anti-Uribist) parties, after controlling for income, education, age, region, rural-urban location, employment status, marital status, and sector of employment. In 2018, nonreligious voters were 19 percentage points more likely to vote for anti-Uribists.

church and new religious groups thus consolidated their influence on the low-educated and low-income groups. Even though left-wing candidates openly declare themselves to be atheists, they have gradually made their rhetoric more flexible and avoided entering into discussions about religion. This explains why the difference in the left vote between nonreligious and religious voters (mainly Catholics and Protestants) has progressively declined (Figure 15.12).

Colombia also had a historical gender gap according to which women were more conservative than men. This gap has been closed since 2014, likely due to a gradual decline in religiosity and the introduction of new social issues on the political agenda that address gender concerns, such as abortion access and gender violence. Finally, in contrast to other Latin American countries, ethnic cleavages are weak in Colombia: Afro-Colombians, the largest ethnic minority, have been only slightly more left-wing relative to the rest of the population (Figure 15.13).

## Mexico

Since its independence from Spain in 1821, the United Mexican States has had a long and rich political history that extends from two empires in the nineteenth century to the one-party system of the hegemonic Institutional Revolutionary Party (Partido Revolucionario Institucional, PRI) and the first transfer of power after democratic elections in the 2000s.[77] The rule of the PRI as the hegemonic party of the twentieth century started at the end of the Mexican Revolution (1910–1917). The initial aim of this armed conflict was to put an end to the dictatorship of Porfirio Díaz (1876–1911). After Díaz left Mexico in 1911, elections were organized and Francisco Madero was elected president.

The PRI was created in 1929 as the direct heir of the revolutionary movement and immediately became the dominant party. Plurality of parties was accepted only with broad limitations in the lower house of the congress from 1963 onward. From 1946 to 1976, the party exhibited its greatest authoritarian control over the electoral process. As a result, repression and violence rose in the 1960s, culminating in the infamous Tlatelolco massacre of 1968.[78] This period ended with the presidential election of 1976, the only election in Mexican history with a single candidate, José López Portillo.

Political plurality in Mexico was confirmed with the electoral reform of 1977, which sought to include groups previously banned and promoted the creation of new political parties. However, the reform did not appease the public, which was increasingly discontented with corruption and electoral fraud; their dissatisfaction provided the basis for a succession of strong left-leaning parties that would play a key role in the following decades.[79]

Two strategies exploited during the heyday of the one-party system deserve special attention. First, many labor union leaders were themselves members of the PRI.[80] However, the PRI lost its monopoly on support

77. V. A. Espinoza and A. Monsiváis, *El deterioro de la democracia: Consideraciones sobre el régimen político, lo público y la ciudadanía en México* (Colegio de la Frontera Norte, 2012): 39.

78. L. J. Molina, *Monitor democrático 2019: Causas y efectos jurídicos del viraje electoral (2018) vs el pluripartidismo en México* (Procesos Editoriales Don José, 2019): 71.

79. F. Cantú, "The Fingerprints of Fraud: Evidence from Mexico's 1988 Presidential Election," *American Political Science Review* 113, no. 3 (2019): 710–726.

80. C. Bazdresch and S. Levy, "Populism and Economic Policy in Mexico, 1970–1982," in *The Macroeconomics of Populism in Latin America*, ed. R. Dornbusch and S. Edwards (University of Chicago Press, 1991), 223–262.

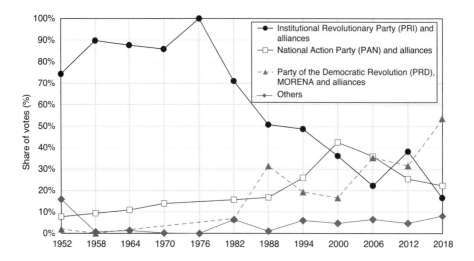

FIGURE 15.13. Election results in Mexico, 1952–2018
*Data Source:* Authors' computations using official election results (see wpid.world).
*Note:* The figure shows the share of votes received by selected groups of Mexican political parties in presidential elections between 1952 and 2018. The Institutional Revolutionary Party (PRI) received 16% of the vote in 2018.

from labor unions in the 1980s, when technocrats who increasingly favored neoliberal reforms replaced the old guard of the party and unions began to lose influence within the PRI structure.[81] Second, the political establishment used the so-called para-state parties to stage competitive elections that were actually controlled by the PRI. Real opposition came only from the National Action Party (Partido Acción Nacional, PAN) and the Mexican Communist Party (Partido Comunista Mexicano, PCM), both of which were illegal and persecuted until the electoral reform of 1977.

The creation of an independent body with the mandate to organize elections in 1990 was followed by increasing transparency and competitiveness in the electoral process. In the subsequent elections, the PRI saw its share of votes decrease until finally it lost the presidency to the PAN in 2000 (Figure 15.13).[82] Simultaneously, violence and drug

81. F. J. Aguilar, *Historia de la CTM 1936–2006* (UNAM, 2009).
82. J. L. Klesner, "The End of Mexico's One-Party Regime," *Political Science and Politics* 34, no. 1 (2001): 107–114.

trafficking dominated the 1990s, prompting some authors to call Mexico a "narco-democracy."[83] Therefore, the quick recognition of the electoral results by PRI president Ernesto Zedillo and the subsequent peaceful transfer of power was a milestone in Mexican political history. Nevertheless, the ghost of electoral fraud reappeared after the 2006 and 2012 elections.[84]

The last decade saw the return of the PRI in 2012 after twelve years of PAN governments, but also its worst defeat in the country's history in 2018. Simultaneously, left-wing forces continued to crystallize during this period. The left first organized itself behind the National Democratic Front during the 1988 elections, led by Cuauhtémoc Cárdenas. The party was known as the Party of the Democratic Revolution (Partido de la Revolución Democrática, PRD) thereafter, and Cárdenas was replaced by his protégé Andrés Manuel López Obrador (AMLO) for the 2006 elections. With the National Regeneration Movement (Movimiento Regeneración Nacional, MORENA), AMLO became the first left-wing president in Mexican history in 2018.

### Mexico's Multi-elite Party System

We now turn to studying the changing relationship between left-right party choice and socioeconomic characteristics during Mexico's transition since 1952 from a one-party to a multiparty system.[85] The main parties on the right are the PRI and the PAN, while the main parties on the left are the PRD and, more recently, Morena (Figure 15.13). Although the PRI was initially a center-left party that drew inspiration from the ideals of the Mexican Revolution, its orientation can be considered center-right in recent years.[86] In the late 1970s the party moved to the center-right following a series of reforms, such as the privatization of state-owned companies and the reestablishment of relations with the church. The party is still part of the Socialist International, but it is not currently considered socialist or social democratic by most contemporary analysts.

83. S. Patenostro, "Mexico as a Narco-Democracy," *World Policy Journal* 12, no. 1 (1995): 41–47.

84. BBC, "Mexico Faces Partial Recount in Presidential Election," BBC News, July 5, 2012, https://www.bbc.com/news/world-18717146.

85. See appendix Table ED1, wpid.world, for data sources.

86. Coppedge, "Classification of Latin American Political Parties"; Huber and Stephens, "Latin America and the Caribbean Political Dataset."

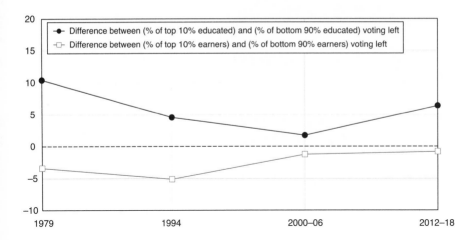

FIGURE 15.14. The social democratic vote by income and education in Mexico, 1979–2018

*Data Source:* Authors' computations using Mexican political attitudes surveys (see wpid.world).

*Note:* The figure shows the relative support of highest-educated and top-income voters for social democratic parties (PRD/MORENA/Other social democrats and progressives), after controlling for age, gender, religion, employment status, marital status, occupation, perceived class, union membership, rural-urban location, region, and ethnicity. Over the period 2012–2018, university graduates were 6 percentage points more likely to vote for social democratic and progressive parties.

Despite Mexico's profound transformation from a one-party to a multiparty system since the 1970s, the country seems to have maintained during this process a reasonably stable multi-elite party system: higher education is associated with a generally greater propensity to vote for the left, whereas higher income is associated with slightly lower support for the left (Figure 15.14). This pattern is largely due to the greater popularity of the PAN and left-wing parties among top-income earners and the highest educated, respectively (Figures 15.15 and 15.16). The PRI's traditional base, in contrast, are the lower educated living in poor rural areas and, in recent years, older voters who remember the years of the "Mexican miracle" (1940–1970).[87] The latter benefited from the support of the PRI through political clientelism and, more recently, social programs such as *Progresa.*

87. See appendix Figure EC14, wpid.world.

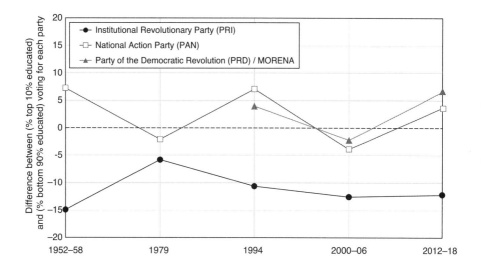

FIGURE 15.15. Vote and education in Mexico, 1952–2018

*Data Source:* Authors' computations using Mexican political attitudes surveys (see wpid.world).

*Note:* The figure shows the difference between the share of top 10% educated voters and the share of bottom 90% educated voters voting for the main Mexican political parties. Over the period 2012–2018, top 10% educated voters were 12 percentage points less likely to vote for the Institutional Revolutionary Party (PRI).

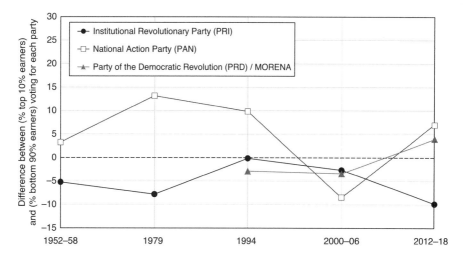

FIGURE 15.16. Vote and income in Mexico, 1952–2018

*Data Source:* Authors' computations using Mexican political attitudes surveys (see wpid.world).

*Note:* The figure shows the difference between the share of top 10% earners and the share of bottom 90% earners voting for the main Mexican political parties. Over the 2012–2018 period, top 10% income earners were 10 percentage points less likely to vote for the Institutional Revolutionary Party (PRI).

The education gradient weakened during the 1990s and 2000s with the decline in the PRI's vote share and the overall increase in support for the PAN and the left. The influence of the "useful" vote to oust the PRI after seventy-one years of political domination may have contributed to this tendency.[88] Despite genuine electoral competition, however, alternation of power did not improve public satisfaction after fiscal and monetary orthodoxy failed to solve urgent problems such as unemployment and poverty.[89] Dissatisfaction reached its peak under the term of PRI president Enrique Peña Nieto (2012–2018).[90] As the left attracted unprecedented support in 2018, especially among the higher educated and low-income earners, these last elections were marked by a return of the educational divide and at the same time, a reduction in the link between income and voting.

### The Decadence of the PRI and the Rise of the Mexican Left

Support for the left in Mexico has increased from less than 10 percent in the 1970s to more than 50 percent in the 2010s. This transition coincided with a series of iterations of electoral fraud, opposition protests, and electoral reforms, which leveled the political playing field and opened new opportunities for electoral competition.[91] The freedoms and opportunities brought about by democratization were responsible for the emergence of a figure like AMLO and his ascent to the presidency. To understand the drivers behind the rise of the Mexican left, it is useful to analyze other socioeconomic and demographic characteristics of voters (Table 15.4).

First, the left has managed to attract an increasing share of Indigenous voters.[92] Recent studies have challenged the idea of an "Indigenous vote" and its distinctiveness from other sociodemographic factors.[93] We

88. Klesner, "End of Mexico's One-Party Regime."

89. D. Crow, "The Party's Over: Citizen Conceptions of Democracy and Political Dissatisfaction in Mexico," *Comparative Politics* 43, no. 1 (2010): 41–61.

90. A. García Magos, "López Obrador in Democratic Mexico," *Oxford Research Encyclopedia of Latin American History*, ed. W. Beesley (Oxford University Press, 2018).

91. García, "López Obrador in Democratic Mexico."

92. Persons of Indigenous background are those who descend from the populations that inhabited the country, or a geographical region to which the country belongs, at the time of conquest or colonization. Persons of Mestizo background are those who have both Spanish and Indigenous roots.

93. W. Sonnleitner, "Participación, representación e inclusión política: Existe un voto indígena en México?" *Política y Gobierno* 27, no. 2 (2020).

*Table 15.4*   The Structure of Political Cleavages in Mexico, 2018

| | \multicolumn{3}{c}{Share of Votes Received (%)} | | |
| --- | --- | --- | --- |
| | PRI | PAN | PRD/Morena |
| **Education** | | | |
| Primary | 25% | 19% | 48% |
| Secondary | 17% | 18% | 57% |
| Tertiary | 13% | 26% | 50% |
| **Income** | | | |
| Bottom 50% | 19% | 19% | 54% |
| Middle 40% | 18% | 20% | 55% |
| Top 10% | 14% | 26% | 53% |
| **Age** | | | |
| 20–39 | 16% | 21% | 52% |
| 40–59 | 20% | 20% | 54% |
| 60+ | 21% | 19% | 53% |
| **Region** | | | |
| North | 20% | 22% | 53% |
| Center West | 15% | 25% | 46% |
| Center | 22% | 20% | 49% |
| South | 12% | 14% | 69% |
| **Ethnic Group** | | | |
| White | 25% | 30% | 39% |
| Mestizo | 18% | 17% | 56% |
| Indigenous | 6% | 14% | 74% |
| Other | 19% | 28% | 48% |

*Data Source:* Authors' computations using Mexican political attitudes surveys (see wpid.world).

*Note:* The table shows the average share of votes received by the main Mexican political parties by selected individual characteristics in the 2018 election. The Institutional Revolutionary Party (PRI) was supported by 25% of primary-educated voters in 2018, compared to only 13% of university graduates. PAN: National Action Party; PRD: Party of the Democratic Revolution.

document that Indigenous voters have progressively shifted toward the left, with support reaching its highest level in 2018, when 74 percent of Indigenous voters voted for Morena after AMLO's promise of more protection and security in Indigenous communities.

Second, there was also an increase in farmers' support for the left in the 2010s. Poor farmers traditionally supported the PRI, based on patronage

politics, and their vote share was still the highest of any group during the 2000s.[94] But farmers went from being the biggest supporters of the PRI to being the biggest supporters of the left in the 2010s, with 71 percent of them voting for Morena.[95]

Third, the left has managed to attract votes from outside the national capital, in particular in the north and south, the old strongholds of the PRI since the Mexican Revolution. The PRI is the only party that is proportionally stronger in rural areas, while both the PAN and the PRD have traditionally drawn most of their support from urban areas.[96] However, strictly rural areas are only a small part of the vast Mexican population, and links between rural, semi-urban, and urban areas are increasingly closer.[97] While support for the left used to come mainly from the national capital, the preference for the left in the north and the south surpassed support from the center in the 2018 election.

Finally, growing support for the left has also come from a mobilized young population. Younger voters were slightly more supportive of the left in the 1990s, and the PAN in the 2000s, than the PRI.[98] Support for the left increased among all age groups in 2018, but this rise was most prominent among the young. Younger cohorts, born after the democratic transition and with no recollection of the hegemonic PRI, therefore seemed to have been particularly hostile to the preservation of the common practices of corruption and clientelism of the PRI.

## Peru

### *From Colonial Rule to Independence*

The political history of Peru has been very turbulent and dates back to the almost 300 years of Spanish colonial rule, which gave rise to the economic, ethnic, and geographic divisions that characterize Peruvian society today. After its independence in 1821, the country took much longer

---

94. A. Díaz, B. Magaloni, J. Olarte, and E Franco, "La geografía electoral de 2012" (Stanford Center on Democracy, Development and the Rule of Law Policy Brief, October 2012), https://cddrl.fsi.stanford.edu/publications/la_geograf%C3%ADa_electoral _de_2012_m%C3%A9xico.

95. See appendix Figure EC45, wpid.world.

96. Magaloni et al., "Geografía electoral de 2012."

97. FAO, "México Rural del Siglo XXI" (FAO technical report, 2018), 5, http://www .fao.org/publications/card/es/c/I9548ES/.

98. See appendix Figures EC7 and EC24, wpid.world.

than most Latin American countries to evolve toward a reasonably stable political and economic system, and it faced alternating periods of democratic and authoritarian rule.

The 1823 Constitution assumed a culturally homogenous nation in which Spanish was the sole official language and Catholicism the sole official religion.[99] Inspired by the ideals of the Enlightenment, liberators recognized the Indigenous as citizens and attempted to provide to them the same rights as Whites and Mestizos (people of mixed descent). In spite of these declarations, the oligarchic republic that emerged in Peru after independence was based on restricted citizenship, slavery, forced labor, and ethnic discrimination.

The exclusion of a majority of the country from the life of the republic was a major source of the failure of state building, and the need for integration remained the main theme of Peruvian politics over the twentieth century.[100] The lack of integration was also reflected in the limited political participation of the Indigenous. The Electoral Law of 1896 restricted voting rights to male literates older than twenty-one and married male literates who had not reached that age, thereby excluding the majority of Indigenous people, who were illiterate. According to the 1876 census, 58 percent of Peruvians were of Indigenous origin.[101] This amendment to the Electoral Law was included in the subsequent constitutions and only modified in the 1979 constitution that gave illiterates the right to vote for the first time in national and municipal elections.

### The Emergence of the Multiparty System

After independence, Peru and its neighbors engaged in intermittent territorial disputes, and numerous brief aristocratic and authoritarian governments followed one another. It was only in the first decades of the twentieth century that left-wing ideologies emerged. In 1924, Peruvian leaders exiled in Mexico founded the Peruvian Aprista Party (Partido Aprista Peruano, APRA); the movement led by Haya de la Torre drew its influences from the Mexican Revolution and, to a lesser extent, from the

99. R. Stavenhagen, "Universal Human Rights and the Cultures of Indigenous Peoples and Other Ethnic Groups: The Critical Frontier of the 1990s," in *Human Rights in Perspective: A Global Assessment,* ed. A. Eide and B. Hagtvet (Basil Blackwell, 1992), 134–151.

100. J. Crabtree, review of *Toledo's Peru: Vision and Reality,* by Ronald Bruce St. John, *Journal of Latin American Studies* 43, no. 2 (2011): 397–399.

101. D. J. Yashar, *Contesting Citizenship in Latin America: The Rise of Indigenous Movements and the Postliberal Challenge* (Cambridge University Press, 2005).

Russian Revolution. In 1928, the Socialist Party of Peru, later the Peruvian Communist Party (Partido Comunista Peruano, PCP), was founded under the leadership of José Carlos Mariátegui, himself a former member of APRA. The two parties were the first to tackle the social and economic problems of the country. Although Mariátegui died at a young age, Haya de la Torre was elected president twice, but prevented by the military from taking office.

In the 1950s and 1960s, two important right-wing parties were founded, Popular Action (Acción Popular, AP) in 1956 and the Christian People's Party (Partido Popular Cristiano, PPC) in 1966. Moreover, old members from APRA and the PCP gave birth to rebel political organizations. In 1959, in particular, a clandestine faction within the PCP emerged in Ayacucho, one of the nation's poorest departments, where until midcentury, bankrupt landowners had used Indigenous people as slaves. This new political group aligned with the Maoist faction of the PCP and defended a new social order where peasant communities would have the same opportunities as people from urban areas in Lima.[102] It was not until the beginning of the 1970s that this faction became the PCP—Shining Path (Sendero Luminoso), and only in 1980 did it move to violence.

### From Authoritarian Rule to Redemocratization

Peru's most recent transition to democracy occurred in 1980 after more than a decade of military rule. The candidate from the center-right AP, Fernando Belaúnde, served as president from 1980 to 1985. After a promising beginning, however, Belaúnde's popularity eroded, due mainly to a prolonged economic crisis and the government's unsuccessful struggle to quell a radical guerrilla insurgency promoted by Sendero Luminoso.

Belaúnde's inability to reactivate the economy and stop the violence led to a rise in support for the APRA. After years of repression and clandestine activity during the period of military rule, the oldest surviving party of Peru was finally legalized in 1980. In 1985, the leader of the APRA since the death of Haya de la Torre, Alan García, was elected president. His term was characterized by a continuation of the severe economic crisis, social unrest, and violence.

By 1990, many Peruvians had found in the independent candidate from the party Change 90 (Cambio 90), Alberto Fujimori, the transformation they were looking for. Fujimori was initially applauded for his

102. D. S. Palmer, *The Shining Path of Peru* (St. Martin's Press, 1992).

aggressive economic reform program and for stepping up counterinsurgency efforts. Nonetheless, with the passing of time, he displayed increasing autocratic tendencies. He dissolved the legislature in 1992, launched a new constitution in 1993 that allowed him to run again and win in 1995, and engaged in military tactics to eradicate Sendero Luminoso, incurring human rights abuses. Fujimori was reelected in 2000, but his government collapsed after revelations of electoral fraud and high-level corruption, forcing him into exile that same year.

Peru then underwent a period of relative political stability, economic growth, and poverty reduction, led by Peru's first president of Indigenous descent, Alejandro Toledo (2001–2006), the candidate from the center-left party Possible Peru (Perú Posible, PP). Former president García launched a political comeback and won the presidential race in 2006 against his left-wing opponent, Ollanta Humala, from the Peruvian Nationalist Party (Partido Nacionalista Peruano, PNP). Economic growth continued under García, but it was not inclusive enough to improve the social conditions of Peru's poorest people. Humala moderated his stance to a more center-left position and won the presidency in 2011 against the conservative Keiko Fujimori, daughter of former president Alberto Fujimori.

In 2016, the center-right bloc Peruvians for Change (Peruanos por el Kambio, PPK), led by Pedro Pablo Kuczynski, won against two other large blocs, the right-wing coalition Popular Force led by Keiko Fujimori and the left-wing coalition Broad Front (Frente Amplio). After some corruption scandals, Kuczynski announced his resignation in 2018 and his vice president Martín Vizcarra took office. He dissolved the congress in September 2019 and issued a decree for legislative elections to be held in January 2020. The election was one of the most divisive in Peruvian history, due largely to the corruption scandals of current and previous members of the two right-wing coalitions, and it opened a new political era in the country.[103] Fujimorists lost most of their seats, while the APRA made the worst result in its history, failing to win a seat for the first time since 1963. Vizcarra was, however, impeached by the Peruvian Congress in November 2020, accused of corruption and mishandling the COVID-19 pandemic. Vizcarra's impeachment led to social unrest, and Manuel Merino, president of the Peruvian Congress who succeeded him as president

103. F. Tuesta, *Perú: Elecciones 2016: Un país dividido y un resultado inesperado* (Fondo Editorial de la PUCP, 2017)

of Peru, resigned on November 15. Francisco Sagasti was then elected president of Congress the next day and became president of Peru on November 17.

### Socioeconomic Cleavages during Redemocratization

The return to constitutional government in 1980 facilitated the institutionalization of procedures for participation in political life, and political parties—some new and some old—emerged from the years of military rule. In what follows, we analyze how this process of redemocratization shaped political polarization along social dimensions, using postelectoral surveys for all presidential elections held from 1995 to 2016.[104]

Figure 15.17 summarizes election results for the most important parties since 1995. Right-wing parties include the Fujimorists, the PPC, the Christian democratic alliance National Unity (2000–2008), the AP, and since 2016, the PPK. Left-wing parties include the Union for Peru (Unión por Perú, UPP), the PNP, Peru Wins (Gana Perú, GP), the PP, and APRA.[105]

Until the mid-twentieth century, Peru was mainly characterized by multiclass electoral constituencies mobilized by oligarchic leaders based on clientelistic networks. Strong class divisions in voting patterns did not emerge until the 1980s, following the rise of labor unions and urban social organizations.[106] The strength of labor unions and popular organizations had already eroded by the end of the 1980s, due to the deep economic crisis and political violence. This process made space for a new type of personalist leadership initiated by Fujimori, which broke with traditional class-based voting patterns and continues with all other leaders to the present.[107] Peru thus has had strong divisions among education

---

104. See appendix Table FE1, wpid.world, for data sources.

105. There is some controversy with respect to the classification of APRA. We follow P. Planas, *La democracia volátil: Movimientos, partidos, líderes políticos y conductas electorales en el Perú contemporáneo* (Fundación Friedrich Ebert, 2000) and classify the party on the center-left. Nonetheless, we conduct the whole analysis excluding APRA and show that it barely affects the results. To categorize other parties, we use the classification of C. Meléndez, "Los ejes de la derecha en el Perú preelectoral," *Revista Argumentos* 3, no. 1 (2015): 3–8.

106. M. A. Cameron, *Democracy and Authoritarianism in Peru: Political Coalitions and Social Change* (Palgrave Macmillan, 1994).

107. K. M. Roberts and M. Arcee, "Neoliberalism and Lower-Class Voting Behavior in Peru," *Comparative Political Studies* 31, no. 2 (1998): 217–246.

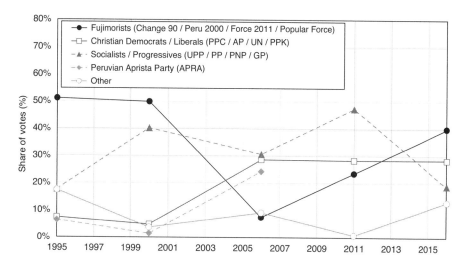

FIGURE 15.17. Election results in Peru, 1995–2016
*Data Source:* Authors' computations using official election results (see wpid.world).
*Note:* The figure shows the share of votes received by selected Peruvian political parties or groups of parties in presidential elections between 1995 and 2016. Note that the APRA still exists in the 2010s but does not appear separately in the survey. Fujimorists (Keiko Fujimori, Popular Force) received 40% of the vote in 2016.

and income groups since the mid-1990s, but they have fluctuated, rather than persisting over time (Figure 15.18).

The education gradient for right-wing parties has been quite stable throughout the whole period. Even though Fujimorism is a multiclass political coalition, it attracts relatively more of the lowest-educated vote, while the other right-wing parties (PPC, UN, AP, and PPK) are more popular among the highest educated (Figure 15.19). Fujimori attracted massive support based not on class solidarity, but on hard work and individual initiative.[108] The education cleavage turned negative between 1995–2000 and 2006–2011, due mainly to a substantial reduction in support for Fujimorism after revelations of electoral fraud and corruption, to the benefit of the APRA, UPP, and GP; this happened among all education groups but was more pronounced among the lower educated.[109] Following Humala's corruption scandals, in the 2016 election the education cleavage

108. Roberts and Arcee, "Neoliberalism and Lower-Class Voting."
109. See appendix Figures FC1 and FC17, wpid.world.

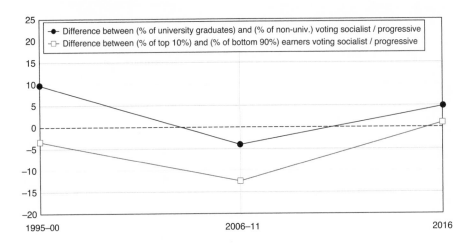

FIGURE 15.18. The socialist/progressive vote by income and education in Peru, 1995–2016

*Data Source:* Authors' computations using Peruvian political attitudes surveys (see wpid.world).

*Note:* The figure shows the relative support of highest-educated and top-income voters for center-left and left-wing parties (UPP/PP/PNP/GP/APRA/Other left), after controlling for age, gender, religious affiliation, employment status, marital status, rural-urban location, ethnicity, and region. In 2016, university graduates were 5 percentage points more likely to vote for socialists/progressives.

turned positive again, as the reduction in the left vote share was more intense among lowest-educated voters than among the highest educated.

Voting differences between income groups have been more pronounced. Support for Fujimorism during the 1990s was nearly the same between top 10 percent and bottom 90 percent earners, but the loss in support since the 2000s was larger among top-income earners, who are better represented among the other right (Figure 15.20). Hence, the Fujimorist Popular Front became in 2016 the most important party among the low-educated and low-income electorate. Keiko Fujimori's success relied on a political platform that emphasized significant measures to tackle violent crime and distanced her from the legacy of authoritarianism and graft of her father.[110] Taken together, recent fluctuations in class-based cleavages are largely determined by changes in the electoral behaviors of

110. Tuesta, *Perú: Elecciones 2016.*

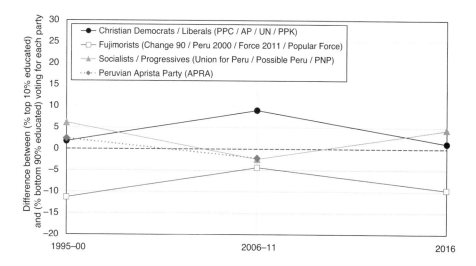

FIGURE 15.19. Vote and education in Peru, 1995–2016
*Data Source:* Authors' computations using Peruvian political attitudes surveys (see wpid.world).
*Note:* The figure shows the difference between the share of top 10% educated voters and the share of bottom 90% educated voters voting for the main Peruvian political parties. In 2016, the top 10% educated were 10 percentage points less likely to vote for Fujimorists (Keiko Fujimori, Popular Force).

the lower educated and the poor, whose vote seems to be driven more by specific leaders than by party ideology.

### The Recent Politicization of Ethnic Identities

When compared to neighboring and ethnically similar Andean countries like Ecuador and Bolivia, Peru appears to be an exceptional case, characterized by the weak activism of nationally organized Indigenous movements and parties.[111] Since redemocratization, however, Indigenous issues have been gradually incorporated into the political process, but their salience for party competition only recently emerged during the presidential campaign of Alberto Fujimori in 1990.

Although of Japanese origin, Alberto Fujimori managed to attract with a pro-ethnic and pro-poor discourse a substantial share of the poor Indigenous and Asian vote in the 1990 presidential runoff elections

111. Yashar, "Contesting Citizenship."

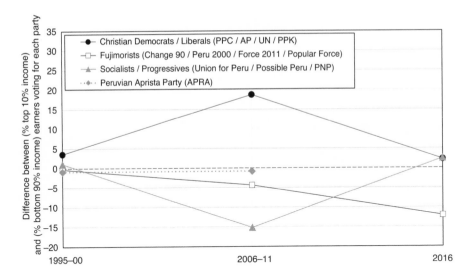

FIGURE 15.20. Vote and income in Peru, 1995–2016

*Data Source:* Authors' computations using Peruvian political attitudes surveys (see wpid.world).

*Note:* The figure shows the difference between the share of top 10% earners and the share of bottom 90% earners voting for the main Peruvian political parties. In 2016, top 10% income earners were 12 percentage points less likely to vote for Fujimorists (Keiko Fujimori, Popular Force).

against Mario Vargas Llosa, who symbolized the White Lima upper class.[112] Fujimorism continued attracting a large share of the Asian vote, but the Indigenous support shifted toward Alejandro Toledo in the 2001 election, when he became the first elected president with Andean roots. He frequently used Indigenous symbols and discussed issues relevant to Indigenous voters during his presidential campaign. In line with Toledo, Humala also referred to ethnic issues during his campaign. Hence, the two presidential left-wing campaigns politicized ethnic divisions to attract more votes in Indigenous areas.[113] This strategy proved to be successful, as the share of votes for Humala grew significantly after 2006 in the south, where the share of Indigenous people is larger (Figure 15.21).

112. R. L. Madrid, "Ethnic Proximity and Ethnic Voting in Peru," *Journal of Latin American Studies* 43, no. 2 (2011): 267–297.
113. C. Raymond and M. Arce, "The Politicization of Indigenous Identities in Peru," *Party Politics* 19, no. 4 (2013): 555–576.

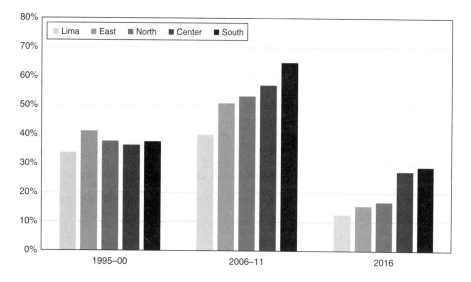

FIGURE 15.21. The socialist/progressive vote by region in Peru, 1995–2016
*Data Source:* Authors' computations using Peruvian political attitudes surveys (see wpid.world).
*Note:* The figure shows the share of votes received by Peruvian center-left and left-wing parties (UPP/PP/PNP/GP/APRA/Other left) by region. The socialists and progressives received 29% of the vote in the South in 2016.

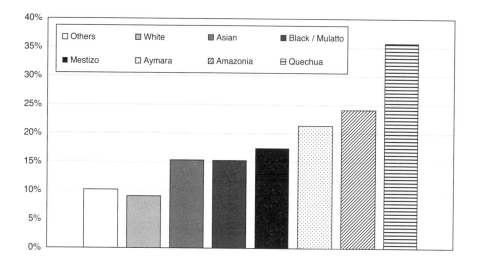

FIGURE 15.22. The ethnic cleavage in Peru, 2016
*Data Source:* Authors' computations using Peruvian political attitudes surveys (see wpid.world).
*Note:* The figure shows the share of votes received by Peruvian center-left/left-wing parties (UPP/PP/PNP/GP/APRA/Other left) by ethnic affiliation. In 2016, 36% of Quechua voters voted for the socialists and progressives, compared to 9% of White voters.

Progressive parties were also significantly more popular among Indigenous voters in the 2016 election, in particular the Quechuas (Figure 15.22). As the Indigenous population is poorer and less educated than the Mestizo and White populations, this politicization of ethnic identities is clearly behind the fluctuations in the education and income cleavages since Fujimori.[114] Overall, these findings show that ethnic cleavages have gained increasing importance in recent decades, and the pro-poor Asian and Indigenous coalitions have contributed to blurring class cleavages in Peru.

114. Appendix Figures FD2 and FD11, wpid.world, show the composition of income and education groups by ethnicity.

16

# Extreme Inequality, Elite Transformation, and the Changing Structure of Political Cleavages in South Africa, 1994–2019

AMORY GETHIN

## Introduction

This chapter draws on political attitudes surveys to study the changing relationships between party support, economic inequality, and racial cleavages in democratic South Africa. The legacy of the apartheid regime has left a marking imprint on social identities, party politics, and access to economic opportunities. It has crystallized South Africa's party system along racial divides, with the ruling African National Congress (ANC), mainly supported by Black voters, opposing the Democratic Alliance (DA), mainly supported by White voters. Behind the persistent dominance of the ANC, however, long-term transformations of sociopolitical structures have opened new potentials for voter realignments. Rising inequalities in a stagnating economy have come with the emergence of a new Black middle class, yet have left a large share of the population in a state of mass unemployment and poverty. Intraparty factionalism and government corruption have posed a growing threat to the ANC, along with difficulties containing latent ethnic, regional, and ideological tensions.

This chapter focuses on the evolution of political cleavages in South Africa by combining and harmonizing survey data on electoral behav-

I am grateful to Goolam Aboobaker, Aroop Chatterjee, Léo Czajka, Halfdan Lynge-Mangueira, Clara Martínez-Toledano, and Thomas Piketty for their useful advice. I also wish to thank the teams of Datafirst and of the South African Social Attitudes Survey for making the data used in this chapter available. This chapter is partly based on A. Gethin, "Cleavage Structures and Distributive Politics" (master's thesis, Paris School of Economics, 2018), chapter 4.

iors since the first national election of 1994. What are the social and ideological coalitions underlying the strength of the ANC and its decline in recent years? What can configurations of ethnicity, class, and political competition tell us about the future of the South African party system? The study of electoral cleavages in South Africa provides unique insights into the relationships between democratization, colonial legacies, and deep inherited racial divides. All dominant parties have in common the need to adapt their appeals to changing social structures by reinventing new cross-class coalitions, at the risk of breaking apart and, in some cases, creating new unsustainable tensions. Comparing the ANC's trajectory to those of other historical dominant parties, such as the Indian National Congress (see Chapter 9), the Liberal Democratic Party in Japan (see Chapter 11), and the Barisan Nasional in Malaysia (see Chapter 12), can therefore prove to be particularly fruitful for better understanding the evolution of one-party dominant systems and the future of South African politics.

### From Apartheid to Democracy

The emergence of the modern South African state goes back to the turn of the twentieth century.[1] Following the defeat of the South African Republic and the Orange Free State in the Second Boer War (1899–1902), the territory was united under British rule, with the Union of South Africa officially bringing together the Cape Colony, the Natal Colony, the Transvaal, and the Orange River Colony in 1910. South African White settlers were at the time divided into two main groups: Afrikaners, who were mostly descendants of Dutch and French immigrants of the eighteenth and nineteenth centuries, and the English-speaking communities who came from more recent waves of immigration following the colonization of southern Africa by the British throughout the nineteenth century.

The unification of South Africa announced the beginning of a process of dispossessing Africans from their rights, access to land, and political participation. At the same time, the new Union of South Africa came with

---

1. For the discussion presented in this section, see, for instance, E. S. Lieberman, *Race and Regionalism in the Politics of Taxation in Brazil and South Africa* (Cambridge University Press, 2003); H. Marais, *South Africa Pushed to the Limit: The Political Economy of Change* (Zed Books, 2011); C. H. Feinstein, *An Economic History of South Africa* (Cambridge University Press, 2005).

the formation of a modern state exclusively reserved for the White population. This outcome was not the result of a deterministic process. In the Cape, the Cape Qualified Franchise had since 1853 allowed all male citizens with property exceeding £25 to vote and to be elected to Parliament, regardless of race. Accordingly, the participation of Blacks and Coloureds in the war on the side of the British had raised hopes of a new order with enhanced political rights. But the 1902 British-Afrikaner Treaty of Vereeniging, by promoting a vision of White national unity, marked a decisive moment in the racial definition of citizenship. Legislators and political leaders saw this unity as crucial to avoiding new conflicts between the Afrikaners and the British. It would also soon be envisioned as a solution to growing class cleavages within the White community.[2] Cross-class alliances were finally successful in 1924, when the National Party founded by Afrikaner nationalists came to power in coalition with the Labour Party, which represented White working-class interests and advocated for protective measures against competition from Black labor.

In 1913, the Natives Land Act delineated the land available for Black occupancy to 7 percent of the national territory. The 1927 Immorality Act made it illegal to have sexual intercourse across the color line. The Cape Qualified Franchise was progressively amended in the 1930s, until all Black voters were finally excluded from political representation in 1960. The apartheid regime was the culmination of these policies aimed at restricting the movements of the Black population and enforcing strict boundaries between the races. From 1948 onward, following the election of the National Party, successive administrations extended the existing segregation system through a series of legislative measures. The 1970 Homeland Citizens Act, completing the Natives Land Act of 1913, thus created "homelands" or "reserves" to which thousands of Africans were forcibly transferred. It would take years of resistance, growing international pressures, and eventually the end of the Cold War to bring about the end of racial segregation in 1994.

Political opposition to White domination had a long history. The African National Congress originated from the South African Native National Congress (SANNC), founded in 1912 by a small group of moderate middle-class Africans aiming to bring together the African population. After years of low activity, it became a major organization in the 1950s

2. Lieberman, *Race and Regionalism*.

and 1960s, organizing passive resistance acts in the spirit of Gandhi's Indian liberation movement. Nevertheless, ideological disagreements within the ANC in the 1950s led to the creation of the Pan-Africanist Congress (PAC), which advocated for a specifically African vision of the new nation, as compared to the ANC, which sought to promote a South Africa for all the races. Mangosuthu Buthelezi, a former ANC Youth League member, further opened new space for internal ethnic-based divisions by creating the Inkatha National Cultural Liberation Movement, which in 1994 became the Inkatha Freedom Party (IFP), an organization exclusively based in KwaZulu-Natal and supported by traditional Zulu chiefs. Internal divisions within the PAC and the limited scope of the IFP, however, prevented these two organizations from becoming serious contenders against the domination of the opposition movement guided by the African National Congress. Just as the Indian National Congress had become the single dominant candidate for ruling independent India, the ANC of Nelson Mandela was by the mid-1990s the only organization with sufficient mass support to bring about the transition from apartheid to a new political regime.

### South Africa's Party System since Democratization

The general elections of 1994 were the first multiracial democratic elections held in South Africa's history. The ANC won the election by a landslide, receiving 63 percent of popular votes as compared to 20 percent for the National Party of F. W. de Klerk. Since then, the ANC has won every general election by a substantial margin (see Figure 16.1). The share of voters supporting the ANC grew during the years of Thabo Mbeki (1999–2008), reaching 70 percent in 2004. It has followed a declining trend since then, moving back to just above 60 percent for the second term of Jacob Zuma in 2014, and reaching a historically low level of 57.5 percent in 2019. Therefore, while the last three elections have shown slow signs of erosion in support for the government, the ANC remains by far the dominant party today. Its hegemony draws in part on its Tripartite Alliance with the powerful Congress of South African Trade Unions (COSATU) and the South African Communist Party (SACP), which have not contested any democratic election separately from the ANC since democratization.

Opposition to the ANC since 1994 has remained weak and diverse. The main serious contenders to the ruling party have been parties bringing

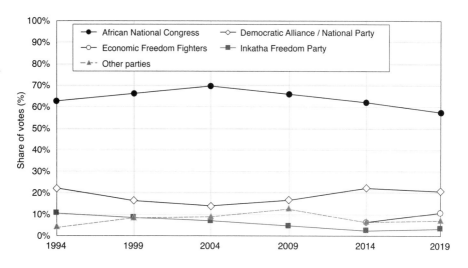

FIGURE 16.1. Election results in South Africa, 1994–2019
*Data Source:* Author's computations using official election results (see wpid.world).
*Note:* The figure shows the share of votes received by selected South African political parties between 1994 and 2019. In 2019, the African National Congress (ANC) received 58% of votes, while the Democratic Alliance received 21%.

together the majority of White South Africans. These have included the National Party (NP) and its successor the New National Party (NNP), which represented the legacy of apartheid governments and lost significance at the end of the 1990s. They were replaced by the newly created Democratic Alliance (DA) in 2003, resulting from a merger between the more liberal Democratic Party and the NNP.[3] The DA has since then represented the main opposition to the ANC in Parliament and in local elections, especially in the Western and Eastern Cape, where it has successfully conquered a number of localities. Ideologically, the DA can generally be considered centrist, promoting a mixed economy combining increased social spending, fiscal sustainability, and deregulation of the labor market. Together, the group of parties consisting in the NP, the NNP, and the DA received between 15 percent and 20 percent of votes from 1994 to 2019.

3. The merger between the NNP and the DP was aborted, but a number of members of the NNP remained in the organization, whose new name (Democratic Alliance) was kept.

Other opposition parties have mainly consisted in regional parties or in splits from the ANC. In 1994, the Inkatha Freedom Party (IFP) of Mangosuthu Buthelezi received 10.5 percent of popular votes, campaigning on a platform of Zulu localism and greater autonomy for traditional African communities. It has seen its support decrease in general elections since then, reaching only 3.3 percent of votes in 2019. The Congress of the People (COPE) was founded following internal divisions between the factions of Jacob Zuma and those of Thabo Mbeki at the fifty-second ANC national conference held at Polokwane in 2007. The conference revealed two forms of divisions within the African National Congress: a difference in economic policies, with Zuma being generally more left-wing than Mbeki, and a difference in ethnic backgrounds manifesting divides between Xhosa-speaking (following Mbeki) and Zulu-speaking (following Zuma) constituencies. The conference led to the victory of Zuma and eventually to his election as president of South Africa. The COPE ran against the ANC in 2009 but received only 7.4 percent of votes. It has become insignificant since then, joining the Democratic Alliance in a number of local elections.

The 2019 elections were another turning point in South Africa's contemporary electoral history. Following allegations of corruption linking Zuma and his administration to the wealthy Gupta family, opposition parties and mass protests joined in accusing the government of "state capture." Dissension grew within the ANC too, and in August 2017 Zuma narrowly survived the eighth motion of no confidence brought against him during his presidency. The fifty-fourth national conference of the African National Congress held in December 2017 finally put an end to Zuma's leadership: Cyril Ramaphosa was elected the party's presidential candidate against Jacob Zuma's wife Nkosazana Dlamini-Zuma, with 52 percent of votes.

The Zuma crisis eroded popular support for the ANC and played a key role in the strengthening of a new far-left opposition to the ANC, the Economic Freedom Fighters (EFF). The EFF was founded by the former African National Congress Youth League president Julius Malema, who was expelled from the ANC in 2013. It claims to follow Marxism-Leninism and proposes policies such as free health care, nationalization of key industries, expropriation of land, and large increases in the minimum wage. Its ideology includes both radical left-wing economic policies as well as Pan-Africanist elements aiming at promoting the Black

majority. According to available evidence, its supporters are predominantly Black, male, young, and urban.[4] The EFF reached a vote share of 6.3 percent in the 2014 general elections and grew to 10.8 percent in 2019, making in the third-most important party in Parliament after the Democratic Alliance at the time of writing.

## Race and Inequality: Continuity and Change

South Africa has always been one of the most unequal countries in the world. The top 1 percent of the population received 22 percent of the national income is 1914.[5] These inequalities at the top end of the distribution came with extreme income gaps between population groups. At about the same period, in 1917, Africans' average incomes were estimated to be about ten times lower than those of Whites, and those of Coloureds and Asians were five times lower. This gap remained approximately constant until the transition to democracy.[6] Non-Whites were systematically excluded from upper layers of society: from 1960 to the mid-1980s, the share of White South Africans in the top 1 percent of the income distribution always exceeded 95 percent.[7]

The particularly high levels of economic inequalities in South Africa, combined with their predominantly racial dimension, implied that the postapartheid era came with a dual economy lacking any significant middle class. The end of institutionalized segregation in the middle of the 1990s did create new opportunities for previously marginalized groups. Yet, income and wealth inequalities did not decrease. Quite the contrary: a number of empirical studies have converged in documenting a rise in overall income disparities at least since 1993.[8] This rise has been driven by

---

4. Citizen Surveys, "How Many White EFF Supporters Exist, and 11 Other Stats," Citizen Surveys, November 1, 2018, https://citizensurveys.net/citizen-surveys-how-many-white-eff-supporters-exist-and-11-other-stats/.

5. F. Alvaredo and A. B. Atkinson, "Colonial Rule, Apartheid and Natural Resources: Top Incomes in South Africa, 1903–2007" (CEPR Discussion Paper Series No. 8155, 2010), https://cepr.org/active/publications/discussion_papers/dp.php?dpno=8155.

6. M. Leibbrandt, I. Woolard, A. Finn, and J. Argent, "Trends in South African Income Distribution and Poverty since the Fall of Apartheid" (OECD Social, Employment and Migration Working Paper No. 101, 2010), https://opendocs.ids.ac.uk/opendocs/bitstream/handle/20.500.12413/11861/Trends_in_South_African.pdf?sequence=1&isAllowed=y.

7. Alvaredo and Atkinson, "Colonial Rule."

8. See, for instance, Leibbrandt et al., "Trends in South African Income Distribution"; M. Wittenberg, "Wages and Wage Inequality in South Africa 1994–2011: The Evidence

the top end of the distribution, with the top 1 percent and the top 0.1 percent benefiting from more pronounced increases in average incomes.[9] Available evidence does not suggest that wealth inequality has declined either: the top 10 percent of the wealth distribution have consistently held over 85 percent of aggregate household wealth since 1993, the highest level of wealth inequality observed in the world today.[10]

Growing income and wealth disparities did come, however, with important changes in the racial composition of middle- and upper-income groups. Average income gaps have significantly decreased, especially between Black and White South Africans. The rise in top income groups was therefore driven by higher inequality *within* racial groups, and in particular within the African population.[11] Put differently, the postapartheid era came with the cooptation of a new, more racially diverse elite, while leaving the overall socioeconomic structure mostly unchanged. Even these changes should, nonetheless, not be exaggerated: the share of Blacks in the top 10 percent increased from 25 percent in 1995 to 35 percent in 2008, while their share in the top 1 percent did not exceed 16 percent in 2008.[12]

Sociologically, the changing shape of South African inequality implied a growing separation between the new non-White middle class and the rest of the population. Politically, it meant a potential for new divisions within the predominantly Black electorate of the ANC. Several studies have accordingly attempted to study the new Black middle class, revealing

from Household Survey Data" (Southern Africa Labour and Development Research Unit Working Paper Series 135, 2014), http://www.opensaldru.uct.ac.za/handle/11090/767.

9. I. Bassier and I. Woolard, "Exclusive Growth: Rapidly Increasing Top Incomes amidst Low National Growth in South Africa" (REDI3x3 Working Paper 47, 2018), http://www.redi3x3.org/paper/exclusive-growth-rapidly-increasing-top-incomes-amidst-low-national-growth-south-africa.

10. A. Chatterjee, L. Czajka, and A. Gethin, "Estimating the Distribution of Household Wealth in South Africa" (WID.world Working Paper 2020/06, 2020).

11. S. van der Berg and M. Louw, "Changing Patterns of South African Income Distribution: Towards Time Series Estimates of Distribution and Poverty" (paper presented at the Conference of the Economic Society of South Africa, Stellenbosch, 2003), https://sarpn.org/documents/d0000727/P800-Poverty_trends_vdBerg_Louw.pdf; Statistics South Africa, "Inequality Trends in South Africa: A Multidimensional Diagnosis of Inequality" (Statistics South Africa Report No. 03-10-19, 2017), http://www.statssa.gov.za/publications/Report-03-10-19/Report-03-10-192017.pdf.

12. E. Morival, "Top Incomes and Racial Inequality in South Africa: Evidence from Tax Statistics and Household Surveys, 1993–2008" (master's thesis, Paris School of Economics, 2011).

a significant and continuous increase in its overall size since 1993.[13] When it comes to political attitudes, however, studies have obtained much more contrasting results. Carlos García-Rivero, for instance, showed that closeness to the ANC in the 1990s gradually became stronger among Blacks whose standards of living were improving, opening the possibility of a realignment dividing voters with lower income levels and the new middle class, with the latter being more supportive of the ruling party.[14] Almost ten years later, Robert Mattes found the exact opposite: Blacks with higher material welfare tend to value different types of government action—and in particular "higher-order goods"—and to identify less with the ANC than poorer Black individuals.[15] However, both studies converged in documenting no concrete electoral consequence of these diverging social values: social class did not predict higher or lower support for the ruling party. This is in line with evidence showing that South African citizens' identification with the ANC has strongly decreased since the mid-1990s, despite the party's continuous success when it comes to competing in general elections.[16]

## The Persistent Intersectionality of Racial and Social Divides

I now turn to studying the structure of political cleavages in South Africa using political attitudes surveys available from two sources. The Institute for Democratic Alternatives in South Africa (IDASA) conducted the first national election study in 1994, a few months after the election took place. In 1998 and 1999, IDASA again surveyed South African voters in a series of opinion polls prior to the 1999 election.[17] Since 2004, other postelectoral surveys have been conducted in the context of the Compara-

13. See, for instance, R. Southall, "Political Change and the Black Middle Class in Democratic South Africa," *Canadian Journal of African Studies* 38, no. 3 (2004): 521–542; R. Mattes, "South Africa's Emerging Black Middle Class: A Harbinger of Political Change?," *Journal of International Development* 27 (2015): 665–692. On methodological issues with defining the new middle class, see J. Visagie and D. Posel, "A Reconsideration of What and Who Is Middle Class in South Africa," *Development South Africa* 30, no. 2 (2013): 149–167.

14. C. García-Rivero, "Race, Class and Underlying Trends in Party Support in South Africa," *Party Politics* 12, no. 1 (2006): 57–75.

15. Mattes, "South Africa's Emerging Black Middle Class."

16. A. Butler, "Considerations on the Erosion of One-Party Dominance," *Representation* 45, no. 2 (2009): 159–171.

17. To increase the reliability of estimates, I use the fourth wave of the 1998–1999 IDASA polls, which took place shortly before the election.

tive National Elections Project (2004, 2009, 2014) and the Comparative Study of Electoral Systems (2014). However, due to limitations in the number of available sociodemographic variables and low sample sizes, I choose instead to rely on the 2004, 2009, 2014, and 2017 South African Social Attitudes Surveys (SASAS) to cover the more recent elections.[18] In the following analysis, I focus on the structure of the vote for the ANC. Detailed figures on support for the Democratic Alliance and on the determinants of electoral turnout can be found in the appendix.[19]

Race has remained the primary determinant of political representation and inequality in the contemporary history of South Africa. The South African census, as well as the majority of household surveys, ask the population to self-categorize into five population groups: "Black/African," "White/European," "Coloured," "Asian/Indian," and "Other." In 2018, Black South Africans represented about 74 percent of the voting-age population, compared to Whites about 13 percent, Coloureds 10 percent, Asians 3 percent, and Others less than 1 percent (see Table 16.1). Black individuals correspond to "African" or "Indigenous" populations, which include a large variety of languages and ethnic groups. Asians are in majority the descendants of Indian indentured laborers brought during the nineteenth century by British authorities to work on plantations. Coloureds are a very diverse group, which can more or less be defined as the residual of the three other categories. It is important to insist on the historically and politically constructed nature of these categories, which are in large part inherited from the rigid classification that the apartheid regime attempted to force on the South African population. As such, "population groups" are to be

---

18. The 2019 SASAS survey was not available at the time of writing, and neither were other postelectoral surveys that could be used to cover the 2019 election. I used the 2017 SASAS survey to get a sense of changes in electoral behaviors from 2014 to 2019. These results should be considered preliminary. An important limitation to the results presented below is "desirability bias": respondents tend to provide socially desirable responses and overreport voting for the winner of the election, especially if there are group pressures. In the case of the United States, see, for instance, A. Brownback and A. Novotny, "Social Desirability Bias and Polling Errors in the 2016 Presidential Election," *Journal of Behavioral and Experimental Economics* 74 (2018): 38–56. Unfortunately, there is no information available to correct this bias, so I uniformly reweight respondents to match official elections results, as in other chapters of this book.

19. See appendix Figures B1 to B18 for the DA/NP/NNP/Freedom Front Plus, and appendix Figures D1 to D11 for the determinants of abstention in general elections (World Political Cleavages and Inequality Database, http://wpid.world). The Freedom Front Plus is a small right-wing national party promoting Afrikaner interests.

*Table 16.1* The Composition of the South African Electorate, 1994–2019

|  | 1994 | 1999 | 2004 | 2009 | 2014 | 2019 |
|---|---|---|---|---|---|---|
| **Population Groups** | | | | | | |
| Black/African | 69% | 71% | 72% | 72% | 74% | 76% |
| White/European | 19% | 17% | 15% | 14% | 13% | 11% |
| Coloured | 10% | 9% | 10% | 11% | 10% | 10% |
| Indian/Asian | 3% | 3% | 3% | 3% | 3% | 3% |
| **Languages** | | | | | | |
| Afrikaans | 19% | 18% | 18% | 18% | 16% | 14% |
| English | 12% | 11% | 11% | 11% | 10% | 10% |
| Zulu | 23% | 20% | 24% | 22% | 20% | 22% |
| Xhosa | 14% | 16% | 14% | 16% | 16% | 14% |
| North Sotho | 7% | 10% | 9% | 7% | 9% | 10% |
| South Sotho | 8% | 9% | 8% | 7% | 8% | 9% |
| Tswana | 8% | 9% | 7% | 8% | 9% | 9% |
| Other | 9% | 8% | 10% | 11% | 12% | 12% |
| **Regions** | | | | | | |
| Eastern/Western/Northern Cape | 31% | 27% | 27% | 29% | 27% | 25% |
| Free State | 6% | 7% | 6% | 6% | 5% | 5% |
| KwaZulu-Natal | 22% | 21% | 21% | 20% | 18% | 19% |
| Other provinces | 40% | 45% | 46% | 45% | 50% | 51% |

*Data Source:* Author's computations using South African political attitudes surveys (see wpid.world).

*Note:* The table shows descriptive statistics for selected variables. In 2014, 74% of the voting-age population self-described as "Black/African," compared to 13% "White/European."

understood primarily in terms of self-assigned social constructs rather than preexisting rigid identities.

Figure 16.2 decomposes the share of popular votes received by the ANC by population group. Racial identification is an exceptionally strong predictor of voting behaviors, with no major change since 1994. From 1994 to 2019, more than 70 percent of Blacks/Africans voted for the ANC in every general election, compared to less than 10 percent of Whites. Support for the ruling party among Coloureds and Asians fell in between, with fluctuations from election to election and no clear trend over time. Black South Africans have been the only population group voting in majority for the ANC.

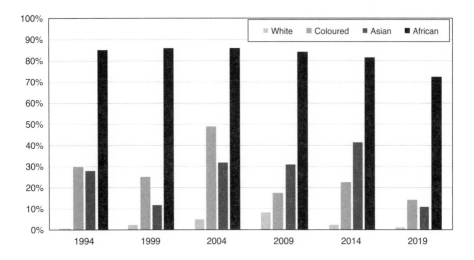

FIGURE 16.2. The racial cleavage in South Africa, 1994–2019: Vote for the ANC by population group
*Data Source:* Author's computations using South African political attitudes surveys (see wpid.world).
*Note:* The figure shows the share of votes received by the African National Congress (ANC) among voters belonging to different population groups between 1994 and 2019. The ANC was supported by more than 70% of African voters, compared to less than 10% of White voters in all years.

Figure 16.3 provides another perspective on the strength and evolution of this cleavage by plotting the difference between the share of Africans voting ANC and the share of other population groups voting ANC, before and after controls. Africans have been more likely to vote for the ANC by 65 to 75 percentage points in all elections, with fluctuations but no clear long-run evolution. Controlling for other available variables slightly reduces this gap, as the ANC tends to receive greater support among lower income groups, from poorer provinces such as Gauteng or Limpopo, and in rural areas, independent of racial affiliations. However, the effect of racial identity on electoral behaviors remains substantial even after controls.

The highly polarized racial structure of political conflicts in South Africa has therefore proved to be very resilient in the past twenty-five years, reflecting the legacy of the transition from apartheid to democracy, which directly shaped South Africa's party system along divisions inherited from a century of legal, institutional, and ideological codifications of race. The

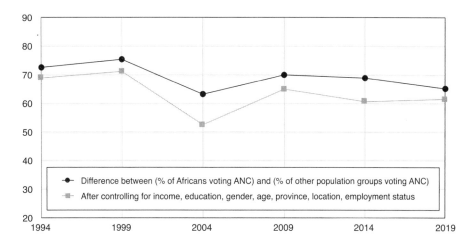

FIGURE 16.3. The racial cleavage in South Africa, 1994–2019: Vote for the ANC among Africans

*Data Source:* Author's computations using South African political attitudes surveys (see wpid.world).

*Note:* The figure shows the difference between the share of votes received by the African National Congress (ANC) among Africans and among other population groups between 1994 and 2019, before and after controls. Africans have always been more likely to support the ANC than other population groups by over 60 percentage points.

reasons underlying enduring support for the ANC in a context of rising inequality, low growth, and increasing corruption, however, are more complex to identify. Karen Ferree has suggested that three different potential frameworks could contribute to explaining this persistence.[20] First, according to the *expressive voting framework,* individuals view their support for ethnically homogeneous parties as a collective, psychologically rewarding affirmation of their social identity. Second, in the *straight policy framework,* voters rationally and independently choose the party that best represents their policy interests. In the *informational framework,* finally, voters are still driven by interests, but the presence of uncertainty implies that they evaluate the ethnic characteristics of candidates as a shortcut for their ideological affiliation. Ferree provides evidence that the latter framework may be the most relevant when it

20. K. E. Ferree, "The Micro-Foundations of Ethnic Voting: Evidence from South Africa" (Afrobarometer Working Paper No. 40, 2006), https://afrobarometer.org/publications /wp40-micro-foundations-ethnic-voting-evidence-south-africa.

comes to understanding voting behaviors in South Africa. In particular, Black voters tend to believe that the ANC represents all population groups (invalidating the expressive voting framework), but that opposition parties (the DP or the NP) represent exclusively White South Africans. The exact opposite is true of White South Africans, who tend to perceive the ANC as being an organization embodying only Black interests. This is consistent with the informational theory: voters tend to identify with the party that they believe best represents the interests of their group, or rather, in this context they tend to vote against the party they feel does not include theirs.

These different motives, however, should not be treated as exclusive. To the extent that social experiences shape collective beliefs, the lack of interactions between population groups create the sociological foundations for policy and partisan identifications based on race. Accordingly, the party system itself, which limits contenders to mainly the ANC and the DA, reinforces voters' expectations and perceptions of the racial nature of party politics. Furthermore, the predominance of race should not prevent us from studying more closely other determinants of electoral behaviors. A large majority of Africans support the ANC, but 15 to 20 percent of them do not, and this share has been rising since 2009. Understanding the factors behind these changes is of great interest for thinking about the future of South Africa's party system.

### Inequality, Identity, and the New Black Middle Class

Race and social class were closely intertwined throughout the twentieth century and continue to be today. How do these two variables interact when it comes to voting behaviors? And do we observe changes in the link between class and party support when evening out the racial dimension of inequality? Figure 16.4 provides some insights into these questions by decomposing the share of votes received by the ANC by income quintile and among the top 10 percent of income earners. Two facts clearly stand out. First, income differences in support for the ANC have remained extremely strong over the entire period: more than 70 percent of the poorest 20 percent of earners have voted for the ruling party, compared to less than 35 percent of voters belonging to the top decile. This gap is, in comparative perspective, the highest observed of all the case studies compiled in this volume (see Chapter 1). Second, the link between income and support for the ANC seems to have gradually become more linear.

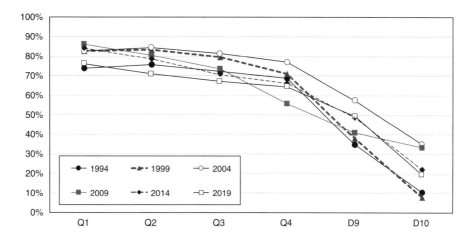

FIGURE 16.4. The ANC vote by income in South Africa, 1994–2019
*Data Source:* Author's computations using South African political attitudes surveys (see wpid.world).
*Note:* The figure shows the share of voters supporting the African National Congress (ANC) in general elections by income quintile (Q1 to Q4) and among the ninth and tenth deciles of income (D9 and D10). The vote for the ANC declines strongly with income in all elections held between 1994 and 2019. Between 74% and 86% of bottom 20% earners (Q1) have supported the ANC in all years, as compared to between 8% and 35% of those belonging to the top 10% (D10).

In 1994, the main divide was between the bottom 80 percent and the top 20 percent. In 2019, by contrast, support for Ramaphosa declined more monotonically with income.

Accordingly, the difference in ANC votes between the bottom 50 percent and the top 50 percent of South African earners has always been very strong and positive, fluctuating between 15 and 30 percentage points (Figure 16.5). After controlling for population group, however, this difference boils down to almost zero. This is a striking yet not surprising result: as poor voters are overwhelmingly Black, and top-income voters are in majority White, there is little space for income to have any independent effect on vote choice. Class cleavages in South Africa therefore remain in large part the joint manifestation of extreme racial cleavages and extreme racial inequalities.

While the independent effect of income remains weak, Figure 16.5 does hint at underlying changes in party identifications. After control-

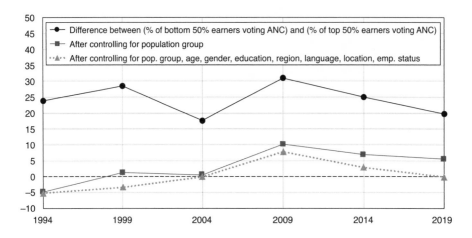

FIGURE 16.5. The ANC vote and income in South Africa, 1994–2019: The role of racial inequalities

*Data Source:* Author's computations using South African political attitudes surveys (see wpid.world).

*Note:* The figure shows the difference between the share of bottom 50% earners and the share of top 50% earners voting African National Congress (ANC) in general elections, before and after controls. Bottom 50% earners have been more likely to support the ANC than other voters by 15–30 percentage points in all years. This difference is strongly reduced after controlling for population group, indicating that the link between vote and income in South Africa is to a large extent driven by racial inequalities, as Africans have the lowest income levels and vote massively for the ANC.

ling for all available variables, the bottom 50 percent show slightly increasing support for the ANC as compared to the rest of the population: they were less likely to vote for the ANC by 5 percentage points in 1994, while they were more likely to do so by 3 percentage points in 2014. The same result holds for wealth: all other things being equal, the bottom 50 percent of wealth holders were more likely to vote for the ANC by 5 percentage points in the last election.[21]

In order to better capture these changes, it is useful to focus on the evolution of class divides within specific population groups. According to the available data, richer Africans were slightly more likely to support the ANC than low-income Black voters in 1994: 87 percent of top 10 percent African earners voted for the party, compared to 80 percent

21. See appendix Figures A2 and A3, wpid.world.

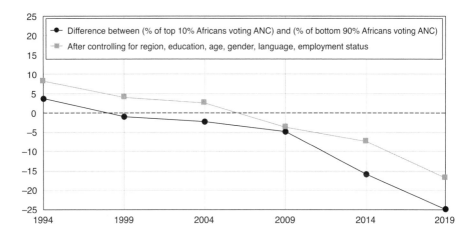

FIGURE 16.6. Vote for the ANC among African top-income earners in South Africa, 1994–2019

*Data Source:* Author's computations using South African political attitudes surveys (see wpid.world).

*Note:* The figure shows the difference between the share of top 10% African earners and the share of bottom 90% African earners voting for the African National Congress (ANC) in general elections, before and after controls. The top 10% of African earners were 4 percentage points more likely to support the ANC in 1994, while they were 25 percentage points less likely to do so in 2019.

of the bottom quintile.[22] Since then, support for the ANC has remained remarkably high among low-income African voters, with some 75 to 90 percent of Africans belonging to the first four quintiles voting in favor of the ruling party in all elections. By contrast, there has been a continuous, significant decline in support for the ANC among top 10 percent Black voters, from 87 percent in 1994 to only 51 percent in 2019. A significant share of the new Black middle class therefore seems to have been moving toward opposition parties.

Figure 16.6 documents this transformation by plotting the difference in ANC vote shares between the top 10 percent of African voters and the bottom 90 percent of African voters, before and after controls. A complete reversal is clearly visible: the top 10 percent were more supportive of the ANC by about 4 percentage points in 1994; in 2019, they had become less likely to vote ANC by 25 percentage points. Accounting for

22. See appendix Figure A14, wpid.world.

*Table 16.2*  Political Opinions of Black South Africans by Income Group, 2017

|  | Bottom 50% | Middle 40% | Top 10% |
|---|---|---|---|
| Most important issue: HIV/AIDS | 14% | 20% | 12% |
| Most important issue: Unemployment | 70% | 67% | 59% |
| Most important issue: Racism/Xenophobia | 2% | 1% | 5% |
| Most important issue: Crime and Safety | 7% | 8% | 16% |
| Most important issue: Other | 7% | 4% | 8% |
| Agrees government should redistribute land to Blacks | 81% | 82% | 73% |
| Trusts national governments | 31% | 30% | 40% |
| Knows no White people, even as acquaintances | 56% | 45% | 38% |

*Data Source:* Author's computations using South African political attitudes surveys (see wpid.world).

*Note:* The table decomposes the political opinions of Black South Africans by income group in 2017 (SASAS survey). Unemployment was the most important problem of South Africa according to 70% of the poorest 50% Black South Africans, compared to 59% of top 10% Black South African earners.

the effects of other variables changes slightly the level of this gap, but the trend remains unchanged. Similar dynamics are also visible when looking at Coloureds and Asians. Low sample sizes prevent us from precisely identifying election-to-election changes, but it is clear that more affluent Coloured and Asian voters have also become more likely to support opposition parties.[23] These dynamics are suggestive of a slow reconfiguration of political cleavages in South Africa: richer South Africans, regardless of their racial identity, have increasingly moved toward the opposition, while poorer Black voters have kept their support for the government broadly unchanged.

How can we interpret these changes in light of theories differentially emphasizing the roles of voters' ideological visions, policy positions, and group identifications? Looking at the link between income and political attitudes can help us understand the relative importance of these factors. This is done in Table 16.2, which decomposes by income group the opinions of Black South Africans on a selected number of questions asked in the 2017 South African Social Attitudes Survey. There are significant differences in policy positions across income groups. Low-income Blacks

23. See appendix Figure A1, wpid.world.

are more likely to consider HIV and unemployment to be the most important problems of the country, while the top 10 percent tend to put relatively greater value on crime, safety, and other issues. This divergence of priorities across social classes, and in particular the gap in the relative importance given to economic issues as compared to issues related to "higher-order" goods, is consistent with Robert Mattes's findings and comparable to similar evidence from Brazil's 2018 election (see Chapter 14). Poorer Africans are also more in favor of redistribution of land to the Black population. Interestingly, the richest 10 percent clearly stand out on these two questions (issue priorities and land redistribution), compared to other income groups, which have on average closer opinions. Finally, there are also major differences across income groups when it comes to social relations with other population groups. Among low- and middle-income Blacks, 56 percent and 45 percent of respondents, respectively, declare knowing no White person, even as an acquaintance. When looking at the top 10 percent of Black voters, this share drops to 38 percent.

Together, these results suggest that an independent social group, with different social and economic priorities, could well be emerging from the upper layers of the Black population. However, the size of this group remains limited, which may explain why ANC support has only moderately declined in the last elections. This group is also significantly more likely to have socialized with other population groups, which is consistent with the information theory of ethnic voting: as new middle-class Black voters get to interact with voters from other backgrounds, they become less and less likely to view opposition parties as exclusive to their group. This opens new potentials for realignment as the opposition is increasingly viewed as "acceptable" and voters are more prone to consider the policy positions of competing candidates.

### The Role of Linguistic and Regional Ties

I conclude this chapter by looking at another potential division within South African society: that of ethnolinguistic identities. Race has been at the heart of politics, but population groups are by no means homogeneous. There is no dominant language or ethnic group within the Black electorate, which is divided into speakers of Zulu (20 percent), Xhosa (16 percent), Sotho (17 percent), Tswana (9 percent), and a number of other local languages (see Table 16.1). About 60 percent of White voters speak Afrikaans and 40 percent English. The same more or less holds

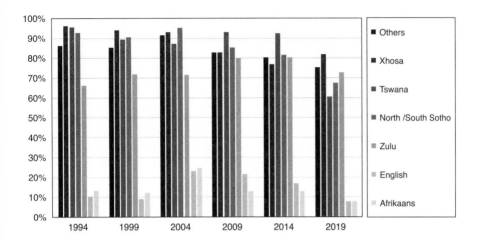

FIGURE 16.7. The ethnolinguistic cleavage in South Africa, 1994–2019: Vote for the ANC by language

*Data Source:* Author's computations using South African political attitudes surveys (see wpid.world).

*Note:* The figure shows the share of voters supporting the African National Congress (ANC) in general elections decomposed by the first language spoken at home. Less than 25% of Afrikaans and English speakers supported the ANC in every election since 1994, compared to more than 75% of Xhosa speakers.

for Coloureds,[24] while the majority of Indians and Asians are native English speakers. Racial and ethnolinguistic identities are therefore closely intertwined, but they should not be seen as synonymous.

Figure 16.7 plots the share of votes received by the ANC by linguistic group from 1994 to 2019. Several findings emerge from these figures. First, the ANC has always received massive support from all the ethnolinguistic groups of the African population: support for the ANC never exceeded 25 percent among Afrikaans- and English-speaking voters, while it was systematically higher than 60 percent among native speakers of Sotho, Tswana, and Xhosa languages. However, some differences between groups do stand out: Zulu voters, in particular, used to be between these two extremes, but then slowly moved closer to the second group. This transformation mirrors the decline of the Inkatha Freedom Party,

24. See appendix Figures C1 to C10, wpid.world, for detailed information on the composition of the South African population and the relationships between race, regional locations, education, income, and language.

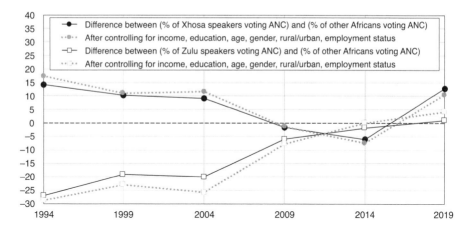

FIGURE 16.8. The ethnolinguistic cleavage in South Africa, 1994–2019: Vote for the ANC among Xhosa and Zulu speakers
*Data Source:* Author's computations using South African political attitudes surveys (see wpid.world).
*Note:* The figure shows the difference between the share of Zulu-speaking African voters and the share of other African voters voting for the African National Congress (ANC) in general elections, and the same difference between Xhosa speakers and other African voters, before and after controls. In 1994, Zulu speakers were less likely to vote for the ANC than other African voters by 27 percentage points. This difference has progressively disappeared over time.

the only serious ethnic-based contender to the ANC within the Black population. Meanwhile, an opposite trend is visible among Xhosa-speaking voters, who used to overwhelmingly vote for Mandela's party in the mid-1990s but have gradually become less supportive of the ANC since then. These two parallel dynamics have led to a significant decline in ethnic-based electoral divides in South Africa, which is robust to controls (see Figure 16.8) and is also visible when looking at differences in voting behaviors across provinces.[25] This transformation coincides with shifts in the ethnic background of party leaders: ANC candidates in 1994 (Nelson Mandela), 1999, and 2004 (Thabo Mbeki) were from Xhosa backgrounds, while Jacob Zuma, elected in 2009 and 2014, is from a Zulu background. Together, these results point to the ANC's remarkable success at continuously unifying a majority of Black South Africans since democ-

25. See appendix Figures A9, A10, and A11, wpid.world.

ratization, while overcoming the potential cleavages that could emerge from ethnolinguistic diversity within the Black population.

## Conclusion

South Africa remains haunted by the shadow of institutionalized racial segregation. More than twenty-five years after the end of the apartheid regime, race continues to determine access to social mobility and economic opportunities. Blacks and Whites still mostly live in separate neighborhoods; they diverge hugely in their living standards; they share only extremely limited common experiences. The compartmentalization of South African society has cultivated the persistence of electoral divides structured by racial affiliations. The new Black middle class stands out as the exception. Its access to the upper layers of society has come with new beliefs, common interactions with other population groups, and greater diversity in political attitudes. Yet, its size remains limited and, in electoral terms, too small to trigger any substantial transformation of South Africa's party system.

One-party dominance in South Africa differs significantly from most of the other cases studied in this volume. Dominant parties indeed often depend on unstable coalitions representing a diversity of interests. In Japan, the Liberal Democratic Party's dominance relied on a unique coalition between business elites and poorer rural areas (see Chapter 11). In India, the Congress was also a "coalition of extremes" bringing together Brahmins, lower castes, and Muslims (see Chapter 9). By contrast, while African National Congress leaders were careful to insist on the nonracial foundation of their legitimacy, electoral politics and political attitudes have in practice said otherwise. The strength of the ANC relies, paradoxically, on the racial contextualization of social experiences. Such experiences have reinforced voters' visions of political parties' racial exclusivism at the same time as they have helped to performatively enforce it. In this context, greater social equality would be a precondition for a realignment of voters on other dimensions of political conflict. Whether such realignment would be based on social class, ethnolinguistic diversity, or other forms of ideological divides yet remains an open question.

The lack of substantial transformation of South Africa's social structure may also explain why voters have been increasingly disillusioned with the democratic process: electoral turnout decreased from 87 percent in 1994 to a record low 66 percent in 2019. This drop in participation

has been associated with growing political inequality; abstention has remained stable among university graduates, while it has been multiplied by three among primary-educated citizens.[26] Surprisingly, opposition parties across the political spectrum seem to have been incapable of mobilizing the low-income, lower-educated electorate, instead mostly attracting urban, higher-educated, and wealthier voters among the Black population.[27] In this context, the future transformation of South Africa's party system will crucially depend on the ability of the African National Congress, or new political organizations, to respond to the aspirations of the disenchanted poor.

26. See appendix Figures D1 to D11, wpid.world.

27. See appendix Table A3, wpid.world, for the detailed structure of the vote for the DA and the EFF, among both the overall population and among Blacks over the 2014–2019 period. Results for the EFF should be interpreted with great caution, given the small sample sizes.

# 17

# Social Inequalities and the Politicization of Ethnic Cleavages in Botswana, Ghana, Nigeria, and Senegal, 1999–2019

### JULES BALEYTE, AMORY GETHIN, YAJNA GOVIND, AND THOMAS PIKETTY

## Introduction

International observers often perceive electoral politics in Sub-Saharan Africa as plagued by ethnic factionalism, patronage, and nepotism. A common, related view holds that African political parties do not have distinct ideological visions, but are instead convenient vehicles for mobilizing resources and group identities. Unlike Western democracies, where electoral behaviors continue to manifest deep-seated cleavages and clearly identifiable social conflicts, African democracies would primarily have opposing charismatic leaders whose success would depend on their ability to be perceived as competent by both their electorate and political elites; valence issues would be at least as important as position issues.[1] The necessity of experience in power—together with the roles played by political finance, patronage networks, electoral manipulation, and use of violence—does explain in part why incumbent African presidents rarely lose elections. It also explains why opponents need access to state resources—sometimes gained by renouncing their ideological principles—to join the ruling party and implement policies that may

We are very grateful to Catherine Lena Kelly, Dominika Koter, Clara Martínez-Toledano, Paul Nugent, Anja Osei, Amy Poteete, and Nicolas van de Walle for their useful advice.

1. J. Bleck and N. van de Walle, *Electoral Politics in Africa since 1990: Continuity and Change* (Cambridge University Press, 2018).

depend more on international aid than on ideological choices or pro-grammatic platforms.

These factors cannot be ignored, but they sometimes tend to obliterate other important dimensions of democratic conflicts. To what extent do political parties represent longer-lasting social divides beyond vote-seeking strategies and valence issues? How strong are ethnic cleavages in Africa when it comes to the electoral arena, and how do these cleavages interact with the structure of inequalities, the history of political party formation, and the legacies of colonialism? Do socioeconomic issues play any role in distinguishing political actors and determining electoral be-haviors, and could class cleavages be emerging?

This chapter aims to provide some insights into these questions by documenting the determinants of the vote in four countries that held mul-tiparty elections from 1999 to 2019: Botswana, Ghana, Nigeria, and Senegal. These countries are, among Sub-Saharan African countries, some of the highest ranked in terms of quality of democracy, fairness of elections, and competitiveness, which allows us to capture variations in the structure of the vote with a reasonable degree of confidence.[2] To do so, we use the Afrobarometer surveys, which since the late 1990s have col-lected information on identification with political parties or coalitions, electoral behaviors, and the main sociodemographic characteristics of voters. While our results should be interpreted with care, given impor-tant issues of misreporting and mismeasurement of political attitudes, we believe that they can still be useful in identifying key distinguishing factors and broad patterns of change. By definition, our focus on four countries with some of the most competitive elections in Africa precludes any con-clusion with respect to why democracies prevail in some countries and not in others.[3] Instead, our objective is to understand how democratization, when it succeeds, leads political parties to mobilize voters on issues that are rooted in deeper ethnic, regional, and socioeconomic transformations.

2. See, for instance, The Economist Intelligence Unit, "Democracy Index 2018: Me Too? Political Participation, Protest and Democracy" (Economist Intelligence Unit, 2019), https://275rzy1ul4252pt1hv2dqyuf-wpengine.netdna-ssl.com/wp-content/uploads/2019/01/Democracy_Index_2018.pdf. On the role of authoritarian incumbents' strategies in shaping multiparty systems in Africa, see R. B. Riedl, *Authoritarian Origins of Demo-cratic Party Systems in Africa* (Cambridge University Press, 2014).

3. To be sure, the four countries considered here are not the only ones holding com-petitive multiparty elections in Sub-Saharan Africa, and this study could be extended to countries such as Benin, Mauritius, and Mali.

Our analysis, organized in four case studies, leads us to two main findings.

First, we document large variations, both across countries and across time, in the strength of ethnic cleavages. Ethnolinguistic affiliations have a strong impact on the vote in Nigeria, a moderate impact in Ghana, and a weak impact in Botswana and Senegal. We argue that these variations mirror major differences in the strength of ethnic inequalities and spatial segregation. In Nigeria, extreme disparities between the primarily Muslim north and the Christian south, reinforced by the British during the colonial period, have been associated with rising ethnoreligious polarization. Ethnolinguistic affiliations also play a role in Ghana through the opposition between the poorer north and the wealthier Ashanti region, but all parties have had to rely on cross-ethnic coalitions to win elections, limiting political polarization along ethnic or regional lines. In Botswana and Senegal, finally, we find both low levels of ethnic inequalities and only weak associations between ethnic identities and voting behaviors.

Second, turning to other determinants of electoral behaviors, we identify two other strong electoral cleavages common to all four countries: a rural-urban cleavage and what we interpret as an emerging class divide, as education—one of the only comparable, though imperfect, measures of socioeconomic status at our disposal—has had an exceptionally strong and growing effect on vote choice. Crucially, we find that parties supported by underprivileged ethnic groups also receive greater support from the lower educated, *beyond* ethnic affiliations. Even in Nigeria, where party politics seem to be drifting toward a unidimensional Christian-Muslim cleavage, a significant share of lower-educated Christians still vote for the All Progressives Congress. Educational and rural-urban cleavages have also been on the rise in Botswana and Senegal, as highest-educated voters have massively turned toward parties opposing the incumbent, while rural areas have favored the continuity of patronage and have been more supportive of the development policies implemented by the ruling coalitions.[4]

Together, these findings point to relatively clear relationships between social inequalities and political representation, with poorer ethnic groups,

4. See, for instance, M. Wachman and C. Boone, "Captured Countryside? Stability and Change in Sub-national Support for African Incumbent Parties," *Comparative Politics* 50, no. 2 (2018): 189–208.

underdeveloped regions, rural areas, and lower-educated individuals often voting for the same parties or coalitions. We interpret this as evidence that inequalities do matter in structuring partisan affiliations in these four countries, albeit with interesting variations in the respective roles of clientelism, issue-based evaluations, and ethnic identities in shaping these divides. While it may be too early to talk about class cleavages or class consciousness, our results clearly suggest that socioeconomic status is playing a growing role in electoral politics, partly, but not only, through its congruence with ethnic, regional, or rural-urban cleavages, and that political competition could well be moving closer toward class-based divides in the future.[5]

Studying democratization through the lens of the political representation of these inequalities can, we believe, be useful in identifying potential trajectories of political cleavages and party systems on the African continent. It also paves the way for renewed attention to parties' platforms and how programmatic linkages contribute to organizing and transforming these political conflicts.

## Botswana

Botswana stands out in the economic and political context in Africa. Since its independence in 1966, it has progressed into a sound economic position in parallel with democratic stability, fair and recurrent multiparty elections, and high voter turnouts. Yet, its political scene is not devoid of challenges—single-party dominance since independence, a weak and fragmented opposition, and an unleveled playing field for the different parties. On the economic side, its growth "miracle," in part due to the discovery of diamonds in the 1970s, did not benefit all sections of society, and it remains marked by high levels of poverty and inequality.[6] This section provides an insight into the political evolution of

5. These findings resonate well with studies on reasons for supporting democracy or on trust in the government across social classes, e.g., D. C. Moehler, "Free and Fair or Fraudulent and Forged: Elections and Legitimacy in Africa" (Afrobarometer Working Paper, 2005); N. W. Letsa and M. Wilfahrt, "Popular Support for Democracy in Autocratic Regimes: A Micro-level Analysis of Preferences," *Comparative Politics* 50, no. 2 (2018): 231–273.

6. L. Chancel, D. Cogneau, A. Gethin, and A. Myczkowski, "How Large Are African Inequalities? Towards Distributional National Accounts in Africa, 1990–2017" (WID.world Working Paper 2019/13, 2019).

Botswana by analyzing the dominance of the Botswana Democratic Party (BDP) since independence and its gradual loss of the upper hand in recent elections. While party fragmentation and within-party factionalism are often cited as the leading explanations for the transformation of Botswana's party system, we show that political cleavages related to rural-urban divides, education, and occupation are also crucial, and increasingly so.

## The Emergence and Political Dominance of the BDP

Unlike South Africa, Botswana had been indirectly ruled by the British, in the form of the Bechuanaland Protectorate, through the close collaboration of the colonial and native elites and the chiefdom system, until the early 1960s saw growing political movements and demands for independence. This led to the creation of various parties, namely the Bechuanaland People's Party (BPP) in 1960, the Bechuanaland Independence Party (BIP), a split from the former, the Bechuanaland Democratic Party (BDP) in 1962, and the Botswana National Front (BNF) in 1965. While there were no strong ideological conflicts between the different existing parties,[7] they clearly differed from one another on several dimensions.

Initially formed as a nationalist movement with a radical anticolonial position, the BPP strongly advocated for the end of colonial rule and White domination.[8] This garnered wide support from the urban areas and the working class, although they were a minority in the country's population. On the other hand, the elites, who consisted of the colonial cattle-owning class, the rich peasantry, and intellectual circles, created an alliance in the form of the BDP, tacitly supported by the colonial government, which gave it a decisive edge in its establishment as a dominant party in the postcolonial period.[9]

---

7. J. H. Polhemus, "Botswana Votes: Parties and Elections in an African Democracy," *Journal of Modern African Studies* 21, no. 3 (1983): 397–430; R. Nengwekhulu, "Some Findings on the Origins of Political Parties in Botswana," *Pula: Botswana Journal of African Studies* 1, no. 2 (1979): 47–76.

8. D. Acemoglu, S. Johnson, and J. A. Robinson, "An African Success Story: Botswana" (CEPR Discussion Paper, 2001), https://econpapers.repec.org/paper/cprceprdp/3219.htm; G. Somolekae, "Political Parties in Botswana" (EISA Research Report No. 27, 2005), https://www.africaportal.org/publications/political-parties-in-botswana/.

9. J. L. Comaroff and J. Comaroff, "Postcolonial Politics and Discourses of Democracy in Southern Africa: An Anthropological Reflection on African Political Modernities," *Journal of Anthropological Research* 53, no. 2 (1997): 123–146.

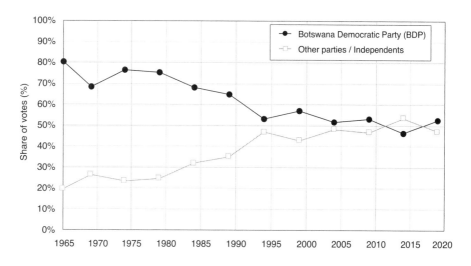

FIGURE 17.1. Election results in Botswana, 1965–2019
*Data Source:* Authors' computations using official election results (see wpid.world).
*Note:* The figure shows the share of votes received by selected groups of political parties in Botswana in general elections between 1965 and 2019. The Botswana Democratic Party received 53% of votes in 2019.

In 1965, in the first election held under universal suffrage, the BDP thus won 80 percent of popular votes, compared to only 14 percent for the BPP. The BNF, a split from the BPP, later emerged as the leading opposition party with an initial aim to fight against the "neo-colonialist regime of the BDP."[10] Despite the absence of strong ideological demarcations, the BDP has been characterized as moderate and embracing liberalism, while the BPP and the BNF were closer to socialism. The opposition parties held a stronghold at the regional level, without posing a real threat to the BDP as the main national party.

Despite the progress of the BNF from the 1984 election onward, it was not until the 1994 elections that a major turning point took place, as urbanization and redrawing of electoral boundaries increased the importance of urban votes, putting the BDP in a difficult position given its traditional reliance on rural areas (see Figure 17.1). The BNF has since then been a serious contender in the political arena, hinting at the end of the one-party dominant system.

10. Polhemus, "Botswana Votes."

*An Uneven Playing Field between the BDP and Opposition Parties*

Despite the decline in support for the BDP, it has managed to remain in power for more than fifty years since independence. The first-past-the-post (FPTP) system in constituencies has given a huge advantage to the BDP: in the 2000s, for instance, the BDP secured around 78 percent of the seats in Parliament with only half of the votes.[11] Moreover, the inability of the opposition parties to obtain a majority in the elections has been attributed to the vast number of challenges and issues they have faced. Above all, the opposition is plagued with internal struggles that have resulted in various important splits, preventing unification of the opposition for the elections.

Party funding, finally, has played a significant role in allowing the BDP to keep the upper hand over the opposition parties. The electoral system in Botswana does not require transparency of electoral financing and does not provide public financial support. Hence, being financially stronger thanks to both higher membership and generous private donors allows the BDP to have a permanent organization across the country and field candidates in all constituencies, unlike the opposition parties. Exploiting its position, the BDP has politicized public services[12] by rewarding or punishing private actors based on loyalty. Contracts for the state-owned diamond mining industry are controlled by the BDP and used as a quid pro quo to retain support. The BDP also enjoys other benefits from its incumbency, such as unequal media coverage.

*The Lack of Ethnic Cleavage in Botswana*

Strikingly, unlike in Nigeria and Ghana (see below), both ethnic inequalities (Figure 17.2) and ethnic cleavages (Figure 17.3) appear to be remarkably low in Botswana, with the share of votes received by the BDP varying little across major ethnolinguistic groups. This lack of ethnic cleavage has often been interpreted as resulting from the country's relative ethnic and religious homogeneity;[13] in the postcolonial era, the main religion has been Christianity and the main ethnic group the Tswana (about 80 percent of the population). However, the depoliticization of

---

11. In addition, Botswana has a system of special nominations, initially put in place to ensure seats for experts but mostly used by the BDP to obtain additional seats (Somolekae, "Political Parties in Botswana," 25).

12. R. Doorenspleet and L. Nijzink, eds. *Party Systems and Democracy in Africa* (Springer, 2014), 73.

13. Acemoglu, Johnson, and Robinson, "African Success Story."

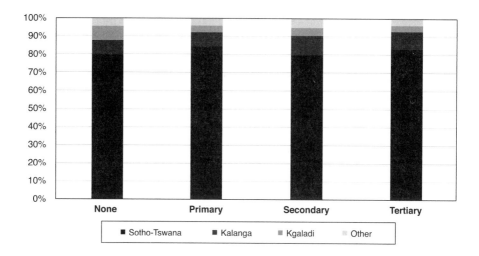

FIGURE 17.2. Ethnolinguistic educational inequalities in Botswana
*Data Source:* Authors' computations using Afrobarometer surveys (see wpid.world).
*Note:* The figure shows the composition of education groups by language in Botswana in 2019. Speakers of Sotho-Tswana languages represented 80% of voters with no diploma and 83% of tertiary-educated voters. Illiterates represented about 11% of the electorate, primary-educated respondents 18%, secondary-educated respondents 49%, and tertiary-educated respondents 22%.

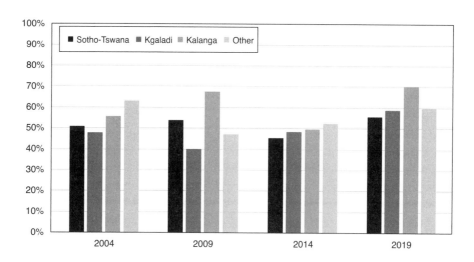

FIGURE 17.3. Vote for the Botswana Democratic Party by language, 2004–2019
*Data Source:* Authors' computations using Afrobarometer surveys (see wpid.world).
*Note:* The figure shows the share of votes received by the Botswana Democratic Party (BDP) by language. In 2019, 55% of speakers of Sotho-Tswana languages voted BDP, compared to 70% of Kalanga speakers. Sotho-Tswana then represented about 81% of the electorate, Kalanga 10%, Kgaladi 5%, and other languages 5%.

group identities in Botswana must also be located in the context of broader historical processes and political choices. The BDP indeed always represented traditional elites beyond ethnic and religious lines, adopted a nonracial and nonethnic policy (for instance, excluding questions related to ethnicity in the census), and developed policies deliberately downplaying social divisions.[14] This arguably contributed to both limiting the political salience of ethnic identities and moderating interethnic inequalities.

On the other hand, the different parties draw support from different regions, even if regional gaps in voting behaviors in Botswana are also relatively low in comparative perspective.[15] The BDP traditionally derives greater support from the northern areas, in contrast to the opposition parties, whose support bases are relatively more scattered, with the BNF stronger in southern regions, the BIP in northwestern regions, and the BPP in northeastern areas.[16]

### Toward Class Cleavages?

While no marked ethnic cleavage can be discerned, the BDP has historically gathered much stronger support from the rural areas than from cities. At the time of independence, the party managed to secure and maintain the support of the rural population through patronage. The BDP has also made large investments in the rural areas to ensure continued support. State resources have been disproportionately spent on public services for the sections of the population that support the BDP.[17]

However, rapid urbanization since the 1980s has meant the continued gradual erosion of the BDP's electoral base. It still receives more of its support from the rural electorate, while urban workers have predominantly supported the opposition parties due to acute dissatisfaction with employment conditions, wages, unemployment, and housing access in cities (Figure 17.4). The egalitarian stance of the BNF, in particular, has appealed to the working class, which explains its popularity in the urban

---

14. A. R. Poteete, "The Absence of Intergroup Violence in Botswana: An Assessment of the Role of Development Strategies," in *The Economic Roots of Conflict and Cooperation in Africa*, ed. W. Ascher and N. Mirovitskaya (Palgrave Macmillan, 2013), 183–219.

15. See appendix Figure AB4, World Political Cleavages and Inequality Database, http://wpid.world.

16. D. Sebudubudu and B. Z. Osei-Hwedie, "In Permanent Opposition: Botswana's Other Political Parties," *South African Journal of International Affairs* 17, no. 1 (2010): 85–102.

17. Acemoglu, Johnson, and Robinson, "African Success Story."

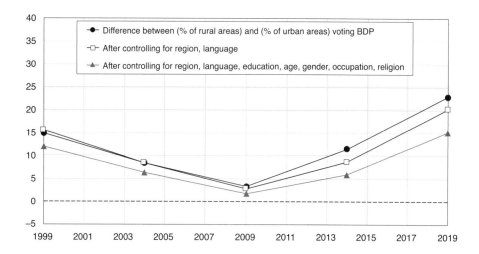

FIGURE 17.4. The rural-urban cleavage in Botswana, 1999–2019
*Data Source:* Authors' computations using Afrobarometer surveys (see wpid.world).
*Note:* The figure shows the difference between the share of voters from rural areas and
the share of voters living in cities voting for the Botswana Democratic Party (BDP),
before and after controls. The BDP garnered a higher share of votes in rural areas than
in urban areas throughout the period considered. Rural areas represented about 32% of
the electorate in 2019, down from 55% in 1999.

areas. Despite not performing well in parliamentary elections, the BNF
has achieved better results in urban local government elections.[18]

Urbanization and educational expansion have also decreased the importance of traditional structures, and as a result, their influence on political choices.[19] Accordingly, as Figure 17.5 shows, a growing cleavage
along educational lines has emerged in recent elections.[20] Higher-educated
voters have gradually reduced their support for the BDP, with the most
diverging point being the 2019 elections, when barely 30 percent of
tertiary-educated voters supported the BDP, compared to more than
70 percent of illiterates, a gap that is robust to controls. The BDP also
still draws massive support from farmers, as was historically the case,

18. B. Z. Osei-Hwedie, "The Political Opposition in Botswana: The Politics of Factionalism and Fragmentation," *Transformation* 45 (2001): 57–77.

19. A. R. Poteete, "Electoral Competition, Factionalism, and Persistent Party Dominance in Botswana," *Journal of Modern African Studies* 50, no. 1 (2012): 75–102.

20. See also appendix Figure AB1, wpid.world.

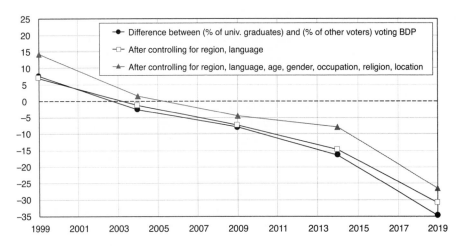

FIGURE 17.5. The educational cleavage in Botswana, 1999–2019
*Data Source:* Authors' computations using Afrobarometer surveys (see wpid.world).
*Note:* The figure shows the difference between the share of university graduates and the
share of nonuniversity graduates voting for the Botswana Democratic Party (BDP),
before and after controls. In 2019, university graduates were less likely to vote BDP by
35 percentage points. Tertiary-educated voters represented about 22% of the electorate
in 2019, compared to 9% in 1999.

but the gap between farmers and professionals or employers has been
widening over time.[21]

Together, these results suggest that Botswana could well be moving
toward class cleavages, as the BDP's decline has increasingly forced the
party to rely on poorer rural areas and lower-educated citizens for continued support. This trajectory bears similarities with the transformation
of other dominant-party systems studied in this book, such as those in
South Africa (Chapter 16), Malaysia (Chapter 12), and India (Chapter 9),
where the weakening of ruling parties' dominance came with a restriction of their voting base to disadvantaged social groups.

## Ghana

Since 1992 and the establishment of the Fourth Republic, the Ghanaian
party system has mainly had two opposing political parties, the National

21. See appendix Figures AB10 and AC7, wpid.world.

Democratic Congress (NDC) and the New Patriotic Party (NPP). This section documents a strong and stable ethnoregional cleavage between wealthier, higher-educated Akan populations living in urbanized central regions, who overwhelmingly support the NPP and are closer to the Danquah-Busia democratic tradition, and supporters of the NDC and the legacy of its founder John Rawlings, overrepresented in the Ewe ethnic group of the Volta region as well as in the marginalized rural northern areas of the country. We also find evidence of rural-urban and educational divides, with poorer rural areas and less-educated voters being more favorable to the NDC beyond ethnoregional affiliations. These results are consistent with the idea that while economic ideologies of the NDC and the NPP may appear quite similar in view of the continuity of their policies pursued since the 1980s, the NDC appears more social-oriented compared to the NPP with its more economically liberal ideology, observable for example in the positions adopted with regard to budgetary rigor and state expenditure. These divides could pave the way for the stabilization of independent class cleavages in the future.

## The Making of a Two-Party System

The origins of party politics in Ghana can be traced back to the independence process of the 1950s. On the one hand, the Danquah-Busia tradition, now claimed by the NPP,[22] historically pushed for a multiparty parliamentary democracy with economic liberalization and cooperation with Western institutions. On the other hand, the Nkrumah tradition called for increased social and economic state intervention and for nonaligned Pan-Africanism.[23] Unlike in Nigeria, however, in Ghana the separation of these two movements in 1949 was based on Kwame Nkrumah's desire for more radical independence, rather than on ethnic identities. In 1960, in the first direct elections held in Ghanaian history, Nkrumah was elected with nearly 90 percent of votes against the United Party of J. B. Danquah, bringing together the opposition, in a context of low turnout and rigged results in rural constituencies (see Figure 17.6).[24] What followed was a period of political instability, including multiple coups d'état, until Flight

22. K. Fordwor, *The Danquah-Busia Tradition in the Politics of Ghana* (Unimax Macmillan, 2010).
23. K. Skinner, *The Fruits of Freedom in British Togoland: Literacy, Politics and Nationalism, 1914–2014* (Cambridge University Press, 2015).
24. R. Gocking, *The History of Ghana* (Greenwood Press, 2005), chapter 7.

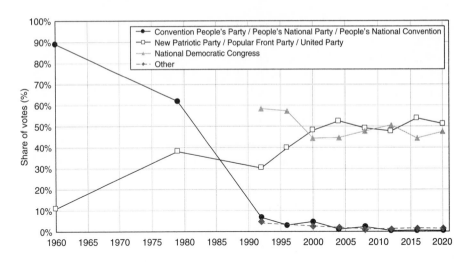

FIGURE 17.6. Presidential election results in Ghana, 1960–2020
*Data Source:* Authors' computations using official election results (see wpid.world).
*Note:* The figure shows the share of votes received by selected groups of political parties in Ghana in the first round of presidential elections between 1960 and 2020. The National Democratic Congress (NDC) received 44% of votes in 2016.

Lieutenant Jerry Rawlings seized power in June 1979 and enabled the organization of new elections. The victory of the People's National Party (PNP) revealed the continued strength of the Nkrumah tradition in the face of an opposition partly divided by ethnic power struggles.[25]

In 1981, a new coup by Rawlings in the name of a "holy war" against corruption nonetheless put an end to the short-lived Third Republic. In the following decade, in a context of serious economic difficulties, he embarked on the development of the country with the help of the International Monetary Fund (IMF), while banning parties and exercising tight control over the media, religious groups, and the justice system. Internal and external political pressure eventually forced him to democratize the country, culminating in the 1992 presidential elections. Rawlings, at the head of the NDC and partly recuperating Nkrumah's legacy,[26] took advantage of incumbency and greater resources and was elected against the NPP representing the Danquah-Busia tradition, with 58 percent of votes.

25. R. Jeffries, "The Ghanaian Elections of 1979," *African Affairs* 79, no. 316 (1980): 397–414.
26. Gocking, *History of Ghana*, chapter 10.

What followed was a cycle of political alternations: after Rawlings left at the end of his two-term limit stipulated by the constitution, the NPP took over the presidency in 2000, before losing in 2008 and 2012 but returning to power in 2016 and 2020. Demands from within society for a multiparty system, as well as investments and efforts made by these two parties to reorganize themselves after electoral defeats and to survive the departure of their emblematic historical leaders, played a key role in the stabilization of this two-party system, making the power of incumbency exceptionally nuanced in Ghana compared to most African countries.[27]

### The Role of Ethnic Cleavages

Ghanaian democratization has therefore led to the emergence of a clear divide between two camps, in large part inherited from the two Ghanaian political traditions: the NDC representing a more social democratic tradition, and the NPP adopting a more liberal perspective. What have been the key factors distinguishing these two parties in the past three decades? Unlike in Botswana, ethnic cleavages have been relatively strong in Ghana: in particular, the NPP is often perceived as defending the interests of the Ashanti community, a wealthier and educated Akan subgroup (Akans represent close to half of the Ghanaian population), while the NDC is seen as favoring the Ewe population and garnering anti-Akan votes.[28] This distinction is clearly visible in voting behaviors: Ewe speakers have indeed always been substantially more supportive of the NDC, while Akan speakers have voted massively for the NPP (Figure 17.8). Ethnicity has therefore represented an important dimension of political conflicts in Ghana. While generally not claiming ethnic favoritism explicitly, parties have often stirred up local rivalries and have been quick to criticize the actions of their opponents, accusing them of endangering national unity. The NPP, for instance, was accused of negligence following the assassination of the King of Dagbon in 2002 amid a crisis between the Dagbon Abudu and Dagbon Andani clans, due to a strong presence of Abudu members in the government.[29]

---

27. Bleck and van de Walle, *Electoral Politics,* chapter 4.

28. P. Nugent, "Living in the Past: Urban, Rural and Ethnic Themes in the 1992 and 1996 Elections in Ghana," *Journal of Modern African Studies* 37, no. 2 (1999): 287–319.

29. P. Nugent, "The 2004 Elections in Ghana: Anatomy of a Two-Party System," *Politique Africaine* 97, no. 1 (2005): 133–150.

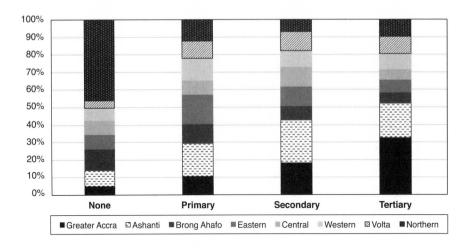

FIGURE 17.7. Regional educational inequalities in Ghana
*Data Source:* Authors' computations using Afrobarometer surveys (see wpid.world).
*Note:* The figure shows the composition of education groups by region in Ghana in 2016. The Northern region includes the Upper East and the Upper West. In 2016, 46% of voters with no diploma lived in the Northern region, compared to 10% of tertiary-educated individuals. Illiterates then represented 18% of the electorate, primary-educated respondents 16%, secondary-educated respondents 38%, and post-secondary-educated respondents (including high school graduates) 28%.

As ethnic groups are concentrated in specific regions, moreover, ethnic divides have naturally been reflected by equally strong regional cleavages: the Ashanti and Brong-Ahafo regions have systematically supported the NPP, while the Volta region, home to the majority of Ewe, has overwhelmingly voted for the NDC (Figure 17.9).[30] Also noteworthy is the support for the NDC in the northern regions, made up in part of Gur populations, which is related more to socioeconomic inequalities than to ethnicity. Indeed, the north concentrates over 45 percent of Ghana's illiterates but only 10 percent of its university graduates (Figure 17.7), as well as a

30. Due to low sample sizes, we include the Upper East and Upper West with the Northern region. Notice that a number of regions have been further divided, but not Ashanti, following a 2018 referendum held under the NPP government, which could be interpreted as an attempt to further splinter the NDC vote.

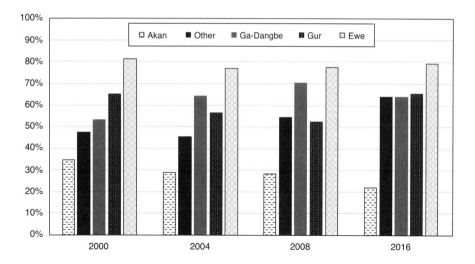

FIGURE 17.8. The NDC vote by linguistic group in Ghana, 2000–2016
*Data Source:* Authors' computations using Afrobarometer surveys (see wpid.world).
*Note:* The figure shows the share of votes received by the National Democratic Congress (NDC) by language. In 2016, 22% of Akan speakers voted NDC, compared to 79% of Ewe speakers. Ewe speakers then represented about 15% of the electorate, speakers of Gur languages 19%, speakers of Ga-Dangbe languages 8%, and Akan speakers 53%.

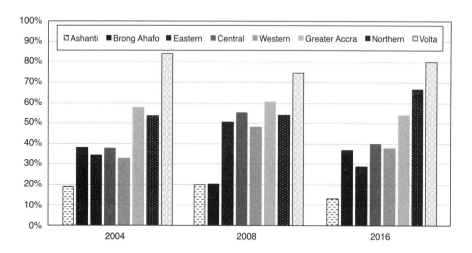

FIGURE 17.9. The NDC vote by region in Ghana, 2004–2016
*Data Source:* Authors' computations using Afrobarometer surveys (see wpid.world).
*Note:* The figure shows the share of votes received by the National Democratic Congress (NDC) by region. The Northern region includes the Upper East and the Upper West. In 2016, the NDC received 80% of votes in the Volta region, compared to 13% of votes in the Ashanti region. The Ashanti region then represented about 19% of the electorate, Brong Ahafo 9%, Eastern 10%, Central 9%, Western 9%, Greater Accra 18%, Northern 16%, and Volta 9%.

larger share of the very poor, in part because of its very arid climate.[31] The NPP therefore seems to have represented the wealthier Akan, while the NDC has been more popular among marginalized ethnic groups since democratization.

This ethnic perspective, however, remains limited. The two block-voting regions, Ashanti and Volta, are indeed not ethnically homogenous;[32] the regional cleavage thus goes beyond ethnic identities. The sizes of the Ashanti and Ewe groups, furthermore, do not constitute a sufficient political majority that could be used by a single party, given Ghana's important ethnic diversity. This has forced the two parties to rely on broader ethnic coalitions, which has arguably played a role in allowing the functioning of Ghana's more peaceful and less violent form of democracy, especially when compared to Nigeria (see below). While spatial cleavages are strong, finally, a number of regions have had close results that decided the outcomes of elections. This is especially the case in the populated Greater Accra region, which has the largest concentration of elites (Figure 17.7) and has experienced significant swings. All these limitations call for a closer inspection of other dimensions of socioeconomic inequalities and social divides.

### Rural-Urban and Educational Cleavages

Other socioeconomic differences overlap regional disparities in Ghana, in particular a rural-urban divide, with more than 70 percent of the illiterate population living in rural areas.[33] In the 1990s, development policies pursued by the NDC government enabled electrification in the countryside, improved access to drinking water, and support for cocoa farmers. At the same time, liberalization and privatization policies affected the mainly urban public sector and came with higher taxation of urban residents.[34] As a result of these dynamics, the NDC has historically won much larger majorities in rural areas, even if this rural-urban cleavage seems to have declined following the NPP's rise to power, especially after controlling for region and language (Figure 17.10).

---

31. Ghana Statistical Service, "Ghana Poverty Mapping Report" (Ghana Statistical Service Report, 2015), https://www2.statsghana.gov.gh/docfiles/publications/POVERTY%20MAP%20FOR%20GHANA-05102015.pdf.

32. See appendix Figure BA16, wpid.world.

33. See in appendix Figure BA12, wpid.world.

34. Nugent, "Living in the Past."

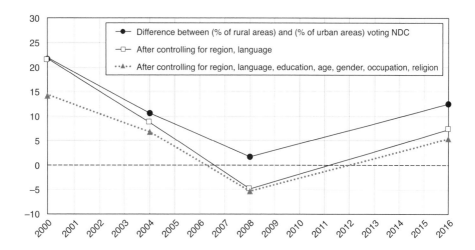

FIGURE 17.10. The rural-urban cleavage in Ghana, 2000–2016
*Data Source:* Authors' computations using Afrobarometer surveys (see wpid.world).
*Note:* The figure shows the difference between the share of voters living in rural areas
and the share of voters living in cities voting for the National Democratic Congress
(NDC), before and after controls. In 2016, rural areas were more likely to vote NDC by
12 percentage points. Rural areas then represented about 46% of the electorate, down
from 63% in 2000.

Rapid urbanization has led to a deterioration in living conditions in
urban areas, with more than a third of Ghanaian urbanites living in shan-
tytowns in 2015, and to an increase in urban unemployment.[35] This
growing precariousness of cities was accompanied by the rise of the NDC
vote, which is consistent with the fact that this party is more popular
among disadvantaged voters. Moreover, migrants from the north often
remain loyal to the NDC, for example in Asawase in the Ashanti region[36] or in the *zongos,* historically Muslim neighborhoods in southern
cities, which are generally underdeveloped. Therefore, rural-urban divides seem to have represented an additional socioeconomic dimension
of political differentiation in Ghana, with poorer rural areas and marginalized workers in cities being more favorable to the NDC.

35. S. Garba and U. Benna, *Population Growth and Rapid Urbanization in the Developing World* (IGI Global, 2016), 95.
36. P. Nugent, "2004 Elections."

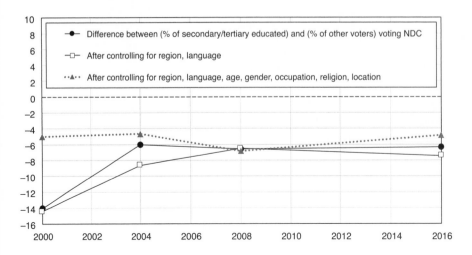

FIGURE 17.11. The educational cleavage in Ghana, 2000–2016
*Data Source:* Authors' computations using Afrobarometer surveys (see wpid.world).
*Note:* The figure shows the difference between the share of secondary/tertiary-educated voters and the share of other voters voting for the National Democratic Congress (NDC), before and after controls. In 2016, higher-educated voters were less likely to vote NDC by 6 percentage points. They then represented about 28% of the electorate.

The NDC, finally, has not only represented poorer ethnic groups, marginalized regions, and rural areas; an educational cleavage also seems to have emerged, with highest-educated voters consistently being less likely to vote NDC by 5 to 10 percentage points, even after controlling for region, language, and other sociodemographic variables (Figure 17.11). This could be because wealthy and educated urban Ghanaian elites were more sensitive to the NPP's rhetoric denouncing the authoritarianism and the lack of democracy of Rawlings's NDC.[37] This educational cleavage is less strong than in the other countries studied in this chapter, but it clearly suggests that socioeconomic status, beyond ethnoregional affiliations, is playing an additional role in framing political cleavages in Ghana. If ethnic inequalities are to decrease in the future, this could well open a potential for the emergence of stronger independent class cleavages, as seems to have been the case in Botswana.

37. Gocking, *History of Ghana*, chapters 11 and 12.

## Nigeria

Nigeria's Fourth Republic was inaugurated in 1999 after three decades of turbulent political events, including short democratic experiences interrupted by military interventions, frequent communal violence, and a major civil war. Since then, Africa's most populated and most diverse country, comprising more than 250 ethnic groups in thirty-six semiautonomous states, has witnessed six elections and a peaceful handover from the People's Democratic Party (PDP) to the opposition All Progressives Congress (APC) in 2015.

In this section, we analyze how democratization and the consolidation of a two-party system in Nigeria has crystallized preexisting ethnic, regional, and religious divides, and how these emerging political cleavages have mirrored long-lasting social inequalities. Three main findings emerge: the persistence of extreme ethnoregional inequalities, the emergence of a sharp religious cleavage, and the rise of educational divides beyond religious, ethnic, or regional specificities. This latter evolution points to the possibility of new class coalitions across religious groups, which could potentially play a role in moderating ethnoreligious tensions and moving Nigerian politics away from communal conflicts.

### From Independence to the Fourth Republic:
### A Turbulent Political History

In 1914, the British created "Nigeria" by amalgamating a number of West African territories with no common political or historical origin. The integration of this large and diverse territory under a single polity was the result of a colonial arbitrary process. It had no foundations in previous political regimes or shared historical narratives. If anything, the British had reinforced preexisting ethnoregional differences between the mostly Christian southern regions and the poorer Muslim northern regions, maintaining indigenous systems of government and law, limiting the penetration of southern Christian missionaries in the Muslim north, and insulating the north from the effects of modern economic development. This was an integral part of their strategy of "indirect rule."[38]

---

38. On the following historical overview, see, for instance, R. L. Sklar, *Nigerian Political Parties: Power in an Emergent African Nation* (Princeton University Press, 1963); R. Bourne, *Nigeria: A New History of a Turbulent Century* (Zed Books, 2015); O. Agbu,

The result was an almost complete absence of a pan-Nigerian national movement. The Nigerian Youth Movement (NYM), founded in 1934 in Lagos, aimed to bring together the different ethnicities under a unified territory independent from the British Empire. The protection of the Muslim emirates by the British, increasingly perceived as a tactic of divide and rule by the nascent nationalist forces, yet prevented the organization from building membership in the north. The north eventually came to view the NYM as representing southern interests. As the British split the southern protectorate into South West and South East in 1938, divisions grew between Yoruba and Igbo factions until the NYM broke apart in 1941.

The political parties that emerged in independent Nigeria, most of them with roots in the colonial period, were all regionally and ethnically based. The Northern People's Congress (NPC), formed in 1949, was supported by traditional Hausa and Fulani rulers of the northern states. The National Council of Nigeria and the Cameroons (NCNC) was stronger among the Igbo people of the eastern region. The Action Group (AG), formed in 1951 from a Yoruba cultural organization, had its roots in the west. Most other small parties and independents were based on sectional local interests.

What followed was a long period of political instability, marked by several coups and growing secessionist sentiments, which led to the deadly Nigerian Civil War (1967–1970). Democracy was finally restored with the organization of the first elections of the Fourth Republic in 1999. The elections suggested that Nigeria would be moving toward a dominant party system, as the People's Democratic Party managed to build a large multi-ethnic and multiregional coalition. Alliances with local elites, distribution of patronage, ballot rigging, and vote buying indeed gave the PDP a substantial incumbent advantage.[39] Crucially, the party was able to accommodate regional interests through an informal arrangement: key positions would alternate between the six geopolitical regions and across north and south. All these factors contributed to the victories of the PDP by large margins in the first four elections (see Figure 17.12).

---

"An Overview of Party Formation in Nigeria, 1960–1999," in *Elections and Governance in Nigeria's Fourth Republic*, ed. O. Agbu (Codesria, 2016), 27–36.

39. J. Herskovits, "Nigeria's Rigged Democracy," *Foreign Affairs* 86, no. 4 (2007): 115–130; M. Dauda, A. Adamu, and L. Ahmodu-Tijani, "Vote Trading in Nigeria Politics," *Asian People Journal* 2, no. 2 (2019): 42–51.

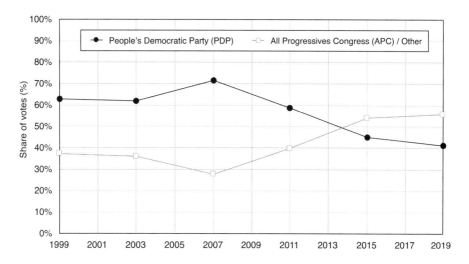

FIGURE 17.12. Presidential election results in Nigeria, 1999–2019
*Data Source:* Authors' computations using official election results (see wpid.world).
*Note:* The figure shows the share of votes received by selected groups of Nigerian political parties in presidential elections between 1999 and 2019. The People's Democratic Party received 41% of votes in 2019, down from 63% in 1999.

Several events, however, contributed to the decline of the PDP until its defeat in 2015. In 2010, after the death of the northern Muslim president Umaru Yar'Adua, Vice President Goodluck Jonathan, a Christian from the Niger Delta, ran as PDP candidate in the 2011 presidential election. This led to growing dissatisfaction and defection of northern elites to opposition parties, as they had expected the PDP to field a northern candidate given that Yar'Adua's mandate had lasted less than three years, after eight years of southern domination of the executive. Corruption, economic mismanagement, and rising insecurity due to the escalation of violence by the neo-Salafist sect Boko Haram in the northeast further reduced support for the PDP.[40] The All Progressives Congress (APC), formed in 2013 as the result of a merger between the three biggest opposition parties, received 54 percent of votes in the 2015 general election. Key to its success was the leadership of General Muhammadu Buhari, who had already headed the country from 1983 to 1985 and was per-

40. P. Lewis and D. Kew, "Nigeria's Hopeful Election," *Journal of Democracy* 26, no. 3 (2015): 94–109.

ceived as more competent to address corruption and the Boko Haram crisis.[41] As Goodluck Jonathan conceded defeat, Nigeria witnessed for the first time in its history a peaceful transfer of power from one political party to another.

## The Structure of Social Inequalities in Nigeria

Before turning to our analysis of the structure of political cleavages, it is worth providing a brief overview of ethnic, religious, and regional affiliations in Nigeria. Geographically, Nigeria is a federation of thirty-six states and a Federal Capital Territory (Abuja). Northern regions are home to about half of the Nigerian electorate and to the majority of Muslims speaking Hausa and Fulani languages. Southern regions are home to the majority of Christians, in particular the Igbo people mostly living in the South East and the Yoruba people concentrated in the South West. These three ethnolinguistic groups together amount to about three-quarters of the adult population. It is also important to stress that regions, ethnicities, and religions do not perfectly overlap: for instance, there are sizable Christian minorities in the northern regions, and a significant share of Yoruba people are Muslims.[42]

Ethnoregional affiliations in Nigeria are tightly linked to economic resources. This is the outcome of a long-run process of uneven development that has its roots in colonial expansion. The British not only chose to limit the sociocultural integration of the poorer Muslim states by keeping in place local elites and systems of government. They also deliberately prevented economic development and educational expansion in the North, as the emergence of new educated elites in the South had been a powerful catalyzer for the birth of a national movement.[43] The result was a long-lasting legacy of regional inequality. The democratization of 1999 and the growth of the Nigerian economy failed to reduce existing income disparities. Instead, the last twenty years have been characterized by growing income polarization, driven by the South South and South West regions concentrating a greater share of output, and the North East

41. Bleck and van de Walle, *Electoral Politics,* 156. Valence issues therefore played a particularly important role in recent elections in Nigeria compared to other countries in Sub-Saharan Africa. See Bleck and van de Walle, *Electoral Politics,* 212.

42. See appendix Figures CA1 to CA18, wpid.world.

43. Bourne, *Nigeria,* chapter 1; H. Onapajo and A. A. Usman, "Fuelling the Flames: Boko Haram and Deteriorating Christian-Muslim Relations in Nigeria," *Journal of Muslim Affairs* 35, no. 1 (2015): 106–122.

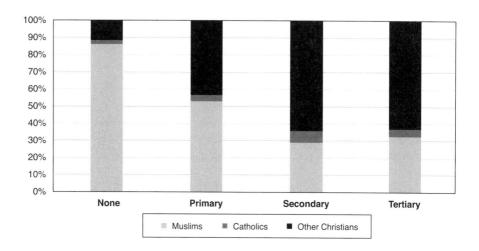

FIGURE 17.13. Ethnoreligious educational inequalities in Nigeria
*Data Source:* Authors' computations using Afrobarometer surveys (see wpid.world).
*Note:* The figure shows the composition of education groups by religion in Nigeria in
2019. Muslims then represented over 85% of voters with no diploma, compared to 32%
of university graduates. Overall, Muslims represented about 41% of the electorate,
Catholics 5%, and other Christians 53%. Illiterates represented 14% of the electorate,
primary-educated respondents 13%, secondary-educated respondents 45%, and
tertiary-educated respondents 28%.

and North West lagging behind.[44] This has fueled the rise of Boko Haram,
which has become increasingly attractive to the destitute youths and
children.[45]

This persistently skewed regional distribution of resources is visible
in the link between educational achievements and religious affiliations.
In 2019, Muslims represented about 40 percent of the adult population,
but more than 80 percent of illiterates (Figure 17.13). Meanwhile, nearly
seven out of ten tertiary-educated citizens were Christians. Religion, ethnolinguistic affiliations, and inequality therefore have remained strongly
if not increasingly associated in contemporary Nigeria.

44. F. Clementi, A. L. Dabalen, V. Molini, and F. Schettino, "When the Centre Cannot
Hold: Patterns of Polarization in Nigeria," *Review of Income and Wealth* 63, no. 4 (2017):
608–632; T. T. Awoyemi, I. Oluwatayo, and O. Obayelu, "Inequality, Polarization and
Poverty in Nigeria" (PMMA Working Paper 2010-04, 2010).
45. O. J. David, L. E. Asuelime, and R. A. Adekoye, "Is Boko Haram Poverty Driven?,"
*African Renaissance* 12, no. 1 (2015): 129–150.

## The Rise of Ethnoreligious Cleavages

How has the rise of the opposition to the People's Democratic Party affected political cleavages in Nigeria? Figures 17.14 and 17.15 show that there has been a surge in religious divides since 2003. In the elections of 2003, 2007, and 2011, support for the PDP varied little across religious groups. The two most recent elections marked a clear rupture: the share of Muslims voting for the PDP dropped from 53 percent in 2011 to only 12 percent in 2019, while Christians became more likely to vote for the PDP.

Controlling for other sociodemographic variables, in particular region and language, reduces the upward trend in religious voting, reflecting the spatial separation of religious groups in Nigeria. However, the fact that the Muslim-Christian cleavage remains very high even after controlling for region and language suggests that growing religious polarization has gone beyond the North-South divide: in particular, Christian minorities of the North have continued to vote for the PDP, while Yoruba Muslims of the South West have shifted their support to the APC.[46]

Therefore, it seems that Nigeria has been dangerously moving toward a "bipolar, Muslim-Christian political identity that overlays a two-party system."[47] This political polarization was triggered by the defection of Muslim leaders from the PDP following the candidacy of Goodluck Jonathan in 2011. It was arguably strengthened by widening regional inequalities and extreme poverty in the North, which have reinforced discontent with the PDP among Muslims. The rise of Boko Haram has also fueled ethnic tensions; many Christians view Boko Haram as having been created by Nigerian Muslims to wipe out Christians, while conspiracy theories depicting Boko Haram as a deliberate attempt to discredit their religion are widespread among Muslims.[48] Resorts to hate speech and ethnoregional appeals by candidates, pre-election violence, vote buying,

46. See appendix Figures CB13 and CB14, wpid.world.

47. F. D. Cox, C. R. Orsborn, and T. D. Sisk, "Religion and Social Cohesion in Nigeria: Frustration, Polarization, and Violence" (Sié Chéou Kang Center for International Security and Diplomacy, 2014).

48. A. Olaniyan and L. Asuelime, "Boko Haram Insurgency and the Widening of Cleavages in Nigeria," *African Security* 7, no. 2 (2014): 91–109; Onapajo and Usman, "Fuelling the Flames."

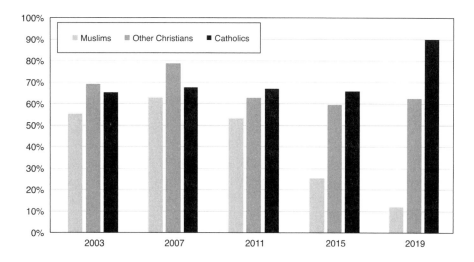

FIGURE 17.14. The PDP vote by religion in Nigeria, 2003–2019
*Data Source:* Authors' computations using Afrobarometer surveys (see wpid.world).
*Note:* The figure shows the share of votes received by the People's Democratic Party
(PDP) by religious affiliation. In 2019, the PDP was supported by 12% of Muslims,
compared to 90% of Catholics. Muslims then represented about 41% of the electorate,
Catholics 5%, and other Christians 53%.

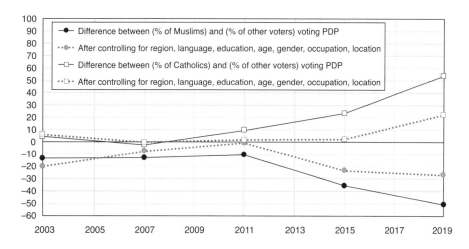

FIGURE 17.15. The ethnoreligious cleavage in Nigeria, 2003–2019
*Data Source:* Authors' computations using Afrobarometer surveys (see wpid.world).
*Note:* The figure shows the difference between the share of Muslim voters and the share
of non-Muslim voters voting for the People's Democratic Party (PDP), and the same
difference for Catholics, before and after controls. In 2019, Muslims were less likely to
vote PDP by 51 percentage points. Muslims then represented about 41% of the electorate,
Catholics 5%, and other Christians 53%.

and the escalation of communal conflicts in the Middle-Belt have also played roles in inflaming religious tensions.[49]

### Beyond Ethnoreligious Identities: Toward Class Cleavages?

To what extent have ethnoreligious cleavages represented class cleavages since democratization, and to what extent have class cleavages developed beyond religion and ethnicity? Figure 17.16 documents a dramatic shift of highest-educated voters toward the PDP. From 1999 to 2011, education did not appear to clearly influence voting behaviors; in 2019, secondary- and tertiary-educated voters had become more likely to vote for the PDP by 34 percentage points. This partly reflects the fact that less-educated Muslims have shifted to the APC: growing religious tensions have mechanically created differential voting behaviors among education groups through preexisting ethnoregional inequalities. However, this divide cannot be explained solely by these inequalities: even after controls, highest-educated voters were still more likely to support the APC by 17 percentage points in 2019. In spite of the emergence of extreme religious polarizations, education has therefore increasingly distinguished voting behaviors within religious groups. In 2019, support for the PDP among Christians varied from 63 percent among tertiary-educated individuals to only 35 percent among illiterates.[50]

How can we interpret the emergence of what seems to be a new class cleavage in Nigeria? On the one hand, we cannot exclude the possibility that it might represent a form of mismeasured ethnic divide. Very localized ethnic tensions, which we cannot perfectly capture in this analysis, might be politicized by the parties, with the PDP generally representing "wealthier" or "dominant" groups. On the other hand, another possibility is that an independent class cleavage could be genuinely emerging, overarching existing ethnic, religious, or regional identities. Educational expansion has been associated with higher political mobilization and electoral turnout among those who most benefited from it, which suggests

49. L. Hamalai, S. Egwu, and J. S. Omotola, *Nigeria's 2015 Election: Continuity and Change in Electoral Democracy* (Palgrave Macmillan, 2017), chapter 2; F. Bagga, *Central Nigeria: Overcoming Dangerous Speech and Endemic Religious Divides* (United States Commission on International Religious Freedom, 2019); O. O. Ayeni, "Commodification of Politics: Party Funding and Electoral Contest in Nigeria," *SAGE Open* 9, no. 2 (2019): 1–8.

50. See appendix Figures CB11 and CB12, wpid.world. Higher support for the PDP among higher-educated voters within each religious group already existed in 2003, but to a lesser extent.

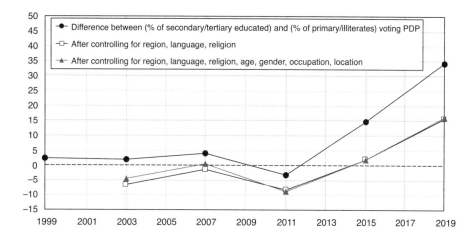

FIGURE 17.16. The educational cleavage in Nigeria, 1999–2019
*Data Source:* Authors' computations using Afrobarometer surveys (see wpid.world).
*Note:* The figure shows the difference between the share of secondary- and tertiary-educated voters and the share of primary-educated and illiterate voters voting for the People's Democratic Party (PDP), before and after controls. In 2019, highest-educated voters were more likely to vote PDP by 34 percentage points. Illiterates then represented 14% of the electorate, primary-educated respondents 13%, secondary-educated respondents 45%, and tertiary-educated respondents 28%.

that development has indeed become a political object.[51] As noted by Ayo Obe, although "it is common to hear the lament that the two parties are 'just the same,' there is in fact a discernible ideological difference between them. . . . On the one side are broadly conservative, promarket forces, today represented by the PDP; on the other is a progressive tendency that stresses social welfarism and policies directly aimed at the poor, which today's APC seeks to embody."[52] If educational divides do partly represent these differences in policy orientations, this would pave the way for the emergence of a cross-cutting cleavage, with the APC representing not only Muslims, but also poorer Christians. Future elections will tell us whether Nigeria will be moving toward an all-encompassing bipolar

51. H. Larreguy and J. Marshall, "The Effect of Education on Civic and Political Engagement in Non-consolidated Democracies: Evidence from Nigeria," *Review of Economics and Statistics* 99, no. 3 (2017): 387–401.
52. A. Obe, "Aspirations and Realities in Africa: Nigeria's Emerging Two-Party System?" *Journal of Democracy* 30, no. 3 (2019): 109–123.

religious divide, or whether these new cleavages could on the contrary allow the political space to move toward nonsectarian socioeconomic issues.

## Senegal

Having never experienced any coup d'état or ethnic conflict in its history,[53] Senegal, with its early democratic opening, is often regarded as an example for African democracies. Since 1978, political pluralism has indeed enabled the setup of multiparty elections, marked by peaceful government changes. However, the Senegal of the 1990s and 2000s is sometimes referred to as a "competitive authoritarian" regime because of the limitation of civil liberties and the uneven playing field constraining the opposition.[54] In this section, we show that ethnic and religious differences play only a moderate role in comparison to a significant cleavage dividing the Dakar region, with a young and better educated population, and the rest of the country, with poor and less urbanized populations that prefer the continuity of patronage from the incumbent.

### A Political History Marked by the Power of Incumbents

At the time of independence in 1960, the founders of the nation, Léopold Sédar Senghor and Mamadou Dia, shared a common vision of a Senegalese national identity beyond regional, ethnic, or religious cleavages. A single party, the Senegalese Progressive Union (Union Progressiste Sénégalaise, UPS), initially ruled the country with Senghor as president, before a gradual transition to a multiparty system. In 1976, three political parties were allowed, assigned to defined ideologies. The UPS, rebranded as the Socialist Party (Parti Socialiste, PS), occupied the socialist-democratic position, whereas the liberal position was taken by the Senegalese Democratic Party (Parti Démocratique Sénégalais, PDS), even though it originally claimed to be a socialist workers' party based on the work ethic of the Mouride brotherhood and the economic development

53. With the notable exception of the armed conflict that pitted the separatist Movement of Democratic Forces of Casamance against the Senegalese government from 1982 to the mid-2010s.

54. C. Kelly, *Party Proliferation and Political Contestation in Africa: Senegal in Comparative Perspective* (Palgrave Macmillan, 2020).

of agricultural production.[55] This doctrinal discrepancy between the categorization imposed by the constitution and the socialist references retained in the party's statutes may help to explain the PDS's ideological ambiguities observed to date, and indirectly those of the entire Senegalese political class.

In 1981, a multiparty system was completely authorized. This led to the fragmentation of the opposition and to a remarkable proliferation of political parties, two-thirds of which had never run on their own individual party labels in presidential or legislative elections as of 2010.[56] These parties, sometimes without electoral objectives or ideological commitment, are generally used to gain reputation and legitimacy in order to negotiate a place in power. These strategies of alliance, union, and cooptation were illustrated by, for example, the participation of the opposition leader of the PDS, Abdoulaye Wade, in several PS governments in the 1990s. Another specificity of Senegalese party politics is "political transhumance," with politicians switching party affiliations, for example after an electoral defeat, mainly in order to access state resources.[57]

Having gained experience in political governance and the recognition that comes with it, along with foreign funding that the government could not limit (unlike local funding), Wade took advantage of struggles over succession within the PS to be elected in the second round in 2000, and capitalized on the advantages of incumbency to be reelected in 2007. Similarly, he was defeated in 2012 by his former prime minister, Macky Sall, who founded his own party, the Alliance for the Republic (Alliance pour la République, APR), following a dispute with Wade. With support from an opportunistic all-party alliance against the PDS, including former members of past PDS coalitions, Sall was elected president in the second round. In 2019, the PS and the PDS did not field their desired candidates due to the polemical imprisonment of their leaders, which Sall took advantage of to get easily reelected.

Figure 17.17 shows the evolution of the vote shares received by the main parties in the first round of presidential elections since 2000. We

55. A. Osei, "Party-Voter Linkage in Senegal: The Rise and Fall of Abdoulaye Wade and the Parti Démocratique Sénégalais," *Journal of African Elections* 12 (2013): 84–108; C. Desouches, *Le Parti démocratique sénégalais, une opposition légale en Afrique* (Berger-Levrault, 1983).

56. Kelly, *Party Proliferation.*

57. Kelly, *Party Proliferation,* chapter 6.

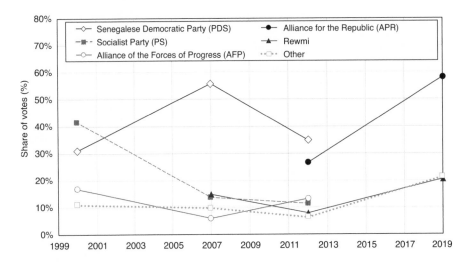

FIGURE 17.17. Presidential election results in Senegal, 2000–2019
*Data Source:* Authors' computations using official election results (see wpid.world).
*Note:* The figure shows the share of votes received by the main parties and groups of parties in presidential elections in Senegal between 2000 and 2019. The Alliance for the Republic (Macky Sall) received 58% of votes in 2019.

have chosen to consider jointly the PDS and the APR, even if they were in direct competition in 2012, for two main reasons. First, we observe some similarities between the voters of these two parties. A number of voters indeed followed Sall in his choice to separate from Wade in 2008, as the president faced public discontent and major demonstrations.[58] The personalization of the party behind the figure of Wade and the lack of prospects for advancement for its other cadres explain the rifts with certain members such as Sall, but also the departure of voters once Wade's unpopularity became too strong.[59] The second reason for our choice is our objective to analyze the structure of political cleavages with respect to the power of incumbency, particularly salient in Senegal, focusing on the commonalities of the incumbents and the common characteristics of their voters.

58. D. Koter, "Urban and Rural Voting Patterns in Senegal: The Spatial Aspects of Incumbency 1978–2012," *Journal of Modern African Studies* 51, no. 4 (2013): 653–679.
59. Osei, "Party-Voter Linkage."

*The Limited Political Salience of Ethnic and Religious Cleavages*

Ethnic inequalities are much less pronounced in Senegal than in Ghana and Nigeria. Educational inequalities between the different ethnic groups appear to be relatively limited (Figure 17.18), in particular between the Wolofs (44 percent of the population) and the Fulani (28 percent). As in Botswana, furthermore, ethnic cleavages are not the main determining factor when it comes to voting in Senegal. Ethnic groups display relatively similar voting behaviors, despite an advantage for candidates from voters of one's own ethnicity—for instance, Macky Sall's advantage among Fulani speakers in 2012 and 2019 (Figure 17.19).

The absence of an ethnic divide in Senegal is a well-known fact.[60] It partly stems from the desire of the founders of the Senegalese nation, Senghor and Dia, to build a state above ethnic differences, assimilating all groups into a national consensus. This objective was reinforced by interethnic marriages, significant migration between regions, and the development of multilingualism. Many Senegalese from different ethnic backgrounds speak Wolof as a second or third language, and Wolof could even be seen as "the irreducible core of the state," even if tensions have arisen when Wolofization attempts were too aggressive for reluctant groups, notably in Casamance.[61] The low levels of interethnic inequalities in Senegal arguably both resulted from and helped to enhance this process of peaceful coexistence and incorporation.

With respect to religion, the vast majority of Senegalese people are Muslim (95 percent), divided into different brotherhoods, the main ones being the Tijaniya (about one-third of the electorate) and the Mouridiya (about one-quarter).[62] The role of religion in politics is generally weak in Senegal, a country known for its religious tolerance, although brotherhoods can play a role through the recommendations of their leaders, khalifs, and marabouts.[63] Initially, despite being Christian, Senghor relied

60. M. Diouf, *Sénégal: Les ethnies et la nation* (L'Harmattan, 2000); Koter, *Beyond Ethnic Politics in Africa* (Cambridge University Press, 2016)

61. D. O'Brien, "The Shadow-Politics of Wolofisation," *Journal of Modern African Studies* 36, no. 1 (1998): 25–46; P. Diédhiou, "Les Intellectuels Sénégalais et la Question des Identités Ethniques au Sénégal," *REFSICOM*, November 13, 2017, http://www.refsicom.org /295.

62. See appendix Figure DA3, wpid.world.

63. M. Diouf, *Tolerance, Democracy, and Sufis in Senegal* (Columbia University, 2013); M. Monjib, "Comportement électoral, politique et socialisation confrérique au Sénégal," *Politique Africaine* 68 (1998): 53–61.

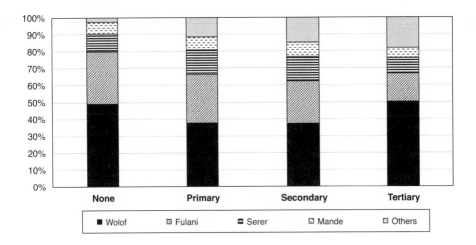

FIGURE 17.18. Ethnolinguistic educational inequalities in Senegal
*Data Source:* Authors' computations using Afrobarometer surveys (see wpid.world).
*Note:* The figure shows the composition of education groups by linguistic group in
Senegal in 2019. Fulani speakers then represented 31% of voters with no diploma,
compared to 17% of university graduates. Overall, Wolof represented about 44% of the
electorate, Fulani 28%, Serer 12%, Mande 7%, and other languages 8%. Illiterates
represented 51% of the electorate, primary-educated respondents 18%, secondary-
educated respondents 23%, and tertiary-educated respondents 9%.

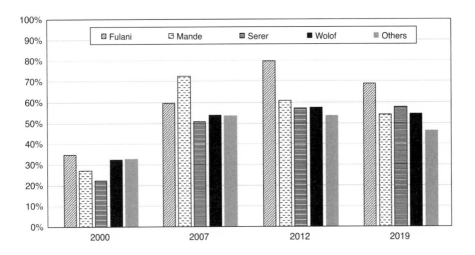

FIGURE 17.19. The PDS/APR vote by language in Senegal, 2000–2019
*Data Source:* Authors' computations using Afrobarometer surveys (see wpid.world).
*Note:* The figure shows the share of votes received by the Senegalese Democratic Party
(PDS) and the Alliance for the Republic (APR) by language. In 2019, 69% of Fulani
speakers voted APR, compared to 55% of Wolof speakers. Wolof then represented about
44% of the electorate, Fulani 28%, Serer 12%, Mande 7%, and other languages 8%.

on the support of Muslim leaders to build a coalition across religious divides, and at the same time forged strong links between citizens and the state through religious brotherhoods. This could explain the limited role of religion in contemporary Senegalese politics; support for the incumbent has varied little across religious groups, especially in recent years.[64] As in the case of ethnicity, moreover, we do not find evidence of strong inequalities between religious groups, even if the Mouridiya are slightly less educated than the rest of Senegalese citizens. The small Christian minority, about 5 percent of the electorate, has been more supportive of the opposition, but this is mainly because it is integrated into the educated and urbanized elite of the Western cities. Therefore, while religion could be a strong determinant of socioeconomic and sociopolitical differentiation in Nigeria and to some extent in Ghana, this has not been the case in Senegal.

### The Advantage of Incumbency and the Rural-Urban Cleavage

Senegalese electoral politics, instead of opposing ethnic or religious groups, is based on the strong persistence of political power over time and on the considerable importance of incumbency advantages.[65] These advantages are larger in rural areas, where information is less readily available; the strongest parties, the PDS and then the APR, obtain their best results in these areas (Figure 17.20). For example, in rural counties such as Linguère or Matam in northern Senegal, Wade won 10 percent of the vote in 2000 as an opposition candidate, while he received 60 percent of votes in 2007 as president; thus he relied on an urban electoral base when he was in the opposition and then on a rural base once in power. Conversely, incumbents do not perform well in Dakar, where their results have been lower than in the rest of the country by 14 percentage points since 1978.[66]

Dominika Koter explains this cleavage as due to the greater efficiency of clientelism in rural areas rather than the implementation of policies that are particularly favorable to the countryside. Indeed, urban citizens

---

64. See appendix Figure DB8, wpid.world. Religious recommendations, in particular the *ndigel* of the Great Khalif of the Mourides, can have an impact (Abdoulaye Wade emphasized his Mouride membership to get the leader's approval). In 2019, however, religious leaders and the khalif did not make any general recommendations, which increased the influence of local marabouts without a common religious approach.

65. Kelly, *Party Proliferation*, chapter 4.

66. Koter, "Urban and Rural Voting Patterns."

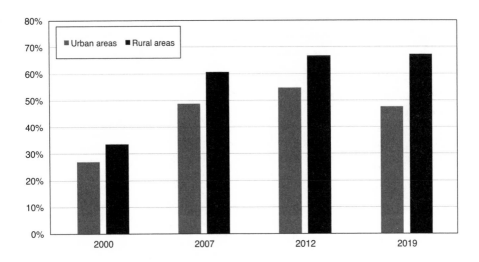

FIGURE 17.20. The rural-urban cleavage in Senegal, 2000–2019
*Data Source:* Authors' computations using Afrobarometer surveys (see wpid.world).
*Note:* The figure shows the share of votes received by the Senegalese Democratic Party
(PDS) and the Alliance for the Republic (APR) by rural-urban location. In 2019, the
APR received 48% of votes in urban areas, compared to 67% of votes in rural areas.
Rural areas then represented about 54% of the electorate.

are more independent from local leaders, unlike in small communities
where monitoring small polling stations is easier. It is also easier to cater
to the financial needs of less-developed areas and conditionally reward
these villages based on election results.[67]

In that sense, patronage plays an important role in structuring cleavages, as in the cases of Thailand and the Philippines (see Chapter 12).[68]
The upper classes tend to denounce patronage and denigrate the behaviors of the poor, who are perceived as ignoring the common good of the
nation as they focus on their immediate personal interests. However, patronage has a real economic and distributive dimension, as transfers
received by low-income voters do effectively contribute to poverty reduction and economic security for the beneficiaries. Poorer voters in rural areas
may thus fear that government changes would jeopardize clientelistic

67. Koter, "Urban and Rural Voting Patterns."
68. M. Thompson, "The Moral Economy of Electoralism and the Rise of Populism in
the Philippines and Thailand," *Journal of Developing Societies* 32, no. 3 (2016): 246–269.

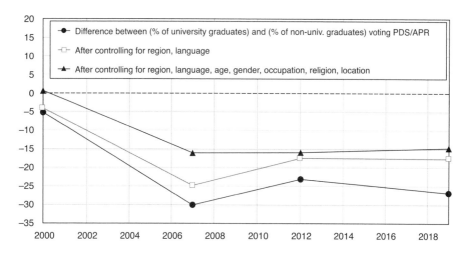

FIGURE 17.21. The educational cleavage in Senegal, 2000–2019
*Data Source:* Authors' computations using Afrobarometer surveys (see wpid.world).
*Note:* The figure shows the difference between the share of university graduates and the share of non-university graduates voting for the Senegalese Democratic Party (PDS) or the Alliance for the Republic (APR), before and after controls. In 2019, university graduates were less likely to vote APR by 27 percentage points. University graduates then represented about 9% of the electorate, up from 6% in 2000.

networks and the regular flow of transfers established by the ruling party, which helps to explain their electoral support for incumbents.

## The Educational Cleavage

The rural-urban cleavage is profoundly linked to an educational cleavage between rural and urban areas, given the higher education levels of young people studying at universities, which are necessarily located in cities, as well as observed migrations from the countryside to the attractive cities. Higher education itself constitutes an even greater electoral divide: highest-educated voters have been much less likely to vote for the incumbent, by a difference of 15 percentage points, after controls, in 2019 (Figure 17.21).

Lower-educated citizens are indeed more likely to be bought, to vote for known candidates, and to vote for candidates closest to victory and with political experience.[69] The educational cleavage therefore lies at the

69. Koter, "Urban and Rural Voting Patterns."

heart of a more general cleavage: young people are generally better educated and more urbanized,[70] and they vote in majority against the incumbent. Wade, for example, managed to mobilize them under the Sopi (change in Wolof) coalition in 2000.[71] This electoral cleavage also naturally appeared between regions, as the western region, including the capital Dakar, concentrates the most-educated and urban populations, and consequently votes less for the incumbent party.[72]

Such support for opposition forces among higher-educated and younger voters corresponds to a rejection of undemocratic methods and corrupt candidates among the political class, as mirrored for example in 2019 by the emergence of Ousmane Sonko at the head of the PASTEF (Patriotes du Sénégal pour le Travail, l'Éthique et la Fraternité). Faced with a shaky democracy, Sonko proposed solutions to fight against corruption and advocated a radical change in the system, claiming his integrity and liberation from the colonial legacy.[73] Raised in Casamance, he also mobilized part of the local electorate, which is sometimes considered marginalized because of its geographical remoteness. This region could be seen as out of tune with the rest of the country, alienated from the rest of Senegal, and it has not yet participated in the electoral arena due to the lack of a coherent political party of its own.

Unlike Ghana and Nigeria, therefore, and more like Botswana, Senegal does not seem to have developed particularly marked ethnic or religious cleavages that would systematically determine the outcome of elections. This absence was partly the legacy of the nonethnic dimension of the independence movement, and was likely reinforced by the weakness of interethnic and interreligious inequalities in the contemporary era. The growing authoritarianism of the Wade and then Sall governments has been associated with democratic demands from the urban and educated youth, while the rural areas, benefiting from the patronage of political elites, prefer the continuity of well-known incumbents with experience in power. This cleavage could well be the deciding factor in the next elections if democratic competition is not too distorted.

70. See appendix Figures DA20 and DA22, wpid.world.

71. See Figure DC10 in appendix, wpid.world.

72. See appendix Figures DA14 and DB4, wpid.world.

73. L. Marfaing and Dirk Kohnert, "Les élections présidentielles de 2019 au Sénégal ou la lente ascension des nouvelles générations," *Canadian Journal of African Studies / Revue canadienne des études africaines* 53, no. 2 (2019): 355–366.

## 18

# Inequality, Identity, and the Long-Run Evolution of Political Cleavages in Israel, 1949–2019

## YONATAN BERMAN

### Introduction

This chapter draws on pre- and postelection surveys to study the long-run evolution of voting patterns in Israel from 1949 to 2019. The heterogenous ethnic, cultural, educational, and religious backgrounds of Israelis created a range of political cleavages that evolved throughout Israel's history and continue to shape its political climate and its society today. Studying these cleavages, their historical origins, and their evolution through the lens of the socioeconomic context is the goal of this chapter.

Within a broader, international context, studying Israel is motivated specifically by its uniqueness in several key issues, compared to other high-income economies:

1. The influence of the Arab-Israeli conflict on Israeli politics, and the importance of a large minority of Palestinian citizens in Israel, both ethnically and religiously
2. The governance of a strong labor party in the thirty years that followed the creation of Israel in 1948
3. The high levels of income inequality and their exceptional evolution
4. The nation's geographical isolation and its unique immigration pattern (essentially accepting all Jewish immigrants and rejecting the rest)

I wish to thank Itai Artzi, Dror Feitelson, Amory Gethin, Clara Martínez-Toledano, and Thomas Piketty for helpful discussions and comments, and Leah Ashuah and Raz Blanero from Tel Aviv-Yafo Municipality for historical data on parliamentary elections in Tel Aviv. I also want to thank Israel National Election Studies for making all their data publicly available online.

5. The role of religion and Jewish heritage in Israeli politics (as well as no separation of religion and state)

These unique issues seemingly make the political cleavages in Israel less likely to be driven by the factors observed in other high-income countries. Yet, as this chapter shows, the most dramatic change in the structure of political cleavages in Israel is similar to that observed in other high-income democracies such as France or the United States: in the 1960s and 1970s, the vote for left-wing (labor and allied) parties was associated with lower-education and lower–social class voters.[1] It has gradually become associated with high–social class voters. This chapter also highlights the weak political response to inequality in Israel.

Despite its geographical, ethnic, and religious peculiarities, Israel can be compared to other high-income countries that tend to be more ethnically and religiously homogenous (see Chapter 1). The long-run trajectory of the interaction between political cleavages and socioeconomic aspects is therefore rather similar. It reinforces the claim that in the long run, global effects are more important to political outcomes than country-specific circumstances.[2]

## A Short Political History of Israel

Israel is a parliamentary republic with proportional representation, in which the parliament (the Knesset) is elected every four years or less. The prime minister is usually the leader of the biggest party. So far, there have been twenty-three parliamentary elections, the first in 1949 and the last in 2020.

Understanding political cleavages in Israel requires contextualizing them in the history that precedes independence. The Land of Israel was under Ottoman rule for 400 years until it was conquered by the British Empire during World War I. It was a British colony until 1948, when Israel declared its independence, following the 1947 United Nations Partition Plan for Palestine. During the first half of the twentieth century, much of the Jewish population in Mandatory Palestine was of Eastern

---

1. The focus in this chapter is on social class, and not on income or other measures of social status.

2. See G. Merom, "Israel's National Security and the Myth of Exceptionalism," *Political Science Quarterly* 114, no. 3 (1999): 409–434; G. Garrett, *Partisan Politics in the Global Economy* (Cambridge University Press, 1998).

European origin,[3] and its Zionist leadership was deeply influenced by socialist ideas. The Holocaust and, later, the Palestinian exodus and the exodus of Jews from Muslim countries in North Africa and Asia, substantially changed the demographic composition of Israel. Despite government efforts to impose a "melting pot" approach, many of the large differences between the various groups persist to this day—religious, economic, and educational differences, among others, contributing to the political cleavages described below.

From 1948 to 1977, a single party—Mapai (Workers' Party of the Land of Israel), which would later merge to become the Israeli Labor Party—was in power, and after 1977, the liberal-right party Likud also regularly imposed itself. Yet, until 2009 the parties on either side of the political map had difficulties forming stable coalitions to rule, forcing a grand coalition of the two largest parties—Likud and Labor—from 1984 to 1990 and again, for shorter periods, in the early 2000s. Figure 18.1 presents the evolution of the parliamentary seat shares of different political blocs.[4]

This evolution also reflects the transformation over time of a multiple elites system, somewhat similar to that described by Maman and Piketty (see Chapters 1 and 2).[5] Politically, the dominance of the socialist left was gradually replaced by the dominance of the right: the Israeli Labor Party (Ha'avoda) has not won a parliamentary election since 1999, and at the time of writing, following the election in March 2020, it has only 3 out of 120 seats in the Knesset. This chapter also shows the gradual rapprochement of the economic and financial elite to the Labor Party. In the 1949 election, the share of left votes in Tel Aviv, the economic center of Israel, was lower than the share of left votes in other regions by 10 percentage points. In 2019 it was higher by 23 percentage points.

---

3. Based on data from *A Survey of Palestine Prepared in December 1945 and January 1946 for the Information of the Anglo-American Committee of Inquiry* (Government Printer, Palestine, 1946).

4. The definition of each party by bloc is given in the appendix, World Political Cleavages and Inequality Database, http://wpid.world. In Israel the difference between the share of seats and the popular vote is small compared to other countries. This is due to proportional representation and a historically low electoral threshold.

5. D. Maman, "The Elite Structure in Israel: A Socio-historical Analysis," *Journal of Political and Military Sociology* 25, no. 1 (1997): 25–46; T. Piketty, "Brahmin Left vs Merchant Right: Rising Inequality and the Changing Structure of Political Conflict" (WID. world Working Paper, 2018).

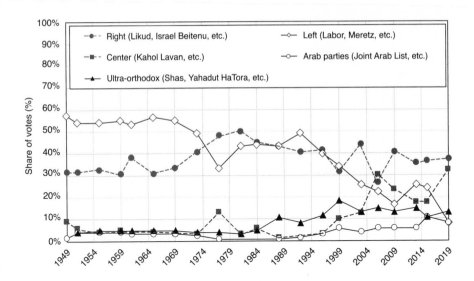

FIGURE 18.1. Legislative election results in Israel, 1949–2019

*Data Source:* Author's computations using official election results (see wpid.world).
*Note:* The figure shows the share of votes received by different political blocs in Israel. The definition of each party by bloc and a historical breakdown of blocs by party are given in appendix Table A1 (see wpid.world).

The decay of the Labor Party went hand in hand with the rise of major center parties, appealing to many disappointed Labor voters. Center parties were always part of the political landscape in Israel. Yet, they became particularly influential during the past two decades, with Kadima being the biggest party after the 2006 and 2009 elections, and Blue and White in the September 2019 election.[6]

This is also an indicator for an evolution in the ideological differences between left, center, and right-wing parties in Israel, which were initially rather large. They became narrower over time. This is true from an economic perspective as well as from other perspectives, such as the Arab-Israeli conflict. For example, Mapam, the second-largest party in the first Israeli parliament, was a socialist party that identified with the Soviet

6. R. Y. Hazan, "Kadima and the Centre: Convergence in the Israeli Party System," *Israel Affairs* 13, no. 2 (2007): 266–288; M. Shamir, R. Ventura, A. Arian, and O. Kedar, "Kadima—Forward in a Dealigned Party System," in *The Elections in Israel 2006*, ed. A. Arian and M. Shamir (Routledge, 2017), 15–43; E. Knoller, *The Center Parties in Israel: Between the Right and the Left* [in Hebrew] (Resling Publishing, 2017).

Union during the late 1940s and early 1950s. Over the years, Mapam has evolved into Meretz, a party that sees itself as a Western European–influenced social democratic party, with an ideology that focuses on human rights and liberal values, and on the Israeli-Palestinian conflict. In addition, the peace agreement between Israel and Egypt, the first between Israel and an Arab country, was achieved during the first right-wing led government, in 1979, despite a common view of the right as being hawkish. Similarly, the major liberalization of the Israeli economy, started in the late 1970s, was continued under the Labor prime minister Shimon Peres in the mid-1980s, and under the Labor-led coalition of 1992–1996. These examples share similarities with processes visible in other countries, in similar periods,[7] including the Thatcher era and the Blair era in the United Kingdom and the Reagan era and the Clinton era in the United States.

This chapter focuses on the division between left and right. This is the dominant political rivalry in Israel. Yet, a large share of the population in Israel does not take a direct part in this rivalry. The ultra-Orthodox community, about 10 percent of the population, traditionally votes for its own parties and is characterized by relatively high turnout rates. The Arab population, about 20 percent of Israel's population, primarily votes for Arab sectarian parties and is characterized by relatively low turnout rates.

A division into political blocs (see Figure 18.1) generally includes the Arab parties in the same bloc with the left-wing and center parties, and the ultra-Orthodox parties with the right-wing parties.[8] Yet, up until the 2010s, political alliances between left-wing parties and ultra-Orthodox parties were common, whereas some center parties were closer to the right. The division into blocs helps in the analysis of long-run trends and is useful for understanding specific cleavages, as it allows dividing the political map into two blocs that have been almost equal since 1977. I therefore choose to focus on these two blocs to study the evolution of political cleavages. Without this strict division, the main results remain largely unchanged.[9]

This chapter focuses on Israeli politics from the late 1960s onward. Yet, it is worth pointing out that political cleavages within the Zionist

7. Knoller, *Center Parties in Israel*.
8. See also appendix Figure A1, wpid.world.
9. See appendix Figure A3, wpid.world.

movement had already existed since the late nineteenth century, both in Europe and in Palestine. During the British Mandate for Palestine, the Assembly of Representatives was a parliamentary institution for the Jewish population in Palestine, with little authority and power, but it was still elected through democratic elections. In all elections from 1920 to 1944, the left-wing parties won by large margins. In parallel, the World Zionist Organization, holding congresses attended by representatives of various Zionist movements, reflected, more than one hundred years ago, some of the cleavages characterizing Israel today: clashes between secular and religious movements, socialists and liberals, and moderates and extremists.[10]

## Inequality and Structural Reforms

The second half of the twentieth century saw Israel becoming a rich country, with income per capita comparable to Western European countries. This development has also been accompanied by a sharp rise in income inequality. As in other Western countries, inequality started rising in the 1970s. It reached its highest levels in the mid-2000s and has been decreasing since then.[11] The long-run evolution of inequality is however rather smooth, making it difficult to identify the impacts of various political outcomes. Specifically, from 1977 to 2003, years characterized by increasing inequality, almost every election led to a change in power between the left and the right.

The major political change of 1977 led to reforms aimed at liberalizing the economy, which was heavily regulated and centralized before then. A major set of such reforms was implemented in 1985[12] by a grand coalition led by Labor prime minister Shimon Peres. This is a standard explanation for the increasing income inequality during the 1980s and 1990s.[13] Yet, the transition process into a market economy and the privatization of numerous government-owned corporations lasted

10. I. Cohen, *A Short History of Zionism* (Frederick Muller, 1951).

11. See appendix Figure A2, wpid.world.

12. S. Fischer, "The Israeli Stabilization Program, 1985–86," *American Economic Review* 77, no. 2 (1987): 275–278.

13. T. Kristal and Y. Cohen, "Decentralization of Collective Agreements and Rising Wage Inequality in Israel," *Industrial Relations: A Journal of Economy and Society* 46, no. 3 (2007): 613–635; M. Dahan, "Income Inequality in Israel: A Distinctive Evolution" (CESifo Working Paper No. 6542, 2017).

through the 2000s under multiple governments from both sides of the political map.

During 2001–2002, following the dot-com crash and amid the Second Intifada, a period of intense violent clashes between Israelis and Palestinians, the Israeli economy faced a severe recession. This led to a series of reforms that included tax cuts, wage cuts in the public sector, and reductions in transfers. These, in turn, led to a decrease in unemployment and a sharp increase in labor force participation. This is seen as the main explanation for the decrease in pretax income inequality.[14] Thus, while major fiscal and structural reforms may have dominated the evolution of income inequality in Israel, they do not seem to stem from particularly identifiable political changes.

The opposite direction of causality can be tested. These reforms, announced during 2002 and early 2003 by the Likud-led government to help the Israeli economy recover from a deep recession, were criticized for their impact on economically disadvantaged groups, and they sparked social protests during the summer of 2003. One of the major reforms, in particular, was child benefit cuts.[15] This reform had no direct effect on adults with no children, or on adults whose children were above the age of eighteen, but substantially affected families with many young children, due to the nonlinear child benefit scheme. Many families who depended on welfare benefits were substantially hurt, mainly through changes that made the criteria for receiving welfare benefits stricter. Thus, lower classes were seemingly hurt the most by the reforms. I use this to test whether self-identified lower-class voters were more likely to move away from the right in general, and specifically toward the left, given that in the 2006 election the Labor Party was led by Amir Peretz, perceived at the time as "the leader of the redistributors."[16]

Strikingly, according to available data, there is no evidence that people who were hurt relatively more by the economic reforms were more likely

---

14. Dahan, "Income Inequality in Israel."

15. The 2003 child benefit reforms consisted of three main changes:
- A nominal reduction in all child benefits
- The cancellation of the increasing benefits by child number (prior to the reform, the more children a family had, the higher the benefit per child was)
- The cancellation of the birth stipend from the second birth onward (this is now a one-time benefit, whereas prior to the reform it was paid after each birth)

16. N. Lochery, "No Longer Dominant, Playing for Second: The Israel Labour Party in the 2006 Election," *Israel Affairs* 13, no. 2 (2007): 305–324.

to move away from the right than the rest of the population. In fact, self-identified lower-class voters were significantly more likely to move from the left to the right from 2003 to 2006 and less likely to move from the right to the left. In addition, despite the dramatic effect of the reforms on families with many children, such families did not seem to "retaliate" against the right: the probability of changing a vote from right to non-right did not increase with household size.[17] These results provide clear evidence for the lack of democratic response to inequality.[18]

There could be many reasons for the weak electoral impact of the reforms. First, they were implemented almost immediately after the formation of the government following the 2003 election. By 2006 their negative impact had diminished substantially. In addition, and perhaps more importantly, the reforms proved to be successful for the recovery of the Israeli economy. By 2006, the unemployment rate was down to pre-recession levels and wage growth in 2004 and 2005 was high. Furthermore, Israel withdrew from the Gaza Strip in the summer of 2005. This significant landmark in the Israeli-Palestinian conflict was (and still is) controversial with the Israeli public and may have reduced the importance of socioeconomic topics in the 2006 election. In addition to these, identity politics, or "tribal voting," plays a major role in Israel.[19]

### From the People's Party to Elitism

The weak political response to changes in inequality suggests that the evolution of socioeconomic cleavages occurs on long time scales. Figure 18.2 plots the difference between left and right votes by social

---

17. The results of this analysis are presented in Figure A5 and Table A2 of the appendix, wpid.world. They show that the probability of a right voter in 2003 switching to non-right or left in 2006 is independent of either household size or belonging to the lower class, after controlling for other sociodemographic variables.

18. This is thoroughly discussed in the Israeli context with a focus on the ethnicity cleavage in N. Mizrachi, "Beyond the Garden and the Jungle: On the Social Limits of Human Rights Discourse in Israel" [in Hebrew], *Ma'asei Mishpat* 4 (2011): 51–74.

19. Mizrachi, "Beyond the Garden and the Jungle." See also T. Mehager, "Genealogy of Tribal Voting in Israel," interview with Lev Luis Grinberg [in Hebrew], Haokets, March 29, 2019, https://www.haokets.org/2019/03/29/%D7%92%D7%A0%D7%90%D7%9C%D7%95%D7%92%D7%99%D7%94-%D7%A9%D7%9C-%D7%94%D7%A6%D7%91%D7%A2%D7%94-%D7%A9%D7%91%D7%98%D7%99%D7%AA-%D7%91%D7%99%D7%A9%D7%A8%D7%90%D7%9C/.

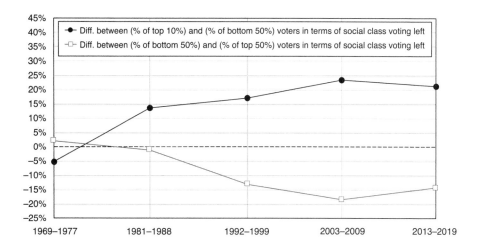

FIGURE 18.2. Class cleavages in Israel, 1969–2019

*Data Source:* Author's computations using INES election surveys (see wpid.world).

*Note:* The figure shows how the vote for left-wing parties in Israel depends on self-reported social class, after controlling for age, gender, education, and household size. Until the late 1980s, lower classes were as likely to vote left (including center and Arab parties) as other voters. Lower classes became much less likely to vote left during the last three decades, while the opposite occurred, to a lesser extent, among top 10% upper classes.

class.[20] It depicts a transition. The bottom 50 percent used to be slightly more left-leaning than the general public before the 1980s. This has changed gradually during the past forty years, and voters who self-identify as lower class are much more likely to vote right than the general public in recent years. At the same time, the top 10 percent became more left-leaning. Self-identified middle-class respondents were almost as likely to vote left as the entire population.

Figure 18.2 shows that the transition mainly occurred during the 1980s and 1990s. Politically, the initial dominance of the left was gradu-

20. This uses data from Israel National Election Studies (INES, see below). The class definitions vary in the INES surveys used in the analysis in different years. Lower class included respondents answering "lower class" or "working class." Upper-middle class and upper class are grouped into a single class defined as upper class. Also, the share of respondents in each class changed over time and an adjustment is necessary for standardization (see also Piketty, "Brahmin Left"). I assume that within each class, left and right voting shares are fixed, which leads to an underestimation of the steepness observed. This adjustment also reduces substantially the uncertainty of the results.

ally replaced by the dominance of the right. The economic elite took an opposite route. They were initially estranged from the Labor Party leadership,[21] but that changed gradually over time. In the 2019 parliamentary election, the most educated and those of high social class were significantly more likely to vote left and significantly less likely to vote right than the rest of the population.

Our data do not go back to the 1940s and 1950s, but the available data shows that this transition becomes even more striking when comparing the population of Tel Aviv, as representing more of the socioeconomic elite, to the general public in Israel. The reason for such a comparison is that Tel Aviv is perceived as representing the rich and well educated in Israel, and its metropolitan area is responsible for about 50 percent of the economic output of Israel.[22] Using the electoral results in Tel Aviv it is possible to observe the evolution of left and right vote shares in Tel Aviv and to compare them to that in Israel as a whole.[23] Assuming Tel Aviv indeed represents the rich and well educated, the data show a transition among this elite from right to left, with respect to the entire country (see Figure 18.3). Figure 18.3 suggests that the transition illustrated in Figure 18.2 potentially started right after the creation of Israel.

Figure 18.3 is only a basic comparison, of course. It ignores the changes in the sociodemographic composition of Tel Aviv. Yet, it strengthens our previous observation: Israel, despite its inherent differences with other high-income countries, shows long-run political patterns somewhat similar to those detected in the United Kingdom, the United States, and France.

I also use the Israel National Election Studies database to test this pattern.[24] Figure 18.4 shows that even after controlling for age, gender,

21. A. Goldstein, "Who Represented the Israeli Middle Class? The Crystallization of the General Zionists from 1948 to 1949," *Middle Eastern Studies* 54, no. 3 (2018): 400–414.

22. See A. Berube, J. L. Trujillo, T. Ran, and J. Parilla, "Global Metro Monitor," Brookings, January 22, 2015, https://www.brookings.edu/research/global-metro-monitor/.

23. Data for the 1949 election was taken from *Haaretz* newspaper archive. See Ha'aretz, *Political Parties in Israel on the Eve of the 2nd Knesset Election* (Ha'aretz Publications, 1951). Data for the 1977 election was obtained from Israel Social Science Data Center, "Election Results for the 9th Knesset 1977," ISDC, Hebrew University of Jerusalem, May 7, 2021, https://isdc.huji.ac.il. Through the Tel Aviv municipality it was possible to obtain the results from 1984 onward. See appendix Figure A4, wpid.world, for a similar comparison of New York City and the United States.

24. The database can be accessed at Israeli National Election Studies, accessed April 8, 2021, https://www.tau.ac.il/~ines/. In all the figures that are based on the surveys, some

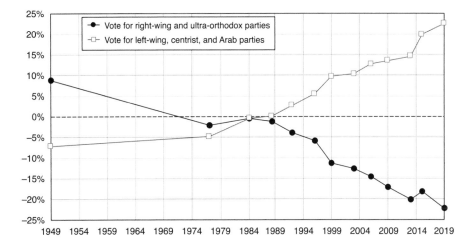

FIGURE 18.3. Vote for right and left in Tel Aviv, Israel, 1949–2019
*Data Source:* Author's computations using historical election results (multiple sources)
(see wpid.world).
*Note:* The figure shows the difference between the share of votes received by right-wing
(including ultra-orthodox) parties in Tel Aviv and the share of votes received by right-wing parties in Israel as a whole, as well as the same difference for left-wing (including center and Arab) parties. Tel Aviv was more right-leaning than Israel as a whole in the first election but gradually became more left-leaning.

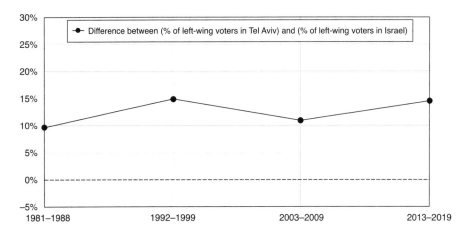

FIGURE 18.4. Residual identity component in Tel Aviv, Israel, 1981–2019
*Data Source:* Author's computations using INES election surveys (see wpid.world).
*Note:* The figure shows the difference between the share of votes received by left-wing parties in Tel Aviv and in the rest of Israel, after controlling for self-reported social class, ethnicity, religiosity, gender, education, household size, and age. The figure illustrates a stable residual left-leaning identity component in Tel Aviv.

household size, social class, education, religiosity. and ethnic origin, residents of Tel Aviv are generally more left-leaning. I consider this as a residual identity dimension of Tel Aviv. These results do not pick up the trend observed in Figure 18.3. It is possible that the residual dimension is fairly stable over time, with much of the trend observed in Figure 18.3 being due to changes in the composition of the population of Tel Aviv, which became gradually richer and more secular with respect to Israel in general.

A recent literature on the rise of radical right parties in high-income countries has identified a relationship between unemployment and right-wing voting. This is particularly true for the United Kingdom in explaining the success of UKIP prior to the EU referendum, for Germany and the rise of the AfD, and for Sweden and the rise of the Sweden Democrats.[25] In these countries there is an additional impact of immigration and exposure to globalization that affects voting. In Israel, these aspects do not play a large role in politics. Immigration to Israel is essentially limited to Jews, and many of them already have families in Israel. Therefore, it does not create the same type of social impact as in many Western countries.

Figure 18.5 shows an increasing trend in the difference in right voting between unemployed or inactive voters and employed voters. In 2003, unemployed or inactive voters were as likely to vote for the right as other voters. They then became slightly more right-leaning than employed voters.[26] This, again, resonates with current trends in other high-income countries. Yet, the unemployment rate in Israel is low in recent years and has been almost monotonically decreasing from about 10 percent to 3.5 percent

---

elections are missing. Unless noted otherwise, this is because not all questions needed for the analyses were asked in all surveys.

25. For the United Kingdom, see S. O. Becker, T. Fetzer, and D. Novy, "Unemployment, Reliance on Factory Jobs and Low Income Explain the Brexit Vote," London School of Economics blog, July 25, 2017, https://blogs.lse.ac.uk/businessreview/2017/07/25/unemployment-reliance-on-factory-jobs-and-low-income-explain-the-brexit-vote/. For Germany, see C. Franz, M. Fratzscher, and A. S. Kritikos, "German Right-Wing Party AfD Finds More Support in Rural Areas with Aging Populations," *DIW Weekly Report* 8, no. 7/8 (2018): 69–79. For Sweden, see E. Dal Bó, F. Finan, O. Folke, T. Persson, and J. Rickne, "Economic Losers and Political Winners: Sweden's Radical Right" (unpublished, 2019), https://oritkedar.huji.ac.il/sites/default/files/oritkedar/files/rise_of_radical_right_feb_2019.pdf.

26. An unemployed or inactive respondent was defined as any respondent who is not working. This definition is much more inclusive than the real definition of unemployment. The real effect is thus probably even larger and more significant than what is found—i.e., there is a sharper increasing trend in the likelihood of the unemployed to vote right.

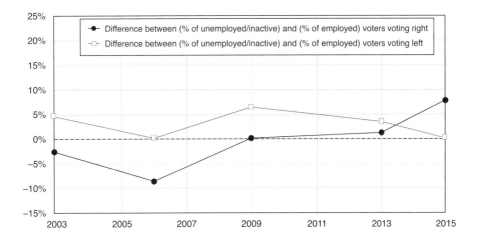

FIGURE 18.5. Vote for right-wing and left-wing parties among unemployed and inactive voters in Israel, 2003–2015

*Data Source:* Author's computations using INES election surveys (see wpid.world).

*Note:* The figure shows the difference between the share of unemployed/inactive voters and the share of employed voters voting for left-wing and right-wing parties. There is a mild trend of increasing support for right-wing parties among unemployed and inactive voters in recent years.

from 2003 to 2019. Thus, despite the noticeable trend, the practical influence of employment or unemployment on Israeli politics is small.

## From Class to Education and Ethnicity and Back

Class is traditionally linked to education. The growing tendency of the upper classes to vote for the left, observed previously, is therefore also visible when looking at education. Figure 18.6 shows the support for left parties in Israel among higher-educated voters.[27] During the 1970s, 1980s, and 1990s, education seemed to have a significant association with left voting that may not have existed previously. Despite a noticeable reduc-

27. I assume that for each year, left and right voting shares are fixed for respondents with a college degree (a college degree or fifteen+ years of schooling—in some of the survey years, respondents were only asked for their number of years of schooling) and for those without a degree (or less than fifteen years of schooling). This is used to adjust for the growing share of people with college degrees.

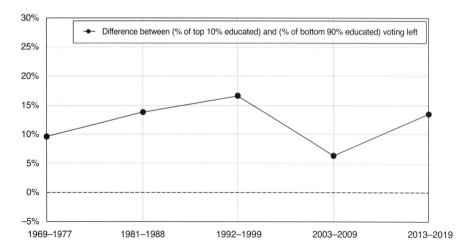

FIGURE 18.6. The educational cleavage in Israel, 1969–2019
*Data Source:* Author's computations using INES election surveys (see wpid.world).
*Note:* The figure shows the difference between the share of top 10% educated voters and the share of bottom 90% educated voters voting for left-wing parties, after controlling for age, social class, religiosity, ethnic origin, household size, and gender. In 2013–2019, higher-educated voters were more likely to vote for left-wing parties by 14 percentage points.

tion in the importance of education in the 2000s, there has been a clear upward trend in its importance during the 2010s, so that the most educated voters seem to have gradually become more left-leaning than the least educated.

The evolution of the link between education and the vote resembles the evolution of voting by ethnic origin. The ethnic cleavage has played a major role in Israeli politics.[28] Figure 18.7 presents the relative support for right-wing parties among Sephardic voters. Since the 1970s, Sephardic Jews (or Mizrachim—Jews who immigrated from Muslim countries in North Africa and Asia, and their descendants; the term "Sephardic" may also refer to Jews whose origin is in Southern Europe—Greece, Bulgaria, Italy, Spain, and Portugal—the dichotomy between the definitions is debatable) have been more likely to vote right, while Ashkenazi Jews (or Ashkenazim—Jews whose origin is in Central or Eastern Europe) have

28. N. Mizrachi, "Beyond the Garden."

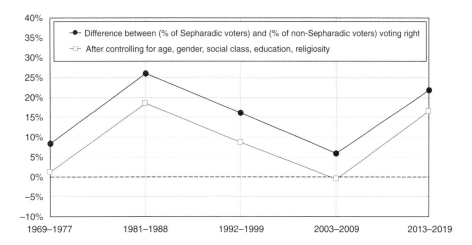

FIGURE 18.7. Vote for right-wing parties among Sephardic voters in Israel, 1969–2019
*Data Source:* Author's computations using INES election surveys (see wpid.world).
*Note:* The figure shows the difference between the share of Sephardic (or Mizrachi) voters and the share of non-Sephardic voters voting for right-wing parties, before and after controls. In 2013–2019, Sephardic voters were more likely to vote for right-wing parties by 22 percentage points.

been more likely to vote left. This is a well-known and well-studied cleavage that is very present in the public discourse and in the media, partially due to long-lasting socioeconomic gaps between Ashkenazim and Mizrachim. Despite those gaps, the differences in voting patterns between Mizrachim and non-Mizrachim exist and are statistically significant even after taking into account the gaps in education, social class, and level of religiosity.

In the cases of the education and ethnicity cleavages there is an increasing polarization in recent years after a period of possible convergence. Yet, the results on the ethnic cleavage should be treated with caution. The data do not allow us to make a clear identification between Ashkenazim, Mizrachim, and other Jewish ethnic groups until the last decade; origin was only inferred from the ethnic origin of respondents. For earlier years, Ashkenazim are defined as those who were born in Europe and North America, or whose father was born there. Mizrachim are defined similarly for Asia and Africa. The large immigration wave

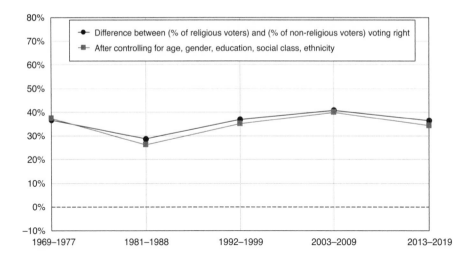

FIGURE 18.8. The religious cleavage in Israel, 1969–2019
*Data Source:* Author's computations using INES election surveys (see wpid.world).
*Note:* The figure shows the difference between the share of religious voters and the share of non-religious voters voting for right-wing parties. In 2013–2019, religious voters were more likely to vote for right-wing parties by 36 percentage points.

from the Soviet Union in the late 1980s and through the 1990s therefore increased the share of Ashkenazim in the surveys.[29]

Religiosity has a large impact on voting that is almost unaffected by controls, as seen in Figure 18.8.[30] Secular voters are more likely to vote

29. See appendix Figure A6, wpid.world. The share of either Ashkenazim or Mizrachim decreases over time in our data. A large and growing share of the population is people born in Israel whose parents were also born in Israel. Such people, neither Ashkenazim nor Mizrachim according to our definition, would likely still consider themselves as belonging to one of these groups. The current data do not allow a more accurate definition. In addition, including immigrants from the Soviet Union as Ashkenazim may potentially lead to an underestimation of ethnic cleavages. Many immigrants vote for immigrant parties or other parties whose base is Russian-speaking Israelis, and they are generally associated with the right, whereas the general Ashkenazi population is relatively more left-leaning.

30. The definition of level of religiosity was based on the survey question: "To what extent do you observe religious tradition?" The survey respondents were given four options: "not at all," "a little," "a lot," "I observe all of it." Subjects who answered either "not at all" or "a little" were classified as secular.

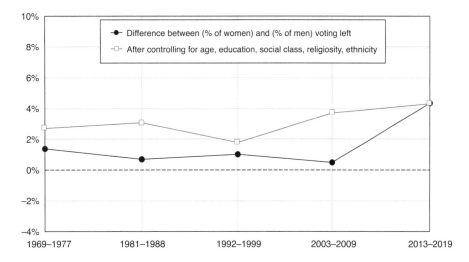

FIGURE 18.9. The gender cleavage in Israel, 1969–2019
*Data Source:* Author's computations using INES election surveys (see wpid.world).
*Note:* The figure shows the difference between the share of women and the share of
men voting for left-wing parties. Women have consistently been more left-leaning than
men, but only to a rather small degree, and only when controlling for other effects.

left and less likely to vote right than religious voters. This also did not
change substantially in the long run.

### Gender Differences in Voting

An additional important cleavage is gender. In many countries, including
in Europe and North America, it was found that women have become
more left-wing over time.[31] Figure 18.9 shows that in the case of Israel,
men tend to be more right-leaning than women after controlling for age,
religiosity, social class, education, and ethnicity. Yet, the differences are
small compared to the cleavages described above. They also do not have
a noticeable long-run trend.

In general, the effect of gender on the vote is smaller in Israel than
what was found in other countries. Yet, since 2006, center parties in Israel have received particularly large support from women—initially

31. See Piketty, "Brahmin Left." See also Chapter 1 for a comparison of the gender
gap in all high-income countries.

Kadima in 2006 and especially in 2009, HaTnua'a in 2013, and Yesh Atid in 2013 and 2015. Michal Shamir and Einat Gedalya-Levy discuss in detail the "gender gap in voting" of the 2009 and 2013 elections in Israel. They find that "in the 2009 Knesset elections, a gender gap was evident among Jews in voting for Kadima and among Arabs in voting for Balad: Jewish women voted more than Jewish men for Kadima, which was led by a woman, Tzipi Livni; and Arab women voted more than Arab men for Balad, which assigned a realistic slot to a woman, Haneen Zoabi—the first time an Arab party has done so."[32]

## Conclusion

The long-run evolution of political cleavages in Israel resembles some of the long-run trends identified in other high-income countries, in particular the gradual shift over time of elites, in terms of self-reported social class, toward the left. This is despite Israel's political, social, and geopolitical uniqueness. The dominance of the Arab-Israeli conflict in the public discourse in Israel, and the way it influences voters, may have a strong short-term impact. Yet, the long-run dynamics may obey a rather universal trajectory that has deeper socioeconomic drivers (see Chapter 1).

Tel Aviv serves as another example, as Israel's economic and cultural center. Voters in Tel Aviv used to be more right-leaning than the general public but are now more left-leaning. A comparison of these trends between Tel Aviv and New York City serves as additional evidence for the similarity in voting patterns between Israel and other high-income economies.[33]

The cleavage between religious and secular voters in Israel is also similar to that observed in other Western countries. Indeed, practicing Jews are substantially more right-leaning than secular Jews. This is similar, for example, to the results found in France for practicing Catholics and voters with no religion,[34] even if the importance of this cleavage in determining actual political outcomes is stronger in Israel than in other Western countries, due to the large share of practicing Jews in the population.

---

32. M. Shamir and E. Gedalya-Lavy, "A Gender Gap in Voting? Women and Men in the 2013 Elections," in *The Elections in Israel 2013*, ed. M. Shamir (Taylor and Francis, 2015), 231.

33. See appendix Figure A4, wpid.world.

34. Piketty, "Brahmin Left."

A subtler observation, which is unique to Israel, is related to the ethnic cleavage between Ashkenazim and Mizrachim. Since the 1970s, Mizrachim have been generally more likely to vote right, while Ashkenazim have been generally more likely to vote left. I find an increasing polarization in voting between Ashkenazim and Mizrachim over the past fifteen years that followed a period of convergence.

There is no evidence, finally, of a strong political response to inequality in Israel. For example, the direct electoral impact of the major economic reforms of 2002–2003 is weak. While the reforms led to a short-run increase in income inequality (in the long run they are thought to have led to a reduction in after-tax inequality), they did not seem to have mattered for the election results.

These results have implications for the interpretation of similar processes in other countries. Israel, due to its uniqueness discussed above, did not experience globalization in the same way as other high-income countries, and also did not see a strong rise in antiestablishment parties in the last decade. Thus, the similarities in the evolution of political cleavages related to education and class in different countries reflect mechanisms that need further exploration, and are likely to reflect deeper long-run processes.

## 19

# Political Cleavages and Social Inequalities in Algeria, Iraq, and Turkey, 1990–2019

LYDIA ASSOUAD, AMORY GETHIN, THOMAS PIKETTY,
AND JULIET-NIL URAZ

## Introduction

Shaken by civil wars, interstate conflicts, and intifada, the Middle East and Northern Africa (MENA) region sometimes finds its unicity around the predominance of violence and authoritarianism. To explain such a political turmoil, a common view consists in reducing all conflicts in the region to their ethnoreligious dimension. The area would be devastated by a cultural divide between Sunni and Shia Islam and/or between ethnic communities. The rivalry of states, affiliated to either Shia Iran or Sunni Saudi Arabia, in the context of heightened tensions around hydrocarbon resources as much as clientelism and corruption, would foster the role of nonstate actors defined along clear identity lines.[1]

Without denying the importance of the identity lens, such an approach, however, pays little attention to underlying inequality dynamics. This grid of analysis also often goes hand in hand with an orientalism bias that overlooks the electoral competition process and the programmatic positions of political parties in the region. While most MENA countries have held regular elections for several decades, little is known about the interactions between the evolution of social disparities and election outcomes.

We are grateful to Ishac Diwan, Dalia Ghanem, and Clara Martínez-Toledano for their useful advice. This chapter is based on J.-N. Uraz, "Political Cleavages and Social Inequality in the Middle East: Turkey, Iraq and Algeria 1990–2019" (master's thesis, Paris School of Economics, 2020).

1. F. Wehrey, ed., *Beyond Sunni and Shia* (Hurst Publishers, 2017).

Yet, despite concerns over electoral irregularities, multiparty elections keep playing an important role, especially in terms of distributive policies and local provision of public goods.[2]

The different waves of mass protests that have shaped the political agenda of the region for almost a decade shed new light on the role that socioeconomic factors play in political conflicts. From the Arab Springs of 2011 to the 2019–2020 street demonstrations in Algeria, Lebanon, and Iraq, as well as the Gezi Park protests in Istanbul in 2013, several movements uniting different social groups called as much for further democratization as for fairer redistribution of national income, in one of the most unequal regions in the world.[3] Does this reveal a redefinition of political cleavages in terms of socioeconomic determinants? And retrospectively, to what extent did socioeconomic determinants interact with the identity vote?

This chapter suggests highlighting the multidimensional aspect of political cleavages in the MENA region by investigating the cases of Algeria, Iraq, and Turkey from 1990 to 2019. These countries, with radically different recent histories, encompass various institutional configurations but face similar types of tensions and inequality levels. Algeria has a strong executive regime with limited power left to the parliament. Iraq set up a semifederal parliamentary system based on an ethnoreligious sharing of power in the early 2000s. Turkey, by contrast, has a long-established multiparty system but recently experienced a strengthening of its executive.[4]

All three also share some features common to the whole region. In each country, the army is a major actor that influences the trajectory with respect to political Islam. The three countries host important ethnic minorities that found political resonance on a national scale. All three went through liberalization reforms in the 1980s–1990s that signaled a reinvention of the "populist" features of their respective regimes. And in

2. R. Hinnebusch, "Political Parties in MENA," *British Journal of Middle Eastern Studies* 44, no. 2 (2017): 159–175; L. Blaydes, "Distributive Politics in the Middle East," in *Routledge Handbook of Middle East Politics,* ed. L. Sadiki (Routledge, 2020), 471–479.

3. L. Assouad, "Inequality and Its Discontents in the Middle East," Carnegie Middle East Center, March 12, 2020, https://carnegie-mec.org/2020/03/12/inequality-and -its-discontents-in-middle-east-pub-81266; F. Alvaredo, L. Assouad, and T. Piketty, "Measuring Inequality in the Middle East 1990–2016: The World's Most Unequal Region?," *Review of Income and Wealth* 65, no. 4 (2019): 685–711.

4. M. Cammett, I. Diwan, A. Richards, and J. Waterbury, *A Political Economy of the Middle East* (Western Press, 2015).

each country, the rise of "crony capitalism" defined new alliances between the government, the powerful security apparatus, and a politically connected business elite, at the expense of the majority.[5]

Four main findings emerge from our analysis. First, income plays a differentiated role in voting divides that remains highly dependent on the historical and institutional context. Both the Algerian and Turkish regimes display cross-class features uniting poorest and richest voters, which may explain the stability of their respective ruling parties. In Iraq, the extremely strong sectarian pattern of the vote overrides intra-sect inequalities but has been recently questioned by the reconfiguration of the opposition and mass mobilizations outside of the electoral arena.

Second, we find that the presence of important ethnic minorities does not necessarily overlap with sociospatial inequalities, but always translates into differentiated voting behavior. The Kurds in Turkey and the Berbers in Algeria have been significantly less supportive of the incumbents over the period of study, with a clear class dimension in the first case only.

Third, we identify other dimensions of identity that mirror inequality dynamics and translate into political cleavages. In Turkey, the salient religious divide has to be understood as part of a broader cultural cleavage opposing voters with different education levels. In Iraq and Algeria, the potential of a generational cleavage requires special attention. Youth discontent seems to be channeled mostly through abstention in both countries. Lastly, the recent mass protests invite specific attention to modes of political participation other than the vote, which have exhibited interclass and cross-sectarian dynamics in Iraq and Algeria.

While our results should be interpreted with great care given important issues of survey misreporting and comparability, we hope that they can contribute to a first attempt at documenting electoral cleavages in these three countries, and spur further data collection efforts in the future.

## Turkey

### A Multiparty System Challenged by New Players

Turkey became an independent nation-state in 1923 after the collapse of the Ottoman Empire. The new regime, led by Mustafa Kemal, implemented

---

5. I. Diwan, A. Malik, and I. Atiyas, eds., *Crony Capitalism in the Middle East* (Oxford University Press, 2019).

a set of radical and authoritarian nation-building policies to create a secular and Westernized nation. Despite the setting up of a representative body and universal suffrage, the Republican People's Party (Cumhuriyet Halk Partisi, CHP) was the only party ruling until 1946. Political opposition and minority movements were heavily repressed, preventing any multiparty system until the start of the Cold War.[6]

The first free and fair elections of 1950 marked the success of an opposition party that managed to rally the private sector and rural discontent. The original matrix of Turkish politics was born: on one hand, the old establishment, represented by the state-founding party CHP, nationalist, urban, secular, and interventionist, thereby often positioned on the left of the political spectrum; on the other hand, the center-right, representing the previously excluded rural pious and the conservative bourgeoisie, corresponding to the culturally dominated "periphery."[7] Three decades of alternations between the CHP and its challenger followed.

The military constitutes a third major actor in Turkish politics. Two direct coups, in 1960 and 1980, and two indirect ones, by means of memorandum in 1971 and 1997, led to government changes, notably preserving the secular aspect of the state.[8] The 1980 coup, in a context of increasing street violence between far-right and far-left activists, may have been the one with the longest-lasting effect. All previously existing parties, including the CHP, were banned from the political scene, and a new electoral law introduced a crucial electoral threshold, preventing any extremist parties from getting into the parliament. The state ideology was redefined toward a "Turkish Islamic Synthesis" to unite Islamism and Turkish nationalism in a broad right bloc.[9]

The 1980s paved the way for a multiparty system split into three to four main actors governing through coalitions. The center-right, while internally divided, concentrated the majority of votes (Figure 19.1). The center-left split into a social democratic branch and a more traditional one, until the reborn CHP replaced them as the main challenger. This equilibrium was broken in 1995 when an Islamic party crossed the 10 percent electoral threshold and became the first party in terms of vote

6. E. J. Zürcher, *Turkey: A Modern History,* (I. B. Tauris, 2017).

7. S. Mardin, "Center-Periphery Relations: A Key to Turkish Politics?," *Daedalus* 102, no. 1 (1973): 169–190.

8. W. Hale, *Turkish Politics and the Military* (Routledge, 1994).

9. E. Kaya, *Secularism and State Religion in Modern Turkey: Law, Policy-Making and the Diyanet* (I. B. Tauris, 2017).

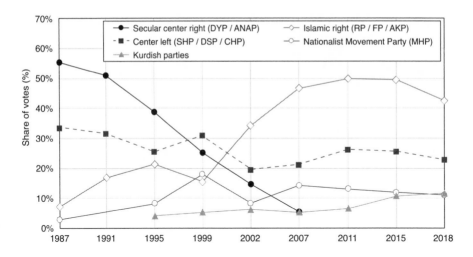

FIGURE 19.1. Legislative election results in Turkey, 1987–2018
*Data Source:* Authors' computations using official election results (see wpid.world)
*Note:* The figure shows the share of votes received by selected groups of Turkish
political parties in legislative elections between 1987 and 2018.

share. At the same time, Kurdish parties, representing the country's main
ethnic minority, entered the electoral arena. The two "structural fears"
of the republic, ethnic division and political Islam, had until then aligned
within the left-right divide that prevailed during the Cold War.[10]

Despite military interventions and the successive bans of the Islamic
parties, another Islamic party, the Justice and Development Party (Adalet
ve Kalkınma Partisi, AKP), captured all discontented voters in 2002, in
the aftermath of the country's most severe economic crisis to date.[11]
Against all expectations, the party ruled by Recep Tayyip Erdoğan, the
former mayor of Istanbul, has managed to remain in power to the present. During its first years in power, the AKP presented itself as the party
that would integrate the country into the EU, while initiating a notable
open-policy dialogue with the Kurdish dissidents.

The disappearance of any EU adhesion prospects, coupled with economic difficulties and geopolitical changes in the region, led the AKP to

10. A. Özerdem and M. Whiting, eds., *The Routledge Handbook of Turkish Politics*
(Routledge, 2019).

11. Ş. Pamuk, *Uneven Centuries: Economic Development of Turkey since 1820*
(Princeton University Press, 2018).

gradually shift toward a combination of ultranationalism and political Islam. In 2015, the first loss of majority for the incumbent meant that it had to ally with far-right nationalists. This initiated an authoritarian drift that was further accentuated by the failed putsch attempt of 2016. A referendum in 2017 institutionalized the shift to a strong presidential system and the Kurdish question was militarized in light of the fight against the Islamic State in Syria and Iraq (ISIS).

### A New Role for the Religious Cleavage in the Secular Republic?

The advent of an Islamic party as the major incumbent in the oldest secular republic of the Middle East raised debates on the potential rise of the role of religion in voting behavior. Yet, data suggest that the increased support for Islamic parties was not concomitant with an increase in religiosity.[12] While religiosity, captured through survey respondents' self-descriptions as religious, does have an impact on vote choice, Figure 19.2 points to the persistence of a religious divide that predated AKP's electoral success. Since 1991, religious voters have consistently been more likely to vote for right-wing parties than nonreligious voters by 25 to 35 percentage points after controls.

The mainstream center-right thus had already captured the more religious and conservative part of the electorate. Moreover, the AKP initially claimed affinities with Christian democratic parties and embodied a moderate approach in a fragmented Islamic landscape.[13] Research paying specific attention to parties' discourses and practices also reveals that Islamic parties have not been emphasizing religious matters in electoral campaigns before getting access to power.[14]

The perceived increase in the importance of the religiosity dimension may denote a mutation of "Islamic identity" aligned with interests in economic liberalization. Far from the traditional vision of the rural pious, such an identity would be cultivated by the modern devout Muslim, giving

---

12. A. Livny, *Trust and the Islamic Advantage* (Cambridge University Press, 2020).

13. W. Hale and E. Özbudun, *Islamism, Democracy and Liberalism in Turkey* (Routledge, 2011).

14. F. M. Wuthrich, *National Elections in Turkey: People, Politics, and the Party System* (Syracuse University Press, 2015).

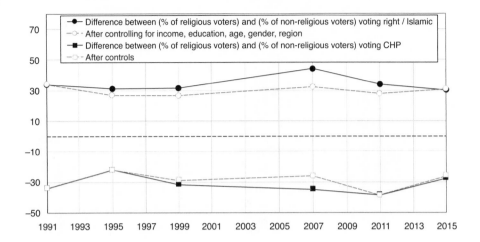

FIGURE 19.2. The religious cleavage in Turkey, 1991–2015
*Data Source:* Authors' computations using Turkish political attitudes surveys
(see wpid.world).
*Note:* The figure shows the difference between the share of religious voters and the share
of non-religious voters voting for right-wing and Islamic parties, and the same difference
for the Republican People's Party (CHP), before and after controls. In 2015, religious
voters were more likely to vote for these parties by 30 percentage points. Religious voters
are defined as those who declare themselves to be "a religious person" (World Values
Survey) or "very religious/somewhat religious" (Comparative Study of Electoral Systems).

him access to business and social connections.[15] The interaction of religiosity with other socioeconomic dimensions, and the subsequent intra-elite conflict between the secular apparatchik and an openly devout new business elite, may be key for understanding Turkish dynamics.

### The Rise of "Inverted" Class Cleavages?

Political analysts quickly noticed the AKP's singular ability to rally diverse electoral bases such as the "poor and the pious" from rural areas and the rising liberal bourgeoisie of central Anatolia, amplifying an electoral bridge initiated by the Islamic parties throughout the 1990s. This success would not have been possible without also gaining the support

15. M. Hakan Yavuz, *Islamic Political Identity in Turkey* (Oxford University Press 2003); A. Buğra and O. Savaşkan, *New Capitalism in Turkey: The Relationships between Politics, Religion and Business* (Edward Elgar, 2014).

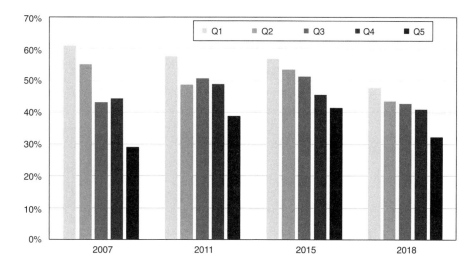

FIGURE 19.3. The AKP vote by income in Turkey, 2007–2018
*Data Source:* Authors' computations using Turkish political attitudes surveys (see wpid.world).
*Note:* The figure shows the share of votes received by the Justice and Development Party (AKP) by income quintile. In 2018, 48% of the poorest 20% of voters (Q1) voted AKP, compared to 32% of the top 20% (Q5).

of poor workers and especially those from the *gecekondu* (built at night), poor urban dwellings resulting from the massive internal migration movement in the 1960s.[16]

What is clearly shown in Figure 19.3 is that the AKP received more than 40 percent of votes in all income quintiles except the highest one. The AKP confirmed its comparative advantage among low-income groups over time, despite an apparent lack of change in the high level of income inequality in the past decades.[17] Regarding top-income voters, data suggests an intra-elite conflict with roughly equal support for the CHP and the AKP among the economic elite.[18] Several factors help to explain this cross-class success.

16. S. Bermek, *The Rise of Hybrid Political Islam in Turkey* (Palgrave Macmillan, 2019).

17. Alvaredo, Assouad, and Piketty, "Measuring Inequality in the Middle East."

18. See appendix Figure AB2, World Political Cleavages and Inequality Database, http://wpid.world.

On the one hand, the AKP was able to leverage the "Islamic trust advantage" built by previous movements and their strong ties with social civil organizations.[19] The discrediting of all mainstream parties, due to several major financial crises in the 1990s and to their perceived collusion, arguably also helped the AKP to impose itself as a coalition of both the losers and the winners of globalization. The greater fiscal discipline and the unprecedented low levels of inflation may have pleased exporting small and medium enterprises as much as poorer workers.

On the other hand, the factors that fueled the growth, namely a massive credit expansion and a boom in the construction sector, renewed clientelistic schemes beyond religious networks. The housing policy made possible the construction of many low-income dwellings, while public procurement contracts and credit lending facilities went to politically connected firms.[20] The AKP might also be a political response to a long-lasting rural-urban divide. Poor urban workers were persistently associated with their rural roots and their differing values and practices, especially their religiosity. The reduction in poverty and the real estate boom under the AKP coincided with the upward mobility of this working class, which may have translated into a new generation of politicians proud of their rural origins.[21]

Strikingly, highest-educated voters have also consistently been less supportive of the incumbent, and more supportive of the CHP, than the lower educated since the early 1990s (Figure 19.4). The effect of education appears to be highly robust to controls and strong enough to revert the impact of religiosity.[22] Such-defined "intellectual elites" therefore seem to relate more to the Kemalist tradition of secularism. Education was indeed at the core of Kemal's modernization reforms, which initiated a long-lasting cultural cleavage in the country.[23]

19. M. Cammett and P. J. Luong, "Is There an Islamist Political Advantage?," *Annual Review of Political Science* 17, no. 10 (2014): 1–20.

20. E. Ç. Gürakar, *Politics of Favoritism in Public Procurement in Turkey: Reconfigurations of Dependency Networks in the AKP Era* (Springer, 2016); Ç. Bircan and O. Saka, "Elections and Economic Cycles: What Can We Learn from the Recent Turkish Experience?," in Diwan, A. Malik, and Atiyas, *Crony Capitalism in the Middle East*, 291–308.

21. T. Erman, "Urbanization and Urbanism," in *The Routledge Handbook of Modern Turkey*, ed. M. Heper and S. Sayari (Routledge, 2017), 293–302.

22. See appendix Figure AB31, wpid.world.

23. L. Assouad, "Charismatic Leaders and Nation Building" (working paper, 2020), https://halshs.archives-ouvertes.fr/halshs-02873520v2/document; O. Sakalli, "Secularization

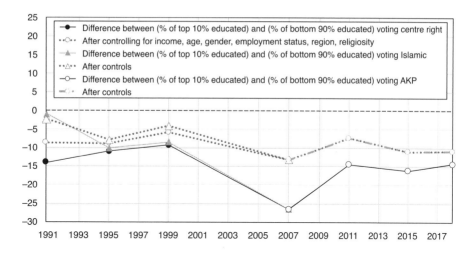

FIGURE 19.4. The educational cleavage in Turkey, 1991–2017
*Data Source:* Authors' computations using Turkish political attitudes surveys (see wpid.world).
*Note:* The figure shows the difference between the share of top 10% educated voters and the share of bottom 90% educated voters voting for right-wing (DYP/ANAP) and Islamic (RP/FP) parties before 2007 or for the AKP after 2007, before and after controls. In 2018, highest-educated voters were less likely to vote AKP by 14 percentage points.

The education divide also recently took on a generational dimension when the AKP put an end to the marginalization of religious schooling.[24] Interestingly, the youth voted less for the AKP than older voters, but controlling for education significantly reverses this trend starting in 2015.[25] While the party may have lost the young graduates who were overrepresented in the 2013 Gezi Park protest, it was not massively rejected by the new generation at large, despite a rising youth unemployment rate. Moreover, in contrast with other MENA countries, Turkey exhibits an extremely high level of electoral participation, including among the youth.

All in all, the AKP appears to have been much more popular among low-income and especially lower-educated voters since the 1990s, while

and Religious Backlash: Evidence from Turkey" (working paper, 2019), https://cepr.org /sites/default/files/Orcan_Sakalli_Religious_backlash_last.pdf.

24. D. Lüküslü, "Creating a Pious Generation: Youth and Education Policies of the AKP in Turkey," *Southeast European and Black Sea Studies* 16, no. 4 (2016): 637–649.

25. See appendix Figure AC3, wpid.world.

top-income and higher-educated voters have been more supportive of the CHP. While partly congruent to the religious cleavage, this divide appears to have a strong socioeconomic dimension. This class cleavage differs significantly from that observed in other Muslim-majority countries studied in this volume, such as Pakistan, where it is the secular Pakistan Peoples Party, not Islamic parties, that has historically been supported by low-income voters (see Chapter 10).

### The Regional Cleavage and the "Kurdish Question"

Turkey's landscape is clearly divided between on one side, the richer West Aegean coast and the urban centers of Istanbul and Ankara, and on the other, the historically most deprived Eastern and Southeastern regions, where the majority of Kurds live.[26] As a consequence, the Kurdish question is often framed as a "class cleavage."[27]

While Kurdish dissent took different forms, from demands for cultural recognition to quest for self-determination, its qualification as a proper political matter is a recent phenomenon. Until the mid-1990s, the cleavage took the form of alternate phases of "tacit" coexistence and self-reinforcing cycles of state repression and escalation of violence.[28] The first unilateral cease-fire of the Kurdistan Worker's Party (PKK) in 1993 and the abandonment of its separatist quest paved the way for openly Kurdish political parties to emerge in the electoral arena. Yet, Kurdish parties were successively banned, despite major electoral gains in Southeastern regions.

The AKP's rise to power in 2002 led to an interesting change in regional voting patterns. Because it shared with the Kurdish parties a somewhat similar history of state repression, the AKP attracted the more pious and socially conservative electorate of the Southeastern regions. Moreover, its first terms were notable for its exceptional recognition of Kurdish sub-identity, which led the party to gain significant political support in the two predominantly Kurdish regions.[29]

26. See appendix maps and Figure AA17, wpid.world.

27. M. Hakan Yavuz, "Five Stages of the Construction of Kurdish Nationalism in Turkey," *Nationalism and Ethnic Politics* 7, no. 3 (2001): 1–24.

28. H. Barkey, "The Transformation of Turkey's Kurdish Question," in *The Kurdish Question Revisited,* ed. G. Stansfield and M. Shareef (Oxford University Press, 2017), 211–224.

29. See appendix Figure AB7, wpid.world.

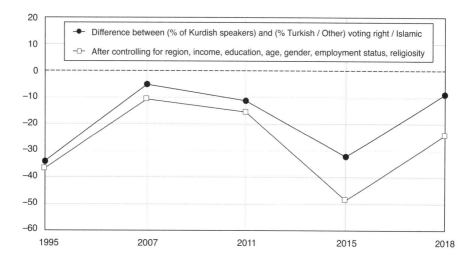

FIGURE 19.5. The Turkish-Kurdish cleavage in Turkey, 1995–2018
*Data Source:* Authors' computations using Turkish political attitudes surveys (see wpid.world).
*Note:* The figure shows the difference between the share of Kurdish speakers and the share of speakers of Turkish and other languages voting for right-wing and Islamic parties before 2007 and the Justice and Development Party (AKP) after 2007, before and after controls. Kurdish speakers were less likely to vote AKP by 32 percentage points in 2015.

Yet, the reversal of the regional and international context put an end to this parenthesis in 2015. The empowerment of the Syrian Kurdish organization in the fight over ISIS led to the resurgence of Kurdish ethnonationalism.[30] In line with these changes, our findings suggest that Kurdish speakers have massively voted against the AKP in the past decade, with a peak in 2015 (Figure 19.5).[31]

At the same time, a new Kurdish party, the Peoples' Democratic Party (Halkların Demokratik Partisi, HDP), appeared as a daunting electoral opponent in 2015, adopting an inclusive radical left stance.[32] For the

30. Z. Kaya and M. Whiting, "The Kurdish Question," in Özerdem and Whiting, *Routledge Handbook of Turkish Politics*, 231–241.

31. Note that not all Kurds speak Kurdish as their first language, so it is likely that our results underestimate this divide.

32. M. Kaya, "The Potentials and Challenges of Left Populism in Turkey: The Case of Peoples' Democratic Party (HDP)," *British Journal of Middle Eastern Studies* 46, no. 5 (2019): 787–812.

first time, Kurdish MPs were entering the parliament as a party, while the HDP succeeded in securing support that was not exclusively from the Southeast region.[33] Overall, the Turkish ethnoregional cleavage remains deeply rooted in socioeconomic inequalities but is not fully frozen. The Kurds have supported ruling parties when they met both their cultural and social demands, while Kurdish parties have managed to attract votes beyond their ethnic group when adopting inclusive platforms.

## Iraq

### A Democratic Transition Shaped by Ethnoreligious Sectarianism

Iraq found its modern territorial form after the collapse of the Ottoman Empire. Britain administered the country after World War I, and Iraq became fully independent only in 1932. Under the influence of pan-Arabism, promoted by the Egyptian Gamal Abdel Nasser, a coup overthrew the monarchy in place in 1958 and established a nationalist republic under military rule. Social and agrarian reforms were implemented, backed by one of the most prominent communist parties of the Middle East. In 1968, the Ba'ath Party took power and imposed a secular dictatorship. Quickly embodied by its leader Saddam Hussein, the Ba'athist regime signaled the political dominance of Sunni Muslims from central Iraq over the poorer Shia and incarnated an Arabic nationalism hostile to the Kurdish part of the population.[34]

While the first decades were marked by significant improvement in human development outcomes, the two Gulf Wars (with Iran in 1980–1988 and the attempted annexation of Kuwait in 1991), followed by ravaging international economic sanctions, left the country devastated. The US-led invasion in 2003, supposedly to prevent nuclear armament, ended with the unraveling of the former regime. The post-2003 period saw a profound institutional reconfiguration and opened an era of extreme violence. The disbanding of the Iraqi army and the systematic de-Ba'athification of the institutions put more than half a million Iraqis out of work and led to an insurgency in Sunni areas. The conflict quickly turned into all-out

33. See appendix Figure AC6, wpid.world.

34. A. Dawisha, *Iraq: A Political History from Independence to Occupation* (Princeton University Press, 2009).

civil war between violent militia, often aligned with tribal and religious interests.[35]

A sectarian mode of governance, sharing power equitably between the various ethnic and religious groups of the country—primarily Sunni, Shia, and Kurds, but also Turkmen and Christians—emerged under the aegis of the United States. This system, the *muhasassa,* appeared as the preferred way to end the capture of power by a politico-military minority. All communities united in apparently monolithic blocs and only few secular parties imposed themselves in the political landscape, while the Ba'ath Party was banned.

Despite tensions and a new war in 2014 due to ISIS expansion in the northwest of the territory, the Islamic-dominated system has been remarkably stable since 2005, and elections have been held consistently. The higher demographic weight of the Shia led their coalitions to gain the highest vote share, while Sunni Arabs initially boycotted the electoral process (Figure 19.6). Yet, the quota-sharing system ensured that the government would be made of coalitions, with a rotating allocation of positions among the three groups. Secular and antisectarian alliances also took on a growing importance. United against the autocratic drift of the Shia prime minister Al-Maliki, the secular al-Iraqiya List notably came first in the 2010 elections but rallied mostly Sunni votes.

Political elites gradually moved from fractionalization to collusion around power sharing, while popular discontent increasingly transcended identity boundaries. Growing street protests arose throughout the country, primarily in Shia areas since 2015.[36] Moving on from demands for provision of basic services, the social movement quickly denounced the failures of the state at large, questioning the legitimacy of its identity mode of governance. For the first time, the antisectarian stance deeply resonated in the Shia political bloc in the elections of 2018, and a new coalition managed to reshuffle the cards, reflecting the call for outside-the-system alliances. Yet, record abstention as much as sustained protests since October 2019 have cast doubt on the ability of the 2003 regime to reinvent itself.[37]

35. P. Marr, *The Modern History of Iraq* (Routledge, 2018).

36. I. Costantini, "The Iraqi Protest Movement: Social Mobilization amidst Violence and Instability," *British Journal of Middle Eastern Studies* (2020): 1–18.

37. T. Dodge and R. Mansour, "Sectarianization and De-sectarianization in the Struggle for Iraq's Political Field," *Review of Faith and International Affairs* 18, no.1 (2020): 58–69.

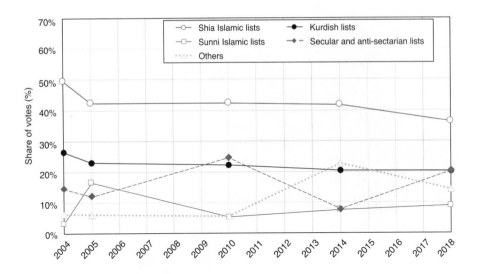

FIGURE 19.6. Legislative election results in Iraq, 2005–2018
*Data Source:* Authors' computations using official election results (see wpid.world).
*Note:* The figure shows the share of votes received by selected groups of Iraqi political parties in legislative elections between 2005 and 2018. The January 2005 election is represented as 2004; the December 2005 election is represented as 2005.

## Spatial Inequalities and Sectarian Voting

More than three decades of conflicts severely deteriorated Iraqis' social conditions. With infrastructures and institutions in tatters, poverty has exploded in an economy dominated by the resource curse.[38] The salient security issue of the post-2003 era, the collapse of oil prices, and poor governance further delayed any improvement of the situation for a population still lacking basic services.[39] This extreme poverty is unevenly distributed over the territory, which impacts ethnic inequality. The three main ethnoreligious groups are largely concentrated in defined areas: the

38. Oxford Poverty and Human Development Initiative, *Iraq Country Briefing, Multidimensional Poverty Index Data Bank* (University of Oxford, 2017). The resource curse refers to the paradoxical situation of countries characterized by unstable and weak economic and political institutions in spite of their rich natural resources, due among other factors to overspecialization in the resource-dependent sector of the economy.

39. World Bank, *Republic of Iraq Public Expenditure Review* (World Bank Publications, 2014).

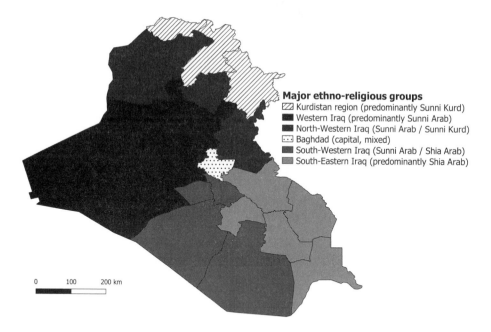

**Major ethno-religious groups**

- Kurdistan region (predominantly Sunni Kurd)
- Western Iraq (predominantly Sunni Arab)
- North-Western Iraq (Sunni Arab / Sunni Kurd)
- Baghdad (capital, mixed)
- South-Western Iraq (Sunni Arab / Shia Arab)
- South-Eastern Iraq (predominantly Shia Arab)

0     100     200 km

FIGURE 19.7. Geographical distribution of main ethnoreligious groups in Iraq
*Data Source:* Authors' elaboration.

north is mostly Kurdish, the center Sunni, and the south of the country
Shia (Figure 19.7).[40]

Regional inequalities, however, have reverted over time. While Shia
and Kurdish provinces have been historically the most deprived, the latter
experienced a reversal of fortune.[41] After having suffered from state repression and ethnic-cleansing campaigns, the Kurdistan Region has benefited from a rather peaceful and prosperous time under a de facto autonomous regime since 1991, institutionalized with the 2005 semifederal
constitution.[42] In contrast, the succession of conflicts hurt the Sunni
northwest the most. Increasing geographical disparities deepened the
ethnic cleavage, which took the form of an independence referendum in
2017 for the Kurdistan Region, whose legality was rejected by the federal government. United as opponents to Saddam's regime, the alliance

40. See appendix maps, wpid.world.

41. See appendix Figures BA8 and BA9, wpid.world.

42. D. Natali, *The Kurdish Quasi-state: Development and Dependency in Post–Gulf
War Iraq* (Syracuse University Press, 2010).

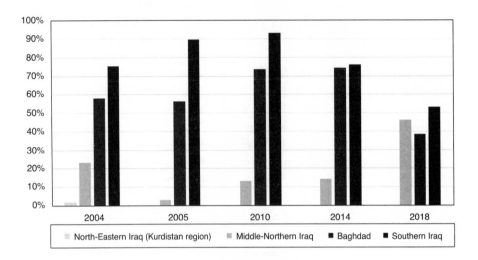

FIGURE 19.8. The regional cleavage in Iraq, 2005–2018: Vote for Shia Islamic lists by region
*Data Source:* Authors' computations using Iraqi political attitudes surveys (see wpid.world).
*Note:* The figure shows the share of votes received by Shia Islamic lists by region. In 2018, Shia Islamic lists received 53% of votes in Southern Iraq, compared to 0% in North-Eastern Iraq. Middle-Northern Iraq is predominantly Sunni, Baghdad is mixed, Southern Iraq is predominantly Shia. The January 2005 election is represented as 2004; the December 2005 election is represented as 2005.

between the Kurds and the Shia has been increasingly called into question with the war against ISIS.[43]

The sectarian feature of the Iraqi system, by construction, leads to extremely high regional cleavages, among the highest observed in this volume (see Chapter 1). The regional variable captures almost perfectly the ethnoreligious divide (Figure 19.8). Yet, decomposing Iraq into three major groups occupying distinct territories remains a simplified misrepresentation. Mixed provinces, such as the capital Baghdad and the disputed province of Kirkuk, remain important, and only one-third to one-half of Iraqi governorates are demographically dominated by a single community. The geographical decomposition of political outcomes also confirms that intersectarian votes exist beyond support for secular and antisectarian

43. J. McEvoy and E. W. Aboultaif, "Power-Sharing Challenges: From Weak Adoptability to Dysfunction in Iraq," *Ethnopolitics,* March 2020, 1–20.

coalitions. Kurdish votes, nonetheless, display a dissimilar pattern, with almost no national list interfering in the Kurdish political scene.[44]

### What Place for the Income Gradient in a Sectarian Vote?

Decomposing the vote along the income dimension confirms the importance of regional and sectarian disparities: controlling for ethnoreligious identity almost completely cancels out the effect of income on the vote from 2005 to 2014.[45] Yet, the sectarian divide is not without deep intra-sect inequalities. A poverty-mapping exercise by district notably reveals that pockets of extreme poverty are side by side with areas enriched by oil windfalls, including within regions predominantly populated by one sect.[46]

This might be partly due to a supply-side shortage. The fall of Saddam Hussein's regime was accompanied by a ban of the socialist pan-Arabist ideology. Few parties openly identified themselves on a left-right spectrum or aimed at drawing poor voters in the post-2003 era. Secular coalitions, which usually adopted a more socialist tone, struggled to find an effective cross-sectarian resonance and initially appealed more to richer Iraqis.[47]

The sectarianization of Iraqi politics also coincided with a struggle over oil resources and their redistribution, which notably channeled through public-sector appointments.[48] Civil servants are much richer, while the poor are concentrated in informal jobs. In a country often ranked among the world's top ten most corrupt, patronage defined on an ethnoreligious basis continued to play a prominent electoral role.[49]

It is only in 2018 that poorer voters became significantly more supportive of antisectarian lists, when the alternative took the form of an unprecedented alliance between the secular communists and a faction of the Islamic Shia, the Saadrists (Figure 19.9). Decried as a tactical alliance with no future, this coalition revealed the importance of the interactions

44. See appendix Figure BB5, wpid.world.

45. See appendix Figures BC1, BC2, and BC3, wpid.world.

46. T. Vishwanath, D. Sharma, N. Krishnan, and B. Blankespoor, *Where Are Iraq's Poor: Mapping Poverty in Iraq* (World Bank, 2017).

47. See appendix Tables B3 to B7, wpid.world.

48. A. Al-Mawlawi, *Public Payroll Expansion in Iraq: Causes and Consequences* (LSE Middle East Centre, 2019).

49. S. Abdullah, T. Gray, and E. Clough, "Clientelism: Factionalism in the Allocation of Public Resources in Iraq after 2003," *Middle Eastern Studies* 54, no. 4 (2018): 665–682.

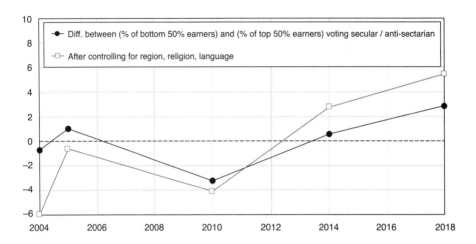

FIGURE 19.9. Vote for secular and antisectarian lists among low-income voters in Iraq, 2005–2018

*Data Source:* Authors' computations using Iraqi political attitudes surveys (see wpid.world).
*Note:* The figure shows the difference between the share of bottom 50% earners and the share of top 50% earners voting for secular and antisectarian lists, before and after controlling for ethnoreligious identity. In 2018, low-income voters were more likely to vote for secular and antisectarian lists by 3 percentage points. The January 2005 election is represented as 2004; the December 2005 election is represented as 2005.

between left-wing movements and Islamic movements on social grounds.[50] By redefining the boundaries of the "antisectarian" camp suddenly prone to incorporate Islamic components, this novel coalition may have reintroduced a class cleavage while transforming the social composition of the opposition.

At the same time, the 2018 elections illustrated how a system based on sectarian lines failed to equally benefit all members of a same sect. It was in the mostly Shia province of Basra that social protests began in mid-2015. Demonstrators held their own Shia leaders accountable for the worsening of public services and lack of electricity in one of the country's most oil-rich governorates.

50. B. Robin-D'Cruz, "Social Brokers and Leftist-Sadrist Cooperation in Iraq's Reform Protest Movement: Beyond Instrumental Action," *International Journal of Middle East Studies* 51, no. 2 (2019): 257–280.

*An Absence of Alternate Cleavages in a System in Crisis?*

Decades of conflicts severely damaged public institutions and infrastructures in Iraq, especially education and health care, which used to be ranked near the top of the region in the late 1970s. In that context, one might have expected that the collapse of the Iraqi educational system would have impacted the political choices of Iraqi. Nonetheless, as with income, education does not seem to impact voting patterns after having controlled for ethnosectarian dynamics.[51]

The absence of a salient education divide may relate to the continuous and massive exodus of the former educated middle class. Having begun during the war decades, the brain drain intensified with the sectarian violence and the de-Ba'athification process, leading to the near disappearance of this class in Iraq demographics today.[52] Interestingly, antisectarian lists were initially more supported by higher-educated voters (Figure 19.10). Yet, by reinventing themselves, antisectarian alliances managed to diversify their electorate beyond the former elite of the Saddam regime. Moreover, while schooling inequality partly overlaps with a generational effect in one of the youngest countries in the world, the vote choices of the young do not reveal any clear cleavage either.[53]

Rather than being channeled through votes for antisectarian lists, social discontent may be expressed mostly in the form of abstention, which is especially high among young and female voters. Strikingly, although vote boycotts were at first aligned with the Sunni identity, refusing to cast a vote has become what may be the clearest cross-sectarian and cross-class mode of political expression.[54] The deficit of trust in the government has also reached across all social and ethnoreligious groups in recent years (Figure 19.11).

To some extent, the rising abstention and ongoing protest movements may invite the conclusion that the antisectarian lists are not necessarily perceived by discontent voters as embodying an opposition to a political system that little mirrors the evolution of social cleavages.[55]

51. See appendix Figures BC7 and BC8, wpid.world.
52. J. Sassoon, "The Brain Drain in Iraq after the 2003 Invasion," in *Writing the Modern History of Iraq*, ed. J. Tejel, P. Sluglett, and R. Bocco (World Scientific, 2012), 379–389.
53. See appendix Figure BC9, wpid.world.
54. See appendix Figures BD1 and BD4, wpid.world.
55. F. A. Jabar, *The Iraqi Protest Movement: From Identity Politics to Issue Politics* (LSE Middle East Centre, 2018).

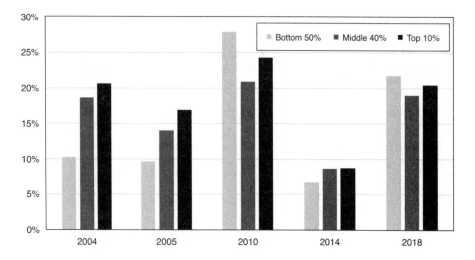

FIGURE 19.10. Vote for secular and antisectarian lists by education group in Iraq, 2005–2018

*Data Source:* Authors' computations using Iraqi political attitudes surveys (see wpid.world).
*Note:* The figure shows the share of votes received by secular and antisectarian lists by education group. In 2018, 22% of the 50% least educated voters supported secular or anti-sectarian lists. The January 2005 election is represented as 2004; the December 2005 election is represented as 2005.

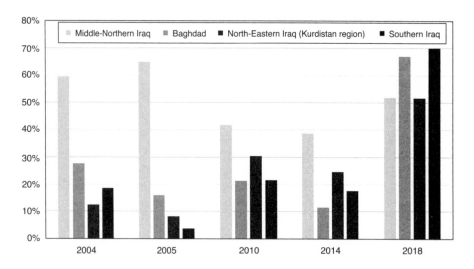

FIGURE 19.11. Trust deficit toward the government by region in Iraq, 2005–2018
*Data Source:* Authors' computations using Iraqi political attitudes surveys (see wpid.world).
*Note:* The figure decomposes distrust expressed toward the government by region. Middle-Northern Iraq is predominantly Sunni, Baghdad is mixed, Southern Iraq is predominantly Shia. The January 2005 election is represented as 2004; the December 2005 election is represented as 2005.

## Algeria

*From Postcolonial Authoritarianism to an "Electoral Autocracy"*

Algeria gained its independence from France in 1962. The new regime, divested of its former French and Algerian-born European bureaucrats, replaced them with trusted war veterans, enshrining from the start the deep connections between the state and the military.[56] The National Liberation Front (Front de Libération Nationale, FLN), which had united revolutionary dissidents during the Algerian War of Independence (1954–1962), imposed itself as the new state party. The FLN established an authoritarian system promoting state socialism and Arabic nationalism that prevailed for almost three decades, until nationwide riots forced the regime to adopt governance reforms in 1988.

Calling for ending corruption in a context of deteriorating socioeconomic conditions, the popular unrest was met by the adoption of a new constitution that paved the way for a democratization process, raising hopes in the whole Arab world. The experience was however cut short when a fundamentalist party, the Islamic Salvation Front (Front Islamique du Salut, FIS), won the first pluralist elections of 1991, triggering military intervention.[57]

With the National Assembly dissolved and the FIS banned, the military took effective control of the country. State repression coupled with a violent radicalization of part of the Islamists triggered a decade of bloody civil war. It was only after this "Black Decade" that there was a second attempt at democratization. In 1999, Bouteflika, a long-standing FLN member backed by the military, was elected president. He would remain in place for nearly two decades, relying on a new pro-government coalition between the FLN and a technocratic movement, the Democratic National Rally (Rassemblement National Démocratique, RND).[58]

The political landscape in Algeria remained dominated by the alliance of the FLN and RND, despite the lack of strong popular backing in general elections (Figure 19.12). The extremely high vote shares going to other marginal parties did not translate into the allocation of parliamen-

56. B. Stora, *Histoire de l'Algérie depuis l'Indépendance 1962–1988* (La Découverte, 2004).

57. J.-P. Peyroulou, *Histoire de l'Algérie depuis 1988* (La Découverte, 2020).

58. J. McDougall, *A History of Algeria* (Cambridge University Press, 2017).

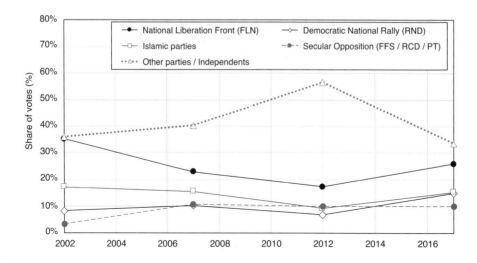

FIGURE 19.12. Legislative election results in Algeria, 2002–2017
*Data Source:* Authors' computations using official election results (see wpid.world).
*Note:* The figure shows the share of votes received by the main parties or groups of political parties in legislative elections held in Algeria between 2002 and 2017. FFS: Front des forces socialistes; RCD: Rassemblement pour la culture et la démocratie; PT: Parti des travailleurs.

tary seats.[59] While the multiparty electoral system was preserved during the civil war, relatively fairer elections took place only after 2002, and were blamed for only perpetuating the status quo with limited democratization.[60] In 2008, a contested constitutional modification ruling out presidential term limits also strengthened the executive.

The Arab Spring wave in 2011 had relatively few repercussions in Algerian politics. Consumption subsidies, pay raises for civil servants, and youth unemployment schemes mitigated the protests.[61] New political parties were legalized but stayed out of the parliament due to the electoral threshold. Nonfundamentalist Islamic parties also united in 2012

59. See appendix Figure CA1, wpid.world.
60. A. Aghrout and Y. Zoubir, "Algeria: Reforms without Change?," in *North African Politics: Change and Continuity,* ed. Y. Zoubir and G. White (Routledge, 2015), 145–155.
61. F. Volpi, "Algeria versus the Arab Spring," *Journal of Democracy* 24, no. 3 (2013): 104–115; L. Achy, "The Price of Stability in Algeria" (Carnegie Middle East Center Papers, April 2013), https://carnegieendowment.org/files/price_stability_algeria.pdf.

but did not manage to replicate the success of political Islam encountered elsewhere in the MENA region.[62] Overall, the opposition remained weak and divided and the rate of abstention was high, exceeding 50 percent over the period.

Instead, localized riots had an increased role in the political agenda in a context of worsening socioeconomic conditions. They gained an unprecedented national dimension in February 2019, following the announcement of Bouteflika's candidacy for a fifth mandate.[63] Despite the president's renunciation of the riots and the organization of new elections, which were massively boycotted, the so-called Hirak protests were still mobilizing a year after they began, with unclear political consequences at the time of writing.[64]

### Spatial Disparities and Ethnic Cleavages in Algeria

Algeria is a middle-income country that relies mostly on its reserves of hydrocarbons and gas, all located in its southern part. The coast, though comprising only 4 percent of the country's area, concentrates almost half of its inhabitants and companies. This massive coastal settlement has come with important spatial disparities, especially between the north and the poorer south.[65] However, while new regional claims have taken on a growing importance in the 2010s in the form of movements against unemployment and youth marginalization in the south, they do not seem to have found a resonance in the electoral arena, as there is no major party representing the distinct interests of the south.

The picture is quite different in the Berber-populated region of Kabylia, in the north of the country. The Berbers, or self-named Amazigh, represent about one-quarter of the Algerian population. Distinct in their language and culture, they were initially not recognized by the newly in-

---

62. D. Ghanem, "The Decline of Islamist Parties in Algeria," Carnegie Middle East Center, February 2014, https://carnegie-mec.org/sada/54510; D. Ghanem, "The Shifting Foundation of Political Islam in Algeria" (Carnegie Middle East Center Papers, Mary 2019), https://carnegie-mec.org/2019/05/03/shifting-foundations-of-political-islam-in-algeria-pub-79047.

63. T. Serres, *L'Algérie face à la catastrophe suspendue* (Karthala, 2019).

64. F. Volpi, "Algeria: When Elections Hurt Democracy," *Journal of Democracy* 31, no. 2 (2020): 152–165.

65. N. Khaoua, "Ecodevelopment in the Light of Euro Mediterranean Partnership: Cases of Coastal Territories of Algeria and Morocco" (MPRA Paper No. 60128, 2014), https://ideas.repec.org/p/pra/mprapa/60128.html. See appendix maps, wpid.world.

dependent state that promoted the Arabization of the country. The so-called Berber question came on the political scene in 1980 when popular uprisings took place in Kabylia. Although it was contained to that region, this first large-scale unrest endorsed socioeconomic and democratic requests at large.

No regional or ethnic Berber political party was launched with the introduction of multiparty elections in 1991. Two of the main secular opposition parties, the Socialist Forces Front (Front des forces socialistes, FFS) and the Rally for Culture and Democracy (Rassemblement pour la culture et la démocratie, RCD), were more successful than others in the region, even if they did not incorporate any ethnic claims into their platform (Figure 19.13). The Kabyle vote appears to be a protest vote that may be explained by their potential exclusion from power and clientelist networks organized by the government. Unlike the situation of the Kurds in Turkey, however, the Algerian "ethnic question" does not have a clear

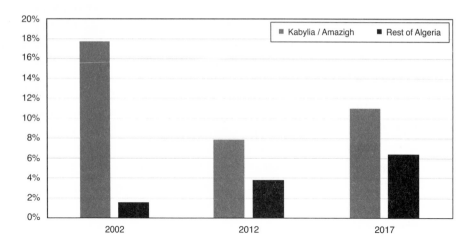

FIGURE 19.13. Vote for the secular opposition by region/language in Algeria, 2002–2017
*Data Source:* Authors' computations using Algerian political attitudes surveys (see wpid.world).
*Note:* The figure shows the share of votes received by secular opposition parties (Front des forces socialistes, FFS and Rassemblement pour la culture et la démocratie, RCD) by region. In 2017, 11% of Kabyle voters supported the secular opposition, compared to 6% of other voters. In 2002, speaking Amazigh at home is taken as a proxy, as the regional decomposition is not available.

class dimension, as Kabylia does not appear to be significantly poorer or richer than the rest of the country.[66]

### A Renewed Cross-class Alliance in a Two-Party Ruling System

Since the end of the Black Decade, two parties, the FLN and the RND, have been effectively running the country, despite their apparently opposite ideological positions. The FLN had a strong socialist component, while the RND initially embodied a new liberal economic view, uniting technocrats behind the structural adjustment reforms defended by the International Monetary Fund.[67] The income gradient of these two parties reflects this divide. The FLN seems to have been relatively more successful among low-income voters, while the RND has appealed to higher-income voters (Figure 19.14).

This pattern recalls the characteristics of so-called neopatrimonial states with cartel ruling, in which blurry frontiers between politics and the economic sector foster clientelistic loyalties among a socially diverse electorate.[68] On one hand, the regime adopted a strong welfare component in the 1970s and kept up high levels of spending and redistributive policies with respect to MENA standards, ensuring poverty reduction.[69] The hydrocarbon rents were distributed through housing or interest rate subsidies and important state jobs. On the other hand, the RND also is the party of the new entrepreneurs and globalization, as liberalization in the 1990s led to a rapid expansion of the private sector and marked a new stage for the crony capitalism system.[70] Each party in the ruling cartel therefore attracted one side of the income distribution, reconciling—or eliminating—class cleavages, thus contributing to maintaining the political status quo.

66. M. Willis, *Politics and Power in the Maghreb* (Oxford University Press, 2014). See appendix Figures CA12 and CA13, wpid.world.

67. L. Hamadouche and Y. Zoubir, "Power and Opposition in Algeria: Toward a Protracted Transition?," *L'Année du Maghreb* 5 (2009): 111–127.

68. S. Eisenstadt, *Traditional Patrimonialism and Modern Neopatrimonialism* (Sage Publications, 1973).

69. F. Eibl, *Social Dictatorships: The Political Economy of the Welfare State in the Middle East and North Africa* (Oxford University Press, 2020).

70. S. Belguidoum, "Transnational Trade and New Types of Entrepreneurs in Algeria," in *The Politics of Algeria: Domestic Issues and International Relations*, ed. Y. Zoubir (Routledge, 2020), 226–236.

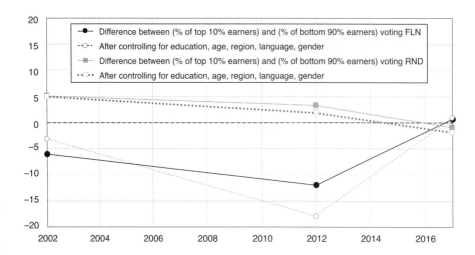

Legend:
- Difference between (% of top 10% earners) and (% of bottom 90% earners) voting FLN
- After controlling for education, age, region, language, gender
- Difference between (% of top 10% earners) and (% of bottom 90% earners) voting RND
- After controlling for education, age, region, language, gender

FIGURE 19.14. Vote for FLN/RND and income in Algeria, 2002–2017
*Data Source:* Authors' computations using Algerian political attitudes surveys (see wpid.world).
*Note:* The figure shows the difference between the share of top 10% earners and the share of bottom 90% earners voting for the ruling parties (Front de libération nationale, FLN and Rassemblement national démocratique, RND), before and after controls. In 2002, top-income voters were less likely to vote FLN by 6 percentage points.

## The Relevance of a Generational Cleavage

The Algerian population is very young, with more than 40 percent aged below twenty-five. This group is one of the most fragile in the country, with an unemployment rate two to three times higher than the national average over the period. In the absence of socioeconomic opportunities, and with the decline of targeted policies that became too costly after the drop in oil prices in 2014, almost two-thirds of Algerian youths in 2019 reported having thought about emigrating.[71]

In this context, the relationship between the youth and the regime has been especially scrutinized. Young Algerians were one of the main actors in the 1988 riots and they joined Islamist armed groups in substantial numbers during the civil war.[72] The historical legitimacy of the

71. UNICEF, "MENA Generation 2030" (United Nations Children's Fund Publications, 2019); see appendix Figure CD7, wpid.world.
72. M. Willis, *The Islamist Challenge in Algeria: A Political History* (New York University Press, 1999).

FLN, derived from its participation in the country's war of independence, has faded away among the new generations—a scenario played out in many other postcolonial countries. Thus, Algerian youth has significantly rejected the regime party, while older voters have been much more likely to support the FLN, except in 2017 (Figure 19.15).

This relative surge in the youth's support for the FLN should nonetheless be interpreted with care. The results are mostly driven by increased abstention, with less than one-fifth of voters younger than thirty-five declaring having voted in the 2017 legislative elections, in a context where aggregate turnout reached only 35 percent.[73]

### A Discredited Electoral System

The extremely high abstention over the period casts doubt on the ability of the multiparty system to reach discontented voters and echoes the continuing calls by parts of the opposition to boycott elections. While presidential elections draw a higher turnout, the appointment of presidential candidates does not answer to a party system mechanism. The ruling parties (FLN, RND) and some opposition parties back the candidate endorsed by the military. The incumbent therefore faces almost no real challengers and with the notable exception of 2019, is reelected with more than 80 percent of votes.

Abstention, together with street protests, has been seen as a new form of political participation in Algeria since the early 2000s.[74] In fact, political activism, indicated by the share of respondents who signed a petition or attended an organized demonstration, has seen increasing involvement from the more disadvantaged social strata over time (Figure 19.16). Civil movements have also been seen as a way to potentially bring the democratic opposition together with increasing participation in various forms of civil society beyond political parties and labor unions.[75] As the movement of the unemployed in the south of the country, the Hirak movement claimed its independence from any political parties.[76]

73. See appendix Figure CD1, wpid.world.

74. L. Hamadouche, "Abstention in Algeria: Another Form of Political Protest," *L'Année du Maghreb* 5 (2009): 263–273.

75. J. Northey, *Civil Society in Algeria, Activism, Identity and the Democratic Process* (I. B. Tauris, 2018).

76. L. Hamadouche and C. Dris, "The Face to Face Hirak-Power: The Crisis of Representation," *L'Année du Maghreb* 21 (2019): 57–68.

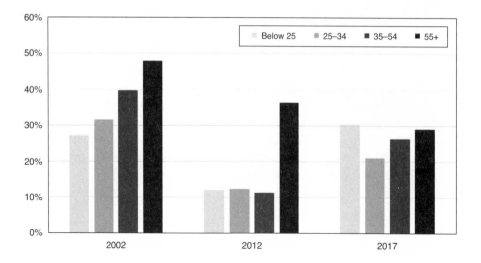

FIGURE 19.15. The generational cleavage in Algeria, 2002–2017. Vote for FLN by age group
*Data Source:* Authors' computations using Algerian political attitudes surveys (see wpid.world).
*Note:* The figure shows the share of votes received by the National Liberal Front (FLN) by age group. In 2002, 27% of voters aged below 25 voted for the FLN, compared to 48% of those aged over 55.

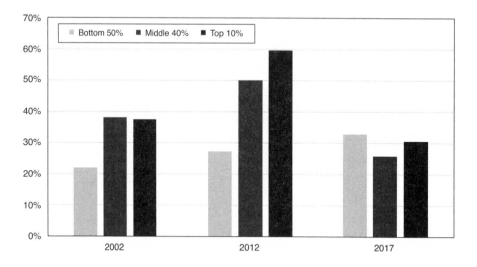

FIGURE 19.16. Political activism by income group in Algeria, 2002–2017
*Data Source:* Authors' computations using Algerian political attitudes surveys (see wpid.world).
*Note:* The figure shows the share of Algerians declaring that they have already attended a demonstration or signed a petition, by income group. This share grew from 22% to 33% among the poorest 50% between 2002 and 2017.

In a striking parallel, the 2019 Iraqi and Algerian protests took place in rentier states that avoided their own Arab Springs in 2011 but were increasingly weakened by the drastic declines in their oil revenues. The two movements, adopting anti-elite and anticorruption rhetoric, revealed that high inequality levels have become part of political conflicts. Transcending existing cleavages and displaying interclass and intersectarian dynamics, they appear as momentums susceptible to reversing previous equilibria, leaving the future of both regimes uncertain.

# Conclusion

AMORY GETHIN, CLARA MARTÍNEZ-TOLEDANO, AND THOMAS PIKETTY

We would like to conclude this volume by insisting once more on the limitations of our project. We have attempted to develop an analytical framework to study the evolution of the socioeconomic structure of electorates in fifty countries from 1948 to 2020. While multiple lessons have emerged from the different chapters of this volume, it is quite clear that the sources, methods, and capacities brought together remain insufficient to satisfactorily answer the interrogations that have motivated our work. We hope first and foremost that this book will help to inspire further research on these questions among the social sciences research community, and that it will have allowed the reader-citizen interested in them to better understand the interaction between political cleavages and social inequalities in comparative and historical perspective. We encourage interested readers to visit the website accompanying this volume (wpid.world), which also includes for each country a large number of supplementary data series and figures that we have not been able to present in this volume for reasons of length.

How do political parties and electoral blocs succeed in aggregating voters from different backgrounds or ethnoreligious identities within large coalitions? What is the relative importance of "class-based" and "identity-based" cleavages in determining the structure of cleavages, electoral behaviors, and political affiliations? As we progressively covered a large variety of countries, experiences, and trajectories, we discovered how crucial multiplying points of view, and more importantly, decentering and de-Westernizing our perspective, were to answering these questions. Nostalgia for the class-based structure of electoral conflicts in postwar Western democracies is not a good guide. The era of the comforting opposition between social democratic (and affiliated) parties

and conservative (and affiliated) parties, once perceived as seemingly eternal, is long gone. It was tied to politico-ideological and sociohistorical circumstances that will not come back, or at least not in the same form. And within European nation-states, it also came with a homogeneity of origins and ethnoreligious identities that should not be idealized. The postcommunist and postcolonial world of the late twentieth and early twenty-first centuries brings into play other cleavages and requires building other platforms of social and economic transformation if it is to succeed in overcoming the divisions of people from diverse origins and convincing them that what unites them is more important than what divides them.

Throughout this volume, we have had a tendency to express a certain preference for "class-based" cleavages over "identity-based" cleavages. The reason for this is quite simple: conflicts mediated by social class are always potentially soluble into social and economic change, whether in the form of redistribution of income and wages, circulation of wealth and power, improvements in working conditions and participation, or egalitarian access to education and health. It is admittedly not always easy to position the cursor at the right level. Yet, a straightforward democratic confrontation between different class-based parties offering complementary viewpoints and experiences can contribute to moving in this direction. In contrast, conflicts over national origin or ethnoreligious identities do not often admit solutions other than further exacerbation or persecution of one side by the other. We would, however, be mistaken to dismiss all identity-based conflicts as forms of irresolvable tribalism. Recognizing the multiplicity of sociocultural and ethnoreligious identities requires inventing new policies based on the respect of diversity and common rules, the fight against discrimination, and in some instances, compensation for past injustices. Such issues have been neglected far too long by Western democracies, which were quick to forget their colonial pasts and the international insertion that was once key to their enrichment. At a theoretical level, one might also imagine a democratic world where class-based and identity-based cleavages would have both disappeared, and where diverging opinions and beliefs would depend entirely on the deliberative process itself rather than on socioeconomic or ethnoreligious determinants. Yet, nothing indicates that this configuration could materialize in a foreseeable future. In this context, it seems more reasonable to take the persisting importance of class-based and identity-based cleavages as given, and envision the conditions of

their transformation within concrete coalitions and tangible political prospects.

Perhaps more relevant to our purpose, one may also imagine a democratic universe structured by new forms of cleavages, starting with the future of the environment and the conditions of a durable cohabitation between humans and nature. We have encountered green and environmentalist parties in several instances in the course of our enquiry, and we have seen the role that they played in accelerating the decline of class cleavages and the rise of "multi-elite" party systems. This, however, represents only the first visible steps of a much longer process. Environmental issues will most likely continue to gain prominence in the coming decades. As the consequences of the current deterioration of the environment on the conditions of social life eventually unfold, they will likely play a structuring role in generating new coalitions with constructive political visions.

To move beyond the research program developed in this volume, it is not enough to simply wait for the next elections and electoral surveys. Other sources and methods, far beyond those we have used here, need to be mobilized. Let us say it once again: this volume relies on a quasi-unique source, namely electoral surveys conducted in fifty electoral democracies from 1948 to 2020. The advantage of this approach is that it has allowed us to apply homogeneous methods to a large number of countries and to reveal a certain number of regularities and transformations. Its disadvantages are equally evident: the complexity of the questions asked calls for the exploitation of many other forms of research materials. We have naturally relied on many studies conducted by researchers in the social sciences, and in particular in political science, to specify the historical contexts and the origins of the party systems of the different countries considered. Our characterizations of the various parties and movements we encountered, however, remain in many cases extremely schematic, if not impressionistic. To go further, one would need to assemble and use in a systematic manner a number of other sources, related for instance to political discourses and electoral platforms,[1] to the policies implemented by parties when they assume power, and to their mobilizational and funding strategies, to name a few. This would arguably require limiting the scope to a smaller number of countries.

---

1. See, for instance, the impressive database assembled in the context of the Manifesto Project (Manifesto Research on Political Representation, https://manifesto-project.wzb.eu/).

Lastly, one should highlight the importance of broadening even further the historical perspective and the nature of the electoral data used. The surveys exploited in this volume have a major advantage: they allow us to observe, for the same voters, both their electoral behaviors and their socioeconomic characteristics. They also suffer from two significant drawbacks. First, no survey of this kind existed before the 1940s or 1950s, or even the 1980s or 1990s in a large number of electoral democracies. Second, even when they do exist, they pose a number of challenges related to self-reporting[2] and, more importantly, to the limited size of the samples used. The electoral surveys exploited in this volume indeed rely on samples of a few thousand voters. This is sufficient to reveal major trends at the national level, but forbids more refined analyses. Small election-to-election variations, for instance, are often not statistically significant, especially when one tries to interact several explanatory variables or if one aims to study narrow regional variations. This also prevents us from precisely identifying the impact of a given proposition or public policy on the perceptions of various groups of voters.

Engaging in more granular analyses, as well as gaining historical depth, requires going back to localized election results (whether at the level of districts, constituencies, or even polling stations) and matching them with administrative, tax, or social data available at this same level (such as census data). This methodology poses multiple challenges related to the inference process too, as it does not cover electoral behaviors and socioeconomic characteristics at the individual level, but only provides averages at a given local level. However, it has the immense benefit of allowing us to adopt a much larger temporal perspective, as data have generally been preserved since the nineteenth century and the first elections held by universal suffrage.[3] This would make it possible to examine even more diversified politico-ideological families and situate the study of political cleavages and social inequalities within a considerably

2. Even if this should not be a major problem, at least when it comes to self-reporting of voting behaviors. We have reweighted electoral surveys to make them representative of official election results, but generally this has very minor implications. See Chapter 1. Biases linked to self-reporting of income and wealth sometimes create more serious difficulties, notably at the top of the distribution, particularly given the imprecision of survey questionnaires.

3. For a particularly fruitful (yet unfortunately not often followed) example, see the classic study by André Siegfried, *Tableau politique de la France de l'ouest sous la Troisième République* (Armand Colin, 1913).

wider historical scope. The lessons arising from such study would likely lead us to relativize even further the supposedly universal character of the postwar Western class-based cleavage, and thereby to better apprehend the conditions of the construction, deconstruction, and reconstruction of more complex political coalitions. Here again, such an initiative could only be reasonably conducted in a first step at the level of monographs focusing on a small number of countries, if not a single country. We hope that the results presented in this volume will contribute to stimulating new research in these multiple directions.

# ACKNOWLEDGMENTS

This volume greatly benefited from the comments of colleagues and friends, who generously agreed to review some of its sections and whose suggestions were particularly useful in revising its different chapters. We are deeply indebted to Jules Baleyte, whose careful examination of the book proved invaluable, and we wish to thank Carmen Durrer de la Sota for her excellent research assistance throughout this project. We are also grateful to Goolam Aboobaker, Lavih Abraham, Ronald Alfaro-Redondo, Itai Artzi, Kentaro Asai, Nitin Bharti, Harry Blain, María Julia Blanco, Francesco Bogliacino, Joel Campbell, Aroop Chatterjee, David Chiavacci, Kevin Cunningham, Federico Curci, Jennifer Curtin, Léo Czajka, Ishac Diwan, Nicolás Dvoskin, Dror Feitelson, Gustavo García, Gabriel Gazeau, Dalia Ghanem, Saad Gulzar, Karl Ho, Christophe Jaffrelot, Eui-Young Jung, Catherine Lena Kelly, Dominika Koter, Wai-Man Lam, Sébastien Lechevalier, Gedeão Locks, Halfdan Lynge-Mangueira, Gary Marks, Kyong Mazzaro, Sidney Michelini, Jules Naudet, Paul Nugent, Anja Osei, Javier Padilla, Amy Poteete, Aidan Regan, Paolo Santini, Thiago Scarelli, Carmen Schmidt, Ferenc Szűcs, Dirk Tomsa, Yoshida Toru, Andreas Ufen, Nicolas van de Walle, and Sebastian Veg.

Many colleagues also provided priceless feedback and valuable insights during the completion of this project. We are notably grateful to Thomas Blanchet, Lucas Chancel, Ignacio Flores, Rowaida Moshrif, Tom Raster, and Olivia Ronsain. This book grew within the friendly and stimulating atmosphere of the World Inequality Lab at the Paris School of Economics, and we want to thank all members of the Lab for these shared moments and their generosity.

Finally, we thank all scholars and colleagues who trusted us in this project and agreed to write or co-write one or several chapters of this

book. Without their support, we would never have been able to offer the little world tour in fifty electoral democracies that we are happy to present to the reader in this volume.

A. Gethin, C. Martínez-Toledano, and T. Piketty

# CONTRIBUTORS

Lydia Assouad is a Research Fellow at the World Inequality Lab.

Jules Baleyte is the head of the international section of the département de la conjoncture at the Institut national de la statistique et des études économiques (INSEE).

Abhijit Vinayak Banerjee is the Ford Foundation International Professor of Economics at the Massachusetts Institute of Technology and Research Fellow at the World Inequality Lab.

Oscar Barrera is a Research Fellow at the World Inequality Lab.

Luis Bauluz is a Postdoctoral Research Fellow at the University of Bonn and Wealth Aggregates Coordinator at the World Inequality Lab.

Yonatan Berman is a fellow at the London Mathematical Laboratory and Research Fellow at the World Inequality Lab.

Carmen Durrer de la Sota is a PhD candidate in Economics at UC Berkeley and Research Assistant at the World Inequality Lab.

Amory Gethin (editor) is a Research Fellow at the World Inequality Lab.

Yajna Govind is Assistant Professor of Economics at Copenhagen Business School and Research Fellow at the World Inequality Lab.

Thanasak Jenmana is a Research Fellow at the World Inequality Lab.

Fabian Kosse is Professor of Applied Economics at LMU Munich.

Ana Leiva is a PhD candidate in Economics at the University of Oslo.

Attila Lindner is Assistant Professor of Economics at University College London.

Clara Martínez-Toledano (editor) is Assistant Professor of Financial Economics at Imperial College London and Wealth Distribution Coordinator at the World Inequality Lab.

Sultan Mehmood is Assistant Professor of Economics at New Economic School in Moscow.

Marc Morgan is Assistant Professor at the Department of History, Economics and Society at the University of Geneva and Western Europe Coordinator at the World Inequality Lab.

Filip Novokmet is a Postdoctoral Research Fellow at the University of Bonn and Research Fellow at the World Inequality Lab.

Thomas Piketty (editor) is Professor at the École des Hautes Études en Sciences Sociales and at the Paris School of Economics and Co-director at the World Inequality Lab.

Alice Sodano is a Research Assistant at the World Inequality Lab.

Juliet-Nil Uraz is a PhD candidate in Social Policy at the London School of Economics.

Tom Zawisza is a British Academy Postdoctoral Fellow at University College London.

Álvaro Zúñiga-Cordero is a Research Fellow at the World Inequality Lab.

# INDEX

Note: Figures and tables are denoted by f and t, respectively, following the page number; footnote information is denoted with an n and note number following the page number.

MW00612070